Microsoft® Word 2002

Illustrated Complete

Jennifer A. Duffy
Carol M. Cram

APPROVED COURSEWARE

COURSE
TECHNOLOGY
THOMSON LEARNING

Australia • Canada • Mexico • Singapore • Spain • United Kingdom • United States

**COURSE
TECHNOLOGY**
—————✦————— ™
THOMSON LEARNING

Microsoft Word 2002 - Illustrated Complete

Jennifer A. Duffy, Carol M. Cram

Managing Editor:
Nicole Jones Pinard

Product Manager:
Emily Heberlein

Associate Product Manager:
Emeline Elliott

Production Editor:
Aimee Poirier

Developmental Editor:
Pamela Conrad

Editorial Assistant:
Christina Kling Garrett

QA Manuscript Reviewers:
John Freitas, Ashlee Welz, Alex White, Harris Bierhoff, Serge Palladino, Holly Schabowski, Jeff Schwartz

Text Designer:
Joseph Lee, Black Fish Design

Composition House:
GEX Publishing Services

The Illustrated Series Vision

Teaching and writing about computer applications can be extremely rewarding and challenging. How do we engage students and keep their interest? How do we teach them skills that they can easily apply on the job? As we set out to write this book, our goals were to develop a textbook that:

▶ works for a beginning student

▶ provides varied, flexible and meaningful exercises and projects to reinforce the skills

▶ serves as a reference tool

▶ makes your job as an educator easier, by providing resources above and beyond the textbook to help you teach your course

Our popular, streamlined format is based on advice from instructional designers and customers. This flexible design presents each lesson on a two-page spread, with step-by-step instructions on the left, and screen illustrations on the right. This signature style, coupled with high-caliber content, provides a comprehensive yet manageable introduction to Microsoft Word 2002 — it is a teaching package for the instructor and a learning experience for the student.

ACKNOWLEDGMENTS

Jennifer Duffy

I wish to express particular thanks to Pam Conrad for her tireless help and keen editorial sensibilities. I am also deeply grateful for the support of my husband, Fred Eliot, and our daughter, Isabella, who patiently waited to be born until this book was nearly finished.

Carol M. Cram

I too wish to thank Pam Conrad, who provided so much encouragement, support, and intelligence throughout the editorial process. She is truly beyond compare! I also wish to thank my husband, Gregg Simpson, for his ongoing support and encouragement, and our daughter Julia for her enthusiastic help. Finally, I'd like to thank my students at Capilano College in North Vancouver. They are what it's all about.

Thanks to the reviewers who provided invaluable feedback and ideas to us, especially Janis Cox and Joe LaMontagne.

Preface

Welcome to *Microsoft Word 2002–Illustrated Complete*. Each lesson in the book contains elements pictured to the right in the sample two-page spread.

▶ How is the book organized?

Two units on Windows 2000 introduce students to basic operating system skills. The book is then organized into sixteen units on Word, covering creating, editing, and formatting text and documents. Students also learn how to create tables and Web sites, merge Word documents, and use graphics, styles, charts, forms, and macros.

▶ What kinds of assignments are included in the book? At what level of difficulty?

The lesson assignments use MediaLoft, a fictional chain of bookstore cafés, as the case study. The assignments on the blue pages at the end of each unit increase in difficulty. Project files and case studies, with many international examples, provide a great variety of interesting and relevant business applications for skills. Assignments include:

- **Concepts Reviews** include multiple choice, matching, and screen identification questions.
- **Skills Reviews** provide additional hands-on, step-by-step reinforcement.
- **Independent Challenges** are case projects requiring critical thinking and application of the skills learned in the unit. The Independent Challenges increase in difficulty, with the first Independent Challenge in each unit being the easiest (most step-by-step with detailed instructions). Independent Challenges 2 and 3 become increasingly open-ended, requiring more independent thinking and problem solving.
- **E-Quest Independent Challenges** are case projects with a Web focus. E-Quests require the use of the World Wide Web to conduct research to complete the project.
- **Visual Workshops** show a completed file and require that the file be created without any step-by-step guidance, involving problem solving and an independent application of the unit skills.

Each 2-page spread focuses on a single skill.

Concise text that introduces the basic principles in the lesson and integrates the brief case study (indicated by the paintbrush icon).

Unit D — Word 2002
Editing Headers and Footers

To change header and footer text or to alter the formatting of headers and footers you must first open the Header and Footer areas. You can open headers and footers using the Header and Footer command on the View menu, or by double-clicking a header or footer in Print Layout view. Alice modifies the header by adding a small circle symbol between "Buzz" and the date. She also adds a border under the header text to set it off from the rest of the page. Finally, she removes the header and footer text from the first page of the document.

Steps

Trouble?
If the Header and Footer toolbar is in the way, click its title bar and drag it to a new location.

1. Place the insertion point at the top of page 2, position the ▷ pointer over the header text at the top of page 2, then double-click
   The Header and Footer areas open.

2. Place the insertion point between the two spaces after Buzz, click **Insert** on the menu bar, then click **Symbol**
   The Symbol dialog box opens and is similar to Figure D-13. **Symbols** are special characters, such as graphics, shapes, and foreign language characters, that you can insert into a document. The symbols shown in Figure D-13 are the symbols included with the (normal text) font. You can use the Font list arrow on the Symbols tab to view the symbols included with each font on your computer.

3. Scroll the list of symbols if necessary to locate the black circle symbol shown in Figure D-13, select the **black circle symbol**, click **Insert**, then click **Close**
   A circle symbol is added at the location of the insertion point.

QuickTip
You can enter different text in the First Page Header and First Page Footer areas.

4. With the insertion point in the header text, click **Format** on the menu bar, then click **Borders and Shading**
   The Borders and Shading dialog box opens.

TABLE D-3: Buttons on the Header and Footer toolbar

button	function
Insert AutoText ▾	Inserts an AutoText entry, such as a field for the filename, or the author's name
Insert Page Number	Inserts a field for the page number so that the pages are numbered automatically
Insert Number of Pages	Inserts a field for the total number of pages in the document
Format Page Number	Opens the Page Number Format dialog box; use to change the numbering format or to begin automatic page numbering with a specific number
Insert Date	Inserts a field for the current date
Insert Time	Inserts a field for the current time
Page Setup	Opens the Page Setup dialog box
Switch Between Header and Footer	Moves the insertion point between the Header and Footer areas

▶ WORD D-12 **FORMATTING DOCUMENTS**

Hints as well as troubleshooting advice, right where you need it – next to the step itself.

Quickly accessible summaries of key terms, toolbar buttons, or keyboard alternatives connected with the lesson material. Students can refer easily to this information when working on their own projects at a later time.

Every lesson features large, full-color representations of what the screen should look like as students complete the numbered steps.

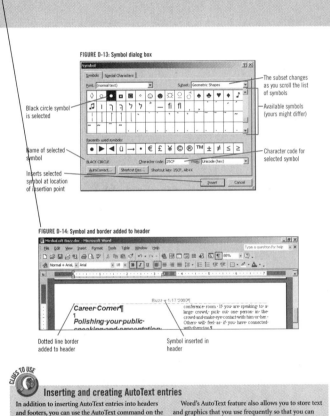

FIGURE D-13: Symbol dialog box

Black circle symbol is selected

The subset changes as you scroll the list of symbols

Available symbols (yours might differ)

Name of selected symbol

Inserts selected symbol at location of insertion point

Character code for selected symbol

FIGURE D-14: Symbol and border added to header

Dotted line border added to header

Symbol inserted in header

Word 2002

Inserting and creating AutoText entries

In addition to inserting AutoText entries into headers and footers, you can use the AutoText command on the Insert menu to insert AutoText entries into any part of a document. Word includes a number of built-in AutoText entries, including salutations and closings for letters, as well as information for headers and footers. To insert a built-in AutoText entry at the location of the insertion point, point to AutoText on the Insert menu, point to a category on the AutoText menu, then click the AutoText entry you want to insert. You can also use the Insert AutoText button on the Header and Footer toolbar to insert an AutoText entry from the Header/Footer category into a header or footer.

Word's AutoText feature also allows you to store text and graphics that you use frequently so that you can easily insert them in a document. To create a custom AutoText entry, enter the text or graphic you want to store—such as a company name or logo—in a document, select it, point to AutoText on the Insert menu, and then click New. In the Create AutoText dialog box, type a name for your AutoText entry, then click OK. The text or graphic is saved as a custom AutoText entry. To insert a custom AutoText entry in a document, point to AutoText on the Insert menu, click AutoText, select the entry name on the AutoText tab in the AutoCorrect dialog box, click Insert, then click OK.

FORMATTING DOCUMENTS WORD D-13

Clues to Use boxes provide concise information that either expands on the major lesson skill or describes an independent task that in some way relates to the major lesson skill.

The pages are numbered according to unit. D indicates the unit, 13 indicates the page.

► Is this book MOUS Certified?

Microsoft Word 2002 – Illustrated Complete covers both the Core and Expert objectives for Word and has received certification approval as courseware for the MOUS program. See the inside front cover for more information on other Illustrated titles meeting MOUS certification.

The first page of each unit includes ⌐MOUS⌐ symbols to indicate which unit skills are MOUS skills. A grid in the back of the book lists all the exam objectives and cross-references them with the lessons and exercises.

► What online content solutions are available to accompany this book?

Visit www.course.com for more information on our online content for Illustrated titles. Options include:

MyCourse.com

Need a quick, simple tool to help you manage your course? Try MyCourse.com, the easiest to use, most flexible syllabus and content management tool available. MyCourse.com offers you brand new content, including Topic Reviews, Extra Case Projects, and Quizzes, to accompany this book.

WebCT

Course Technology and WebCT have partnered to provide you with the highest quality online resources and Web-based tools for your class. Course Technology offers content for this book to help you create your WebCT class, such as a suggested Syllabus, Lecture Notes, Practice Test questions, and more.

Blackboard

Course Technology and Blackboard have also partnered to provide you with the highest quality online resources and Web-based tools for your class. Course Technology offers content for this book to help you create your Blackboard class, such as a suggested Syllabus, Lecture Notes, Practice Test questions, and more.

Instructor Resources

The Instructor's Resource Kit (IRK) CD is Course Technology's way of putting the resources and information needed to teach and learn effectively into your hands. All the components are available on the IRK, (pictured below), and many of the resources can be downloaded from www.course.com.

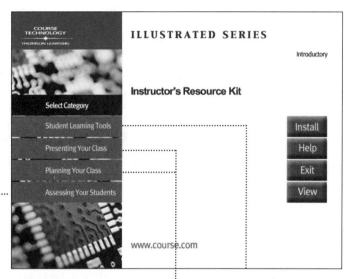

ASSESSING YOUR STUDENTS

Solution Files
Solution Files are Project Files completed with comprehensive sample answers. Use these files to evaluate your students' work. Or, distribute them electronically or in hard copy so students can verify their own work.

ExamView
ExamView is a powerful testing software package that allows you to create and administer printed, computer (LAN-based), and Internet exams. ExamView includes hundreds of questions that correspond to the topics covered in this text, enabling students to generate detailed study guides that include page references for further review. The computer-based and Internet testing components allow students to take exams at their computers, and also save you time by grading each exam automatically.

PRESENTING YOUR CLASS

Figure Files
Figure Files contain all the figures from the book in .jpg format. Use the figure files to create transparency masters or in a PowerPoint presentation.

STUDENT TOOLS

Project Files and Project Files List
To complete most of the units in this book, your students will need **Project Files**. Put them on a file server for students to copy. The Project Files are available on the Instructor's Resource Kit CD-ROM, the Review Pack, and can also be downloaded from www.course.com.

Instruct students to use the **Project Files List** at the end of the book. This list gives instructions on copying and organizing files.

PLANNING YOUR CLASS

Instructor's Manual
Available as an electronic file, the Instructor's Manual is quality-assurance tested and includes unit overviews, detailed lecture topics for each unit with teaching tips, comprehensive sample solutions to all lessons and end-of-unit material, and extra Independent Challenges. The Instructor's Manual is available on the Instructor's Resource Kit CD-ROM, or you can download it from www.course.com.

Sample Syllabus
Prepare and customize your course easily using this sample course outline (available on the Instructor's Resource Kit CD-ROM).

SAM, Skills Assessment Manager for Microsoft Office XP
SAM is the most powerful Office XP assessment and reporting tool that will help you gain a true understanding of your students' proficiency in Microsoft Word, Excel, Access, and PowerPoint 2002. (Available separately from the IRK CD.)

TOM, Training Online Manager for Microsoft Office XP
TOM is Course Technology's MOUS-approved training tool for Microsoft Office XP. Available via the World Wide Web and CD-ROM, TOM allows students to actively learn Office XP concepts and skills by delivering realistic practice through both guided and self-directed simulated instruction.

Brief Contents

Contents

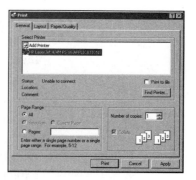
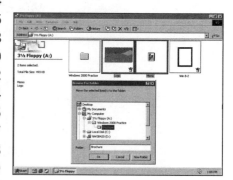

Word 2002

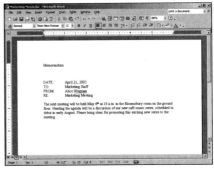

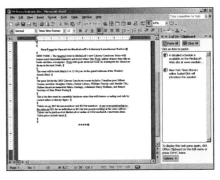

Contents

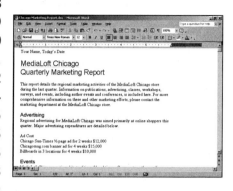

Formatting Documents WORD D-1

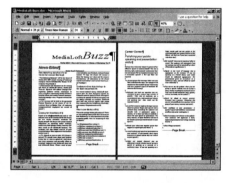

Creating and Formatting Tables WORD E-1

Illustrating Documents with Graphics   WORD F-1

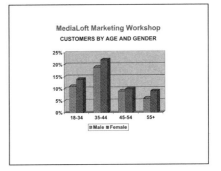

Creating a Web Site   WORD G-1

Contents

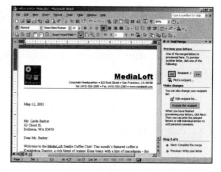

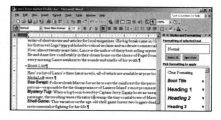

Integrating Word with Other Programs
WORD K-1

Exploring Advanced Graphics
WORD L-1

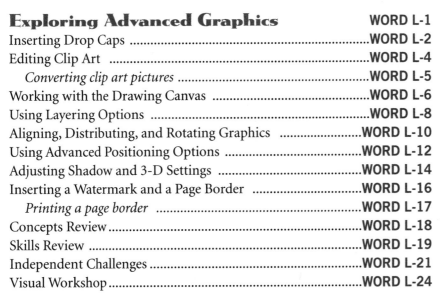

Contents

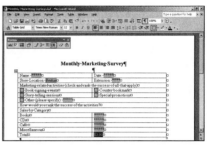

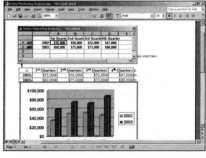

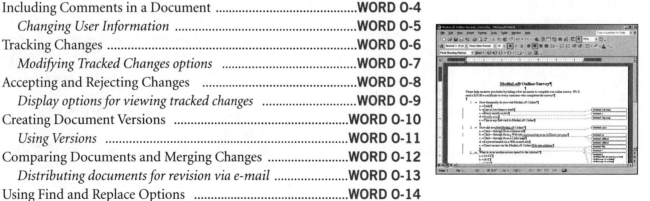

Windows 2000 Appendix A

Appendix A: Formatting a Disk   **WINDOWS 2000 1**

Read This Before You Begin

Software Information and Required Installation

This book was written and tested using Microsoft Office XP - Professional Edition, with a typical installation on Microsoft Windows 2000, with Internet Explorer 5.0 or higher.

What are Project Files?

To complete many of the units in this book, you need to use Project Files. You use a Project File, which contains a partially completed document used in an exercise, so you don't have to type in all the information you need in the document. Your instructor will either provide you with a copy of the Project Files or ask you to make your own copy. Detailed instructions on how to organize you files, as well as a complete listing of all the files you'll need and will create, can be found in the back of the book (look for the yellow pages) in the Project Files List.

Why is my screen different from the book?

1. Your Desktop components and some dialog box options might be different if you are using an operating system other than Windows 2000

2. Depending on your computer hardware capabilities and the Windows Display settings on your computer, you may notice the following differences:
   - Your screen may look larger or smaller because of your screen resolution (the height and width of your screen)
   - The colors of the title bar in your screen may be a solid blue

3. Depending on your Office settings, your toolbars may display on a single row and your menus may display with a shortened list of frequently used commands. Office menus and toolbars can modify themselves to your working style by displaying only the most frequently used buttons and menu commands.

To view buttons not currently displayed, click a Toolbar Options button  at the end of either the Standard or Formatting toolbar. To view the full list of menu commands, click the double arrow at the bottom of the menu.

Toolbars on one row

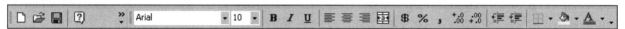

In order to have your toolbars display on two rows, showing all buttons, and to have the full menus display, you must turn off the personalized menus and toolbars feature. Click tools on the menu bar, Click Customize, select the show Standard and Formatting toolbars on two rows and Always show full menus check boxes on the Options tab, then click Close. This book assumes you are displaying toolbars on two rows and full menus.

Toolbars on two rows

Unit A

Getting
Started with Windows 2000

Objectives

- ► **Start Windows and view the Active Desktop**
- ► **Use the mouse**
- ► **Start a program**
- ► **Move and resize windows**
- ► **Use menus, keyboard shortcuts, and toolbars**
- ► **Use dialog boxes**
- ► **Use scroll bars**
- ► **Use Windows Help**
- ► **Close a program and shut down Windows**

Microsoft Windows 2000 is an **operating system**, a computer **program**, or set of instructions, that controls how the computer carries out basic tasks such as displaying information on your computer screen and running programs. Windows 2000 helps you save and organize the results of your work as **files**, which are electronic collections of data. Windows 2000 also coordinates the flow of information among the programs, printers, storage devices, and other components of your computer system, as well as among other computers on a network. When you work with Windows 2000, you will notice many **icons**, small pictures intended to be meaningful symbols of the items they represent. You will also notice rectangular-shaped work areas known as **windows**, thus the name of the operating system. These icons, windows, and various other words and symbols create what is referred to as a **graphical user interface** (**GUI**, pronounced "gooey"), through which you interact with the computer. ⬤ This unit introduces you to basic skills that you can use in all Windows programs.

Windows 2000

Starting Windows and Viewing the Active Desktop

When you turn on your computer, Windows 2000 automatically starts and the Active Desktop appears. The **Active Desktop**, shown in Figure A-1, is where you organize all the information and tools you need to accomplish your computer tasks. You can access, store, share, and explore information seamlessly, whether it resides on your computer, a network, or the **Internet**, a worldwide collection of over 40 million computers linked together to share information. The desktop is called "active" because it offers an interactive link between your computer and the Internet, so that Internet content displayed on your desktop, such as stock prices or weather information, is always up to date. When you start Windows for the first time, the desktop appears with the **default** settings, those preset by the operating system. For example, the default color of the desktop is blue. If any of the default settings have been changed on your computer, your desktop will look different than the one in the figures, but you should be able to locate all the items you need. The bar at the bottom of your screen is called the **taskbar**, which shows what programs are currently running. You use the Start menu, accessed by clicking the **Start button** at the left end of the taskbar, to perform such tasks as starting programs, finding and opening files, and accessing Windows Help. The **Quick Launch toolbar** is next to the Start button; it contains several buttons you can click to start Internet-related programs quickly, and another that you can click to show the desktop when it is not currently visible. Table A-1 identifies the icons and other elements you see on your desktop. If Windows 2000 is not currently running, follow the steps below to start it now.

Trouble?

If you don't know your password, see your instructor or technical support person.

1. Turn on your computer and monitor

You might see a "Please select the operating system to start" prompt. Don't worry about selecting one of the options; Microsoft Windows 2000 Professional automatically starts after 30 seconds. When Windows starts and the desktop appears, you may see a Log On to Windows dialog box. If so, continue to Step 2. If not, view Figure A-1, then continue on to the next lesson.

Trouble?

If the Getting Started with Windows 2000 dialog box opens, move your mouse pointer over the Exit button in the lower-right corner of the dialog box and press the left mouse button once to close the dialog box.

2. Enter the correct user name, type your password, then press [Enter]

Once the password is accepted, the Windows desktop appears on your screen. See Figure A-1.

Accessing the Internet from the Active Desktop

Windows 2000 provides a seamless connection between your desktop and the Internet with Internet Explorer. Internet Explorer is an example of a **browser,** a program designed to access the **World Wide Web** (also known as the **WWW**, or simply the **Web**). Internet Explorer is integrated with the Windows 2000 operating system. You can access it by clicking its icon on the desktop or on the Quick Launch toolbar. You can access Web pages, and place Web content such as weather or stock updates on the desktop for instant viewing. This information is updated automatically whenever you connect to the Internet, making your desktop truly active. You can also communicate electronically with other Internet users, using the Windows e-mail and newsreader program, Outlook Express.

FIGURE A-1: Windows Active Desktop

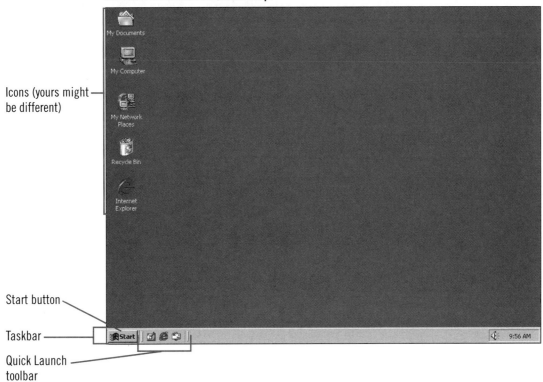

Icons (yours might be different)

Start button

Taskbar

Quick Launch toolbar

TABLE A-1: Elements of the Windows desktop

desktop element	icon	allows you to
My Documents folder		Store programs, documents, graphics, or other files
My Computer		Work with different disk drives and printers on your computer
My Network Places		Open files and folders on other computers and install network printers
Recycle Bin		Delete and restore files
Internet Explorer		Start Internet Explorer to access the Internet
Connect to the Internet		Set up Internet access
Start button	Start	Start programs, open documents, search for files, and more
Taskbar		Start programs and switch among open programs
Quick Launch toolbar		Start Internet Explorer, start Outlook Express, and display the desktop

Using the Mouse

A **mouse** is a hand-held **input or pointing device** that you use to interact with your computer. Input or pointing devices come in many shapes and sizes; some, like a mouse, are directly attached to your computer with a cable; others function like a TV remote control and allow you to access your computer without being right next to it. Figure A-2 shows examples of common pointing devices. Because the most common pointing device is a mouse, this book uses that term. If you are using a different pointing device, substitute that device whenever you see the term "mouse." When you move the mouse, the **mouse pointer** on the screen moves in the same direction. The **mouse buttons** are used to select icons and commands, which is how you communicate with the computer. Table A-2 shows some common mouse pointer shapes that indicate different activities. Table A-3 lists the five basic mouse actions. Begin by experimenting with the mouse now.

Steps

1. **Locate the mouse pointer on the desktop, then move the mouse across your desk or mousepad**
   Watch how the mouse pointer moves on the desktop in response to your movements; practice moving the mouse pointer in circles, then back and forth in straight lines.

2. **Position the mouse pointer over the My Computer icon**
   Positioning the mouse pointer over an item is called **pointing**.

Trouble?

If the My Computer window opens during this step, your mouse isn't set with the Windows 2000 default mouse settings. See your instructor or technical support person for assistance. This book assumes your computer is set to all Windows 2000 default settings.

3. **With the pointer over the My Computer icon, press and release the left mouse button**
   Pressing and releasing the left mouse button is called **clicking** (or single-clicking, to distinguish it from double-clicking, which you'll do in Step 7). When you position the mouse pointer over an icon or any item and click, you select that item. When an item is **selected**, it is **highlighted** (shaded differently from other items), and the next action you take will be performed on that item.

4. **With the My computer icon selected, press and hold down the left mouse button, then move the mouse down and to the right and release the mouse button**
   The icon becomes dimmed and moves with the mouse pointer; this is called **dragging**, which you do to move icons and other Windows elements. When you release the mouse button, the item is positioned at the new location.

5. **Position the mouse pointer over the My Computer icon, then press and release the right mouse button**
   Clicking the right mouse button is known as **right-clicking**. Right-clicking an item on the desktop produces a **pop-up menu**, as shown in Figure A-3. This menu lists the commands most commonly used for the item you have clicked. A **command** is a directive that provides access to a program's features.

6. **Click anywhere outside the menu to close the pop-up menu**

QuickTip

When a step tells you to "click," use the left mouse button. If it says "right-click," use the right mouse button.

7. **Position the mouse pointer over the My Computer icon, then quickly press and release the left mouse button twice**
   Clicking the mouse button twice quickly is known as **double-clicking**, which, in this case, opens the My Computer window. The **My Computer** window contains additional icons that represent the drives and system components that are installed on your computer.

8. **Click the Close button ⊠ in the upper-right corner of the My Computer window**

TABLE A-2: Common mouse pointer shapes

shape	used to
↖	Select items, choose commands, start programs, and work in programs
I	Position mouse pointer for editing or inserting text; called the insertion point
⧖	Indicate Windows is busy processing a command
↔	Change the size of a window; appears when mouse pointer is on the border of a window
↑	Select and open Web-based data

FIGURE A-2: Common pointing devices

Trackball

Trackpoint

Right mouse button

Left mouse button

Mouse

Intellimouse

FIGURE A-3: Displaying a pop-up menu

Selected icon

Pop-up menu

CLUES TO USE

More about the mouse: Classic style and Internet style

Because Windows 2000 integrates the use of the Internet with its other functions, it allows you to extend the way you click in a Web browser program on the Internet to the way you click in other computer programs. With the default Windows 2000 settings, you click an item to select it and double-click an item to open it. In a Web browser program, however, you point to an item to select it and single-click to open it. Windows 2000 gives you two choices for clicking: with the **Classic style**, you double-click to open items, and with the **Internet style**, you single-click to open items. To switch between styles, double-click the My Computer icon (or click if you are currently using the Internet style), click Tools on the menu bar, click Folder Options, click the General tab if necessary, click the Single-click to Open an Item option or the Double-click to Open an Item option in the Click items as follows section, and then click OK.

TABLE A-3: Basic mouse techniques

technique	what to do
Pointing	Move the mouse to position the mouse pointer over an item on the desktop
Clicking	Press and release the left mouse button
Double-clicking	Press and release the left mouse button twice quickly
Dragging	Point to an item, press and hold the left mouse button, move the mouse to a new location, then release the mouse button
Right-clicking	Point to an item, then press and release the right mouse button

Starting a Program

Clicking the Start button on the taskbar opens the Start menu, which lists submenus for a variety of tasks described in Table A-4. As you become familiar with Windows, you might want to customize the Start menu to include additional items that you use most often. Windows 2000 comes with several built-in programs, called **accessories**. Although not as feature-rich as many programs sold separately, Windows accessories are useful for completing basic tasks. ✍ In this lesson, you start a Windows accessory called **WordPad**, which is a word-processing program you can use to create and edit simple documents.

Steps

1. Click the **Start button** on the taskbar
The Start menu opens.

2. Point to **Programs**
The Programs submenu opens, listing the programs and categories for programs installed on your computer. WordPad is in the category called Accessories.

QuickTip

Windows 2000 features personalized menus, which list only the commands you've most recently used. Whenever you want to view other commands available on the menu, rest the mouse pointer over the double arrows ☒ at the bottom of the menu.

3. Point to **Accessories**
The Accessories menu, shown in Figure A-4, contains several programs to help you complete common tasks. You want to start WordPad. If you do not see WordPad, rest the mouse pointer over the double arrows at the bottom of Programs submenu and wait. The full menu will open after a few seconds.

4. Click **WordPad**
WordPad opens with a blank document window open, as shown in Figure A-5. Don't worry if your window does not fill the screen; you'll learn how to maximize it in the next lesson. Note that a **program button** appears on the taskbar and is highlighted, indicating that WordPad is open.

TABLE A-4: Start menu categories

category	description
Windows Update	Connects to a Microsoft Web site and updates your Windows 2000 files as necessary
Programs	Displays a menu of programs included on the Start menu
Documents	Displays a menu of the most recently opened and recently saved documents
Settings	Displays a menu of tools for selecting settings for your system
Search	Locates programs, files, folders, people, or computers on your computer network, or finds information and people on the Internet
Help	Provides Windows Help information by topic, alphabetical index, or search criteria
Run	Opens a program or file based on a location and filename that you type or select
Shut Down	Provides options to log off, shut down, or restart the computer

FIGURE A-4: Cascading menus

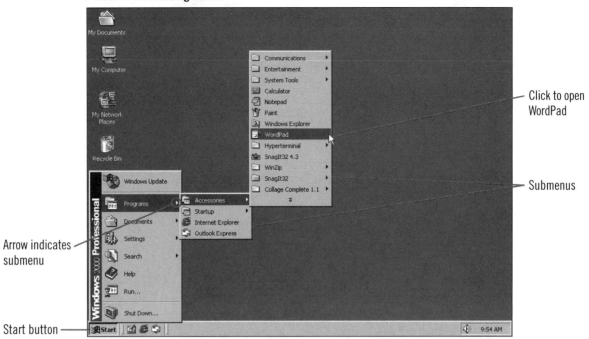

Click to open
WordPad

Submenus

Arrow indicates
submenu

Start button

FIGURE A-5: WordPad program window

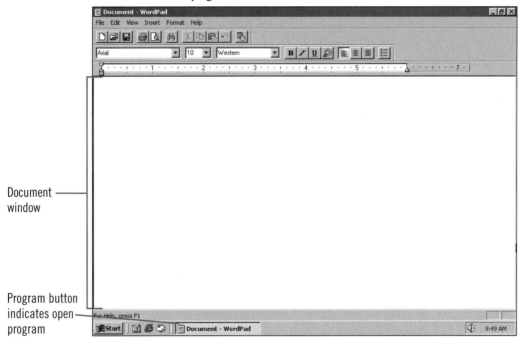

Document
window

Program button
indicates open
program

The Startup Folder

You can specify one or more programs to open each time you start Windows 2000 by placing shortcuts in the Startup Folder. This might be useful if you know you will be working in the same programs first thing every day. To place a program in the Startup Folder, click the Start button, point to Settings, then click

Taskbar & Start Menu. Click the Advanced tab of the Taskbar and Start Menu Properties dialog box, click Advanced, and then, in the Start Menu folder, locate the shortcut to the program you want to specify, and drag it to the Startup folder.

Moving and Resizing Windows

One of the powerful features of Windows is the ability to open more than one window or program at once. This means, however, that the desktop can get cluttered with the various programs and files you are using. You can keep your desktop organized by changing the size of a window or moving it. You can do this by clicking the sizing buttons in the upper-right corner of any window and dragging a corner or border of any window that does not completely fill the screen. Practice sizing and moving the WordPad window now.

Steps

1. **If the WordPad window does not already fill the screen, click the Maximize button in the WordPad window**
   When a window is **maximized**, it takes up the whole screen.

2. **Click the Restore button in the WordPad window**
   To **restore** a window is to return it to its previous size, as shown in Figure A-6. The Restore button only appears when a window is maximized.

3. **Position the pointer on the right edge of the WordPad window until the pointer changes to ↔, then drag the border to the right**
   The width of the window increases. You can size the height or width of a window by dragging any of the four sides individually.

> **QuickTip**
>
> You can resize windows by dragging any corner. You can also drag any border to make the window taller, shorter, wider, or narrower.

4. **Position the pointer in the lower-right corner of the WordPad window until the pointer changes to ↖, as shown in Figure A-6, then drag down and to the right**
   The height and width of the window increase proportionally when you drag a corner instead of a side. You can also position a restored window wherever you wish on the desktop by dragging its title bar. The **title bar** is the area along the top of the window that displays the file name and program used to create it.

5. **Drag the title bar on the WordPad window up and to the left, as shown in Figure A-6**
   The window is repositioned on the desktop. At times, you might wish to close a program window, yet keep the program running and easily accessible. You can accomplish this by minimizing a window.

> **QuickTip**
>
> If you have more than one window open and you want to quickly access something on the desktop, you can click the Show Desktop button on the Quick Launch toolbar. All open windows are minimized so the desktop is visible.

6. **In the WordPad window, click the Minimize button**
   When you **minimize** a window, it shrinks to a program button on the taskbar, as shown in Figure A-7. WordPad is still running, but it is out of your way.

7. **Click the WordPad program button on the taskbar to reopen the window**
   The WordPad program window reopens.

8. **Click the Maximize button in the upper-right corner of the WordPad window**
   The window fills the screen.

FIGURE A-6: Restored program window

Title bar

Sizing buttons

Drag to resize
height and width
proportionately

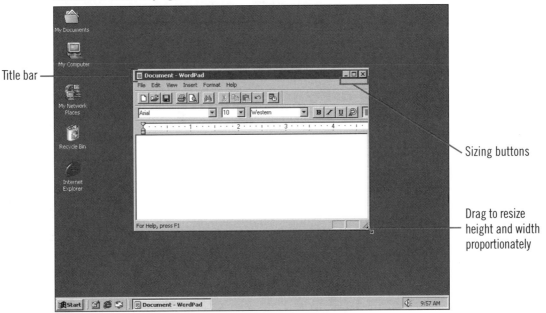

FIGURE A-7: Minimized program window

Indicates program
is running but not
in use

More about sizing windows

Keep in mind that many programs contain two sets of
sizing buttons: one that controls the program window
itself and another that controls the window for the
file with which you are working. The program sizing
buttons are located in the title bar and the file sizing
buttons are located below them. See Figure A-8. When
you minimize a file window within a program, the file
window is reduced to an icon in the lower-left corner
of the program window, but the size of the program
window remains intact.

FIGURE A-8: Program and file sizing buttons

Program window
sizing buttons

File window sizing
buttons

Using Menus, Keyboard Shortcuts, and Toolbars

A **menu** is a list of commands that you use to accomplish certain tasks. You've already used the Start menu to start WordPad. Each Windows program also has its own set of menus, which are located on the **menu bar** under the title bar. The menus organize commands into groups of related operations. See Table A-5 for a description of items on a typical menu. **Toolbar buttons** offer another method for executing menu commands; instead of clicking the menu and then the menu command, you simply click the button for the command. A **toolbar** is a set of buttons usually positioned below the menu bar in a Windows program. In Windows 2000, you can customize a toolbar by adding buttons to or removing buttons from toolbars to suit your preferences. ✎ You will open the Control Panel, then use a menu and toolbar button to change how the contents of the window appear, and then add and remove a toolbar button.

QuickTip

You now have two windows open: WordPad and the Control Panel. The Control Panel is the active window (or active program) because it is the one with which you are currently working. WordPad is inactive because it is open but you are not working with it. Working with more than one window at a time is called multitasking.

1. **Click the Start button on the taskbar, point to Settings, then click Control Panel**
The Control Panel window opens over the WordPad window. The **Control Panel** contains icons for various programs that allow you to specify how your computer looks and performs.

2. **Click View on the menu bar**
The View menu appears, listing the View commands, as shown in Figure A-9. On a menu, a **check mark** identifies a feature that is currently enabled or "on." To disable or turn "off" the feature, you click the command again to remove the check mark. A **bullet mark** can also indicate that an option is enabled. To disable a bulleted option, you must select another option in its place.

3. **Click Small Icons**
The icons are now smaller than they were before, taking up less room in the window.

4. **Press [Alt][V] to open the View menu, then press [T] to execute the Toolbars command**
The View menu appears again, and then the Toolbars submenu appears, with checkmarks next to the commands that are currently selected. You opened these menus using the keyboard. Notice that a letter in each command on the View menu is underlined. These are **keyboard navigation indicators**, indicating that you can press the underlined letter, known as a **keyboard shortcut**, instead of clicking to execute the command.

5. **Press [C] to execute the Customize command**
The Customize Toolbar dialog box opens. A dialog box is a window in which you make specifications for how you want a task performed; you'll learn more about working in a dialog box shortly. In the Customize Toolbar dialog box, you can add toolbar buttons to the current toolbar, or remove buttons already on the toolbar. The list on the right shows which buttons are currently on the toolbar, and the list on the left shows which buttons are available to add.

6. **Click the Favorites button in the Available toolbar buttons section, then click the Add button**
As shown in Figure A-10, the Favorites button is added to the Standard toolbar of the Control Panel window.

7. **Click Favorites in the Current toolbar buttons section, click the Remove button, then click Close on the Customize Toolbar dialog box**
The Favorites button disappears from the Standard toolbar, and the Customize Toolbar dialog box closes.

8. **On the Control Panel toolbar, click the Views button list arrow** ▦▾
Some toolbar buttons have an arrow, which indicates the button contains several choices. Clicking the button shows the choices.

QuickTip

When you rest the pointer over a button without clicking, a Screentip appears, telling you the name of the button.

9. **In the list of View choices, click Details**
The Details view includes a description of each program in the Control Panel.

Check mark

Menu bar

Commands in View menu

FIGURE A-9: Opening a menu

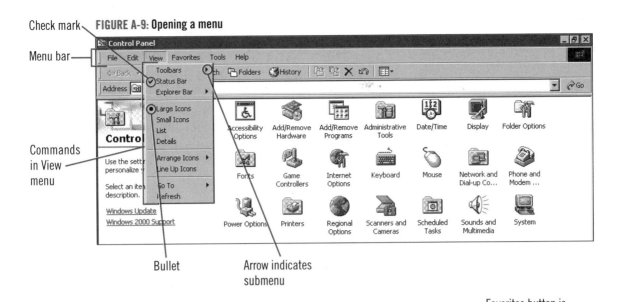

Bullet

Arrow indicates submenu

Favorites button is added to the toolbar

FIGURE A-10: Customize Toolbar dialog box

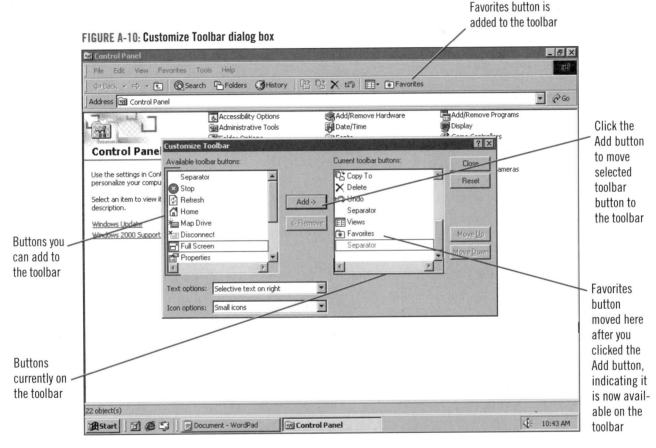

Click the Add button to move selected toolbar button to the toolbar

Buttons you can add to the toolbar

Favorites button moved here after you clicked the Add button, indicating it is now available on the toolbar

Buttons currently on the toolbar

TABLE A-5: Typical items on a menu

item	description	example
Dimmed command	Indicates the menu command is not currently available	Undo Ctrl+Z
Ellipsis	Opens a dialog box that allows you to select different or additional options	Save As...
Triangle	Opens a cascading menu containing an additional list of commands	Zoom ▶
Keyboard shortcut	Executes a command using the keyboard instead of the mouse	Paste Ctrl+V
Underlined letter	Indicates the letter to press for the keyboard shortcut	Print Preview

Windows 2000

Using Dialog Boxes

A **dialog box** is a window that opens when you choose a menu command that is followed by an ellipsis (…), or any command that needs more information before the program can carry out the command you selected. Dialog boxes open in other situations as well, such as when you open a program in the Control Panel. See Figure A-11 and Table A-6 for some of the typical elements of a dialog box. Practice using a dialog box to control your mouse settings.

Trouble?

If you can't see the Mouse icon, resize the Control Panel window.

1. In the Control Panel window, double-click the Mouse icon

The Mouse Properties dialog box opens, as shown in Figure A-12. **Properties** are characteristics of a specific computer element (in this case, the mouse) that you can customize. The options in this dialog box allow you to control the way the mouse buttons are configured, select the types of pointers that appear, choose the speed of the mouse movement on the screen, and specify what type of mouse you are using. **Tabs** at the top of the dialog box separate these options into related categories.

2. Click the Motion tab if necessary to make it the front-most tab

This tab contains three options for controlling the way your mouse moves. Under Speed, you can set how fast the pointer moves on the screen in relation to how you move the mouse. You drag a **slider** to specify how fast the pointer moves. Under Acceleration, you can click an **option button** to adjust how much your pointer accelerates as you move it faster. When choosing among option buttons, you can select only one at a time. Under Snap to default, there is a **check box**, which is a toggle for turning a feature on or off—in this case, for setting whether or not you want your mouse pointer to move to the default button in dialog boxes.

3. Under Speed, drag the slider all the way to the left for Slow, then move the mouse pointer across your screen

Notice how slowly the mouse pointer moves. After you select the options you want in a dialog box, you need to select a **command button**, which carries out the options you've selected. The two most common command buttons are OK and Cancel. Clicking OK accepts your changes and closes the dialog box; clicking Cancel leaves the original settings intact and closes the dialog box. The third command button in this dialog box is Apply. Clicking the Apply button accepts the changes you've made and keeps the dialog box open so that you can select additional options. Because you might share this computer with others, it's important to return the dialog box options back to the original settings.

QuickTip

You can also use the keyboard to carry out commands in a dialog box. Pressing [Enter] is the same as clicking OK; pressing [Esc] is the same as clicking Cancel.

4. Click Cancel

The original settings remain intact and the dialog box closes.

FIGURE A-11: Elements of a typical dialog box

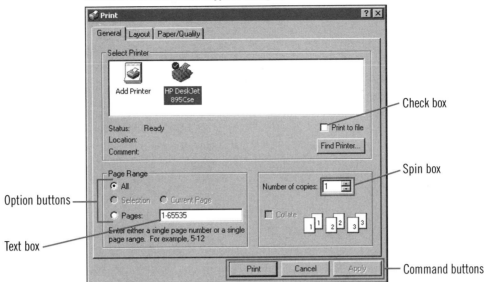

Option buttons

Text box

Check box

Spin box

Command buttons

FIGURE A-12: Mouse Properties dialog box

Tabs

Slider

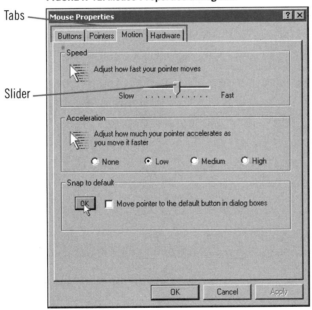

TABLE A-6: Typical items in a dialog box

item	description	item	description
Check box	A box that turns an option on (when the box is checked) and off (when it is unchecked)	List box	A box containing a list of items; to choose an item, click the list arrow, then click the desired item
Text box	A box in which you type text	Spin box	A box with two arrows and a text box; allows you to scroll in numerical increments or type a number
Option button	A small circle that you click to select a single dialog box option; you cannot check more than one option button in a list	Slider	A shape that you drag to set the degree to which an option is in effect
Command button	A rectangular button in a dialog box with the name of the command on it	Tab	A place in a dialog box where related commands and options are organized

Using Scroll Bars

When you cannot see all of the items available in a window, scroll bars appear on the right and/or bottom edges of the window. **Scroll bars** allow you to view the additional contents of the window. There are several ways you can scroll in a window. When you need to scroll only a short distance, you can use the scroll arrows. To scroll the window in larger increments, click in the scroll bar above or below the scroll box. Dragging the scroll box moves you quickly to a new part of the window. See Table A-7 for a summary of the different ways to use scroll bars. ▬▬ With the Control Panel window in Details view, you can use the scroll bars to view all of the items in this window.

Steps

1. **In the Control Panel window, drag the lower-right corner of the dialog box up toward the upper-left corner until the scroll bars appear, as shown in Figure A-13**
   Scroll bars appear only when the window is not large enough to include all the information. After you resize the dialog box, they appear along the bottom and right side of the dialog box. You may have to size your window smaller than the one in the figure for your scroll bars to appear.

2. **Click the down scroll arrow, as shown in Figure A-13**
   Clicking this arrow moves the view down one line.

3. **Click the up scroll arrow in the vertical scroll bar**
   Clicking this arrow moves the view up one line.

4. **Click anywhere in the area below the scroll box in the vertical scroll bar**
   The view moves down one window's height. Similarly, you can click in the scroll bar above the scroll box to move up one window's height.

5. **Drag the scroll box all the way down to the bottom of the vertical scrollbar**
   The view now includes the items that appear at the very bottom of the window.

6. **Drag the scroll box all the way up to the top of the vertical scroll bar**
   This view shows the items that appear at the top of the window.

7. **Click the area to the right of the scroll box in the horizontal scroll bar**
   The far right edge of the window comes into view. The horizontal scroll bar works the same as the vertical scroll bar.

8. **Click the area to the left of the scroll box in the horizontal scroll bar**
   You should return the Control Panel to its original settings.

9. **Maximize the Control Panel window, click the Views button list arrow** 🔳▾ **on the Control Panel toolbar, then click Large Icons**

FIGURE A-13: Scroll bars

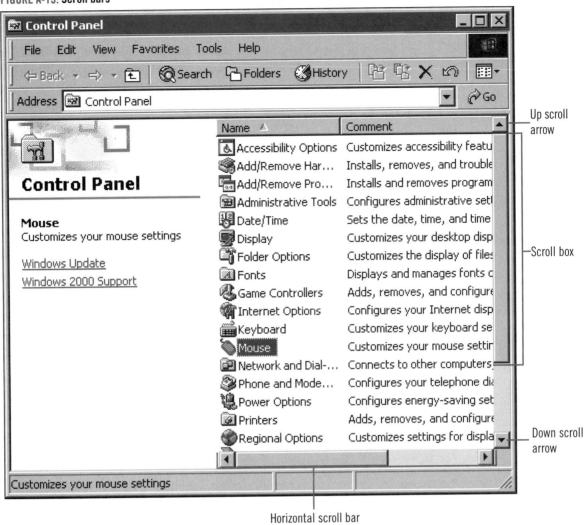

TABLE A-7: Using scroll bars in a window

to	do this
Move down one line	Click the down arrow at the bottom of the vertical scroll bar
Move up one line	Click the up arrow at the top of the vertical scroll bar
Move down one window height	Click in the area below the scroll box in the vertical scroll bar
Move up one window height	Click in the area above the scroll box in the vertical scroll bar
Move up a large distance in the window	Drag the scroll box up in the vertical scroll bar
Move down a large distance in the window	Drag the scroll box down in the vertical scroll bar
Move a short distance side-to-side in a window	Click the left or right arrows in the horizontal scroll bar
Move to the right one window width	Click in the area to the right of the scroll box in the horizontal scroll bar
Move to the left one window width	Click in the area to the left of the scroll box in the horizontal scroll bar
Move left or right a large distance in the window	Drag the scroll box in the horizontal scroll bar

Windows 2000

Using Windows Help

When you have a question about how to do something in Windows 2000, you can usually find the answer with a few clicks of your mouse. **Windows Help** works like a book stored on your computer, with a table of contents and an index to make finding information easier. Help provides guidance on many Windows features, including detailed steps for completing procedures, definitions of terms, lists of related topics, and search capabilities. You can browse or search for information in the Help window, or you can connect to a Microsoft Web site on the Internet for the latest technical support on Windows 2000. You can also access **context-sensitive help**, help specifically related to what you are doing, using a variety of methods such as right-clicking an object or using the question mark button in a dialog box. ▉ In this lesson, you get Help on starting a program. You also get information on the taskbar.

Steps 1234

1. **Click the Start button on the taskbar, then click Help**
   The Windows Help window opens with the Contents tab in front, as shown in Figure A-14. The Contents tab provides you with a list of Help categories. Each category contains two or more topics that you can see by clicking the book or the category next to it.

QuickTip

Click the Glossary category on the Contents tab to access definitions for hundreds of computer terms.

2. **Click the Contents tab if it isn't the front-most tab, click Working with Programs, then view the Help categories that are displayed**
   The Help window contains a selection of topics related to working with programs.

3. **Click Start a Program**
   Help information for this topic appears in the right pane, as shown in Figure A-15. **Panes** divide a window into two or more sections. At the bottom of the text in the right pane, you can click Related Topics to view a list of topics that may also be of interest to you. Some Help topics also allow you to view additional information about important words; these words are underlined, indicating that you can click them to display a pop-up window with the additional information.

4. **Click the underlined word taskbar, read the definition, then press [Enter] or click anywhere outside the pop-up window to close it**

5. **In the left pane, click the Index tab**
   The Index tab provides an alphabetical list of all the available Help topics, like an index at the end of a book. You can type a topic in the text box at the top of the pane. As you type, the list of topics automatically scrolls to try to match the word or phrase you type. You can also scroll down to the topic. In either case, the topic appears in the right pane.

6. **In the left pane, click the Search tab**
   You can use the Search tab to locate a Help topic using keywords. You enter a word or phrase in the text box and click List Topics; a list of matching topics appears below the text box. To view a topic, double-click it or select the topic, then click Display.

7. **In the left pane, click the Favorites tab**
   You can add the To Start a Program topic, or any other displayed topic, to the Favorites tab of the Help window by simply clicking the Favorites tab, then clicking the Add button.

8. **Click the Web Help button 🌐 on the toolbar**
   Information on the Web site for Windows 2000 Help appears in the right pane (a **Web site** is a document or related documents that contain highlighted words, phrases, and graphics that link to other sites on the Internet). To access online support or information, click one of the available options.

QuickTip

To get help on a specific Windows program, click Help on the program's menu bar.

9. **Click the Close button ☒ in the upper-right corner of the Windows Help window**
   The Help window closes.

FIGURE A-14: Windows Help window

Help toolbar

Help tabs

Click to view alphabetical list of Help topics

Click to search for words and phrases in Help topics

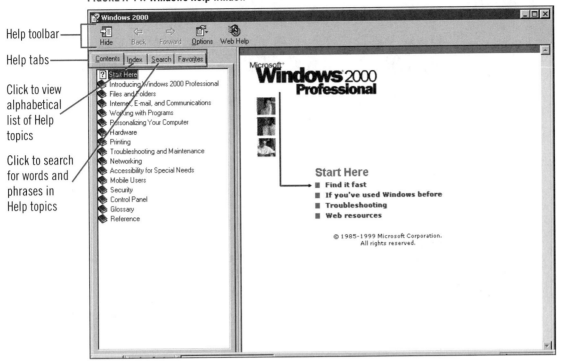

FIGURE A-15: Viewing a Help topic

Help topic

Pointer changes to hand pointer when a topic is selected

Left pane contains Help categories and topics

Right pane contains help on the topic you select

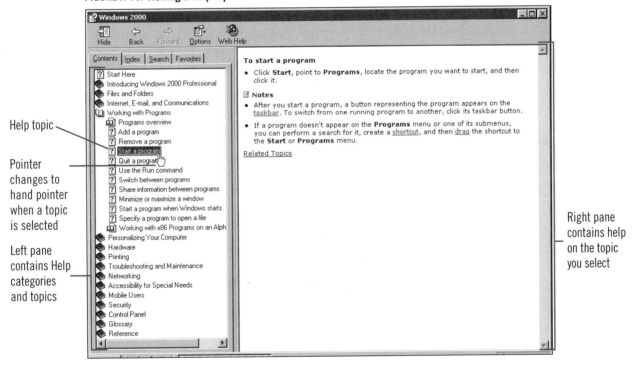

Context-sensitive help

To receive help in a dialog box, click the Help button in the upper-right corner of the dialog box; the mouse pointer changes to ▷?. Click the Help pointer on the item for which you need additional information. A pop-up window provides a brief explanation of the selected feature. You can also right-click the button on an item in a dialog box, then click the What's This? button to view the Help explanation.

Closing a Program and Shutting Down Windows

When you are finished working on your computer, you need to make sure you shut it down properly. This involves several steps: saving and closing all open files, closing all the open programs and windows, shutting down Windows, and finally, turning off the computer. If you turn off the computer while Windows is running, you could lose important data. To **close** programs, you can click the Close button in the window's upper-right corner or click File on the menu bar and choose either Close or Exit. To shut down Windows after all your files and programs are closed, click Shut Down from the Start menu, then select the desired option from the Shut Down dialog box, shown in Figure A-16. See Table A-8 for a description of shut down options. ✎ Close all your open files, windows, and programs, then exit Windows.

Steps

1. **In the Control Panel window, click the Close button ⊠ in the upper-right corner of the window**
   The Control Panel window closes.

2. **Click File on the WordPad menu bar, then click Exit**
   If you have made any changes to the open file, you will be prompted to save your changes before the program quits. Some programs also give you the option of choosing the Close command on the File menu in order to close the active file but leave the program open, so you can continue to work in it with a different file. Also, if there is a second set of sizing buttons in the window, the Close button on the menu bar will close the active file only, leaving the program open for continued use.

3. **If you see a message asking you to save changes to the document, click No**
   WordPad closes and you return to the desktop.

4. **Click the Start Button on the taskbar, then click Shut Down**
   The Shut Down Windows dialog box opens, as shown in Figure A-16. In this dialog box, you have the option to log off, shut down the computer, or restart the computer.

5. **Click the What do you want the computer to do? list arrow**

6. **If you are working in a lab, click the list arrow again and click Cancel to leave the computer running; if you are working on your own machine or if your instructor told you to shut down Windows, click Shut down, then click OK**

7. **If you see the message "It is now safe to turn off your computer," turn off your computer and monitor**
   On some computers, the power shuts off automatically, so you may not see this message.

FIGURE A-16: Shut Down Windows dialog box

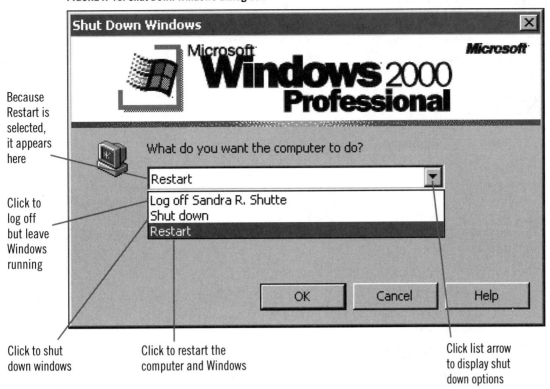

Because Restart is selected, it appears here

Click to log off but leave Windows running

Click to shut down windows

Click to restart the computer and Windows

Click list arrow to display shut down options

The Log Off command

To change users on the same computer quickly, you can choose the Log Off command from the Shut Down Windows dialog box. When you choose this command, the current user is logged off and Windows 2000 shuts down and automatically restarts, stopping at the point where you need to enter a password. When the new user enters a user name and password, Windows restarts and the desktop appears as usual.

TABLE A-8: Shut down options

shut down option	function	when to use it
Shut down	Prepares the computer to be turned off	When you are finished working with Windows and you want to shut off your computer
Restart	Restarts the computer and reloads Windows	When you want to restart the computer and begin working with Windows again (your programs might have frozen or stopped working)
Log off	Ends your session, then reloads Windows for another user	When you want to end your session but leave the computer running for another user

Practice

► Concepts Review

Identify each of the items labeled in Figure A-17.

FIGURE A-17

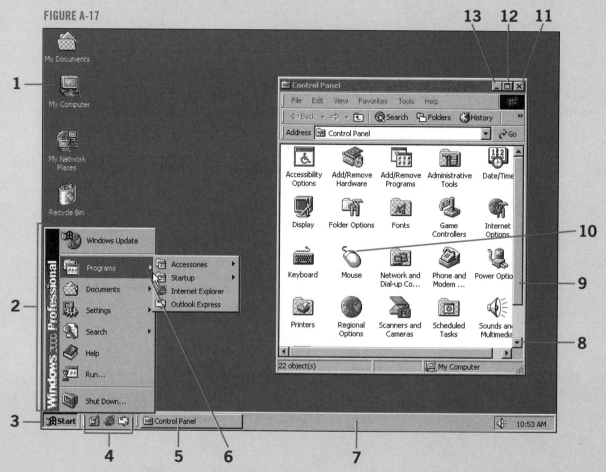

Match each of the statements with the term it describes.

14. Shrinks a window to a button on the taskbar
15. Shows the name of the window or program
16. The taskbar item you first click to start a program
17. Requests more information that you supply before carrying out command
18. Shows the Start button, Quick Launch toolbar, and any currently open programs
19. An input device that lets you point to and make selections
20. Graphic representation of program

a. Taskbar
b. Dialog box
c. Start button
d. Mouse
e. Title bar
f. Minimize button
g. Icon

Select the best answer from the list of choices.

21. The acronym GUI stands for
    a. Grayed user information.
    b. Group user icons.
    c. Graphical user interface.
    d. Group user interconnect.

22. **Which of the following is NOT provided by Windows 2000?**
    a. The ability to organize files
    b. Instructions to coordinate the flow of information among the programs, files, printers, storage devices, and other components of your computer system
    c. Programs that allow you to specify the operation of the mouse
    d. Spell checker for your documents

23. **All of the following are examples of using a mouse, EXCEPT**
    a. clicking the Maximize button.
    c. double-clicking to start a program.
    b. pressing [Enter].
    d. dragging the My Computer icon.

24. **The term for moving an item to a new location on the desktop is**
    a. pointing.   **b.** clicking.   **c.** dragging.   **d.** restoring.

25. **The Maximize button is used to**
    a. return a window to its previous size.
    c. scroll slowly through a window.
    b. expand a window to fill the computer screen.
    d. run programs from the Start menu.

26. **What appears if a window contains more information than can be viewed in the window?**
    a. Program icon   **b.** Cascading menu   **c.** Scroll bars   **d.** Check boxes

27. **A window is active when**
    a. you can only see its program button on the taskbar.
    c. it is open and you are currently using it.
    b. its title bar is dimmed.
    d. it is listed in the Programs submenu.

28. **You can exit Windows by**
    a. double-clicking the Control Panel application.
    b. double-clicking the Program Manager control menu box.
    c. clicking File, then clicking Exit.
    d. selecting the Shut Down command from the Start menu.

▶ Skills Review

1. **Start Windows and view the Active Desktop.**
   a. Turn on the computer, if necessary.
   b. After Windows starts, identify as many items on the desktop as you can, without referring to the lesson material.
   c. Compare your results to Figure A-1.

2. **Use the mouse.**
   a. Double-click the Recycle Bin icon.
   b. Drag the Recycle Bin window to the upper-right corner of the desktop.
   c. Right-click the title bar of the Recycle Bin, then click Close.

3. **Start a program.**
   a. Click the Start button on the taskbar, then point to Programs.
   b. Point to Accessories, then click Calculator (rest your pointer on the double arrows to display more menu commands if necessary).
   c. Minimize the Calculator window.

4. **Move and resize windows.**
   a. Drag the Recycle Bin icon to the bottom of the desktop.
   b. Double-click the My Computer icon to open the My Computer window.
   c. Maximize the window, if it is not already maximized.

    d. Restore the window to its previous size.

    e. Resize the window until you see the vertical scroll bar.

    f. Minimize the My Computer window.

    g. Drag the Recycle Bin back to the top of the desktop.

5. Use menus, keyboard shortcuts, and toolbars.

    a. Click the Start button on the taskbar, point to Settings, then click Control Panel.

    b. Click View on the menu bar, point to Toolbars, then click Standard Buttons to deselect the option and hide the toolbar.

    c. Redisplay the toolbar.

    d. Press [Alt][V] to display the View menu, then press [L] to view the Control Panel as a list.

    e. Note the change, then use keyboard shortcuts to change the view back.

    f. Click the Up One Level button to view My Computer.

    g. Click the Back button to return to the Control Panel.

    h. Click View, click Toolbars, then click Customize.

    i. Add a button to the toolbar, remove it, then close the Customize the Toolbar dialog box.

    j. Click the Restore button on the Control panel window.

6. Use dialog boxes.

    a. Double-click the Display icon, then click the Screen Saver tab.

    b. Click the Screen Saver list arrow, click any screen saver in the list, then view it in the Preview box above the list.

    c. Click the Effects tab.

    d. In the Visual effects section, click the Use large icons check box to select it, then click Apply.

    e. Note the change in the icons on the desktop and in the Control Panel window.

    f. Click the Use large icons check box to deselect it, click the Screen Saver tab, return the screen saver to its original setting, then click Apply.

    g. Click the Close button in the Display Properties dialog box, but leave the Control Panel open.

7. Use scroll bars.

    a. Click View on the Control Panel toolbar, then click Details.

    b. Resize the Control Panel window, if necessary, so that both scroll bars are visible.

    c. Drag the vertical scroll box down all the way.

    d. Click anywhere in the area above the vertical scroll box.

    e. Click the down scroll arrow until the scroll box is back at the bottom of the scroll bar.

    f. Drag the horizontal scroll box so you can read the descriptions for the icons.

8. Get Help.

    a. Click the Start button on the taskbar, then click Help.

    b. Click the Contents tab, then click Introducing Windows 2000 Professional.

    c. Click Tips for New Users, click the Use the Personalized Menus feature, then click Overview of Personalized Menus.

    d. Read the topic contents, then click Related Topics.

9. Close a program and shut down Windows.

    a. Click the Close button to close the Help topic window.

    b. Click File on the menu bar, then click Close to close the Control Panel window.

    c. Click the Calculator program button on the taskbar to restore the window.

    d. Click the Close button in the Calculator window to close the Calculator program.

    e. Click the My Computer program button on the taskbar, then click the Close button to close the window.

    f. If you are instructed to do so, shut down your computer.

▶ Independent Challenges

1. Windows 2000 has an extensive help system. In this independent challenge, you will use Help to learn about more Windows 2000 features and explore the help that's available on the Internet.

    a. Open Windows Help and locate help topics on adjusting the double-click speed of your mouse and displaying Web content on your desktop.

If you have a printer, print a Help topic for each subject. If you do not have a printer, write a summary of each topic.

    b. Follow these steps below to access help on the Internet. If you don't have Internet access, you can't do this step.

        i. Click the Web Help button on the toolbar.

        ii. Click the link <u>Windows 2000 home page</u>. A browser opens and prompts you to connect to the Internet if you are not already connected.

        iii. Write a summary of what you find.

        iv. Click the Close button in the title bar of your browser, then disconnect from the Internet and close Windows Help.

2. You may need to change the format of the clock and date on your computer. For example, if you work with international clients it might be easier to show the time in military (24-hour) time and the date with the day before the month. You can also change the actual time and date on your computer, to accomodate such things as time zone changes.

    a. Open the Control Panel window, then double-click the Regional Options icon.

    b. Click the Time tab to change the time to show a 24-hour clock rather than a 12-hour clock.

    c. Click the Date tab to change the Short date format to show the date, followed by the month, followed by the year (e.g., 30/3/01).

    d. Change the time to one hour later using the Date/Time icon in the Control Panel window.

    e. Return the settings to the original time and format, then close all open windows.

3. Calculator is a Windows program on the Accessories menu that you can use for calculations you need to perform while using the computer. Follow these guidelines to explore the Calculator and the Help that comes with it:

    a. Start the Calculator from the Accessories menu.

    b. Click Help on the menu bar, then click Help Topics. The Calculator Help window opens, showing several help topics.

    c. View the help topic on how to perform simple calculations, then print it if you have a printer connected.

    d. Open the Perform a scientific calculation category, then view the definition of a number system.

    e. Determine how many months you have to work to earn an additional week of vacation if you work for a company that provides one additional day of paid vacation for every 560 hours you work. (*Hint:* Divide 560 by the number of hours you work per month.)

    f. Close all open windows.

4. You can customize many Windows features to suit your needs and preferences. One way you do this is to change the appearance of the taskbar on the desktop. In this challenge, try the guidelines described to explore the different ways you can customize the appearance of the taskbar.

    a. Position the pointer over the top border of the taskbar. When the pointer changes shape, drag up an inch.

    b. Resize the taskbar back to its original size.

    c. Click the Start button on the taskbar, point to Settings, then click Taskbar & Start Menu.

    d. In the upper-right corner of the General tab, click the Help button, then click the first check box to view the pop-up window describing it. Repeat this for each check box.

    e. Click each check box and observe the effect in the preview area. (*Note:* Do not click OK.)

    f. Click Cancel.

▶ Visual Workshop

Use the skills you have learned in this unit to customize your desktop so it looks like the one in Figure A-18. Make sure you include the following:

- Calculator program minimized
- Vertical scroll bar in Control Panel window
- Large icons view in Control Panel window
- Rearranged icons on desktop; your icons may be different (*Hint:* If the icons *snap* back to where they were, they are set to be automatically arranged. Right-click a blank area of the desktop, point to Arrange Icons, then click Auto Arrange to deselect this option.)

Use the Print Screen key to make a copy of the screen, then print it from the Paint program. (To print from the Paint program, click the Start button on the taskbar, point to Programs, point to Accessories, then click Paint; in the Paint program window, click Edit on the menu bar, then click Paste; click Yes to fit the image on the bitmap, click the Print button on the toolbar, then click Print in the Print dialog box. See your instructor or technical support person for assistance.)

When you have completed this exercise, be sure to return your settings and desktop back to their original arrangement.

FIGURE A-18

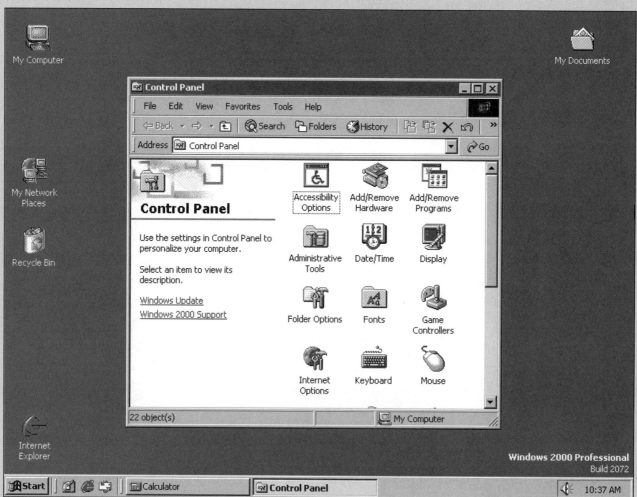

Working
with Programs, Files, and Folders

Objectives

► **Create and save a WordPad document**
► **Open, edit, and save an existing Paint file**
► **Work with multiple programs**
► **Understand file management**
► **View files and create folders with My Computer**
► **Move and copy files with My Computer**
► **Manage files with Windows Explorer**
► **Delete and restore files**
► **Create a shortcut on the desktop**

Most of your work on a computer involves using programs to create files. For example, you might use WordPad to create a resumé or Microsoft Excel to create a budget. The resumé and the budget are examples of **files**, electronic collections of data that you create and save on a disk. In this unit, you learn how to work with files and the programs you use to create them. You create new files, open and edit an existing file, and use the Clipboard to copy and paste data from one file to another. You also explore the file management features of Windows 2000, using My Computer and Windows Explorer. Finally, you learn how to work more efficiently by managing files directly on your desktop.

Creating and Saving a WordPad Document

As with most programs, when you start WordPad a new, blank **document** (or file) opens. To create a new file, such as a memo, you simply begin typing. Your work is automatically stored in your computer's **random access memory (RAM)** until you turn off your computer, at which point anything stored in the computer's RAM is erased. To store your work permanently, you must save your work as a file on a disk. You can save files either on an internal **hard disk**, which is built into your computer, usually the C: drive, or on a removable 3.5" or 5.25" **floppy disk**, which you insert into a drive on your computer, usually the A: or B: drive. Before you can save a file on a floppy disk, the disk must be formatted. (See the Appendix, "Formatting a Disk," or your instructor or technical support person for more information.) When you name a file, you can use up to 255 characters including spaces and punctuation in the File Name box, using either upper- or lowercase letters. ✎ In this lesson, you start WordPad and create a file that contains the text shown in Figure B-1. Then you save the file to Project Disk 1.

1. **Click the Start button** on the taskbar, point to **Programs**, point to **Accessories**, click **WordPad**, then click the **Maximize button** if the window does not fill your screen
   The WordPad program window opens with a new, blank document in the document window. The blinking **insertion point** I indicates where the text you type will appear.

Trouble?

If you make a mistake, press [Backspace] to delete the character to the left of the insertion point.

2. **Type Memo**, then press **[Enter]**
   Pressing [Enter] inserts a new line and moves the insertion point to the next line.

3. **Press [Enter]** again, then type the remaining text shown in Figure B-1, pressing **[Enter]** at the end of each line
   Now that the text is entered, you can format it. **Formatting** changes the appearance of text to make it more readable or attractive.

QuickTip

Double-click to select a word or triple-click to select a paragraph.

4. **Click to the left of the word Memo**, drag the mouse to the right to highlight the word, then release the mouse button
   The text is now **selected** and any action you make will be performed on the text.

5. **Click the Center button** 🖹 on the Formatting toolbar, then click the **Bold button** on the Formatting toolbar
   The text is centered and bold.

6. **Click the Font Size list arrow** `10 ▾`, then click **16** in the list
   A **font** is a particular shape and size of type. The text is enlarged to 16 point. One **point** is 1/72 of an inch in height. Now that your memo is complete, you are ready to save it to your Project Disk.

7. **Click File** on the menu bar, then click **Save As**
   The Save As dialog box opens, as shown in Figure B-2. In this dialog box, you specify where you want your file saved and also give your document a name.

Trouble?

This unit assumes that the Project Disk is in the A: drive. If not, substitute the correct drive any time you are instructed to use the 3½ Floppy (A:) drive. See your instructor or technical support person for help.

8. **Click the Save in list arrow**, and then click **3½ Floppy (A:)**, or whichever drive contains your Project Disk 1
   The drive containing your Project Disk is now active, meaning that any files currently on the disk appear in the list of folders and files and that the file you save now will be saved on the disk in this drive.

9. **Click the text** in the File name text box, type **Memo**, then click **Save**
   Your memo is now saved as a WordPad file with the name "Memo" on your Project Disk. Notice that the WordPad title bar contains the name of the file.

FIGURE B-1: Text to enter in WordPad

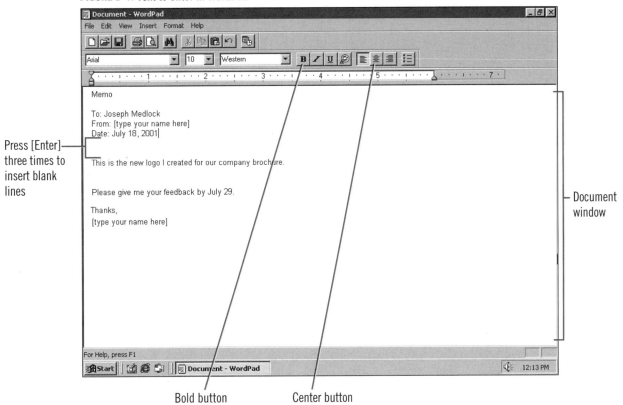

Press [Enter] three times to insert blank lines

Document window

Bold button   Center button

FIGURE B-2: Save As dialog box

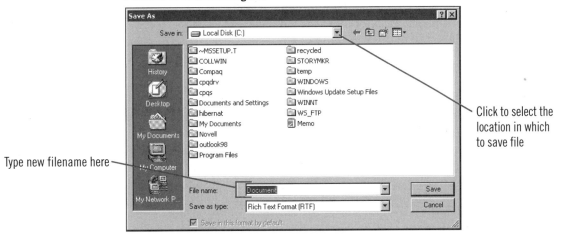

Click to select the location in which to save file

Type new filename here

Creating a new document

When you want to create a new document in WordPad once the program is already open and another document is active, you can click the New button on the Standard toolbar. A dialog box opens from which you can choose to create a new Rich Text, Word 6, Text, or Unicode Text document. **Rich Text** documents, the WordPad default document format, can include text formatting and tabs, and be available for use in a variety of other word-processing programs; **Word 6** documents can be opened, edited, and enhanced in Microsoft Word version 6.0 or later without conversion; **Text** documents can be used in numerous other programs because they contain no formatting; and **Unicode Text** documents can contain text from any of the world's writing systems, such as Roman, Greek, and Chinese. You select one of the options by clicking it, and then clicking OK.

Windows 2000

Opening, Editing, and Saving an Existing Paint File

Sometimes you create files from scratch, but often you may want to use a file you or someone else has already created; to do so, you need to **open** the file. Once you open a file, you can **edit** it, or make changes to it, such as adding or deleting text. After editing a file, you can save it with the same filename, which means that you no longer will have the file in its original form, or you can save it with a different filename, so that the original file remains unchanged. ✒️ In this lesson, you use **Paint**, a drawing program that comes with Windows 2000, to open a file, edit it by changing a color, then save the file with a new filename to leave the original file unchanged.

1. Click the **Start button** on the taskbar, point to **Programs**, point to **Accessories**, click **Paint**, then click the **Maximize button** if the window doesn't fill the screen
   The Paint program opens with a blank work area. If you wanted to create a file from scratch, you would begin working now.

2. Click **File** on the menu bar, then click **Open**
   The Open dialog box works similarly to the Save As dialog box.

3. Click the **Look in list arrow**, then click **3½ Floppy (A:)**
   The Paint files on your Project Disk 1 are listed in the Open dialog box, as shown in Figure B-3.

QuickTip

You can also open a file by double-clicking it in the Open dialog box.

4. Click **Win B-1** in the list of files, and then click **Open**
   The Open dialog box closes and the file named Win B-1 opens. Before you make any changes to a file, you should save it with a new filename, so that the original file is unchanged.

5. Click **File** on the menu bar, then click **Save As**

6. Make sure **3½ Floppy (A:)** appears in the Save in text box, select the text **Win B-1** in the File name text box if necessary, type **Logo**, then click **Save**
   The Logo file appears in the Paint window, as shown in Figure B-4. Because you saved the file with a new name, you can edit it without changing the original file. You will now use buttons in the **Tool Box**, a toolbar of illustration tools available in Windows Paint, and the **Color Box**, a palette of colors from which you can choose, to modify the graphic.

7. Click the **Fill With Color button** 🎨 in the Tool Box, then click the **Blue color box**, which is the fourth from the right in the first row
   Notice how clicking a button in the Tool Box changes the mouse pointer. Now when you click an area in the image, it will be filled with the color you selected in the Color Box. See Table B-1 for a description of the tools in the Tool Box.

8. Move the pointer into the **white area that represents the sky** until the pointer changes to 🎨, then click
   The sky is now blue.

9. Click **File** on the menu bar, then click **Save**
   The change you made is saved to disk.

FIGURE B-3: **Open dialog box**

List of files

Look in list arrow;
click to select the
location of the file

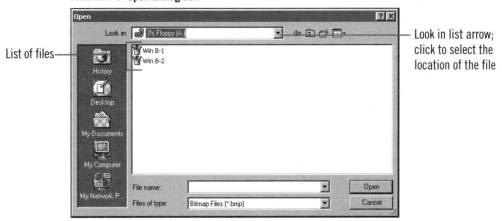

FIGURE B-4: **Paint file saved with new filename**

Name of file
appears in
title bar

Tool Box

Choose this
blue color

Color box

Sky area to fill
with color

Fill With Color
button

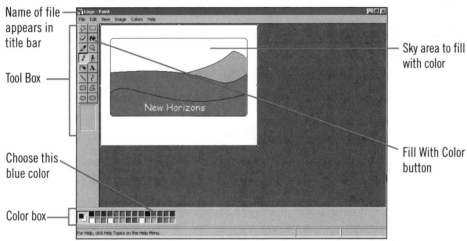

TABLE B-1: **Paint Tool Box buttons**

tool	description	tool	description
Free-Form Select button	Selects a free-form section of the picture to move, copy, or edit	**Airbrush button**	Produces a circular spray of dots
Select button	Selects a rectangular section of the picture to move, copy, or edit	**Text button**	Inserts text into the picture
Eraser button	Erases a portion of the picture using the selected eraser size and foreground color	**Line button**	Draws a straight line with the selected width and foreground color
Fill With Color button	Fills closed shape or area with the current drawing color	**Curve button**	Draws a wavy line with the selected width and foreground color
Pick Color button	Picks up a color off the picture to use for drawing	**Rectangle button**	Draws a rectangle with the selected fill style; also used to draw squares by holding down [Shift] while drawing
Magnifier button	Changes the magnification; lists magnifications under the toolbar	**Polygon button**	Draws polygons from connected straight-line segments
Pencil button	Draws a free-form line one pixel wide	**Ellipse button**	Draws an ellipse with the selected fill style; also used to draw circles by holding down [Shift] while drawing
Brush button	Draws using a brush with the selected shape and size	**Rounded Rectangle button**	Draws rectangles with rounded corners using the selected fill style; also used to draw rounded squares by holding down [Shift] while drawing

Working with Multiple Programs

A powerful feature of Windows is its capability to run more than one program at a time. For example, you might be working with a document in WordPad and want to search the Internet to find the answer to a question. You can start your browser, a program designed to access information on the Internet, without closing WordPad. When you find the information, you can leave your browser open and switch back to WordPad. Each open program is represented by a program button on the taskbar that you click to switch between programs. You can also copy data from one file to another, (whether the files were created with the same Windows program or not), using the **Clipboard**, a temporary area in your computer's memory, and the Cut, Copy, and Paste commands. See Table B-2 for a description of these commands. In this lesson, you copy the logo graphic you worked with in the previous lesson into the memo you created in WordPad.

Steps

Trouble?

If some parts of the image or text are outside the dotted rectangle, click anywhere outside the image, then select the image again, making sure you include everything.

1. **Click the Select button** ▫ **on the Tool Box, and then drag a rectangle around the entire graphic**
   When you release the mouse button, the dotted rectangle surrounds the selected area, as shown in Figure B-5. Make sure the entire image is inside the rectangle. The next action you take affects the entire selection.

2. **Click Edit on the menu bar, and then click Copy**
   The logo is copied to the Clipboard. When you **copy** an object onto the Clipboard, the object remains in its original location and is also available to be pasted into another location.

QuickTip

To switch between programs using the keyboard, press and hold down [Alt], press [Tab] until the program you want is selected, then release [Alt].

3. **Click the WordPad program button on the taskbar**
   WordPad becomes the active program.

4. **Click in the first line below the line that ends "for our company brochure."**
   The insertion point indicates where the logo will be pasted.

5. **Click the Paste button** 🖻 **on the WordPad toolbar**
   The contents of the Clipboard, in this case the logo, are pasted into the WordPad file, as shown in Figure B-6.

6. **Click the Save button** 🖫 **on the toolbar**
   The Memo file is saved with the logo inserted.

7. **Click the WordPad Close button**
   Your WordPad document and the WordPad program close. Paint is now the active program.

8. **Click the Paint Close button; if you are prompted to save changes, click Yes**
   Your Paint document and the Paint program close. You return to the desktop.

TABLE B-2: Overview of cutting, copying and pasting

Toolbar button	function	keyboard shortcut
✂ Cut	Removes selected information from a file and places it on the Clipboard	[Ctrl][X]
🖻 Copy	Places a copy of selected information on the Clipboard, leaving the file intact	[Ctrl][C]
🖻 Paste	Inserts whatever is currently on the Clipboard into another location within the same file, or in a different file	[Ctrl][V]

FIGURE B-5: Selecting the logo to copy and paste into the Memo file

Select button

Dotted line indicates selected area

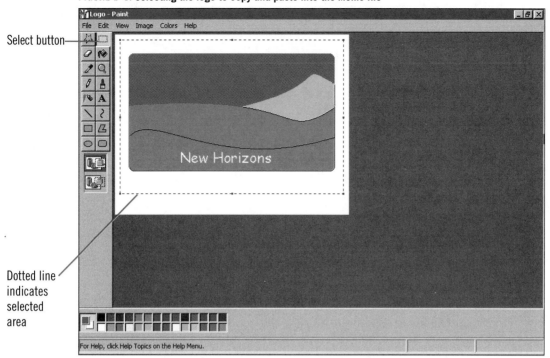

FIGURE B-6: Memo with pasted logo

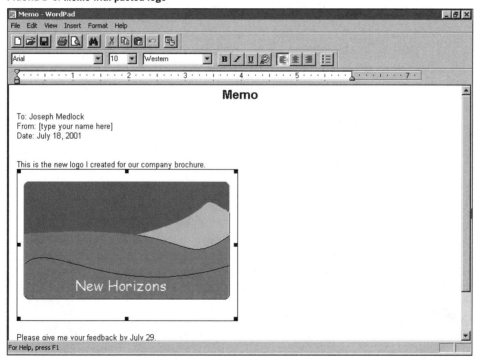

Understanding File Management

After you have created and saved numerous files using various programs, **file management**, the process of organizing and keeping track of all of your files, can be a challenge. Fortunately, Windows 2000 provides tools to keep everything organized so you can easily locate the files you need, move files to new locations, and delete files you no longer need. There are two main tools for managing your files: My Computer and Windows Explorer. In this lesson, you preview the ways you can use My Computer and Windows Explorer to manage your files.

Details

Windows 2000 gives you the ability to:

 Create folders in which you can save your files

Folders are areas on a floppy disk or hard disk in which you can store files. For example, you might create a folder for your documents and another folder for your graphic files. Folders can also contain additional folders, which creates a more complex structure of folders and files, called a **file hierarchy**. See Figure B-7 for an example of how files can be organized.

Examine and organize the hierarchy of files and folders

You can use either My Computer or Windows Explorer to see the overall structure of your files and folders. By examining your file hierarchy with these tools, you can better organize the contents of your computer and adjust the hierarchy to meet your needs. Figures B-8 and B-9 illustrate how My Computer and Windows Explorer list folders and files.

Copy, move, and rename files and folders

If you decide that a file belongs in a different folder, you can move it to another folder. You can also rename a file if you decide a different name is more descriptive. If you want to keep a copy of a file in more than one folder, you can copy it to new folders.

Delete files and folders you no longer need, as well as restore files you delete accidentally

Deleting files and folders you are sure you don't need frees up disk space and keeps your file hierarchy more organized. The **Recycle Bin**, a space on your computer's hard disk that stores deleted files, allows you to restore files you deleted by accident. To free up disk space, you should occasionally empty the Recycle Bin by deleting the files permanently from your hard drive.

Locate files quickly with the Windows 2000 Search feature

As you create more files and folders, you may forget where you placed a certain file or you may forget what name you used when you saved a file. With Search, you can locate files by providing only partial names or other factors, such as the file type (for example, a WordPad document or a Paint graphic) or the date the file was created or modified.

Use shortcuts

If a file or folder you use often is located several levels down in your file hierarchy (in a folder within a folder, within a folder), it might take you several steps to access it. To save time accessing the files and programs you use frequently, you can create shortcuts to them. A **shortcut** is a link that gives you quick access to a particular file, folder, or program.

FIGURE B-7: Sample file hierarchy

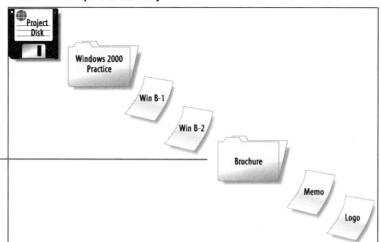

In this hierarchy,
Brochure folder is a
subfolder of
Windows 2000
Practice folder

FIGURE B-8: Brochure folder shown in My Computer

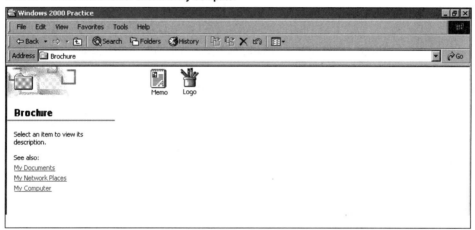

FIGURE B-9: Brochure folder shown in Windows Explorer

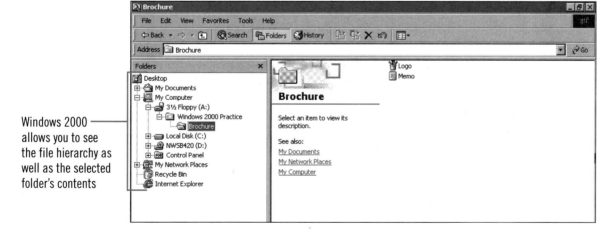

Windows 2000
allows you to see
the file hierarchy as
well as the selected
folder's contents

Viewing Files and Creating Folders with My Computer

My Computer shows the contents of your computer, including files, folders, programs, disk drives, and printers. You can click the icons representing these various parts of your computer to view their contents or properties. You can manage your files using the My Computer menu bar and toolbar. See Table B-3 for a description of the toolbar buttons. ◄━━ In this lesson, you begin by using My Computer to move around in your computer's file hierarchy, then you create two new folders on your Project Disk 1 for the files you created.

Steps 1 2 3 4

Trouble?

If you do not see the toolbar, click View on the menu bar, point to Toolbars, and then click Standard Buttons. If you do not see the Address Bar, click View, point to Toolbar, and then click Address Bar.

1. **Double-click the My Computer icon** on your desktop, then click the **Maximize button** if the My Computer window does not fill the screen
   My Computer opens and displays the contents of your computer, as shown in Figure B-10. Your window may contain icons for different folders, drives, and printers.

2. **Make sure your Project Disk 1 is in the floppy disk drive, then double-click the 3½ Floppy (A:) icon**
   The contents of your Project Disk 1 appear in the window. These are the project files and the files you created using WordPad and Paint. Each file is represented by an icon, which indicates the program that was used to create the file. If Microsoft Word is installed on your computer, the Word icon appears for the WordPad files; if not, the WordPad icon appears.

Trouble?

This book assumes that your hard drive is the C: drive. If yours differs, substitute the appropriate drive for the C: drive wherever it is referenced. See your instructor or technical support person for assistance.

3. Click the **Address list arrow** on the Address Bar, as shown in Figure B-10, then click **Local Disk (C:)** or the letter for the main hard drive on your computer
   The window changes to show the contents of your hard drive. The **Address Bar** allows you to open and view a drive, folder, or even a Web page. You can also type in the Address Bar to go to a different drive, folder, or Web page. For example, typing "C:\" will display drive C:; typing "E:\Personal Letters" will display the Personal Letters folder on the E: drive, and typing "http://www.microsoft.com" opens Microsoft's Web site if your computer is connected to the Internet.

4. Click the **Back button** on the toolbar
   The Back button displays the previous location, in this case, your Project Disk.

5. Click the **Views button** 📊 on the toolbar, then click **Details**
   Details view shows not only the files and folders, but also the sizes of the files, the types of files, folders, or drives and the date the files were last modified.

6. Click 📊 , then click **Thumbnails**
   This view offers less information but provides a preview of graphics and a clear view of the contents of the disk.

7. Click **File** on the menu bar, point to **New**, then click **Folder**
   A new folder is created on your Project Disk 1, as shown in Figure B-11. The folder is called "New Folder" by default. It is selected and ready to be renamed. You can also create a new folder by right-clicking in the blank area of the My Computer window, clicking New, then clicking Folder.

QuickTip

To rename a folder, click the folder to select it, click the folder name so it is surrounded by a rectangle, type the new folder name, then press [Enter].

8. Type **Windows 2000 Practice**, then press **[Enter]**
   Choosing descriptive names for your folders helps you remember their contents.

9. Double-click the **Windows 2000 Practice folder**, repeat Step 7 to create a new folder in the Windows 2000 Practice folder, type **Brochure** for the folder name, then press **[Enter]**

10. Click the **Up button** 📁 to return to your Project Disk 1

FIGURE B-10: My Computer window

Menu bar

Toolbar

Address bar

Status bar

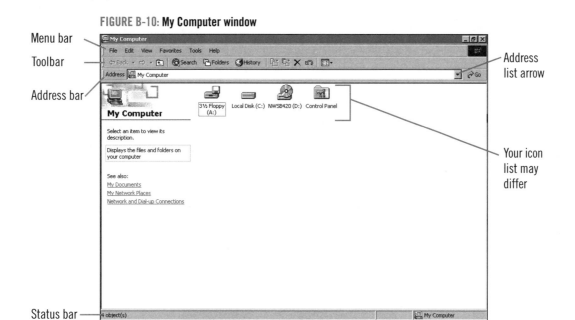

Address list arrow

Your icon list may differ

FIGURE B-11: Creating a new folder

Back button

Folder is located on disk in the A: drive

Type new name here

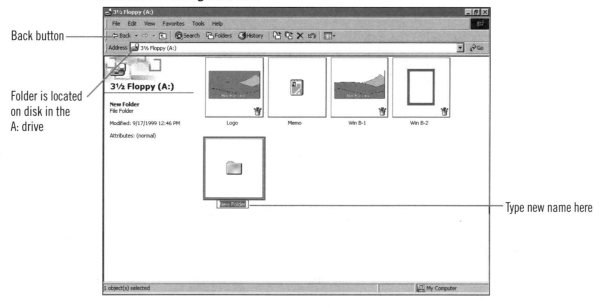

TABLE B-3: Buttons on the My Computer toolbar

button	function
⇐	Moves back to the previous location you have already visited
⇒	Moves forward to the previous location you have already visited
🔼	Moves up one level in the file hierarchy
📋	Opens the Browse For Folder dialog box, to move the selected file to a new location
📋	Opens the Browse For Folder dialog box, to copy the selected file to a new location
↶	Undoes the most recent My Computer operation
✕	Deletes a folder or file permanently
▦▾	Lists the contents of My Computer using different views

Moving and Copying Files with My Computer

You can move a file or folder from one location to another using a variety of methods in My Computer or Windows Explorer. If the file or folder and the location to which you want to move it are both visible on the desktop, you can simply drag the item from one location to the other. You can also use the cut, copy, and paste commands on the Edit menu or the corresponding buttons on the toolbar. Finally you can right-click the file or folder and choose the Send to command to "send" it to another location—most often a floppy disk for **backing up** files. Backup copies are made in case you have computer trouble, which may cause you to lose files. ✒ In this lesson, you move your files into the folder you created in the last lesson.

Steps 1 2 3 4

1. **Click View, point to Arrange Icons, then click by Name**
   In this view, folders are listed first in alphabetical order, followed by files, also in alphabetical order.

2. **Click the Win B-1 file, hold down the mouse button and drag the file onto the Windows 2000 Practice folder, as shown in Figure B-12, then release the mouse button**
   Win B-1 is moved into the Windows 2000 Practice folder.

3. **Double-click the Windows 2000 Practice folder and confirm that it contains the Win B-1 file as well as the Brochure folder**

4. **Click the Up button ⬆ on the My Computer toolbar, as shown in Figure B-12**
   You return to your Project Disk. The Up button shows the next level up in the folder hierarchy.

5. **Click the Logo file, press and hold down [Shift], then click the Memo file**
   Both files are selected. Table B-4 describes methods for selecting multiple objects.

6. **Click the Move To button ⬆ on the 3½ Floppy (A:) toolbar**
   The filenames turn gray, and the Browse For Folder dialog box opens, as shown in Figure B-13.

7. **Click the plus sign ⊞ next to My Computer if you do not see 3½ Floppy (A:) listed, double-click the 3½ Floppy (A:) drive, double-click the Windows 2000 Practice folder, double-click the Brochure folder, then click OK**
   The two files are moved to the Brochure folder. Only the Windows 2000 Practice folder and the Win B-2 file remain.

8. **Click the Close button in the 3½ Floppy (A:) window**

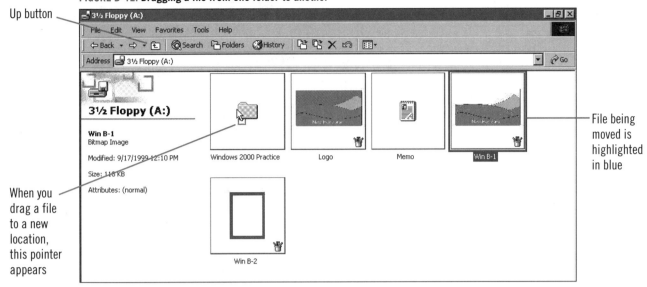
FIGURE B-12: Dragging a file from one folder to another

Up button

When you
drag a file
to a new
location,
this pointer
appears

File being
moved is
highlighted
in blue

FIGURE B-13: Moving files

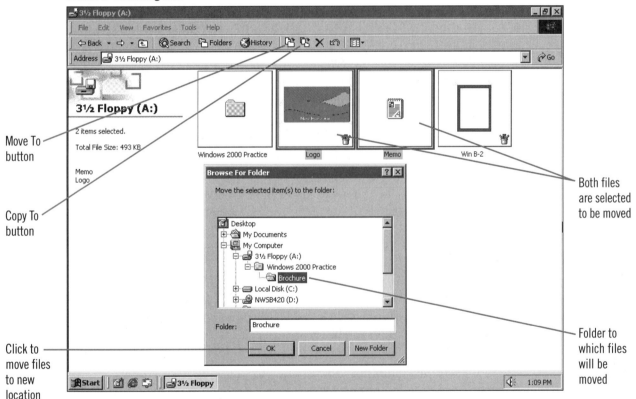

Move To
button

Copy To
button

Click to
move files
to new
location

Both files
are selected
to be moved

Folder to
which files
will be
moved

TABLE B-4: Techniques for selecting multiple files and folders

to select	do this
Individual objects not grouped together	Click the first object you want to select, then press and hold down [Ctrl] as you click each additional object you want to add to the selection
Objects grouped together	Click the first object you want to select, then press and hold down [Shift] as you click the last object in the list of objects you want to select; all the objects listed between the first and last objects are selected

Unit B

Windows 2000

Managing Files with Windows Explorer

As with My Computer, you can use Windows Explorer to copy, move, delete, and rename files and folders. However, Windows Explorer is more powerful than My Computer: it allows you to see the overall structure of the contents of your computer or network, (the file hierarchy), while you work with individual files and folders within that structure. This means you can work with more than one computer, folder, or file at once. ◢◣ In this lesson, you copy a folder from your Project Disk 1 onto the hard drive and then rename the folder.

Steps

Trouble?

If you do not see the toolbar, click View on the menu bar, point to Toolbars, then click Standard Buttons. If you do not see the Address Bar, click View, point to Toolbars, then click Address Bar.

1. **Click the Start button, point to Programs, point to Accessories, click Windows Explorer, then click the Maximize button if the Windows Explorer window doesn't already fill the screen**
   Windows Explorer opens, as shown in Figure B-14. The window is divided into two areas called **panes**. The left pane, called the **Explorer Bar**, displays the drives and folders on your computer in a hierarchy. The right pane displays the contents of whatever drive or folder is currently selected in the left pane. Each pane has its own set of scroll bars, so that changing what you can see in one pane won't affect what you can see in the other. Like My Computer, Windows Explorer has a menu bar, toolbar, and Address Bar.

2. **Click View on the menu bar, then click Details if it is not already selected**
   Remember that a bullet point next to a command on the menu bar indicates that it's selected.

Trouble?

If you cannot see the A: drive, you may have to click the plus sign (+) next to My Computer to view the available drives on your computer.

3. **In the left pane, scroll to and click 3½ Floppy (A:)**
   The contents of your Project Disk 1 appear in the right pane.

4. **In the left pane, click the plus sign (+) next to 3½ Floppy (A:)**
   You can click the plus sign (+) or minus sign (-) next to any item in the left pane to show or hide the different levels of the file hierarchy, so that you don't always have to look at the entire structure of your computer or network. A plus sign (+) next to a computer, drive, or folder indicates there are additional folders within that object. A minus sign (-) indicates that all the folders of the next level of hierarchy are shown. Clicking the + displays (or "expands") the next level; clicking the - hides (or "collapses") them.

QuickTip

When neither a + nor a – appears next to an icon, it means that the item does not have any folders in it, although it may have files, which you can see listed in the right pane by clicking the icon.

5. **In the left pane, double-click the Windows 2000 Practice folder**
   The contents of the Windows 2000 Practice folder appear in the right pane of Windows Explorer, as shown in Figure B-15. Double-clicking an item in the left pane that has a + next to it displays its contents in the right pane and also expands the next level in the hierarchy in the left pane.

Trouble?

If you are working in a lab setting, you may not be able to add items to your hard drive. Skip Steps 6, 7, and 8 if you are unable to complete them.

6. **In the left pane, drag the Windows 2000 Practice folder on top of the C: drive icon, then release the mouse button**
   When you drag files or folders to a different drive, they are copied rather than moved. The Windows 2000 Practice folder and the files in it are copied to the hard disk.

7. **In the left pane, click the C: drive icon**
   The Windows 2000 Practice folder should now appear in the list of folders in the right pane. You may have to scroll to see it. Now you should rename the folder so you can distinguish the original folder from the copy.

QuickTip

You can also rename a selected file by pressing [F2], or using the Rename command on the File menu.

8. **Right-click the Windows 2000 Practice folder in the right pane, click Rename in the pop-up menu, type Practice Copy, then press [Enter]**

FIGURE B-14: Windows Explorer window

Left pane, also known as Explorer Bar

Your list of folders and files will vary

Contents of the C: drive

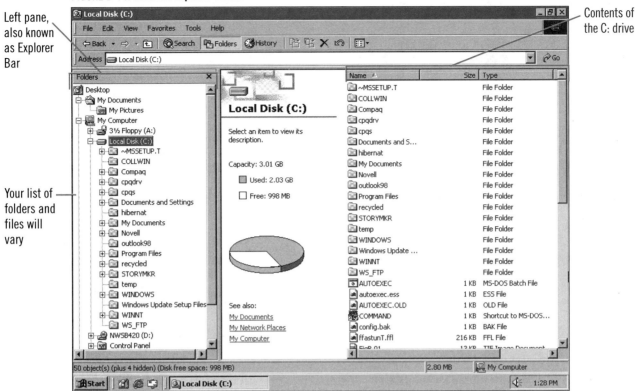

FIGURE B-15: Contents of Windows 2000 Practice folder

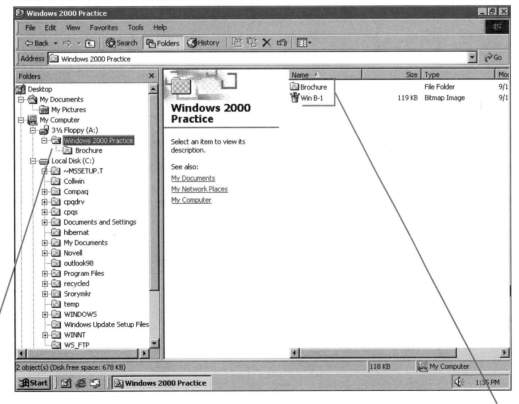

Windows 2000 Practice folder selected in left pane

Contents of Windows 2000 Practice folder appear in right pane

Deleting and Restoring Files

To save disk space and manage your files more effectively, you should **delete** (or remove) files you no longer need. Because files deleted from your hard drive are stored in the Recycle Bin until you remove them permanently by emptying the Recycle Bin, you can restore any files you might have deleted accidentally. However, if you delete a file from your floppy disk it will not be stored in the Recycle Bin—it will be permanently deleted. See Table B-5 for an overview of deleting and restoring files. There are many ways to delete files and folders from the My Computer and Windows Explorer windows, as well as from the Windows 2000 desktop. ◆━━ In this lesson, you delete a file by dragging it to the Recycle Bin, restore it, and delete a folder by using the Delete command in Windows Explorer.

Steps 1 2 3 4

1. **Click the Restore button** 🗗 **on the Windows Explorer title bar**
   You should be able to see the Recycle Bin icon on your desktop. If you can't see it, resize or move the Windows Explorer window until it is visible. See Figure B-16.

2. **If necessary, scroll until you see the Practice Copy folder in the right pane of Windows Explorer**

QuickTip

If you are unable to delete the file, it might be because your Recycle Bin is full, or too small, or the properties have been changed so that files are not stored in the Recycle Bin but are deleted instead. See your instructor or technical support person for assistance.

3. **Drag the Practice Copy folder from the right pane to the Recycle Bin on the desktop, as shown in Figure B-16, then click Yes to confirm the deletion if necessary**
   The folder no longer appears in Windows Explorer because you have moved it to the Recycle Bin.

4. **Double-click the Recycle Bin icon on the desktop**
   The Recycle Bin window opens, as shown in Figure B-17. Depending on the number of files already deleted on your computer, your window might look different. Use the scroll bar if you can't see the files.

5. **Click Edit on the Recycle Bin menu bar, then click Undo Delete**
   The Practice Copy folder is restored and should now appear in the Windows Explorer window. You might need to minimize your Recycle Bin window if it blocks your view of Windows Explorer, and you might need to scroll to the bottom of the right pane to find the restored folder.

6. **Click the Practice Copy folder in the right pane, click the Delete button** ☒ **on the Windows Explorer toolbar (resize the window as necessary to see the button), then click Yes**
   When you are sure you no longer need files you've moved into the Recycle Bin, you can empty the Recycle Bin. You won't do this now, in case you are working on a computer that you share with other people. But, when you're working on your own machine, simply right-click the Recycle Bin icon, then click Empty Recycle Bin in the pop-up menu.

7. **Close the Recycle Bin**
   If you minimized the Recycle Bin in Step 4, click its program button to open the Recycle Bin window, and then click the Close button.

FIGURE B-16: **Dragging a folder to delete it**

Drag the
folder here

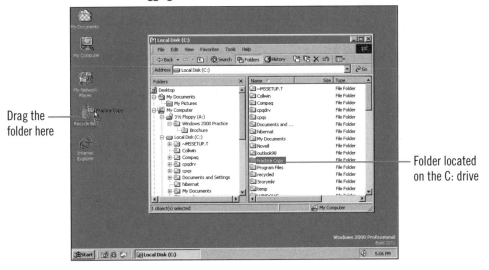

Folder located
on the C: drive

FIGURE B-17: **Recycle Bin window**

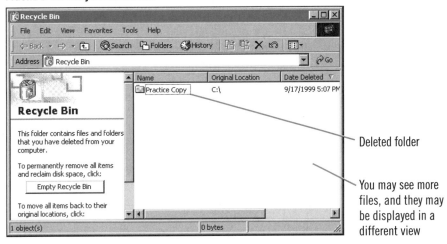

Deleted folder

You may see more
files, and they may
be displayed in a
different view

TABLE B-5: **Methods for deleting and restoring files**

ways to delete a file	ways to restore a file from the Recycle Bin
Select the file, then click the Delete button on the toolbar	Click the Undo button on the toolbar
Select the file, then press [Delete]	Select the file, click File, then click Restore
Right-click the file, then click Delete on the pop-up menu	Right-click the file, then click Restore
Drag the file to the Recycle Bin	Drag the file from the Recycle Bin to any other location

Customizing your Recycle Bin

You can set your Recycle Bin according to how you like to delete and restore files. For example, if you do not want files to go to the Recycle Bin but rather want them to be immediately and permanently deleted, right-click the Recycle Bin, click Properties, then click the Do Not Move Files to the Recycle Bin check box. If you find that the Recycle Bin fills up too fast and you are not ready to delete the files permanently, you can increase the amount of disk space devoted to the Recycle Bin by moving the Maximum Size of Recycle Bin slider to the right. This, of course, reduces the amount of disk space you have available for other things. Also, you can choose not to have the Confirm File Delete dialog box open when you send files to the Recycle Bin. See your instructor or technical support person before changing any of the Recycle Bin settings.

Windows 2000

Creating a Shortcut on the Desktop

When you frequently use a file, folder, or program that is located several levels down in the file hierarchy, you may want to create a shortcut to the object. You can place the shortcut on the desktop or in any other location, such as a folder, that you find convenient. To open the file, folder, or program using the shortcut, double-click the icon. ◤━━━ In this lesson, you use Windows Explorer to create a shortcut on your desktop to the Memo file.

Steps 1 2 3 4

1. In the left pane of the Windows Explorer window, click the **Brochure folder**
The contents of the Brochure folder appear in the right pane.

2. In the right pane, right-click the **Memo file**
A pop-up menu appears, as shown in Figure B-18.

3. Click **Create Shortcut** in the pop-up menu
The file named Shortcut to Memo file appears in the right pane. Now you need to move it to the desktop so that it will be accessible whenever you need it.

Trouble?

Make sure to use the right mouse button in Step 4. If you used the left mouse button by accident, right-click the Shortcut to Memo file in the right pane of Windows Explorer, click Delete, and repeat Step 4.

4. Click the **Shortcut to Memo file** with the right-mouse button, then drag the **shortcut** to an empty area of the desktop
Dragging an icon using the left mouse button copies it. Dragging an icon using the right mouse button gives you the option to copy it, move it, or create a shortcut to it. When you release the mouse button a pop-up menu appears.

5. Click **Move Here** in the pop-up menu
A shortcut to the Memo file now appears on the desktop, as shown in Figure B-19. You might have to move or resize the Windows Explorer window to see it.

6. Double-click the **Shortcut to Memo file icon**
WordPad starts and the Memo file opens (if you have Microsoft Word installed on your computer, it will start and open the file instead). Using a shortcut eliminates the many steps involved in starting a program and locating and opening a file.

7. Click the **Close button** in the WordPad or Word title bar
Now you should delete the shortcut icon in case you are working in a lab and share the computer with others.

QuickTip

Deleting a shortcut deletes only the link; it does not delete the original file or folder to which it points.

8. On the desktop, click the **Shortcut to Memo file**, press **[Delete]**, then click **Yes** to confirm the deletion
The shortcut is removed from the desktop and is now in the Recycle Bin.

9. Close all windows, then shut down Windows

FIGURE B-18: **Creating a shortcut**

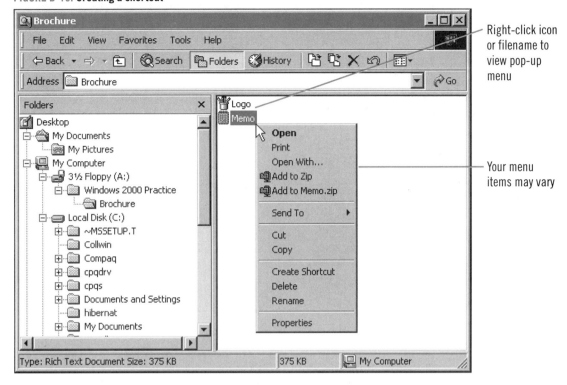

Right-click icon or filename to view pop-up menu

Your menu items may vary

FIGURE B-19: **Shortcut on desktop**

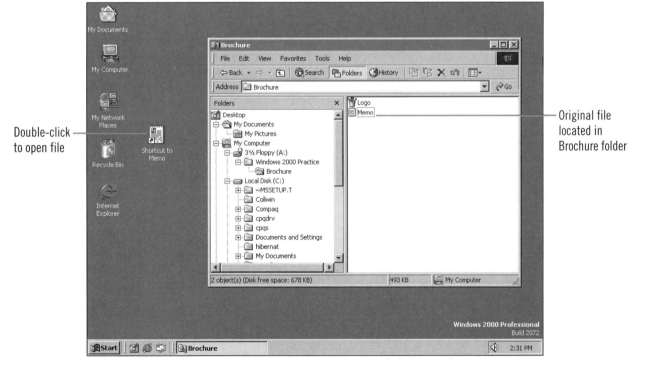

Double-click to open file

Original file located in Brochure folder

Adding shortcuts to the Start menu

If you do not want your desktop to get cluttered with icons but you would still like easy access to certain files, programs, and folders, you can create a shortcut on the Start menu. Drag the file, program, or folder that you want to add to the Start menu from the Windows Explorer window to the Start button. The file, program, or folder will appear on the first level of the Start menu.

Practice

► Concepts Review

Label each of the elements of the Windows Explorer window shown in Figure B-20.

FIGURE B-20

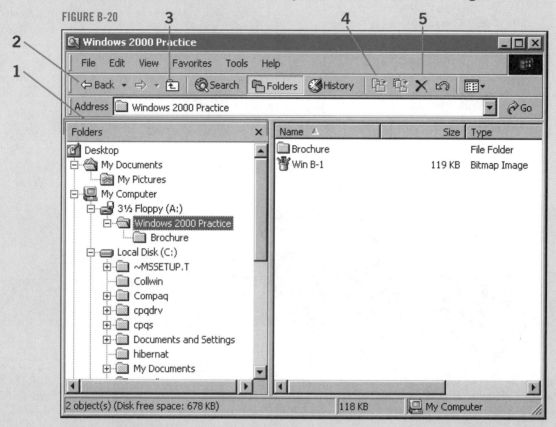

Match each of the statements with the term it describes.

6. Electronic collections of data
7. Your computer's temporary storage area
8. Temporary location of information you wish to paste into another program
9. Storage areas on your hard drive for files, folders, and programs
10. Structure of files and folders

a. RAM
b. Folders
c. Files
d. File hierarchy
e. Clipboard

Select the best answer from the list of choices.

11. To prepare a floppy disk to save your files, you must first do which of the following?
    a. Copy work files to the disk
    b. Format the disk
    c. Erase all the files that might be on the disk
    d. Place the files on the Clipboard
12. You can use My Computer to
    a. create a drawing of your computer.
    b. view the contents of a folder.
    c. change the appearance of your desktop.
    d. add text to a WordPad file.
13. Which of the following best describes WordPad?
    a. A program for organizing files
    b. A program for performing financial analysis
    c. A program for creating basic text documents
    d. A program for creating graphics

14. **Which of the following is NOT a way to move files from one folder to another?**
    a. Open the file and use the Save As command to save the file in a new location
    b. In My Computer or the Windows Explorer, drag the selected file to the new folder
    c. Use the Move To button on the Standard toolbar in the My Computer or the Windows Explorer window
    d. Use the [Ctrl][X] and [Ctrl][V] keyboard shortcuts while in the My Computer or the Windows Explorer window

15. **In which of the following can you view the hierarchy of drives, folders, and files in a split pane window?**
    a. Windows Explorer
    b. Programs
    c. My Computer
    d. WordPad

16. **To restore files that you have sent to the Recycle Bin,**
    a. click File, then click Empty Recycle Bin.
    b. click Edit, then click Undo Delete.
    c. click File, then click Undo.
    d. You cannot retrieve files sent to the Recycle Bin.

17. **To select files that are not grouped together, select the first file, then**
    a. press [Shift] while selecting the second file.
    b. press [Alt] while selecting the second file.
    c. press [Ctrl] while selecting the second file.
    d. click on the second file.

18. **Pressing [Backspace]**
    a. deletes the character to the right of the cursor.
    b. deletes the character to the left of the cursor.
    c. moves the insertion point one character to the right.
    d. deletes all text to the left of the cursor.

19. **The size of a font is measured in**
    a. centimeters.
    b. points.
    c. places.
    d. millimeters.

20. **The Back button on the My Computer toolbar**
    a. starts the last program you used.
    b. displays the next level of the file hierarchy.
    c. backs up the currently selected file.
    d. displays the last location you visited.

▶ Skills Review

Use Project Disk 2 to complete the exercises in this section.

1. **Create and save a WordPad file.**
   a. Start Windows, then start WordPad.
   b. Type **My Drawing Ability**.
   c. Press [Enter] three times.
   d. Save the document as *Drawing Ability* to your Project Disk 2.

2. **Open, edit, and save an existing Paint file.**
   a. Start Paint and open the file Win B-2 on your Project Disk 2.
   b. Inside the picture frame, use the ellipses tool to create a circle filled with purple and then use the rectangle tool to place a square filled with yellow inside the circle.
   c. Save the picture as *First Unique Art* to your Project Disk 2.

3. **Work with multiple programs.**
   a. Select the entire graphic and copy it to the Clipboard, then switch to WordPad.
   b. Place the insertion point in the last blank line, paste the graphic into your document, then deselect the graphic.
   c. Save the changes to your WordPad document.
   d. Switch to Paint.
   e. Using the Fill With Color button, change the color of a filled area of your graphic.
   f. Save the revised graphic with the new name *Second Unique Art* to Project Disk 2.
   g. Select the entire graphic and copy it to the Clipboard.
   h. Switch to WordPad, move the insertion point to the line below the graphic by clicking below the graphic and press [Enter], type **This is another version of my graphic.** below the first picture, then press [Enter].

   i. Paste the second graphic under the text you just typed.

   j. Save the changed WordPad document as *Two Drawing Examples* to your Project Disk 2.

   k. Exit Paint and WordPad.

4. View files and create folders with My Computer.

   a. Open My Computer.

   b. Double-click the drive that contains your Project Disk 2.

   c. Create a new folder on your Project Disk 2 by clicking File, New, then Folder, and name the new folder *Review*.

   d. Open the folder to display its contents (it is empty).

   e. Use the Address Bar to view your hard drive, usually (C:).

   f. Create a folder on the hard drive called *Temporary*, then use the Back button to view the Review folder.

   g. Create two new folders in it, one named *Documents* and the other named *Artwork*.

   h. Click the Forward button as many times as necessary to move up in the file hierarchy and view the contents of the hard drive.

   i. Change the view to Details.

5. Move and copy files with My Computer.

   a. Use the Address Bar to view your Project Disk 2.

   b. Use the [Shift] key to select *First Unique Art* and *Second Unique Art*, then cut and paste them into the Artwork folder.

   c. Use the Back button as many times as necessary to view the contents of Project Disk 2.

   d. Select the two WordPad files, *Drawing Ability* and *Two Drawing Examples*, then move them into the Review folder.

   e. Open the Review folder, select the two WordPad files again, then drag them into the Documents folder.

6. Manage files with Windows Explorer.

   a. Open Windows Explorer and view the contents of the Artwork folder in the right pane.

   b. Select the two Paint files.

   c. Drag the two Paint files from the Artwork folder to the Temporary folder on the hard drive to copy them.

   d. View the contents of the Documents folder in the right pane.

   e. Select the two WordPad files.

   f. Repeat Step c to copy the files to the Temporary folder on the hard drive.

   g. View the contents of the Temporary folder in the right pane to verify that the four files are there.

7. Delete and restore files and folders.

   a. Resize the Windows Explorer window so you can see the Recycle Bin icon on the desktop, then scroll in Windows Explorer so you can see the Temporary folder in the left pane.

   b. Delete the Temporary folder from the hard drive by dragging it to the Recycle Bin.

   c. Click Yes if necessary to confirm the deletion.

   d. Open the Recycle Bin, restore the Temporary folder and its files to your hard disk, and then close the Recycle Bin. (*Note:* If your Recycle Bin is empty, your computer is set to automatically delete items in the Recycle Bin.)

   e. Delete the Temporary folder again by pressing [Delete]. Click Yes if necessary to confirm the deletion.

8. Create a shortcut on the desktop.

   a. Use the left pane of Windows Explorer to locate the Windows folder on your hard drive. Select the folder to view its contents in the right pane. (*Note:* If you are in a lab setting, you may not have access to the Windows folder.)

   b. In the right pane, scroll through the list of objects until you see a file called Explorer.

   c. Drag the Explorer file with the right mouse button to the desktop to create a shortcut.

   d. Close Windows Explorer.

   e. Double-click the new shortcut to make sure it starts Windows Explorer. Then close Windows Explorer again.

   f. Delete the shortcut for Windows Explorer and exit Windows.

▶ Independent Challenges

If you are doing all of the Independent Challenges, you may need to use additional floppy disks. Label the first new disk Project Disk 3, and the next Project Disk 4.

1. You have decided to start a bakery business and you want to use Windows 2000 to organize the files for the business.

   a. Create two new folders on your Project Disk 3, one named *Advertising* and one named *Customers*.

   b. Use WordPad to create a letter inviting new customers to the open house for the new bakery, then save it as *Open House Letter* and place it in the Customers folder.

   c. Use WordPad to create a list of five tasks that need to get done before the business opens (such as purchasing equipment, decorating the interior, and ordering supplies), then save it as *Business Plan* to your Project Disk 3, but don't place it in a folder.

   d. Use Paint to create a simple logo for the bakery, save it as *Bakery Logo*, and then place it in the Advertising folder.

   e. Print the file Bakery Logo, then delete it from your Project Disk 3.

2. On your computer's hard drive, create a folder called *IC2*. Follow the guidelines listed here to create the file hierarchy shown in Figure B-21.

   a. Start WordPad, create a new file that contains a list. Save the file as *To Do List* to your Project Disk 3 (Project Disk 4 if you are out of space on Project Disk 3).

   b. Start My Computer and copy the Open House Letter file on your Project Disk 3 to the IC2 folder. Rename the file *Article*.

   c. Copy the Memo file again to the IC2 folder on your hard drive and rename the second copy of the file *Article Two*.

   d. Use My Computer to copy any Paint file to the IC2 folder and rename the file *Sample Logo*, then delete the Sample Logo file.

   e. Copy the To Do List from your Project Disk 3 to the IC2 folder and rename the file *Important List*.

   f. Move the files into the folders shown in Figure B-21.

   g. Copy the IC2 folder to your Project Disk 3. Then delete the IC2 folder on your hard drive. Using the Recycle Bin, restore the file called IC2. To remove all your work on the hard drive, delete this folder again.

FIGURE B-21

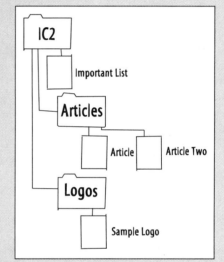

3. With Windows 2000, you can access the Web from My Computer and Windows Explorer, allowing you to search for information located not only on your computer or network, but also on any computer on the Internet.

   a. Start Windows Explorer, then click in the Address Bar so the current location (probably your hard drive) is selected, type **www.microsoft.com**, then press [Enter].

   b. Connect to the Internet if necessary. The Microsoft Web page appears in the right pane of Windows Explorer.

   c. Click in the Address Bar, then type **www.course.com**, press [Enter], and then wait a moment while the Course Technology Web page opens.

   d. Make sure your Project Disk is in the floppy disk drive, then click 3½ Floppy (A:) in the left pane.

   e. Click the Back button list arrow, then click Welcome to Microsoft's Homepage.

   f. Capture a picture of your desktop by pressing [Print Screen] located on the upper-right side of your keyboard. (This stores the picture on the Clipboard.) Open the Paint program, paste the contents of the Clipboard into the drawing window, then print it.

   g. Close Paint without saving your changes.

   h. Close Windows Explorer and disconnect from the Internet.

4. Create a shortcut to the drive that contains your Project Disk 3. Then capture a picture of your desktop showing the new shortcut by pressing [Print Screen], located on the upper-right side of your keyboard. The picture is stored temporarily on the Clipboard. Then open the Paint program and paste the contents of the Clipboard into the drawing window. Click No when asked to enlarge the Bitmap. Print the screen, close Paint without saving your changes, then delete the shortcut when you are finished.

▶ Visual Workshop

Recreate the screen shown in Figure B-22, which contains the Brochure window in My Computer, two shortcuts on the desktop, and two open files. Press [Print Screen] to make a copy of the screen, (a copy of the screen is placed on the Clipboard), open Paint, click Paste to paste the screen picture into Paint, then print the Paint file.

FIGURE B-22

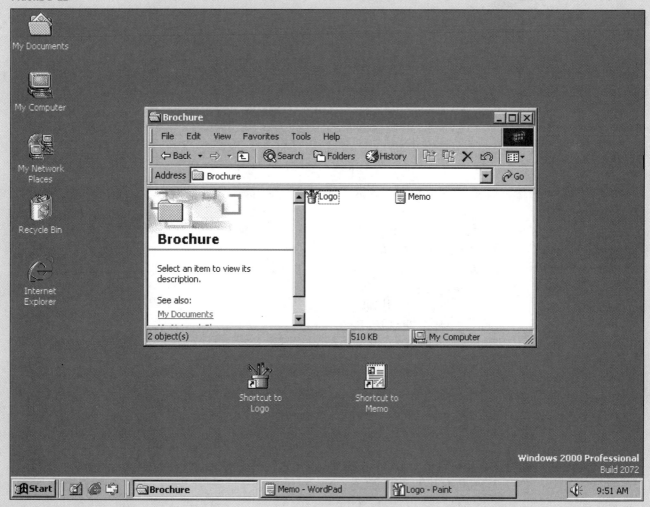

Getting
Started with Word 2002

Objectives

- ► **Understand word processing software**
- ► **Start Word 2002**
- ► **Explore the Word program window**
- ► **Start a document**
- ► **Save a document**
- ► **Print a document**
- ► **Use the Help system**
- ► **Close a document and exit Word**

Microsoft Word 2002 is a word processing program that makes it easy to create a variety of professional-looking documents, from simple letters and memos to newsletters, research papers, Web pages, business cards, resumes, financial reports, and other documents that include multiple pages of text and sophisticated formatting. In this unit, you will explore Word's editing and formatting features and learn how to start Word and create a document. Alice Wegman is the marketing manager at MediaLoft, a chain of bookstore cafés that sells books, music, and videos. Alice familiarizes herself with Word and uses it to create a memo to the marketing staff. You will work with Alice as she creates her memo.

Word 2002

Understanding Word Processing Software

A **word processing program** is a software program that includes tools for entering, editing, and formatting text and graphics. Microsoft Word is a powerful word processing program that allows you to create and enhance a wide range of documents quickly and easily. Figure A-1 shows the first page of a report created using Word and illustrates some of the Word features you can use to enhance your documents. The electronic files you create using Word are called **documents**. One of the benefits of using Word is that document files are stored on a disk, making them easy to transport and revise. Alice needs to write a memo to the marketing staff to inform them of an upcoming meeting. Before beginning her memo, she explores Word's editing and formatting capabilities.

You can use Word to accomplish the following tasks:

► **Type and edit text**

Word's editing tools make it simple to insert and delete text in a document. You can add text to the middle of an existing paragraph, replace text with other text, undo an editing change, and correct typing, spelling, and grammatical errors with ease.

► **Copy and move text from one location to another**

Using Word's more advanced editing features you can copy or move text from one location and insert it in a different location in a document. You also can copy and move text between documents. Being able to copy and move text means you don't have to retype text that is already entered in a document.

► **Format text and paragraphs with fonts, colors, and other elements**

Word's sophisticated formatting tools allow you to make the text in your documents come alive. You can change the size, style, and color of text, add lines and shading to paragraphs, and enhance lists with bullets and numbers. Using text-formatting features creatively helps you highlight important ideas in your documents.

► **Format and design pages**

Word's page-formatting features give you power to design attractive newsletters, create powerful resumes, and produce documents such as business cards, CD labels, and books. You can change the paper size and orientation of your documents, add headers and footers to pages, organize text in columns, and control the layout of text and graphics on each page of a document.

► **Enhance documents with tables, charts, diagrams, and graphics**

Using Word's powerful graphic tools you can spice up your documents with pictures, photographs, lines, shapes, and diagrams. You also can illustrate your documents with tables and charts to help convey your message in a visually interesting way.

► **Create Web pages**

Word's Web page design tools allow you to create documents that others can read over the Internet or an intranet. You can enhance Web pages with themes and graphics, add hyperlinks, create online forms, and preview Web pages in your Web browser.

► **Use Mail Merge to create form letters and mailing labels**

The Word Mail Merge feature allows you to easily send personalized form letters to many different people. You can also use Mail Merge to create mailing labels, directories, e-mail messages, and many other types of documents.

FIGURE A-1: A report created using Word

Format the size and appearance of text

Insert graphics

Create columns of text

Add bullets to lists

Create tables

Add headers to every page

Align text in paragraphs evenly

Add lines

Create charts

Add page numbers

MediaLoft Marketing Report, April 2003

MediaLoft Book Buyer Survey

In an effort to develop an economic profile of the MediaLoft book buyers, the marketing department hired the market research firm Takeshita Consultants, Inc. to create and administer a survey of the MediaLoft customer base. A secondary goal of the survey was to identify the areas in which MediaLoft can improve its service and products in the book department. Over 20,000 people completed the survey, which was distributed at MediaLoft stores, the Chicago Book Fair, the Modern Language Association annual meeting, the San Diego Literary Festival, and other events.

Book-buyer Profile

A typical MediaLoft book-buyer is a 42-year-old professional with an annual household income between $40,000 and $60,000. He or she has graduated from college and has one child. The typical book-buyer works in the city and owns a home in an urban or suburban area.

- 42% graduated from college.
- 32% have a graduate level degree.
- 26% have completed high school.
- 60% earn more than $40,000 per year.
- 8% earn more than $70,000 per year.
- 60% are employed as professionals.
- 20% work in clerical/service industries.
- 20% work in trades.

Survey Methods

The survey was distributed to purchasing and non-purchasing customers at MediaLoft stores during January and February 2003. Surveys were distributed at other events as they were held. The table below shows the distribution of surveys by location and by sex. Roughly equal numbers of surveys were completed at the eight MediaLoft stores.

Survey Location	Male	Female
MediaLoft stores	6,657	7,801
Chicago Book Fair	1,567	1,238
MLA annual meeting	563	442
SD Literary Festival	398	487
Other	865	622
Total	**10,050**	**10,590**
	Grand Total	**20,640**

Purchasing Habits

Respondents report they purchase one or two books a month. 80% purchase books online, but 68% prefer to shop for reading material in bookstores.

Preferred Genres

14% 25% 18% 16% 19% 8%

■ Fiction   ■ Non-Fiction
■ Biography/Memoir   ■ Technical
□ Professional   ■ Children's

Customer Satisfaction

On the whole, MediaLoft book customers gave the book department a favorable review. Customers rated the quality of book offerings as excellent, the quantity of titles as very good, and the subject coverage as excellent. Equally favorable ratings were given to the sales staff and the physical appearance of MediaLoft stores. Book-buyers did express interest in seeing a wider selection of non-fiction titles and deeper discounts for computer and professional titles. The organization and variety of titles in the children's and juvenile departments could also be improved.

1▶

Planning a document

Before you create a new document, it's a good idea to spend time planning it. Identify the message you want to convey, the audience for your document, and the elements, such as tables or charts, you want to include. You should also think about how you want your document to sound and look—is it a business letter, which should be written in a pleasant, but serious tone and have a formal appearance, or are you creating a flyer that must be colorful, eye-catching, and fun to read?

The purpose and audience for your document will determine the appropriate design. Planning the layout and design of a document involves deciding how to organize the text, selecting the fonts to use, identifying the graphics to include, and selecting the formatting elements that will enhance its message and appeal. For longer documents, such as newsletters, it can be useful to sketch the layout and design of each page before you begin.

Word 2002

Starting Word 2002

Before starting Word, you must start Windows by turning on your computer. Once Windows is running, you can start Word or any other application by using the Start button on the Windows taskbar. You can also start Word by clicking the Word icon on the Windows desktop or the Word icon on the Microsoft Office Shortcut bar, if those items are available on your computer. Alice uses the Start button to start Word so she can familiarize herself with its features.

1. Click the **Start button** 🏁Start on the Windows taskbar
The Start menu opens on the desktop.

2. Point to **Programs** on the Start menu
The Programs menu opens, as shown in Figure A-2. The Programs menu displays the list of programs installed on your computer. If you are using personalized menus in Windows, your Programs menu might display only the most frequently used programs; click the double arrow at the bottom of the Programs menu to expand the menu and display the complete list of programs.

3. Click **Microsoft Word** on the Programs menu
The **Word program window** opens and displays a blank document and the New Document task pane, as shown in Figure A-3. The blank document opens in the most recently used view. **Views** are different ways of displaying a document in the document window. Figure A-3 shows a blank document in Print Layout view. The lessons in this unit will use Print Layout view.

4. Click the **Print Layout View button** 📄 as shown in Figure A-3
If your blank document opened in a different view, the view changes to Print Layout view.

5. Click the **Zoom list arrow** on the Standard toolbar as shown in Figure A-3, then click **Page Width**
The blank document fills the document window. Your screen should now match Figure A-3. The blinking vertical line in the upper-left corner of the document window is the **insertion point**. It indicates where text will appear when you type.

6. Move the mouse pointer around in the Word program window
The mouse pointer changes shape depending on where it is in the Word program window. In the document window in Print Layout view, the mouse pointer changes to an **I-beam pointer** I or a **click and type pointer** I≡. You use these pointers to move the insertion point in the document or to select text to edit. Table A-1 describes common mouse pointers.

7. Place the mouse pointer over a toolbar button
When you place the pointer over a button or some other element of the Word program window, a ScreenTip appears. A **ScreenTip** is a label that identifies the name of the button or feature.

Trouble?
If Microsoft Word is not on your Programs menu, ask your technical support person for assistance.

Trouble?
If your toolbars are on one row, click the Toolbar Options button 》 at the end of the Formatting toolbar, then click Show Buttons on Two Rows.

TABLE A-1: Common Word pointers

pointer	use to
I	Move the insertion point in a document or to select text
I≡ or I≡	Move the insertion point in a blank area of a document in Print Layout or Web Layout view; automatically applies the paragraph formatting required to position text at that location in the document
↖	Click a button, menu command, or other element of the Word program window; appears when you point to elements of the Word program window
⇗	Select a line or lines of text; appears when you point to the left edge of a line of text in the document window
🖑	Open a hyperlink; appears when you point to a hyperlink in the task pane or a document

FIGURE A-2: Starting Word from the Programs menu

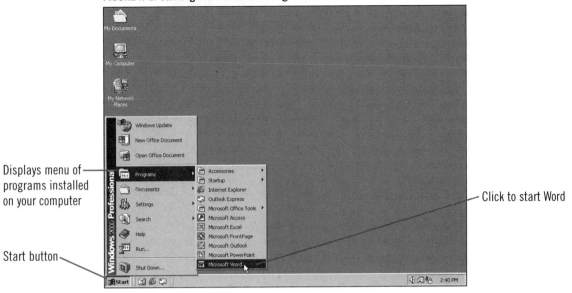

Displays menu of programs installed on your computer

Start button

Click to start Word

FIGURE A-3: Word program window in Print Layout view

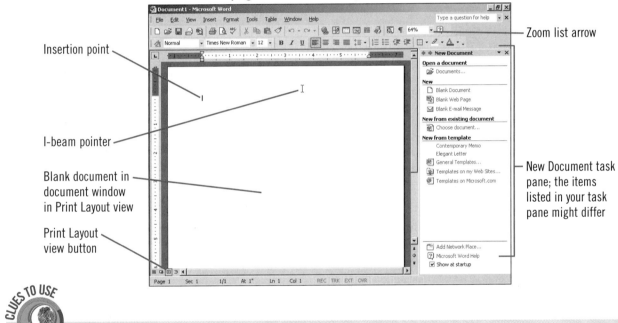

Insertion point

Zoom list arrow

I-beam pointer

Blank document in document window in Print Layout view

Print Layout view button

New Document task pane; the items listed in your task pane might differ

Using Word document views

Each Word view provides features that are useful for working on different types of documents. The default view, **Print Layout view**, displays a document as it will look on a printed page. Print Layout view is helpful for formatting text and pages, including adjusting document margins, creating columns of text, inserting graphics, and formatting headers and footers. Also useful is **Normal view**, which shows a simplified layout of a document, without margins, headers and footers, or graphics. When you want to quickly type, edit, and format text, it's often easiest to work in Normal view. **Web Layout view** allows you to accurately format Web pages or documents that will be viewed on a computer screen. In Web Layout view, a document appears just as it will when viewed with a Web browser. Finally, **Outline view** is useful for editing and formatting longer documents that include multiple headings. Outline view allows you to reorganize text by moving the headings.

You switch between views by clicking the view buttons on the horizontal scroll bar or by using the commands on the View menu. Changing views does not affect how the printed document will appear. It simply changes the way you view the document in the document window.

Word 2002

Exploring the Word Program Window

When you start Word, a blank document appears in the document window and the New Document task pane appears. ![] Alice examines the elements of the Word program window.

Details

Using Figure A-4 as a guide, find the elements described below in your program window.

▶ The **title bar** displays the name of the document and the name of the program. Until you give a new document a different name, its temporary name is Document1. The title bar also contains resizing buttons and the program Close button, common to all Windows programs.

▶ The **menu bar** contains the names of the Word menus. Clicking a menu name opens a list of commands from which you can choose. The menu bar also contains the Ask a Question box and the Close Window button. You use the **Ask a Question box** to access the Word Help system.

▶ The **toolbars** contain buttons for the most commonly used commands. The **Standard toolbar** contains buttons for frequently used operating and editing commands, such as saving a document, printing a document, and cutting, copying, and pasting text. The **Formatting toolbar** contains buttons for commonly used formatting commands, such as changing font type and size, applying bold to text, and changing paragraph alignment. The Clues to Use in this lesson provides more information about working with Word's toolbars.

▶ The **New Document task pane** contains shortcuts for opening a document and for creating new documents. The blue words in the New Document task pane are **hyperlinks** that provide quick access to existing documents, document templates, and dialog boxes used for creating and opening documents. As you learn more about Word, you will work with other task panes that provide shortcuts to Word formatting and editing features. Clicking a hyperlink in a task pane can be quicker than using menu commands and toolbar buttons to accomplish a task.

▶ The **document window** displays the current document. You enter text and format your document in the document window.

▶ The horizontal and vertical rulers appear in the document window in Print Layout view. The **horizontal ruler** displays left and right document margins as well as the tab settings and paragraph indents, if any, for the paragraph in which the insertion point is located. The **vertical ruler** displays the top and bottom document margins.

▶ The **vertical and horizontal scroll bars** are used to display different parts of the document in the document window. The scroll bars include **scroll boxes** and **scroll arrows**, which you can use to easily move through a document.

▶ The **view buttons** at the left end of the horizontal scroll bar allow you to display the document in Normal, Web Layout, Print Layout, or Outline view.

▶ The **status bar** displays the page number and section number of the current page, the total number of pages in the document, and the position of the insertion point in inches, lines, and characters. The status bar also indicates the on/off status of several Word features, including tracking changes, overtype mode, and spelling and grammar checking.

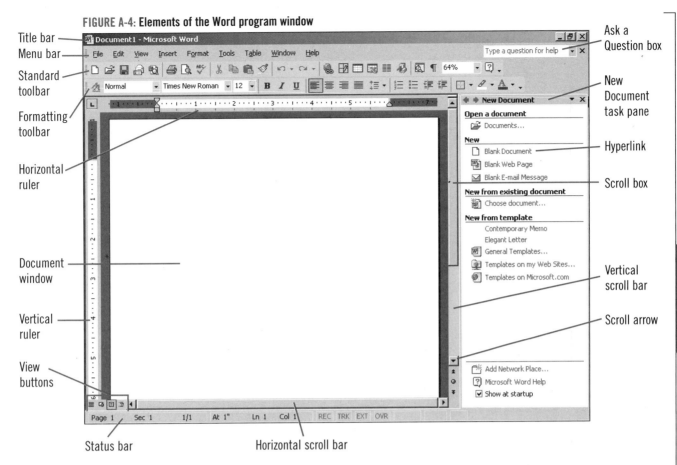

FIGURE A-4: Elements of the Word program window

Title bar
Menu bar
Standard toolbar
Formatting toolbar
Horizontal ruler
Document window
Vertical ruler
View buttons
Status bar
Horizontal scroll bar

Ask a Question box
New Document task pane
Hyperlink
Scroll box
Vertical scroll bar
Scroll arrow

Working with toolbars and menus in Word 2002

The lessons in this book assume you are working with full menus and toolbars visible, which means the Standard and Formatting toolbars appear on two rows and display all the buttons, and the menus display the complete list of menu commands.

You can also set Word to use personalized toolbars and menus that modify themselves to your working style. When you use personalized toolbars, the Standard and Formatting toolbars appear on the same row and display only the most frequently used buttons. To use a button that is not visible on a toolbar, click the Toolbar Options button ⁞ at the end of the toolbar, and then click the button you want on the Toolbar Options list. As you work, Word adds the

buttons you use to the visible toolbars, and moves the buttons you haven't used recently to the Toolbar Options list. Similarly, Word menus adjust to your work habits, so that the commands you use most often appear on shortened menus. You click the double arrow at the bottom of a menu to view additional menu commands.

To work with full toolbars and menus visible, you must turn off the personalized toolbars and menus features. To turn off personalized toolbars and menus, click Tools on the menu bar, click Customize, select the Show Standard and Formatting toolbars on two rows and Always show full menus check boxes on the Options tab, and then click Close.

Word 2002

Starting a Document

You begin a new document by simply typing text in a blank document in the document window. Typing with a word processor is easy because word processors include a **word-wrap** feature, which means as you reach the edge of the page when you type, Word automatically moves the insertion point to the next line of the document. You need only press [Enter] when you want to start a new paragraph or insert a blank line. Also, you can easily edit text in a document by inserting new text or by deleting existing text. ✎ Alice types a quick memo to the marketing staff to inform them of the agenda and schedule for the next marketing meeting.

Steps

1. Click the Close button in the New Document task pane
The task pane closes and the blank document fills the screen.

2. Type Memorandum, then press [Enter] four times
Each time you press [Enter] the insertion point moves to the start of the next line.

3. Type DATE:, then press [Tab] twice
Pressing [Tab] moves the insertion point several spaces to the right. You can use the [Tab] key to align the text in a memo header or to indent the first line of a paragraph.

4. Type April 21, 2003, then press [Enter]
When you press [Enter], a purple dotted line appears under the date. This dotted underline is a **smart tag**. It indicates that Word recognizes the text as a date. If you move the mouse pointer over the smart tag, a **Smart Tag Actions button** ⓘ appears above the date. Smart tags are just one of many automatic features you will encounter as you type. Table A-2 describes other automatic features available in Word. You can ignore the smart tags in your memo.

5. Type:
> **TO: [Tab] [Tab] Marketing Staff [Enter]**
> **FROM: [Tab] Your Name [Enter]**
> **RE: [Tab] [Tab] Marketing Meeting [Enter] [Enter]**

Red or green wavy lines may appear under the words you typed. A red, wavy line means the word is not in Word's dictionary and might be misspelled. A green, wavy line indicates a possible grammar error. You can correct any typing errors you make later.

6. Type The next marketing meeting will be held May 6th at 10 a.m. in the Bloomsbury room on the ground floor.
As you type, notice that the insertion point moves automatically to the next line of the document. You also might notice that Word corrects typing errors or makes typographical adjustments as you type. This feature is called **AutoCorrect**. AutoCorrect automatically detects and adjusts typos, certain misspelled words (such as "taht" for "that"), and incorrect capitalization as you type. For example, in the memo, Word automatically changed "6th" to "6ᵗʰ."

7. Type Heading the agenda will be a discussion of our new cafe music series, scheduled for August. Please bring ideas for promoting this exciting new series to the meeting.
When you type the first few characters of "August," Word's AutoComplete feature displays the complete word in a ScreenTip. **AutoComplete** suggests text to insert quickly into your documents. You can ignore AutoComplete for now. Your memo should resemble Figure A-5.

8. Position the pointer I after for (but before the space) in the second sentence, then click
Clicking moves the insertion point after "for."

9. Press [Backspace] three times, then type to debut in
Pressing [Backspace] removes the character before the insertion point.

10. Move the insertion point before marketing in the first sentence, then press [Delete] ten times to remove the word marketing and the space after it
Pressing [Delete] removes the character after the insertion point. Figure A-6 shows the revised memo.

FIGURE A-5: Memo text in the document window

Blank lines between paragraphs

Purple dotted underline indicates a smart tag

Red, wavy underline indicates a possible misspelled word (your memo will show your name)

Text wraps to the next line (yours might differ)

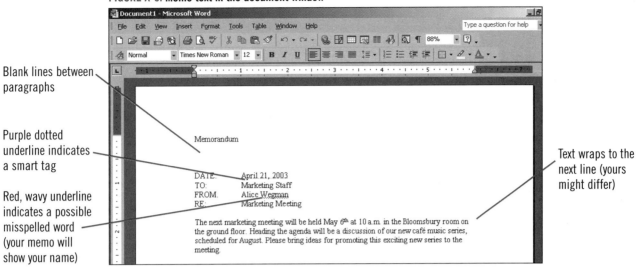

FIGURE A-6: Edited memo text

Text inserted in the memo

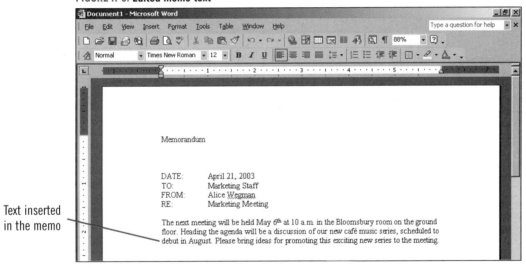

TABLE A-2: Word's automatic features

feature	what appears	to use
AutoComplete	A ScreenTip suggesting text to insert appears as you type	Press [Enter] to insert the text suggested by the ScreenTip; continue typing to reject the suggestion
Spelling and grammar	A red, wavy line under a word indicates a possible misspelling; a green wavy line under text indicates a possible grammatical error	Right-click red- or green-underlined text to display a shortcut menu of correction options; click a correction to accept it and remove the wavy underline
AutoCorrect	A small blue box appears when you place the pointer under text corrected by AutoCorrect; an AutoCorrect Options button appears when you point to the corrected text	Word automatically corrects typos, minor spelling errors, and capitalization, and adds typographical symbols (such as © and ™) as you type; to reverse an AutoCorrect adjustment, click the AutoCorrect Options button, then click Undo
Smart tag	A purple dotted line appears under text Word recognizes as a date, name, address, or place; a Smart Tag Actions button appears when you point to a smart tag	Click the Smart Tag Actions button to display a shortcut menu of options (such as adding a name to your address book in Outlook or opening your Outlook calendar to a date); to remove a smart tag, click Remove this Smart Tag on the shortcut menu

Word 2002

Saving a Document

To store a document permanently so you can open and edit it in the future, you must save a document as a **file** on your computer. When you **save** a document you give it a name, called a **filename**, and indicate the location where you want to store the file. Files can be saved to your computer's internal hard disk, to a floppy disk, or to a variety of other locations. You can save a document using the Save button on the Standard toolbar or the Save command on the File menu. Once you have saved a document for the first time, you should save it again every few minutes and always before printing so that the saved file is updated to reflect your latest changes. ✍️ Alice saves her memo with the filename Marketing Memo.

Steps 1 2 3 4

Trouble?

If you don't see the extension .doc on the filenames in the Save As dialog box, don't worry. Windows can be set to display or not to display the file extensions.

▶ **1.** Click the **Save button** 🖬 on the Standard toolbar

The first time you save a document, the Save As dialog box opens, as shown in Figure A-7. The default filename, Memorandum, appears in the File name text box. The default filename is based on the first few words of the document. The ".doc" extension is assigned automatically to all Word documents to distinguish them from files created in other software programs. To save the document with a different filename, type a new filename in the File name text box, and use the Save in list arrow to select where you want to store the document file. You do not need to type .doc when you type a new filename. Table A-3 describes the functions of the buttons in the Save As dialog box.

2. Type **Marketing Memo** in the File name text box

The new filename replaces the default filename. It's a good idea to give your documents brief filenames that describe the contents.

Trouble?

This book assumes your Project Files are stored in drive A. Substitute the correct drive or folder if this is not the case.

▶ **3.** Click the **Save in list arrow**, then navigate to the drive or folder where your Project Files are located

The drive or folder where your Project Files are located appears in the Save in list box. Your Save As dialog box should resemble Figure A-8.

4. Click **Save**

The document is saved to the location you specified in the Save As dialog box, and the title bar displays the new filename, "Marketing Memo."

5. Place the insertion point before **August** in the second sentence, type **early**, then press **[Spacebar]**

You can continue to work on a document after you have saved it with a new filename.

6. Click 🖬

Your change to the memo is saved. Saving a document after you give it a filename saves the changes you make to a document. You also can click File on the menu bar, and then click Save to save a document.

Recovering lost document files

Sometimes while you are working on a document, Word might freeze, making it impossible to continue working, or you might experience a power failure that shuts down your computer. Should this occur, Word has a built-in recovery feature that allows you to open and save the files that were open during the interruption. When you restart Word after an interruption, the Document Recovery task pane opens on the left side of your screen and lists both the original and the recovered versions of the Word files. If you're not sure which file to open (original or recovered), it's usually better to open the recovered file because it includes your latest changes to the document. You can, however, open and review all the versions of the file that were recovered and select the best one to save. Each file listed in the Document Recovery task pane has a list arrow with options that allow you to open the file, save the file, delete the file, or show repairs made to the file.

FIGURE A-7: Save As dialog box

Active folder or drive

Folders and files in the active folder or drive (yours will differ)

Default filename and file extension are selected

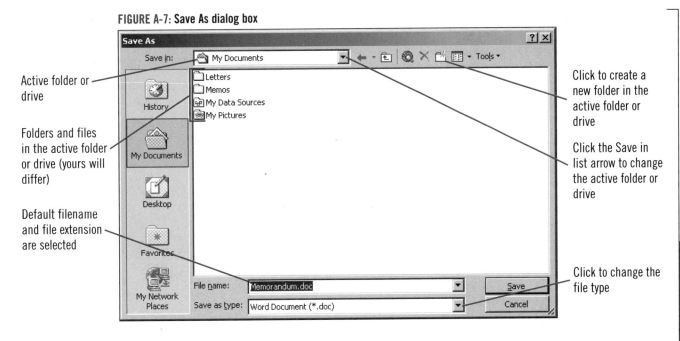

Click to create a new folder in the active folder or drive

Click the Save in list arrow to change the active folder or drive

Click to change the file type

FIGURE A-8: File to be saved to drive A

Location of Project Files (yours might differ)

New filename

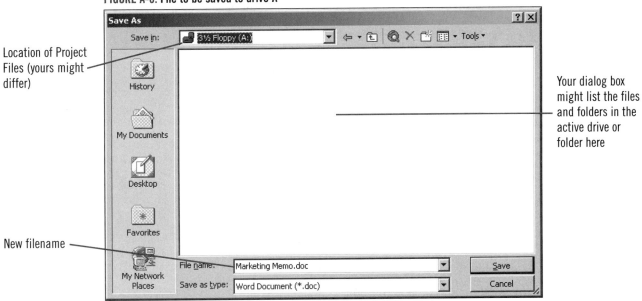

Your dialog box might list the files and folders in the active drive or folder here

TABLE A-3: Save As dialog box buttons

button	use to
⬅ **Back**	Navigate to the drive or folder previously shown in the Save in list box; click the Back list arrow to navigate to a recently displayed drive or folder
🔼 **Up One Level**	Navigate to the next highest level in the folder hierarchy (to the drive or folder that contains the current folder)
🔍 **Search the Web**	Connect to the World Wide Web to locate a folder or file
✕ **Delete**	Delete the selected folder or file
📁 **Create New Folder**	Create a new folder in the current folder or drive
▦ ▾ **Views**	Change the way folder and file information is shown in the Save As dialog box
Tools ▾ **Tools**	Open a menu of commands related to the selected drive, folder, or file

Word 2002

Printing a Document

Before you print a document, it's a good habit to examine it in Print Preview to see what it will look like when printed. When you are ready, you can print a document using the Print button on the Standard toolbar or the Print command on the File menu. When you use the Print button, the document prints using the default print settings. If you want to print more than one copy of a document or select other printing options, you must use the Print command. ✒ Alice displays her memo in Print Preview and then prints a copy.

Steps

1. Click the Print Preview button 🔍 on the Standard toolbar
The document appears in Print Preview. It is useful to examine a document carefully in Print Preview so that you can correct any problems before printing it.

QuickTip

You can also use the Zoom list arrow on the Print Preview toolbar to change the magnification in the Print Preview window.

2. Move the pointer over the memo text until it changes to 🔍, then click the memo
Clicking with the ⊕ pointer magnifies the document in the Print Preview window and changes the pointer to 🔍. The memo appears in the Print Preview window exactly as it will look when printed, as shown in Figure A-9. Clicking with 🔍 reduces the size of the document in the Print Preview window.

3. Click the Magnifier button 🔍 on the Print Preview toolbar
Clicking the Magnifier button turns off the magnification feature and allows you to edit the document in Print Preview. In edit mode, the pointer changes to I. The Magnifier button is a **toggle button**, which means you can use it to switch back and forth between magnification mode and edit mode.

4. Compare the text on your screen with the text in Figure A-9, examine your memo carefully for typing or spelling errors, correct any mistakes, then click the Close Preview button Close on the Print Preview toolbar
Print Preview closes and the memo appears in the document window.

5. Click the Save button 💾 on the Standard toolbar
If you made any changes to the document since you last saved it, the changes are saved.

6. Click File on the menu bar, then click Print
The Print dialog box opens, as shown in Figure A-10. Depending on the printer installed on your computer, your print settings might differ slightly from those in the figure. You can use the Print dialog box to change the current printer, change the number of copies to print, select what pages of a document to print, and modify other printing options.

7. Click OK
The dialog box closes and a copy of the memo prints using the default print settings. You can also click the Print button 🖨 on the Standard toolbar or the Print Preview toolbar to print a document using the default print settings.

FIGURE A-9: Memo in the Print Preview window

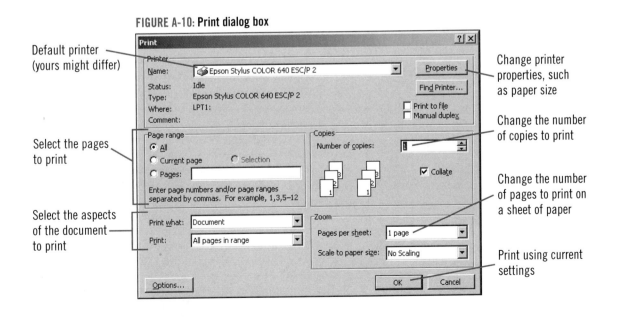

Magnifier button

Close Preview button

Memorandum

DATE: April 21, 2003
TO: Marketing Staff
FROM: Alice Wegman
RE: Marketing Meeting

The next meeting will be held May 6th at 10 a.m. in the Bloomsbury room on the ground floor. Heading the agenda will be a discussion of our new café music series, scheduled to debut in early August. Please bring ideas for promoting this exciting new series to the meeting.

FIGURE A-10: Print dialog box

Default printer (yours might differ)

Change printer properties, such as paper size

Change the number of copies to print

Select the pages to print

Change the number of pages to print on a sheet of paper

Select the aspects of the document to print

Print using current settings

Print
Printer
Name: Epson Stylus COLOR 640 ESC/P 2   Properties
Status: Idle   Find Printer...
Type: Epson Stylus COLOR 640 ESC/P 2
Where: LPT1:   ☐ Print to file
Comment: ☐ Manual duplex

Page range   Copies
● All   Number of copies: 1
○ Current page   ○ Selection
○ Pages: ☑ Collate
Enter page numbers and/or page ranges
separated by commas. For example, 1,3,5–12

Print what: Document   Zoom
Print: All pages in range   Pages per sheet: 1 page
                                    Scale to paper size: No Scaling

Options...   OK   Cancel

Using the Help System

Word includes an extensive Help system that provides immediate access to definitions, instructions, and useful tips for working with Word. You can quickly access the Help system by typing a question in the Ask a Question box on the menu bar, or by clicking the Microsoft Word Help button on the Standard toolbar. Table A-4 describes the many ways to get help while using Word. Alice is curious to learn more about typing with AutoCorrect and viewing a document in Print Preview. She searches the Word Help system to discover more about these features.

Steps

1. Type AutoCorrect in the Ask a Question box on the menu bar, then press [Enter]

A drop-down menu of help topics related to AutoCorrect opens. You can select a topic from this menu or click See more… to view additional help topics related to your query.

2. Click About automatic corrections on the drop-down menu

> **QuickTip**
>
> Click the Print button on the Help window toolbar to print the current help topic.

The Microsoft Word Help window opens, as shown in Figure A-11. The left pane of the Help window contains the Contents, Answer Wizard, and Index tabs, which you can use to search for and display information on help topics. The right pane of the Help window displays the "About automatic corrections" help topic you selected. The blue text in the Help window indicates a link to a definition or to more information about the topic. Notice that the pointer changes to ↑ when you move it over the blue text.

3. Read the information in the Help window, then click the blue text hyperlinks

Clicking the link expands the help topic to display more detailed information. A definition of "hyperlink" appears in green text in the Help window.

4. Read the definition, then click hyperlinks again to close the definition

5. Click Using AutoCorrect to correct errors as you type, then read the expanded information, clicking the down scroll arrow as necessary to read the entire help topic

Clicking the up or down scroll arrow allows you to navigate through the help topic when all the text does not fit in the Help window. You can also **scroll** by clicking the scroll bar above and below the scroll box, or by dragging the scroll box up or down in the scroll bar.

6. Click the Answer Wizard tab in the left pane if necessary, type print a document in the What would you like to do? text box, then click Search

> **QuickTip**
>
> Click the Back and Forward buttons on the Help window toolbar to navigate between the help topics you have viewed.

When you click Search, a list of help topics related to your query appears in the Select topic to display box on the Answer Wizard tab, as shown in Figure A-12. The active help topic—the topic selected in the Select topic to display box—appears in the right pane.

7. Click the Index tab, type print preview in the Type keywords text box, then click Search

As you type, notice that Word automatically supplies possible keywords in the Type keywords box. When you click Search, a list of help topics related to Print Preview appears in the Choose a topic box. You can use the Index tab to narrow the scope of the help topics related to your query by searching for topics related to specific words or phrases.

8. Click Edit text in print preview in the Choose a topic box

The help topic appears in the right pane of the Help window.

9. Click the Close button on the Help window title bar to close Help

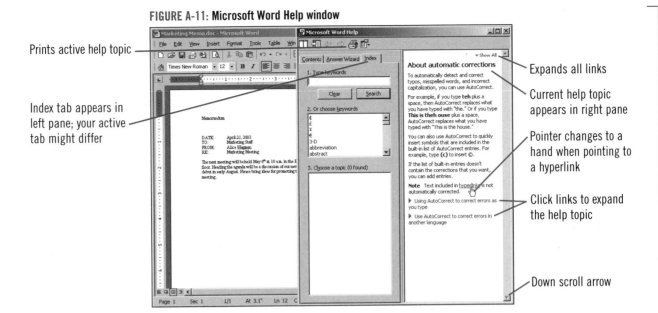

FIGURE A-11: Microsoft Word Help window

Prints active help topic

Index tab appears in left pane; your active tab might differ

Expands all links

Current help topic appears in right pane

Pointer changes to a hand when pointing to a hyperlink

Click links to expand the help topic

Down scroll arrow

FIGURE A-12: Answer Wizard tab in the Microsoft Word Help window

Query used to search for topic

Close button

Active help topic

List of help topics related to query

Word 2002

TABLE A-4: Word resources for getting Help

resource	function	to use
Ask a Question box	Provides quick access to the Help system	Type a word or question in the Ask a Question box, then press [Enter]
Office Assistant	Displays tips and Help topics related to your current task and provides access to the Help system	Press [F1] or click the Microsoft Word Help button [?] on the Standard toolbar, select a Help topic or type a word or question in the Office Assistant dialog box, then click Search
Microsoft Word Help window	Catalogs and displays the detailed Help topics included in the Help system	Browse the table of contents on the Contents tab, type a question in the text box on the Answer Wizard tab, or search for topics related to a keyword on the Index tab
What's This?	Displays information about elements of the Word program window in ScreenTips	Press [Shift][F1] or click the What's This? command on the Help menu, then use the ⬉? pointer to click the element for which you want help
Help on the World Wide Web	Connects to the Microsoft Office Web site, where you can search for information on a topic	Click the Office on the Web command on the Help menu

Word 2002

Closing a Document and Exiting Word

When you finish working on a document and have saved your changes, you can close the document using the Close Window button on the menu bar or the Close command on the File menu. Closing a document closes the document only, it does not close the Word program window. To close the Word program window and exit Word, you can use the Close button on the title bar or the Exit command on the File menu. Using the Exit command closes all open documents. It's good practice to save and close your documents before exiting Word. Figure A-14 shows the Close buttons on the title bar and menu bar. ✎ Alice closes the memo and exits Word.

Steps

1. **Click File on the menu bar, then click Close**
   If you saved your changes to the document before closing it, the document closes. If you did not save your changes, an alert box opens asking if you want to save the changes.

QuickTip

Click the New Blank Document button 🗋 on the Standard toolbar to create a new blank document.

2. **Click Yes if necessary**
   The document closes, but the Word program window remains open, as shown in Figure A-15. You can create or open another document, access Help, or close the Word program window.

3. **Click File on the menu bar, then click Exit**
   The Word program window closes. If any Word documents were still open when you exited Word, Word would close all open documents, prompting you to save changes to those documents if necessary.

Using the Office Assistant to get Help

The **Office Assistant**, shown in Figure A-13, is an animated character that appears on your screen to provide tips while you work. For example, when you begin typing a letter, the Office Assistant anticipates what you are doing and opens to offer help writing a letter. You can accept this help or continue working on your own. The Office Assistant also appears when you use the Microsoft Word Help button 🔲 to access the Word Help system. In this case, the Office Assistant displays a list of help topics related to tasks you have recently completed and provides space for you to search for information on other topics. Selecting a help topic in the Office Assistant displays that topic in the Microsoft Help window. When you finish working with the Office Assistant, right-click it and then click Hide to close it. You also can turn off the Office Assistant: right-click it, click Options, deselect the Use the Office Assistant check box on the Options tab in the Office Assistant dialog box, and then click OK. To turn it on again, click Show Office Assistant on the Help menu.

FIGURE A-13: Office Assistant

FIGURE A-14: Close and Close Window buttons

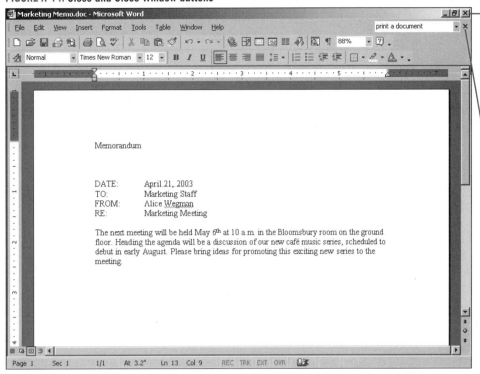

Close button on title bar closes all open documents and exits Word

Close Window button closes the current document

FIGURE A-15: Word program window with no documents open

New Blank Document button

Practice

► Concepts Review

Label the elements of the Word program window shown in Figure A-16.

FIGURE A-16

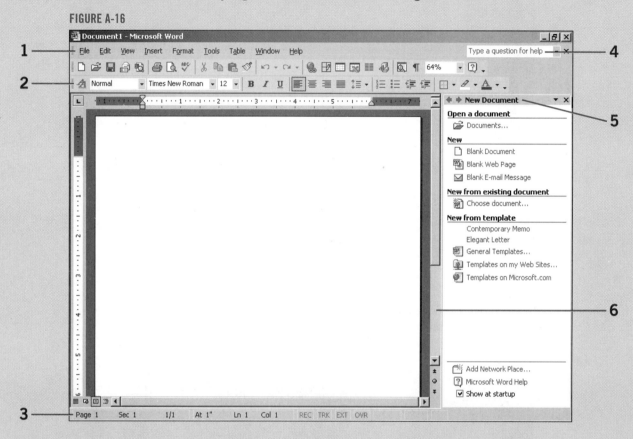

Match each term with the statement that best describes it.

7. Print Preview
8. Office Assistant
9. Status bar
10. Menu bar
11. AutoComplete
12. Horizontal ruler
13. AutoCorrect
14. Normal view

a. Suggests text to insert into a document
b. Provides access to Word commands
c. Displays the document exactly as it will look when printed
d. Provides tips on using Word and displays Help topics
e. Fixes certain errors as you type
f. Displays the number of pages in the current document
g. Displays a simple layout view of a document
h. Displays tab settings and document margins

Select the best answer from the list of choices.

15. Which element of the Word program window contains hyperlinks to help you quickly accomplish a task?

a. Formatting toolbar

b. Menu bar

c. New Document task pane

d. Status bar

16. Which button is found on the Formatting toolbar?

a. Underline button

b. Drawing button

c. Format Painter button

d. Tables and Borders button

17. What is the function of the Exit command on the File menu?

a. To save changes to and close the current document

b. To close the current document without saving changes

c. To close all open documents and the Word program window

d. To close all open programs

18. Which view would you use if you want to adjust the margins in a document?

a. Outline view

b. Print Layout view

c. Normal view

d. Web Layout view

19. Which of the following does *not* appear on the status bar?

a. The current page number

b. The current line number

c. The Overtype mode status

d. The current tab settings

20. Which of the following is *not* used to access Word Help topics?

a. The Ask a Question box

b. The Search task pane

c. The Office Assistant

d. The Answer Wizard

▶ Skills Review

1. Start Word 2002.

   a. Start Word using the Programs menu.

   b. Switch to Print Layout view if necessary.

   c. Change the zoom level to Page Width if necessary.

2. Explore the Word program window.

   a. Identify as many elements of the Word program window as you can without referring to the unit material.

   b. Click each menu name on the menu bar and drag the pointer through the menu commands.

   c. Point to each button on the Standard and Formatting toolbars and read the ScreenTips.

   d. Point to each hyperlink in the New Document task pane.

   e. Click the view buttons to view the blank document in Normal, Web Layout, Print Layout, and Outline view.

   f. Return to Print Layout view.

3. Start a document.

   a. Close the New Document task pane.

   b. In a new blank document, begin typing a fax to one of your customers at Plateau Tours and Travel in Montreal.

   c. Type **FAX** at the top of the page, then press [Enter] four times.

d. Type the following, pressing [Tab] as indicated and pressing [Enter] at the end of each line:
To: [Tab] **Dr. Monique Lacasse**
From: [Tab] **Your Name**
Date: [Tab] **Today's Date**
Re: [Tab] **Travel arrangements**
Pages: [Tab] **1**
Fax: [Tab] **(514) 555-3948**

e. Press [Enter], then type **I have reserved a space for you on the February 4-18 Costa Rica Explorer tour. You are scheduled to depart Montreal's Dorval Airport on Plateau Tours and Travel charter flight 234 at 7:45 a.m. on February 4th, arriving in San Jose at 4:30 p.m. local time.**

f. Press [Enter] twice, then type **Please call me at (514) 555-4983 or stop by our offices on rue St-Denis.**

g. Insert this sentence at the beginning of the second paragraph: **I must receive full payment within 48 hours to hold your reservation.**

h. Using the [Backspace] key, delete **Travel** in the Re: line, then type **Costa Rica tour.**

i. Using the [Delete] key, delete **48** in the last sentence, then type **72.**

4. Save a document.

a. Click File on the menu bar, then click Save.

b. Save the document as **Lacasse Fax** to the drive and folder where your Project Files are located.

c. After your name, type a comma, a space, and then type **Plateau Tours and Travel**.

d. Click the Save button to save your changes to the document.

5. Print a document.

a. Click the Print Preview button to view the document in Print Preview.

b. Click the word FAX to zoom in on the document, then proofread the fax.

c. Click the Magnifier button to switch to edit mode, then correct any typing errors in your document.

d. Close Print Preview, then save your changes to the document.

e. Print the fax using the default print settings.

6. Use the Help system.

a. Click the Microsoft Word Help button to open the Office Assistant. (*Hint*: If the Help window opens instead of the Office Assistant, close the Help window, click Help on the menu bar, click Show the Office Assistant, then click the Microsoft Word Help button again.)

b. Type **save a document** in the Office Assistant text box, then click Search.

c. Click the topic Save a document.

d. Read about saving documents in Word by clicking the links to expand the help topic.

e. Click the Contents tab, then double-click the topic Viewing and Navigating Documents.

f. Click the topic Zoom in on or out of a document, then read the help topic.

g. Close the Microsoft Word Help window.

7. Close a document and exit Word.

a. Close the Lacasse Fax document, saving your changes if necessary.

b. Exit Word.

▶ Independent Challenge 1

You are a performance artist, well known for your innovative work with computers. The Missoula Arts Council president, Jeb Zobel, has asked you to be the keynote speaker at an upcoming conference in Missoula, Montana, on the role of technology in the arts. You are pleased at the invitation, and write a letter to Mr. Zobel accepting the invitation and confirming the details. Your letter to Mr. Zobel should reference the following information:

- The conference will be held October 10–12, 2003 at the civic center in Missoula.
- You have been asked to speak for one hour on Saturday, October 11, followed by a half hour for questions.
- Mr. Zobel suggested the lecture topic "Technology's Effect on Art and Culture."
- Your talk will include a 20-minute slide presentation.
- The Missoula Arts Council will make your travel arrangements.
- Your preference is to arrive in Missoula on Friday, October 10, and depart on Sunday, October 12.
- You want to fly in and out of the airport closest to your home.

a. Start Word.

b. Save a new blank document as **Zobel Letter** to the drive and folder where your Project Files are located.

c. Model your letter to Mr. Zobel after the sample business letter shown in Figure A-17: there are 3 blank lines after the date, 1 blank line after the inside address, 1 blank line after the salutation, 1 blank line after each body paragraph, and 3 blank lines between the closing and your typed name.

d. Begin the letter by typing today's date.

e. Type the inside address. Be sure to include Mr. Zobel's title and the name of the organization. Make up a street address.

f. Type a salutation.

g. Using the information listed above, type the body of the letter:
- In the first paragraph, accept the invitation to speak and confirm the important conference details.
- In the second paragraph, confirm your lecture topic and provide any relevant details.
- In the third paragraph, state your travel preferences.
- Type a short final paragraph.

h. Type a closing, then include your name in the signature block.

i. Save your changes.

j. Preview and print the letter, then close the document and exit Word.

FIGURE A-17

July 8, 2003

Dr. Amanda Russell
Department of Literature and Creative Writing
Nashua State College
Nashua, NH 03285

Dear Dr. Russell:

Thank you for the invitation to speak at your upcoming seminar on "The Literature of Place." I will be happy to do so. I understand that the seminar will be held from 2:30 p.m. to 4:30 p.m. on September 17 in the Sanders Auditorium. As you suggested, I will address the topic "Writers of the Monadonock Region."

I appreciate your invitation and I look forward to working with you on September 17.

Sincerely,

Jessica Grange

Independent Challenge 2

Your company has recently installed Word 2002 on its company network. As the training manager it's your responsibility to teach employees how to use the new software productively. Since installing Word 2002, several employees have asked you about smart tags. In response to their queries, you decide to write a memo to all employees and explain how to use the smart tag feature. You know that smart tags are designed to help users perform tasks in Word that normally would require opening a different program, such as Microsoft Outlook (a desktop information-management program that includes e-mail, calendar, and address book features). Before writing your memo, you'll learn more about smart tags by searching the Word Help system.

FIGURE A-18

WORD TRAINING MEMORANDUM

To: All employees
From: Your Name, Training Manager
Date: Today's date
Re: Smart tags in Word 2002

a. Start Word and save a new blank document as **Smart Tags Memo** to the drive and folder where your Project Files are located.

b. Type **WORD TRAINING MEMORANDUM** at the top of the document, press [Enter] four times, then type the memo heading information shown in Figure A-18. Make sure to include your name in the From line and the current date in the Date line.

c. Press [Enter] twice to place the insertion point where you will begin typing the body of your memo.

d. Search the Word Help system for information on working with smart tags.

e. Type your memo after completing your research. In your memo, define smart tags, then explain what they look like, how to use smart tags, and how to remove smart tags from a document.

f. Save your changes, preview and print the memo, then close the document and exit Word.

Independent Challenge 3

Yesterday you interviewed for a job as marketing director at Komata Web Designs. You spoke with several people at Komata, including Hiro Kobayashi, Director of Operations, whose business card is shown in Figure A-19. You need to write a follow-up letter to Mr. Kobayashi, thanking him for the interview and expressing your interest in the company and the position. He also asked you to send him some samples of your marketing work, which you will enclose with the letter.

FIGURE A-19

Hiro Kobayashi
Director of Operations

Komata Web Designs

5-8, Edobori 4-chome
Minato-ku
Tokyo 108-0034 Japan

Phone: (03) 5555-3299
Fax: (03) 5555-7028
Email: hkoba@komata.co.jp

a. Start Word and save a new blank document as **Komata Letter** to the drive and folder where your Project Files are located.

b. Begin the letter by typing today's date.

c. Four lines below the date, type the inside address, referring to Figure A-19 for the address information. Be sure to include the recipient's title, company name, and full mailing address in the inside address. (*Hint*: When typing a foreign address, type the name of the country in capital letters by itself on the last line.)

d. Two lines below the inside address, type the salutation.

e. Two lines below the salutation, type the body of the letter according to the following guidelines:

- In the first paragraph, thank him for the interview. Then restate your interest in the position and express your desire to work for the company. Add any specific details you think will enhance the power of your letter.

- In the second paragraph, note that you are enclosing three samples of your work and explain something about the samples you are enclosing.
- Type a short final paragraph.

f. Two lines below the last body paragraph, type a closing, then four lines below the closing, type the signature block. Be sure to include your name in the signature block.

g. Two lines below the signature block, type an enclosure notation. (*Hint*: An enclosure notation usually includes the word "Enclosures" or the abbreviation "Enc." followed by the number of enclosures in parentheses.)

h. Save your changes.

i. Preview and print the letter, then close the document and exit Word.

 # Independent Challenge 4

Unlike personal letters or many e-mail messages, business letters are formal in tone and format. The World Wide Web is one source for information on writing styles, proper document formatting, and other business etiquette issues. In this independent challenge, you will research guidelines and tips for writing effective and professional business letters. Your online research should seek answers to the following questions: What is important to keep in mind when writing a business letter? What are the parts of a business letter? What are some examples of types of business letters? What are some useful tips for writing business letters?

a. Use your favorite search engine to search the Web for information on writing and formatting business letters. Use the keywords **business letters** to conduct your search. If your search does not result in links to information on business letters, try looking at the following Web sites: www.eHow.com, www.business-letters.com, or www.about.com.

b. Review the Web sites you find. Print at least two Web pages that offer useful guidelines for writing business letters.

c. Start Word and save a new blank document as **Business Letters** to the drive and folder where your Project Files are located.

d. Type your name at the top of the document, then press [Enter] twice.

e. Type a brief report on the results of your research. Your report should answer the following questions:
- What are the URLs of the Web sites you visited to research guidelines for writing a business letter? (*Hint*: A URL is a Web page's address. An example of a URL is www.eHow.com.)
- What is important to keep in mind when writing a business letter?
- What are the parts of a business letter?
- In what situations do people write business letters? Provide as many examples as you can think of.

f. Save your changes to the document, preview and print it, then close the document and exit Word.

► Visual Workshop

Create the cover letter shown in Figure A-20. Since you plan to print the letter on your letterhead, you do not need to include your return address. Save the document with the name **Publishing Cover Letter** to the drive and folder where your Project Files are stored, print a copy of the letter, then close the document and exit Word.

FIGURE A-20

June 16, 2003

Ms. Olivia Johansen
Managing Editor
Conway Press
483 Grove Street
Wellesley, MA 02181

Dear Ms. Johansen:

I read of the opening for an editorial assistant on the June 15 edition of Boston.com, and I would like to be considered for the position. A recent graduate of Whitfield College, I am interested in pursuing a career in publishing.

My desire for a publishing career springs from my interest in writing and editing. At Whitfield College, I was a frequent contributor to the student newspaper and was involved in creating a Web site for student poetry and short fiction.

I have a wealth of experience using Microsoft Word in professional settings. For the past several summers I worked as an office assistant for Packer Investment Consultants, where I used Word to create newsletters and financial reports for clients. During the school year, I also worked part-time in the Whitfield College admissions office. Here I used Word's mail merge feature to create form letters and mailing labels.

My enclosed resume details my talents and experience. I would welcome the opportunity to discuss the position and my qualifications with you. I can be reached at 617-555-3849.

Sincerely,

Your Name

Enc.

Editing

Documents

Objectives

- ⌈MOUS⌉ ► **Open a document**
- ⌈MOUS⌉ ► **Select text**
- ⌈MOUS⌉ ► **Cut and paste text**
- ⌈MOUS⌉ ► **Copy and paste text**
- ⌈MOUS⌉ ► **Use the Office Clipboard**
- ⌈MOUS⌉ ► **Use the Spelling and Grammar checker and the Thesaurus**
- ⌈MOUS⌉ ► **Find and Replace text**
- ⌈MOUS⌉ ► **Use wizards and templates**

Word's sophisticated editing features make it easy to revise and polish your documents. In this unit, you learn how to open an existing file, revise it by replacing, copying, and moving text, and then save the document as a new file. You also learn to perfect your documents using Word's proofing tools, and to quickly create attractive, professionally designed documents using wizards and templates. ◢▬ Alice Wegman needs to create a press release about a new MediaLoft lecture series in New York. The press release should provide information about the series so that newspapers, radio stations, and other media outlets can announce it to the public. Alice also needs to create a fax coversheet to use when she faxes the press release to her list of press contacts. You will work with Alice as she creates these documents.

Opening a Document

Sometimes the easiest way to create a document is to edit an existing document and save it with a new filename. To modify a document, you must first **open** it so that it displays in the document window. Word offers several methods for opening documents, described in Table B-1. Once you have opened a file, you can use the Save As command to create a new file that is a copy of the original. You can then edit the new file without making changes to the original. ✒ Rather than write her press release from scratch, Alice decides to modify a press release written for a similar event. She begins by opening the press release document and saving it with a new filename.

Steps

Trouble?

If the New Document task pane is not open, click File on the menu bar, then click New.

QuickTip

You also can use the Open button 📂 on the Standard toolbar or the Open command on the File menu to open the Open dialog box.

QuickTip

You also can double-click a filename in the Open dialog box to open the file.

1. Start **Word**

Word opens and a blank document and the New Document task pane appear in the program window, as shown in Figure B-1. The New Document task pane contains links for opening existing documents and for creating new documents.

2. Click the **Documents** or **More Documents** hyperlink under Open a document in the New Document task pane

The Open dialog box opens. You use the Open dialog box to locate and select the file you want to open. The Look in list box displays the current drive or folder.

3. Click the **Look in list arrow**, then click the **drive** containing your Project Files

A list of Project Files appears in the Open dialog box, as shown in Figure B-2. If your Project Files are located in a folder, double-click the folder to display its contents.

4. Click the filename **WD B-1** in the Open dialog box, then click **Open**

The document opens. Notice that the filename WD B-1 appears in the title bar. Once you have opened a file, you can edit it and use the Save or the Save As command to save your changes. You use the **Save** command when you want to save the changes you make to a file, overwriting the file that is stored on a disk. You use the **Save As** command when you want to create a new file with a different filename, leaving the original file intact.

5. Click **File** on the menu bar, then click **Save As**

The Save As dialog box opens. By saving a file with a new filename, you create a document that is identical to the original document. The original filename is selected (highlighted) in the File name text box. Any text you type will replace the selected text.

6. Type **NY Press Release** in the File name text box, then click **Save**

The original file closes and the NY Press Release file is displayed in the document window. Notice the new filename in the title bar. You can now make changes to the press release file without affecting the original file.

TABLE B-1: Methods for opening documents

use	to	if you want to
The Open button 📂 on the Standard toolbar, Open command on the File menu, or [Ctrl][O]	Open the Open dialog box	Open an existing file; a fast way to open a document when the New Document task pane is not displayed
The Documents or More Documents hyperlink in the New Document task pane	Open the Open dialog box	Open an existing file; a fast way to open a document when the New Document task pane is displayed
A filename hyperlink in the New Document task pane	Open the file in the document window	Open the file; a fast way to open a file that was recently opened on your computer
The Choose a document hyperlink in the New Document task pane	Open the New From Existing Document dialog box	Create a copy of an existing file; a fast way to open a document you intend to save with a new filename

FIGURE B-1: New Document task pane

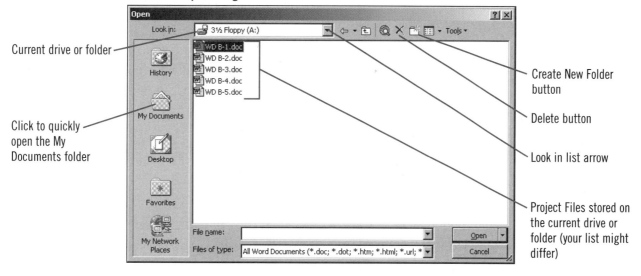

Open button

Your task pane might also include hyperlinks to recently opened files here

Documents hyperlink (yours might be the More Documents hyperlink)

Click to open an existing file as a new file

FIGURE B-2: Open dialog box

Current drive or folder

Click to quickly open the My Documents folder

Create New Folder button

Delete button

Look in list arrow

Project Files stored on the current drive or folder (your list might differ)

Managing files and folders

The Open and Save As dialog boxes include powerful tools for navigating, creating, and deleting files and folders on your computer, a network, or the Web. By selecting a file or folder and clicking the Delete button ⊠, you can delete the item and send it to the Recycle Bin. You can also create a new folder for storing files by clicking the Create New Folder button 🗂 and typing a name for the folder. The new folder is created in the current folder.

Using the Save As dialog box, you can also create new files that are based on existing files. You can

create a new file by saving an existing file with a different filename or by saving it in a different location on your system. You also can save a file in a different file format so that it can be opened in a different software program. To save a file in a different format, click the Files of type list arrow, then click the type of file you want to create. For example, you can save a Word document (which has a .doc file extension) as a plain text file (.txt), as a Web page file (.htm), or in a variety of other file formats.

Selecting Text

Before deleting, editing, or formatting text, you must **select** the text. Selecting text involves clicking and dragging the I-beam pointer across text to highlight it. You also can click with the ∕ᴬ pointer in the blank area to the left of text to select lines or paragraphs. Table B-2 describes the many ways to select text. ◢▬▬ Alice revises the press release by selecting text and replacing it with new text.

Steps 123⁴

1. **Click before December 9, 2002 and drag the ⌶ pointer over the text to select it**
   The date is selected, as shown in Figure B-3.

2. **Type January 13, 2003**
   The text you type replaces the selected text.

3. **Double-click James, type your first name, double-click Callaghan, then type your last name**
   Double-clicking a word selects the entire word.

4. **Place the pointer in the margin to the left of the phone number so that the pointer changes to ∕ᴬ, click to select the phone number, then type (415) 555-8293**
   Clicking to the left of a line of text with the ∕ᴬ pointer selects the entire line.

5. **Click the down scroll arrow at the bottom of the vertical scroll bar until the headline Guy Fogg to Speak ... is at the top of your document window**
   The scroll arrows or scroll bars allow you to **scroll** through a document. You scroll through a document when you want to display different parts of the document in the document window.

6. **Select SAN FRANCISCO, then type NEW YORK**

7. **In the fourth body paragraph, select the sentence All events will be held at the St. James Hotel., then press [Delete]**
   Selecting text and pressing [Delete] removes the text from the document.

8. **Select and replace text in the second and last paragraphs using the following table:**

select	type
February 12	March 6
St. James Hotel in downtown San Francisco	Waldorf-Astoria Hotel
National Public Radio's Helen DeSaint	New York Times literary editor Isabel Eliot

   The edited press release is shown in Figure B-4.

9. **Click the Save button 💾 on the Standard toolbar**
   Your changes to the press release are saved. Always save before and after editing text.

Replacing text in Overtype mode

Normally you must select text before typing to replace the existing characters, but by turning on **Overtype mode** you can type over existing characters without selecting them first. To turn Overtype mode on and off on your computer, double-click OVR in the status bar.

On some computers you also can turn Overtype mode on and off by pressing [Insert]. When Overtype mode is on, OVR appears in black in the status bar. When Overtype mode is off, OVR is dimmed.

FIGURE B-3: Date selected in the press release

Selected text

Left document margin

Down scroll arrow

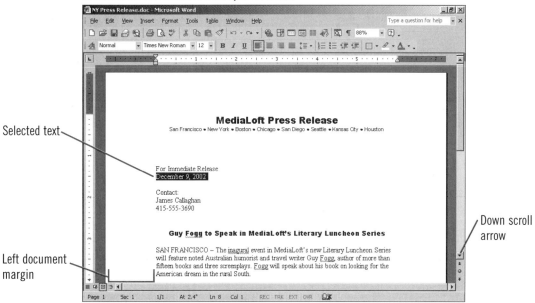

FIGURE B-4: Edited press release

Replacement text

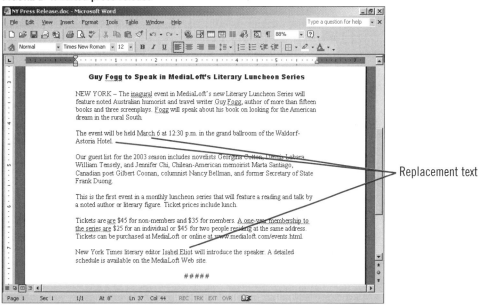

TABLE B-2: Methods for selecting text

to select	use the mouse pointer to
Any amount of text	Drag over the text
A word	Double-click the word
A line of text	Click with the pointer to the left of the line
A sentence	Press and hold [Ctrl], then click the sentence
A paragraph	Triple-click the paragraph or double-click with the pointer to the left of the paragraph
A large block of text	Click at the beginning of the selection, press and hold [Shift], then click at the end of the selection
Multiple nonconsecutive selections	Select the first selection, then press and hold [Ctrl] as you select each additional selection
An entire document	Triple-click with the pointer to the left of any text, click Select All on the Edit menu, or press [Ctrl][A]

Cutting and Pasting Text

Word's editing features allow you to move text from one location to another in a document. The operation of moving text is often called **cut and paste**. When you cut text from a document, you remove it from the document and add it to the **Clipboard**, a temporary storage area for text and graphics that you cut or copy from a document. You cut text by selecting it and using the Cut button or the Cut command on the Edit menu. To insert the text from the Clipboard into the document, you place the insertion point where you want to insert the text, and then use the Paste button or the Paste command on the Edit menu to paste the text at that location. You also can move text by dragging it to a new location using the mouse. ✏ Alice reorganizes the information in the press release by moving text using the cut and paste and dragging methods.

Steps 1 2 3 4

1. **Click the Show/Hide ¶ button ¶ on the Standard toolbar**
   Formatting marks appear in the document window. **Formatting marks** are special characters that appear on your screen and do not print. Common formatting marks include the paragraph symbol (¶), which shows the end of a paragraph—wherever you press [Enter]; the dot symbol (•), which represents a space—wherever you press [Spacebar]; and the arrow symbol (→), which shows the location of a tab stop—wherever you press [Tab]. Working with formatting marks turned on can help you to select, edit, and format text with precision.

> **Trouble?**
> If the Clipboard task pane opens, close it.

2. **In the third paragraph, select Canadian poet Gilbert Coonan, (including the comma and the space after it), then click the Cut button ✂ on the Standard toolbar**
   The text is removed from the document and placed on the Clipboard. Word uses two different clipboards: the **system Clipboard** (the Clipboard), which holds just one item, and the **Office Clipboard**, which holds up to 24 items. The last item you cut or copy is always added to both clipboards. You'll learn more about the Office Clipboard in a later lesson.

3. **Place the insertion point before novelists (but after the space) in the first line of the third paragraph, then click the Paste button 📋 on the Standard toolbar**
   The text is pasted at the location of the insertion point, as shown in Figure B-5. The Paste Options button 📋 appears below text when you first paste it in a document. You'll learn more about the Paste Options button in the next lesson. For now, you can ignore it.

4. **Press [Ctrl], then click the sentence Ticket prices include lunch. in the fourth paragraph**
   The entire sentence is selected.

> **Trouble?**
> If you make a mistake, click the Undo button 🔙 on the Standard toolbar, then try again.

5. **Press and hold the mouse button over the selected text until the pointer changes to ▷, then drag the pointer's vertical line to the end of the fifth paragraph (between the period and the paragraph mark) as shown in Figure B-6**
   The pointer's vertical line indicates the location the text will be inserted when you release the mouse button.

6. **Release the mouse button**
   The selected text is moved to the location of the insertion point. It's convenient to move text using the dragging method when the locations of origin and destination are both visible on the screen. Text is not removed to the Clipboard when you move it using the dragging method.

7. **Deselect the text, then click the Save button 💾 on the Standard toolbar**
   Your changes to the press release are saved.

FIGURE B-5: **Moved text with Paste Options button**

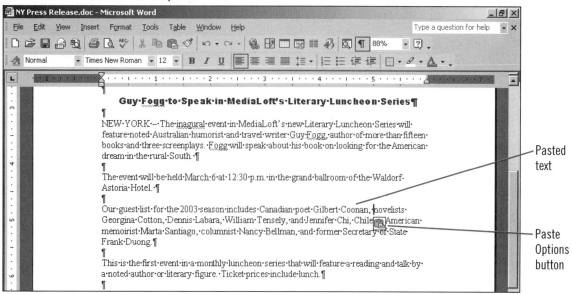

Pasted text

Paste Options button

FIGURE B-6: **Text being dragged to a new location**

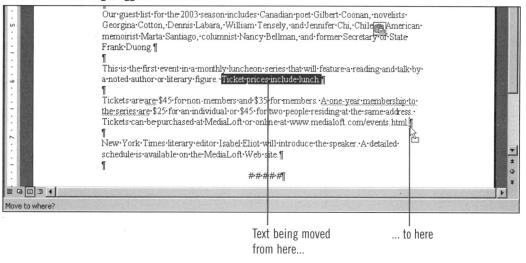

Text being moved from here...

... to here

Using keyboard shortcuts

Instead of using the Cut, Copy, and Paste commands to edit text in Word, you can use the keyboard shortcuts [Ctrl][X] to cut text, [Ctrl][C] to copy text, and [Ctrl][V] to paste text. A **shortcut key** is a function key, such as [F1], or a combination of keys, such as [Ctrl][S], that you press to perform a command. For example, pressing [Ctrl][S] saves changes to a document just as clicking the Save button or using the Save command on the File menu saves a document. Becoming skilled at using keyboard shortcuts can help you to quickly accomplish many of the tasks you perform frequently in Word. If a keyboard shortcut is available for a menu command, then it is listed next to the command on the menu. To find a more extensive list of shortcut keys, search the Help system using the keyword "shortcuts."

Copying and Pasting Text

Copying and pasting text is similar to cutting and pasting text, except that the text you copy is not removed from the document. Rather, a copy of the text is placed on the Clipboard, leaving the original text in place. You can copy text to the Clipboard by using the Copy command on the Edit menu or the Copy button, or you can copy text by pressing [Ctrl] as you drag the selected text from one location to another. ✎ Alice continues to edit the press release by copying text from one location to another.

Trouble?

If the Clipboard task pane opens, close it.

1. In the headline, select **Literary Luncheon**, then click the **Copy button** 📋 on the Standard toolbar
   A copy of the text is placed on the Clipboard, leaving the text you copied in place.

2. Place the insertion point before **season** in the third body paragraph, then click the **Paste button** 📋 on the Standard toolbar
   "Literary Luncheon" is inserted before "season," as shown in Figure B-7. Notice that the pasted text is formatted differently than the paragraph in which it was inserted.

QuickTip

If you don't like the result of a paste option, try another option or click the Undo button and then paste the text again.

3. Click the **Paste Options button** 📋▾, then click **Match Destination Formatting**
   The Paste Options button allows you to change the formatting of pasted text. The formatting of "Literary Luncheon" is changed to match the rest of the paragraph. The options available on the Paste Options menu depend on the format of the text you are pasting and the format of the surrounding text. Table B-3 summarizes the commands used for pasting text.

4. Scroll down if necessary so that the last two paragraphs are visible on your screen

5. In the fifth paragraph, select **www.medialoft.com**, press and hold **[Ctrl]**, then press the mouse button until the pointer changes to ▯

6. Drag the pointer's vertical line to the end of the last paragraph, placing it between **site** and the period, release the mouse button, then release [Ctrl]
   The text is copied to the last paragraph. Since the formatting of the text you copied is the same as the formatting of the paragraph in which you inserted it, you can ignore the Paste Options button. Text is not copied to the Clipboard when you copy it using the dragging method.

7. Place the insertion point between **site** and **www.medialoft.com** in the last paragraph, type **at** followed by a space, then click the **Save button** 💾 on the Standard toolbar
   Compare your document with Figure B-8.

Using the Undo, Redo, and Repeat commands

Word remembers the editing and formatting changes you make so that you can easily reverse or repeat them. You can reverse the last action you took by clicking the Undo button 🔙 on the Standard toolbar, or you can undo a series of actions by clicking the Undo list arrow 🔙▾ and selecting the action you want to reverse. When you undo an action using the Undo list arrow, you also undo all the actions above it in the list; that is, all actions that were performed after the action you selected. Similarly, you can keep the changes you just reversed by using the Redo button 🔜 and the Redo list arrow 🔜▾.

If you want to repeat a change you just made, use the Repeat command on the Edit menu. The name of the Repeat command changes depending on the last action you took. For example, if you just typed "thank you," the name of the command will be Repeat Typing. Clicking the Repeat Typing command will insert "thank you" at the location of the insertion point. You also can repeat the last action you took by pressing [F4].

FIGURE B-7: Text pasted in document

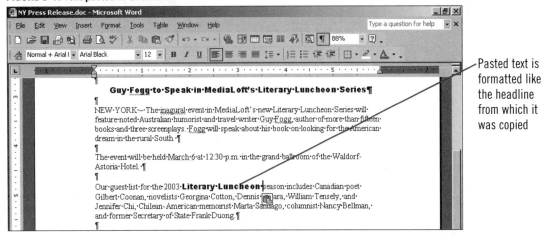

Pasted text is formatted like the headline from which it was copied

FIGURE B-8: Copied text in press release

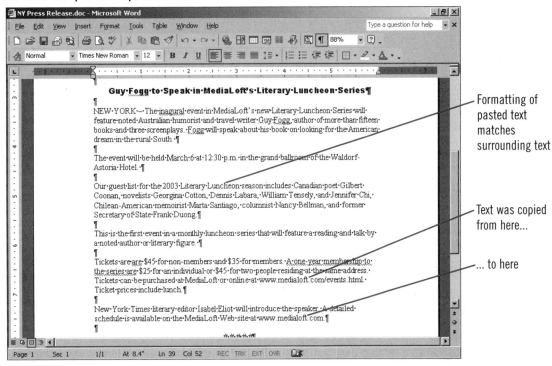

Formatting of pasted text matches surrounding text

Text was copied from here...

... to here

TABLE B-3: Commands used for pasting text

command	use to
Paste command on the Edit menu, Paste button on the Standard toolbar, or [Ctrl][V]	Insert the last item you cut or copied at the location of the insertion point; use the Paste Options button to change the format of the pasted text
Paste Special command on the Edit menu	Insert an item copied or cut from another Office program into a Word document; allows you to embed the object so that you can edit it in its original program; also allows you to create a link to the source file so that changes to the source file are reflected in the Word document
Paste as Hyperlink command on the Edit menu	Paste text so that it is formatted as a hyperlink that jumps to the location from where text was copied; can be used only in conjunction with the Copy command

Using the Office Clipboard

The Office Clipboard allows you to collect text and graphics from files created in any Office Program and insert them into your Word documents. It holds up to 24 items and, unlike the system Clipboard, the items on the Office Clipboard can be viewed. By default, the Office Clipboard opens automatically when you cut or copy two items consecutively. You can also use the Office Clipboard command on the Edit menu to manually display the Office Clipboard if you prefer to work with it open. You add items to the Office Clipboard using the Cut and Copy commands. The last item you collect is always added to both the system Clipboard and the Office Clipboard. Alice uses the Office Clipboard to move several sentences in her press release.

Steps

1. In the last paragraph, select the sentence **New York Times literary editor...** (including the space after the period), then click the **Cut button** on the Standard toolbar
   The sentence is cut to the Clipboard.

2. Select the sentence **A detailed schedule is...** (including the ¶ mark), then click
   The Office Clipboard opens in the Clipboard task pane, as shown in Figure B-9. It displays the items you cut from the press release. The icon next to each item indicates the items are from a Word document.

3. Place the insertion point at the end of the second paragraph (before the ¶ mark after Hotel.), then click the **New York Times literary editor...** item on the Office Clipboard
   Clicking an item on the Office Clipboard pastes the item in the document at the location of the insertion point. Notice that the item remains on the Office Clipboard even after you pasted it. Items remain on the Office Clipboard until you delete them or close all open Office programs. Also, if you add a 25th item to the Office Clipboard, the first item is deleted.

4. Place the insertion point at the end of the third paragraph (after Duong.), then click the **A detailed schedule is...** item on the Office Clipboard
   The sentence is pasted in the document.

5. Select the fourth paragraph, which contains the sentence **This is the first event...** (including the ¶ mark), then click
   The sentence is cut to the Office Clipboard. Notice that the last item collected displays at the top of the Clipboard task pane. The last item collected is also stored on the system Clipboard.

6. Place the insertion point at the beginning of the third paragraph (before Our...), click the **Paste button** on the Standard toolbar, then press **[Backspace]**
   The "This is the first ..." sentence is pasted at the beginning of the "Our guest list ..." paragraph. You can paste the last item collected using either the Paste command or the Office Clipboard.

7. Place the insertion point at the end of the third paragraph (before the ¶ mark), then press **[Delete]** twice
   The ¶ symbols and the blank line between the third and fourth paragraphs are deleted.

8. Click the **Show/Hide ¶ button** on the Standard toolbar
   Compare your press release with Figure B-10.

9. Click the **Clear All button** on the Office Clipboard to remove the items from it, close the Clipboard task pane, press **[Ctrl][Home]**, then click the **Save button**
   Pressing [Ctrl][Home] moves the insertion point to the top of the document.

FIGURE B-9: Office Clipboard in Clipboard task pane

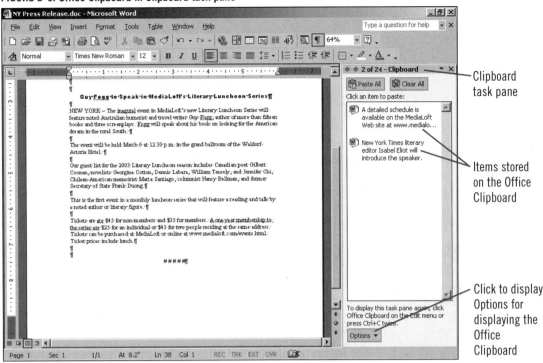

Clipboard task pane

Items stored on the Office Clipboard

Click to display Options for displaying the Office Clipboard

FIGURE B-10: Revised press release

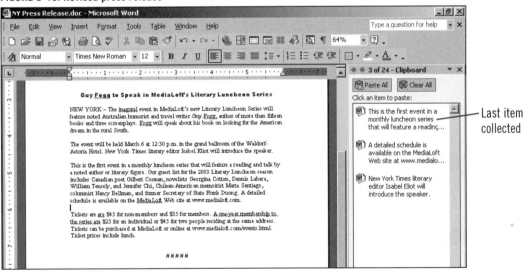

Last item collected

Copying and moving items between documents

The system and Office Clipboards also can be used to copy and move items between Word documents. To copy or cut text from one Word document and paste it into another, first open both documents in the program window. When a document is open in the program window, a Word program button labeled with its filename appears on the taskbar. With multiple documents open, you can copy and move text between documents by copying or cutting the item(s) from one document and then switching to another document and pasting the item(s). To switch between open documents, click the button on the taskbar for the document you want to appear in the document window. The Office Clipboard stores all the items collected from all files, regardless of which document is displayed in the document window. The system Clipboard stores the last item collected from any file.

Using the Spelling and Grammar Checker and the Thesaurus

When you finish typing and revising a document, you can use the Spelling and Grammar command to search the document for misspelled words and grammatical errors. The Spelling and Grammar checker flags possible mistakes, suggests correct spellings, and offers remedies for grammatical errors such as subject-verb agreement, repeated words, and punctuation. Word also includes a Thesaurus, which you can use to look up synonyms for awkward or repetitive words. Alice uses the Spelling and Grammar checker to search her press release for errors. Before beginning the search, she sets the Spelling and Grammar checker to ignore words, such as Fogg, she knows are spelled correctly. She also uses the Thesaurus to find a synonym for "noted."

Trouble?

If Word flags your name or "MediaLoft" as misspelled, right-click those words, then click Ignore All.

QuickTip

To change the language used by Word's proofing tools, click Tools on the menu bar, point to Language, then click Set Language.

Trouble?

You might need to correct other spelling and grammatical errors.

QuickTip

If Word does not offer a valid correction, correct the error yourself.

QuickTip

You also can right-click a word and point to Synonyms on the shortcut menu to see a list of synonyms for a word.

1. Right-click **Fogg** in the headline

A shortcut menu that includes suggestions for correcting the spelling of "Fogg"opens. You can correct individual spelling and grammar errors by right-clicking text that is underlined with a red or green wavy line and selecting a correction. Although "Fogg" is not in Word's dictionary, it is spelled correctly in the document.

2. Click **Ignore All**

Clicking Ignore All tells Word not to flag "Fogg" as misspelled.

3. Press **[Ctrl][Home]**, then click the **Spelling and Grammar button** on the Standard toolbar

The Spelling and Grammar: English (U.S.) dialog box opens, as shown in Figure B-11. The dialog box identifies "inagural" as misspelled and suggests possible corrections for the error. The word selected in the Suggestions box is the correct spelling.

4. Click **Change**

Word replaces the misspelled word with the correctly spelled word. Next, the dialog box indicates "are" is repeated in a sentence.

5. Click **Delete**

Word deletes the second occurrence of the repeated word. Next, the dialog box flags a subject-verb agreement error and suggests using "is" instead of "are," as shown in Figure B-12. The phrase selected in the Suggestions box is correct.

6. Click **Change**

The word "is" replaces the word "are" in the sentence and the Spelling and Grammar dialog box closes. Keep in mind that the spelling and grammar feature identifies many common errors, but you cannot rely on it to find and correct all spelling and grammatical errors in your documents. Always proofread your documents carefully.

7. Click **OK** to complete the spelling and grammar check, then scroll up until the headline is displayed at the top of your screen

8. In the first sentence of the third paragraph, select **noted**, click **Tools** on the menu bar, point to **Language**, then click **Thesaurus**

The Thesaurus: English (U.S.) dialog box opens, as shown in Figure B-13. Possible synonyms for "noted" appear in the dialog box.

9. Click **distinguished** in the Replace with Synonym list box, then click **Replace**

The dialog box closes and "distinguished" replaces "noted" in the press release.

10. Press **[Ctrl][Home]**, then click the **Save button** on the Standard toolbar

FIGURE B-11: Spelling and Grammar: English (U.S.) dialog box

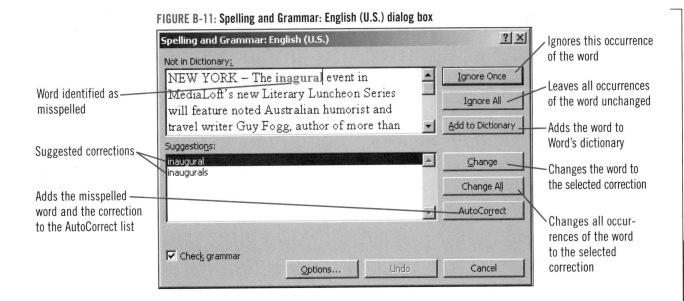

Word identified as misspelled

Suggested corrections

Adds the misspelled word and the correction to the AutoCorrect list

Ignores this occurrence of the word

Leaves all occurrences of the word unchanged

Adds the word to Word's dictionary

Changes the word to the selected correction

Changes all occurrences of the word to the selected correction

FIGURE B-12: Grammar error identified in Spelling and Grammar dialog box

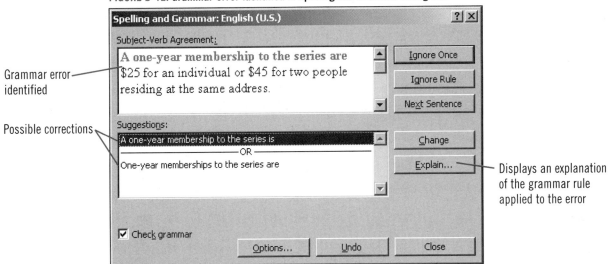

Grammar error identified

Possible corrections

Displays an explanation of the grammar rule applied to the error

FIGURE B-13: Thesaurus: English (U.S.) dialog box

Word in the document

Possible meanings for the word

Replaces the word with the selected synonym

Synonyms for the selected meaning of the word

Finding and Replacing Text

Word's Find and Replace feature allows you to automatically search for and replace all instances of a word or phrase in a document. For example, you might need to substitute "bookstore" for "store," and it would be very time-consuming to manually locate and replace each instance of "store" in a long document. Using the Replace command you can automatically find and replace all occurrences of specific text at once, or you can choose to find and review each occurrence individually. You also can use the Find command to locate and highlight every occurrence of a specific word or phrase in a document. MediaLoft has decided to change the name of the New York series from "Literary Luncheon Series" to "Literary Limelight Series." Alice uses the Replace command to search the document for all instances of "Luncheon" and replace them with "Limelight."

Steps

1. **Click Edit on the menu bar, click Replace, then click More in the Find and Replace dialog box**
   The Find and Replace dialog box opens, as shown in Figure B-14.

2. **Click the Find what text box, then type Luncheon**
   "Luncheon" is the text that will be replaced.

3. **Press [Tab], then type Limelight in the Replace with text box**
   "Limelight" is the text that will replace "Luncheon."

4. **Click the Match case check box in the Search Options section to select it**
   Selecting the Match case check box tells Word to find only exact matches for the uppercase and lowercase characters you entered in the Find what text box. You want to replace all instances of "Luncheon" in the proper name "Literary Luncheon Series." You do not want to replace "luncheon" when it refers to a lunchtime event.

5. **Click Replace All**
   Clicking Replace All changes all occurrences of "Luncheon" to "Limelight" in the press release. A message box reports three replacements were made.

6. **Click OK to close the message box, then click Close to close the Find and Replace dialog box**
   Word replaced "Luncheon" with "Limelight" in three locations, but did not replace "luncheon."

7. **Click Edit on the menu bar, then click Find**
   The Find and Replace dialog box opens with the Find tab displayed. The Find command allows you to quickly locate all instances of text in a document. You can use it to verify that Word did not replace "luncheon."

8. **Type luncheon in the Find what text box, click the Highlight all items found in check box to select it, click Find All, then click Close**
   The Find and Replace dialog box closes and "luncheon" is selected in the document.

9. **Deselect the text, click the Save button on the Standard toolbar, then click the Print button on the Standard toolbar**
   A copy of the finished press release prints. Compare your document to Figure B-15.

10. **Click File on the menu bar, then click Close**

> **QuickTip**
> Click Find Next to find, review, and replace each occurrence individually.

FIGURE B-14: Replace tab in the Find and Replace dialog box

Replace only exact matches of uppercase and lowercase characters

Find only complete words

Use wildcards (*) in a search string

Find words that sound like the Find what text

Find and replace all forms of a word

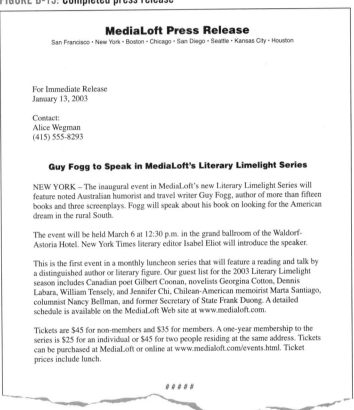

FIGURE B-15: Completed press release

MediaLoft Press Release

San Francisco • New York • Boston • Chicago • San Diego • Seattle • Kansas City • Houston

For Immediate Release
January 13, 2003

Contact:
Alice Wegman
(415) 555-8293

Guy Fogg to Speak in MediaLoft's Literary Limelight Series

NEW YORK – The inaugural event in MediaLoft's new Literary Limelight Series will feature noted Australian humorist and travel writer Guy Fogg, author of more than fifteen books and three screenplays. Fogg will speak about his book on looking for the American dream in the rural South.

The event will be held March 6 at 12:30 p.m. in the grand ballroom of the Waldorf-Astoria Hotel. New York Times literary editor Isabel Eliot will introduce the speaker.

This is the first event in a monthly luncheon series that will feature a reading and talk by a distinguished author or literary figure. Our guest list for the 2003 Literary Limelight season includes Canadian poet Gilbert Coonan, novelists Georgina Cotton, Dennis Labara, William Tensely, and Jennifer Chi, Chilean-American memoirist Marta Santiago, columnist Nancy Bellman, and former Secretary of State Frank Duong. A detailed schedule is available on the MediaLoft Web site at www.medialoft.com.

Tickets are $45 for non-members and $35 for members. A one-year membership to the series is $25 for an individual or $45 for two people residing at the same address. Tickets can be purchased at MediaLoft or online at www.medialoft.com/events.html. Ticket prices include lunch.

# # # # #

Inserting text with AutoCorrect

As you type, AutoCorrect automatically corrects many commonly misspelled words. By creating your own AutoCorrect entries, you also can set Word to quickly insert text that you type often, such as your name or contact information, or to correct words you frequently misspell. For example, you could create an AutoCorrect entry so that "Alice Wegman" is automatically inserted whenever you type "aw" followed by a space. To create an AutoCorrect entry, click AutoCorrect Options on the Tools menu. On the AutoCorrect tab in the AutoCorrect dialog box, type the text you want to be automatically corrected in the Replace text box (such as "aw"), type the text you want to be automatically inserted in its place in the With text box (such as "Alice Wegman"), then click Add. The AutoCorrect entry is added to the list. Note that Word inserts an AutoCorrect entry in a document only when you press [Spacebar] after typing the text you want Word to correct. For example, Word will insert "Alice Wegman" when you type "aw" followed by a space, but not when you type "awful."

Using Wizards and Templates

Word includes many templates that you can use to quickly create memos, faxes, letters, reports, brochures, and other professionally designed documents. A **template** is a formatted document that contains placeholder text. To create a document that is based on a template, you replace the placeholder text with your own text and then save the document with a new filename. A **wizard** is an interactive set of dialog boxes that guides you through the process of creating a document. A wizard prompts you to provide information and select formatting options, and then it creates the document for you based on your specifications. You can create a document with a wizard or template using the New command on the File menu. Alice will fax the press release to her list of press contacts, beginning with the *New York Times*. She uses a template to create a fax coversheet for the press release.

Steps

1. Click **File** on the menu bar, then click **New**
   The New Document task pane opens.

2. Click the **General Templates hyperlink** in the New Document task pane
   The Templates dialog box opens. The tabs in the dialog box contain icons for the Word templates and wizards.

3. Click the **Letters & Faxes tab**, then click the **Professional Fax** icon
   A preview of the Professional Fax template appears in the Templates dialog box, as shown in Figure B-16.

4. Click **OK**
   The Professional Fax template opens as a new document in the document window. It contains placeholder text, which you can replace with your own information.

   > **QuickTip**
   > Double-clicking an icon in the Templates dialog box also opens a new document based on the template.

5. Drag to select **Company Name Here**, then type **MediaLoft**

6. Click the **Click here and type return address and phone and fax numbers placeholder**
   Clicking the placeholder selects it. When a placeholder says Click here… you do not need to drag to select it.

7. Type **MediaLoft San Francisco**, press **[Enter]**, then type **Tel: (415) 555-8293**
   The text you type replaces the placeholder text.

   > **QuickTip**
   > Delete any placeholder text you do not want to replace.

8. Replace the remaining placeholder text with the text shown in Figure B-17
   Word automatically inserted the current date in the document. You do not need to replace the current date with the date shown in the figure.

9. Click **File** on the menu bar, click **Save As**, use the Save in list arrow to navigate to the drive or folder where your Project Files are located, type **NYT Fax** in the File name text box, then click **Save**
   The document is saved with the filename NYT Fax.

10. Click the **Print button** 🖨 on the Standard toolbar, click **File** on the menu bar, then click **Exit**
    A copy of the fax coversheet prints and the document and Word close.

FIGURE B-16: Letters & Faxes tab in Templates dialog box

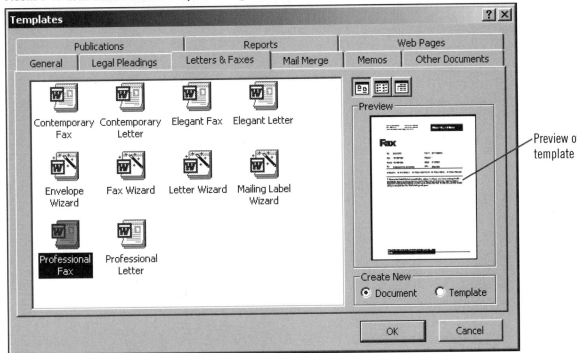

Preview of selected template

FIGURE B-17: Completed fax coversheet document

MediaLoft San Francisco
Tel: (415) 555-8293

MediaLoft

Fax

To:	Arts Editor, New York Times	**From:**	Your Name
Fax:	(212) 555-3948	**Pages:**	2, including cover sheet
Phone:	(212) 555-3000	**Date:**	1/13/2003
Re:	Literary Limelight Series	**CC:**	Isabel Eliot, Literary Editor

☐ **Urgent**   ☐ **For Review**   ☐ **Please Comment**   ☐ **Please Reply**   ☐ **Please Recycle**

• **Comments:** Please see the attached press release regarding the launch of MediaLoft's Literary Limelight Series. This March 6 event will be hosted by Isabel Eliot, New York Times literary editor, at the Waldorf-Astoria Hotel. Please include notice of the event in your Arts Calendar.

Your document will show the current date

Practice

► Concepts Review

Label the elements of the Open dialog box shown in Figure B-18.

FIGURE B-18

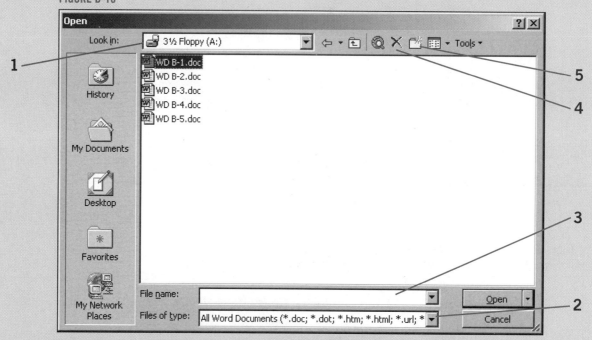

Match each term with the statement that best describes it.

6. **System Clipboard**
7. **Show/Hide**
8. **Select**
9. **Thesaurus**
10. **Undo**
11. **Template**
12. **Office Clipboard**
13. **Paste**
14. **Replace**

a. Feature used to suggest synonyms for words
b. Command used to insert text stored on the Clipboard into a document
c. Command used to reverse the last action you took in a document
d. Temporary storage area for only the last item cut or copied from a document
e. Document that contains placeholder text
f. Temporary storage area for up to 24 items collected from any Office file
g. Command used to locate and replace occurrences of specific text in a document
h. Action that must be taken before text can be cut, copied, or deleted
i. Command used to display formatting marks in a document

Select the best answer from the list of choices.

15. Which of the following is *not* used to open an existing document?
    a. Documents or More documents hyperlink in the New Document task pane
    b. Open command on the Edit menu
    c. Blank document hyperlink in the New Document task pane
    d. Open button on the Standard toolbar

16. To locate and change all instances of a word in a document, which command do you use?
    - **a.** Replace
    - **b.** Find
    - **c.** Search
    - **d.** Paste

17. Which of the following statements is *not* true?
    - **a.** The last item cut or copied from a document is stored on the system Clipboard.
    - **b.** The Office Clipboard can hold more than one item.
    - **c.** You can view the contents of the Office Clipboard.
    - **d.** When you move text by dragging it, a copy of the text you move is stored on the system Clipboard.

18. Which Word feature corrects errors as you type?
    - **a.** AutoCorrect
    - **b.** Thesaurus
    - **c.** Spelling and Grammar
    - **d.** Undo and Redo

19. Which command do you use to paste an item created in a different Office program into a Word document so that changes to the source file are reflected in the Word document?
    - **a.** Paste
    - **b.** Paste Special
    - **c.** Paste as Hyperlink
    - **d.** Office Clipboard

20. What does the symbol ¶ represent when it is displayed in the document window?
    - **a.** Text that is pasted
    - **b.** A space
    - **c.** The end of a paragraph
    - **d.** A tab stop

▶ Skills Review

1. **Open a document.**
    - **a.** Start Word, click the Open button, then open the file WD B-2 from the drive and folder where your Project Files are located.
    - **b.** Save the document with the filename **CAOS Press Release**.

2. **Select text.**
    - **a.** Select **Today's Date** and replace it with the current date.
    - **b.** Select **Your Name** and **Your Phone Number** and replace them with the relevant information.
    - **c.** Scroll down, then select and replace text in the body of the press release using the following table as a guide:

in paragraph	select	replace with
1	16 and 17	13 and 14
1	fifth	eighth
4	open his renovated Pearl St studio for the first time this year	offer a sneak-preview of his Peace sculpture commissioned by the city of Prague

    - **d.** In the fourth paragraph, delete the sentence **Exhibiting with him will be sculptor Francis Pilo**.
    - **e.** Save your changes to the press release.

3. Cut and paste text.

a. Display paragraph and other formatting marks in your document if they are not already displayed.

b. Use the Cut and Paste buttons to switch the order of the two sentences in the fourth paragraph (which begins New group shows...).

c. Use the drag method to switch the order of the second and third paragraphs.

d. Adjust the spacing if necessary so that there is one blank line between paragraphs, then save your changes.

4. Copy and paste text.

a. Use the Copy and Paste buttons to copy **CAOS 2000** from the headline and paste it before the word **map** in the third paragraph.

b. Change the formatting of the pasted text to match the formatting of the third paragraph, then insert a space between **2000** and **map** if necessary.

c. Use the drag method to copy **CAOS** from the third paragraph and paste it before the word **group** in the second sentence of the fourth paragraph, then save your changes.

5. Use the Office Clipboard.

a. Use the Office Clipboard command on the Edit menu to open the Office Clipboard in the task pane.

b. Scroll so that the first body paragraph is displayed at the top of the document window.

c. Select the **fifth paragraph** (which begins Studio location maps...) and cut it to the Office Clipboard.

d. Select the **third paragraph** (which begins Cambridgeport is easily accessible...) and cut it to the Office Clipboard.

e. Use the Office Clipboard to paste the Studio location maps... item as the new fourth paragraph.

f. Use the Office Clipboard to paste the Cambridgeport is easily accessible... item as the new fifth paragraph.

g. Use any method to switch the order of the two sentences in the fourth paragraph (which begins Studio location maps...).

h. Adjust the spacing if necessary so that there is one blank line between each of the six body paragraphs.

i. Turn off the display of formatting marks, clear and close the Office Clipboard, then save your changes.

6. Use the Spelling and Grammar checker and the Thesaurus.

a. Set Word to ignore the spelling of Cambridgeport, if necessary. (*Hint*: Right-click Cambridgeport.)

b. Move the insertion point to the top of the document, then use the Spelling and Grammar command to search for and correct any spelling and grammatical errors in the press release.

c. Use the Thesaurus to replace **thriving** in the second paragraph with a different suitable word.

d. Save your changes to the press release.

7. Find and replace text.

a. Using the Replace command, replace all instances of **2000** with **2003**.

b. Replace all instances of the abbreviation **St** with **Street**, taking care to replace whole words only when you perform the replace. (*Hint*: Click More to expand the Find and Replace dialog box.)

c. Use the Find command to find all instances of **st** in the document, and make sure no errors occurred when you replaced St with Street.

d. Proofread your press release, correct any errors, save your changes, print a copy, then close the document.

8. Use wizards and templates.

    a. Use the New command to open the New Documents task pane.

    b. Use the General Templates hyperlink to open the Templates dialog box.

    c. Create a new document using the Elegant Fax template.

    d. Replace the placeholder text in the document using Figure B-19 as a guide. Delete any placeholders that do not apply to your fax. The date in your fax will be the current date.

    e. Scroll to the bottom of the document and replace the placeholder text with your return address.

    f. Save the document as **CAOS Fax**, print a copy, close the document, then exit Word.

FIGURE B-19

CAOS 2003

FACSIMILE TRANSMITTAL SHEET

TO:	FROM:
Pat Zabko, Listings Editor	Your Name
COMPANY:	DATE:
Boston Phoenix	9/12/2003
FAX NUMBER :	TOTAL NO. OF PAGES INCLUDING COVER:
(617) 555-2980	2
PHONE NUMBER:	SENDER'S REFERENCE NUMBER:
RE:	YOUR REFERENCE NUMBER:
Cambridgeport Artists Open Studios	

☐ URGENT   ☐ FOR REVIEW   ☐ PLEASE COMMENT   ☐ PLEASE REPLY   ☐ PLEASE RECYCLE

NOTES/COMMENTS:

    A press release regarding the 2003 Cambridgeport Artists Open Studios is included with this fax. Please include this information in the Phoenix Listings.

▶ Independent Challenge 1

Because of your success in revitalizing a historic theatre in Hobart, Tasmania, you were hired as the director of The Wellington Lyric Theatre in Wellington, New Zealand, to breathe life into its theatre revitalization efforts. After a year on the job, you are launching your first major fund-raising drive. You'll create a fund-raising letter for the Lyric Theatre by modifying a letter you wrote for the theatre in Hobart.

    a. Start Word, open the file WD B-3 from the drive and folder where your Project Files are located, then save it as **Lyric Theatre Letter**.

    b. Replace the theatre name and address, the date, the inside address, and the salutation with the text shown in Figure B-20.

    c. Use the Replace command to replace all instances of **Hobart** with **Wellington**.

    d. Use the Replace command to replace all instances of **Tasmanians** with **New Zealanders**.

    e. Use the Find command to locate the word **considerable**, then use the Thesaurus to replace the word with a synonym.

    f. Create an AutoCorrect entry that inserts **Wellington Lyric Theatre** whenever you type **wlt**.

    g. Select each XXXXX and the space that follows it, then type **wlt** followed by a space.

    h. Move the fourth body paragraph so that it becomes the second body paragraph.

FIGURE B-20

The Wellington Lyric Theatre
72-74 Hobson Street, Thorndon, Wellington, New Zealand

September 12, 2003

Mr. Colin Fuller
168 Cuba Street
Wellington

Dear Mr. Fuller,

i. Replace Your Name with your name in the signature block.

j. Use the Spelling and Grammar command to check for and correct spelling and grammar errors.

k. Proofread the letter, correct any errors, save your changes, print a copy, close the document, then exit Word.

▶ Independent Challenge 2

An advertisement for job openings in Scotland caught your eye and you have decided to apply. The ad, shown in Figure B-21, was printed in last weekend's edition of your local newspaper. You'll use the Letter Wizard to create a cover letter to send with your resume.

a. Read the ad shown in Figure B-21 and decide which position to apply for. Choose the position that most closely matches your qualifications.

b. Start Word and open the Templates dialog box.

c. Double-click Letter Wizard on the Letters & Faxes tab, then select Send one letter in the Office Assistant balloon or Letter Wizard dialog box.

d. In the Letter Wizard—Step 1 of 4 dialog box, choose to include a date on your letter, select Elegant Letter for the page design, select Modified block for the letter style, include a header and footer with the page design, then click Next.

e. In the Letter Wizard—Step 2 of 4 dialog box, enter the recipient's name (Ms. Hillary Price) and the delivery address, referring to the ad for the address information. Also enter the salutation **Dear Ms. Price** using the business style, then click Next.

f. In the Letter Wizard—Step 3 of 4 dialog box, include a reference line in the letter, enter the appropriate position code (see Figure B-21) in the Reference line text box, then click Next.

g. In the Letter Wizard—Step 4 of 4 dialog box, enter your name as the sender, enter your return address (including your country), and select an appropriate complimentary closing. Then, because you will be including your resume with the letter, include one enclosure. Click Finish when you are done.

h. Click Cancel to close the Office Assistant, if necessary. Then save the letter with the filename **Global Dynamics Letter** to the drive and folder where your Project Files are located.

i. Replace the placeholder text in the body of the letter with three paragraphs that address your qualifications for the job:

- In the first paragraph, specify the job you are applying for, indicate where you saw the position advertised, and briefly state your qualifications and interest in the position.

FIGURE B-21

GlobalDynamics

Career Opportunities in Scotland

Global Dynamics, an established software development firm with offices in North America, Asia, and Europe, is seeking candidates for the following positions in its new Edinburgh facility:

Instructor
Responsible for delivering software training to our expanding European customer base. Duties include delivering hands-on training, keeping up-to-date with product development, and working with the Director of Training to ensure the high quality of course materials. Successful candidate will have excellent presentation skills and be proficient in Microsoft PowerPoint and Microsoft Word. **Position B12C6**

Administrative Assistant
Proficiency with Microsoft Word a must! Administrative office duties include making travel arrangements, scheduling meetings, taking notes and publishing meeting minutes, handling correspondence, and ordering office supplies. Must have superb multi-tasking abilities, excellent communication, organizational, and interpersonal skills, and be comfortable working with e-mail and the Internet. **Position B16F5**

Copywriter
The ideal candidate will have marketing or advertising writing experience in a high tech environment, including collateral, newsletters, and direct mail. Experience writing for the Web, broadcast, and multimedia is a plus. Fluency with Microsoft Word required. **Position C13D4**

Positions offer salary, excellent benefits, moving expenses, and career growth opportunities.

Send resume and cover letter referencing position code to:

**Hillary Price
Director of Recruiting
Global Dynamics
24 Castle Terrace
Edinburgh EH3 9SH
United Kingdom**

- In the second paragraph, describe your work experience and skills. Be sure to relate your experience and qualifications to the position requirements listed in the ad.
- In the third paragraph, politely request an interview for the position and provide your phone number and e-mail address.

j. When you are finished typing the letter, check it for spelling and grammar errors and correct any mistakes.

k. Save your changes to the letter, print a copy, close the document, then exit Word.

▶ Independent Challenge 3

As administrative director of continuing education, you drafted a memo to instructors asking them to help you finalize the course schedule for next semester. Today you'll examine the draft and make revisions before printing it.

a. Start Word and open the file WD B-4 from the drive and folder where your Project Files are located.

b. Open the Save As dialog box, navigate to the drive and folder where your Project Files are located, use the Create New Folder button to create a new folder called **Memos**, then save the document as **Computer Memo** in the Memos folder.

c. Replace Your Name with your name in the From line.

d. Use the Cut and Paste buttons to move the sentence **If you are planning to teach …** from the first body paragraph to become the first sentence in the last paragraph of the memo.

e. Use the [Delete] key to merge the first two paragraphs into one paragraph.

f. Use the Office Clipboard to reorganize the list of twelve-week courses so that the courses are listed in alphabetical order. (*Hint*: Use the Zoom list arrow to enlarge the document as needed.)

g. Use the dragging method to reorganize the list of one-day seminars so that the seminars are listed in alphabetical order.

h. Use the Spelling and Grammar command to check for and correct spelling and grammar errors.

i. Clear and close the Office Clipboard, save your changes, print a copy, close the document, then exit Word.

e Independent Challenge 4

Reference sources—dictionaries, thesauri, style and grammar guides, and guides to business etiquette and procedure—are essential for day-to-day use in the workplace. Much of this reference information is available on the World Wide Web. In this independent challenge, you will locate reference sources on the Web and use some of them to look up definitions, synonyms, and antonyms for words. Your goal is to familiarize yourself with online reference sources so you can use them later in your work.

a. Start Word, open the file WD B-5 from the drive and folder where your Project Files are located, and save it as **Web References**. This document contains the questions you will answer about the Web reference sources you find. You will type your answers to the questions in the document.

b. Replace the placeholder text at the top of the Web References document with your name and the date.

c. Use your favorite search engine to search the Web for grammar and style guides, dictionaries, and thesauri. Use the keywords **grammar**, **usage**, **dictionary**, **glossary**, and **thesaurus** to conduct your search. If your search does not result in links to appropriate reference sources, try the following Web sites: www.bartleby.com, www.dictionary.com, or www.thesaurus.com.

d. Complete the Web References document, then proofread it and correct any mistakes.

e. Save the document, print a copy, close the document, then exit Word.

► Visual Workshop

Using the Contemporary Letter template, create the letter shown in Figure B-22. Save the document as **Visa Letter**. Check the letter for spelling and grammar errors, then print a copy.

FIGURE B-22

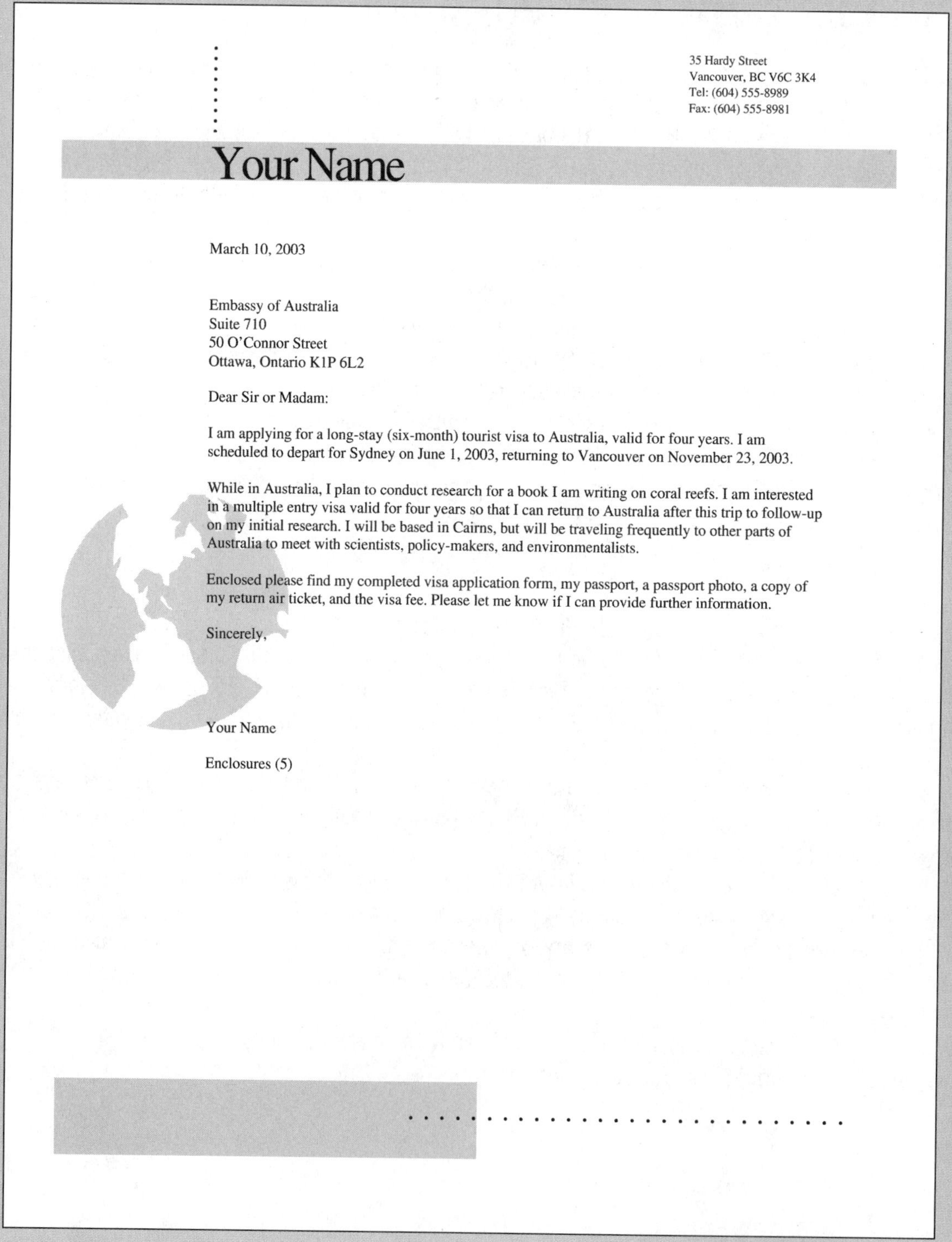

35 Hardy Street
Vancouver, BC V6C 3K4
Tel: (604) 555-8989
Fax: (604) 555-8981

Your Name

March 10, 2003

Embassy of Australia
Suite 710
50 O'Connor Street
Ottawa, Ontario K1P 6L2

Dear Sir or Madam:

I am applying for a long-stay (six-month) tourist visa to Australia, valid for four years. I am scheduled to depart for Sydney on June 1, 2003, returning to Vancouver on November 23, 2003.

While in Australia, I plan to conduct research for a book I am writing on coral reefs. I am interested in a multiple entry visa valid for four years so that I can return to Australia after this trip to follow-up on my initial research. I will be based in Cairns, but will be traveling frequently to other parts of Australia to meet with scientists, policy-makers, and environmentalists.

Enclosed please find my completed visa application form, my passport, a passport photo, a copy of my return air ticket, and the visa fee. Please let me know if I can provide further information.

Sincerely,

Your Name

Enclosures (5)

Formatting

Text and Paragraphs

Objectives

- ▶ **Format with fonts**
- ▶ **Change font styles and effects**
- ▶ **Change line and paragraph spacing**
- ▶ **Align paragraphs**
- ▶ **Work with tabs**
- ▶ **Work with indents**
- ▶ **Add bullets and numbering**
- ▶ **Add borders and shading**

Formatting can enhance the appearance of a document, create visual impact, and help illustrate a document's structure. The formatting of a document can also add personality and lend a degree of professionalism to your document. In this unit you learn how to format text using different fonts and font-formatting options. You also learn how to change the alignment, indentation, and spacing of paragraphs, and how to spruce up documents with borders, shading, bullets, and other paragraph-formatting effects. Isaac Robinson is the marketing director at the MediaLoft Chicago store. Isaac has drafted a quarterly marketing report to send to MediaLoft's headquarters. He now needs to format the report so it is attractive and highlights the significant information. You will work with Isaac as he formats the report.

Formatting with Fonts

Formatting text with different fonts is a quick and powerful way to enhance the appearance of a document. A **font** is a complete set of characters with the same typeface or design. Arial, Times New Roman, Comic Sans, Courier, and Tahoma are some of the more common fonts, but there are hundreds of others, each with a specific design and feel. Another way to alter the impact of text is to increase or decrease its **font size**, which is measured in points. A **point** is ½ of an inch. When formatting a document with fonts, it's important to pick fonts that augment the document's purpose. You can apply fonts and font sizes to text by selecting the text and using the Formatting toolbar. ✏ Isaac changes the font and font size of the title and headings in his report, selecting a font that enhances the business tone of the document. By formatting the title and headings in a font different from the body text, he helps to visually structure the report for readers.

Steps 1 2 3 4

1. Start **Word**, open the file **WD C-1** from the drive and folder where your Project Files are located, then save it as **Chicago Marketing Report**
   The file opens in Print Layout view.

2. Click the **Normal View button** 📄 on the horizontal scroll bar, click the **Zoom list arrow** on the Standard toolbar, then click **100%** if necessary
   The document switches to Normal view, a view useful for simple text formatting. The name of the font used in the document, Times New Roman, is displayed in the Font list box on the Formatting toolbar. The font size, 12, appears next to it in the Font Size list box.

3. Select the title **MediaLoft Chicago Quarterly Marketing Report**, then click the **Font list arrow** on the Formatting toolbar
   The Font list showing the fonts available on your computer opens, as shown in Figure C-1. Fonts you have used recently appear above the double line. All the fonts on your computer are listed in alphabetical order below the double line.

4. Click **Arial**
   The font of the report title changes to Arial.

5. Click the **Font Size list arrow** on the Formatting toolbar, then click **20**
   The font size of the title increases to 20 points.

6. Click the **Font Color list arrow** 🅰▾ on the Formatting toolbar
   A palette of colors opens.

7. Click **Dark Blue** on the Font Color palette as shown in Figure C-2, then deselect the text
   The color of the report title text changes to dark blue. The active color on the Font Color button also changes to dark blue.

8. Select the heading **Advertising**, click the **Font list arrow**, click **Arial**, click the **Font Size list arrow**, click **14**, click the **Font Color button** 🅰, then deselect the text
   The heading is formatted in 14-point Arial with a dark blue color.

9. Scroll down the document and format each of the following headings in 14-point Arial with a dark blue color: **Events**, **Classes & Workshops**, **Publications**, and **Surveys**

10. Press **[Ctrl][Home]**, then click the **Save button** 💾 on the Standard toolbar
    Pressing [Ctrl][Home] moves the insertion point to the beginning of the document. Compare your document to Figure C-3.

FIGURE C-1: Font list

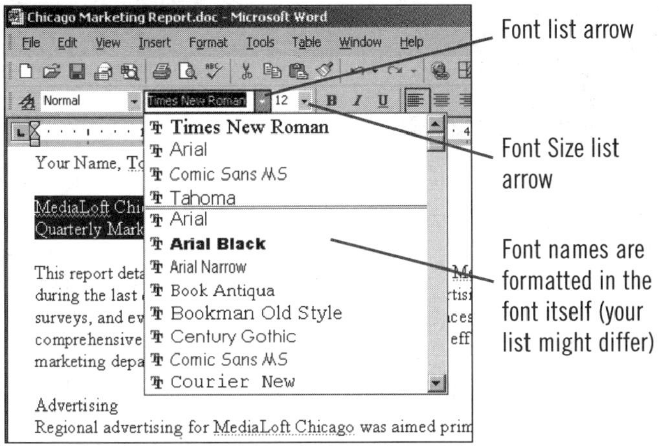

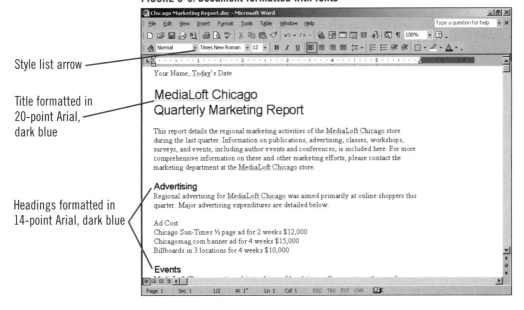

Font list arrow

Font Size list arrow

Font names are formatted in the font itself (your list might differ)

FIGURE C-2: Font Color palette

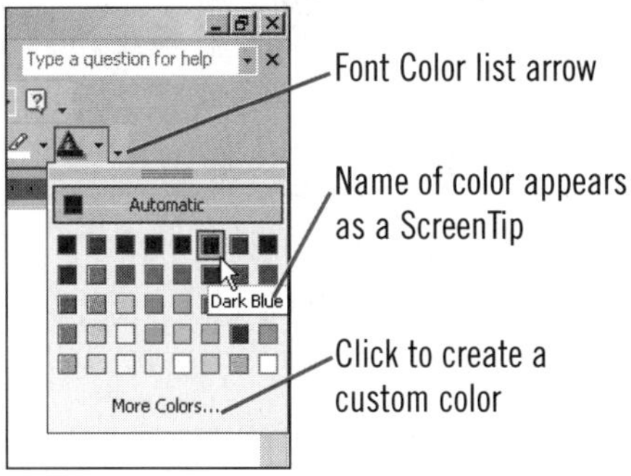

Font Color list arrow

Name of color appears as a ScreenTip

Click to create a custom color

FIGURE C-3: Document formatted with fonts

Style list arrow

Title formatted in 20-point Arial, dark blue

Headings formatted in 14-point Arial, dark blue

Clearing text formatting

If you are unhappy with the way text is formatted, you can use the Clear Formats command to return the text to the default format settings. By default, text is formatted in 12-point Times New Roman and paragraphs are left-aligned and single-spaced. To clear formatting from text, select the text you want to clear, point to Clear on the Edit menu, then click Formats. Alternately, click the Styles list arrow on the Formatting toolbar, then click Clear Formatting. Clearing formatting from text does not delete or change the text itself; it simply formats the text with the default format settings.

Word 2002

Changing Font Styles and Effects

You can dramatically change the appearance of text by applying different font styles, font effects, and character-spacing effects. For example, you can use the buttons on the Formatting toolbar to make text darker by applying **bold**, or to slant text by applying *italic*. You can also use the Font command on the Format menu to apply font effects and character-spacing effects to text. Isaac spices up the appearance of the text in his document by applying different font styles and effects.

QuickTip

Click the Underline button [U] on the Formatting toolbar to underline text.

1. Select **MediaLoft Chicago Quarterly Marketing Report**, then click the **Bold button** [B] on the Formatting toolbar

Applying bold makes the characters darker and thicker.

2. Select the **paragraph** under the title, then click the **Italic button** [I] on the Formatting toolbar

The paragraph is formatted in italic.

QuickTip

To quickly apply bold to multiple headings, press and hold [Ctrl] as you select each heading, then click [B].

3. Scroll down and apply bold to each dark blue heading

The headings all have a darker, thicker appearance.

4. Scroll up until the subheading Author Events is at the top of your screen, select **Author Events**, click **Format** on the menu bar, then click **Font**

The Font dialog box opens, as shown in Figure C-4. You can use the Font tab to change the font, font style, size, and color of text, and to add an underline and apply font effects to the selected text.

5. Scroll up the Font list, click **Arial**, click **Bold Italic** in the Font style list box, select the **Small caps check box**, then click **OK**

The subheading is formatted in Arial, bold, italic, and small caps. When you change text to small caps, the lowercase letters are changed to uppercase letters in a smaller font size.

QuickTip

If you apply formats one by one, then pressing [F4] repeats only the last format you applied.

6. Select **Travel Writers & Photographers Conference**, then press **[F4]**

Pressing [F4] repeats the last action you took. Because you last applied Arial, bold, italic, and small caps together in one action (using the Font dialog box), the subheading is formatted in Arial, bold, italic, and small caps.

7. Under Author Events, select the book title **Just H20 Please: Tales of True Adventure on the Environmental Frontline**, click [I], select **2** in the book title, click **Format** on the menu bar, click **Font**, click the **Subscript check box**, click **OK**, then deselect the text

As shown in Figure C-5, the book title is formatted in italic and the character 2 is subscript.

QuickTip

To animate the selected text, click the Text Effects tab in the Font dialog box, then select an animation style. The animation appears only when a document is viewed in Word; animation effects do not print.

8. Press **[Ctrl][Home]**, select the **report title**, click **Format** on the menu bar, click **Font**, then click the **Character Spacing tab** in the Font dialog box

You use the Character Spacing tab to change the scale, or width, of the selected characters, to alter the spacing between characters, or to raise or lower the position of the characters.

9. Click the **Scale list arrow**, click **150%**, click **OK**, deselect the text, then click the **Save button** [⊞] on the Standard toolbar

Increasing the scale of the characters makes them wider and gives the text a shorter, squat appearance, as shown in Figure C-6.

FIGURE C-4: Font tab in Font dialog box

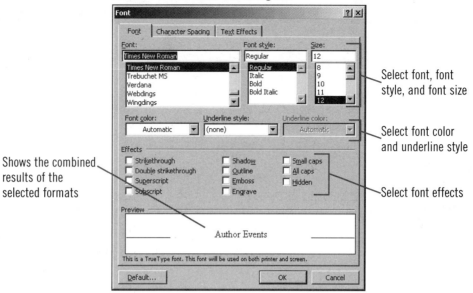

Select font, font style, and font size

Select font color and underline style

Shows the combined results of the selected formats

Select font effects

FIGURE C-5: Font effects applied to text

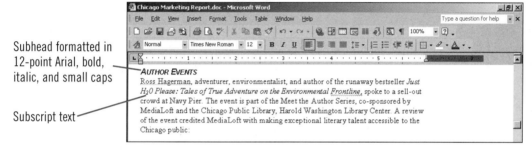

Subhead formatted in 12-point Arial, bold, italic, and small caps

Subscript text

FIGURE C-6: Character-spacing effects applied to text

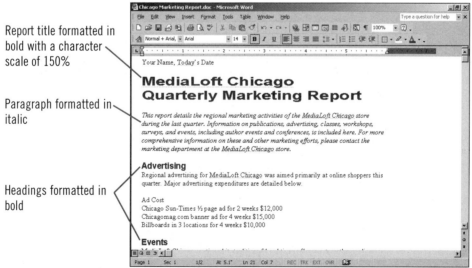

Report title formatted in bold with a character scale of 150%

Paragraph formatted in italic

Headings formatted in bold

Changing the case of letters

The Change Case command on the Format menu allows you to quickly change letters from uppercase to lowercase—and vice versa—saving you the time it takes to retype text you want to change. To change the case of selected text, use the Change Case command to open the Change Case dialog box, then select the case style you want to use. Sentence case capitalizes the first letter of a sentence, title case capitalizes the first letter of each word, and toggle case switches all letters to the opposite case.

Changing Line and Paragraph Spacing

Increasing the amount of space between lines adds more white space to a document and can make it easier to read. Adding space between paragraphs can also open up a document and improve its appearance. You can change line and paragraph spacing using the Paragraph command on the Format menu. You can also use the Line Spacing button to quickly change line spacing. ✎ Isaac increases the line spacing of several paragraphs and adds extra space under each heading to give the report a more open feel.

Steps

QuickTip

The checkmark on the Line Spacing list indicates the current line spacing.

1. Place the insertion point in the italicized paragraph under the report title, then click the **Line Spacing list arrow** 📄▾ on the Formatting toolbar
   The Line Spacing list opens. This list includes options for increasing the space between lines.

2. Click **1.5**
   The space between the lines in the paragraph increases to 1.5 lines. Notice that you do not need to select an entire paragraph to change its paragraph formatting; simply place the insertion point in the paragraph you want to format.

QuickTip

Word recognizes any string of text that ends with a paragraph mark as a paragraph, including titles, headings, and single lines in a list.

3. Scroll down until the heading Advertising is at the top of your screen, select the **four-line list** that begins with Ad Cost, click 📄▾, then click **1.5**
   The line spacing between the selected paragraphs changes to 1.5. To change the paragraph-formatting features of more than one paragraph, you must select the paragraphs.

4. Place the insertion point in the heading **Advertising**, click **Format** on the menu bar, then click **Paragraph**
   The Paragraph dialog box opens, as shown in Figure C-7. You can use the Indents and Spacing tab to change line spacing and the spacing above and below paragraphs. Spacing between paragraphs is measured in points.

QuickTip

Adjusting the space between paragraphs is a more precise way to add white space to a document than inserting blank lines.

5. Click the **After up arrow** in the Spacing section so that 6 pt appears, then click **OK**
   Six points of space are added below the paragraph—the Advertising heading.

6. Select **Advertising**, then click the **Format Painter button** 🖌 on the Standard toolbar
   The pointer changes to 🖌I. The **Format Painter** is a powerful Word feature that allows you to copy all the format settings applied to the selected text to other text that you want to format the same way. The Format Painter is especially useful when you want to copy multiple format settings, but you can also use it to copy individual formats.

QuickTip

Using the Format Painter is not the same as using [F4]. Pressing [F4] repeats only the last action you took. You can use the Format Painter at any time to copy multiple format settings.

7. Select **Events** with the 🖌I pointer, then deselect the text
   Six points of space are added below the Events heading paragraph and the pointer changes back to the I-beam pointer. Compare your document with Figure C-8.

8. Select **Events**, then double-click 🖌
   Double-clicking the Format Painter button allows the Format Painter to remain active until you turn it off. By keeping the Format Painter turned on you can apply formatting to multiple items.

9. Scroll down, select the headings **Classes & Workshops**, **Publications**, and **Surveys** with the 🖌I pointer, then click 🖌 to turn off the Format Painter
   Six points of space are added below each heading paragraph.

10. Press **[Ctrl][Home]**, then click the **Save button** 🖫 on the Standard toolbar

FIGURE C-7: Indents and Spacing tab in Paragraph dialog box

Change the spacing
above and below
paragraphs

Change the line spacing

Spacing After up
arrow

Preview of selected
settings

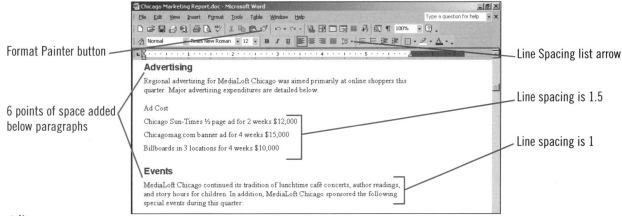

FIGURE C-8: Line and paragraph spacing applied to document

Format Painter button

6 points of space added
below paragraphs

Line Spacing list arrow

Line spacing is 1.5

Line spacing is 1

Formatting with styles

You can also apply multiple format settings to text in one step by applying a style. A **style** is a set of formats, such as font, font size, and paragraph alignment, that are named and stored together. To work with styles, click the Styles and Formatting button ▨ on the Formatting toolbar to open the Styles and Formatting task pane, shown in Figure C-9. The task pane displays the list of available styles and the formats you have created for the current document, if any. To view all the styles available in Word, click the Show list arrow at the bottom of the task pane, then click All Styles.

A **character style**, indicated by a **ā** character in the list of styles, includes character format settings, such as font and font size. A **paragraph style**, indicated by a ¶ character in the list, is a combination of character and paragraph formats, such as font, font size, paragraph alignment, and paragraph spacing. To apply a style, select the text or paragraph you want to format, then click the style name in the Pick formatting to apply list box.

FIGURE C-9: Styles and Formatting task pane

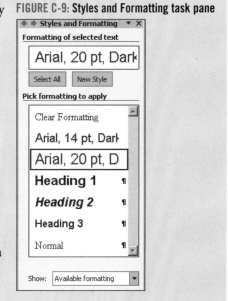

Aligning Paragraphs

Changing paragraph alignment is another way to enhance a document's appearance. Paragraphs are aligned relative to the left and right margins in a document. By default, text is **left-aligned**, which means it is flush with the left margin and has a ragged right edge. Using the alignment buttons on the Formatting toolbar, you can **right-align** a paragraph—make it flush with the right margin—or **center** a paragraph so that it is positioned evenly between the left and right margins. You can also **justify** a paragraph so that both the left and right edges of the paragraph are flush with the left and right margins. Isaac changes the alignment of several paragraphs at the beginning of the report to make it visually more interesting.

1. Replace **Your Name, Today's Date** with your name, a comma, and the date

2. Select your name and the date, then click the **Align Right button** 📄 on the Formatting toolbar

   The text is aligned with the right margin. In Normal view, the junction of the white and shaded sections of the horizontal ruler indicates the location of the right margin. The left end of the ruler indicates the left margin.

3. Place the insertion point between your name and the comma, press **[Delete]** to delete the comma, then press **[Enter]**

   The new paragraph containing the date is also right-aligned. Pressing [Enter] in the middle of a paragraph creates a new paragraph with the same text and paragraph formatting as the original paragraph.

4. Select the **report title**, then click the **Center button** 📄 on the Formatting toolbar

   The two paragraphs that make up the title are centered between the left and right margins.

5. Place the insertion point in the **Advertising** heading, then click 📄

   The Advertising heading is centered.

6. Place the insertion point in the italicized paragraph under the report title, then click the **Justify button** 📄

   The paragraph is aligned with both the left and right margins, as shown in Figure C-10. When you justify a paragraph, Word adjusts the spacing between words so that each line in the paragraph is flush with the left and the right margins.

7. Place the insertion point in **MediaLoft** in the report title, click **Format** on the menu bar, then click **Reveal Formatting**

   The Reveal Formatting task pane opens in the Word program window, as shown in Figure C-11. The task pane shows the formatting applied to the text and paragraph where the insertion point is located. You can use the Reveal Formatting task pane to check or change the formatting of any character, word, paragraph, or other aspect of a document.

8. Select **Advertising**, then click the **Alignment** hyperlink in the Reveal Formatting task pane

   The Paragraph dialog box opens with the Indents and Spacing tab displayed. It shows the settings for the selected text.

9. Click the **Alignment list arrow**, click **Left**, click **OK**, then deselect the text

   The Advertising heading is left-aligned.

10. Close the Reveal Formatting task pane, then click the **Save button** 💾 on the Standard toolbar

FIGURE C-10: Modified paragraph alignment

Right margin in Normal view

Right-aligned

Justified

Center-aligned

Left-aligned

FIGURE C-11: Reveal Formatting task pane

Reveal Formatting task pane

Format settings for the selected text

Click hyperlinks to change format settings

Click - to hide information

Click + to display information

Select to show underlying style

Select to show formatting marks in document

Working with Click and Type

Word's Click and Type feature allows you to automatically apply the paragraph formatting necessary to insert text (or graphics or tables) in a blank area of a document in Print Layout or Web Layout view. As you move the pointer around in a blank area of a document, the pointer changes depending on its location. Double-clicking with a click and type pointer in a blank area of a document automatically applies the appropriate alignment and indentation for that location, so that when you begin typing, the text is already formatted.

The pointer shape indicates which formatting will be applied at each location when you double-click. For example, if you click with the ⟂̲ pointer, the text you type will be center-aligned. Clicking with I⁼ creates a left tab stop at the location of the insertion point so that the text you type is left-aligned at the tab stop. Clicking with ⁼I right-aligns the text you type. The I⁼ pointer creates left-aligned text with a first line indent. The best way to learn how to use Click and Type is to experiment in a blank document.

Word 2002

Working with Tabs

Tabs allow you to align text vertically at a specific location in a document. A **tab stop** is a point on the horizontal ruler that indicates the location at which to align text. By default, tab stops are located every ½" from the left margin, but you can also set custom tab stops. Using tabs, you can align text to the left, right, or center of a tab stop, or you can align text at a decimal point or bar character. You set tabs using the horizontal ruler or the Tabs command on the Format menu. Isaac uses tabs to format the information on advertising expenditures so it is easy to read.

1. Scroll down until the heading Advertising is at the top of your screen, then select the **four-line list** beginning with Ad Cost

Before you set tab stops for existing text, you must select the paragraphs for which you want to set tabs.

Trouble?

If the horizontal ruler is not visible, click Ruler on the View menu.

2. Point to the **tab indicator** L at the left end of the horizontal ruler

The icon that appears in the tab indicator indicates the active type of tab; pointing to the tab indicator displays a ScreenTip with the name of the active tab type. By default, left tab is the active tab type. Clicking the tab indicator scrolls through the types of tabs.

3. Click the **tab indicator** to see each of the available tab types, make **left tab** L the active tab type, then click the **1" mark** on the horizontal ruler

A left tab stop is inserted at the 1" mark on the horizontal ruler. Clicking the horizontal ruler inserts a tab stop of the active type for the selected paragraph or paragraphs.

4. Click the **tab indicator** twice so the **Right Tab icon** ⊐ is active, then click the **4½" mark** on the horizontal ruler

A right tab stop is inserted at the 4½" mark on the horizontal ruler, as shown in Figure C-12.

QuickTip

Don't use the Spacebar to vertically align text in columns; always use tabs or a table.

5. Place the insertion point before **Ad** in the first line in the list, press **[Tab]**, place the insertion point before **Cost**, then press **[Tab]**

Inserting a tab before Ad left-aligns the text at the 1" mark. Inserting a tab before Cost right-aligns Cost at the 4½" mark.

6. Insert a tab at the beginning of each remaining line in the list, then insert a tab before each **$** in the list.

The paragraphs left-align at the 1" mark. The prices right-align at the 4½" mark.

7. Select the four lines of tabbed text, drag the right tab stop to the **5" mark** on the horizontal ruler, then deselect the text

Dragging the tab stop moves it to a new location. The prices right-align at the 5" mark.

QuickTip

Place the insertion point in a paragraph to see the tab stops for that paragraph on the horizontal ruler.

8. Select the last three lines of tabbed text, click **Format** on the menu bar, then click **Tabs**

The Tabs dialog box opens, as shown in Figure C-13. You can use the Tabs dialog box to set tab stops, change the position or alignment of existing tab stops, clear tab stops, and apply tab leaders to tabs. **Tab leaders** are lines that appear in front of tabbed text.

9. Click **5"** in the Tab stop position list box, click the **2 option button** in the Leader section, click **OK**, deselect the text, then click the **Save button** 🖫 on the Standard toolbar

A dotted tab leader is added before each 5" tab stop, as shown in Figure C-14.

FIGURE C-12: Left and right tab stops on the horizontal ruler

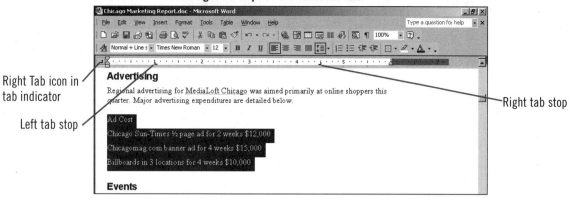

Right Tab icon in tab indicator

Left tab stop

Right tab stop

FIGURE C-13: Tabs dialog box

Select the tab stop you want to modify

FIGURE C-14: Tab leaders

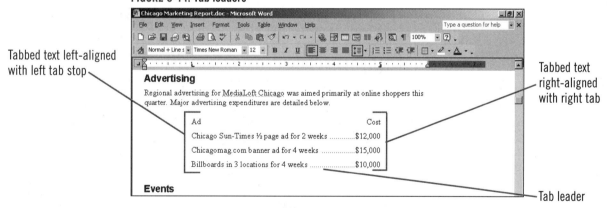

Tabbed text left-aligned with left tab stop

Tabbed text right-aligned with right tab

Tab leader

Creating a table

In addition to using tabs to organize text in rows and columns, you can create a table and then enter the text in rows and columns. To create a simple table, place the insertion point where you want to insert the table, click the Insert Table button 🔲 on the Standard toolbar, then, on the grid that appears, drag to select the number of columns and rows you want for the table. When you release the mouse button, an empty table is inserted in the document. To enter or edit text in the table, place the insertion point in a table cell, then type. To move the insertion point from cell to cell, press [Tab] or click in a cell. To format text in a table, select the text, then use the buttons on the Formatting toolbar. The Table menu also includes commands for modifying and formatting tables.

Word 2002

Working with Indents

When you **indent** a paragraph, you move its edge in from the left or right margin. You can indent the entire left or right edge of a paragraph or just the first line. The **indent markers** on the horizontal ruler indicate the indent settings for the paragraph in which the insertion point is located. Dragging the indent markers to a new location on the ruler is one way to change the indentation of a paragraph; using the indent buttons on the Formatting toolbar is another. You can also use the Paragraph command on the Format menu to indent paragraphs. Table C-1 describes different types of indents and the methods for creating each. ✎ Isaac indents several paragraphs in the report.

1. Press **[Ctrl][Home]**, click the **Print Layout View button** 🔳 on the horizontal scroll bar, click the **Zoom list arrow** on the Standard toolbar, then click **Page Width**
   The document is displayed in Print Layout view, making it easier to see the document margins.

QuickTip

Press [Tab] at the beginning of a paragraph to indent the first line ½". You can also set a custom indent using the Indents and Spacing tab in the Paragraph dialog box.

2. Place the insertion point in the italicized paragraph under the title, then click the **Increase Indent button** 📑 on the Formatting toolbar
   The entire paragraph is indented ½" from the left margin, as shown in Figure C-15. The indent marker ⬓ also moves to the ½" mark on the horizontal ruler. Each time you click the Increase Indent button, the left edge of a paragraph moves another ½" to the right.

3. Click the **Decrease Indent button** 📑 on the Formatting toolbar
   The left edge of the paragraph moves ½" to the left, and the indent marker moves back to the left margin.

Trouble?

Take care to drag only the First Line Indent marker. If you make a mistake, click the Undo button 🔄 , then try again.

4. Drag the **First Line Indent marker** ▽ to the ¼" mark on the horizontal ruler as shown in Figure C-16
   The first line of the paragraph is indented ¼". Dragging the first line indent marker indents only the first line of a paragraph.

5. Scroll to the bottom of page 1, place the insertion point in the **quote** (the last paragraph), then drag the **Left Indent marker** ⬜ to the ½" mark on the horizontal ruler
   When you drag the Left Indent marker, the First Line and Hanging Indent markers move as well. The left edge of the paragraph is indented ½" from the left margin.

6. Drag the **Right Indent marker** △ to the 5½" mark on the horizontal ruler
   The right edge of the paragraph is indented ½" from the right margin, as shown in Figure C-17.

7. Click the **Save button** 💾 on the Standard toolbar

TABLE C-1: Types of indents

indent type	description	to create
Left indent	The left edge of a paragraph is moved in from the left margin	Drag the Left Indent marker ⬜ right to the position where you want the left edge of the paragraph to align, or click the Increase Indent button 📑 to indent the paragraph in ½" increments
Right indent	The right edge of a paragraph is moved in from the right margin	Drag the Right Indent marker △ left to the position where you want the right edge of the paragraph to end
First-line indent	The first line of a paragraph is indented more than the subsequent lines	Drag the First Line Indent marker ▽ right to the position where you want the first line of the paragraph to start
Hanging indent	The subsequent lines of a paragraph are indented more than the first line	Drag the Hanging Indent marker ⬒ right to the position where you want the hanging indent to start
Negative indent (or Outdent)	The left edge of a paragraph is moved to the left of the left margin	Drag the Left Indent marker ⬜ left to the position where you want the negative indent to start

FIGURE C-15: Indented paragraph

First Line Indent marker

Hanging Indent marker

Left Indent marker

Indented paragraph

Decrease Indent button

Increase Indent button

Right Indent marker

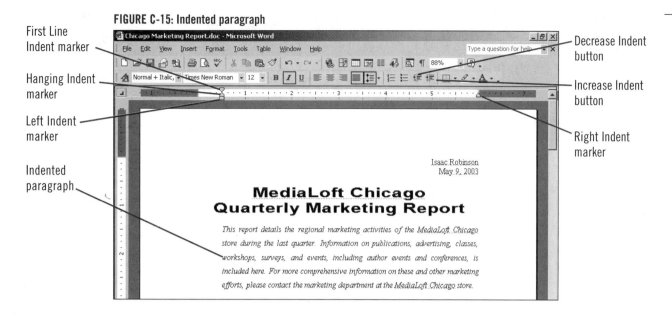

FIGURE C-16: First Line Indent marker being dragged

First Line Indent marker being dragged to the ¼" mark

FIGURE C-17: Paragraph indented from the left and right

Paragraph indented ½" from left

Paragraph indented ½" from right

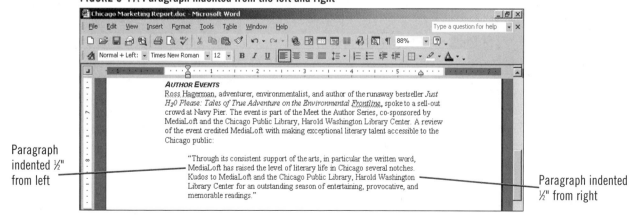

Adding Bullets and Numbering

Formatting a list with bullets or numbering can help to organize the ideas in a document. A **bullet** is a character, often a small circle, that appears before the items in a list to add emphasis. Formatting a list as a numbered list helps illustrate sequences and priorities. You can quickly format a list with bullets or numbering by using the Bullets and Numbering buttons on the Formatting toolbar. You can also use the Bullets and Numbering command on the Format menu to change or customize bullet and numbering styles. ◆ Isaac formats the lists in his report with numbers and bullets.

1. Scroll down until the first paragraph on the second page (Authors on our...) is at the top of your screen

2. Select the **three-line list of names** under the paragraph, then click the **Numbering button** 📋 on the Formatting toolbar
   The paragraphs are formatted as a numbered list.

3. Place the insertion point after **Jack Seneschal**, press **[Enter]**, then type **Polly Flanagan**
   Pressing [Enter] in the middle of the numbered list creates a new numbered paragraph and automatically renumbers the remainder of the list. Similarly, if you delete a paragraph from a numbered list, Word automatically renumbers the remaining paragraphs.

4. Click 1 in the list
   Clicking a number in a list selects all the numbers, as shown in Figure C-18.

5. Click the **Bold button** 📋 on the Formatting toolbar
   The numbers are all formatted in bold. Notice that the formatting of the items in the list does not change when you change the formatting of the numbers. You can also use this technique to change the formatting of bullets in a bulleted list.

6. Select the **list of classes and workshops** under the Classes & Workshops heading, scrolling down if necessary, then click the **Bullets button** 📋 on the Formatting toolbar
   The five paragraphs are formatted as a bulleted list.

7. With the list still selected, click **Format** on the menu bar, then click **Bullets and Numbering**
   The Bullets and Numbering dialog box opens with the Bulleted tab displayed, as shown in Figure C-19. You use this dialog box to apply bullets and numbering to paragraphs, or to change the style of bullets or numbers.

8. Click the **Square bullets box** or select another style if square bullets are not available to you, click **OK**, then deselect the text
   The bullet character changes to a small square, as shown in Figure C-20.

9. Click the **Save button** 📋 on the Standard toolbar

QuickTip

To change the numbers to letters, Roman numerals, or another numbering style, right-click the list, click Bullets and Numbering, then select a new numbering style on the Numbered tab.

QuickTip

To remove a bullet or number, select the paragraph(s), then click 📋 or 📋.

FIGURE C-18: Numbered list

Numbers selected in numbered list

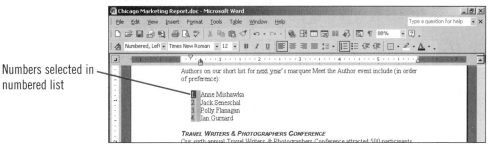

FIGURE C-19: Bulleted tab in the Bullets and Numbering dialog box

Numbered tab contains options for numbered lists

Outline Numbered tab contains options for outlines

Square bullets (your bullet styles might differ)

Click to select different characters and pictures to use as bullets

FIGURE C-20: Square bullets applied to list

Numbers are bold

Square bullets applied to list

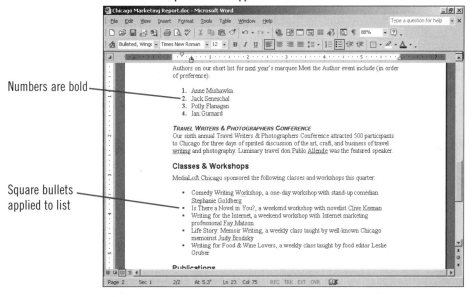

Creating outlines

You can create lists with hierarchical structures by applying an outline numbering style to a list. To create an outline, begin by applying an outline numbering style from the Outline Numbered tab in the Bullets and Numbering dialog box, then type your outline, pressing [Enter] after each item. To demote items to a lower level of importance in the outline, place the insertion point in the item, then click the Increase Indent button 🔲 on the Formatting toolbar. Each time you indent a paragraph, the item is demoted to a lower lever in the outline. Similarly, you can use the Decrease Indent button 🔲 to promote an item to a higher level in the outline. You can also create a hierarchical structure in any bulleted or numbered list by using 🔲 and 🔲 to demote and promote items in the list. To change the outline numbering style applied to a list, select a new style from the Outline Numbered tab in the Bullets and Numbering dialog box.

Adding Borders and Shading

Borders and shading can add color and splash to a document. **Borders** are lines you add above, below, to the side, or around words or a paragraph. You can format borders using different line styles, colors, and widths. **Shading** is a color or pattern you apply behind words or paragraphs to make them stand out on a page. You apply borders and shading using the Borders and Shading command on the Format menu. ✐ Isaac enhances the advertising expenses table by adding shading to it. He also applies a border under every heading to visually punctuate the sections of the report.

Steps

1. Scroll up until the heading Advertising is at the top of your screen

2. Select the **four paragraphs** of tabbed text under the Advertising heading, click **Format** on the menu bar, click **Borders and Shading**, then click the **Shading tab**
   The Shading tab in the Borders and Shading dialog box is shown in Figure C-21. You use this tab to apply shading to words and paragraphs.

3. Click the **Pale Blue box** in the bottom row of the Fill section, click **OK**, then deselect the text
   Pale blue shading is applied to the four paragraphs. Notice that the shading is applied to the entire width of the paragraphs, despite the tab settings.

4. Select the **four paragraphs**, drag the **Left Indent marker** ▭ to the ¾" mark on the horizontal ruler, drag the **Right Indent marker** △ to the 5¼" mark, then deselect the text
   The paragraphs are indented from the left and right, making the shading look more attractive.

5. Select **Advertising**, click **Format** on the menu bar, click **Borders and Shading**, then click the **Borders tab**
   The Borders tab is shown in Figure C-22. You use this tab to add boxes and lines to words or paragraphs.

6. Click the **Custom box** in the Setting section, click the **Width list arrow**, click ¾ pt, click the **Bottom Border button** ⊞ in the Preview section, click **OK**, then deselect the text
   A ¾-point black border is added below the Advertising paragraph.

7. Click **Events**, press **[F4]**, then scroll down and use [F4] to add a border under each blue heading
   The completed document is shown in Figure C-23.

8. Click the **Save button** 🖫 on the Standard toolbar, click the **Print button** 🖨, close the document, then exit Word
   A copy of the report prints. Depending on your printer, colors might appear differently when you print. If you are using a black and white printer, colors will print in shades of gray.

Highlighting text in a document

You can mark important text in a document with highlighting. **Highlighting** is transparent color that is applied to text using the Highlight pointer ⫍. To highlight text, click the Highlight list arrow 🖉▾ on the Formatting toolbar, select a color, then use the I-beam part of the ⫍ pointer to select the text. Click 🖉 to turn off the Highlight pointer. To remove highlighting, select the highlighted text, click 🖉▾, then click None. Highlighting prints, but it is used most effectively when a document is viewed online.

FIGURE C-21: Shading tab in Borders and Shading dialog box

Name of active color appears here

Pale Blue

Click to select a shading pattern

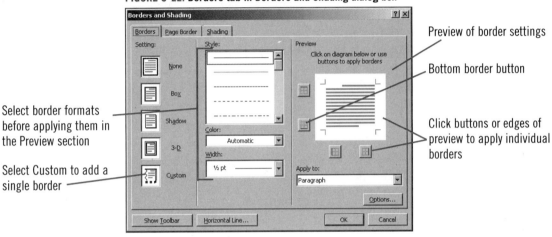

Preview of shading settings

Click to choose to apply the settings to the paragraph or to the selected text

FIGURE C-22: Borders tab in Borders and Shading dialog box

Select border formats before applying them in the Preview section

Select Custom to add a single border

Preview of border settings

Bottom border button

Click buttons or edges of preview to apply individual borders

FIGURE C-23: Borders and shading applied to the document

Border under headings

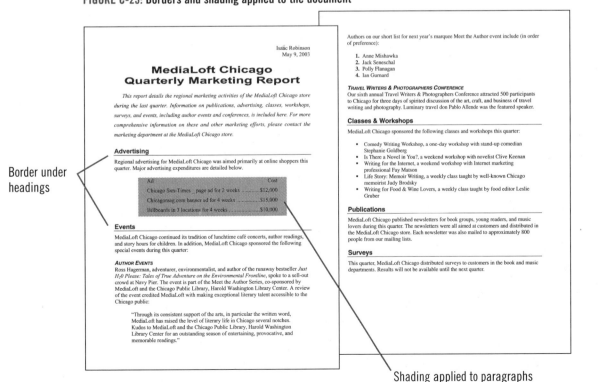

Shading applied to paragraphs

Practice

► Concepts Review

Label each element of the Word program window shown in Figure C-24.

FIGURE C-24

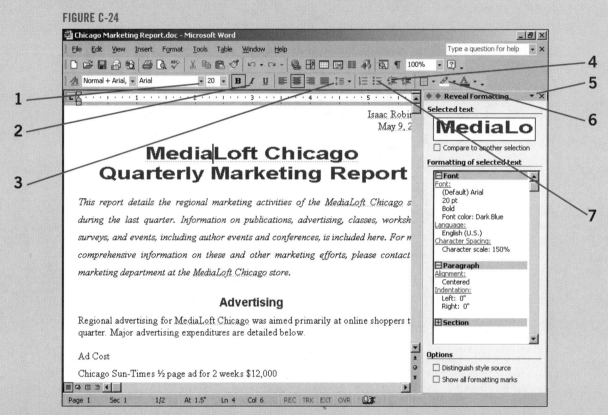

Match each term with the statement that best describes it.

8. Italic
9. Bullet
10. Style
11. Bold
12. Point
13. Highlight
14. Shading
15. Border

a. A character that appears at the beginning of a paragraph to add emphasis
b. Transparent color that is applied to text to mark it in a document
c. A text style in which characters are slanted
d. Color or a pattern that is applied behind text to make it look attractive
e. A set of format settings
f. A unit of measurement equal to ½ of an inch
g. A line that can be applied above, below, or to the sides of a paragraph
h. A text style in which characters are darker and thicker

Select the best answer from the list of choices.

16. Which button is used to align a paragraph with both the left and right margins?
    a. ▤
    b. ▤

    c. ▤
    d. ▤

Word 2002

17. **What is Times New Roman?**
    a. A character format
    b. A font
    c. A style
    d. A text effect

18. **What is the most precise way to increase the amount of white space between two paragraphs?**
    a. Indent the paragraphs.
    b. Insert an extra blank line between the paragraphs.
    c. Use the Paragraph command to change the spacing below the first paragraph.
    d. Change the line spacing of the paragraphs.

19. **What element of the Word program window can be used to check the font effects applied to text?**
    a. Standard toolbar
    b. Formatting toolbar
    c. Styles and Formatting task pane
    d. Reveal Formatting task pane

20. **Which command would you use to apply color behind a paragraph?**
    a. Borders and Shading
    b. Background
    c. Paragraph
    d. Styles and Formatting

 ## Skills Review

1. **Format with fonts.**
   a. Start Word, open the file WD C-2 from the drive and folder where your Project Files are located, save it as **EDA Report**, then scroll through the document to get a feel for its contents.
   b. Press [Ctrl][Home], format the report title **Concord Springs Economic Development Report Executive Summary** in 22-point Tahoma. Choose a different font if Tahoma is not available to you.
   c. Change the font color of the report title to Blue-Gray.
   d. Format each of the following headings in 14-point Tahoma with the Blue-Gray font color: **Mission Statement**, **Guiding Principles**, **Issues**, **Proposed Actions**.
   e. Press [Ctrl][Home], then save your changes to the report.

2. **Change font styles and effects.**
   a. Apply bold to the report title and to each heading in the report.
   b. Format the paragraph under the Mission Statement heading in italic.
   c. Format the third paragraph under the Issues heading, **Years Population Growth**, in bold small caps, with a Blue-Gray font color.
   d. Change the font color of the two paragraphs under Years Population Growth to Blue-Gray.
   e. Format the paragraph **Source: Office of State Planning** in italic.
   f. Scroll to the top of the report, change the character scale of **Concord Springs Economic Development Report** to 80%, then save your changes.

3. **Change line and paragraph spacing.**
   a. Change the line spacing of the three-line list under the first body paragraph to 1.5 lines.
   b. Add 12 points of space before the Executive Summary paragraph.
   c. Add 12 points of space after each heading in the report.
   d. Add 6 points of space after each paragraph in the list under the Guiding Principles heading.
   e. Add 6 points of space after each paragraph under the Proposed Actions heading.
   f. Press [Ctrl][Home], then save your changes to the report.

4. **Align paragraphs.**

    a. Press [Ctrl][A] to select the entire document, then justify all the paragraphs.

    b. Center the two-paragraph report title.

    c. Press [Ctrl][End], type your name, press [Enter], type the current date, then right-align your name and the date.

    d. Save your changes to the report.

5. **Work with tabs.**

    a. Scroll up and select the four-line list of blue-gray population information.

    b. Set left tab stops at the 1¾"-mark and the 3" mark.

    c. Insert a tab at the beginning of each paragraph in the list.

    d. In the first paragraph, insert a tab before Population. In the second paragraph, insert a tab before 4.5%. In the third paragraph, insert a tab before 53%.

    e. Select the first three paragraphs, then drag the second tab stop to the 2¾" mark on the horizontal ruler.

    f. Press [Ctrl][Home], then save your changes to the report.

6. **Work with indents.**

    a. Indent the first line of the first body paragraph ½".

    b. Indent the paragraph under the Mission Statement heading ½" from the left and ½" from the right.

    c. Indent the first line of the paragraph under the Guiding Principles heading ½".

    d. Indent the first line of the three body paragraphs under the Issues heading ½".

    e. Press [Ctrl][Home], then save your changes to the report.

7. **Add bullets and numbering.**

    a. Apply bullets to the three-line list under the first body paragraph.

    b. Change the bullet style to small circles (or choose another bullet style if small circles are not available to you).

    c. Change the font color of the bullets to Blue-Gray.

    d. Scroll down until the Guiding Principles heading is at the top of your screen.

    e. Format the five-paragraph list under Guiding Principles as a numbered list.

    f. Format the numbers in 12-point Tahoma bold, then change the font color to Blue-Gray.

    g. Scroll down until the Proposed Actions heading is at the top of your screen, then format the paragraphs under the heading as a bulleted list using checkmarks as the bullet style (or choose another bullet style).

    h. Change the font color of the bullets to Blue-Gray, press [Ctrl][Home], then save your changes to the report.

8. **Add borders and shading.**

    a. Change the font color of the report title to Light Yellow, then apply Blue-Gray shading.

    b. Apply Light Yellow shading to the Mission Statement heading, then add a 1-point Blue-Gray border below the Mission Statement heading.

    c. Use the Format Painter to copy the formatting of the Mission Statement heading to the other headings in the report.

    d. Under the Issues heading, select the first three lines of tabbed text, which are formatted in Blue-Gray.

    e. Apply Light Yellow shading to the paragraphs, then add a 1-point Blue-Gray box border around the paragraphs.

    f. Indent the paragraphs 1½" from the left and 1½" from the right.

    g. Press [Ctrl][Home], save your changes to the report, view the report in Print Preview, then print a copy. The formatted report is shown in Figure C-25.

    h. Close the file and exit Word.

FIGURE C-25

Concord Springs Economic Development Report

Executive Summary

The Concord Springs Economic Development Authority (EDA) has written an economic policy plan for the Town of Concord Springs. The plan is intended to advance dynamic and interactive discussion. It will be used to continuously assess and foster decision-making about the town's:

- Development
- Infrastructure
- Quality of life

Mission Statement

The purpose of the EDA is to foster a sustainable economy consistent with the town's planning objectives. The mix of industry, commerce, open space, residential development, and the arts in Concord Springs results in the town's vitality and an excellent quality of life for its citizens. Maintaining this balance is important.

Guiding Principles

Five basic principles guide Concord Springs' economic policy. These principles seek to safeguard the special features that give the town its character while embracing appropriate economic opportunities.

1. Concord Springs should remain a major economic center of the region.
2. Economic activity must respect Concord Springs' natural, cultural, and historic heritage.
3. A pedestrian-friendly core commercial center is essential.
4. Sustained economic prosperity requires a balance between residential development, industrial/commercial development, and open space.
5. Investing in the infrastructure is necessary to maintain and expand the existing tax and job base.

Issues

Of Concord Springs' approximately 64,000 acres of land, 12% is zoned for business, commercial, or industrial use, and 88% for residential development. Historically the town has relied upon business and industry to provide 35%-40% of the tax base, as well as employment opportunities. Concord Springs does not have a great deal of non-residential development potential. Non-residential development has traditionally been the backbone of the Concord Springs economy.

The population of Concord Springs is expected to rise dramatically over the next decade. The following chart shows the expected change:

YEARS	POPULATION GROWTH
1980-2000	4.5%
2000-2020	53% (projected)

Source: Office of State Planning

At issue is the town's ability to continue to support increasing public costs (most importantly, education) with a tax base shifting toward residential taxpayers. The EDA believes Concord Springs should remain the market center of the region and avoid becoming a bedroom community. Concord Springs has maintained a sense of community in part because more than 50% of working residents are able to earn a living within the town. Jobs must be continuously created to sustain the percentage of residents who live and work in Concord Springs.

Proposed Actions

- ✓ Implement a business retention program that focuses on the growth and expansion of businesses already operating in Concord Springs.
- ✓ Build a consortium of technical and skill development resources to assist companies with educational and training needs.
- ✓ Sponsor an e-commerce workshop.
- ✓ Allocate funds for expanded downtown parking.
- ✓ Develop a strategic open space plan.

Your Name
Today's Date

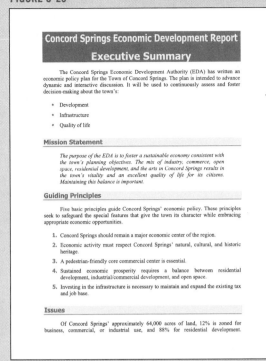

► Independent Challenge 1

You are an estimator for Zakia Construction in the Australian city of Wollongong. You have drafted an estimate for a home renovation job, and need to format it. It's important that your estimate have a clean, striking design, and reflect your company's professionalism.

FIGURE C-26

ZAKIAConstruction
73 Corrimal Street
Wollongong, NSW 2500
Tel: 02-4225-3202
www.zabel.com.au

a. Start Word, open the file WD C-3 from the drive and folder where your Project Files are located, save it as **Zakia Construction**, then read the document to get a feel for its contents. Figure C-26 shows how you will format the letterhead.
b. In the first paragraph, format **ZAKIA** in 24-point Arial Black. (*Hint*: Select a similar font if Arial Black is not available to you.)
c. Format **Construction** in 24-point Arial, then change the character scale to 90%.
d. Format the next four lines in 9-point Arial, right-align them, then add a 1-point border below the last line.
e. In the body of the document, format the title **Proposal of Renovation** in 16-point Arial Black, then center the title.
f. Format the following headings (including the colons) in 12-point Arial Black: **Date**, **Work to be performed for and at**, **Scope of work**, **Payment schedule** and **Agreement**.
g. Format the 14-paragraph list under Scope of work as a numbered list, then apply bold to the numbers.
h. Change the paragraph spacing to add 4 points of space after each paragraph in the list.
i. With the list selected, set a right tab stop at the 5¾" mark, then insert tabs before every price in the list.
j. Apply bold to the two paragraphs—**Total estimated job cost** and **Approximate job time**—below the list.
k. Replace Your Name with your name in the signature block, select the signature block, set a left tab stop at the 3½" mark, then indent the signature block.
l. Examine the document carefully for formatting errors and make any necessary adjustments.
m. Save and print the document, then close the file and exit Word.

Independent Challenge 2

Your employer, The Lange Center for Contemporary Arts in Halifax, Nova Scotia, is launching a membership drive. Your boss has written the text for a flyer advertising Lange membership, and asks you to format it so that it is eye-catching and attractive.

a. Open the file WD C-4 from the drive and folder where your Project Files are located, save it as **Membership Flyer**, then read the document. Figure C-27 shows how you will format the first several paragraphs of the flyer.

FIGURE C-27

b. Select the entire document and format it in 10-point Arial Narrow.

c. Format the first paragraph, **Membership Drive**, in 26-point Arial Narrow, bold, with a white font color. Expand the character spacing by 7 points. Center the paragraph and apply plum shading to the paragraph.

d. Format the second paragraph, **2003**, in 36-point Arial Black, 80% gray font color, with a shadow effect. Expand the character spacing by 25 points and change the character scale to 200%. Center the paragraph.

e. Format each **What we do for…** heading in 12-point Arial, bold, with a plum font color. Add a single line ½-point border under each heading.

f. Format each subheading (**Gallery, Lectures, Library, All members…**, and **Membership Levels**) in 10-point Arial, bold. Add 3 points of spacing before each paragraph.

g. Indent each body paragraph ¼", except for the paragraphs under the What we do for YOU heading.

h. Format the four paragraphs under the All members… subheading as a bulleted list. Use a bullet symbol of your choice and format the bullets in the plum color.

i. Indent the five paragraphs under the Membership Levels heading ¼". For these five paragraphs, set left tab stops at the 1¼" mark and the 2" mark on the horizontal ruler. Insert tabs before the price and before the word **All** in each of the five paragraphs.

j. Format the name of each membership level (**Artistic, Conceptual**, etc.) in 10-point Arial, bold, italic, with a plum font color.

k. Format the **For more information** paragraph in 14-point Arial, bold, with a plum font color. Center the paragraph and add a 6-point dotted black border above the paragraph.

l. Format the last two paragraphs in 11-point Arial Narrow, and center the paragraphs. In the contact information, replace **Your Name** with your name, then apply bold to your name.

m. Examine the document carefully for formatting errors and make any necessary adjustments.

n. Save and print the flyer, then close the file and exit Word.

 Independent Challenge 3

One of your responsibilities as program coordinator at Solstice Mountain Sports is to develop a program of winter outdoor learning and adventure workshops. You have written a memo to your boss to update her on your progress. You need to format the memo so it is professional-looking and easy to read.

a. Start Word, open the file WD C-5 from the drive and folder where your Project Files are located, then save it as **Solstice Memo**.

b. Format the heading **Solstice Mountain Sports Memorandum** in 26-point Impact, then center it.

c. In the memo header, replace Today's Date and Your Name with the current date and your name.

d. Select the four-line memo header, set a left tab stop at the ¾" mark, then insert tabs before the date, the recipient's name, your name, and the subject of the memo.

e. Select **Date:**, then apply the character style Strong to it. FIGURE C-28
(*Hint:* Open the Styles and Formatting task pane, click the Show list arrow, click All Styles if necessary, scroll through the alphabetical list of styles to locate the style Strong, then click Strong.)

f. Apply the Strong style to **To:**, **From:**, and **Re:**, then double-space the four lines in the memo header.

g. Apply a 3-point dotted border below the blank line under the memo header. (*Hint:* Turn on formatting marks, select the paragraph symbol below the memo header, then apply a border below it.)

h. Apply the paragraph style Heading 3 to the headings **Overview**, **Workshops**, **Accommodation**, **Fees**, and **Proposed winter programming**.

i. Under the Fees heading, format the words **Workshop fees** and **Accommodation fees** using the Strong style.

j. Add 6 points of space after the Workshop fees paragraph.

k. In the Fees section, apply green highlighting to these sentences: **Workshop fees include materials and equipment.** and **This is a discounted rate.**

l. On the second page of the document, format the list under the Proposed winter programming heading as an outline. Figure C-28 shows the hierarchical structure of the outline. (*Hint:* Format the list as an outline numbered list, then use the Increase Indent and Decrease Indent buttons to change the level of importance of each item.)

m. Change the outline numbering style to the bullet numbering style shown in Figure C-28, if necessary.

n. Save and print the document, then close the file and exit Word.

Proposed winter programming
- ❖ Skiing, Snowboarding, and Snowshoeing
  - ➤ Skiing and Snowboarding
    - ▪ Cross-country skiing
      - • Cross-country skiing for beginners
      - • Intermediate cross-country skiing
      - • Inn-to-inn ski touring
      - • Moonlight cross-country skiing
    - ▪ Telemarking
      - • Basic telemark skiing
      - • Introduction to backcountry skiing
      - • Exploring on skis
    - ▪ Snowboarding
      - • Backcountry snowboarding
  - ➤ Snowshoeing
    - ▪ Beginner
      - • Snowshoeing for beginners
      - • Snowshoeing and winter ecology
    - ▪ Intermediate and Advanced
      - • Intermediate snowshoeing
      - • Guided snowshoe trek
      - • Above tree line snowshoeing
- ❖ Winter Hiking, Camping, and Survival
  - ➤ Hiking
    - ▪ Beginner
      - • Long-distance hiking
      - • Winter summits
      - • Hiking for women
  - ➤ Winter camping and survival
    - ▪ Beginner
      - • Introduction to winter camping
      - • Basic winter mountain skills
      - • Building snow shelters
    - ▪ Intermediate
      - • Basic winter mountain skills II
      - • Ice climbing
      - • Avalanche awareness and rescue

Independent Challenge 4

The fonts you choose for a document can have a major effect on the document's tone. Not all fonts are appropriate for use in a business document, and some fonts, especially those with a definite theme, are appropriate only for specific purposes. The World Wide Web includes hundreds of Web sites devoted to fonts and text design. Some Web sites sell fonts, others allow you to download fonts for free and install them on your computer. In this independent challenge, you will research Web sites related to fonts and find examples of fonts you could use in your work.

a. Start Word, open the file WD C-6 from the drive and folder where your Project Files are located, and save it as **Fonts**. This document contains the questions you will answer about the fonts you find.

b. Use your favorite search engine to search the Web for Web sites related to fonts. Use the keyword **font** to conduct your search. If your search does not result in appropriate links, try looking at the following Web sites: www.1001freefonts.com, www.fontsnthings.com, and www.fontfreak.com.

c. Explore the fonts available for downloading. As you examine the fonts, notice that fonts fall into two general categories: serif fonts, which have a small stroke, called a serif, at the ends of characters, and sans serif fonts, which do not have a serif. Times New Roman is an example of a serif font and Arial is an example of a sans serif font.

d. Type your answers in the Fonts document, save it, print a copy, then close the file and exit Word.

► Visual Workshop

Using the file WD C-7 found in the drive and folder where your Project Files are located, create the menu shown in Figure C-29. (*Hints*: Use Georgia for the font. Change the font size of the heading to 72 points, scale the font to 66%, and expand the spacing by 2 points. For the rest of the text, change the font size to 11 points. Indent all the text ½" from the left and the right. Use paragraph spacing to adjust the spacing between paragraphs so that all the text fits on one page. If the Georgia font is not available to you, choose a different font.) Save the menu as **Rosebud Specials**, then print a copy.

FIGURE C-29

Rosebud Café

DAILY SPECIALS

MONDAY
Veggie Chili
Hearty veggie chili with melted cheddar in our peasant French bread bowl. Topped with sour cream & scallions.
$5.95

TUESDAY
Greek Salad
Our large garden salad with kalamata olives, feta cheese, and garlic vinaigrette. Served with an assortment of rolls.
$5.95

WEDNESDAY
French Dip
Lean roast beef topped with melted cheddar on our roasted garlic roll. Served with a side of au jus and red bliss mashed potatoes.
$6.95

THURSDAY
Chicken Cajun Bleu
Cajun chicken, chunky blue cheese, cucumbers, leaf lettuce, and tomato on our roasted garlic roll.
$6.50

FRIDAY
Clam Chowder
Classic New England thick, rich, clam chowder in our peasant French bread bowl. Served with a garden salad.
$5.95

SATURDAY
Hot Chicken and Gravy
Delicious chicken and savory gravy served on a thick slice of toasted honest white. Served with red bliss mashed potatoes.
$6.95

SUNDAY
Turkey-Bacon Club
Double-decker roasted turkey, crisp bacon, leaf lettuce, tomato, and sun-dried tomato mayo on toasted triple seed.
$6.50

Your Name

Formatting

Documents

- ⌐MOUS⌐ ► **Set document margins**
- ⌐MOUS⌐ ► **Divide a document into sections**
- ⌐MOUS⌐ ► **Add page breaks**
- ⌐MOUS⌐ ► **Add page numbers**
- ⌐MOUS⌐ ► **Insert headers and footers**
- ⌐MOUS⌐ ► **Edit headers and footers**
- ⌐MOUS⌐ ► **Format columns**
- ⌐MOUS⌐ ► **Insert clip art**

Word's page formatting features allow you to creatively lay out and design the pages of your documents. In this unit, you learn how to change the document margins, determine the page orientation of a document, add page numbers, and insert headers and footers. You also learn how to format text in columns and how to illustrate your documents with clip art. ⟍⟍ Alice Wegman has written and formatted the text for a quarterly newsletter for the MediaLoft marketing staff. She is now ready to lay out and design the pages of the newsletter. She plans to organize the articles in columns and to illustrate the newsletter with clip art. You will work with Alice as she formats the newsletter.

Setting Document Margins

Changing a document's margins is one way to change the appearance of a document and control the amount of text that fits on a page. The **margins** of a document are the blank areas between the edge of the text and the edge of the page. When you create a document in Word, the default margins are 1" at the top and bottom of the page, and 1.25" on the left and right sides of the page. You can adjust the size of a document's margins using the Page Setup command on the File menu, or using the rulers. Alice plans the newsletter to be a four-page document when finished. She reduces the size of the document margins so that more text fits on each page.

Steps

1. Start **Word**, open the file **WD D-1** from the drive and folder where your Project Files are located, then save it as **MediaLoft Buzz**
   The newsletter opens in Print Layout view.

2. Scroll through the newsletter to get a feel for its contents, then press **[Ctrl][Home]**
   The newsletter is currently six pages long. Notice the status bar indicates the page where the insertion point is located and the total number of pages in the document.

3. Click **File** on the menu bar, click **Page Setup**, then click the **Margins tab** in the Page Setup dialog box if necessary
   The Margins tab in the Page Setup dialog box is shown in Figure D-1. You can use the Margins tab to change the width of the top, bottom, left, or right document margins, to change the orientation of the pages from portrait to landscape, and to alter other page layout settings. **Portrait orientation** means a page is taller than it is wide; **landscape orientation** means a page is wider than it is tall. This newsletter uses portrait orientation.

4. Click the **Top down arrow** three times until 0.7" appears, then click the **Bottom down arrow** until 0.7" appears
   The top and bottom margins of the newsletter will be .7". Notice that the margins in the Preview section of the dialog box change as you adjust the margin settings.

5. Press **[Tab]**, type **.7** in the Left text box, press **[Tab]**, then type **.7** in the Right text box
   The left and right margins of the newsletter will also be .7". You can change the margin settings by using the arrows or by typing a value in the appropriate text box.

6. Click **OK**
   The document margins change to .7", as shown in Figure D-2. The bar at the intersection of the white and gray areas on the horizontal and vertical rulers indicates the location of the margin. You can also change a document's margins by dragging the bar to a new location. Notice that the status bar indicates the total number of pages in the document is now five.

7. Click the **Zoom list arrow** on the Standard toolbar, then click **Two Pages**
   The first two pages of the document appear in the document window.

8. Scroll down to view all five pages of the newsletter, press **[Ctrl][Home]**, click the **Zoom list arrow**, click **Page Width**, then click the **Save button** 🖫 on the Standard toolbar to save the document

FIGURE D-1: Margins tab in Page Setup dialog box

Default margin settings

Set gutter margin

Select gutter position

Select page orientation

Set mirror margins and other page layout options

Preview of margin settings

Select part of document to apply settings to

FIGURE D-2: Newsletter with smaller margins

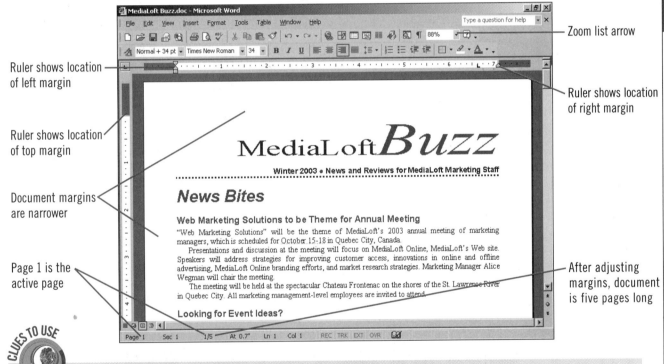

Zoom list arrow

Ruler shows location of left margin

Ruler shows location of right margin

Ruler shows location of top margin

Document margins are narrower

After adjusting margins, document is five pages long

Page 1 is the active page

CLUES TO USE

Changing paper size, orientation, and margin settings

By default, the documents you create in Word use an 8½" x 11" paper size in portrait orientation with the default margin settings, but you can adjust these settings in the Page Setup dialog box to create documents of any size, shape, and layout. On the Margins tab, change the orientation of the pages by selecting Portrait or Landscape. To change the layout of multiple pages, use the Multiple pages list arrow to create pages that use mirror margins, include two pages per sheet of paper, or are formatted like a folded booklet. **Mirror margins** are used in documents with facing pages, such as a magazine, where the margins on the left page of the document are a mirror image of the margins on

the right. Documents with mirror margins have inside and outside margins, rather than right and left margins. Another type of margin is a gutter margin, which is used in documents that are bound, such as books. A **gutter** adds extra space to the left or top margin so that the binding does not obscure text. Add a gutter to a document by adjusting the setting in the Gutter text box on the Margins tab. If you want to change the size of the paper used in a document, use the Paper tab in the Page Setup dialog box. Use the Paper size list arrow to select a standard paper size, or enter custom measurements in the Width and Height text boxes.

Word 2002

Dividing a Document into Sections

Dividing a document into sections allows you to format each section of the document with different page layout settings. A **section** is a portion of a document that is separated from the rest of the document by section breaks. **Section breaks** are formatting marks that you insert in a document to show the end of a section. Once you have divided a document into sections, you can format each section with different column, margin, page orientation, header and footer, and other page layout settings. By default, a document is formatted as a single section, but you can divide a document into as many sections as you like. Alice wants to format the body of the newsletter in two columns, but leave the masthead and the headline "News Bites" as a single column. She inserts a section break before the body of the newsletter to divide the document into two sections, then she changes the number of columns in the second section to two.

1. **Click the Show/Hide ¶ button ¶ on the Standard toolbar to display formatting marks if they are not visible**
Turning on formatting marks allows you to see the section breaks you insert in a document.

QuickTip
When you insert a section break at the beginning of a paragraph, Word inserts the break at the end of the previous paragraph. A section break stores the formatting information for the preceding section.

2. **Place the insertion point before the headline Web Marketing Solutions to be..., click Insert on the menu bar, then click Break**
The Break dialog box opens, as shown in Figure D-3. You use this dialog box to insert different types of section breaks. Table D-1 describes the different types of section breaks.

3. **Click the Continuous option button, then click OK**
Word inserts a continuous section break, shown as a dotted double line, above the headline. A continuous section break begins a new section of the document on the same page. The document now has two sections. Notice that the status bar indicates that the insertion point is in section 2.

4. **With the insertion point in section 2, click the Columns button ▦ on the Standard toolbar**
A grid showing four columns opens below the button. You use the grid to select the number of columns you want to create.

QuickTip
To change the margins or page orientation of a section, place the insertion point in the section, change the margin or page orientation settings on the Margins tab in the Page Setup dialog box, click the Apply to list arrow on the Margins tab, click This section, then click OK.

5. **Point to the second column on the grid, then click**
Section 2 is formatted in two columns, as shown in Figure D-4. The text in section 1 remains formatted in a single column. Notice the status bar now indicates the document is four pages long. Formatting text in columns is another way to increase the amount of text that fits on a page. You'll learn more about columns in a later lesson.

6. **Click the Zoom list arrow on the Standard toolbar, click Two Pages, then scroll down to examine all four pages of the document**
The text in section 2—all the text below the continuous section break—is formatted in two columns. Text in columns flows automatically from the bottom of one column to the top of the next.

7. **Press [Ctrl][Home], click the Zoom list arrow, click Page Width, then save the document**

TABLE D-1: Types of section breaks

section break	function
Next page	Begins a new a section and moves the text following the break to the top of the next page
Continuous	Begins a new section on the same page
Even page	Begins a new section and moves the text following the break to the top of the next even-numbered page
Odd page	Begins a new section and moves the text following the break to the top of the next odd-numbered page

FIGURE D-3: Break dialog box

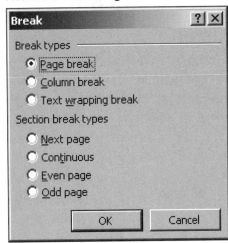

FIGURE D-4: Continuous section break and columns

Text in section 1 is formatted in one column

Insertion point is in section 2

Text in section 2 is formatted in two columns

Section 2 is the active section

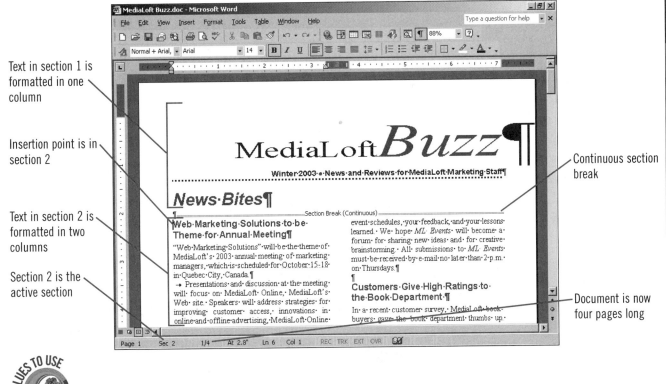

Continuous section break

Document is now four pages long

CLUES TO USE

Changing page layout settings for a section

Dividing a document into sections allows you to vary the layout of a document. In addition to applying different column settings to sections, you can apply different margins, page orientation, paper size, vertical alignment, header and footer, page numbering, and other page layout settings. For example, if you are formatting a report that includes a table with many columns, you might want to change the table's page orientation to landscape so that it is easier to read. To do this, you would insert a section break before and after the table to create a section that contains only the table. Then you would use the Margins tab in the Page Setup dialog box to change the page orientation of the table section to landscape.

To change the page layout settings for an individual section, place the insertion point in the section, open the Page Setup (or Columns) dialog box, select the options you want to change, click the Apply to list arrow, click This section, then click OK. When you select This section in the Apply to list box, the settings are applied to the current section only. If you select Whole document in the Apply to list box, the settings are applied to all the sections in the document.

Adding Page Breaks

As you type text in a document, Word automatically inserts a **soft page break** when you reach the bottom of a page, allowing you to continue typing on the next page. You can also force text onto the next page of a document by using the Break command to insert a **hard page break**. ✐ Alice inserts hard page breaks where she knows she wants to begin each new page of the newsletter.

Steps

1. **Scroll down to the bottom of page 1, place the insertion point before the headline Career Corner, click Insert on the menu bar, then click Break**
   The Break dialog box opens. You also use this dialog box to insert page, column, and text-wrapping breaks. Table D-2 describes these types of breaks.

QuickTip

Hard and soft page breaks are always visible in Normal view.

2. **Make sure the Page break option button is selected, then click OK**
   Word inserts a hard page break before "Career Corner" and moves all the text following the page break to the beginning of the next page, as shown in Figure D-5. The page break appears as a dotted line in Print Layout view. Page break marks are visible on the screen but do not print.

3. **Scroll down to the bottom of page 2, place the insertion point before the headline Webcasts Slated for May, press and hold [Ctrl], then press [Enter]**
   Pressing [Ctrl][Enter] is a fast way to insert a hard page break. The headline is forced to the top of the third page.

4. **Scroll down to the bottom of page 3, place the insertion point before the headline Staff News, then press [Ctrl][Enter]**
   The headline is forced to the top of the fourth page.

5. **Press [Ctrl][Home], click the Zoom list arrow on the Standard toolbar, then click Two Pages**
   The first two pages of the document are displayed, as shown in Figure D-6.

6. **Scroll down to view pages 3 and 4, click the Zoom list arrow, click Page Width, then save the document**

CLUES TO USE

Vertically aligning text on a page

By default, text is vertically aligned with the top margin of a page, but you can change the vertical alignment of text so that it is centered between the top and bottom margins, justified between the top and bottom margins, or aligned with the bottom margin of the page. You would vertically align text on a page only when the text does not fill the page; for example, if you are creating a flyer or a title page for a report. To change the vertical alignment of text in a section (or a document), place the insertion point in the section you want to align, open the Page Setup dialog box, use the Vertical alignment list arrow on the Layout tab to select the alignment you want—top, center, justified, or bottom—use the Apply to list arrow to select the part of the document you want to align, then click OK.

FIGURE D-5: Hard page break in document

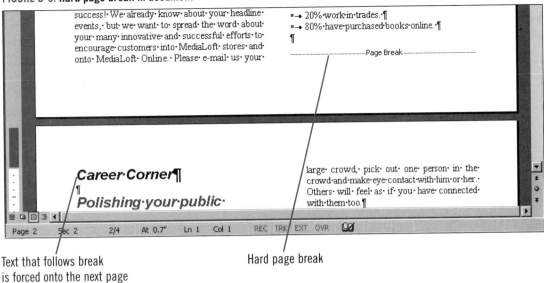

Text that follows break
is forced onto the next page

Hard page break

FIGURE D-6: Pages 1 and 2

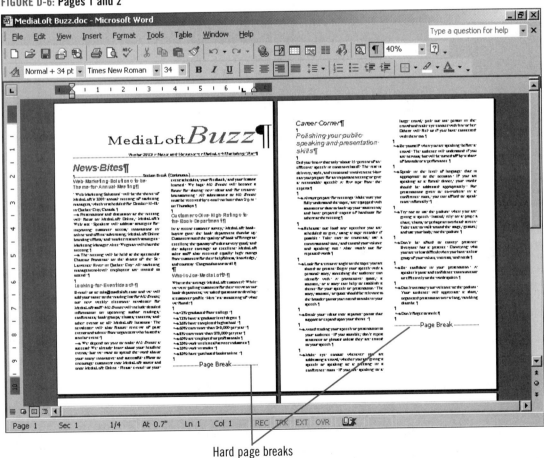

Hard page breaks

TABLE D-2: Types of breaks

break	function
Page break	Forces the text following the break to begin at the top of the next page
Column break	Forces the text following the break to begin at the top of the next column
Text wrapping break	Forces the text following the break to begin at the beginning of the next line

Adding Page Numbers

If you want to number the pages of a multi-page document, you can insert a page number field at the top or bottom of each page. A **field** is a code that serves as a placeholder for data that changes in a document, such as a page number or the current date. When you use the Page Numbers command on the Insert menu to add page numbers to a document, Word automatically numbers the pages for you. ▬▬▬ Alice adds page numbers to the bottom of each page in the document.

Steps

1. **Click Insert on the menu bar, then click Page Numbers**
   The Page Numbers dialog box opens, as shown in Figure D-7. You use this dialog box to specify the position—top or bottom of the page—and the alignment for the page numbers. Bottom of page (Footer) is the default position.

QuickTip

You can also align page numbers with the left, right, inside, or outside margins of a document.

2. **Click the Alignment list arrow, then click Center**
   The page numbers will be centered between the left and right margins at the bottom of each page.

3. **Click OK, then scroll to the bottom of the first page**
   The page number 1 appears in gray at the bottom of the first page, as shown in Figure D-8. The number is gray, or dimmed, because it is located in the Footer area. When the document is printed, the page numbers appear as normal text. You will learn more about headers and footers in the next lesson.

4. **Click the Print Preview button ⬚ on the Standard toolbar, then click the One Page button ⬚ on the Print Preview toolbar if necessary**
   The first page of the newsletter appears in Print Preview. Notice the page number.

5. **Click the page number with the ⊕ pointer to zoom in on the page**
   The page number is centered at the bottom of the page, as shown in Figure D-9.

6. **Scroll down the document to see the page number at the bottom of each page**
   Word automatically numbered the pages of the newsletter.

QuickTip

To display more than six pages of a document in Print Preview, drag to expand the Multiple Pages grid.

7. **Click the Multiple Pages button ⬚ on the Print Preview toolbar, point to the second box in the bottom row on the grid to select 2 x 2 pages, then click**
   All four pages of the newsletter appear in the Print Preview window.

8. **Click Close on the Print Preview toolbar, then save the document**

Inserting date and time fields

Using the Date and Time command on the Insert menu, you can add a field for the current date or the current time into a document. To insert the current date or time at the location of the insertion point, click Date and Time on the Insert menu, then select the date or time format you want to use from the list of available formats in the Date and Time dialog box. To insert the date or time as a field that will be updated automatically each time you open or print the document, select the Update automatically check box, then click OK. If you want to insert the current date or time as static text that does not change each time you open or print the document, deselect the Update automatically check box, then click OK. Word uses the clock on your computer to compute the current date and time.

Once you have inserted a date or time field, you can modify the format by changing the field code: right-click the field, click Edit Field on the shortcut menu, then select a new format in the Field properties list in the Field dialog box. You can edit static text just as you would any other text in Word.

FIGURE D-7: Page Numbers dialog box

Set location for page number (header or footer)

Set alignment of page number

Clear to hide the page number on the first page

Click to change the numbering format

Preview of page number position

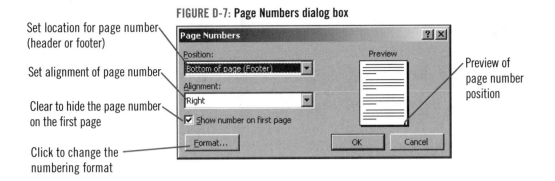

FIGURE D-8: Page number in document

Page number is dimmed

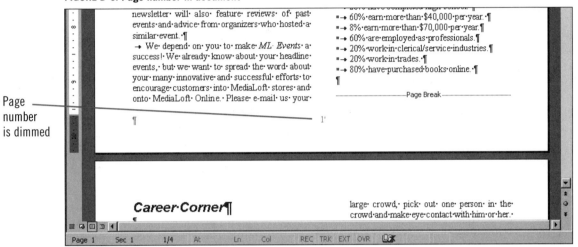

FIGURE D-9: Page number in Print Preview

One Page button

Multiple Pages button

Page number in Print Preview

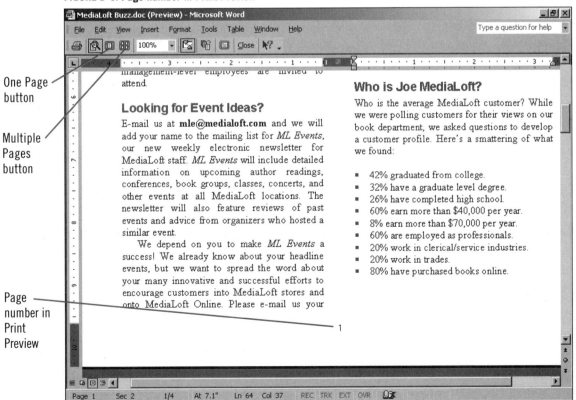

Word 2002

Inserting Headers and Footers

A **header** is text or graphics that appears at the top of every page of a document. A **footer** is text or graphics that appears at the bottom of every page. In longer documents, headers and footers often contain information such as the title of the publication, the title of the chapter, the name of the author, the date, or a page number. You can add headers and footers to a document by using the Header and Footer command on the View menu to open the Header and Footer areas, and then inserting text and graphics in them. Alice creates a header that includes the name of the newsletter and the current date.

1. **Click View on the menu bar, then click Header and Footer**
   The Header and Footer areas open and the document text is dimmed, as shown in Figure D-10. When the document text is dimmed, it cannot be edited. The Header and Footer toolbar also opens. It includes buttons for inserting standard text into headers and footers and for navigating between headers and footers. See Table D-3. The Header and Footer areas of a document are independent of the document itself and must be formatted separately. For example, if you select all the text in a document and then change the font, the header and footer font does not change.

QuickTip

You can change the date format by right-clicking the field, clicking Edit Field on the shortcut menu, and then selecting a new date format in the Field properties list in the Field dialog box.

2. **Type Buzz in the Header area, press [Spacebar] twice, then click the Insert Date button 🗓 on the Header and Footer toolbar**
   Clicking the Insert Date button inserts a date field into the header. The date is inserted using the default date format (usually month/date/year, although your default date format might be different). The word "Buzz" and the current date will appear at the top of every page in the document.

3. **Select Buzz and the date, then click the Center button ▤ on the Formatting toolbar**
   The text is centered in the Header area. You can also use tabs to center and right-align text in the Header and Footer areas. Notice that the center and right tab stops shown on the ruler do not align with the current margin settings. The tab stops are the default tab stops for the Header and Footer areas, based on the default margin settings. If you change the margins in a document, you need to adjust the tab stops in the Header or Footer area to align with the new margin settings.

QuickTip

Unless you set different headers and footers for different sections, the information you insert in any Header or Footer area will appear on every page in the document.

4. **With the text still selected, click the Font list arrow on the Formatting toolbar, click Arial, click the Bold button 𝐁, then click in the Header area to deselect the text**
   The header text is formatted in 12-point Arial bold, as shown in Figure D-11.

5. **Click the Switch Between Header and Footer button 🖼 on the Header and Footer toolbar**
   The insertion point moves to the Footer area. A page number field already appears centered in the Footer area.

6. **Double-click the page number to select the field, click the Font list arrow, click Arial, click 𝐁, then click in the Footer area to deselect the field**
   The page number is formatted in 12-point Arial bold.

QuickTip

To change the distance between the header and footer and the edge of the page, change the From edge settings on the Layout tab in the Page Setup dialog box.

7. **Click Close on the Header and Footer toolbar, save the document, then scroll down until the bottom of page 1 and the top of page 2 appear in the document window**
   The Header and Footer areas close and the header and footer text is dimmed, as shown in Figure D-12. The header text—"Buzz" and the current date—appear at the top of every page in the document, and a page number appears at the bottom of each page.

FIGURE D-10: Header area

Header and Footer toolbar

Insert Date button

Header area is open

Document text is dimmed

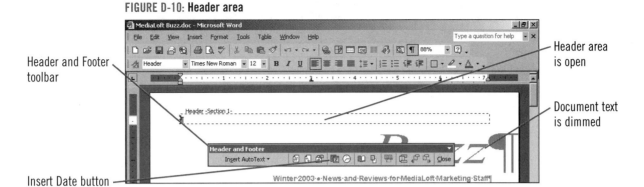

FIGURE D-11: Formatted header text

Information in Header area for section 1 appears on every page

Formatted text is centered in the Header area

Tab stops for the header are set for the default document margins

Switch Between Header and Footer button

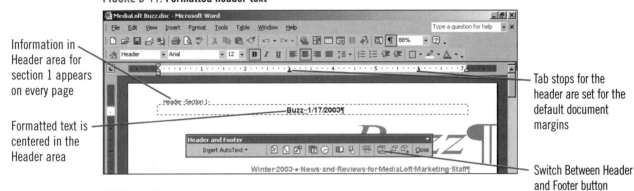

FIGURE D-12: Header and footer in the document

Page number appears in footer on every page

Header text appears in header on every page (your date will differ)

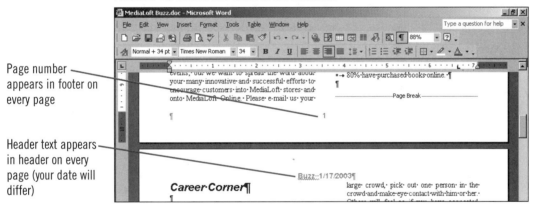

TABLE D-3: Buttons on the Header and Footer toolbar

button	function
Insert AutoText ▾	Inserts an AutoText entry, such as a field for the filename, or the author's name
# Insert Page Number	Inserts a field for the page number so that the pages are numbered automatically
Insert Number of Pages	Inserts a field for the total number of pages in the document
Format Page Number	Opens the Page Number Format dialog box; use to change the numbering format or to begin automatic page numbering with a specific number
Insert Date	Inserts a field for the current date
Insert Time	Inserts a field for the current time
Page Setup	Opens the Page Setup dialog box
Switch Between Header and Footer	Moves the insertion point between the Header and Footer areas

Word 2002

Editing Headers and Footers

To change header and footer text or to alter the formatting of headers and footers you must first open the Header and Footer areas. You can open headers and footers using the Header and Footer command on the View menu, or by double-clicking a header or footer in Print Layout view. Alice modifies the header by adding a small circle symbol between "Buzz" and the date. She also adds a border under the header text to set it off from the rest of the page. Finally, she removes the header and footer text from the first page of the document.

Steps

Trouble?

If the Header and Footer toolbar is in the way, click its title bar and drag it to a new location.

1. Place the insertion point at the top of page 2, position the ⬚ pointer over the header text at the top of page 2, then double-click
The Header and Footer areas open.

2. Place the insertion point between the two spaces after Buzz, click **Insert** on the menu bar, then click **Symbol**
The Symbol dialog box opens and is similar to Figure D-13. **Symbols** are special characters, such as graphics, shapes, and foreign language characters, that you can insert into a document. The symbols shown in Figure D-13 are the symbols included with the (normal text) font. You can use the Font list arrow on the Symbols tab to view the symbols included with each font on your computer.

Trouble?

If you cannot locate the symbol, type 25CF in the Character code text box.

3. Scroll the list of symbols if necessary to locate the black circle symbol shown in Figure D-13, select the **black circle symbol**, click **Insert**, then click **Close**
A circle symbol is added at the location of the insertion point.

4. With the insertion point in the header text, click **Format** on the menu bar, then click **Borders and Shading**
The Borders and Shading dialog box opens.

5. Click the **Borders tab**, click **Custom** in the Setting section, click the **dotted line** in the Style scroll box (the second line style), click the **Width list arrow**, click **2¼ pt**, click the **Bottom border button** in the Preview section, make sure Paragraph is selected in the Apply to list box, click **OK**, then click **Close** on the Header and Footer toolbar
A dotted line border is added below the header text, as shown in Figure D-14.

6. Press **[Ctrl][Home]** to move the insertion point to the beginning of the document
The newsletter already includes the name of the document at the top of the first page, making the header information redundant. You can modify headers and footers so that the header and footer text does not appear on the first page of a document or a section.

7. Click **File** on the menu bar, click **Page Setup** then click the **Layout tab**
The Layout tab of the Page Setup dialog box includes options for creating a different header and footer for the first page of a document or a section, and for creating different headers and footers for odd- and even-numbered pages in a document or a section. For example, in a document with facing pages, such as a magazine, you might want the publication title to appear in the left-page header and the publication date to appear in the right-page header.

QuickTip

You can enter different text in the First Page Header and First Page Footer areas.

8. Click the **Different first page check box** to select it, click the **Apply to list arrow**, click **Whole document**, then click **OK**
The header and footer text is removed from the Header and Footer areas on the first page.

9. Scroll to see the header and footer on pages 2, 3, and 4, then save the document

FIGURE D-13: Symbol dialog box

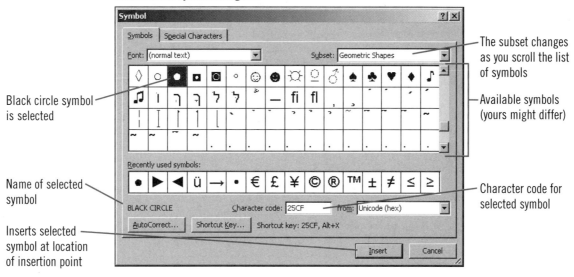

The subset changes as you scroll the list of symbols

Available symbols (yours might differ)

Black circle symbol is selected

Name of selected symbol

Character code for selected symbol

Inserts selected symbol at location of insertion point

FIGURE D-14: Symbol and border added to header

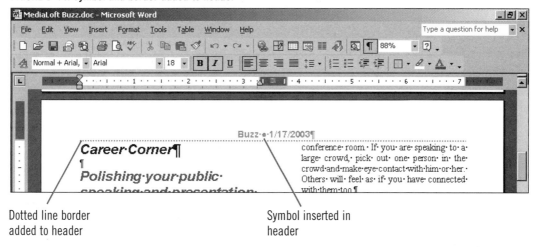

Dotted line border added to header

Symbol inserted in header

CLUES TO USE

Inserting and creating AutoText entries

Word includes a number of built-in AutoText entries, including salutations and closings for letters, as well as information for headers and footers. To insert a built-in AutoText entry at the location of the insertion point, point to AutoText on the Insert menu, point to a category on the AutoText menu, then click the AutoText entry you want to insert. You can also use the Insert AutoText button on the Header and Footer toolbar to insert an AutoText entry from the Header/Footer category into a header or footer.

Word's AutoText feature also allows you to store text and graphics that you use frequently so that you can easily insert them in a document. To create a custom AutoText entry, enter the text or graphic you want to store—such as a company name or logo—in a document, select it, point to AutoText on the Insert menu, and then click New. In the Create AutoText dialog box, type a name for your AutoText entry, then click OK. The text or graphic is saved as a custom AutoText entry. To insert a custom AutoText entry in a document, point to AutoText on the Insert menu, click AutoText, select the entry name on the AutoText tab in the AutoCorrect dialog box, click Insert, then click OK.

Formatting Columns

Formatting text in columns often makes it easier to read. You can apply column formatting to a whole document, to a section, or to selected text. The Columns button on the Standard toolbar allows you to quickly create columns of equal width. In addition, you can use the Columns command on the Format menu to create columns and to customize the width and spacing of columns. To control the way text flows between columns, you can insert a **column break**, which forces the text following the break to move to the top of the next column. You can also balance columns of unequal length by inserting a continuous section break at the end of the last column in a section. ✎ Alice formats the Staff News page in three columns, then she adjusts the flow of text.

Steps

1. Scroll to the top of page 4, place the insertion point before **Boston**, click **Insert** on the menu bar, click **Break**, select the **Continuous option button**, then click **OK**
   A continuous section break is inserted before Boston. The newsletter now contains three sections.

QuickTip

To change the width and spacing of existing columns, you can use the Columns dialog box or drag the column markers on the horizontal ruler.

2. Refer to the status bar to confirm that the insertion point is in section 3, click **Format** on the menu bar, then click **Columns**
   The Columns dialog box opens, as shown in Figure D-15.

3. Select **Three** in the Presets section, click the **Spacing down arrow** twice until 0.3" appears, select the **Line between check box**, then click **OK**
   All the text in section 3 is formatted in three columns of equal width with a line between the columns, as shown in Figure D-16.

QuickTip

To create a banner headline that spans the width of a page, select the headline text, click the Columns button, then click 1 Column.

4. Click the **Zoom list arrow** on the Standard toolbar, then click **Whole Page**
   Notice that the third column of text is much shorter than the first two columns. Page 4 would look better if the three columns were balanced—each the same length.

5. Place the insertion point at the end of the third column, click **Insert** on the menu bar, click **Break**, select the **Continuous option button**, then click **OK**
   The columns in section 3 adjust to become roughly the same length.

6. Scroll up to page 3
   The two columns on page 3 are also uneven. The page would look better if the information about the third webcast did not break across the two columns.

QuickTip

If a section contains a column break, you cannot balance the columns by inserting a continuous section break.

7. Click the **Zoom list arrow**, click **Page Width**, scroll to the bottom of page 3, place the insertion point before **Tuesday, June 10**, click **Insert** on the menu bar, click **Break**, click the **Column break option button**, then click **OK**
   The text following the column break is forced to the top of the next column.

8. Click the **Zoom list arrow**, click **Two Pages**, then save the document
   The columns on pages 3 and 4 are displayed, as shown in Figure D-17.

Hyphenating text in a document

Hyphenating a document is another way to control the flow of text in columns. Hyphens are small dashes that break words that fall at the end of a line. Hyphenation diminishes the gaps between words in justified text and reduces ragged right edges in left-aligned text. If a document includes narrow columns, hyphenating the text can help give the pages a cleaner look. To hyphenate a document automatically, point to Language on the Tools menu, click Hyphenation, select the Automatically hyphenate document check box in the Hyphenation dialog box, and then click OK. You can also use the Hyphenation dialog box to change the hyphenation zone—the distance between the margin and the end of the last word in the line. A smaller hyphenation zone results in a greater number of hyphenated words and a cleaner look to columns of text.

FIGURE D-15: Columns dialog box

Select a preset format for columns

Change the number of columns

Select to add a line between columns

Set custom widths and spacing for columns

Preview of current settings

Select to create columns of equal width

Select part of document to apply format to

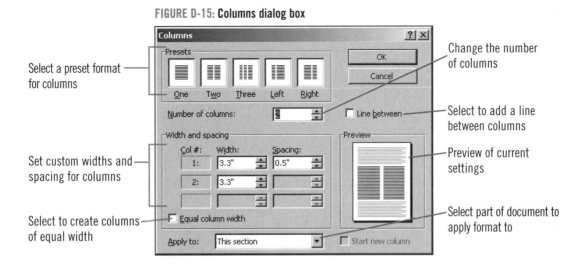

FIGURE D-16: Text formatted in three columns

Column markers show the width and spacing of columns

Text in section 3 is formatted in 3 columns

Section break is at end of section 2

Line added between columns

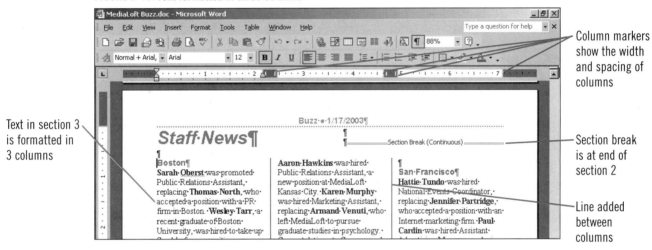

FIGURE D-17: Completed pages 3 and 4 of newsletter

Text following column break is forced to top of next column

Column break

Continuous section break

Columns in section are balanced

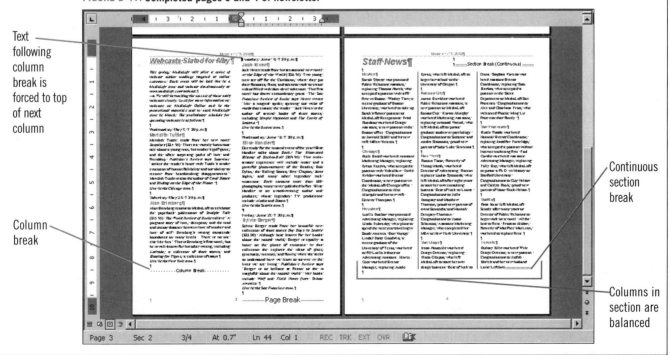

Inserting Clip Art

Illustrating a document with clip art images can give it visual appeal and help to communicate your ideas. **Clip art** is a collection of graphic images that you can insert into a document. Clip art images are stored in the Clip Organizer, a library of the **clips**—media files, including graphics, photographs, sounds, movies, and animations—that come with Word. Clips are organized in collections in the Clip Organizer. You can add a clip to a document using the Clip Art command on the Insert menu. Once you insert a clip art image, you can wrap text around it, resize it, and move it to a different location. Alice illustrates the second page of the newsletter with a clip art image. After she inserts the image, she wraps text around it, enlarges it, and then moves it so that it is centered between the two columns of text.

Steps

1. Click the **Zoom list arrow** on the Standard toolbar, click **Page Width**, scroll to the top of page 2, then place the insertion point before the first body paragraph, which begins **Did you know...**
   You will insert the clip art graphic at the location of the insertion point.

2. Click **Insert** on the menu bar, point to **Picture**, then click **Clip Art**
   The Insert Clip Art task pane opens, as shown in Figure D-18. You can use this task pane to search for clips related to a keyword.

   Trouble?
   If the Add Clips to Organizer message box opens, click Later.

3. Select the text in the Search text text box if necessary, type **communication**, then click **Search**
   Clips with the keyword "communication" appear in the Insert Clip Art task pane, as shown in Figure D-19. When you point to a clip, a ScreenTip showing the first few keywords applied to the clip, the width and height of the clip in pixels, and the file size and file type for the clip appears.

   Trouble?
   Select a different clip if the clip shown in Figure D-19 is not available to you.

4. Point to the **clip** shown in Figure D-19, click the **list arrow** that appears next to the clip, click **Insert** on the menu, then close the Insert Clip Art task pane
   The clip is inserted at the location of the insertion point. You want to center the graphic on the page. Until you apply text wrapping to a graphic, it is part of the line of text in which it was inserted (an **inline graphic**). To move a graphic independently of text, you must wrap the text around it to make it a **floating graphic**, which can be moved anywhere on a page.

5. Double-click the **clip art image**, click the **Layout tab** in the Format Picture dialog box, click **Tight**, then click **OK**
   The text in the first body paragraph wraps around the irregular shape of the clip art image. The white circles that appear on the square edges of the graphic are the **sizing handles**, which appear when a graphic is selected. You can drag a sizing handle to change the size of the image.

   QuickTip
   To verify the size of a graphic or to set precise measurements, double-click the graphic to open the Format Picture dialog box, then adjust the Height and Width settings on the Size tab.

6. Position the pointer over the **lower-right sizing handle**, when the pointer changes to drag down and to the right until the graphic is about 2½" wide and 2½" tall
   As you drag a sizing handle, the dotted lines show the outline of the graphic. Refer to the dotted lines and the rulers as you resize the graphic. When you release the mouse button, the image is enlarged.

7. With the graphic still selected, position the pointer over the graphic, when the pointer changes to drag the graphic down and to the right so it is centered on the page as shown in Figure D-20, release the mouse button, then deselect the graphic
   The graphic is now centered between the two columns of text.

8. Click the **Zoom list arrow**, then click **Two Pages**
   The completed pages 1 and 2 are displayed, as shown in Figure D-21.

   Trouble?
   If page 3 is a blank page or contains text continued from page 2, reduce the size of the graphic on page 2.

9. Press [Ctrl][End], press [Enter], type your name, save your changes, print the document, then close the document and exit Word

FIGURE D-18: Insert Clip Art task pane

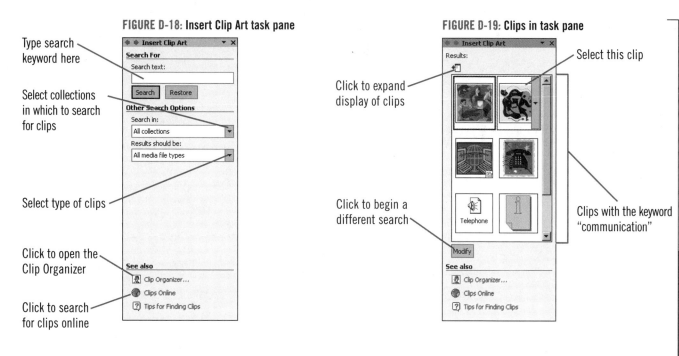

Type search keyword here

Select collections in which to search for clips

Select type of clips

Click to open the Clip Organizer

Click to search for clips online

FIGURE D-19: Clips in task pane

Click to expand display of clips

Click to begin a different search

Select this clip

Clips with the keyword "communication"

FIGURE D-20: Graphic being moved to a new location

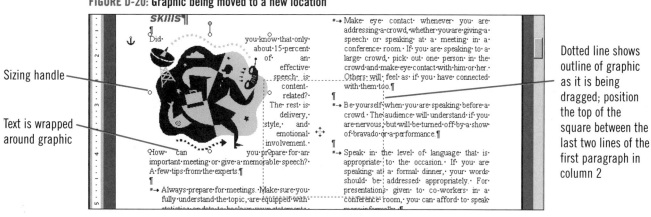

Sizing handle

Text is wrapped around graphic

Dotted line shows outline of graphic as it is being dragged; position the top of the square between the last two lines of the first paragraph in column 2

FIGURE D-21: Completed pages 1 and 2 of newsletter

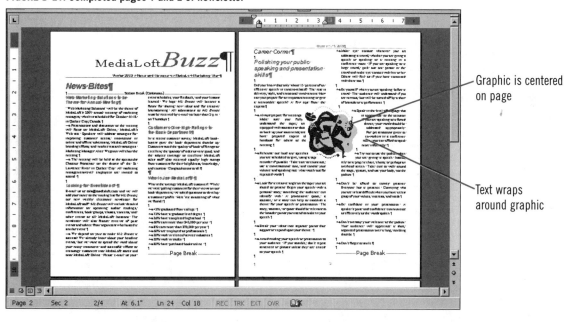

Graphic is centered on page

Text wraps around graphic

Practice

► Concepts Review

Label each element shown in Figure D-22.

FIGURE D-22

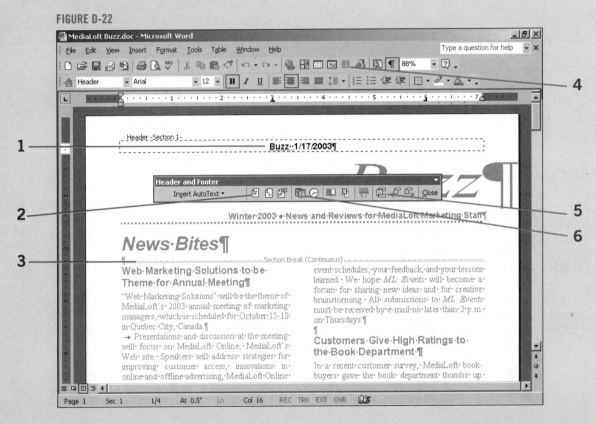

Match each term with the statement that best describes it.

7. Section break	a.	A formatting mark that forces the text following the mark to begin at the top of the next page
8. Header	b.	The blank area between the edge of the text and the edge of the page
9. Footer	c.	A placeholder for information that changes
10. Field	d.	Text or graphics that appears at the top of every page in a document
11. Hard page break	e.	An image to which text wrapping has been applied
12. Margin	f.	A formatting mark that divides a document into parts that can be formatted differently
13. Inline graphic	g.	An image that is inserted as part of a line of text
14. Floating graphic	h.	Text or graphics that appears at the bottom of every page in a document

Select the best answer from the list of choices.

15. **Which of the following do documents with mirror margins always have?**
    a. Landscape orientation
    b. Inside and outside margins
    c. Gutters
    d. Different first page headers and footers

16. **Which button is used to insert a field into a header or footer?**
    a. ▣
    b. ▣
    c. ▣
    d. ▣

17. **Which type of break do you insert if you want to force text to begin on the next page?**
    a. Continuous section break
    b. Soft page break
    c. Hard page break
    d. Text wrapping break

18. **Which type of break do you insert if you want to balance the columns in a section?**
    a. Continuous section break
    b. Soft page break
    c. Column break
    d. Text wrapping break

19. **What must you do to change an inline graphic to a floating graphic?**
    a. Resize the graphic
    b. Move the graphic
    c. Apply text wrapping to the graphic
    d. Anchor the graphic

20. **Pressing [Ctrl][Enter] does which of the following?**
    a. Inserts a soft page break
    b. Inserts a continuous section break
    c. Moves the insertion point to the beginning of the document
    d. Inserts a hard page break

▶ Skills Review

1. **Set document margins.**
   a. Start Word, open the file WD D-2 from the drive and folder where your Project Files are located, then save it as **Amherst Fitness**.
   b. Change the top and bottom margins to 1.2" and the left and right margins to 1".
   c. Save your changes to the document.

2. **Divide a document into sections.**
   a. Scroll down, then insert a continuous section break before the **Facilities** heading.
   b. Format the text in Section 2 in two columns, then save your changes to the document.

3. **Add page breaks.**
   a. Insert a hard page break before the heading **Welcome to the Amherst Fitness Center!**, scrolling up if necessary.
   b. Scroll down and insert a hard page break before the heading **Services**.
   c. Scroll down and insert a hard page break before the heading **Membership**.
   d. Press [Ctrl][Home], then save your changes to the document.

4. **Add page numbers.**
   a. Insert page numbers in the document. Center the page numbers at the bottom of the page.
   b. View the page numbers on each page in Print Preview, then save your changes to the document.

5. **Insert headers and footers.**
   a. Open the Header and Footer areas, then type your name in the Header area.
   b. Press [Tab] twice, then use the Insert Date button on the Header and Footer toolbar to insert the current date.
   c. On the horizontal ruler, drag the right tab stop from the 6" mark to the 6½" mark so that the date aligns with the right margin of the document.
   d. Move the insertion point to the Footer area.
   e. Double-click the page number to select it, then format the page number in bold italic.
   f. Close headers and footers, preview the header and footer on each page in Print Preview, close Print Preview, then save your changes to the document.

6. Edit headers and footers.

   a. Open headers and footers, then apply italic to the text in the header.

   b. Move the insertion point to the Footer area, double-click the page number to select it, then press [Delete].

   c. Click the Align Right button on the Formatting toolbar.

   d. Use the Symbol command on the Insert menu to open the Symbol dialog box.

   e. Insert a black right-pointing triangle symbol, then close the Symbol dialog box.

   f. Use the Insert Page Number button on the Header and Footer toolbar to insert a page number.

   g. Use the Page Setup button on the Header and Footer toolbar to open the Page Setup dialog box.

   h. Use the Layout tab to create a different header and footer for the first page of the document.

   i. Scroll to the beginning of the document. If you want your name on the first page of the document, type your name in the First Page Header area, then apply italic to your name.

   j. Close headers and footers, preview the header and footer on each page in Print Preview, close Print Preview, then save your changes to the document.

7. Format columns.

   a. On page 2, select **Facilities** and the paragraph mark below it, use the Columns button to format the selected text as one column, then center **Facilities** on the page.

   b. Balance the columns on page 2 by inserting a continuous section break at the bottom of the second column.

   c. On page 3, select **Services** and the paragraph mark below it, format the selected text as one column, then center the text.

   d. Balance the columns on page 3.

   e. On page 4, select **Membership** and the paragraph mark below it, format the selected text as one column, then center the text.

   f. Insert a column break before the **Membership Cards** heading, then save your changes to the document.

8. Insert clip art.

   a. On page 1, place the insertion point in the second blank paragraph below **A Rehabilitation and Exercise Facility**. (*Hint*: Place the insertion point to the left of the paragraph mark.)

   b. Open the Insert Clip Art task pane. Search for clips related to the keyword **Victories**.

   c. Insert the clip shown in Figure D-23. Select a different clip if this one is not available to you.

   d. Select the graphic, then drag the lower-right sizing handle up and to the left so that the graphic is about 2" wide and 3" tall. Size the graphic so that all the text and the hard page break fit on page 1. (*Hint*: The sizing handles on inline graphics are black squares.)

   e. Scroll to page 3, then place the insertion point before the **Personal Training** heading.

   f. In the Insert Clip Art task pane, search for an appropriate clip to illustrate this page. You might try searching using the keywords **sports**, **health**, or **heart**.

   g. When you find an appropriate clip, insert it in the document, then close the Insert Clip Art task pane.

   h. Double-click the graphic to open the Format Picture dialog box, then click the Layout tab. Apply the Tight text wrapping style to the graphic.

   i. Move the graphic so that it is centered below the text at the bottom of the page (below the page break mark). Adjust the size and position of the graphic so that the page looks attractive.

   j. Save your changes to the document. Preview the document, print a copy, then close the document and exit Word.

FIGURE D-23

The Amherst
Fitness Center

A Rehabilitation and Exercise Facility

Member Services

► Independent Challenge 1

You are the owner of a small catering business in Latona, Ontario called Bon Appetit Catering Services. You have begun work on the text for a brochure advertising your business and are now ready to lay out the pages and prepare the final copy. The brochure will be printed on both sides of an 8½" × 11" sheet of paper, and folded in thirds.

FIGURE D-24

Bon Appetit
◇
Catering
Services

Complete catering services available
for all types of events. Menus and
estimates provided upon request.

a. Start Word, open the file WD D-3 from the drive and folder where your Project Files are located, then save it as **Bon Appetit**. Read the document to get a feel for its contents.

b. Change the page orientation to landscape, and change all four margins to .6".

c. Format the document in three columns of equal width.

d. Insert a hard page break before the heading **Catering Services**.

e. On page 1, insert column breaks before the headings **Sample Indian Banquet Menu** and **Sample Tuscan Banquet Menu**.

f. On page 1, insert a continuous section break at the end of the third column.

g. Add lines between the columns on the first page, then center the text in the columns.

h. Create a different header and footer for the first page. Type **Call for custom menus designed to your taste and budget** in the First Page Footer area.

i. Center the text in the footer area, format it in 20-point Comic Sans MS, all caps, with a plum font color, then close headers and footers.

j. On page 2, insert a column break before Your Name. Press [Enter] as many times as necessary to move the contact information to the bottom of the second column. Be sure all five lines of the contact information are in column 2 and do not flow to the next column.

k. Replace Your Name with your name, then center the contact information in the column.

l. Insert a column break at the bottom of the second column. Then, type the text shown in Figure D-24 in the third column. Refer to the figure as you follow the instructions for formatting the text in the third column.

m. Format **Bon Appetit Catering Services** in 28-point Comic Sans MS, bold, with a plum font color.

n. Format the remaining text in 12-point Comic Sans MS, with a plum font color. Center the text in the third column.

o. Below Bon Appetit, insert the symbol shown in Figure D-24. (*Hint*: Type the character code 25CA in the Character code text box in the Symbol dialog box to find the symbol.) Change the font color of the symbol to gold.

p. Insert the clip art graphic shown in Figure D-24 or another appropriate clip art graphic. Do not wrap text around the graphic.

q. Add and remove blank paragraphs in the third column of your brochure so that the spacing between elements roughly matches the spacing shown in Figure D-24.

r. Save your changes, preview the brochure in Print Preview, then print a copy. If possible, print the two pages of the brochure back to back so that the brochure can be folded in thirds. Close the document and exit Word.

▶ Independent Challenge 2

You work in the Campus Safety Department at Miller State College. You have written the text for an informational flyer about parking regulations on campus and now you need to format the flyer so it is attractive and readable.

a. Start Word, open the file WD D-4 from the drive and folder where your Project Files are located, then save it as **Parking FAQ**. Read the document to get a feel for its contents.

b. Change all four margins to .7".

c. Insert a continuous section break before **1. May I bring a car to school?** (*Hint*: Place the insertion point before "May.")

d. Scroll down and insert a next page section break before **Sample Parking Permit**.

e. Format the text in section 2 in three columns of equal width with .3" of space between the columns.

f. Hyphenate the document using the automatic hyphenation feature. (*Hint*: If the Hyphenation feature is not installed on your computer, skip this step.)

g. Add a 3-pt dotted line bottom border to the blank paragraph under Miller State College. (*Hint*: Place the insertion point before the paragraph mark under Miller State College, then apply a bottom border to the paragraph.)

h. Add your name to the header. Right-align your name and format it in 10-point Arial.

i. Add the following text to the footer, inserting symbols between words as indicated: **Parking and Shuttle Service Office • 54 Buckley Street • Miller State College • 942-555-2227**.

j. Format the footer text in 10-point Arial Black and center it in the footer. Use a different font if Arial Black is not available to you. If necessary adjust the font and font size so that the entire address fits on one line.

k. Apply a 3-pt dotted line border above the footer text. Make sure to apply the border to the paragraph.

l. Balance the columns in section 2.

m. Add an appropriate clip art image to the upper-right corner of the document, above the border. Make sure the graphic does not obscure the border.

n. Place the insertion point on page 2 (which is section 4). Change the left and right margins in section 4 to 1". Also change the page orientation of section 4 to landscape.

o. Change the vertical alignment of section 4 to Center.

p. Save your changes, preview the flyer in Print Preview, then print a copy. If possible, print the two pages of the flyer back to back. Close the document and exit Word.

▶ Independent Challenge 3

A book publisher would like to publish an article you wrote on stormwater pollution in Australia as a chapter in a forthcoming book called *Environmental Issues for the New Millennium*. The publisher has requested that you format your article like a book chapter before submitting it for publication, and has provided you with a style sheet.

a. Start Word, open the file WD D-5 from the drive and folder where your Project Files are located, then save it as **Stormwater**.

b. Change the font of the entire document to 11-point Book Antiqua. If this font is not available to you, select a different font suitable for the pages of a book. Change the alignment to justified.

c. Change the paper size to 6" × 9".

d. Create mirror margins. (*Hint*: Use the Multiple Pages list arrow.) Change the top and bottom margins to .8", change the inside margin to .4", change the outside margin to .6", and create a .3" gutter to allow room for the book's binding.

e. Change the Zoom level to Two Pages. Create different headers and footers for odd- and even- numbered pages.

f. Change the Zoom level to Page Width. In the odd page header, type **Chapter 7**, insert a symbol of your choice, then type **Stormwater Pollution in the Fairy Creek Catchment**.

g. Format the header text in 9-point Book Antiqua italic, then right-align the text.

h. In the even page header, type your name, insert a symbol of your choice, then insert the current date. (*Hint*: Scroll down or use the Show Next button to move the insertion point to the even page header.)

i. Change the format of the date to include just the month and the year. (*Hint*: Right-click the date field, then click Edit Field.)

j. Format the header text in 9-point Book Antiqua italic. The even page header should be left-aligned.

k. Insert page numbers that are centered in the footer. Format the page number in 10-point Book Antiqua. Make sure to insert a page number field in both the odd and even page footer areas.

l. Format the page numbers so that the first page of Chapter 7 begins on page 53. (*Hint*: Select a page number field, then use the Format Page Number button.)

m. Go to the beginning of the document, press [Enter] 10 times, type **Chapter 7: Stormwater Pollution in the Fairy Creek Catchment**, press [Enter] twice, type your name, then press [Enter] twice.

n. Format the chapter title in 16-point Book Antiqua bold, format your name in 14-point Book Antiqua using small caps, then left-align the text.

o. Save your changes, preview the chapter in Print Preview, print the first three pages of the chapter, then close the document and exit Word.

 # Independent Challenge 4

One of the most common opportunities to use Word's page layout features is when formatting a research paper. The format recommended by the *MLA Handbook for Writers of Research Papers*, a style guide that includes information on preparing, writing, and formatting research papers, is the standard format used by many schools, colleges, and universities. In this independent challenge, you will research the MLA (Modern Language Association) guidelines for formatting a research paper and use the guidelines you find to prepare a sample first page of a research report.

a. Start Word, open the file WD D-6 from the drive and folder where your Project Files are located, then save it as **MLA Style**. This document contains the questions you will answer about MLA style guidelines.

b. Use your favorite search engine to search the Web for information on the MLA guidelines for formatting a research report. Use the keywords **MLA Style** and **research paper format**, to conduct your search. If your search does not result in links to appropriate sources, try the following Web sites: http://webster.commnet.edu/mla.htm or www.mla.org.

c. Look for information on the proper formatting for the following aspects of a research paper: paper size, margins, title page or first page of the report, line spacing, paragraph indentation, page numbers, and works cited.

d. Type your answers to the questions in the MLA Style document, save it, print a copy, then close the document.

e. Using the information you learned, start a new document and create a sample first page of a research report. Use **MLA Format for Research Papers** as the title for your sample report, and make up information about the course and instructor, if necessary. For the body of the report, type several sentences about MLA style. Make sure to format the page exactly as the MLA style dictates.

f. Save the document as **MLA Sample Format** to the drive and folder where your Project Files are located, print a copy, close the document, then exit Word.

▶ Visual Workshop

Use the file WD D-7, found on the drive and folder where your Project Files are located, to create the article shown in Figure D-25. (*Hint*: Change all four margins to .6". Make the width of the first column 2.2" and the width of the second column 4.8". Format the second column with borders and shading, but take care not to apply shading to the blank paragraph before the Clean Up heading. Select a different clip if the clip shown in the figure is not available to you.) Save the document with the filename **Gardener's Corner**, then print a copy.

FIGURE D-25

GARDENER'S CORNER

Putting a Perennial Garden to Bed

By Your Name

A certain sense of peace descends when a perennial garden is put to bed for the season. The plants are safely tucked in against the elements, and the garden is ready to welcome the first signs of life. When the work is done, you can sit back and anticipate the bright blooms of spring. Many gardeners are uncertain of how to close a perennial garden. This week's column demystifies the process.

Clean up

Debris that is left on top of soil invites garden pests to lay their eggs and spend the winter. Garden clean up can be a gradual process—plants will deteriorate at different rates, allowing you to do a little bit each week.

1. Edge beds and borders and remove stakes and other plant supports.
2. Dig and divide irises, daylilies, and other early bloomers.
3. Cut back plants when foliage starts to deteriorate.
4. Rake all debris out of the garden and pull any weeds that remain.

Plant perennials

Fall is the perfect time to plant perennials! The warm, sunny days and cool nights provide optimal conditions for new root growth.

1. Dig deeply and enhance soil with organic matter.
2. Use a good starter fertilizer to speed up new root growth.
3. Untangle the roots of new plants before planting them.
4. Water deeply after planting as the weather dictates.

Add compost

Organic matter is the key ingredient to healthy soil. If you take care of the soil, your plants will become strong and disease resistant.

1. Use an iron rake to loosen the top few inches of soil.
2. Spread a one to two inch layer of compost over the entire garden.
3. Refrain from stepping on the area and compacting the soil.

To mulch or not to mulch?

Winter protection for perennial beds can only help plants survive the winter. Here's what works and what doesn't:

1. Always apply mulch after the ground is frozen.
2. Never apply generic hay because is contains billions of weed seeds. Also, whole leaves and bark mulch hold too much moisture.
3. Straw and salt marsh hay are excellent choices for mulch.

Creating
and Formatting Tables

Objectives

- ► **Insert a table**
- ► **Insert and delete rows and columns**
- ► **Modify table rows and columns**
- ► **Sort table data**
- ► **Split and merge cells**
- ► **Perform calculations in tables**
- ► **Use Table AutoFormat**
- ► **Create a custom format for a table**

Tables are commonly used to display information for quick reference and analysis. In this unit, you learn how to create and modify a table in Word, how to sort table data and perform calculations, and how to format a table with borders and shading. You also learn how to use a table to structure the layout of a page. Alice Wegman is preparing a summary budget for an advertising campaign aimed at the Boston market. The goal of the ad campaign is to promote MediaLoft Online, the MediaLoft Web site. Alice decides to format the budget information as a table so that it is easy to read and analyze. You will work with Alice as she creates the table.

Inserting a Table

A **table** is a grid made up of rows and columns of cells that you can fill with text and graphics. A **cell** is the box formed by the intersection of a column and a row. The lines that divide the columns and rows and help you see the grid-like structure of a table are called **borders**. You can create a table in a document by using the Insert Table button on the Standard toolbar or the Insert command on the Table menu. Once you have created a table, you can add text and graphics to it. Alice begins by inserting a blank table into the document and then adding text to it.

Steps

1. Start **Word**, close the **New Document task pane**, click the **Print Layout View button** on the horizontal scroll bar if necessary, click the **Zoom list arrow** on the Standard toolbar, then click **Page Width**
   A blank document appears in Print Layout view.

2. Click the **Insert Table button** on the Standard toolbar
   A grid opens below the button. You move the pointer across this grid to select the number of columns and rows you want the table to contain. To expand the grid, drag the lower-right corner.

3. Point to the **second box** in the fourth row to select 4 × 2 Table, then click
   A table with two columns and four rows is inserted in the document, as shown in Figure E-1. The insertion point is in the first cell in the first row.

4. Type **Location**, then press **[Tab]**
   Pressing [Tab] moves the insertion point to the next cell in the row.

5. Type **Cost**, press **[Tab]**, then type **Boston Sunday Globe**
   Pressing [Tab] at the end of a row moves the insertion point to the first cell in the next row.

6. Press **[Tab]**, type **27,600**, then type the following text in the table, pressing **[Tab]** to move from cell to cell
Boston.com	25,000
Taxi tops	18,000

7. Press **[Tab]**
   Pressing [Tab] at the end of the last cell of a table creates a new row at the bottom of the table, as shown in Figure E-2. The insertion point is located in the first cell in the new row.

8. Type the following, pressing **[Tab]** to move from cell to cell and to create new rows
Boston Herald	18,760
Townonline.com	3,250
Bus stops	12,000
Boston Magazine	12,400

9. Click the **Save button** on the Standard toolbar, then save the document with the filename **Boston Ad Budget** to the drive and folder where your Project Files are located
   The table is shown in Figure E-3.

FIGURE E-1: **Blank table**

Insert Table button

Column

Row

Cell

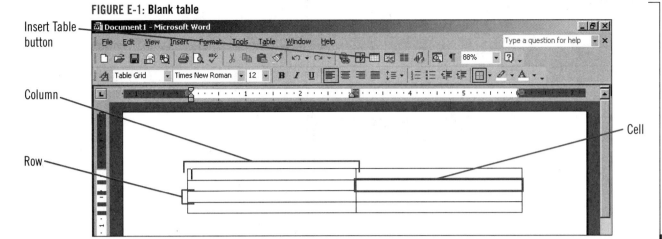

FIGURE E-2: **New row in table**

New row

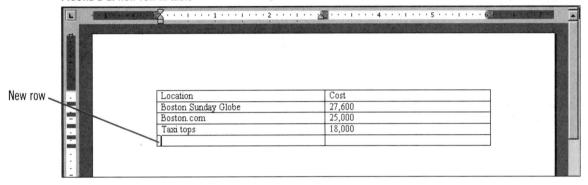

Location	Cost
Boston Sunday Globe	27,600
Boston.com	25,000
Taxi tops	18,000

FIGURE E-3: **Text in the table**

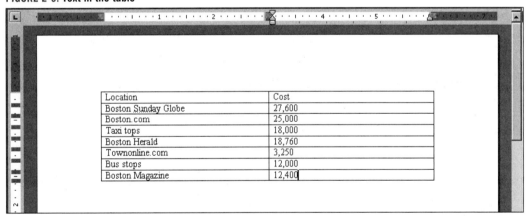

Location	Cost
Boston Sunday Globe	27,600
Boston.com	25,000
Taxi tops	18,000
Boston Herald	18,760
Townonline.com	3,250
Bus stops	12,000
Boston Magazine	12,400

CLUES TO USE

Creating a formatted blank table

When you use the Insert command on the Table menu to create a table, you have the option of formatting the table before you create it. To create a formatted blank table, point to Insert on the Table menu, then click Table to open the Insert Table dialog box. In the dialog box, first select the number of columns and rows you want your table to include. Next, in the AutoFit behavior area, choose an option for sizing the width of the columns in your table: set a specific fixed width, automatically size the columns to fit the text, or resize columns according to the width of the window. Finally, click AutoFormat to open the AutoFormat dialog box. In the AutoFormat dialog box, select a format for the table, then click OK. Click OK in the Insert Table dialog box to insert a table formatted with the options you specified.

Inserting and Deleting Rows and Columns

You can easily modify the structure of a table by adding and removing rows and columns. First, you must select an existing row or column in the table to indicate where you want to insert or delete information. You can select any element of a table using the Select command on the Table menu, but it is often easier to select rows and columns using the mouse: click in the margin to the left of a row to select the row; click the top border of a column to select the column. Alternatively, you can drag across a row or down a column to select it. To insert rows and columns, use the Insert command on the Table menu or the Insert Rows and Insert Columns button on the Standard toolbar. To delete rows and columns, use the Delete command on the Table menu. Alice adds a new row to the table and deletes an unnecessary row. She also adds new columns to the table to provide more detailed information.

1. **Click the Show/Hide/¶ button ¶ on the Standard toolbar to display formatting marks**
   An end of cell mark appears at the end of each cell and an end of row mark appears at the end of each row.

QuickTip

To insert more than one row or column, select the number of rows or columns you want to insert, then click the Insert Rows or Insert Columns button.

2. **Place the pointer in the margin to the left of the Townonline.com row until the pointer changes to ⬁ , then click**
   The entire row is selected, including the end of row mark. If the end of row mark is not selected, you have selected only the text in a row, not the row itself. When a row is selected, the Insert Table button changes to the Insert Rows button.

3. **Click the Insert Rows button ⬚ on the Standard toolbar**
   A new row is inserted above the Townonline.com row, as shown in Figure E-4.

4. **Click in the first cell of the new row, type Boston Phoenix, press [Tab], then type 15,300**
   Clicking in a cell moves the insertion point to that cell.

QuickTip

You can also delete a row or column by using the Delete command on the Table menu or by pressing [Ctrl][X] or [Shift][Delete].

5. **Select the Boston Herald row, right-click, then click Delete Rows on the shortcut menu**
   The selected row is deleted. If you select a row and press [Delete], you delete only the contents of the row, not the row itself.

6. **Place the pointer over the top border of the Location column until the pointer changes to ⬇, then click**
   The entire column is selected. When a column is selected, the Insert Table button changes to the Insert Columns button.

QuickTip

To select a cell, place the ⬛ pointer over the left border of the cell, then click.

7. **Click the Insert Columns button ⬚ on the Standard toolbar, then type Type**
   A new column is inserted to the left of the Location column, as shown in Figure E-5.

8. **Click in the Location column, click Table on the menu bar, point to Insert, click Columns to the Right, then type Details in the first cell of the new column**
   A new column is added to the right of the Location column. You can also use the Insert command to add columns to the left of the active column or to insert rows above or below the active row.

9. **Press [▼] to move the insertion point to the next cell in the Details column, enter the text shown in Figure E-6 in each cell in the Details and Type columns, click ¶ to turn off the display of formatting marks, then save your changes**
   You can use the arrow keys to move the insertion point from cell to cell. Notice that text wraps to the next line in the cell as you type. Compare your table to Figure E-6.

FIGURE E-4: Inserted row

Insert Rows button

New row is inserted and selected by default

End of cell mark

End of row mark

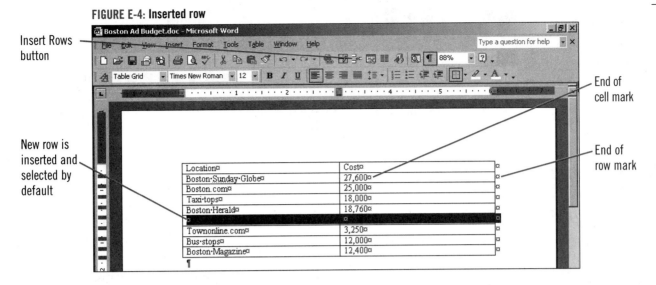

FIGURE E-5: Inserted column

New column

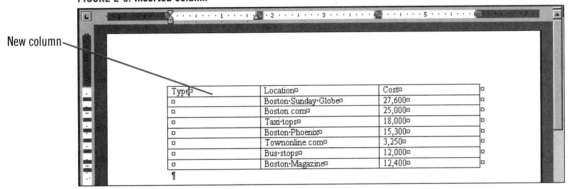

FIGURE E-6: Text in Type and Details columns

Text wraps to the next line

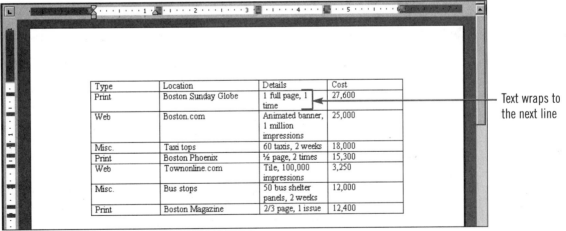

CLUES TO USE

Copying and moving rows and columns

You can copy and move rows and columns within a table in the same manner you copy and move text. Select the row or column you want to move, then use the Copy or Cut button to place the selection on the Clipboard. Place the insertion point in the location you want to insert the row or column, then click the Paste button to paste the selection. Rows are inserted above the row containing the insertion point; columns are inserted to the left of the column containing the insertion point. You can also copy or move columns and rows by selecting them and using the pointer to drag them to a new location in the table.

Modifying Table Rows and Columns

Once you create a table, you can easily adjust the size of columns and rows to make the table easier to read. You can change the size of columns and rows by dragging a border, by using the AutoFit command on the Table menu, or by setting exact measurements for column width and row height using the Table Properties dialog box. Alice adjusts the size of the columns and rows to make the table more attractive and easier to read. She also centers the text vertically in each table cell.

Steps

1. Position the pointer over the **border** between the first and second columns until the pointer changes to ↔, then drag the border to approximately the ½" **mark** on the horizontal ruler
   The dotted line that appears as you drag represents the border. Dragging the column border changes the width of the first and second columns: the first column is narrower and the second column is wider. When dragging a border to change the width of an entire column, make sure no cells are selected in the column. You can also drag a row border to change the width of the row above it.

2. Position the pointer over the **right border** of the Location column until the pointer changes to ↔, then double-click
   Double-clicking a column border automatically resizes the column to fit the text.

3. Use ↔ to double-click the **right border** of the Details column, then use ↔ to double-click the **right border** of the Cost column
   The widths of the Details and Cost columns are adjusted.

4. Move the pointer over the table, then click the **table move handle** ⊞ that appears outside the upper-left corner of the table
   Clicking the table move handle selects the entire table. You can also use the Select command on the Table menu to select an entire table.

5. Click **Table** on the menu bar, point to **AutoFit**, click **Distribute Rows Evenly**, then deselect the table
   All the rows in the table become the same height, as shown in Figure E-7. You can also use the commands on the AutoFit menu to make all the columns the same width, to make the width of the columns fit the text, and to adjust the width of the columns so the table is justified between the margins.

6. Click in the **Details column**, click **Table** on the menu bar, click **Table Properties**, then click the **Column tab** in the Table Properties dialog box
   The Column tab, shown in Figure E-8, allows you to set an exact width for columns. You can specify an exact height for rows and an exact size for cells using the Row and Cell tabs. You can also use the Table tab to set a precise size for the table, to change the alignment of the table on a page, and to wrap text around a table.

7. Select the measurement in the Preferred width text box, type **3**, then click **OK**
   The width of the Details column changes to 3".

8. Click ⊞ to select the table, click **Table** on the menu bar, click **Table Properties**, click the **Cell tab**, click the **Center box** in the Vertical Alignment section, click **OK**, deselect the table, then save your changes
   The text is centered vertically in each table cell, as shown in Figure E-9.

FIGURE E-7: Resized columns and rows

Table move handle: click to select the table; drag to move the table

Rows are all the same height

Table resize handle; drag to change the size of all the rows and columns

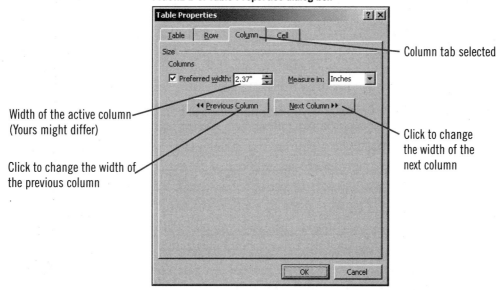

Type	Location	Details	Cost
Print	Boston Sunday Globe	1 full page, 1 time	27,600
Web	Boston.com	Animated banner, 1 million impressions	25,000
Misc.	Taxi tops	60 taxis, 2 weeks	18,000
Print	Boston Phoenix	½ page, 2 times	15,300
Web	Townonline.com	Tile, 100,000 impressions	3,250
Misc.	Bus stops	50 bus shelter panels, 2 weeks	12,000
Print	Boston Magazine	2/3 page, 1 issue	12,400

FIGURE E-8: Table Properties dialog box

Column tab selected

Width of the active column (Yours might differ)

Click to change the width of the previous column

Click to change the width of the next column

FIGURE E-9: Text centered vertically in cells

Column is widened

Text is centered vertically in the cell

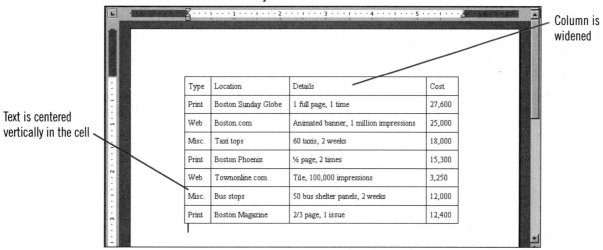

Type	Location	Details	Cost
Print	Boston Sunday Globe	1 full page, 1 time	27,600
Web	Boston.com	Animated banner, 1 million impressions	25,000
Misc.	Taxi tops	60 taxis, 2 weeks	18,000
Print	Boston Phoenix	½ page, 2 times	15,300
Web	Townonline.com	Tile, 100,000 impressions	3,250
Misc.	Bus stops	50 bus shelter panels, 2 weeks	12,000
Print	Boston Magazine	2/3 page, 1 issue	12,400

Sorting Table Data

Tables are often easier to interpret and analyze when the data is **sorted**, which means the rows are organized in alphabetical or sequential order based on the data in one or more columns. When you sort a table, Word arranges all the table data according to the criteria you set. You set sort criteria by specifying the column (or columns) by which you want to sort, and indicating the sort order— ascending or descending—you want to use. **Ascending order** lists data alphabetically or sequentially (from A to Z, 0 to 9, or earliest to latest). **Descending order** lists data in reverse alphabetical or sequential order (from Z to A, 9 to 0, or latest to earliest). You can sort using the data in one column or multiple columns. When you sort by multiple columns you must select primary, secondary, and tertiary sort criteria. You can use the Sort command on the Table menu to sort a table. ◢◤◤◤ Alice sorts the table so that all ads of the same type are listed together. She also adds secondary criteria so that the ads within each type are listed in descending order by cost.

Steps

QuickTip

To quickly sort a table by a single column, click in the column, then click the Sort Ascending ⬆ or Sort Descending ⬇ button on the Tables and Borders toolbar. When you use these buttons, Word does not include the header row in the sort.

1. Place the insertion point anywhere in the table

To sort an entire table, you simply need to place the insertion point anywhere in the table. If you want to sort specific rows only you must select the rows you want to sort.

2. Click **Table** on the menu bar, then click **Sort**

The Sort dialog box opens, as shown in Figure E-10. You use this dialog box to specify the column or columns by which you want to sort, the type of information you are sorting (text, numbers, or dates), and the sort order (ascending or descending). Column 1 is selected by default in the Sort by list box. You want to sort your table first by the information in the first column—the type of ad (Print, Web, or Misc.)—so you won't change the Sort by criteria.

3. Click the **Descending option button** in the Sort by area

The ad type information will be sorted in descending—or reverse alphabetical—order, so that the "Web" ads will be listed first, followed by the "Print" ads, and then the "Misc." ads.

4. In the Then by section click the **Then by list arrow**, click **Column 4**, click the **Type list arrow**, click **Number**, then click the **Descending option button**

Within the Web, Print, and Misc. groups, the rows will be sorted by the cost of the ad—the information contained in the fourth column. The data in the fourth column is numbers, not dates or text. The rows will appear in descending order within each group, with the most expensive ad listed first.

5. Click the **Header row option button** in the My list has section to select it

The table includes a header row that you do not want included in the sort.

6. Click **OK**, then deselect the table

The rows in the table are sorted first by the information in the Type column and second by the information in the Cost column, as shown in Figure E-11. The first row of the table, which is the Header row, is not included in the sort.

7. Save your changes to the document

FIGURE E-10: Sort dialog box

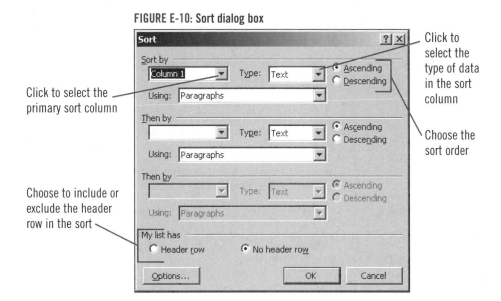

Click to select the
primary sort column

Choose to include or
exclude the header
row in the sort

Click to
select the
type of data
in the sort
column

Choose the
sort order

FIGURE E-11: Sorted table

Header row is not
included in the sort

First, rows are sorted
by type in descending
order

Second,
within each
type, rows are
sorted by cost
in descending
order

Type	Location	Details	Cost
Web	Boston.com	Animated banner, 1 million impressions	25,000
Web	Townonline.com	Tile, 100,000 impressions	3,250
Print	Boston Sunday Globe	1 full page, 1 time	27,600
Print	Boston Phoenix	½ page, 2 times	15,300
Print	Boston Magazine	2/3 page, 1 issue	12,400
Misc.	Taxi tops	60 taxis, 2 weeks	18,000
Misc.	Bus stops	50 bus shelter panels, 2 weeks	12,000

Sorting lists and paragraphs

In addition to sorting table data, you can use the Sort command on the Table menu to sort lists and paragraphs. For example, you might want to sort a list of names alphabetically. To sort lists and paragraphs, select the items you want included in the sort, click Table on the menu bar, and then click Sort. In the Sort Text dialog box, use the Sort by list arrow to select the sort by criteria (paragraphs or fields), use the Type list arrow to select the type of data (text, numbers, or dates), and then click the Ascending or Descending option button to choose a sort order.

When sorting text information in a document, "fields" refers to text or numbers that are separated by a character, such as tabs or commas. For example, if the names are listed in "Lastname, Firstname" order, the last names and first names are each considered a field, and you can choose to sort the list in alphabetical order by last name or by first name. Use the Options button in the Sort Text dialog box to specify the character that separates the fields in your lists or paragraphs, along with other sort options.

Splitting and Merging Cells

A convenient way to change the format and structure of a table is to merge and split the table cells. When you **merge** cells, you combine adjacent cells into a single larger cell. When you **split** a cell, you divide an existing cell into multiple cells. You can merge and split cells using the Merge Cells and Split Cells commands on the Table menu, or the Merge Cells and Split Cells buttons on the Tables and Borders toolbar. ▸ Alice merges cells in the first column to create a single cell for each ad type—Web, Print, and Misc. She also adds a new row to the bottom of the table, and splits the cells in the row to create three new rows with a different structure.

Steps 1 2 3 4

Trouble?

To move the Tables and Borders toolbar, click its title bar and drag it to a new location.

1. Click the **Tables and Borders button** ⊞ on the Standard toolbar, then click the **Draw Table button** ✎ on the Tables and Borders toolbar to turn off the Draw pointer ✎ if necessary
   The Tables and Borders toolbar, which includes buttons for formatting and working with tables, opens. See Table E-1.

2. Select the two **Web cells** in the first column of the table, click the **Merge Cells button** ⊞ on the Tables and Borders toolbar, then deselect the text
   The two Web cells merge to become a single cell. When you merge cells, Word converts the text in each cell into a separate paragraph in the merged cell.

3. Select the first **Web** in the cell, then press **[Delete]**

4. Select the three **Print cells** in the first column, click ⊞, type **Print**, select the two **Misc. cells**, click ⊞, then type **Misc.**
   The three Print cells merge to become one cell and the two Misc. cells merge to become one cell.

5. Click in the **Bus stops cell**, click the **Insert Table list arrow** ⊞▾ on the Tables and Borders toolbar, then click **Insert Rows Below**
   A row is added to the bottom of the table. The Insert Table button on the Tables and Borders toolbar also changes to the Insert Rows Below button. The active buttons on the Tables and Borders toolbar reflect the most recently used commands. You can see a menu of related commands by clicking the list arrow next to a button.

6. Select the **first three cells** in the new last row of the table, click ⊞, then deselect the cell
   The three cells in the row merge to become a single cell.

QuickTip

To split a table in two, click the row you want to be the first row in the second table, click Table on the menu bar, then click Split Table.

7. Click in the **first cell in the last row**, then click the **Split Cells button** ⊞ on the Tables and Borders toolbar
   The Split Cells dialog box opens, as shown in Figure E-12. You use this dialog box to split the selected cell or cells into a specific number of columns and rows.

8. Type **1** in the Number of columns text box, press **[Tab]**, type **3** in the Number of rows text box, click **OK**, then deselect the cells
   The single cell is divided into three rows of equal height. When you split a cell into multiple rows and/or columns, the width of the original column does not change. If the cell you split contains text, all the text will appear in the upper left-most cell.

9. Click in the **last cell** in the Cost column, click ⊞, repeat step 8, then save your changes
   The cell is split into three rows, as shown in Figure E-13. The last three rows of the table now have only two columns.

FIGURE E-12: Split Cells dialog box

Tables and Borders button

Insert Rows Below button

Cells created by merging other cells

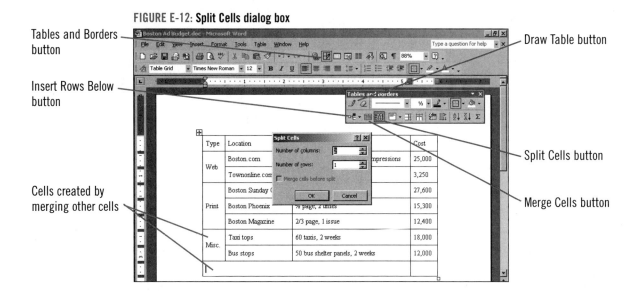

Draw Table button

Split Cells button

Merge Cells button

FIGURE E-13: Cells split into three rows

Cells are split into three rows

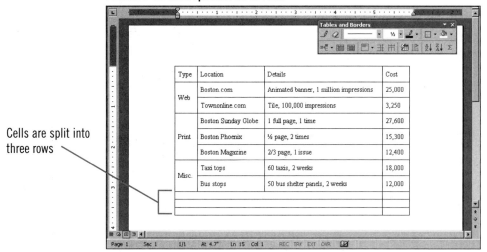

TABLE E-1: Buttons on the Tables and Borders toolbar

button	use to	button	use to
	Draw a table or cells		Divide a cell into multiple cells
	Remove a border between cells		Change the alignment of text in cells
	Change border line style		Make rows the same height
½	Change the thickness of borders		Make columns the same width
	Change the border color		AutoFormat the table
	Add or remove individual borders		Change the orientation of text
	Change shading color of cells		Sort rows in ascending order
	Insert rows, columns, cells, or a table, and AutoFit columns		Sort rows in descending order
	Combine selected cells into a single cell	Σ	Calculate sum of values above or to the left of the active cell

Performing Calculations in Tables

If your table includes numerical information, you can perform simple calculations in the table. Word's AutoSum feature allows you to quickly total the numbers in a column or row. In addition, you can use the Formula command to perform other standard calculations, such as averages. When you calculate data in a table using formulas, you use cell references to refer to the cells in the table. Each cell has a unique **cell reference** composed of a letter and a number; the letter represents its column and the number represents its row. For example, the cell in the third row of the second column is cell B3. Figure E-14 shows the cell references in a simple table. ◆▬▬ Alice uses the AutoSum feature to calculate the total cost of the Boston ad campaign. She also adds information about the budgeted cost and creates a formula to calculate the difference between the actual and budgeted costs.

Steps

QuickTip

If a column or row contains blank cells, you must type a zero in any blank cell before using AutoSum.

1. Click in the **first blank cell** in column 1, type **Total Cost**, press **[Tab]**, then click the AutoSum button Σ on the Tables and Borders toolbar
   Word totals the numbers in the cells above the active cell and inserts the sum. You can use the AutoSum button to quickly total the numbers in a column or a row. If the cell you select is at the bottom of a column of numbers, AutoSum totals the column. If the cell is at the right end of a row of numbers, AutoSum totals the row.

2. Select **12,000** in the cell above the total, then type **13,500**
   If you change a number that is part of a calculation, you must recalculate the result.

QuickTip

When the insertion point is in the cell that contains a formula, pressing [F9] updates the calculation.

3. Press **[↓]**, then press **[F9]**

4. Press **[Tab]**, type **Budgeted**, press **[Tab]**, type **113,780**, press **[Tab]**, type **Difference**, then press **[Tab]**
   The insertion point is in the last cell of the table.

5. Click **Table** on the menu bar, then click **Formula**
   The Formula dialog box opens, as shown in Figure E-15. The SUM formula appears in the Formula text box. Word proposes to sum the numbers above the active cell, but you want to insert a formula that calculates the difference between the actual and budgeted costs.

Trouble?

Cell references are determined by the number of columns in each row, not by the number of columns in the table. Therefore, rows 9 and 10 have only two columns.

6. Select **=SUM(ABOVE)** in the Formula text box, then type **=B9-B10**
   You must type an equal sign ("=") to indicate that the text following it is a formula. You want to subtract the budgeted cost in the second column of row 10 from the actual cost in the second column of row 9; therefore, you type a formula to subtract the value in cell B10 from the value in cell B9.

7. Click **OK**, then save your changes
   The difference appears in the cell, as shown in Figure E-16.

Working with formulas

In addition to the sum function, Word includes formulas for averaging, counting, and rounding data, to name a few. To use a Word formula, click the Paste function list arrow in the Formula dialog box, select a function, then insert the cell references of the cells you want included in the calculation in parentheses after the name of the function. When entering formulas, you must separate cell references by a comma. For example, if you want to average the values in cells A1, B3, and C4, enter the formula =AVERAGE(A1,B3,C4). You must also separate cell ranges by a colon. For example, to total the values in cells A1 through A9, enter the formula =SUM(A1:A9). You can also type simple custom formulas using a plus sign (+) for addition, a minus sign (-) for subtraction, an asterisk (*) for multiplication, and a slash (/) for division. All Word formulas begin with an equal sign.

FIGURE E-14: Cell references in a table

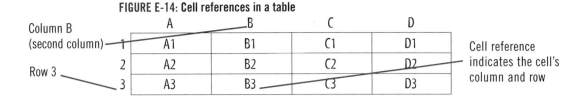

Column B (second column) ——

Row 3 ——

Cell reference indicates the cell's column and row

	A	B	C	D
1	A1	B1	C1	D1
2	A2	B2	C2	D2
3	A3	B3	C3	D3

FIGURE E-15: Formula dialog box

Suggested formula

Suggested range of cells

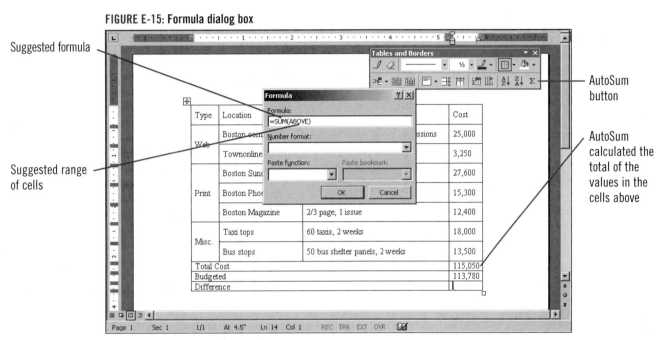

AutoSum button

AutoSum calculated the total of the values in the cells above

FIGURE E-16: Difference calculated in table

Cell A9

Cell A10

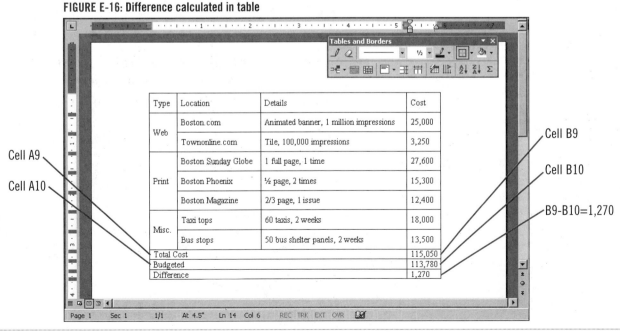

Cell B9

Cell B10

B9-B10=1,270

Word 2002

Using Table AutoFormat

Adding shading and other design elements to a table can help give it a polished appearance and make the data easier to read. Word's Table AutoFormat feature allows you to quickly apply a professional table design to a table. Table format styles include borders, shading, fonts, alignment, colors, and other formatting effects. You can apply a table format style to a table using the Table AutoFormat command on the Table menu or the Table AutoFormat button on the Tables and Borders toolbar. Alice wants to enhance the appearance of the table with shading, borders, and other formats. She uses the Table AutoFormat feature to quickly apply a table format style to the table.

Steps

1. **Click Table on the menu bar, then click Table AutoFormat**
   The Table AutoFormat dialog box opens, as shown in Figure E-17.

2. **Scroll down the list of table styles, then click Table List 7**
   A preview of the Table List 7 style appears in the Preview area.

3. **Clear the Last row and Last column check boxes in the Apply special formats to area**
   The Preview area shows that the formatting of the last row and column of the table now match the formatting of the other rows and columns in the table.

4. **Click Apply**
   The Table List 7 style is applied to the table, as shown in Figure E-18. Because of the structure of the table, this style neither enhances the table nor helps make the data more readable.

QuickTip
Use the Reveal Formatting task pane to view the format settings applied to tables and cells.

5. **With the insertion point in the table, click the Table AutoFormat button 📧 on the Tables and Borders toolbar, scroll down the list of table styles in the Table AutoFormat dialog box, click Table Professional, then click Apply**
   The Table Professional style is applied to the table. This style works with the structure of the table.

6. **Select the Type column, click the Center button 📧 on the Formatting toolbar, select the Cost column, then click the Align Right button 📧 on the Formatting toolbar**
   The data in the Type column is centered, and the data in the Cost column is right-aligned.

7. **Select the last three rows of the table, click 📧, then click the Bold button 📧 on the Formatting toolbar**

8. **Select the first row of the table, click 📧, click the Font Size list arrow on the Formatting toolbar, click 16, click 📧, deselect the row, then save your changes**
   The text in the header row is centered, enlarged, and bold, as shown in Figure E-19.

Using tables to lay out a page

Tables are often used to display information for quick reference and analysis, but you can also use tables to structure the layout of a page. You can insert any kind of information in the cell of a table—including graphics, bulleted lists, charts, and other tables (called nested tables). For example, you might use a table to lay out a resume, a newsletter, or a Web page. When you use a table to lay out a page, you generally remove the table borders to hide the table structure from the reader. When you remove a border, a gridline appears on the screen. Gridlines are light gray lines that show the edges of cells, but do not print. If your document will be viewed online—for example, if you are planning to e-mail your resume to potential employers—you should turn off the display of gridlines so that the document looks the same online as it would look if printed. To turn gridlines off or on, click the Hide Gridlines or Show Gridlines command on the Table menu.

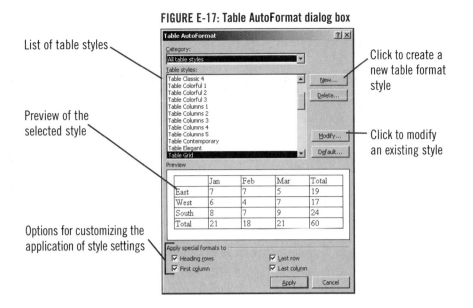

FIGURE E-17: Table AutoFormat dialog box

List of table styles

Preview of the selected style

Options for customizing the application of style settings

Click to create a new table format style

Click to modify an existing style

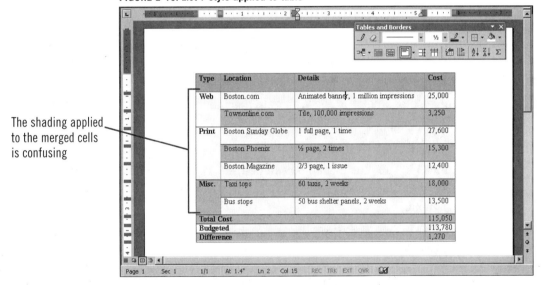

FIGURE E-18: List 7 style applied to table

The shading applied to the merged cells is confusing

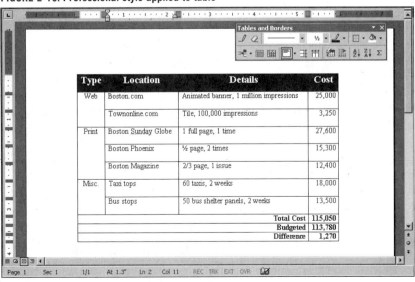

FIGURE E-19: Professional style applied to table

Word 2002

Creating a Custom Format for a Table

You can also use the buttons on the Tables and Borders toolbar to create your own table designs. For example, you can add or remove borders and shading, vary the line style, thickness, and color of borders, change the orientation of text from horizontal to vertical, and change the alignment of text in cells. ✐ Alice adjusts the text direction, shading, and borders in the table to make it easier to understand at a glance.

1. Select the **Type and Location cells** in the first row, click the **Merge Cells button** ▦ on the Tables and Borders toolbar, then type **Ad Location**
The two cells are combined into a single cell containing the text "Ad Location."

QuickTip

In cells with vertical text, the I-beam pointer is rotated 90 degrees.

2. Select the **Web**, **Print**, **and Misc. cells** in the first column, click the **Change Text Direction button** ▥ on the Tables and Borders toolbar twice, then deselect the cells
The text is rotated 270 degrees.

3. Position the pointer over the **right border** of the Web cell until the pointer changes to ◄‖►, then drag the border to approximately the ¼" **mark** on the horizontal ruler
The width of the column containing the vertical text narrows.

4. Place the insertion point in the **Web cell**, then click the **Shading Color list arrow** ▨▾ on the Tables and Borders toolbar
The Shading Color palette opens, as shown in Figure E-20.

5. Click **Gold** on the palette, click the **Print cell**, click ▨▾, click **Aqua**, click the **Misc. cell**, click ▨▾, then click **Orange**
Shading is applied to each cell.

6. Drag to select the **six white cells** in the Web rows (rows 2 and 3), click ▨▾, then click **Light Yellow**

7. Repeat step 6 to apply **Light Turquoise** shading to the Print rows and **Tan** shading to the Misc. rows
Shading is applied to all the cells in rows 1-8.

QuickTip

On the Borders button menu, click the button that corresponds to the border you want to add or remove.

8. Select the **last three rows** of the table, click the **Border list arrow** �▾ on the Tables and Borders toolbar, click the **No Border button** ▦ on the menu that appears, then deselect the rows
The top, bottom, left, and right borders are removed from each cell in the selected rows.

9. Select the **Total Cost row**, click the **Border list arrow** ▦▾, click the **Top Border button** ▦, click the **113,780 cell**, click **the Border list arrow** ▦▾, click the **Bottom Border button** ▦, click **Table** on the menu bar, then click **Hide Gridlines**
A top border is added to each cell in the Total Cost row, and a bottom border is added below 113,780. Hiding the gridlines allows you to see the table as it will appear when printed. The completed table is shown in Figure E-21.

10. Press **[Ctrl][Home]**, press **[Enter]**, type your name, save your changes, print a copy of the document, close the document, then exit Word
Press [Enter] at the beginning of a table to move the table down one line in a document.

FIGURE E-20: Shading Color palette

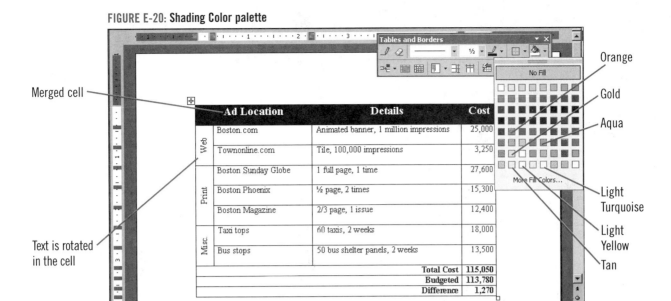

Merged cell

Text is rotated
in the cell

Orange

Gold

Aqua

Light
Turquoise

Light
Yellow

Tan

FIGURE E-21: Completed table

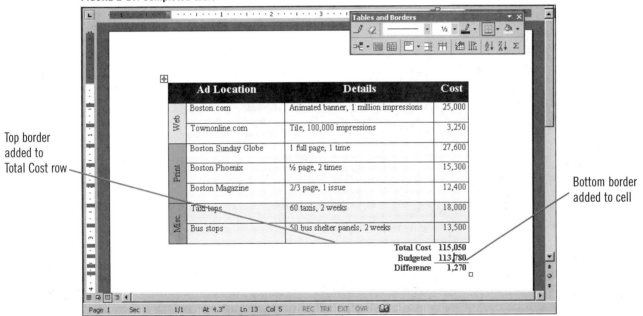

Top border
added to
Total Cost row

Bottom border
added to cell

Drawing a table

Word's Draw Table feature allows you to draw table cells exactly where you want them. To draw a table, click the Draw Table button on the Tables and Borders toolbar to turn on the Draw pointer, then click and drag to draw a cell. Using the same method, draw borders within the cell to create columns and rows, or draw additional cells attached to the first cell. If you want to remove a border from a table, click the Eraser button on the Tables and Borders toolbar to activate the Eraser pointer, then click the border you want to remove. You can use the Draw pointer and the Eraser pointer to change the structure of any table. Click the Draw Table button or the Eraser button again to turn off the draw or erase feature.

Practice

► Concepts Review

Label each element of the Tables and Borders toolbar shown in Figure E-22.

FIGURE E-22

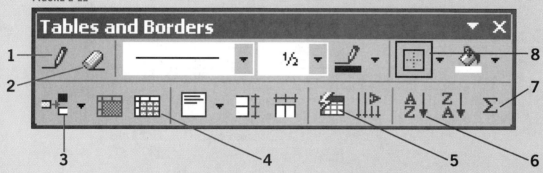

Match each term with the statement that best describes it.

9. Cell
10. Nested table
11. Ascending order
12. Descending order
13. Borders
14. Gridlines
15. Cell reference

a. An object inserted in a table cell
b. Sort order that organizes text from A to Z
c. The box formed by the intersection of a column and a row
d. Lines that show columns and rows in a table, but do not print
e. Lines that separate columns and rows in a table
f. A cell address composed of a column letter and a row number
g. Sort order that organizes text from Z to A

Select the best answer from the list of choices.

16. Which of the following is the cell reference for the third cell in the fourth column?
   a. C4
   b. 4C
   c. 3D
   d. D3

17. Which of the following is *not* a valid way to add a new row to the bottom of a table?
   a. Click in the bottom row, then click the Insert Rows button on the Standard toolbar
   b. Click in the bottom row, then click the Insert Rows Below button on the Tables and Borders toolbar
   c. Click in the bottom row, point to Insert on the Table menu, then click Rows Below
   d. Place the insertion point in the last cell of the last row, then press [Tab]

18. Which button would you use to change the orientation of text in a cell?
   a. 🔲
   b. 🔲
   c. 🔲
   d. 🔲

19. Which of the following is *not* a correct formula for adding the values in cells A1, A2, and A3?
  a. =SUM(A1~A3)
  b. =A1+A2+A3
  c. =SUM(A1:A3)
  d. =SUM(A1, A2, A3)

20. What happens when you double-click a column border?
  a. The columns in the table are distributed evenly.
  b. A new column is added to the right.
  c. A new column is added to the left.
  d. The column width is adjusted to fit the text.

▶ Skills Review

1. Insert a table.

  a. Start Word, open a new blank document, then save it as **Mutual Funds** to the drive and folder where your Project Files are located.
  b. Type your name, press [Enter] twice, type **Mutual Fund Performance**, then press [Enter].
  c. Insert a table that contains four columns and four rows.
  d. Type the information shown in Table E-2, pressing [Tab] to add rows as necessary.
  e. Save your changes.

TABLE E-2

Fund Name	1 Year	5 Year	10 Year
Computers	16.47	25.56	27.09
Europe	-6.15	13.89	10.61
Natural Resources	19.47	12.30	15.38
Health Care	32.45	24.26	23.25
Financial Services	22.18	21.07	24.44
500 Index	9.13	15.34	13.69

2. Insert and delete rows and columns.

  a. Insert a row above the Health Care row, then type the following text in the new row:
  Canada   8.24   8.12   8.56
  b. Delete the Europe row.
  c. Insert a column to the right of the 10 Year column, type **Date Purchased** in the header row, then enter a date in each cell in the column using the format MM/DD/YY (for example, 11/27/91).
  d. Move the Date Purchased column to the right of the Fund Name column, then save your changes.

3. Modify table rows and columns.

  a. Double-click the border between the first and second columns to resize the columns.
  b. Drag the border between the second and third columns to the 2¼" mark on the horizontal ruler.
  c. Double-click the right border of the 1 Year, 5 Year, and 10 Year columns, select the three columns, then distribute the columns evenly.
  d. Select rows 2-7, use the Table Properties dialog box to set the row height to exactly .3", then save your changes.

4. Sort table data.

  a. Sort the table rows in descending order by the information in the 1 Year column.
  b. Sort the rows in ascending order by date purchased.
  c. Alphabetize the table by fund name, then save your changes.

5. Split and merge cells.

  a. Insert a row above the header row.
  b. Merge the first cell in the new row with the Fund Name cell.
  c. Merge the second cell in the new row with the Date Purchased cell.

   d. Merge the three remaining blank cells in the first row into a single cell, then type **Average Annual Returns** in the merged cell.

   e. Add a new row to the bottom of the table.

   f. Merge the first two cells in the new row, then type **Average Return** in the merged cell.

   g. Select the first seven cells in the first column (from Fund Name to Natural Resources), open the Split Cells dialog box, clear the Merge cells before split check box, then split the cells into two columns.

   h. Type **Trading Symbol** as the heading for the new column, then enter the following text in the remaining cells in the column: **FINX**, **CAND**, **COMP**, **FINS**, **HCRX**, **NARS**.

   i. Double-click the right border of the first column to resize the column, double-click the right border of the last column, then save your changes.

6. Perform calculations in tables.

   a. Place the insertion point in the last cell in the 1 Year column, then open the Formula dialog box.

   b. Delete the text in the Formula text box, type **=average(above)**, click the Number Format list arrow, click 0.00%, then click OK.

   c. Repeat step b to insert the average return in the last cell in the 5 Year and 10 Year columns.

   d. Change the value of the 1-year average return for the Natural Resources fund to **10.35**.

   e. Use [F9] to recalculate the average return for 1 year, then save your changes.

7. Use Table AutoFormat.

   a. Open the AutoFormat dialog box, select an appropriate table style for the table, then apply the style to the table. Was the style you chose effective?

   b. Using AutoFormat, apply the Table List 3 style to the table.

   c. Change the font of all the text in the table to 10-point Arial.

   d. Apply bold to the 1 Year, 5 Year, and 10 Year column headings, and to the bottom row of the table.

   e. Center the table between the margins, center the table title **Mutual Funds Performance**, format the title in 14-point Arial bold, then save your changes.

8. Create a custom format for a table.

   a. Select the entire table, then use the Align Center button on the Tables and Borders toolbar to center the text in every cell vertically and horizontally.

   b. Right-align the dates and the numbers in columns 3-6.

   c. Left-align the fund names and trading symbols in columns 1 and 2.

   d. Right-align the text in the bottom row. Make sure the text in the header row is still centered.

   e. Select all the cells in the header row, including the 1 Year, 5 Year, and 10 Year column headings, change the shading color to indigo, then change the font color to white.

   f. Apply light yellow shading to the cells containing the fund names and trading symbols.

   g. Apply pale blue, tan, and lavender shading to the cells containing the 1 Year, 5 Year, and 10 Year data, respectively. Do not apply shading to the bottom row of the table.

   h. Remove all the borders in the table.

   i. Add a ½ pt white bottom border to the Average Annual Returns cell.

   j. Add a 2¼ pt black border around the outside of the table. Also add a top border to the last row of the table.

   k. Examine the table, make any necessary adjustments, then save your changes.

   l. Preview the table in Print Preview, print a copy, close the file, then exit Word.

Independent Challenge 1

You are organizing a series of canoe races on the Murray River in southeastern Australia as part of a river festival. For each race, you need to create a flyer that describes the race for the participants. In this exercise, you will format one flyer.

a. Start Word, open the file WD E-1, then save it as **40K Relay** to the drive and folder where your Project Files are located.

b. In the second blank paragraph below the Relay Details heading, insert a table with 5 columns and 3 rows.

c. Enter the text shown in Table E-3, adding rows as necessary.

d. Resize the columns to fit the text.

e. Add a column between the Start Location and Distance columns. Type **Portages** in the header row, then enter the following information in the Portages column: **0**; **0**; **2 @ 300m**; **1 @ 800m**; **2 @ 200m each** and **1 @ 500m**.

f. Resize the Portages column to fit the text, then distribute the table rows evenly.

g. Using AutoFormat, apply a table style to the table. Select a style that makes the table attractive and easy to read.

h. Center the text in each cell in the table both horizontally and vertically. (*Hint*: Use the Align Center button.)

i. Scroll up, then select the six paragraphs of tabbed text under the Race Details heading.

j. Convert the text to a 2-column table. (*Hint*: Point to Convert on the Table menu, click Text to Table, then click OK.)

k. Remove all the borders from the table, then enhance the flyer with font and paragraph formatting.

l. Press [Ctrl][End], type your name, save your changes, preview the flyer, print it, close the file, then exit Word.

TABLE E-3

Leg	Km	Check-in	Start Location	Distance
1	0	8:30	Echuca Wharf	8 km
2	8	10:00	Rosemount Homestead	8 km
3	16	11:00	Mungo Billabong	4 km
4	20	11:30	Kingfisher Park	9 km
5	29	12:30	Yarrawonga Winery	11 km

 # Independent Challenge 2

You need new business cards with a fresh design that expresses your personality or the character of your business. In this exercise, you will create a page of business cards using a table to lay out the page. The standard size for business cards is 2"33.5". Figure E-23 shows sample business cards.

a. Start Word, open a new blank document, then save it as **Business Cards** to the drive and folder where your Project Files are located.

b. Change the top, bottom, left and right margins to .4".

c. At the top of the document, insert a table with 2 columns and 5 rows.

d. Select the table, then change the height of the rows to exactly 2" and the width of the columns to exactly 3.5".

e. Center the table on the page.

f. In one cell, enter the information you want to include on your business card. Include your name, address, phone and fax numbers, e-mail address, and Web site, if appropriate. Also include your title and the name of your

FIGURE E-23

Top End Web
Web Site Design & Hosting

Luís Vouzikas
General Manager

550 Knuckey Street, Darwin NT 0801
Phone: 08-8555-7634; Fax: 08-8555-3445
www.topendweb.com.au

Vouzikas Construction
Carpentry · Construction · Remodeling

Luís Vouzikas
Owner

300 Yorkshire Street North, Guelph, Ontario NIH 5B7
Tel: 519-555-8229; vouzikas@yahoo.com

company if appropriate. (*Hint*: If Word automatically formats your e-mail or Web site address as a hyperlink, right click the underlined text, then click Remove Hyperlink.)

g. Use fonts, paragraph alignment, paragraph spacing, colors, clip art, borders, shading, symbols, and other formatting features to create an attractive design for your business card.

h. When you are satisfied with your design, double-check to make sure the row height is still 2" and the column width is still 3.5". Make any necessary adjustments.

i. Select the cell containing the business card, then copy the cell contents to each cell in the table. Once the contents are copied, check your column and row measurements again and make any necessary adjustments.

j. Remove all the table borders, save your changes, preview the business cards in Print Preview, print a copy of the document, close the file, then exit Word.

► Independent Challenge 3

You work in the advertising department at a magazine. Your boss has asked you to create a fact sheet on the ad dimensions for the magazine. The fact sheet should include the dimensions for each type of ad as well as a visual representation of the different ad shapes and sizes, shown in Figure E-24. You'll use tables to lay out the fact sheet, present the dimension information, and illustrate the ad shapes and sizes.

a. Start Word, open the file WD E-2 from the drive and folder where your Project Files are located, then save it as **Ad Dimensions**. Read the document to get a feel for its contents.

b. Drag the border between the first and second column to approximately the 2¾" mark on the horizontal ruler, resize the second and third columns to fit the text, then use the Table Properties dialog box to make each row in the table at least .5".

c. Change the alignment of the text in the first column to Center Left, then change the alignment of the text in the Width and Height columns to Center Right.

d. Remove all the borders from the table, then apply a 2¼ point, dark blue, dotted line, inside horizontal border to the entire table.

e. In the second blank paragraph under the table heading, insert a new table with three columns and four rows, then merge the cells in the third column of the new blank table.

f. Drag the border between the first and second columns of the new blank table to the 1¼" mark on the horizontal ruler. Drag the border between the second and third columns to the 1½" mark.

FIGURE E-24

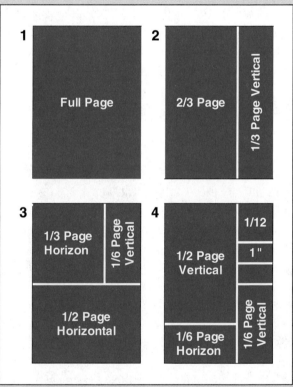

g. Select the table that contains text, cut it to the Clipboard, then paste it in the merged cell in the blank table. The table with text is now a nested table in the main table.

h. Split the nested table above the Unit Size (Bleed) row. (*Hint*: Use the Split Table command on the Table menu.)

i. Merge the cells in the first column of the main table, then merge the cells in the second column.

j. Split the first column into one column and seven rows.

k. Using the Row tab in the Table Properties dialog box, change the row height of each cell in the first column so that the rows alternate between exactly 1.8" and .25" in height. Make the height of the first, third, fifth, and seventh rows 1.8".

l. Add dark blue shading to the first, third, fifth, and seventh cells in the first column, then remove all the borders from the main table.

m. In the first blue cell, type **Full Page**, then center it vertically in the cell.

n. On the Tables and Borders toolbar, change the Line Style to a single line, change the Line Weight to 1, then change the Border Color to white.

o. Activate the Draw Table pointer, then, referring to Figure E-24, draw a vertical border that divides the second blue cell into 2/3 and 1/3. (*Hint*: You can also divide the cell using the Split Cells and Merge Cells buttons.)

p. Label the cells and align the text as shown in the figure. (*Hint*: Change the text direction and alignment before typing text. Take care not to change the size of the cells when you type. If necessary, press [Enter] to start a new line of text in a cell, or reduce the font size of the text.)

q. Referring to Figure E-24, divide the third and fourth blue cells, then label the cells as shown in the figure.

r. Hide the gridlines in the document, examine it for errors, then make any necessary adjustments.

s. Press [Ctrl][End], type your name, save your changes to the document, preview it, print a copy, close the file, then exit Word.

 # Independent Challenge 4

A well-written and well-formatted resume gives you a leg up on getting a job interview. In a winning resume, the content and format support your career objective and effectively present your background and qualifications. One simple way to create a resume is to lay out the page using a table. In this exercise you will research guidelines for writing and formatting resumes. You will then create your own resume using a table for its layout.

a. Use your favorite search engine to search the Web for information on writing and formatting resumes. Use the keywords resume templates. If your search does not result in links to appropriate sources, try the following Web sites: www.jobsonline.com or www.career.vt.edu.

b. Print helpful advice on writing and formatting resumes from at least two Web sites.

c. Think about the information you want to include in your resume. The header should include your name, address, telephone number, and e-mail address. The body should include your career objective and information on your education, work experience, and skills. You may want to add additional information.

d. Sketch a layout for your resume using a table as the underlying grid. Include the table rows and columns in your sketch.

e. Start Word, open a new blank document, then save it as **My Resume** to the drive and folder where your Project Files are located.

f. Set appropriate margins, then insert a table to serve as the underlying grid for your resume. Split and merge cells and adjust the size of the table columns as necessary.

g. Type your resume in the table cells. Take care to use a professional tone and keep your language to the point.

h. Format your resume with fonts, bullets, and other formatting features. Adjust the spacing between sections by resizing the table columns and rows.

i. When you are satisfied with the content and format of your resume, remove the borders from the table, then hide the gridlines.

j. Check your resume for spelling and grammar errors.

k. Save your changes, preview your resume, print a copy, close the file, then exit Word.

▶ Visual Workshop

Create the calendar shown in Figure E-25 using a table to lay out the entire page. (*Hints*: The clip art image is inserted in the table. The top and bottom margins are .5", the left and right margins are .7", the font is Century Gothic, and the clip art image uses the keyword "carnival," but you can use a different clip art image or font if necessary.) Type your name in the last table cell, save the calendar with the filename **March 2003** to the drive and folder where your Project Files are located, then print a copy.

FIGURE E-25

March 2003

Sunday	Monday	Tuesday	Wednesday	Thursday	Friday	Saturday
						1
2	3	4	5	6	7	8
9	10	11	12	13	14	15
16	17	18	19	20	21	22
23	24	25	26	27	28	29
30	31					

Illustrating
Documents with Graphics

Objectives

- ▶ Add graphics
- ▶ Resize graphics
- ▶ Position graphics
- ▶ Create text boxes
- ▶ Create AutoShapes
- ▶ Use the drawing canvas
- ▶ Create WordArt
- ▶ Create charts

Graphics can help illustrate the ideas in your documents, provide visual interest on a page, and give your documents punch and flair. In addition to clip art, you can add graphics created in other programs to a document, or you can use Word's drawing features to create your own images. In this unit, you learn how to insert, modify, and position graphics, how to draw your own images, and how to illustrate a document with WordArt and charts. ✐ Alice Wegman is preparing materials for a workshop for new MediaLoft marketing staff. She uses the graphic features of Word to illustrate three handouts on different MediaLoft marketing issues. You will work with Alice as she creates the handouts.

Adding Graphics

Graphic images you can insert in a document include the clip art that comes with Word, photos taken with a digital camera, scanned art, and graphics created in other graphics programs. When you first insert a graphic it is an **inline graphic**—part of the line of text in which it was inserted. You can move an inline graphic just as you would move text. To be able to move a graphic independently of text, you must apply a text wrapping style to it to make it a **floating graphic**, which can be moved anywhere on a page. You can insert clip art or another graphic file into a document using the Picture command on the Insert menu. Alice has written a handout containing tips for writing and designing ads. She wants to illustrate the handout with the MediaLoft logo, a graphic created in another graphics program. She uses the Picture, From File command to insert the logo in the document. She then wraps the text around the logo.

Steps

1. Start **Word**, open the file **WD F-1** from the drive and folder where your Project Files are located, save it as **Ad Tips**, click the **Zoom list arrow** on the Standard toolbar, click **Page Width** if necessary, then read the document to get a feel for its contents

The document opens in Print Layout view.

2. Click the **Show/Hide ¶ button** ¶ on the Standard toolbar to turn on the display of formatting marks, then click the **Drawing button** on the Standard toolbar to display the Drawing toolbar if it is not already displayed

The Drawing toolbar, located below the document window, includes buttons for inserting, creating, and modifying graphics.

3. Click before the heading **Create a simple layout**, click **Insert** on the menu bar, point to **Picture**, then click **From File**

The Insert Picture dialog box opens. You use this dialog box to locate and insert graphic files. Most graphic files are **bitmap graphics**, which are composed of a series of small dots, called **pixels**, that define color and intensity. Bitmap graphics are often saved with a .bmp, .png, .jpg, .wmf, .tif, or .gif file extension. Use the Files of type list arrow in the Insert Picture dialog box to select the type of graphic file you want to insert. To view all the graphic files in a particular location, select All Pictures.

4. Click the **Files of type list arrow**, click **All Pictures** if necessary, use the Look in list arrow to navigate to the drive and folder where your Project Files are located, click the file **Mloft.jpg**, then click **Insert**

The logo is inserted as an inline graphic at the location of the insertion point. Unless you want a graphic to be part of a line of text, usually the first thing you do after inserting it is to wrap text around it so it becomes a floating graphic. To be able to position a graphic anywhere on a page, you must apply a text wrapping style to it even if there is no text on the page.

5. Click the **logo graphic** to select it

Squares, called **sizing handles**, appear on the sides and corners of the graphic when it is selected, as shown in Figure F-1. The Picture toolbar also opens. The Picture toolbar includes buttons for modifying graphics.

6. Click the **Text Wrapping button** on the Picture toolbar

A menu of text wrapping styles opens.

7. Click **Tight**

The text wraps around the sides of the graphic, as shown in Figure F-2. Notice that the sizing handles change to circles, indicating the graphic is a floating object, and an anchor and a green rotate handle appear. The anchor indicates the floating graphic is **anchored** to the nearest paragraph, so that the graphic will move with the paragraph if the paragraph is moved. The anchor symbol appears only when formatting marks are displayed.

8. Click ¶, deselect the graphic, then click the **Save button** on the Standard toolbar to save your changes

FIGURE F-1: Inline graphic

Picture toolbar

Graphic is part of the same line of text as "Create a simple layout"

Sizing handles; square sizing handles indicate an inline graphic

Drawing toolbar

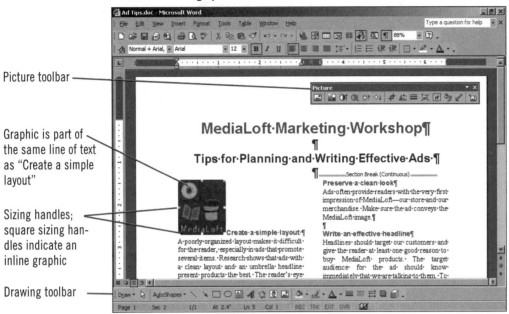

FIGURE F-2: Floating graphic

Text Wrapping button

Rotate handle

Logo is anchored to the paragraph next to it

Circular sizing handles indicate a floating graphic

Text wraps around the shape of the graphic

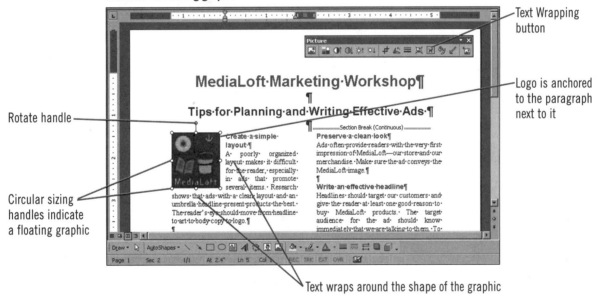

Inserting clips from the Microsoft Design Gallery Live Web site

If you have an Internet connection open when you search for clips using the Insert Clip Art task pane, your search results will automatically include clips from the Microsoft Design Gallery Live Web site, in addition to the clips stored in your Clip Organizer. You can also visit the Microsoft Design Gallery Live Web site to download clips into your Clip Organizer. To visit the Design Gallery Live Web site, click the Clips Online hyperlink in the Insert Clip Art task pane. This opens your browser and connects you to the site, where, after you have read and accepted the License Agreement, you are free to search for and download clips. You can search for clips related to a keyword, in a certain category, or of a particular file type (clip art, photos, sounds, or motion). To download a clip, click the check box under the clip to select it, then click the red arrow to the left of the check box. The clip is automatically downloaded and stored in the appropriate category in your Clip Organizer, making it available for use when you are not connected to the Internet.

Resizing Graphics

Once you insert a graphic into a document, you can change its shape or size by using the mouse to drag a sizing handle, or by using the Picture command on the Format menu to specify an exact height and width for the graphic. Resizing a graphic with the mouse allows you to see how the image looks as you modify it. Using the Picture command to alter a graphic's shape or size allows you to set precise measurements. ✒ Alice enlarges the MediaLoft logo.

QuickTip

Click Ruler on the View menu to display the rulers.

1. Click the **logo graphic** to select it, place the pointer over the **middle-right sizing handle**, when the pointer changes to ↔, drag to the right until the graphic is about 1¾" wide

As you drag, the dotted outline indicates the size and shape of the graphic. You can refer to the ruler to gauge the measurements as you drag. When you release the mouse button, the image is stretched to be wider. Dragging a side, top, or bottom sizing handle changes only the width or height of a graphic.

QuickTip

If you enlarge a bitmap graphic too much, the dots that make up the picture become visible and the graphic is distorted.

2. Click the **Undo button** 🔄 on the Standard toolbar, place the pointer over the **upper-right sizing handle**, when the pointer changes to ↗ drag up and to the right until the graphic is about 2" tall and 1¾" wide as shown in Figure F-3

The image is enlarged. Dragging a corner sizing handle resizes the graphic proportionally so that its width and height are reduced or enlarged by the same percentage. Table F-1 describes other ways to resize objects using the mouse.

3. Double-click the **logo graphic**

The Format Picture dialog box opens. It includes options for changing the coloring, size, scale, text wrapping, and position of a graphic. You can double-click any graphic object or use the Picture command on the Format menu to open the Format Picture dialog box.

4. Click the **Size tab**

The Size tab, shown in Figure F-4, allows you to enter precise height and width measurements for a graphic or to scale a graphic by entering the percentage by which you want to reduce or enlarge it. When a graphic is sized to **scale**, its height to width ratio remains the same.

Trouble?

Your height measurement might differ slightly.

5. Change the measurement in the Width text box in the Size and rotate area to **1.5**, then click the **Height text box** in the Size and rotate area

The height measurement automatically changes to 1.69". When the Lock aspect ratio check box is selected, you need only to enter a height or width measurement. Word calculates the other measurement so that the resized graphic will be proportional.

6. Click **OK**, then save your changes

The logo is resized to be precisely 1.5" wide and approximately 1.69" tall.

TABLE F-1: Methods for resizing an object using the mouse

do this	to
Drag a corner sizing handle	Resize a clip art or bitmap graphic proportionally from a corner
Press [Shift] and drag a corner sizing handle	Resize a drawing object, such as an AutoShape or WordArt object, proportionally from a corner
Press [Ctrl] and drag a side, top, or bottom sizing handle	Resize any graphic object vertically or horizontally while keeping the center position fixed
Press [Ctrl] and drag a corner sizing handle	Resize any graphic object diagonally while keeping the center position fixed
Press [Shift][Ctrl] and drag a corner sizing handle	Resize any graphic object proportionally while keeping the center position fixed

FIGURE F-3: Dragging to resize an image

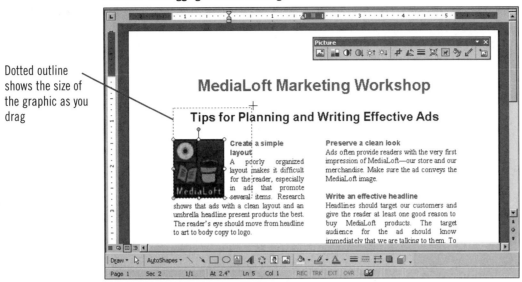

Dotted outline shows the size of the graphic as you drag

FIGURE F-4: Size tab in the Format Picture dialog box

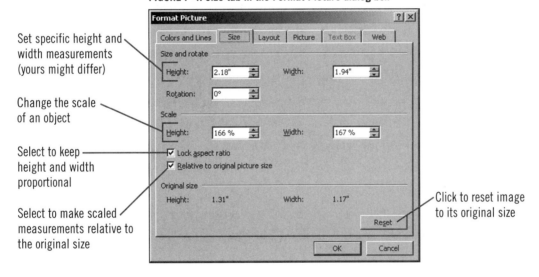

Set specific height and width measurements (yours might differ)

Change the scale of an object

Select to keep height and width proportional

Select to make scaled measurements relative to the original size

Click to reset image to its original size

Clues to Use

Cropping graphics

If you want to use only part of a picture in a document, you can crop the graphic to trim the parts you don't want to use. To crop a graphic, select it, then click the Crop button [⊞] on the Picture toolbar. The pointer changes to the cropping pointer 🔁 and cropping handles (solid black lines) appear on all four corners and sides of the graphic. To crop one side of a graphic, drag a side cropping handle inward to where you want to trim the graphic. To crop two sides at once, drag a corner cropping handle inward to the point where you want the corner of the cropped image to be. When you drag a cropping handle, the shape of the cropping pointer changes to correspond to the shape of the cropping handle you are dragging. When you finish adjusting the parameters of the graphic, click the Crop button again to turn off the crop feature. You can also crop a graphic by entering precise crop measurements on the Picture tab in the Format Picture dialog box.

Positioning Graphics

Once you insert a graphic into a document and make it a floating graphic, you can move it by dragging it with the mouse, nudging it with the arrow keys, or setting an exact location for the graphic using the Picture command on the Format menu. Dragging an object with the mouse or using the arrow keys allows you to position a graphic visually. Using the Picture command to position a graphic allows you to place an object precisely on a page.　　　Alice experiments with different positions for the MediaLoft logo to determine which position enhances the document the most.

Steps

QuickTip

To move an object only horizontally or vertically, press [Shift] as you drag.

1. Select the **logo graphic** if necessary, move the pointer over the graphic, when the pointer changes to 🕂, drag the graphic down and to the right as shown in Figure F-5 so its top aligns with the top of the **Create a simple layout** heading

   As you drag, the dotted outline indicates the position of the graphic. When you release the mouse button, the graphic is moved and the text wraps around the graphic. Notice that the Create a simple layout heading is now above the graphic.

2. With the graphic selected, press [◄] four times, then press [▲] three times

   Each time you press an arrow key the graphic is **nudged**—moved a small amount—in that direction. You can also press [Ctrl] and an arrow key to nudge an object in even smaller (one pixel) increments.

QuickTip

You can place a floating graphic anywhere on a page, including outside the margins.

3. Double-click the **graphic**, click the **Layout tab** in the Format Picture dialog box, then click **Advanced**

   The Advanced Layout dialog box opens. The Picture Position tab, shown in Figure F-6, allows you to specify an exact position for a graphic relative to some aspect of the document, such as a margin, column, or paragraph.

4. Click the **Picture Position tab** if necessary, click the **Alignment Option button** in the Horizontal section, click the **Alignment list arrow**, click **Centered**, click the **relative to list arrow**, then click **Margin**

   The logo will be centered horizontally between the left and right page margins.

5. Change the measurement in the Absolute position text box in the Vertical section to **1.5**, click the **below list arrow**, then click **Margin**

   The top of the graphic will be positioned precisely 1.5" below the top margin.

6. Click the **Text Wrapping tab**

   You can use the Text Wrapping tab to change the text wrapping style, to wrap text around only one side of a graphic, and to change the distance between the edge of the graphic and the edge of the wrapped text. You want to increase the amount of white space between the sides of the graphic and the wrapped text.

7. Select **Square**, select **0.13** in the Left text box, type **.3**, press [**Tab**], then type **.3** in the Right text box

   The distance between the graphic and the edge of the wrapped text will be .3" on either side.

Trouble?

If the Picture toolbar remains open after you deselect the graphic, close the toolbar.

8. Click **OK** to close the Advanced Layout dialog box, click **OK** to close the Format Picture dialog box, deselect the graphic, then save your changes

   The logo is centered between the margins, the top of the graphic is positioned 1.5" below the top margin, and the amount of white space between the left and right sides of the graphic and the wrapped text is increased to .3", as shown in Figure F-7.

FIGURE F-5: Dragging a graphic to move it

Top of graphic aligns with the top of the text

Dotted outline shows the position as you drag

FIGURE F-6: Picture Position tab in the Advanced Layout dialog box

Click to horizontally align a graphic relative to an aspect of the document

Click to position a graphic a precise distance from an aspect of the document

Select the aspect of the document you want to position the graphic in relationship to

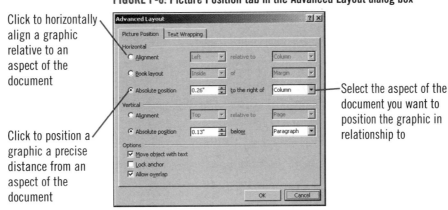

FIGURE F-7: Repositioned logo

Logo is centered and its top is 1.5" from the top margin

1.5" mark on the ruler

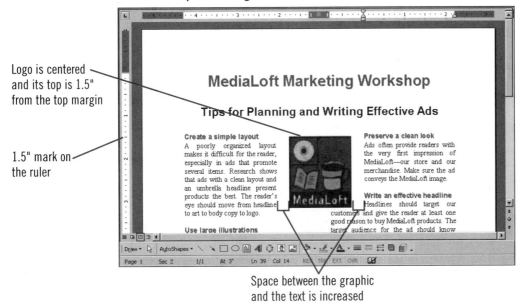

Space between the graphic and the text is increased

Creating Text Boxes

When you want to illustrate your documents with text, you can create a text box. A **text box** is a container that you can fill with text and graphics. Like other drawing objects, text boxes can be resized, formatted with colors, lines, and text wrapping, and positioned anywhere on a page. You can create a text box using the Text Box button on the Drawing toolbar or the Text Box command on the Insert menu. When you insert a text box or another drawing object, a drawing canvas opens in the document. A **drawing canvas** is a workspace for creating your own graphics. You can choose to draw the text box directly in the document, or to draw it in the drawing canvas. ✎ Alice wants to add a pull quote to call attention to the main point of the handout. She draws a text box, adds the pull quote text to it, formats the text, and then positions the text box on the page.

Steps

1. Scroll down, click before the **Use large illustrations** heading, then click the **Text Box button** 🖾 on the Drawing toolbar
   A drawing canvas opens in the document, as shown in Figure F-8, and the pointer changes to +. You'll draw a text box outside the drawing canvas.

2. Move the + pointer directly under the lower-left corner of the MediaLoft logo, then click and drag down and to the right to draw a text box that is about 1½" wide and 2¾" tall
   When you release the mouse button, the drawing canvas disappears and the insertion point is located in the text box, as shown in Figure F-9. The Text Box toolbar also opens.

3. Type **The reader's eye should move from headline to art to body copy to logo**

4. Select the text, click the **Font list arrow** on the Formatting toolbar, click **Arial**, click the **Font size list arrow**, click **14**, click the **Bold button** **B**, click the **Center button** 🖺, click the **Line Spacing list arrow** 🖹▾, click **2.0**, then click outside the text box
   The text is formatted. Notice that the text does not wrap around the text box. By default, text boxes are inserted with the In front of text wrapping style applied.

5. Click the **text box**, double-click the **text box frame**, click the **Size tab** in the Format Text Box dialog box, then change the height to **2.75"** and the width to **1.5"** in the Size and rotate section, if necessary
   When you click a text box with the I pointer, the insertion point moves inside the text box and sizing handles appear. Clicking the frame of a text box with the ⬚ pointer selects the text box object itself. Double-clicking the frame opens the Format Text Box dialog box.

6. Click the **Layout tab**, click **Advanced**, click the **Picture Position tab** if necessary, click the **Alignment option button** in the Horizontal section, click the **Alignment list arrow**, click **Centered**, click the **relative to list arrow**, click **Margin**, click the **Absolute position option button** in the Vertical section if necessary, change the measurement in the Absolute position text box to **3.4**, click the **below list arrow**, then click **Margin**
   The text box will be centered between the left and right margins and its top will be precisely 3.4" below the top margin.

7. Click the **Text Wrapping tab**, click **Square**, change the Top, Bottom, Left, and Right measurements to **.3"** in the Distance from text section, click **OK** twice, then deselect the text box
   The text is wrapped in a square around the text box.

8. Click inside the text box, click the **Line Color list arrow** 🖉▾ on the Drawing toolbar, click **No Line**, then deselect the text box
   The thin black border around the text box is removed, as shown in Figure F-10.

9. Press **[Ctrl][End]**, type your name, save your changes, print, then close the file

FIGURE F-8: Drawing canvas

Drawing canvas

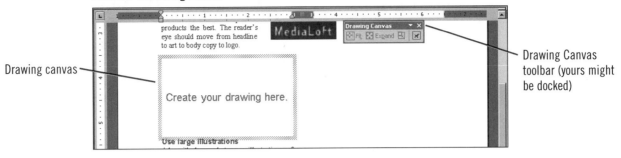

Drawing Canvas toolbar (yours might be docked)

FIGURE F-9: Text box

Insertion point in text box

Text box frame

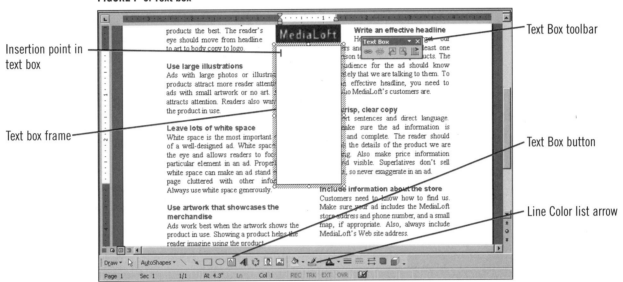

Text Box toolbar

Text Box button

Line Color list arrow

FIGURE F-10: Completed handout with text box

Text wraps around the text box

Formatted text in text box

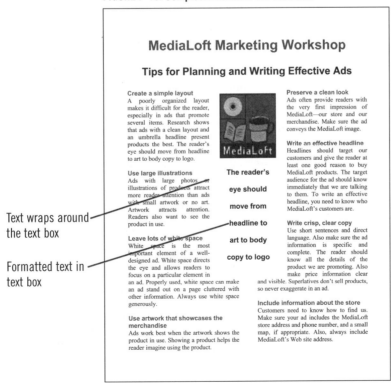

Creating AutoShapes

You can create your own graphics in Word using AutoShapes. **AutoShapes** are the rectangles, ovals, triangles, lines, block arrows, stars, banners, lightning bolts, hearts, suns, and other drawing objects you can create using the tools on the Drawing toolbar. The Drawing toolbar also includes tools for adding colors, shadows, fills, and three-dimensional effects to your images. Table F-2 describes the buttons on the Drawing toolbar. You can choose to draw a line or shape exactly where you want it in a document, or you can create a graphic in a drawing canvas. It's helpful to use a drawing canvas if your graphic includes multiple items. ✐ Alice creates a handout that illustrates MediaLoft book sales by genre. She uses AutoShapes to create a picture of a stack of books, and then adds the text, to the picture.

Steps

1. Click the **New Blank Document button** ▢ on the Standard toolbar, then save the document as **Genre Sales** to the drive and folder where your Project Files are located

2. Click the **Rectangle button** ▢ on the Drawing toolbar
   When you click an AutoShape button, a drawing canvas opens, the Drawing Canvas toolbar appears, and the pointer changes to +. The Drawing Canvas toolbar contains buttons for sizing the graphics you create in the drawing canvas, and for wrapping text around the drawing canvas. You'll learn more about resizing and positioning the drawing canvas in the next lesson.

3. Scroll down until the entire drawing canvas is visible on your screen, place the pointer about ¾" above the lower-left corner of the drawing canvas, then drag down and to the right to create a rectangle that is about **5"** wide and **½"** tall
   You do not need to be exact in your measurements as you drag. When you release the mouse button, sizing handles appear around the rectangle to indicate it is selected. Cropping handles also appear around the edges of the drawing canvas.

4. Click **AutoShapes** on the Drawing toolbar, point to **Basic Shapes**, then click the **Sun**
   The AutoShapes menu contains categories of shapes and lines that you can draw.

5. Place the + pointer in the upper-left corner of the drawing canvas, then drag down and to the right to create a sun that is about ½" wide
   The sun shape includes a yellow diamond-shaped adjustment handle. You can drag an **adjustment handle** to change the shape, but not the size, of many AutoShapes.

6. Position the pointer over the adjustment handle until it changes to ▷, drag the handle to the right about ¼", click the **Fill Color list arrow** ▨▾ on the Drawing toolbar, click **Gold**, click the **rectangle** to select it, click ▨▾, then click **Aqua**
   The sun shape becomes narrower and the shapes are filled with color. Notice that when you select a color, the active color changes on the Fill Color button.

7. Double-click ▢ to activate the rectangle tool, refer to Figure F-11 to draw three more rectangles, click ▢ to turn off the tool, then fill the rectangles with color
   After all four rectangles are drawn, use the sizing handles to resize the rectangles if necessary.

8. Press and hold **[Shift]**, click each **rectangle** to select it, click the **3-D Style button** ▢ on the Drawing toolbar, then click **3-D Style 1** (the first style in the top row)
   The rectangles become three-dimensional, making the group look like a stack of books.

9. Deselect the books, right-click the **top book**, click **Add Text**, click the **Font Size list arrow** on the Formatting toolbar, click **20**, then type **Children's - 17%**
   The 3-D rectangle changes to a text box. You can convert any shape to a text box by right-clicking it and clicking Add Text.

10. Add the 20-point text as shown in Figure F-12, then save your changes

FIGURE F-11: AutoShapes in the drawing canvas

Shape of sun is narrower

Sizing handles indicate rectangle is selected

Cropping handles

Drawing canvas frame

Draw three rectangles in step 7 and fill them with lavender, gold, and pink

Aqua fill

Active color on the Fill Color button is lavender (yours might differ)

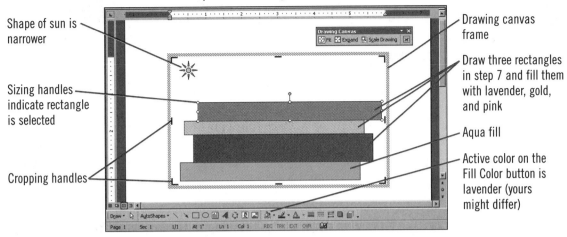

FIGURE F-12: Text added to AutoShapes

Add text in step 10

Rectangles are three-dimensional

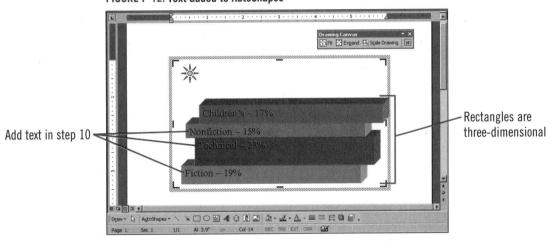

TABLE F-2: Buttons on the Drawing toolbar

button	use to	button	use to
Draw ▾	Open a menu of commands for grouping, positioning, rotating, and wrapping text around graphics, and for changing an AutoShape to a different shape	🖼	Insert a clip art graphic
▚	Select graphic objects	🖼	Insert a picture from a file
AutoShapes ▾	Open a menu of drawing options for lines, shapes, and callouts	🎨 ▾	Fill a shape with a color, a texture, a gradient, or a pattern
╲	Draw a straight line	✐	Change the color of a line, arrow, or line around a shape
↘	Draw a straight line with an arrowhead	A ▾	Change the color of text
▢	Draw a rectangle or square	≡	Change the style and weight of a line, arrow, or line around a shape
○	Draw an oval or circle	⋮⋮⋮	Change the dash style of a line, arrow, or line around a shape
▤	Insert a text box	⇄	Change a line to an arrow; change the style of an arrow
🎼	Insert a WordArt graphic	▢	Add a shadow to a graphic object
🎨	Insert a diagram or an organization chart	▱	Make a graphic object three-dimensional

Using the Drawing Canvas

When multiple shapes are contained in a drawing canvas, you can resize and move them as a single graphic object. The Drawing Canvas toolbar includes buttons for sizing a drawing canvas and for wrapping text around it. Once you apply a text wrapping style to a drawing canvas, you can position it anywhere in a document. ✏ Alice wants to add another three books to the stack. She enlarges the drawing canvas, adds the shapes, sizes the drawing as a single object, and then moves it to the bottom of the page.

Steps 1234

1. Click the **Zoom list arrow** on the Standard toolbar, click **75%**, then click the **stack of books graphic** to make the drawing canvas visible if necessary
   Cropping handles appear around the edges of the drawing canvas.

2. Place the pointer over the **top-middle cropping handle**, when the pointer changes to ⊥, drag the handle to the top of the page, then release the mouse button
   The drawing canvas is enlarged from the top, but the size of the graphic does not change. Dragging a cropping handle resizes the canvas, but not the graphic.

3. Select the **sun**, position the pointer over it until the pointer changes to 🅺, drag the **sun** on top of the right end of the Technical book, then release the mouse button
   The sun shape is moved to the spine of the book, but is hidden beneath the rectangle shape.

4. With the sun shape selected, click the **Draw button** on the Drawing toolbar, point to **Order**, then click **Bring to Front**
   The sun shape is moved on top of the rectangle shape.

5. Double-click the **Rectangle button** 🔲 on the Drawing toolbar, draw three more rectangles on top of the stack of books, click 🔲, then right-click each **rectangle** and add the 20-point text shown in Figure F-13

6. Select each **rectangle**, fill it with any color, then apply the **3D Style 1**

Trouble?
If your Drawing Canvas toolbar is not open, right-click the drawing canvas frame, then click Show Drawing Canvas toolbar on the shortcut menu.

7. Click the **Fit Drawing to Contents button** 🔳 on the Drawing Canvas toolbar
   The drawing canvas is automatically resized to fit the graphic within it.

8. Click the **Zoom list arrow**, click **Whole Page**, then click the **Scale Drawing button** 🔳 on the Drawing Canvas toolbar
   The cropping handles on the drawing canvas change to sizing handles. You can now use the drawing canvas frame to resize the contents of the drawing canvas as a single graphic.

QuickTip
To precisely size or position a drawing canvas, double-click the drawing canvas frame to open the Format Drawing Canvas dialog box.

9. Drag the **bottom-middle sizing handle** down until the graphic is about **6"** tall
   Resizing the drawing canvas resizes all the shapes within it. Dragging a top, bottom, or side handle stretches the graphic. Dragging a corner handle resizes the graphic proportionally.

10. Click the **Text Wrapping button** 🔳 on the Drawing Canvas toolbar, click **Square**, place the pointer over the **drawing canvas frame** so it changes to 🅺, drag the **canvas** down and position it so it is centered in the bottom part of the page, deselect the drawing canvas, then save your changes
    Compare your document to Figure F-14. You must wrap text around a drawing canvas to be able to position it anywhere on a page.

FIGURE F-13: New rectangles in drawing canvas

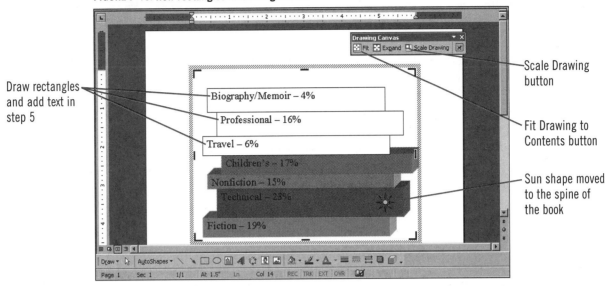

Draw rectangles and add text in step 5

Scale Drawing button

Fit Drawing to Contents button

Sun shape moved to the spine of the book

FIGURE F-14: Resized and repositioned graphic

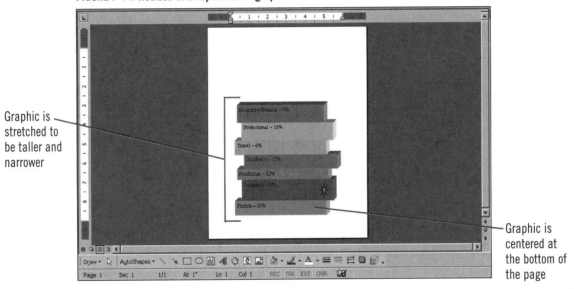

Graphic is stretched to be taller and narrower

Graphic is centered at the bottom of the page

CLUES TO USE

Drawing lines

In addition to drawing straight lines and arrows, you can use the Lines tools on the AutoShapes menu to draw curved, freeform, and scribble lines. Click AutoShapes on the Drawing toolbar, point to Lines, then select the type of line you want to draw. Choose Curve 5 to draw an object with smooth curves, choose Freeform ✎ to draw an object with both freehand and straight-line segments, or choose Scribble ✐ to draw a freehand object that looks like it was drawn with a pencil. The lines you draw include vertexes—a **vertex** is either a point where two straight lines meet or the highest point in a curve. To create a curve or freeform line, click the location you want the line to begin, move the mouse, click to insert a vertex, move the mouse, and so on. Double-click to end a curve or freeform line or click near the starting point to close a shape, if that's what you have drawn. Drawing scribble lines is similar to drawing with a pencil: drag the pointer to draw the line, then release the mouse button when you are finished. The best way to learn about drawing curve, freeform, and scribble lines is to experiment. Once you draw a line, you can modify its shape by right-clicking it, clicking Edit Points, and then dragging a vertex to a different location.

Creating WordArt

Another way to give your documents punch and flair is to use WordArt. **WordArt** is a drawing object that contains text formatted with special shapes, patterns, and orientations. You create WordArt using either the WordArt button on the Drawing toolbar or the Picture, WordArt command on the Insert menu. ✎ Alice uses WordArt to create a fun heading for her handout.

Steps

1. **Press [Ctrl][Home], press [Enter], click the Zoom list arrow on the Standard toolbar, click Page Width, then click the Insert WordArt button ⊿ on the Drawing toolbar**
   The WordArt Gallery opens, as shown in Figure F-15. It includes the styles you can choose for your WordArt.

2. **Click the fourth style in the fourth row, then click OK**
   The Edit WordArt Text dialog box opens. You type the text you want to format as WordArt in this dialog box and, if you wish, change the font and font size of the WordArt text.

QuickTip

You can use the Text Wrapping button on the WordArt toolbar to convert the object to a floating graphic.

3. **Type Genre Sales, then click OK**
   The WordArt object appears at the location of the insertion point. Like other graphic objects, the WordArt object is an inline graphic until you wrap text around it.

4. **Click the WordArt object to select it**
   The WordArt toolbar appears when a WordArt object is selected. It includes buttons for editing and modifying WordArt.

Trouble?

If your page goes blank, click the Undo button 🔄 and repeat step 5. Take care not to make the Word Art object taller than 2".

5. **Drag the lower-right corner sizing handle down and to the right to make the object about 2" tall and 6" wide**
   The WordArt is enlarged to span the page between the left and right margins, as shown in Figure F-16.

6. **Click the WordArt Same Letter Heights button 🅰 on the WordArt toolbar, click the WordArt Character Spacing button ⸯ on the WordArt toolbar, then click Loose**
   First, the uppercase and lowercase letters change to become the same height, and then the spacing between the characters is increased.

QuickTip

To change the color of WordArt, click the Format WordArt button 🎨 on the WordArt toolbar, then use the Colors and Lines tab in the Format WordArt dialog box.

7. **Click the WordArt Shape button 🅰ᵇᶜ on the WordArt toolbar, then click the Curve Up shape (the first shape in the third row)**
   The shape of the WordArt text changes. You can experiment with different shapes, fonts, colors, and other effects to create WordArt that has the impact you desire.

8. **Click the Zoom list arrow, click Whole Page, click the WordArt Gallery button 🖼 on the WordArt toolbar, click the second style in the third row, click OK, then deselect the WordArt object**
   The WordArt changes to a different style. The completed handout is shown in Figure F-17.

Trouble?

Adjust the colors as necessary.

9. **Press [Ctrl][Home], type your name, save your changes, print the document, then close the file**

FIGURE F-15: WordArt Gallery

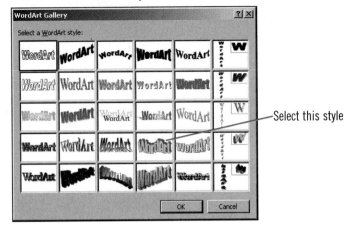

Select this style

FIGURE F-16: Resized WordArt

WordArt toolbar

WordArt Character Spacing button

WordArt Same Letter Heights button

WordArt Shape button

WordArt Gallery button

WordArt object is enlarged

FIGURE F-17: Completed handout with WordArt

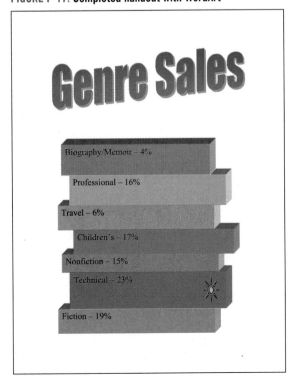

Word 2002

Creating Charts

Adding a chart can be an attractive way to illustrate a document that includes numerical information. A **chart** is a visual representation of numerical data and usually is used to illustrate trends, patterns, or relationships. Word's chart feature allows you to create many types of charts, including bar, column, pie, area, and line charts. You can add a chart to a document using the Picture, Chart command on the Insert menu. ▅▅▅ Alice creates a handout that includes a chart showing the distribution of MediaLoft customers by age and gender.

Steps

1. **Open the file WD F-2** from the drive and folder where your Project Files are located, save it as **Age and Gender**, then press **[Ctrl][End]**
   You will insert a chart at the location of the insertion point, which is centered under the title.

2. **Click Insert** on the menu bar, point to **Picture**, then click **Chart**
   A table opens in a datasheet window and a column chart appears in the document. The datasheet and the chart contain placeholder data that you can replace with your own data. The chart is based on the data in the datasheet. Any change you make to the data in the datasheet is made automatically to the chart. Notice that when a chart object is open, the Standard toolbar includes buttons for working with charts.

3. **Click the datasheet title bar** and drag it so that the chart is visible, then move the pointer over the **datasheet**
   The pointer changes to ✛. You use this pointer to select the cells in the datasheet.

QuickTip

Click the Chart Type list arrow 📊▾ on the Standard toolbar to change the type of chart.

4. **Click the East cell**, type **Male**, click the **West cell**, type **Female**, click the gray **3 cell** to select the third row, then press **[Delete]**
   When you click a cell and type, the data in the cell is replaced with the text you type. As you edit the datasheet, the changes you make are reflected in the chart.

5. **Replace the remaining placeholder text** with the data shown in Figure F-18, then click outside the chart to deselect it

6. **Click the chart** to select the object, press **[Ctrl]**, then drag the **lower-right corner sizing handle** down and to the right until the outline of the chart is approximately 7" wide
   The chart is enlarged and still centered.

QuickTip

Point to any part of a chart to see a ScreenTip that identifies the part. You can also use the Chart Objects list arrow on the Standard toolbar to select a part of a chart.

7. **Double-click the chart** to open it, click the **View Datasheet button** 📋 on the Standard toolbar to close the datasheet, click the **legend** to select it, then click the **Format Legend button** 📄 on the Standard toolbar
   The name of the button is Format Legend because the legend is selected. The Format Legend dialog box opens. It includes options for modifying the legend. Select any part of a chart object and use 📄 to open a dialog box with options for formatting that part of the chart.

8. **Click the Placement tab**, click the **Bottom option button**, then click **OK**
   The legend moves below the chart.

9. **Click the value axis** (the Y-axis), click 📄, click the **Number tab** in the Format Axis dialog box, click **Percentage** in the Category list, click the **Decimal places down arrow** twice so **0** appears, click **OK**, then deselect the chart
   Percent signs are added to the Y-axis. The completed handout is shown in Figure F-19.

10. **Type Prepared by** followed by your name centered in the document footer, save your changes, print the handout, close the document, then exit Word

FIGURE F-18: Datasheet and chart object

Datasheet window

Chart reflects data in datasheet

Value axis

View Datasheet button

Format button

Chart object

Legend

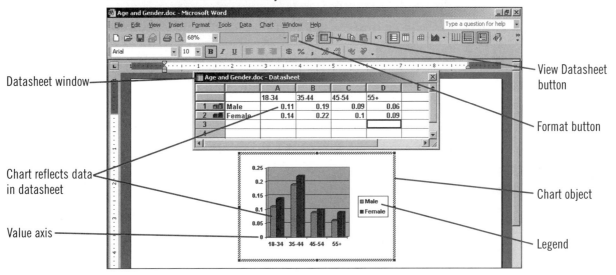

FIGURE F-19: Completed handout with chart

Percent signs added to the value axis

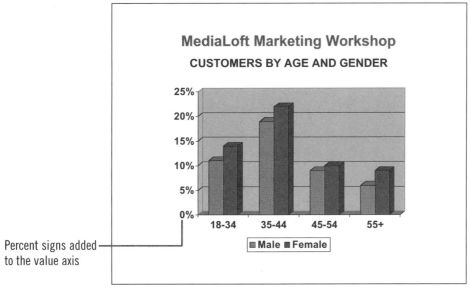

Creating diagrams and organization charts

Diagrams are another way to illustrate concepts in your documents. Word includes a diagram feature that allows you to quickly create and format several types of diagrams, including pyramid, Venn, target, cycle, and radial diagrams, as well as organization charts. To insert a diagram or an organization chart, click the Insert Diagram button 🔲 on the Drawing toolbar or use the Diagram command on the Insert menu to open the Diagram Gallery, shown in Figure F-20. Select a diagram type in the Diagram Gallery, then click OK. The diagram appears in a drawing canvas with placeholder text, and the Diagram toolbar opens. The toolbar contains buttons for customizing and formatting the diagram, and for sizing and positioning the drawing canvas. Use the AutoFormat button on the Diagram toolbar to apply colors and shading to your diagram.

FIGURE F-20: Diagram Gallery

Practice

► Concepts Review

Label the elements shown in Figure F-21.

FIGURE F-21

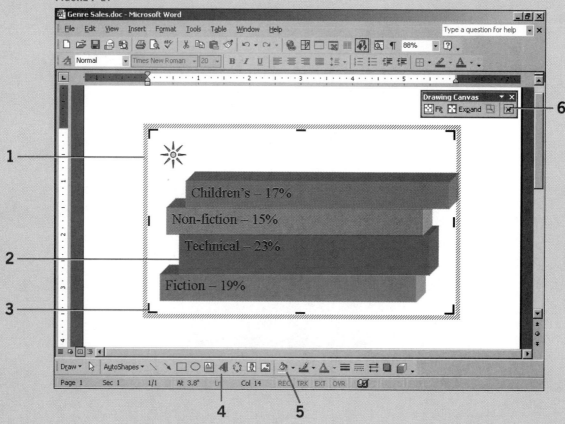

Match each term with the statement that best describes it.

7. **Text box**
8. **Drawing canvas**
9. **AutoShape**
10. **Bitmap graphic**
11. **Chart**
12. **WordArt**
13. **Pixels**
14. **Vertex**

a. A graphic object composed of specially formatted text
b. A graphic that is composed of a series of small dots
c. A graphic object that is a container for text and graphics
d. The intersection of two line sections or the highest point on a curve
e. A workspace for creating graphics
f. Dots that define color and intensity in a graphic
g. A graphic object drawn using the tools on the Drawing toolbar
h. A visual representation of numerical data

Select the best answer from the list of choices.

15. Which button can be used to create a text box?
    a. ▢
    c. ▢
    b. ▢
    d. ▢

16. What must you do to a drawing canvas before moving it to a different location?
    a. Fit the drawing canvas to the contents.
    b. Scale the drawing canvas.
    c. Wrap text around the drawing canvas.
    d. Enter a precise position for the drawing canvas in the Format Drawing Canvas dialog box.

17. What would you drag to change an AutoShape's shape, but not its size or dimensions?
    a. Cropping handle
    c. Sizing handle
    b. Adjustment handle
    d. Rotate handle

18. Which method would you use to nudge a picture?
    a. Select the picture, then drag it to a new location.
    b. Select the picture, then press an arrow key.
    c. Select the picture, then drag a top, bottom, or side sizing handle.
    d. Select the picture, then drag a corner sizing handle.

19. If you want to create an oval that contains formatted text, what kind of graphic object would you create?
    a. WordArt
    c. An AutoShape
    b. A text box
    d. A pie chart

20. What style of text wrapping is applied to a text box by default?
    a. In line with text
    c. Tight
    b. Square
    d. In front of text

▶ Skills Review

1. **Add graphics.**
    a. Start Word, open the file **WD F-3** from the drive and folder where your Project Files are located, then save it as **Farm Flyer**.
    b. Press [Ctrl][End], then insert the file **Farm.jpg** from the drive and folder where your Project Files are located.
    c. Select the photo, apply the Square text wrapping style to it, then save your changes.

2. **Resize graphics.**
    a. Scroll down so that the graphic is at the top of your screen.
    b. Drag the lower-right sizing handle to enlarge the graphic proportionally so that it is about 4" wide and 3" high.
    c. Click the Crop button on the Picture toolbar.
    d. Drag the bottom-middle cropping handle up approximately 1", then click the Crop button again.
    e. Double-click the photo, click the Size tab, then change the width of the photo to 6". (*Hint*: Make sure the Lock aspect ratio check box is selected.)
    f. Save your changes.

3. Position graphics.

   a. Drag the photo up so that its top is aligned with the top margin.

   b. Double-click the photo, click the Layout tab, then click Advanced.

   c. On the Picture Position tab, change the horizontal alignment to centered relative to the margins.

   d. In the Vertical section, change the absolute position to 2" below the margin.

   e. On the Text Wrapping tab, change the wrapping style to Top and bottom, change the Top measurement to 2", then change the Bottom measurement to .3".

   f. Close the Advanced Layout and Format Picture dialog boxes, then save your changes.

4. Create text boxes.

   a. Change the zoom level to Whole Page, then draw a 1.5" x 6" text box at the bottom of the page. (*Note*: Do not draw the text box in the drawing canvas if it opens.)

   b. Change the zoom level to Page Width, type **Mountain Realty** in the text box, format the text in 20-point Arial bold, then center it in the text box.

   c. Press [Enter], type **603-555-3466**, press [Enter], type **www.mountainrealty.com**, then format the text in 11-point Arial bold.

   d. Resize the text box to be 1" high and 4" wide, then move it to the lower-left corner of the page, aligned with the left and bottom margin.

   e. Fill the text box with Blue-Gray, change the font color of the text to White, then remove the line from around the text box.

   f. With the text box selected, click Draw on the Drawing toolbar, point to Change AutoShape, point to Basic Shapes, then click the Oval. (*Note:* Adjust the text size or oval size if necessary)

   g. Deselect the text box, then save your changes.

5. Create AutoShapes.

   a. Click AutoShapes on the Drawing toolbar, point to Basic Shapes, then click the Isosceles Triangle shape.

   b. Draw an isosceles triangle in the drawing canvas, then fill it with Violet. (*Note:* The drawing canvas appears on a new page 2. You will resize and position the drawing canvas after you finish drawing in it.)

   c. Draw three more isosceles triangles in the drawing canvas, then fill them with Lavender, Blue-Gray, and Indigo.

   d. Drag the triangles to position them so they overlap each other to look like mountains.

   e. Draw a sun shape in the drawing canvas, fill it with Gold, then position it so it overlaps the tops of the mountains. Resize the sun if necessary.

   f. Select the sun, click Draw on the Drawing toolbar, point to Order, then click Send to Back.

   g. Use the Order commands to change the order of the triangles and the sun so that the shapes look like a mountain range with the sun setting behind it. Resize and reposition the shapes as necessary to create a mountain effect, then save your changes.

6. Use the drawing canvas.

   a. Fit the drawing canvas to the mountain range graphic.

   b. Apply the Square text wrapping style to the drawing canvas. (*Hint*: You might need to scroll the document to locate the drawing canvas after you apply text wrapping to it.)

   c. Click the Scale Drawing button, then resize the drawing canvas so the graphic is approximately 1.5" wide and 1" tall. Adjust the shapes in the drawing canvas if the graphic looks awkward after resizing it.

   d. Change the zoom level to Whole Page, move the drawing canvas to the lower-right corner of the page, aligned with the right and bottom margins, then deselect the drawing canvas.

   e. Save your changes, then press [Ctrl][Home] to move the insertion point to the top of the document (the beginning of the text).

7. Create WordArt.

   a. Insert a WordArt object, select any horizontal WordArt style, type **Farmhouse**, then click OK.

   b. Apply Square text wrapping to the WordArt object, then move it above the photograph if necessary.

   c. Resize the WordArt object to be 6" wide and 1.25" tall, then position it so it is 1" below the top of the page and centered between the margins.

   d. Open the WordArt Gallery, then change the style to the fifth style in the second row.

   e. Type **Contact** followed by your name in the document footer, center the text, then format it in 12-point Arial.

   f. Save your changes to the flyer, print a copy, then close the file.

8. Create charts.

   a. Open a new, blank document, then save it as **Realty Sales** to the drive and folder where your Project Files are located.

   b. Click the Center button, type **Mountain Realty 2003 Sales**, then format the text in 26-point Arial bold.

   c. Press [Enter] twice, then insert a chart.

   d. Click the Chart Type list arrow on the Standard toolbar, then click Pie Chart.

   e. Select the second and third rows in the datasheet, then press [Delete].

FIGURE F-22

   f. Replace the data in the datasheet with the data shown in Figure F-22, then close the datasheet.

		A	B	C	D	E
		Houses	Land	Farms	Businesses	
1	Pie 1	11.3	4.1	4.4	6.2	
2						

Realty Sales.doc - Datasheet

   g. Select the legend, click the Format Legend button, then change the placement of the legend to Bottom.

   h. Use the Chart Objects list arrow to select the Plot Area, open the Format Plot Area dialog box, then change the Border and Area patterns to None.

   i. Use the Chart Objects list arrow to select Series "Pie 1," open the Format Data Series dialog box, click the Data Labels tab, then make the data labels show the percentage.

   j. Resize the chart object proportionally so it is about 5" wide.

   k. Type **Prepared by** followed by your name centered in the document footer, save your changes, print the document, close the file, then exit Word.

► Independent Challenge 1

You are starting a business and need to design a letterhead. Your letterhead will include a logo, which you'll design using AutoShapes, as well as your name and contact information. Figure F-23 shows a sample letterhead.

FIGURE F-23

Georgia J. McQueeney
Architect/Planner
54 Erie Street _ Syracuse, NY 13219 _ 315-555-3288 _ gjmcq@earthlink.net

   a. Start Word, open a new blank document, then save it as **Letterhead** to the drive and folder where your Project Files are located.

   b. Identify the nature of your business, then examine the shapes available on the AutoShapes menus and decide what kind of logo to create.

   c. Using pencil and paper, sketch a design for your letterhead. Determine the positions for your logo, name, address, and any other design elements you want to include. You will create and organize all the elements of your letterhead in a drawing canvas.

   d. Using AutoShapes, create your logo in a drawing canvas. Use the buttons on the Drawing toolbar to enhance the logo with color, text, lines, shadows, and other effects.

   e. Resize the logo and position it in the drawing canvas.

f. In the drawing canvas, create a text box that includes your name, address, and other important contact information. Format the text and the text box using the buttons on the Formatting and Drawing toolbars.

g. Resize the text box as necessary and position it in the drawing canvas.

h. Add to the drawing canvas any other design elements you want to include.

i. When you are satisfied with the layout of your letterhead in the drawing canvas, fit the drawing canvas to its contents, then resize the drawing canvas as necessary.

j. Wrap text around the drawing canvas, then position it on the page.

k. Save your changes, preview the letterhead, print a copy, close the file, then exit Word.

► Independent Challenge 2

You design ads for GoTroppo.com, a company that specializes in discounted travel to tropical destinations. Your next assignment is to design a full-page ad for a travel magazine. Your ad will contain a photograph of a vacation scene, shown in Figure F-24, the text "Your vacation begins here and now," and the Web address "www.gotroppo.com."

a. Start Word, open a new, blank document, then save it as **GoTroppo Ad** to the drive and folder where your Project Files are located.

b. Change all four page margins to .7".

FIGURE F-24

c. Insert the file **Vacation.jpg** from the drive and folder where your Project Files are located, then examine the photo. Think about how you can use this photo effectively in your ad.

d. Using pencil and paper, sketch the layout for your ad. You can use AutoShapes, lines, text boxes, WordArt, and any other design elements in your ad to make it powerful and eye-catching.

e. Apply a text wrapping style to the photograph to make it a floating graphic, then format the photograph as you planned. You can crop it, resize it, move it, and combine it with other design elements.

f. Using text boxes or WordArt, add the text **Your vacation begins here and now** and the Web address **www.gotroppo.com** to the ad.

g. Use the buttons on the Drawing and Formatting toolbars to format the graphic objects.

h. Adjust the layout and design of the ad: adjust the colors, add or remove design elements, and resize and reposition the objects if necessary.

i. When you are satisfied with your ad, type your name in the document header, save your changes, print a copy, close the document, then exit Word.

Independent Challenge 3

You are a graphic designer. The public library has hired you to design a bookmark for Literacy Week. Their only request is that the bookmark includes the words Literacy Week. You'll create three different bookmarks for the library.

a. Start Word, open a new, blank document, then save it as **Bookmarks** to the drive and folder where your Project Files are located.

b. Change the page orientation to landscape, change all four page margins to .7", and change the zoom level to Whole Page.

c. Draw three rectangles in a drawing canvas. Resize the rectangles to be 2.5" x 6.5" and move them so they do not overlap. Each rectangle will become a bookmark.

d. In the first rectangle, design a bookmark using AutoShapes.

e. In the second rectangle, design a bookmark using WordArt.

f. In the third rectangle, design a bookmark using clip art.

g. Use the buttons on the Drawing toolbar to format the bookmarks with fills, colors, lines, and other effects. Be sure to add the words Literacy Week to each bookmark.

h. Type your name in the document header, save your changes, print, close the document, then exit Word.

Independent Challenge 4

One way to find graphic images to use in your documents is to download them from the Web. Many Web sites feature images that are in the public domain, which means they have no copyright restrictions. You are free to download these images and use them in your documents, although often you must acknowledge the artist or identify the source. Other Web sites include images that are copyrighted and require written permission, and often payment, to use. Before downloading and using graphics from the Web, it's important to research and establish their copyright status and permission requirements. In this exercise you will download photographs from the Web and research their copyright restrictions.

a. Start Word, open the file WD F-4 from the drive and folder where your Project Files are located, then save it as **Copyright Info**. This document contains a table that you will fill with the photos you find on the Web and the copyright restrictions for those photos.

b. Use your favorite search engine to search the Web for photographs. Use the keywords **photo archives** to conduct your search. If your search does not result in appropriate links, try looking at the following Web sites: http://pictures.fws.gov, http://gimp-savvy.com, http://www-pao.ksc.nasa.gov, or http://vulcan.wr.usgs.gov.

c. Find at least three Web sites that contain photos you could use in a document. Save a photo from each Web site to your computer, and note the URL and copyright restrictions. To save an image from a Web page, right-click the image, then click the appropriate command on the shortcut menu.

d. Insert the photos you saved from the Web in the Photo column of the table. Resize the photos proportionally so that they are no more than 1.5" tall or 1.5" wide. Wrap text around the photos and center them in the table cells.

e. For each photo, enter the URL and the copyright restrictions for the photo in the table. In the Copyright Restrictions column, indicate if the photo is copyright or in the public domain, and note the requirements for using that photo in a document.

f. Type your name in the document header, save your changes, print a copy, close the file, then exit Word.

▶ Visual Workshop

Using WD F-5.doc and Surfing.jpg (found in the drive and folder where your Project Files are located), create the flyer shown in Figure F-25. Type your name in the header, save the flyer as **Surf Safe**, then print a copy.

FIGURE F-25

surf safe

NEVER SURF ALONE

Follow the rules
All beginning surfers need to follow basic safety rules before heading into the waves. The key to safe surfing is caution and awareness.

Wear sunscreen
Sunscreen helps prevent skin cancer and aging of the skin. 30+ SPF broad spectrum sunscreen screens out both UVA and UVB rays and provides more than 30 times your natural sunburn protection. Apply sunscreen at least 15 minutes before exposing yourself to the sun, and reapply it every two hours or after swimming, drying with a towel, or excessive perspiration. Zinc cream also helps prevent sunburn and guards against harmful UV rays.

Dress appropriately
Wear a wet suit or a rash vest. Choose a wet suit that is appropriate for the water temperature. Rash vests help protect against UV rays.

Use a safe surfboard
A safe surfboard is a surfboard that suits your ability. Beginners need a big, thick surfboard for stability.

Learn how to escape rips
A rip current is a volume of water moving out to sea: the bigger the surf, the stronger the rips associated with it. Indicators of rips include:

- Brown water caused by stirred up sand
- Foam on the surface of the water that trails past the break
- Waves breaking on both sides of a rip current
- A rippled appearance between calm water
- Debris floating out to sea

If you are dragged out by a rip, don't panic! Stay calm and examine the rip conditions before trying to escape the current. Poor swimmers should ride the rip out from the beach and then swim parallel to the shore for 30 or 40 meters. Once you have escaped the rip, swim toward the shore where the waves are breaking. You can also probe with your feet to see if a sand bar has formed near the edge of the rip. Strong swimmers should swim at a 45 degree angle across the rip.

Study the surf
Always study the surf before going in. Select a safe beach with waves under 1 meter, and pick waves that are suitable for your ability.

Creating
a Web Site

Objectives

- MOUS ► **Plan a Web site**
- MOUS ► **Create a Web page**
- MOUS ► **Format a Web page with themes**
- MOUS ► **Illustrate a Web page with graphics**
- MOUS ► **Save a document as a Web page**
- MOUS ► **Add hyperlinks**
- MOUS ► **Modify hyperlinks**
- MOUS ► **Preview a Web page in a browser**

Creating a Web site and posting it on the Internet or an intranet is a powerful way to share information with other people. The Web page formatting features of Word allow you to easily create professional-looking Web pages from scratch or to save an existing document in HTML format so it can be viewed using a browser. In this unit, you learn how to create a new Web page and how to save an existing document as a Web page. You also learn how to edit and format Web pages, create and modify hyperlinks, and preview a Web page in a browser. ⟋⟍ MediaLoft is sponsoring the Seattle Writers Festival, a major public event featuring prominent writers from around the world. Alice Wegman needs to create a Web site that she will post on the World Wide Web to promote the event and provide information to the public. You will work with Alice as she creates the Seattle Writers Festival Web site.

Planning a Web Site

A **Web page** is a document that can be stored on a computer called a Web server and viewed on the World Wide Web or on an intranet using a **browser**, a software program used to access and display Web pages. A **Web site** is a group of associated Web pages that are linked together with hyperlinks. Before creating a Web page or a Web site, it's important to plan its content and organization. The **home page** is the main page of a Web site, and is the first Web page viewers see when they open a site. Usually, it is the first page you plan and create. The Seattle Writers Festival Web site will include a home page that serves both as an introduction to the festival and as a table of contents for the other Web pages in the site. Before creating the home page, Alice identifies the content she wants to include, plans the organization of the Web site, and sketches the design for each Web page.

Details

▶ **Identify the goal of the Web site**

A successful Web site has a clear purpose. For example, it might promote a product, communicate information, or facilitate a transaction. Alice's Web site will communicate information about the Seattle Writers Festival to the public.

▶ **Sketch the Web site**

Identify the information you want to include on each Web page, sketch the layout and design of each Web page, and map the links between the pages in the Web site. A well-designed Web site is visually interesting and easy for viewers to use. Figure G-1 shows the sketch of Alice's Web site.

▶ **Create each Web page and save it in HTML format**

You can create a Web page from scratch in Word, use a Word template to create a standard type of Web page, or convert an existing document to a Web page. When you create a Web page in Word, you save it in HTML format. **HTML** (Hypertext Markup Language) is the programming language used to describe how each element of a Web page should appear when viewed with a browser. Alice will use a blank Web page template to create her home page. She will create the Program of Events Web page by saving an existing document in HTML format. Files saved in HTML format can be recognized by their .htm or .html file extension.

▶ **Determine the filenaming convention to use**

Different operating systems place various restrictions on Web site filenames. It's safest to name Web pages using the standard eight-dot-three filenaming convention, which specifies that a filename have a maximum of eight letters followed by a period and a three-letter file extension—mypage.htm or chap_1.htm, for example. Alice will use the eight-dot-three naming convention for her Web pages.

▶ **Format each Web page**

You can use the standard Word formatting features to enhance Web pages with fonts, backgrounds, graphics, lines, tables, and other format effects. Word also includes visual themes that you can apply to Web pages to format them quickly. The look of a Web page impacts the viewer as much as its content, so it's important to select fonts, colors, and graphics that complement the goal of your Web site. Alice will apply a theme that expresses the spirit of the writers festival to each Web page. A consistent look between Web pages is an important factor in Web site design.

▶ **Create the hyperlinks between Web pages**

Hyperlinks are text or graphics that viewers can click to open a file, another Web page, or an e-mail message, or click to jump to a specific location in the same file. Hyperlinks are commonly used to link the pages of a Web site to each other. Alice will add hyperlinks that link the home page to other Web pages in her Web site. She will also add links from the home page to other Web sites on the Internet and to an e-mail message to MediaLoft.

▶ **View the Web site using a browser**

Before publishing your Web site to the Web or an intranet, it's important to view your Web pages in a browser to make sure they look and work as you intended. Alice will use the Web Page Preview feature to check the formatting of each Web page in her browser and to test the hyperlinks.

FIGURE G-1: Alice's Web site sketch

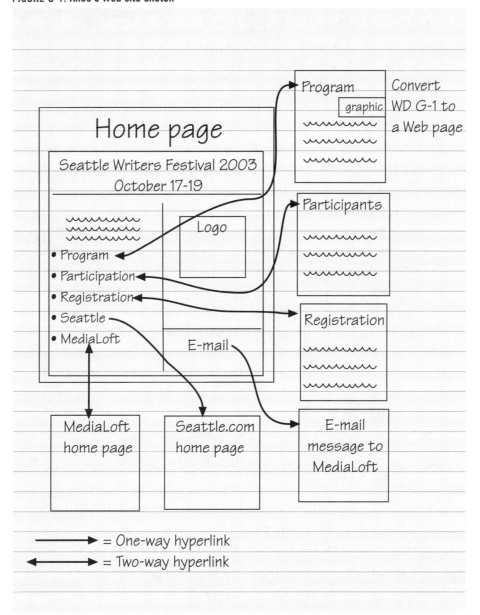

Creating a Web site with the Web Page Wizard

Once you have determined the content and organization of a Web site, one quick way to create it is to use the Web Page Wizard. Through a series of dialog boxes, the Wizard prompts you to: enter a title and save as location for your Web site; choose between using a frame or a separate Web page for the hyperlinks between pages; select the files or templates to include as Web pages; organize and name the Web pages and hyperlinks; and select a common visual theme to apply to each page. When you are finished tailoring your selection, Word creates the Web site for you and the first Web page appears in the document window. You can then use Word's formatting features to customize each page in the Web site. To start the Web Page Wizard, click the General Templates hyperlink in the New Document task pane, click the Web Pages tab in the Templates dialog box, click the Web Page Wizard icon, then click OK to open the Web Page Wizard. Click Next to begin, then answer the questions and choose from the options in each Wizard dialog box, clicking Next to move to the next dialog box. When you are satisfied with your selections, click Finish.

Creating a Web Page

Creating a Web page involves creating a document that uses HTML formatting. HTML places codes, called **tags**, around the elements of a Web page to describe how each element should appear when viewed with a browser. When you create a Web page in Word, you use the usual Word buttons and commands to edit and format it and Word automatically inserts the HTML tags for you. A quick way to create a new Web page is to start with a template. Word includes a template for a new blank Web page, as well as templates for many standard types of Web pages. Because text and graphics align and position differently on Web pages than in Word documents, it's helpful to use a table to structure the layout of a Web page. Alice begins by creating the home page. She starts with a new blank Web page, inserts a table to structure the layout of the home page, adds text, and then saves the Web page in HTML format.

Steps

1. Start **Word**, then click **Blank Web Page** in the New Document task pane
   A blank Web page opens in the document window in Web Layout view, which shows a Web page as it will appear when viewed in a Web browser.

2. Click the **Zoom list arrow** on the Standard toolbar, click **100%** if necessary, click the **Insert Table button** 🔲 on the Standard toolbar, point to the second box in the third row of the grid to create a 3 x 2 Table, then click
   A table with two columns and three rows is inserted. After you finish using the table to help lay out the design of the Web page, you will remove the table borders.

3. Select the **two cells** in the first row, click **Table** on the menu bar, click **Merge Cells**, then deselect the row
   Two cells in the first row merge to become a single cell.

4. Click in the first row, type **Seattle Writers Festival 2003**, press **[Enter]** twice, type **October 17-19**, then press **[Enter]**

5. Select the **two cells** in the second and third rows of the first column, click **Table** on the menu bar, click **Merge Cells**, then deselect the cell
   The two cells in the first column merge to become a single cell.

6. Type the text shown in Figure G-2 in the table cells

7. Click the **Save button** 🔲 on the Standard toolbar
   The Save As dialog box opens. Word assigns a default page title and filename for the Web page and indicates Web Page (*.htm; *html) as the Save as type. Web pages are automatically saved in HTML format.

8. Click **Change Title**, type **Seattle Writers Festival - Home (Your Name)** in the Set Page Title dialog box, then click **OK**
   The page title appears in the title bar when the Web page is viewed with a browser. It's important to assign a page title that describes the Web page for visitors.

9. Drag to select **Seattle Writers Festival 2003.htm** in the File name text box, type **swfhome**, then use the Save in list arrow to navigate to the drive and folder where your Project Files are located
   The filename appears in the title bar when the Web page is viewed in Word. Compare your Save As dialog box with Figure G-3. Word automatically assigns the .htm file extension when Web Page (*.htm; *.html) is selected as the Save as type, so you do not need to type it.

10. Click **Save**
    The filename swfhome appears in the title bar. Depending on your Windows settings, the filename extension may or may not appear after the filename.

FIGURE G-2: Web page in Web Layout view

New Web Page button

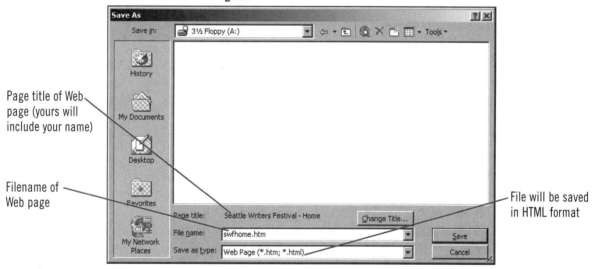

Type the text in these table cells in your table

FIGURE G-3: Save As dialog box

Page title of Web page (yours will include your name)

Filename of Web page

File will be saved in HTML format

Adding frames to a Web page

Many Web pages you visit on the Internet include frames for displaying fixed information. A frame is a section of a Web page window in which a separate Web page can be displayed. Frames commonly contain hyperlinks and other navigation elements that help visitors browse a Web site. A header that remains at the top of the screen while visitors browse a Web site is one example of a frame; a left column that contains hyperlinks to each page in the Web site and stays on the screen while readers visit different pages is another

example. You can add a frame to a Web page by pointing to Frames on the Format menu, and then clicking the type of frame you want to add. Click New Frames Page to open the Frames toolbar, which you can use to select a location (left, right, above, or below) for a new, empty frame. Alternately, if you have applied heading styles to text in the current Web page, you can click Table of Contents in Frame to create a frame that includes hyperlinks to each heading in the Web page.

Formatting a Web Page with Themes

Word includes a multitude of themes that you can apply to Web pages to quickly give them an attractive and consistent look. A **theme** is a set of complementary design elements that you can apply to Web pages, e-mail messages, and other documents that are viewed on-screen. Themes include Web page backgrounds, styles for headings and hyperlinks, picture bullets, horizontal lines, table borders, and other specially designed formats that work well together. You can apply a theme to a Web page using the Theme command on the Format menu. Alice applies a theme to the Web page, formats the text using the theme styles, and adds a horizontal line and bullets. She then experiments with alternate themes to find a design that more closely matches the character of the Writers Festival.

Steps

1. Click **Format** on the menu bar, click **Theme**, scroll down the Choose a Theme list box, then click **Refined**

   A preview of the Refined theme appears in the Theme dialog box, as shown in Figure G-4. The theme includes a background and styles for text, hyperlinks, bullet characters, and horizontal lines.

2. Click **OK**

   The theme background is added to the Web page and the Normal style that comes with the theme is applied to the text.

3. Select **Seattle Writers Festival 2003**, click the **Style list arrow** on the Formatting toolbar, click **Heading 1** in the Style list, then deselect the text

   The Heading 1 style—24-point Times New Roman white—is applied to the heading text.

4. Select **October 17-19**, click the Style list arrow, click **Heading 2**, then deselect the text

   The Heading 2 style—18-point Times New Roman white—is applied to the date text.

5. Select the **heading** and the **date**, click the **Center button** 🔳 on the Formatting toolbar, move the pointer over the table, click the **table move handle** ⊞ to select the table, then click 🔳

   The heading, date, and table are centered on the Web page.

6. Place the insertion point in the blank line between the heading and the date, click the **Outside Border list arrow** 🔲 on the Formatting toolbar, then click the **Horizontal Line button** 🔳

   A horizontal line formatted in the theme design is added below the heading.

7. Select the five-line list at the bottom of the first column, then click the **Bullets button** 🔳 on the Formatting toolbar

   The list is formatted using bullets from the theme design.

8. Click **Format** on the menu bar, click **Theme**, scroll down the Choose a Theme list box, select **Sumi Painting**, then click **OK**

   The background and the text, line, and bullet styles applied to the Web page change to the designs used in the Sumi Painting theme. You do not need to reapply the styles to a Web page when you change its theme.

9. Select **Seattle Writers Festival 2003**, click the **Bold button** 🅱 on the Formatting toolbar, deselect the text, then save your changes

   The heading is formatted in bold. Once you have applied styles to text you can customize the format to suit your purpose. Compare your Web page with Figure G-5.

QuickTip

To create a custom background, point to Background on the Format menu. For a solid color background, select a standard color or click More Colors. For a background with a gradient, texture, pattern, or picture, click Fill Effects.

QuickTip

To change the size or alignment of a line, double-click the line to open the Format Horizontal Line dialog box, then adjust the settings on the Horizontal Line tab.

QuickTip

Backgrounds are visible only in Web Layout view and do not print.

FIGURE G-4: Refined theme in the Theme dialog box

List of available themes (yours might differ)

Options for modifying theme colors

Picture bullets that come with the theme

Horizontal line design

Styles for text and hyperlinks

Theme background

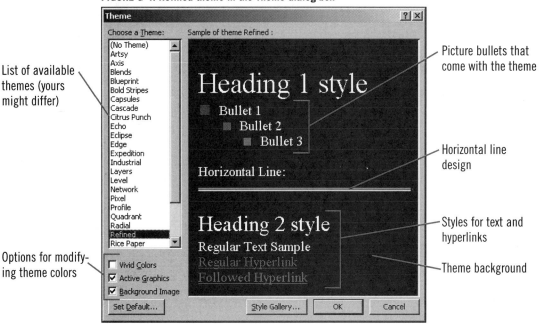

FIGURE G-5: Sumi Painting theme applied to the Web page

Heading 1 style applied

Heading 2 style applied

Picture bullets that come with the Sumi Painting theme

Horizontal line that comes with the Sumi Painting theme

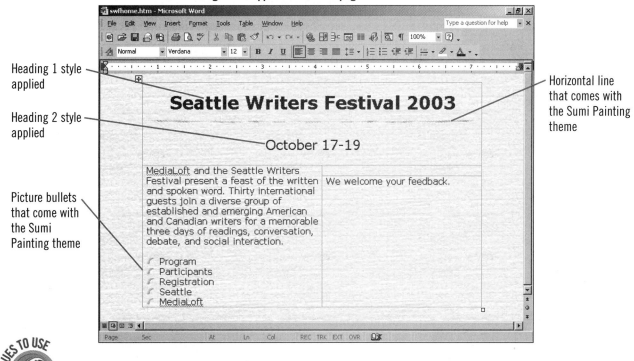

Managing Web page files

When you save a document as a Web page, Word automatically creates a supporting folder in the same location as the .htm file. This folder has the same name as the .htm file plus the suffix _files. It houses the supporting files associated with the Web page. For example, when you create a new Web page or save an existing document as an .htm file, each graphic—including the bullets, background textures, horizontal lines, and other graphics included on the Web page—is automatically converted to a GIF or JPEG format file and saved in the supporting folder. Be aware that if you copy or move a Web page to a different location, it's important that you copy or move the supporting folder (and all the files in it) along with the .htm file, otherwise the links between the .htm file and the supporting files may be broken. If a browser cannot locate the graphic files associated with a Web page, the browser will display a placeholder (often a red X) instead of a graphic.

Illustrating a Web Page with Graphics

You can illustrate your Web pages with pictures, clip art, WordArt, text boxes, AutoShapes, and other graphic objects. When you insert a graphic on a Web page, it is inserted as an inline graphic and you must apply text wrapping to be able to move it independently of the line of text. Floating graphics align and position differently on Web pages than in Word documents, however, because browsers do not support the same graphic formatting options as Word. For example, a floating graphic with square text wrapping can only be left- or right-aligned on a Web page, whereas you can position a floating graphic anywhere in a Word document. For this reason, it's important to use Web Layout view to position graphics on a Web page. If you want to position floating graphics or text precisely on a Web page, you can create a table and then insert the text or graphics in the table cells. ✎ Alice wants the MediaLoft logo to appear to the right of center on the Web page. She inserts the logo in the blank cell in the table, and then adjusts the table formatting to make the Web page attractive.

Steps 1 2 3 4

1. Place the insertion point in the blank cell in the second column of the table, click **Insert** on the menu bar, point to **Picture**, then click **From File**
The Insert Picture dialog box opens.

2. Use the Look in list arrow to navigate to the drive and folder where your Project Files are located, click the file **mloft.jpg**, then click **Insert**
The logo is inserted in the cell as an inline graphic.

3. Click the **logo** to select it, click the **Center button** 🔲 on the Formatting toolbar, press [→], then press **[Enter]**
The graphic is centered in the table cell and a blank line is inserted under the logo.

4. Position the pointer over the border between the first and second columns until the pointer changes to ↔, then drag the border to approximately the **4¼" mark** on the horizontal ruler
The first column widens and the second column narrows. The logo remains centered in the table cell.

5. Select **We welcome your feedback.**, click 🔲, then click in the table to deselect the text
The text is centered in the table cell, as shown in Figure G-6. In Web Layout view, text and graphics are positioned as they are in a Web browser.

6. Click the **table move handle** 🔲 to select the table, click the **Horizontal Line list arrow** 🔲 on the Formatting toolbar, click the **No Border button** 🔲, deselect the table, then save your changes
Removing the table borders masks that the underlying structure of the Web page is a table, as shown in Figure G-7. The text on the left is now a wide column and the logo and text under the logo are positioned to the right of center. By inserting text and graphics in a table, you can position them exactly where you want.

FIGURE G-6: Logo and text centered in the second column

Table move handle

Web Layout
View button

Logo and text are
centered in the
table cells

FIGURE G-7: Web page with table borders removed

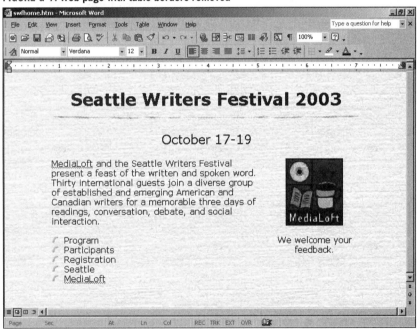

CLUES TO USE

Adding alternate text for graphics

Graphics can take a long time to appear on a Web page, so some people turn off the display of graphics in their browsers so that they can download and view Web pages more quickly. If you don't want visitors to your Web page to see empty space where you intended that they see a graphic, you can add alternate text to appear on the Web page instead of the graphic.

Alternate text will also appear in some browsers while the graphic is loading. To add alternate text to a Web page, select the graphic, then click the Picture command on the Format menu. On the Web tab in the Format Picture dialog box, type the text you want to appear in lieu of the graphic, then click OK.

Saving a Document as a Web Page

When you save an existing document as a Web page, Word converts the content and formatting of the Word file to HTML and displays the Web page as it will appear in a browser. Any formatting that is not supported by Web browsers is either converted to similar supported formatting or removed from the Web page. For example, if you save a document that contains a floating graphic in HTML format, the graphic will be left- or right-aligned on the Web page. Table G-1 describes several common formatting elements that are not supported by Web browsers. You can save a document as a Web page using the Save as Web Page command on the File menu. ✎ Alice wants to add a Web page that includes the festival program of events to her Web site. Rather than create the Web page from scratch, she converts an existing document to HTML format. She then adjusts the formatting of the new Web page and applies the Sumi Painting theme.

Steps

1. **Open the file WD G-1 from the drive and folder where your Project Files are located, click the Zoom list arrow on the Standard toolbar, then click Two Pages**
   The document opens in Print Layout view, as shown in Figure G-8. Notice that the document is two pages long, the text is formatted in three columns, and the graphic on the first page is centered.

2. **Click File on the menu bar, click Save as Web Page, click Change Title, type Seattle Writers Festival – Program of Events (Your Name) in the Set Page Title dialog box, click OK, select WD G-1.htm in the Filename text box, type swfevent, then click Save**
   A dialog box opens and informs you that browsers do not support some of the formatting features of the document. It says the floating graphic will be left- or right-aligned in the Web page. You can click Tell Me More in the dialog box to learn more about features not supported by Web browsers.

3. **Click Continue**
   A copy of the document is saved in HTML format with the filename "swfevent" and the page title "Seattle Writers Festival – Events (Your Name)." The Web page appears in Web Layout view. Notice that the graphic is now left-aligned on the Web page.

4. **Click the Zoom list arrow on the Standard toolbar, click 100% if necessary, then scroll to the bottom of the Web page**
   The text is now formatted in a single column, there are no margins on the Web page, and the document is one long page.

5. **Press [Ctrl][Home], double-click the graphic to open the Format Picture dialog box, click the Size tab, select 3.76 in the Height text box, type 2, then click OK**
   The size of the graphic is reduced.

6 **Drag the graphic to the upper-right corner of the Web page, then deselect the graphic**
   The graphic jumps into place in the upper-right corner when you release the mouse button.

7. **Click Format on the menu bar, click Theme, click Sumi Painting in the Choose a Theme list box, click OK, then save your changes**
   The Sumi Painting theme is applied to the Web page, giving it a look that is consistent with the home page. Notice that the bullet characters change to the picture bullets included with the theme. The font of the body text also changes to the Normal style font used in the theme (12-point Verdana). Compare your Web page with Figure G-9.

FIGURE G-8: Word document in Print Layout view

Floating graphic is centered

Text is formatted in columns

Document is two pages long

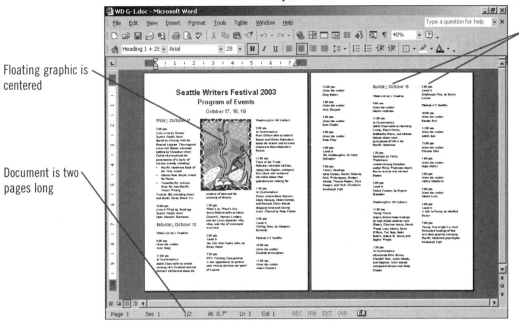

FIGURE G-9: Web page in Web Layout view

Body text changes to Sumi Painting theme Normal style

Bullets change to Sumi Painting theme picture bullets

Graphic is moved to the upper-right corner

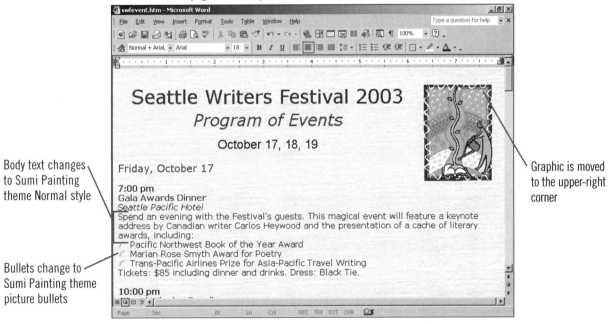

TABLE G-1: Word features that are not supported by Web browsers

feature	result when viewed with a browser
Character formatting	Shadow text becomes bold, small caps become all caps, and embossed, engraved, and outline text becomes solid; character scale changes to 100%; drop caps are removed
Paragraph formatting	Indents are removed, tabs might not align correctly, and border and shading styles might change
Page layout	Margins, columns, page numbers, page borders, and headers and footers are removed; all footnotes are moved to the end of the document
Graphics	Floating graphics, including pictures, AutoShapes, text boxes, and WordArt, are left- or right-aligned
Tables	Decorative cell borders become box borders, diagonal borders are removed, vertical text is changed to horizontal

Adding Hyperlinks

Hyperlinks allow readers to link to (or "jump") to a Web page, e-mail address, file, or a specific location in a document. When you create a hyperlink in a document, you select the text or graphic you want to use as a hyperlink and then specify the location you want to jump to when the hyperlink is clicked. You create hyperlinks using the Insert Hyperlink button on the Standard toolbar. Text that is formatted as a hyperlink appears as colored, underlined text. ✏ To make navigating the Events Web page easier, Alice creates hyperlinks that jump from the dates in the third line of the Web page to the schedule for those dates farther down the Web page. She then inserts several hyperlinks on her home page: one to link to the Events Web page, one to link to the Seattle.com Web site on the Internet, and one to link to an e-mail message to MediaLoft.

Steps 1 2 3 4

1. Select **19** in the third line of the Events Web page, then click the **Insert Hyperlink button** 🖳 on the Standard toolbar

The Insert Hyperlink dialog box opens. You use this dialog box to specify the location of the Web page, file, e-mail address, or position in the current document you want to jump to when the hyperlink—in this case, the text "19"—is clicked.

2. Click **Place in This Document** in the Link to section

All the headings in the Web page are displayed in the dialog box, as shown in Figure G-10. In this context, "heading" is any text to which a heading style has been applied.

QuickTip

Press [Ctrl] and click any hyperlink in Word to follow the hyperlink.

3. Click **Sunday, October 19** in the Select a place in this document section, then click **OK**

The selected text, "19", is formatted in bright blue and underlined, the hyperlink style when the Sumi Painting theme is applied. When the Web page is viewed in a browser, clicking the 19 hyperlink will jump the viewer to the heading "Sunday, October 19" farther down the Web page.

4. Select **18**, click 🖳, click **Saturday, October 18** in the Insert Hyperlink dialog box, click **OK**, select **17**, click 🖳, click **Friday, October 17**, click **OK**, save your changes, then close the file

The numbers 18 and 17 are formatted as hyperlinks to the headings for those dates in the Web page. After you save and close the file, the home page appears in the document window.

5. Select **Program** in the bulleted list, click 🖳, click **Existing File or Web Page** in the Link to section, use the Look in list arrow to navigate to the drive and folder where your Project Files are located, then click **swfevent.htm**

The filename swfevent.htm appears in the Address text box, as shown in Figure G-11.

QuickTip

To create a ScreenTip that appears in a browser, click ScreenTip in the Insert Hyperlink dialog box, then in the Set Hyperlink ScreenTip dialog box, type the text you want to appear.

6. Click **OK**

"Program" is formatted as a hyperlink to the Program of Events Web page. If you point to a hyperlink in Word, the address of the file or Web page it links to appears in a ScreenTip.

7. Select **Seattle** in the list, click 🖳, type **www.seattle.com** in the Address text box in the Insert Hyperlink dialog box, then click **OK**

As you type the Web address, Word automatically adds "http://" in front of "www". A Web address is also called a **URL**, which stands for Uniform Resource Locator. "Seattle" is formatted as a hyperlink to the Seattle.com Web site on the Internet.

QuickTip

By default, Word automatically creates a hyperlink to an e-mail address or URL when you type the address or URL in a document or Web page.

8. Select **feedback** under the logo, click 🖳, then click **E-mail Address** in the Link to section of the Insert Hyperlink dialog box

The Insert Hyperlink dialog box changes so you can create a link to an e-mail message.

9. Type **swf@medialoft.com** in the E-mail address text box, type **Seattle Writers Festival** in the Subject text box, click **OK**, then save your changes

"Feedback" is formatted as a hyperlink, as shown in Figure G-12.

FIGURE G-10: Creating a hyperlink to a heading

Creates a hyperlink to a Web page or file

Creates a hyperlink to a location in the current file

Creates a hyperlink to a new blank document

Creates a hyperlink to an e-mail address

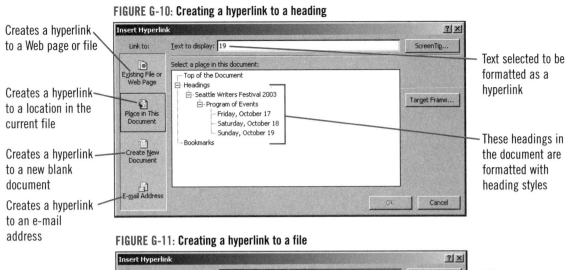

Text selected to be formatted as a hyperlink

These headings in the document are formatted with heading styles

FIGURE G-11: Creating a hyperlink to a file

File to jump to when the hyperlink is clicked

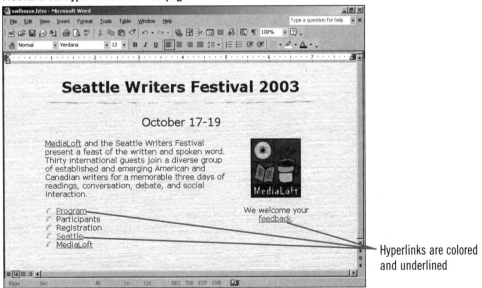

Click to change the default ScreenTip for the hyperlink

Click to browse the Internet for a specific URL to link to

Files and folders in the active drive or folder (yours might differ)

FIGURE G-12: Hyperlinks in the Web page

Hyperlinks are colored and underlined

CLUES TO USE

Pasting text as a hyperlink

You can quickly create a hyperlink to a specific location in any document by copying text from the destination location and pasting it as a hyperlink. To copy and paste text as a hyperlink, select the text you want to jump to, copy it to the Clipboard, place the insertion point in the location you want to insert the hyperlink, click Edit on the menu bar, then click Paste as Hyperlink. The text you copied is pasted and formatted as a hyperlink.

Modifying Hyperlinks

Over time, you might need to edit the hyperlinks on your Web pages with new information or remove them altogether. When you edit a hyperlink, you can change the hyperlink destination, the hyperlink text, or the ScreenTip that displays when a viewer points to the hyperlink. You can easily update or remove a hyperlink by right-clicking it and selecting the Edit Hyperlink or Remove Hyperlink command on the shortcut menu. ✒ Alice changes the hyperlink text for the Program and Seattle hyperlinks to make them more descriptive. She also adds a ScreenTip to the Seattle hyperlink so that visitors to the home page will better understand what the link offers.

Steps 1 2 3 4

1. Right-click **Program**, then click **Edit Hyperlink** on the shortcut menu
   The Edit Hyperlink dialog box opens.

2. Click after **Program** in the Text to display text box, press **[Spacebar]**, type **of Festival Events**, then click **OK**
   The hyperlink text changes to "Program of Festival Events" on the Web page.

3. Right-click **Seattle**, click **Edit Hyperlink**, then click **ScreenTip** in the Edit Hyperlink dialog box
   The Set Hyperlink ScreenTip dialog box opens, as shown in Figure G-14. Any text you type in this dialog box will appear as a ScreenTip when a viewer points to the hyperlink.

4. Type **Hotels, dining, and entertainment in Seattle** in the ScreenTip text box, then click **OK**

5. Click in front of **Seattle** in the Text to display text box in the Edit Hyperlink dialog box, type **Visiting**, press **[Spacebar]**, click **OK**, then save your changes
   The hyperlink text changes to "Visiting Seattle."

6. Point to **Visiting Seattle**
   The ScreenTip you added appears, as shown in Figure G-15.

Adding comments to Web pages and documents

A **comment** is an embedded note that you add to a document or a Web page. Comments appear in a balloon in the right margin of a document in Print Layout or Web Layout view, as shown in Figure G-13, and are generally used to facilitate collaboration when two or more people are working on the same document or Web page.

To insert a comment in a document, select the text you want to comment upon, click Insert on the menu bar, click Comment, type your comment in the comment balloon that appears, then click outside the balloon. To respond to a comment, click in the comment balloon, click Comment on the Insert menu, then type a response in the new comment balloon that opens. To delete a comment, right-click it, then click Delete Comment on the shortcut menu. Note that comments also appear on a Web page when it is viewed in a browser. Comments appear as ScreenTips in a browser when a reader points to a comment mark (usually the author's initials in brackets).

Before you publish Web pages be sure to remove any comments you don't want others to see.

FIGURE G-13: Comment in a document

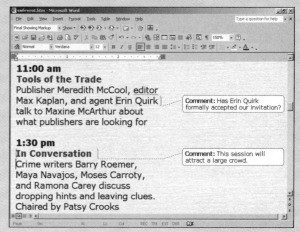

FIGURE G-14: Set Hyperlink ScreenTip dialog box

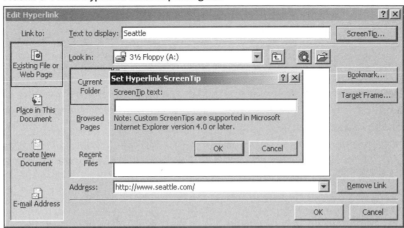

FIGURE G-15: ScreenTip and edited hyperlinks

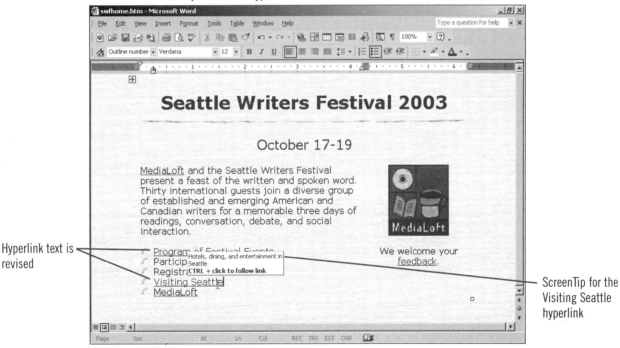

Hyperlink text is revised

ScreenTip for the Visiting Seattle hyperlink

E-mailing a document from Word

Another way to share information online is to e-mail a Word document to others. To e-mail a document directly from Word, open the document, then click the E-mail button 📧 on the Standard toolbar. An e-mail message header opens in the program window. Type the e-mail address(es) of the recipient(s) in the To and Cc text boxes in the message header, separating multiple addresses with a comma or a semicolon. When you are ready to send the file, click Send a Copy on the e-mail header toolbar. Your default e-mail program sends a copy of the document to each recipient.

Preview a Web Page in a Browser

Before you publish Web pages to the Web or an intranet, it's important to preview the pages in a browser to make sure they look as you intended. You can use the Web Page Preview command on the Edit menu to open a copy of a Web page in your default browser. When previewing a Web page, you should check for formatting errors and test each hyperlink. 〜 Alice previews the Web site in her browser and tests the hyperlinks. After viewing the Program Web page, she uses Word to adjust its formatting.

Steps

Trouble?

You must have a Web browser installed on your computer to complete this lesson. If your default browser is not Internet Explorer 5, your screens might not match the figures in the lesson and some features might not be available.

1. Click **File** on the menu bar, click **Web Page Preview**, then click the Maximize button on the browser title bar if necessary
   The browser opens and the home page is displayed in the browser window, as shown in Figure G-16. Notice that the page title—Seattle Writers Festival - Home—appears in the browser title bar. Your page title will also include your name.

2. Click the **Program of Festival Events hyperlink**
   The Seattle Writers Festival – Program of Events Web page opens in the browser window.

3. Click the **19 hyperlink**
   The browser jumps down the page and displays the program for Sunday, October 19 in the browser window.

4. Click the **Back button** ⇐ Back on the browser toolbar
   The top of the Program of Events Web page is displayed in the browser window. The browser toolbar includes buttons for navigating between Web pages, searching the Internet, and printing and editing the current Web page.

Trouble?

If the Edit with Microsoft Word button is not available in your browser, click the Word Program button on the taskbar to switch to Word, then open swfevent.htm.

5. Click the **Edit with Microsoft Word button** 🔳 on the browser toolbar
   The Program of Events Web page appears in a Word document window.

6. Click the **Zoom list arrow** on the Standard toolbar, click **100%** if necessary, select **Tickets** under the bulleted list, press and hold [Ctrl], select **Dress**, release [Ctrl], click the **Bold button** 🔳 on the Formatting toolbar, save your changes, then close the file
   The home page appears in the Word document window. You want to check that your changes to the Program of Events Web page will preview correctly in the browser.

QuickTip

To view or edit the HTML tags for a Web page, click View on the browser title bar, then click Source.

7. Click **File** on the menu bar, click **Web Page Preview**, then click the **Program of Festival Events** hyperlink
   The revised Program of Events Web page appears in the browser, as shown in Figure G-17.

8. Click the **Print button** 🖨 on the browser toolbar to print a copy of the swfevent Web page, click ⇐ Back, then point to the **Visiting Seattle hyperlink**
   The ScreenTip you created for the hyperlink appears. The URL of the Seattle.com Web site also appears in the status bar. If you are connected to the Internet you can click the Visiting Seattle hyperlink to open the Seattle.com Web site in your browser window. Click the Back button on the browser toolbar to return to the Seattle Writers Festival home page when you are finished.

Trouble?

If an e-mail message does not open, continue with step 10.

9. Click the **feedback hyperlink**
   An e-mail message that is automatically addressed to swf@medialoft.com with the subject "Seattle Writers Festival" opens in your default e-mail program.

10. Close the e-mail message, click 🖨 to print the swfhome Web page, exit your browser, then exit Word

FIGURE G-16: Home page in Internet Explorer

Page title (yours will include your name)

Edit with Microsoft Word button

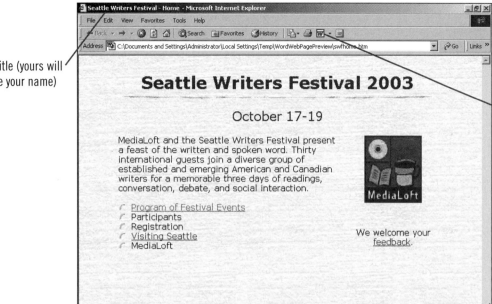

FIGURE G-17: Program of Events page in Internet Explorer

Print button

Text is bold

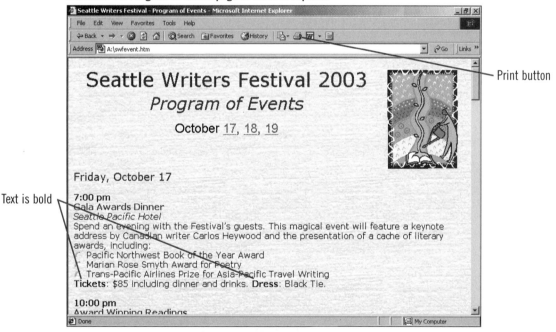

Posting a Web site to the Web or an intranet

To make your Web site available to others, you must post (or publish) it to the Web or to a local intranet. Publishing a Web site involves copying the HTML files and the supporting folders and files to a Web server—either your Internet Service Provider's (ISP) server, if you want to publish it to the Internet, or the server for your local intranet. Check with your ISP or your network administrator for instructions on how to post your Web pages to the correct server.

Practice

► Concepts Review

Label each element shown in Figure G-18.

FIGURE G-18

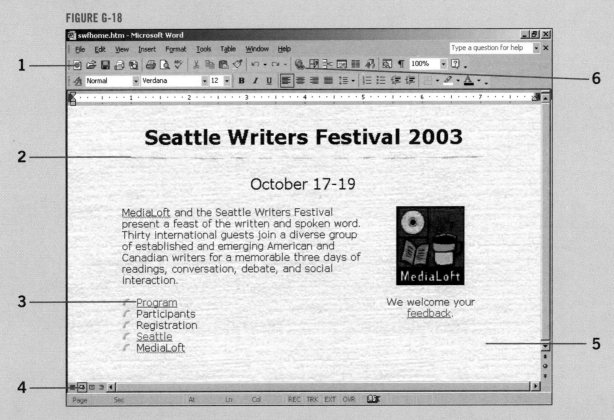

Match each term with the statement that best describes it.

7. **Hyperlink**
8. **Web page**
9. **Home page**
10. **HTML**
11. **Theme**
12. **Web site**
13. **Browser**
14. **URL**

a. The main page of a Web site
b. A software program used to access and display Web pages
c. A document that can be viewed using a browser
d. A group of associated Web pages
e. The address of a Web page on the World Wide Web
f. A programming language used to create Web pages
g. Text or graphic that jumps the viewer to a different location when clicked
h. A set of common design elements that can be applied to a Web page

Select the best answer from the list of choices.

15. **Which of the following is *not* a design element included in a theme?**
    a. Web page background
    b. Horizontal line style
    c. Font effects
    d. Picture bullets

16. Which of the following *cannot* be opened using a hyperlink?
    a. Support folders
    c. E-mail messages
    b. Web pages
    d. Files

17. Which of the following formats is supported by Web browsers?
    a. Headers and footers
    c. Columns of text
    b. Page numbers
    d. Inline graphics

18. What does using the Save as Web Page command accomplish?
    a. Opens the active file in a browser
    c. Applies a Web theme to the active file
    b. Converts the active file to HTML format
    d. Converts floating graphics to inline graphics

19. Where does the page title of a Web page appear?
    a. On the home page
    c. In the name of the supporting folder
    b. In the Word title bar
    d. In the browser title bar

20. Which of the following statements is false?
    a. The supporting folder for a Web page holds GIF and JPEG files.
    b. When you save a document as a Web page, Word adds HTML tags to the file.
    c. You can use the Center button to center a floating graphic in Web Layout view.
    d. Hyperlink text is underlined.

► Skills Review

1. **Create a Web page.**
   a. Study the sketch for the Web site devoted to literacy issues shown in Figure G-19.
   b. Start Word and create a blank Web page.
   c. Create a table with two columns and three rows, select the table, then AutoFit the table to fit the window. (*Hint:* Click Table on the menu bar, point to AutoFit, click AutoFit to window.)
   d. Merge the two cells in the first row of the table, then type **Literacy Facts** in the first row.
   e. Merge the cells in rows 2 and 3 in the second column, click Insert on the menu bar, click File, navigate to the drive and folder where your Project Files are located, select WD G-2, then click Insert.
   f. In the last cell of the first column, type the following three-item list: **What you can do, Literacy Volunteers of America, Contact us**.
   g. Save the file as a Web page to the drive and folder where your Project Files are located with the page title **Literacy Facts – Home** and the filename **literacy**.

2. **Format a Web page with themes.**
   a. Apply the Poetic or Network theme to the Web page. (*Note:* Select a different theme if neither of these themes is available to you.)
   b. Format Literacy Facts in the Heading 1 style, center the text, then press [Enter].
   c. Insert a horizontal line below the heading.
   d. Apply bullets to the list in the last cell of the first column, then save your changes.

3. **Illustrate a Web page with graphics.**
   a. In the blank cell in the first column, insert the graphic file reader.gif from the drive and folder where your Project Files are located.
   b. Center the graphic in the cell, press [Enter], type **Literacy is not just reading and writing; the ability to perform basic math and solve problems is also important.**, press [Enter], then change the font size of the text to 10.
   c. Drag the border between the first and second columns to approximately the 2¼" mark on the horizontal ruler.
   d. Click Format on the menu bar, point to Background, click Fill Effects, click the Gradient tab, select the Two Colors Option button in the Colors section, click the Color 1 list arrow, click Lavender, click the Color 2 list arrow, click Light Yellow, then click OK.

e. Select the table, remove the table borders, then save your changes.

4. Save a document as a Web page.

a. Open the file WD G-3 from the drive and folder where your Project Files are located.

b. Examine the document, then save it as a Web page with the page title **Literacy – what you can do** and the filename **whattodo**.

c. Read the message about formatting changes, then click Continue.

d. Apply the theme you used with the Literacy page to the Web page, then apply the Heading 1 style to the heading.

e. Double-click the graphic, click the Layout tab, change its text wrapping style to In line with text, then move it before Literacy in the heading.

f. Change the background to a lavender and light yellow gradient. (*Hint*: See Step 3d).

g. Save your changes, then close the file.

5. Add hyperlinks.

a. In the Literacy Facts file, select What you can do, then format it as a hyperlink to the whattodo.htm file.

b. Format Literacy Volunteers of America as a hyperlink to the Web address **www.literacyvolunteers.com**.

c. Format Contact us as a hyperlink to your e-mail address with the message subject **Literacy information**. (*Note:* If you do not have an e-mail address, skip this step.)

d. Save your changes.

6. Modify hyperlinks.

a. Right-click the Contact us hyperlink, click Edit Hyperlink, then change the Text to display to **For more information on literacy, contact** followed by your name.

b. Edit the Literacy Volunteers of America hyperlink so that the ScreenTip says **Information on LVA and links to literacy Web sites**.

c. Edit the What you can do hyperlink so that the ScreenTip says **Simple actions you can take to help eliminate illiteracy**.

d. Save your changes.

7. Preview a Web page in a browser.

a. Preview the Literacy Facts Web page in your browser, test all the hyperlinks, then print a copy of the Literacy Facts Web page.

b. Open the whattodo.htm file in Word.

c. Press [Ctrl][End], press [Enter], type **For more information, contact** followed by your name, format your name as a hyperlink to your e-mail address, then save your changes.

d. Preview the Literacy - what you can do Web page in your browser, test the hyperlink, then print the page.

e. Close the browser, close all open Word files, then exit Word.

FIGURE G-19

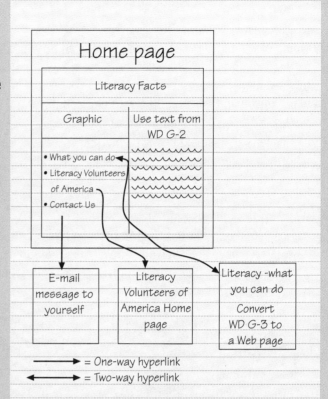

▶ Independent Challenge 1

You have written a story about a recent hiking expedition you took and want to share it and some photos with your family and friends. You decide to create a Web page. Figure G-20 shows how you will arrange the photos.

a. Start Word, open a blank Web page, save the Web page with the page title **A long walk with Jackson** and the filename **longwalk** to the drive and folder where your Project Files are located, then change the zoom level to 100% if necessary.

b. Insert a table with two columns and four rows, merge the two cells in the first row, merge the three cells in the second column, select the table, then AutoFit the table to fit the window.

c. Type **A long walk with Jackson** in the first row of the table, then press [Enter].

d. Click in the second column, then insert the file WD G-4 from the drive and folder where your Project Files are located. (*Hint*: Use the File command on the Insert menu.)

e. Click in the first blank cell in the first column, then insert the graphic file **rwolf.jpg** from the drive and folder where your Project Files are located.

f. Press [Enter], then type **Rising Wolf Mountain (elev. 9513 feet)**.

g. In the last blank cell in the first column, insert the graphic file jackson.jpg from the drive and folder where your Project Files are located, then resize the photo proportionally to be the same width as the Rising Wolf Mountain photo.

h. Press [Enter], then type **Jackson enjoying the view**.

i. Drag the border between the first and second columns left to approximately the 3¼" mark.

j. Apply a theme, then format the Web page using theme elements and other formatting features.

k. Select Glacier National Park in the first paragraph in the second column, format it as a hyperlink to the URL **www.nps.gov/glac/home.htm** with the ScreenTip **Glacier National Park Website Visitor Center**.

l. Press [Ctrl][End], press [Enter], type **E-mail** followed by your name, center the text, then format your name as a hyperlink to your e-mail address, if you have one.

m. Resize the table rows and columns as necessary to make the Web page attractive, remove the borders from the table, save your changes, preview the Web page in your browser, then test the hyperlinks.

n. Switch to Word, make any necessary adjustments, save your changes, preview the Web page in your browser, print a copy, close the browser, close the file in Word, then exit Word.

FIGURE G-20

Rising Wolf Mountain (elev. 9513 feet)

Jackson enjoying the view

▶ Independent Challenge 2

You and your partner have just started a mail-order business called Monet's Garden. You create a small Web site that includes a home page and a list of your products and prices.

a. Start Word, open the Templates dialog box, double-click Web Page Wizard on the Web pages tab, then click Next.

b. Name the Web site **Monet's Garden**, click Browse, navigate to the drive and folder where your Project Files are located, click Open, then click Next.

c. Click Separate Page, then click Next.

d. Click Remove Page three times to remove each Web page, click Add Template Page, select Right-aligned Column, click OK, click Add Existing File, navigate to the drive and folder where your Project Files are located, click WD G-5, click Open, then click Next.

e. Select Right-aligned Column in the list, click Rename, type **Monet's Garden Home**, click OK, click WD G-5, click Rename, type **Products and Prices**, click OK, then click Next.

f. Click Browse Themes, select the Nature theme (or another theme), click OK, click Next, then click Finish.

g. After the wizard creates the Web site, the default contents page of the Web site opens in Word. It has the file-name default.htm. This page provides links to the other pages in the Web site.

h. Select the table on the default.htm page, remove the borders, then save your changes.

i. Press [Ctrl], click the Monet's Garden Home hyperlink on the default.htm page to open the home page in your browser, then open the Monet's Garden Home page in Word.

j. At the top of the home page, type **Order** in the blank table cell, format Order as a hyperlink to the e-mail address **monetsgarden@monad.net**, then remove the table borders.

k. Replace the main heading placeholder with **Monet's Garden**, replace the first section heading placeholder with **Professionally Designed Perennial Gardens!**, then replace the first body paragraph with the following: **If you've admired perennial gardens but thought it would be too complicated or expensive to create your own, here's great news. Our fail-proof garden packages will get you off to a sure-fire start and guarantee you glorious blooms for years to come.**

l. Delete the remaining placeholder text in the first column, delete the caption placeholder in the second column, then replace the graphic with an appropriate clip art image.

m. Adjust the formatting of the Web page to make it attractive, press [Ctrl][End], type **For more information, contact** followed by your name, make your name a hyperlink to your e-mail address, then save your changes.

n. Open the Products and Prices page in Word.

o. At the top of the Products and Prices page, type **Order** in the blank table cell, right-align Order, format it as a hyperlink to the e-mail address **monetsgarden@monad.net**, then remove the table borders.

p. Scroll down the Web page, read the comment, change 60 to 30 in the Web page text, then delete the comment. (*Hint*: Right-click the comment, then click Delete comment.)

q. Apply styles and other formatting to the Web page to make it attractive and give it a look consistent with the Monet's Garden Home page, press [Ctrl][End], type **For more information, contact** followed by your name, make your name a hyperlink to your e-mail address, then save your changes.

r. Preview the Web site in your browser, test the hyperlinks, print a copy of the home page and the Products and Prices page, exit your browser, close all open files, then exit Word.

► Independent Challenge 3

You are in charge of publicity for the Sydney Triathlon 2003 World Cup. One of your responsibilities is to create a Web site to provide details of the event. You have created the content for the Web pages as Word documents, and now need to save and format them as Web pages. Your Web site will include a home page and three other Web pages. One of the Web pages is shown in Figure G-21.

FIGURE G-21

a. Start Word, open the file WD G-6 from the drive and folder where your Project Files are located, then save it as a Web page with the page title **Sydney Triathlon 2003 World Cup - Home** and the filename **tri_home**.

b. Apply the Geared Up Factory or Cascade theme, but first remove the check from the Background Image check box in the Theme dialog box. (*Note*: Use a different theme if neither of these themes is available to you.)

c. Press [Ctrl][A], then change the font size to 10.

d. Apply the Heading 1 style to the heading Sydney Triathlon 2003 World Cup in the first row of the table, right-align the text, apply italic, select Sydney Triathlon 2003 in the heading, apply bold, select Triathlon 2003, then change the font color to a different color.

e. Apply the Heading 4 style to Welcome to the Sydney Triathlon 2003 World Cup! in the upper-left cell of the table, apply bold, then center the text.

f. Read the remaining text on the Web page, then format it with heading styles, fonts, font colors, and other formatting effects to make it look attractive. Preview the Web page in your browser.

g. Remove the table borders from the Web page, press [Ctrl][End], type your name, save your changes, then close the file.

h. Open the files listed in the table from the drive and folder where your Project Files are located, then save them as Web pages with the page titles and filenames listed in the table.

Project File	Page Title	Filename
WD G-7	Sydney Triathlon 2003 World Cup – Best Views	tri_view
WD G-8	Sydney Triathlon 2003 World Cup – Getting There	tri_get
WD G-9	Sydney Triathlon 2003 World Cup – The Athletes	tri_athl

i. In Word, open the tri_home.htm file, then change the zoom level to 100% if necessary.

j. Select Best Views, then format it as a hyperlink to the tri_view.htm file. Format Getting There and The Athletes as hyperlinks to the tri_get.htm and tri_athl.htm files, then save your changes.

k. Open each of the remaining three files—tri_view.htm, tri_get.htm, and tri_athl.htm—and format the text in the left column of each Web page as a hyperlink to the appropriate file. Save your changes, then close each Web page.

l. Preview the home page in your browser. Test each hyperlink on the home page and on the other Web pages.

m. Examine each Web page in your browser, make any necessary formatting adjustments in Word, print a copy of each Web page from your browser, then close your browser, close all open files, and exit Word.

 Independent Challenge 4

In this independent challenge you will use the Personal Web page template to create a Web page that provides information about you and your interests. Your Web page will include hyperlinks to Web sites that you think will be useful to people who share your passions.

a. Start Word, open the Templates dialog box, then create a new Web page based on the Personal Web page template.

b. Save the Web page with the filename **my_page** to the drive and folder where your Project Files are located. Use your name for the page title.

c. Under Contents, delete the Work Information and Current Projects items, then scroll down and delete the placeholders in the Work Information and Current projects sections of the Web page. (*Note:* Delete from the heading for each section to the "Back to top" hyperlink.)

d. Use your favorite search engine to search for Web sites related to your interests. Write down the page titles and URLs of at least three Web sites that you think are worth visiting.

e. Replace the placeholder text in the Favorite Links section with the names of the three Web sites you liked. Format each name as a hyperlink to the Web site, and create a ScreenTip that explains why you think it's a good Web site.

f. Replace the remaining placeholder text in the Web page with information about yourself.

g. Format your e-mail and Web addresses as hyperlinks to those addresses. Edit each Back to top hyperlink so that it jumps to the main heading at the top of the page rather than to the top of the document.

h. Illustrate the Web page with a clip art graphic. Create a table to position the graphic if necessary.

i. Format the Web page with a background, heading styles, lines, bullets, fonts, colors, and any other formatting features.

j. Save your changes, preview the Web page in your browser, test each hyperlink, then make any necessary adjustments.

k. Save your changes, preview the Web page in your browser again, print a copy, close the browser, close the file, then exit Word.

► Visual Workshop

Create the Web pages shown in Figure G-22 using the graphic files rest.jpg, bridge.jpg, and studlamp.jpg, found on the drive and folder where your Project Files are located. Save the home page with the page title **Gallery Azul Home (Your Name)** and the filename **azulhome**. Save the exhibit page with the page title **Gallery Azul Exhibit (Your Name)** and the filename **azulexhb**. On the home page, create a hyperlink to the exhibit page and a hyperlink to the e-mail address **GalleryAzul@ptown.net**. On the Exhibit page, create a hyperlink to the home page. View the Web pages in your browser, then print a copy of each Web page.

FIGURE G-22

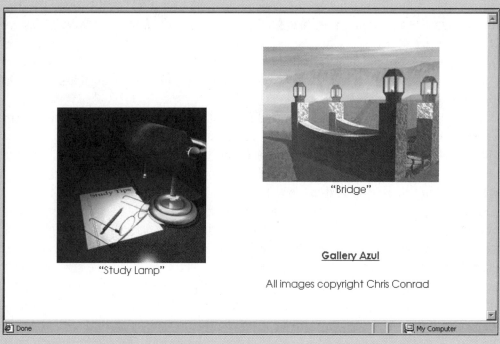

Merging
Word Documents

Objectives

- [MOUS] ► **Understand mail merge**
- [MOUS] ► **Create a main document**
- [MOUS] ► **Design a data source**
- [MOUS] ► **Enter and edit records**
- [MOUS] ► **Add merge fields**
- [MOUS] ► **Merge data**
- [MOUS] ► **Create labels**
- [MOUS] ► **Sort and filter records**

A mail merge operation combines a standard document, such as a form letter, with customized data, such as a set of names and addresses, to create a set of personalized documents. You can perform a mail merge to create documents used in mass mailings, such as letters and labels. You also can use mail merge to create documents that include customized information, such as business cards. In this unit you learn how to use the Mail Merge Wizard to set up and perform a mail merge. Alice Wegman needs to send a welcome letter to the new members of the MediaLoft Coffee Club, a program designed to attract customers to the MediaLoft Café. She also needs to send a brochure to all the members of the club. She uses mail merge to create a personalized form letter and mailing labels for the brochures.

Understanding Mail Merge

When you perform a mail merge, you merge a standard document with a file that contains customized information for many individuals or items. The document with the standard text is called the **main document**. The file with the unique data for individual people or items is called the **data source**. Merging the main document with a data source results in a merged document that contains customized versions of the main document, as shown in Figure H-1. The Mail Merge Wizard steps you through the process of setting up and performing a mail merge. Alice uses the Mail Merge Wizard to create her form letters and mailing labels. Before beginning, she explores the steps involved in performing a mail merge.

► **Create the main document**

The main document contains the text—often called **boilerplate text**—that appears in every version of the merged document. The main document also includes the merge fields, which indicate where the customized information will be inserted when you perform the merge. You insert the merge fields in the main document after you have created or selected the data source.

► **Create a data source or select an existing data source**

The data source is a file that contains the unique information for each individual or item. It provides the information that varies in every version of the merged document. A data source is composed of data fields and data records. A **data field** is a category of information, such as last name, first name, street address, city, or postal code. A **data record** is a complete set of related information for an individual or an item, such as one person's name and address. It is easiest to think of a data source file as a table: the header row contains the names of the data fields (the **field names**), and each row in the table is an individual data record. You can use the Mail Merge Wizard to create a new data source, or you can merge a main document with an existing data source, such as a data source created in Word, an Outlook Contact List, or an Access database.

► **Identify the fields to include in the data source and enter the records**

When you create a new data source, you must first identify the fields to include. It's important to think of and include all the fields before you begin to enter data. For example, if you are creating a data source that will include addresses, you might need to include fields for a person's middle name, title, department name, or country, even though every address in the data source will not include that information. Once you have identified the fields and set up your data source, you are ready to enter the data for each record.

► **Add merge fields to the main document**

A **merge field** is a placeholder that you insert in the main document to indicate where the data from each record should be inserted when you perform the merge. For example, in the location you want to insert a zip code, you insert a zip code merge field. The merge fields in a main document must correspond with the field names in the associated data source. Merge fields must be inserted, not typed, in the main document. The Mail Merge Wizard provides access to the dialog boxes you use to insert merge fields.

► **Merge the data from the data source into the main document**

Once you have established your data source and inserted the merge fields in the main document, you are ready to perform the merge. You can merge to a new file, which will contain a customized version of the main document for each record in the data source, or you can merge directly to a printer, fax, or e-mail message.

FIGURE H-1: Mail merge process

Data source document

Field name

Store	Title	First Name	Last Name	Address Line 1	City	State	Zip Code	Country
Seattle	Ms.	Linda	Barker	62 Cloud St.	Bellevue	WA	83459	US
Boston	Mr.	Bob	Cruz	23 Plum St.	Boston	MA	02483	US
Chicago	Ms.	Joan	Yatco	456 Elm St.	Chicago	IL	60603	US
Seattle	Ms.	Anne	Butler	48 East Ave.	Vancouver	BC	V6F 1AH	CANADA
Boston	Mr.	Fred	Silver	56 Pearl St.	Cambridge	MA	02139	US

Data record

Main document

MediaLoft
Corporate Headquarters • 821 Post Street • San Francisco, CA 94108
Tel: (415) 555-2398 • Fax: (415) 555-2393 • www.medialoft.com

May 12, 2003

««AddressBlock»»

««GreetingLine»»

Welcome to the MediaLoft «Store» Coffee Club! This month's featured coffee is Kealakekua Sunrise, a rich blend of organic Kona beans with a hint of macadamia – the twin flavors of Hawaii.

Your membership entitles you to a free cup of the featured coffee any Saturday morning at the MediaLoft Café. In addition you will receive a 10% discount on all coffees and coffee-related products. We'll hope you'll join us each Saturday at MediaLoft.

Sincerely,

Alice Wegman
Marketing Manager

Merge fields

Boilerplate text

Merged document

MediaLoft
Corporate Headquarters • 821 Post Street • San Francisco, CA 94108
Tel: (415) 555-2398 • Fax: (415) 555-2393 • www.medialoft.com

May 12, 2003

Ms. Linda Barker
62 Cloud St.
Bellevue, WA 83459

Dear Ms. Barker:

Welcome to the MediaLoft Seattle Coffee Club! This month's featured coffee is Kealakekua Sunrise, a rich blend of organic Kona beans with a hint of macadamia – the twin flavors of Hawaii.

Your membership entitles you to a free cup of the featured coffee any Saturday morning at the MediaLoft Café. In addition you will receive a 10% discount on all coffees and coffee-related products. We'll hope you'll join us each Saturday at MediaLoft.

Sincerely,

Alice Wegman
Marketing Manager

Customized information

Understanding compare and merge

The Word compare and merge feature is different from mail merge. Mail merge combines a main document with a file containing customized information to create a set of unique documents. Compare and merge is used to compare any two documents—usually an original document and an edited copy of the original—to create a third document that shows the differences between the two. To compare and merge two documents, open the edited copy of the document, click Tools on the menu bar, then click Compare and Merge Documents. In the Compare and Merge dialog box, select the original document, click the Merge button list arrow, then click Merge into new document. A new merge document showing the differences between the edited document and the original document opens. The differences between the two documents are shown as tracked changes (colored and underlined text). You can then examine the merged document, edit it, and save it with a new filename.

Creating a Main Document

The first step in performing a mail merge is to create the main document—the file that contains the boilerplate text. You can create a main document from scratch, save an existing document as a main document, or use a mail merge template to create a main document. The Mail Merge Wizard walks you through the process of selecting the type of main document to create. Alice uses an existing form letter for her main document. She begins by starting the Mail Merge Wizard.

 **Steps**

QuickTip

You can click an option button in the task pane to read a description of each type of merge document.

1. Start **Word**, click **Tools** on the menu bar, point to **Letters and Mailings**, then click **Mail Merge Wizard**
   The Mail Merge task pane opens, as shown in Figure H-2, and displays information for the first step in the mail merge process: selecting the type of merge document to create.

2. Make sure the **Letters option button** is selected, then click **Next: Starting document** to continue with the next wizard step
   The task pane displays the options for the second step: selecting the main document. You can use the current document, start with a mail merge template, or use an existing file.

QuickTip

If you choose "Use the current document" and the current document is blank, you can create a main document from scratch. Either type the boilerplate text at this wizard step, or wait until the wizard prompts you to do so.

3. Select the **Start from existing document option button**, select **More files** in the Start from existing list box if necessary, then click **Open**
   The Open dialog box opens.

4. Use the Look in list arrow to navigate to the drive and folder where your Project Files are located, select the file **WD H-1**, then click **Open**
   The letter that opens contains the boilerplate text for the main document. Notice the filename in the title bar is Document1. When you create a main document that is based on an existing document, Word gives the main document a default temporary filename.

5. Click the **Save button** 🖫 on the Standard toolbar, then save the main document with the filename **Coffee Letter Main** to the drive and folder where your Project Files are located
   It's a good idea to include "main" in the filename so that you can easily recognize the file as a main document.

6. Click the **Zoom list arrow** on the Standard toolbar, click **Text Width**, select **April 9, 2003** in the letter, type today's date, scroll down, select **Alice Wegman**, type your name, press **[Ctrl][Home]**, then save your changes
   The edited main document is shown in Figure H-3.

7. Click **Next: Select recipients** to continue with the next wizard step
   You will continue with Step 3 of 6 in the next lesson.

 CLUES TO USE

Working with smart tags

Smart tags are labels applied to data (text) that Word recognizes as a date, address, place, name, or other type of data. Text that is labeled with a smart tag is marked with a dotted purple underline. Smart tags allow you to use Word to perform tasks that you would normally need to do in another Office program. For example, in Word you can click a smart tag labeling a person's name to add the person's name and address to one of your contact lists in Outlook, without having to open Outlook first. To find out the kinds of actions you can take with a smart tag, point to the smart tag, click the Smart Tag Actions button that appears, then select from the menu of options.

FIGURE H-2: Step 1 of 6 Mail Merge task pane

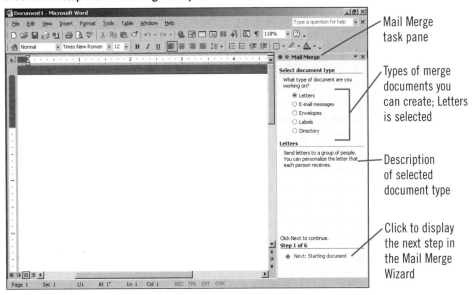

Mail Merge task pane

Types of merge documents you can create; Letters is selected

Description of selected document type

Click to display the next step in the Mail Merge Wizard

FIGURE H-3: Main document with the Step 2 of 6 Mail Merge task pane

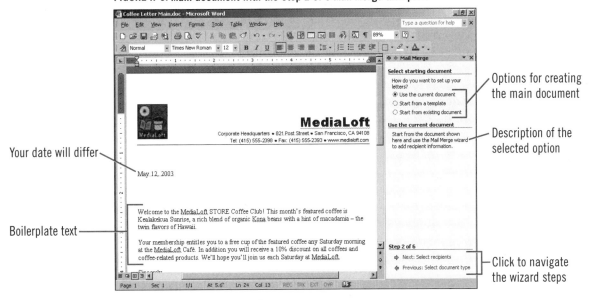

Your date will differ

Boilerplate text

Options for creating the main document

Description of the selected option

Click to navigate the wizard steps

Using a mail merge template

If you are creating a letter, fax, or directory, you can use a mail merge template to start your main document. Each template includes boilerplate text, which you can customize, and merge fields, which you can match to the field names in your data source. To create a main document that is based on a mail merge template, click the Start from a template option button in the Step 2 of 6 Mail Merge task pane, then click Select template. In the Templates dialog box that opens, select a template on the Mail Merge tab, then click OK to create the document. Once you have created the main document, you can customize it with your own information: edit the boilerplate text, change the document format, or add, remove, or modify the merge fields. Before performing the merge, make sure to match the names of the address merge fields used in the template with the field names used in your data source. To match the field names, click the Match Fields button 🔳 on the Mail Merge toolbar, then use the list arrows in the Match fields dialog box to select the field name in your data source that corresponds to each address field component in the main document.

Designing a Data Source

Once you have identified the main document, the next step in the mail merge process is to identify the data source, the file that contains the information that will differ in each version of the merge document. You can use an existing data source that already contains the records you want to include in your merge, or you can create a new data source. When you create a new data source you must determine the fields to include—the categories of information, such as a first name, last name, city, or a zip code—and then add the records. ▰▰▰▰ Alice creates a new data source that includes fields for the name, address, and MediaLoft store location of each new member of the Coffee Club.

Steps 1 2 3 4

1. **Make sure the Mail Merge task pane displays Step 3 of 6 at the bottom**
   Step 3 of 6 involves selecting a data source to use for the merge. You can use an existing data source, a list of contacts created in Microsoft Outlook, or a new data source.

2. **Select the Type a new list option button, then click Create**
   The New Address List dialog box opens, as shown in Figure H-4. You use this dialog box both to design your data source and to enter records. The Enter Address information section of the dialog box includes fields that are commonly used in form letters, but you can customize your data source by adding and removing fields from this list. A data source can be merged with more than one main document, so it's important to design a data source to be flexible. The more fields you include in a data source, the more flexible it is. For example, if you include separate fields for a person's title, first name, middle name, and last name, you can use the same data source to create an envelope addressed to "Mr. John Montgomery Smith" and a form letter addressed to "Dear John."

3. **Click Customize**
   The Customize Address List dialog box opens, as shown in Figure H-5. You use this dialog box to add, delete, rename, and reorder the fields in the data source.

4. **Click Company Name in the list of field names, click Delete, then click Yes in the warning dialog box that opens**
   Company Name is removed from the list of field names. The Company Name field will not be part of the data source.

5. **Repeat step 4 to delete the Address Line 2, Home Phone, Work Phone and E-mail Address fields**
   The fields are removed from the data source.

6. **Click Add, type Store in the Add Field dialog box, then click OK**
   A field called "Store," which you will use to indicate the location of the MediaLoft store where the customer joined the Coffee Club, is added to the data source.

7. **Select Store in the list of field names if necessary, then click Move Up eight times**
   The field name "Store" is moved to the top of the list. Although the order of field names does not matter in a data source, it's convenient to arrange the field names logically to make it easier to enter and edit records.

8. **Click OK**
   The New Address List dialog box shows the customized list of fields, with the Store field first in the list. The next step is to enter each record you want to include in the data source. You will add records to the data source in the next lesson.

FIGURE H-4: New Address List dialog box

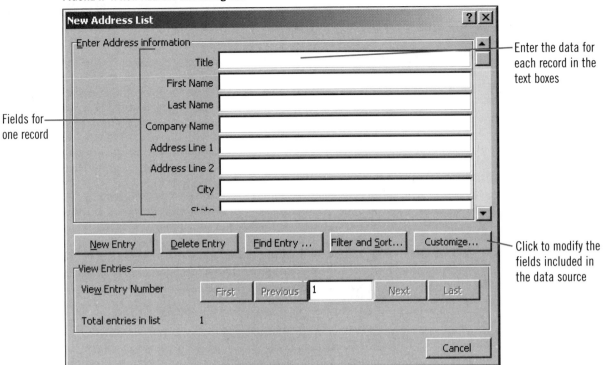

Fields for one record

Enter the data for each record in the text boxes

Click to modify the fields included in the data source

FIGURE H-5: Customize Address List dialog box

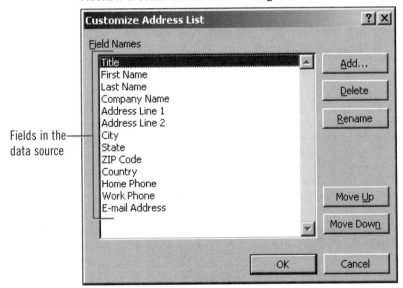

Fields in the data source

Merging with an Outlook data source

If you maintain lists of contacts in Microsoft Outlook, you can use one of your Outlook contact lists as a data source for a merge. To merge with an Outlook data source, click the Select from Outlook contacts option button in the Step 3 of 6 Mail Merge task pane, then click Choose Contacts Folder to open the Select Contact List folder dialog box. In this dia-log box, select the contact list you want to use as the data source, then click OK. All the contacts included in the selected folder appear in the Mail Merge Recipients dialog box. Here you can refine the list of recipients to include in the merge by sorting and fil-tering the records. When you are satisfied, click OK in the Mail Merge Recipients dialog box.

Entering and Editing Records

Once you have established the structure of a data source, the next step is to enter the records. Each record includes the complete set of information for each individual or item you include in the data source. ➤ Alice creates a record for each new member of the Coffee Club.

Steps 1 2 3 4

1. Place the insertion point in the Store text box in the New Address List dialog box, type **Seattle**, then press **[Tab]**

"Seattle" appears in the Store field and the insertion point moves to the next field in the list, the Title field.

2. Type **Ms.**, press **[Tab]**, type **Linda**, press **[Tab]**, type **Barker**, press **[Tab]**, type **62 Cloud St.**, press **[Tab]**, type **Bellevue**, press **[Tab]**, type **WA**, press **[Tab]**, type **83459**, press **[Tab]**, then type **US**

Compare your New Address List dialog box with Figure H-6.

3. Click **New Entry**

The record for Linda Barker is added to the data source and the dialog box displays empty fields for the next record, record 2.

4. Enter the following four records, pressing **[Tab]** to move from field to field, and clicking **New Entry** at the end of each record except the last:

Store	Title	First Name	Last Name	Address Line 1	City	State	ZIP Code	Country
Boston	Mr.	Bob	Cruz	23 Plum St.	Boston	MA	02483	US
Chicago	Ms.	Joan	Yatco	456 Elm St.	Chicago	IL	60603	US
Seattle	Ms.	Anne	Butler	48 East Ave.	Vancouver	BC	V6F 1AH	CANADA
Boston	Mr.	Fred	Silver	56 Pearl St.	Cambridge	MA	02139	US

5. Click **Close**

The Save Address List dialog box opens. Data sources are saved by default in the My Data Sources folder so that you can easily locate them to use in other merge operations. Data sources you create in Word are saved in Microsoft Office Address Lists (*.mdb) format.

6. Type **New Coffee Club Data** in the File name text box, use the Save in list arrow to navigate to the drive and folder where your Project Files are located, then click **Save**

The data source is saved, and the Mail Merge Recipients dialog box opens, as shown in Figure H-7. The dialog box shows the records in the data source in table format. You can use the dialog box to edit, sort, and filter records, and to select the recipients to include in the mail merge. You will learn more about sorting and filtering in a later lesson. The check marks in the first column indicate the records that will be included in the merge.

7. Click the **Joan Yatco record**, click **Edit**, select **Ms.** in the Title text box in the New Coffee Club Data.mdb dialog box, type **Dr.**, then click **Close**

The data in the Title field for Joan Yatco changes from "Ms." to "Dr." and the New Coffee Club Data.mdb dialog box closes.

8. Click **OK** in the Mail Merge Recipients dialog box

The dialog box closes. The file type and filename of the data source attached to the main document now appear under Use an existing list in the Mail Merge task pane, as shown in Figure H-8. The Mail Merge toolbar also appears in the program window when you close the data source. You'll learn more about the Mail Merge toolbar in later lessons.

FIGURE H-6: Record in New Address List dialog box

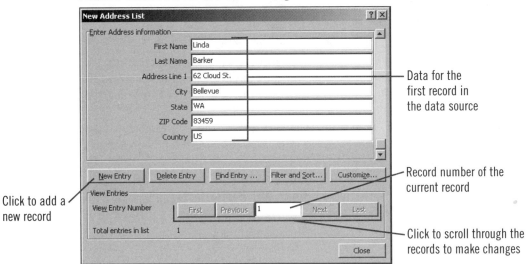

Data for the first record in the data source

Record number of the current record

Click to add a new record

Click to scroll through the records to make changes

FIGURE H-7: Mail Merge Recipients dialog box

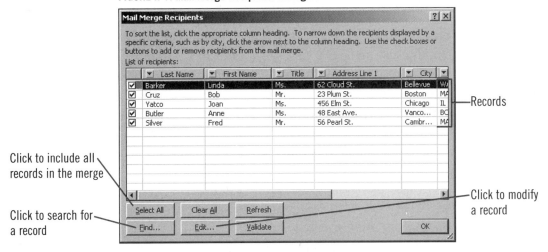

Click to include all records in the merge

Records

Click to modify a record

Click to search for a record

FIGURE H-8: Data source attached to the main document

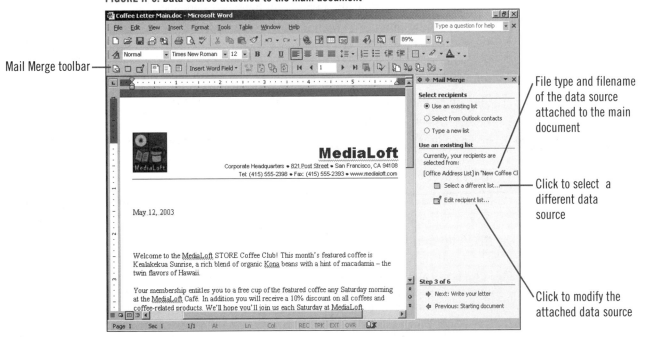

Mail Merge toolbar

File type and filename of the data source attached to the main document

Click to select a different data source

Click to modify the attached data source

Adding Merge Fields

After you have created and identified the data source, the next step is to insert the merge fields in the main document. Merge fields serve as placeholders for text that will be inserted when the main document and the data source are merged. The names of merge fields correspond to the field names in the data source. You can insert merge fields using the Mail Merge task pane or the Insert Merge Field button on the Mail Merge toolbar. You cannot type merge fields into the main document. Alice uses the Mail Merge task pane to insert merge fields for the inside address and greeting of her letter. She also inserts a merge field for the store location in the body of the letter.

1. Click the **Show/Hide ¶ button** ¶ on the Standard toolbar to display formatting marks, then click **Next: Write your letter** in the Mail Merge task pane

   The Mail Merge task pane shows the options for Step 4 of 6: writing the letter and inserting the merge fields in the main document. Since your form letter is already written, you are ready to add the merge fields to it.

2. Place the insertion point in the blank line above the first body paragraph, then click **Address block** in the Mail Merge task pane

   The Insert Address Block dialog box opens, as shown in Figure H-9. You use this dialog box to specify the fields you want to include in an address block. In this merge, the address block is the inside address of the form letter. An address block automatically includes fields for the street, city, state, and postal code, but you can select the format for the recipient's name and indicate whether to include a company name or country in the address.

3. Scroll the list of formats for a recipient's name to get a feel for the kinds of formats you can use, then click **Mr. Joshua Randall Jr.** if necessary

   The selected format uses the recipient's title, first name, and last name.

4. Click the **Only include the country/region if different than: option button**, then type **US** in the text box

   You only need to include the country in the address block if the country is different from the United States, so you indicate that all entries in the Country field except "US" should be included in the printed address.

5. Click **OK**, then press **[Enter]** twice

   The merge field AddressBlock is added to the main document. Chevrons (<< and >>) surround a merge field to distinguish it from the boilerplate text.

6. Click **Greeting line** in the Mail Merge task pane

   The Greeting Line dialog box opens. You want to use the format "Dear Mr. Randall:" (the recipient's title and last name, followed by a colon) for a greeting. The default format uses a comma, so you have to change the comma to a colon.

7. Click the **, list arrow**, click **:**, click **OK**, then press **[Enter]**

   The merge field GreetingLine is added to the main document.

8. In the body of the letter select **STORE**, then click **More items** in the Mail Merge task pane

   The Insert Merge Field dialog box opens and displays the list of field names included in the data source.

9. Select **Store** if necessary, click **Insert**, click **Close**, press **[Spacebar]** to add a space between the merge field and Coffee if necessary, save your changes, then click ¶ to turn off the display of formatting marks

   The merge field Store is inserted in the main document, as shown in Figure H-10. You must type spaces and punctuation between merge fields if you want spaces and punctuation to appear between the data in the merged documents. You will preview the merged data and perform the merge in the next lesson.

FIGURE H-9: Address Block dialog box

Formats for the recipient's name —

Click to match the default address field names to the field names used in your data source

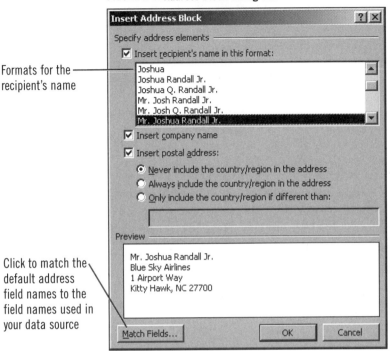

FIGURE H-10: Merge fields in the main document

Merge fields —

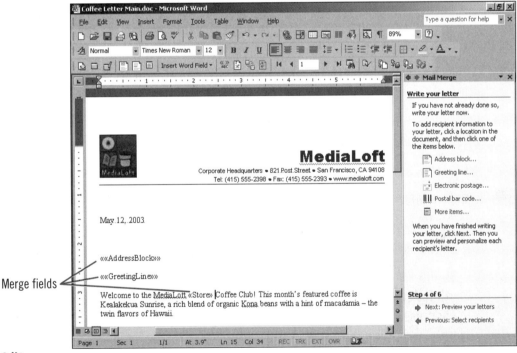

Matching fields

The merge fields you insert in a main document must correspond with the field names in the associated data source. If you are using the Address Block merge field, you must make sure that the default address field names correspond with the field names used in your data source. If the default address field names do not match the field names in your data source, click Match Field in the Insert Address Block dialog box, then use the list arrows in the Match Fields dialog box to select the field name in the data source that corresponds to each default address field name.

Merging Data

Once you have added records to your data source and inserted merge fields in the main document, you are ready to perform the merge. Before merging, it's a good idea to preview the merged data to make sure the printed documents will appear as you want them to. You can preview the merge using the wizard or the View Merged Data button on the Mail Merge toolbar. When you merge the main document with the data source, you must choose between merging to a new file or directly to a printer. ✎ Before merging the form letter with the data source, Alice previews the merge to make sure each customized letter looks as she intended. She then merges the two files to a new document.

Steps 123

1. **Click Next: Preview your letters in the Mail Merge task pane**
   The data from the first record in the data source appears in place of the merge fields in the main document, as shown in Figure H-11. Always check the preview document to make sure the merge fields, punctuation, page breaks, and spacing all appear as you intend before you perform the merge.

2. **Click the Next Recipient button >> in the Mail Merge task pane**
   The data from the second record in the data source appears in place of the merge fields.

3. **Click in the Go to Record text box on the Mail Merge toolbar, press [Backspace], type 4, then press [Enter]**
   The data for the fourth record appears in the document window. The non-US country name, in this case Canada, is included in the address block, just as you specified. You can also use the First Record ⊮, Previous Record ◀, Next Record ▶, and Last Record ⧫ buttons on the Mail Merge toolbar to preview the merged data. Table H-1 describes other buttons on the Mail Merge toolbar.

4. **Click Next: Complete the Merge in the Mail Merge task pane**
   The options for Step 6 of 6 appear in the Mail Merge task pane. Merging to a new file allows you to edit the individual letters.

5. **Click Edit individual letters to merge the data to a new document**
   The Merge to New Document dialog box opens. You can use this dialog box to specify the records to include in the merge.

6. **Make sure the All option button is selected, then click OK**
   The main document and the data source are merged to a new document called Letters1, which contains a customized form letter for each record in the data source. You can now further personalize the letters without affecting the main document or the data source.

7. **Click the Zoom list arrow on the Standard toolbar, click Page Width, scroll to the fourth letter (addressed to Ms. Anne Butler), place the insertion point before V6F in the address block, then press [Enter]**
   The postal code is now consistent with the proper format for a Canadian address.

8. **Click the Save button 🖫 on the Standard toolbar to open the Save As dialog box, then save the merge document as Coffee Letter Merge to the drive and folder where your Project Files are located**
   You may decide not to save a merged file if your data source is large. Once you have created the main document and the data source, you can create the letters by performing the merge again.

9. **Click File on the menu bar, click Print, click the Current Page option button in the Page Range section of the Print dialog box, click OK, then close all open Word files, saving changes if prompted**
   The letter to Anne Butler prints.

FIGURE H-11: Preview of merged data

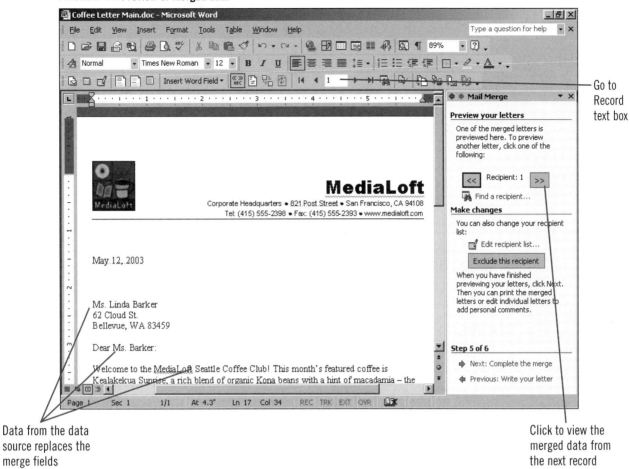

Go to Record text box

Data from the data source replaces the merge fields

Click to view the merged data from the next record

TABLE H-1: Buttons on the Mail Merge toolbar

button	use to
	Change the main document to a different type, or convert it to a normal Word document
	Select an existing data source
	Edit, sort, or filter the associated data source
	Insert an Address Block merge field
	Insert a Greeting Line merge field
	Insert a merge field from the data source
	Switch between viewing the main document with merge fields and with merged data
	Highlight the merge fields in the main document
	Match address fields with the field names used in the data source
	Search for a record in the merged documents
	Check for errors in the merged documents
	Merge the data to a new document and display it on screen
	Print the merged documents without first reviewing them on screen

Creating Labels

You can also use the Mail Merge Wizard to create mailing labels or print envelopes for a mailing. When you create labels or envelopes, you must select a standard label or envelope size to use as the main document, select a data source, and then insert the merge fields in the main document before performing the merge. In addition to mailing labels, you can use mail merge to create labels for diskettes, CDs, videos, and other items, and to create documents that are based on standard or custom label sizes, such as business cards, nametags, and postcards. ✏️ Alice uses the Mail Merge Wizard to create mailing labels for a brochure she needs to send to all members of the Coffee Club. She creates a new label main document and attaches an existing data source.

Steps

1. Click the **New Blank Document button** 🗋 on the Standard toolbar, click the **Zoom list arrow** on the Standard toolbar, click **Page Width**, click **Tools** on the menu bar, point to **Letters and Mailings**, then click **Mail Merge Wizard**
   The Mail Merge task pane opens.

> **Trouble?**
>
> If your dialog box does not show Avery standard, click the Label products list arrow, then click Avery standard.

2. Click the **Labels option button** in the Mail Merge task pane, click **Next: Starting document** to move to step 2 of 6, make sure the **Change document layout option button** is selected, then click **Label options**
   The Label Options dialog box opens, as shown in Figure H-12. You use this dialog box to select a label size for your labels and to specify the type of printer you plan to use. The default brand name Avery standard appears in the Label products list box. You can use the Label products list arrow to select other label products or a custom label. The many standard types of Avery labels for mailings, file folders, diskettes, post cards, and other types of labels are listed in the Product number list box. The type, height, width, and paper size for the selected product is displayed in the Label information section.

> **Trouble?**
>
> If your gridlines are not visible, click Table on the menu bar, then click Show Gridlines.

3. Scroll down the Product number list, click **5161 – Address**, then click **OK**
   A table with gridlines appears in the main document, as shown in Figure H-13. Each table cell is the size of a label for the label product you selected.

4. Save the label main document with the filename **Coffee Labels Main** to the drive and folder where your Project Files are located
   Next you need to select a data source for the labels.

5. Click **Next: Select recipients** to move to Step 3 of 6, click the **Use an existing list option button** if necessary, then click **Browse**
   The Select Data Source dialog box opens.

6. Use the Look in list arrow to navigate to the drive and folder where your Project Files are located, then open the file **WD H-2.mdb**
   The Mail Merge Recipients dialog box opens and displays all the records in the data source. In the next lesson you will sort and filter the records before performing the mail merge.

FIGURE H-12: Label Options dialog box

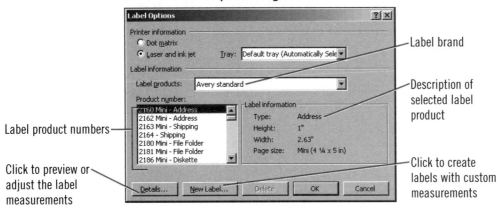

Label brand

Description of selected label product

Label product numbers

Click to preview or adjust the label measurements

Click to create labels with custom measurements

FIGURE H-13: Label main document

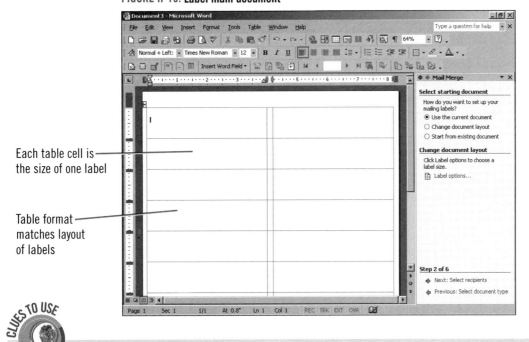

Each table cell is the size of one label

Table format matches layout of labels

Printing individual envelopes and labels

The Mail Merge Wizard allows you to easily print envelopes and labels for mass mailings, but you can also quickly format and print individual envelopes and labels using the Envelopes and Labels dialog box. To open the Envelopes and Labels dialog box, point to Letters and Mailings on the Tools menu, then click Envelopes and Labels. On the Envelopes tab, shown in Figure H-14, type the recipient's address in the Delivery address box and the return address in the Return address box. Click Options to open the Envelope Options dialog box, which you can use to select the envelope size, change the font and font size of the delivery and return addresses, and change the printing options. When you are ready to print the envelope, click Print in the Envelopes and Labels dialog box. The procedure for printing an individual label is similar to printing an individual envelope:

Enter the recipient's address on the Labels tab, click Options to select a label product number, click OK, then click Print.

FIGURE H-14: Envelopes tab in the Envelopes and Labels dialog box

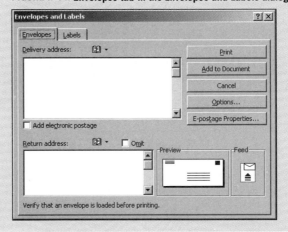

Sorting and Filtering Records

If you are using a large data source, you might want to sort and/or filter the records before performing a merge. **Sorting** the records determines the order in which the records are merged. For example, you might want to sort an address data source so that records are merged alphabetically by last name or in zip code order. **Filtering** the records pulls out the records that meet specific criteria and includes only those records in the merge. For instance, you might want to filter a data source to send a mailing only to people who live in the state of New York. You can use the Mail Merge Recipients dialog box both to sort and to filter a data source. ✏️ Alice applies a filter to the data source so that only United States addresses are included in the merge. She then sorts those records so that they merge in zip code order.

Steps

1. **In the Mail Merge Recipients dialog box, scroll right to display the Country field, click the Country column heading list arrow, then click US on the menu that opens**
   A filter is applied to the data source so that only the records with "US" in the Country field will be merged. You can filter a data source by as many criteria as you like. To remove a filter, click a column heading list arrow, then click "All."

2. **Scroll right, click the ZIP Code column heading, then scroll right again to see the ZIP Code column**
   The Mail Merge Recipients dialog box now displays only the records with a US address sorted in zip code order, as shown in Figure H-15.

3. **Click OK, then click Next: Arrange your labels in the Mail Merge task pane**
   The sort and filter criteria you set are saved for the current merge, and the options for Step 4 of 6 appear in the task pane.

4. **Click Postal Bar Code in the task pane, then click OK in the Insert Postal Bar Code dialog box**
   A merge field for a U.S. postal bar code is inserted in the first label in the main document. When the main document is merged with the data source, a customized postal bar code determined by the recipient's zip code and street address will appear on every label.

5. **Press [→], press [Enter], click Address Block in the task pane, then click OK in the Insert Address Block dialog box**
   The Address Block merge field is added to the first label.

6. **Point to the down arrow at the bottom of the task pane to scroll down, then click Update all labels in the task pane**
   The merge fields are copied from the first label to every label in the main document.

7. **Click Next: Preview your labels in the task pane**
   A preview of the merged label data appears in the main document. Only U.S. addresses are included, and the labels are organized in zip code order.

8. **Click Next: Complete the merge in the task pane, click Edit individual labels, then click OK in the Merge to New Document dialog box**
   The merged labels document is shown in Figure H-16.

9. **In the first label replace Ms. Clarissa Landfair with your name, save the document with the filename US Coffee Labels Zip Code Merge to the drive and folder where your Project Files are located, print the labels, save and close all open files, then exit Word**

FIGURE H-15: US records sorted in zip code order

Click the column heading to sort the records

All records with a US address are sorted by zip code in ascending order

Click the list arrow to filter the records

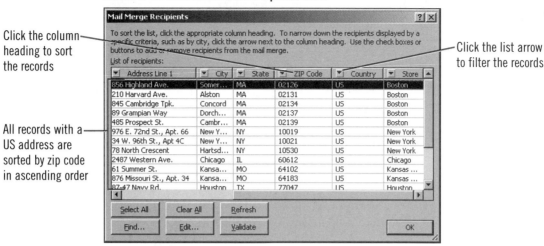

FIGURE H-16: Merged labels

Postal bar code

Labels are sorted by zip code

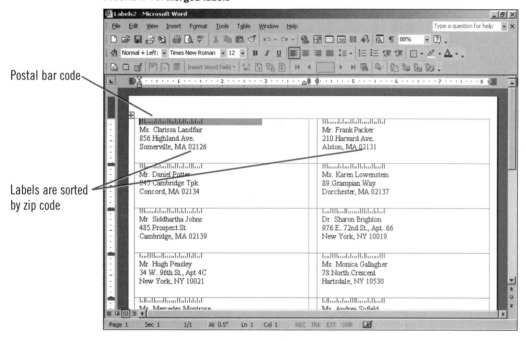

Inserting individual merge fields

You must include proper punctuation, spacing, and blank lines between the merge fields in a main document if you want punctuation, spaces, and blank lines to appear between the data in the merge documents. For example, to create an address line with a city, state, and zip code, you would insert the City merge field, type a comma and a space, insert the State merge field, type a space, and then insert the Zip Code merge field: <<City>>, <<State>> <<Zip Code>>.

You can insert an individual merge field by selecting the field name in the Insert Merge Fields dialog box, clicking Insert, and then clicking Close. You can also insert several merge fields at once by clicking a field name in the Insert Merge Field dialog box, clicking Insert, clicking another field name, clicking Insert, and so on. When you have finished inserting the merge fields, click Close. You can then add spaces, punctuation, and lines between the merge fields you inserted in the main document.

Practice

► Concepts Review

Label each toolbar button shown in Figure H-17.

FIGURE H-17

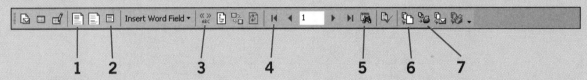

Match each term with the statement that best describes it.

8. Main document   a. The standard text that appears in every version of a merged document
9. Merge field   b. A complete set of information for one item or individual
10. Data field   c. To organize records in a sequence
11. Boilerplate text   d. A file that contains boilerplate text and merge fields
12. Data source   e. A file that contains customized information for each item or individual
13. Data record   f. To pull out records that meet certain criteria
14. Filter   g. A placeholder for merged data in the main document
15. Sort   h. A category of information in a data source

Select the best answer from the list of choices.

16. In a mail merge, which type of file contains the information that varies for each individual or item?
     a. Main document   c. Merge document
     b. Data source   d. Label document

17. Which of the following buttons can be used to insert a merge field for an inside address?
     a.   c.
     b.   d.

18. Which of the following buttons can be used to preview the merged data in the main document?
     a.   c.
     b.   d.

19. Which command is used to merge two documents to create a third document that shows the difference between the two?
     a. AutoSummarize   c. Track Changes
     b. Mail Merge Wizard   d. Compare and Merge Documents

20. Which of the following is included in a data source?
     a. Boilerplate text   c. Merge fields
     b. Records   d. Labels

▶ Skills Review

1. **Create a main document.**
   a. Start Word, then open the Mail Merge task pane.
   b. Use the Mail Merge Wizard to create a letter main document, click Next, then select the current (blank) document.
   c. At the top of the blank document, press [Enter] four times, type today's date, press [Enter] five times, then type **We are delighted to receive your generous contribution of AMOUNT to the New England Humanities Council (NEHC).**
   d. Press [Enter] twice, then type **Whether we are helping adult new readers learn to read or bringing humanities programs into our public schools, senior centers, and prisons, NEHC depends upon private contributions to ensure that free public humanities programs continue to flourish in CITY and throughout the REGION region. I hope we will see you at a humanities event soon.**
   e. Press [Enter] twice, type **Sincerely**, press [Enter] four times, type your name, press [Enter], then type **Executive Director.**
   f. Save the main document as **Donor Thank You Main** to the drive and folder where your Project Files are located.

2. **Design a data source.**
   a. Click Next; in the Step 3 of 6 Mail Merge task pane, select the Type a new list option button, then click Create.
   b. Click Customize in the New Address List dialog box, then remove the fields from the data source: Company Name, Address Line 2, Country, Home Phone, Work Phone, and E-mail Address.
   c. Add an **Amount** field and a **Region** field to the data source. Be sure these fields follow the Zip Code field.
   d. Rename the Address Line 1 field **Street**, then click OK to close the Customize Address List dialog box.

3. **Enter and edit records.**
   a. Add the following records to the data source:

Title	First Name	Last Name	Street	City	State	Zip Code	Amount	Region
Mr.	John	Conlin	34 Mill St.	Exeter	NH	03833	$250	Seacoast
Mr.	Bill	Webster	289 Sugar Hill Rd.	Franconia	NH	03632	$1000	Seacoast
Ms.	Susan	Janak	742 Main St.	Derby	VT	04634	$25	North Country
Mr.	Derek	Gray	987 Ocean Rd.	Portsmouth	NH	03828	$50	Seacoast
Ms.	Rita	Murphy	73 Bay Rd.	Durham	NH	03814	$500	Seacoast
Ms.	Amy	Hunt	67 Apple St.	Northfield	MA	01360	$75	Pioneer Valley
Ms.	Eliza	Perkins	287 Mountain Rd.	Dublin	NH	03436	$100	Pioneer Valley

   b. Save the data source as **Donor Data** to the drive and folder where your Project Files are located.
   c. Change the region for record 2 (Bill Webster) from Seacoast to **White Mountain.**
   d. Click OK to close the Mail Merge Recipients dialog box.

4. **Add merge fields.**
   a. Click Next, then in the blank line above the first body paragraph, insert an Address Block merge field.
   b. In the Insert Address Block dialog box, click Match Fields.
   c. Click the list arrow next to Address 1 in the Match Fields dialog box, click Street, click OK, then click OK in the Insert Address Block dialog box to accept the default address block format.
   d. Press [Enter] twice, insert a Greeting Line merge field using the default greeting line format, then press [Enter].
   e. In the first body paragraph, replace AMOUNT with the Amount merge field.
   f. In the second body paragraph, replace CITY with the City merge field and REGION with the Region merge field. (*Note*: Make sure to insert a space before or after each merge field as needed.)
   g. Save your changes to the main document.

5. Merge data.

a. Click Next to preview the merged data, then scroll through each letter.

b. Click the View Merged Data button on the Mail Merge toolbar, then make any necessary adjustments.

c. Place the insertion point before "I hope" in the second sentence of the second body paragraph, then press [Enter] twice to create a new paragraph.

d. Combine the first and second body paragraphs into a single paragraph, then save your changes.

e. Click Next, click Edit individual letters, then merge all the records to a new file.

f. Save the merged document as **Donor Thank You Merge** to the drive and folder where your Project Files are located, print a copy of the first letter, then save and close all open files.

6. Create labels.

a. Open a new blank document, then start the Mail Merge Wizard.

b. Create a label main document, click Next, then select Change the document layout if necessary in the Step 2 of 6 Mail Merge task pane.

c. Open the Label Options dialog box, select Avery 5162 – Address labels, then click OK, save the label main document as **Donor Labels Main** to the drive and folder where your Project Files are located, then click Next.

d. Use an existing list, click Browse, then open the Donor Data.mdb file you created.

7. Sort and filter records.

a. Filter the records so that only the records with NH in the State field are included in the merge.

b. Sort the records in zip code order, then click OK.

c. Click Next, insert a Postal Bar Code merge field using the default settings, press [→], then press [Enter].

d. Insert an Address Block merge field using the default settings, then click the View Merged Data button.

e. Click the View Merged Data button again, click the Address Block merge field in the upper-left table cell to select it if necessary, then click Address Block in the Mail Merge task pane.

f. Click Match Fields in the Insert Address Block dialog box, click the list arrow next to Address 1, click Street, click OK, then click OK again.

g. Click the View Merged Data button to preview the merged data, click Update All Labels in the Mail Merge task pane, then click Next to move to Step 5 of the Mail Merge Wizard.

h. Preview the merged data, then click Next to move to Step 6 of the Mail Merge Wizard.

i. Click Edit individual labels, merge all the records, then save the merged file as **NH Donor Labels Merge** to the drive and folder where your Project Files are located.

j. In the first label, change Ms. Eliza Perkins to your name, save the document, then print it.

k. Save and close all open Word files, then exit Word.

▶ Independent Challenge 1

You are the director of the Emerson Arts Center (EAC). The EAC is hosting an exhibit of ceramic art in the city of Cambridge, MA, and you want to send a letter advertising the exhibit to all EAC members with a Cambridge address. You'll use Mail Merge to create the letter. If you are able to print envelopes on your printer, you will also use Word to print an envelope for one letter that you need to separate from the mass mailing.

a. Start Word, then use the Mail Merge Wizard to create a letter main document using the file WD H-3, found on the drive and folder where your Project Files are located.

b. Replace Your Name with your name in the signature block, then save the main document as **Member Letter Main** to the drive and folder where your Project Files are located.

c. Use the file WD H-4, found on the drive and folder where your Project Files are located, as the data source. Alternatively, if you maintain a list of contacts in Outlook, use your Outlook contact list as the data source.

d. Sort the data source by last name, then filter the data so that only records with Cambridge as the city are included in the merge. (*Note:* If you are using an Outlook data source, select different filter criteria.)

e. Insert an address block and a greeting line merge field in the main document, preview the merged letters, then make any necessary adjustments. (*Note*: If you are using an Outlook data source, you might need to match the fields.)

f. Merge all the records to a new document, then save it as **Member Letter Merge** to the drive and folder where your Project Files are located. (*Note*: If you are using an Outlook data source, merge only the first four records.)

g. Print the first letter. If you can print envelopes on your printer, continue with the next step. If you cannot print envelopes, close all open Word files, saving changes, and then exit Word.

h. If you can print envelopes, select the inside address in the first merge letter, click Tools on the menu bar, point to Letters and Mailings, then click Envelopes and Labels.

i. On the Envelopes tab, type your name in the Return address text box, type **60 Crandall Street, Concord, MA 01742**, click Options, make sure the Envelope size is set to Size 10, then change the font of the Delivery address and the Return address to 12-point Times New Roman.

j. On the Printing Options tab, select the appropriate Feed method for your printer, then click OK.

k. Click Print, then click No to save the return address as the default.

l. Save the merge document, close it, save the main document, close it, then exit Word.

▶ Independent Challenge 2

One of your responsibilities at DSI Enterprises, a growing computer software company, is to create business cards for the staff. You use mail merge to create the cards so that you can easily produce standard business cards for future employees.

a. Start Word, then use the Mail Merge Wizard to create labels using the current blank document as the main document.

b. Select Avery standard 3612 – Business Card labels.

c. Create a new data source that includes the following fields: Title, First Name, Last Name, Phone, Fax, E-mail, and Hire Date. Add the following records to the data source:

Title	First Name	Last Name	Phone	Fax	E-mail	Hire Date
President	Sandra	Bryson	(312) 555-3982	(312) 555-6654	sbryson@dsi.com	1/12/01
Vice President	Philip	Holm	(312) 555-2323	(312) 555-4956	pholm@dsi.com	1/12/01

d. Add six more records to the data source, including one with your name as the Administrative Assistant.

e. Save the data source with the filename **Employee Data** to the drive and folder where your Project Files are located, then sort the data by Title.

f. In the first table cell, create the DSI Enterprises business card. Figure H-18 shows a sample DSI business card, but you should create your own design. Include the company name, a street address, and the Web site address www.dsi.com. Also include a First Name, Last Name, Title, Phone, Fax, and E-mail merge field. (*Hint*: If your design includes a graphic, insert the graphic before inserting the merge fields. Use the Insert Merge Field dialog box to insert each merge field, adjusting the spacing between merge fields as necessary.)

g. Format the business card with fonts, colors, and other format-ting features. (*Note*: Use the Other Task Panes list arrow to reopen the Mail Merge task pane if necessary.)

FIGURE H-18

h. Update all the labels, preview the data, make any necessary adjustments, then merge all the records to a new document.

i. Save the merge document with the filename **Business Cards Merge** to the drive and folder where your Project Files are located, print a copy, then close the file.

j. Save the main document with the filename **Business Cards Main** to the drive and folder where your Project Files are located, close the file, then exit Word.

Independent Challenge 3

You need to create a team roster for the children's softball team you coach. You use mail merge to create both the team roster and mailing labels.

a. Start Word, then use the Mail Merge Wizard to create a directory using the current blank document.

b. Create a new data source that includes the following fields: First Name, Last Name, Age, Position, Parent First Name, Parent Last Name, Address, City, State, Zip Code, and Home Phone.

c. Enter the following records in the data source:

First Name	Last Name	Age	Position	Parent First Name	Parent Last Name	Address	City	State	Zip Code	Home Phone
Sophie	Wright	8	Shortstop	Kerry	Wright	58 Main St.	Camillus	NY	13031	555-2345
Will	Jacob	7	Catcher	Bob	Jacob	32 North Way	Camillus	NY	13031	555-9827
Brett	Eliot	8	First base	Olivia	Eliot	289 Sylvan Way	Marcellus	NY	13032	555-9724
Abby	Herman	7	Pitcher	Sarah	Thomas	438 Lariat St.	Marcellus	NY	13032	555-8347

d. Add five additional records to the data source using the following last names and positions: O'Keefe, Second base; George, Third base; Goleman, Left field; Siebert, Center field; Choy, Right field. Make up the remaining information for the records.

e. Save the data source as **Softball Team Data** to the drive and folder where your Project Files are located.

f. Sort the records by last name, then click Next in the Mail Merge task pane.

g. Insert a table that includes five columns and one row in the main document.

h. In the first table cell, insert the First Name and Last Name merge fields, separated by a space.

i. In the second cell, insert the Position merge field.

j. In the third cell, insert the Address and City merge fields, separated by a comma and a space.

k. In the fourth cell, insert the Home Phone merge field.

l. In the fifth cell, insert the Parent First Name and Parent Last Name merge fields, separated by a space.

m. Preview the merged data and make any necessary adjustments. (*Hint*: Only the first record will display when you preview the data.)

n. Merge all the records to a new document, then save the document with the filename **Softball Roster Merge** to the drive and folder where your Project Files are located.

o. Press [Ctrl][Home], press [Enter], type **Tigers Team Roster** at the top of the document, press [Enter], type **Coach:**, followed by your name, then press [Enter] twice.

p. Insert a new row at the top of the table, then type the following column headings in the new row: **Name, Position, Address, Phone, Parent Name**.

q. Format the roster to make it attractive and readable, save your changes, print a copy, then close the file.

r. Close the main document without saving changes.

s. Open a new blank document, then use the Mail Merge Wizard to create mailing labels using Avery 5162 – Address labels.

t. Use the Softball Team data source you created, and sort the records in zip code order.

u. In the first table cell, create your own address block using the Parent First Name, Parent Last Name, Address, City, State, and Zip Code merge fields. Be sure to include proper spacing and punctuation.

v. Update all the labels, preview the merged data, merge all the records to a new document, then type your name centered in the document header.

w. Save the document with the filename **Softball Labels Merge** to the drive and folder where your Project Files are located, print a copy, close the file, close the main document without saving changes, then exit Word.

Independent Challenge 4

Your boss has given you the task of purchasing mailing labels for a mass mailing of your company's annual report. Your company plans to use Avery standard 5160 white labels for a laser printer, or their equivalent, for the mailing. The annual report will be sent to 55,000 people. In this independent challenge, you will search for Web sites that sell Avery labels, compare the costs, and then write a memo to your boss detailing your purchasing recommendations.

a. Use your favorite search engine to search for Web sites that sell Avery labels. Use the keywords **Avery labels** to conduct your search. If your search does not result in appropriate links, try looking at the following Web sites: www.staples.com, www.officeworld.com, www.worldlabel.com.

b. Find at least three Web sites that sell Avery 5160 white labels for a laser printer, or their equivalent. Note the URL of the Web sites and the price and quantity of the labels. You need to purchase enough labels for a mailing of 55,000, plus enough extras in case you make mistakes.

c. Start Word, then use the Professional Memo template to create a memo to your boss. Save the memo as **5160 Labels Memo** to the drive and folder where your Project Files are located.

d. In the memo, make up information to replace the placeholder text in the memo header, then type the body of your memo.

e. In the body, include a table that shows the URL of each Web site, the product name, the unit cost, the number of labels in each unit, the number of units you need to purchase, and the total cost of purchasing the labels. Also make a brief recommendation to your boss.

f. Format the memo so it is attractive and readable, save your changes, print a copy, close the file, then exit Word.

▶ Visual Workshop

Using the Mail Merge Wizard, create the post cards shown in Figure H-19. Use Avery standard 3611–Post Card labels for the main document and create a data source that contains at least four records. Save the data source as **Party Data**, save the main document as **Party Card Main**, and save the merge document as **Party Card Merge**, all to the drive and folder where your Project Files are located. (*Hint:* Use a table to lay out the postcard; the clip art graphic uses the keyword "party;" and the font is Comic Sans MS.) Print a copy of the postcards.

FIGURE H-19

You're invited to a
surprise party!

Il.l....l.l..ll...llll..ll.l.l
Grace Pappas
186 Buena Vista Terrace
Apt. 5C
San Francisco, CA 94117

For: Claudette Summer
When: August 3rd, 7:00 p.m.
Where: The Wharf Grill
Given by: Your Name

You're invited to a
surprise party!

Il.l....l.l..ll...llll.l.l..ll
Mika Takeda
456 Parker Ave.
San Francisco, CA 94118

For: Claudette Summer
When: August 3rd, 7:00 p.m.
Where: The Wharf Grill
Given by: Your Name

Working
with Styles and Templates

Objectives

- ► **Explore styles and templates**
- ► **Create paragraph styles**
- ► **Modify paragraph styles**
- ► **Create and modify character styles**
- ► **Create list and table styles**
- ► **Rename, delete, and copy styles**
- ► **Create a template**
- ► **Revise and attach a template**

Word's sophisticated styles and templates allow you to format your documents quickly, efficiently, and professionally. In this unit, you learn how to apply existing styles to selected text in a document and how to create new styles. You also learn how to apply a template to a document and how to create a new template that contains styles.　The Marketing Department has hired Nazila Sharif to produce author profiles for distribution at book-signing events. To save time, Nazila decides to develop a template on which to base each author profile. This template will include several styles for specific types of text. Nazila can periodically update these styles to reflect different topics, seasons, or author preferences. You will help Nazila use styles and templates to create and modify the author profiles.

Exploring Styles and Templates

Word 2002

You use styles and templates to automate document-formatting tasks and to ensure consistency between related documents. A **style** consists of various formats such as font style, font size, and alignment that are combined into one set that you can name. For example, a style called "Main Head" could apply the Arial font, 14-point font size, bold, and a border style to selected text. A **template** is a file that contains the basic structure of a document, such as the page layout, headers and footers, and graphic elements. Nazila wants to include styles in the template she plans to create for the author profiles. She familiarizes herself with how she can use styles to automate formatting tasks and how she can use templates to create unified sets of documents.

Details

▶ Using styles helps you save time because you can update styles quickly and easily. For example, suppose you have applied a style named "Section Head" to each section head in a document. When you change the formatting in the Section Head style, Word automatically updates all the text formatted with that style. Imagine how much time you would save if your document contains 50 or 100 section headings that are all formatted with the Section Head style!

▶ Word includes four style categories: paragraph, character, list, and table. A **paragraph** style includes both character and paragraph formats. You use a paragraph style when you want to format all the text in a paragraph at once. A **character** style includes character formats only. You use a character style to apply character format settings only to selected text within a paragraph. A **list** style allows you to format a series of lines with numbers or bullets and with selected font and paragraph formats. Finally, you create a **table** style to specify how you want both the table grid and the text in a table to appear. Figure I-1 shows a document formatted with the four kinds of styles.

▶ You work in the Styles and Formatting task pane to create, apply, and modify all four types of styles. In this task pane, you can select all text that has been formatted with a specific style, as shown in Figure I-2. Then you can modify the style, delete the style, or create a new style.

▶ Text you type into a blank document is formatted with the paragraph style called **Normal style** until you specify otherwise. By default, text formatted with the Normal style uses the Times New Roman 12 pt font and the text is left-aligned and single-spaced.

▶ Every document you create in Word is based on a template. Most of the time, this template is the **Normal template** because the Normal template is loaded automatically when you start a new document. The styles assigned to the Normal template are available to all documents.

▶ You can create your own template or you can use one of Word's preset templates. When you create a new document based on a template, the styles included with the template are automatically assigned to the new document. You can also attach a template to an existing document and then apply the styles in the attached template to selected text in the document.

Exploring AutoFormats and the Style Gallery

AutoFormat and the Style Gallery are two Word features that allow you to apply styles quickly. When you use the AutoFormat feature, Word analyzes each paragraph in your completed document and then applies an appropriate style, depending on where the paragraph appears in the document.

When you apply a template from the Style Gallery to an existing document, all styles included in that template are applied to text formatted with styles in the existing document. To access the Style Gallery, click Format on the menu bar, click Theme, then click Style Gallery in the Theme dialog box.

FIGURE I-1: Document formatted with styles

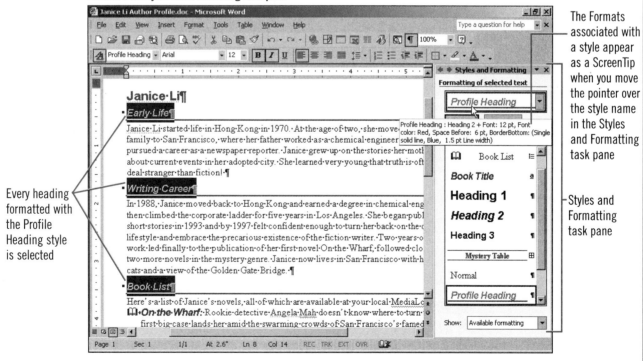

Janice Li

Early Life

Paragraph styles apply formatting to a paragraph, which might be one or more lines of text

Janice Li started life in Hong Kong in 1970. At the age of two, she moved with her family to San Francisco, where her father worked as a chemical engineer and her mother pursued a career as a newspaper reporter. Janice grew up on the stories her mother wrote about current events in her adopted city. She learned very young that truth is often a great deal stranger than fiction!

Writing Career

In 1988, Janice moved back to Hong Kong and earned a degree in chemical engineering, then climbed the corporate ladder for five years in Los Angeles. She began publishing her short stories in 1993 and by 1997 felt confident enough to turn her back on the corporate lifestyle and embrace the precarious existence of the fiction writer. Two years of hard work led finally to the publication of her first novel "On the Wharf," followed closely by two more novels in the mystery genre. Janice now lives in San Francisco with her three cats and a view of the Golden Gate Bridge.

Character style applies formatting to text within a paragraph

Book List

Here's a list of Janice's novels, all of which are available at your local MediaLoft store.

List style adds bullets or numbers to a series of paragraphs

- *On the Wharf*: Rookie detective Angela Mah doesn't know where to turn when her first big case lands her amid the swarming crowds of San Francisco's famed Fisherman's Wharf. She needs to find out who—or what—has been selectively tainting seafood.
- *Silicon Sleuth*: California's Silicon Valley is home to more than its fair share of young millionaires. When one of them crashes his new Ferrari into the back of detective Charles Wendl's Toyota, a simple fender bender turns deadly.
- *Dragon Swindle*: Dragons come in many shapes and sizes. The one that artist Marilyn Leung must find is only three inches long, but with the power to kill if she can't find and destroy it.

Signing Schedule

Table style applies formatting to a table grid and table text

Mystery Book Nights		
May 1, 2003	May 10, 2003	May 12, 2003
Seattle MediaLoft	Chicago MediaLoft	New York MediaLoft

Word 2002

FIGURE I-2: Styles and Formatting task pane

The Formats associated with a style appear as a ScreenTip when you move the pointer over the style name in the Styles and Formatting task pane

Every heading formatted with the Profile Heading style is selected

Styles and Formatting task pane

Creating Paragraph Styles

A **paragraph style** is a combination of character and paragraph formats that you name and store as a set. You can create a paragraph style and then apply it to any paragraph. Remember that any line of text followed by a hard return is considered a paragraph—even if the line consists of only one or two words. ◤━━━ Nazila has written a profile of mystery author Lance Rose. She decides to create her own paragraph styles for the headings and sub-headings included in the profile.

Steps

1. Start Word, open the file **WD I-1** from the drive and folder where your Project Files are located, save the file as **Lance Rose Author Profile**, then click the **Styles and Formatting button** 📄 on the Formatting toolbar
   The Styles and Formatting task pane opens. The Normal paragraph style is applied to the author's name at the top of the document and to the paragraphs of text, and the Heading 2 style is applied to section heads such as Early Life.

2. Click the **New Style button** in the Styles and Formatting task pane
   The New Style dialog box opens, as shown in Figure I-3. In this dialog box, you enter a name for the new style, select a style type, and then select the formatting options you want applied to text formatted with the new style.

3. Type **Profile Title** as the style name in the Name text box, press **[Tab]**, then make sure that "Paragraph" appears in the Style type list box
   The default style type is Paragraph. When you create a new paragraph style, you can base it on another style by selecting a style in the Style based on list box, or you can create a new style that is based on no preset style. When you base a style on an existing style, the settings for the existing style, as well as any changes you make to the settings, are included with the new style. By default, a new style is based on the Normal style.

4. Select **Arial**, **16**, **Bold**, and the **Blue** font color as shown in Figure I-4, then click **OK**
   The Profile Title style appears in the Pick formatting to apply list box.

5. Select **Lance Rose**, then click **Profile Title** in the Pick Formatting to apply list box
   The heading Lance Rose is formatted with the Profile Title style.

6. Click anywhere in the **Early Life** heading, click the **Heading 2 list arrow** in the Pick formatting to apply list box, then click **Select All 4 Instance(s)**
   The four headings formatted with the Heading 2 style are selected.

7. Click the **New Style button**, then type **Profile Heading** as the style name in the Name text box
   Notice that the Profile Heading style is based on the Heading 2 style because this style was applied to the text you selected before opening the New Style dialog box.

8. Change the font size to **12** and the font color to **Red**, then click **OK**

9. Click **Profile Heading** in the Pick formatting to apply list box to apply the Style to the selected headings, click **Lance Rose** at the beginning of the document to deselect the selected text, click the **Show list arrow** at the bottom of the Styles and Formatting task pane, click **Formatting in use**, then save the document
   The document appears as shown in Figure I-5. When you show only the formatting in use, you can quickly identify which styles are used to format your document.

FIGURE I-3: New Style dialog box

By default, a new style is based on the Normal style

By default, after you format a paragraph with the new style, that style is applied to the next paragraph when you press [Enter]

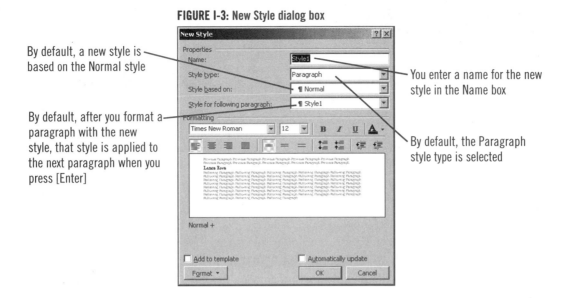

You enter a name for the new style in the Name box

By default, the Paragraph style type is selected

FIGURE I-4: Settings for Profile Title style

Arial font style selected

16-point font size selected

Appearance of text formatted with the Profile Title style

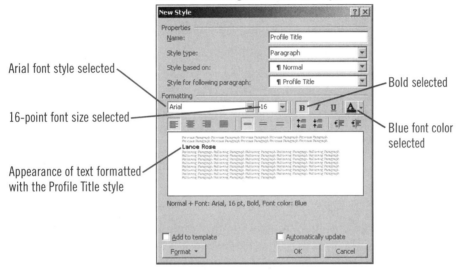

Bold selected

Blue font color selected

FIGURE I-5: Document formatted with new styles

The style applied to the currently selected text appears in the Style list box on the Formatting toolbar

Profile Title style applied

Profile Heading style applied

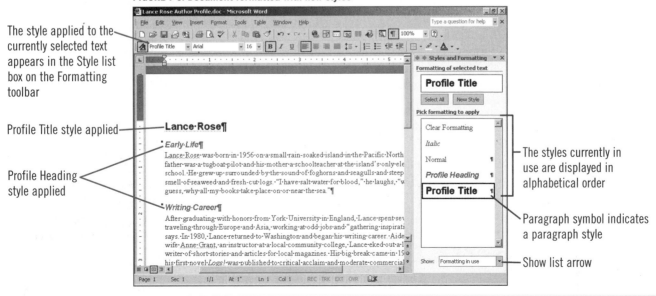

The styles currently in use are displayed in alphabetical order

Paragraph symbol indicates a paragraph style

Show list arrow

Modifying Paragraph Styles

A paragraph style is composed of character formats such as bold and italic and of paragraph formats such as line spacing before and after a paragraph. You can modify a paragraph style to change the set of formats included with the style. For example, you might decide to change the font style to Britannic Bold and add a border line under the paragraph. You can also change paragraph formats such as line spacing and alignment. Finally, you can include numbers or bullets with text formatted with a paragraph style. Nazila decides to modify the Profile Heading style by reducing the Before paragraph spacing to 6 pt and adding a bottom blue border line.

Steps 1234

1. Click the **Profile Heading list arrow** in the Pick formatting to apply list box, click **Modify**, click **Format** at the bottom of the Modify Style dialog box, then click **Paragraph**

   The Paragraph dialog box opens with the Indents and Spacing tab selected.

2. Click the **down arrow** next to the Before text box in the Spacing section **one time** to reduce the Spacing Before a paragraph to **6 pt** as shown in Figure I-6, then click **OK**

3. Click **Format** in the Modify Style dialog box, then click **Border**

   The Borders and Shading dialog box opens. You want to add a single line under each heading formatted with the Profile Heading style.

4. Click the **Color list arrow**, click the **Blue color box**, click the **Width list arrow**, then click the **1½ pt** width

5. Click the bottom of the grid in the Preview Section as shown in Figure I-7 to select the bottom of the paragraph

   Figure I-7 shows the format settings for the bottom border line.

6. Click **OK** to exit the Borders and Shading dialog box, then click **OK**

   All four of the headings formatted with the Profile Heading style are automatically updated. You can view all the format settings included with the Profile Heading style—or any currently selected text—by viewing the Reveal Formatting task pane.

7. Click the word **Early**, click the **Other Task Panes list arrow** at the top of the Styles and Formatting task pane, then click **Reveal Formatting**

   All the formatting associated with the currently selected text appears in the Reveal Formatting task pane, as shown in Figure I-8. Information about text, paragraph, and section formatting is organized into categories in the Reveal Formatting task pane. Use the scroll bar as needed to view all of the formatting assigned to the selected text.

8. Save the document

Clearing formats

To quickly remove all the formatting from selected text, click Clear Formatting in the Pick formatting to apply list box in the Styles and Formatting task pane. All the styles and any other formats that have been applied to the selected text are instantly removed. This feature is most useful when you need to reformat text that has been formatted several times with various styles and options. To avoid unexpected results when working with styles, you may want to get into the habit of clearing the existing styles and then starting with a new style that you have created yourself and which includes only the formats you want.

FIGURE I-6: Before paragraph spacing reduced

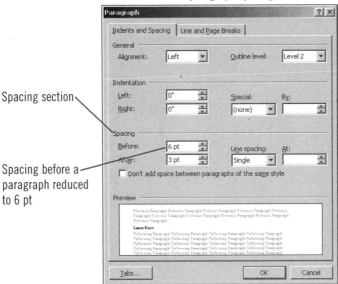

Spacing section

Spacing before a paragraph reduced to 6 pt

FIGURE I-7: Border options selected

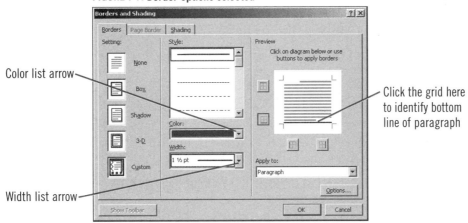

Color list arrow

Click the grid here to identify bottom line of paragraph

Width list arrow

FIGURE I-8: Reveal Formatting task pane with modified Profile Heading style

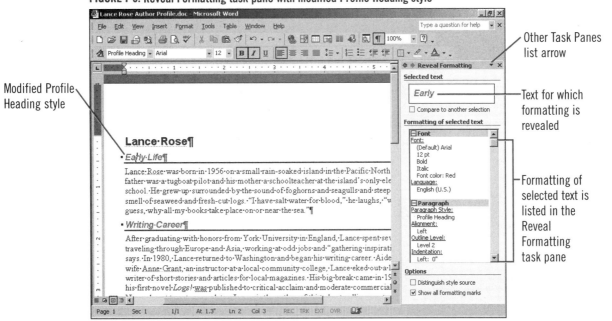

Modified Profile Heading style

Other Task Panes list arrow

Text for which formatting is revealed

Formatting of selected text is listed in the Reveal Formatting task pane

Creating and Modifying Character Styles

A **character style** includes character format settings that you name and store as a set. You apply a character style to selected text within a paragraph. Any text in the paragraph that is not formatted with the character style is formatted with the currently applied paragraph style. You use a character style to apply character formats such as the font and size of text, and bold and italic formats. Nazila wants to create a character style called Book Title to apply to each book title in the Book List section of Lance's profile.

Steps

1. Scroll down the page to the Book List section, then select the book title **Sea Swept:**, including the colon

2. Click the **Other Task Panes list arrow** in the Reveal Formatting task pane, click **Styles and Formatting**, then click the **New Style button** in the Styles and Formatting task pane

3. Type **Book Title** in the Name text box

4. Click the **Style type list arrow**, then select **Character**

5. Select the character formatting settings as shown in Figure I-9: **Arial**, **14**, **Bold**, **Italic**, and the **Blue** font color, then click **OK**
   The Book Title style does not appear in the Pick formatting to apply list box because the Styles and Formatting task pane is set to show the Formatting in use option, and you have not yet applied the Book Title style to text in the document.

6. Click the **Show list arrow**, click **Available styles**, then click **Book Title** in the Pick formatting to apply list box
   Notice that Sea Swept is formatted using the Book Title style.

7. Apply the Book Title style to **Mystery Tug:** and **Shell Game:**
   Notice that the font size assigned to the Book Title style is larger than the font size assigned to the Section Head style. You modify the font size assigned to the Book Title style to follow acceptable design practices.

8. With **Shell Game** still selected, click the **Book Title list arrow** in the Pick formatting to apply list box, click **Modify**, change the font size to **12 pt** and the font color to **Dark Blue**, then click **OK**

9. Click away from **Shell Game** to deselect it, compare the three book titles to Figure I-10, then save the document

FIGURE I-9: Book Title Character style options selected

Character formatting set to Arial font, 14-point font size, Bold, Italic, and Blue font color

Character style type selected

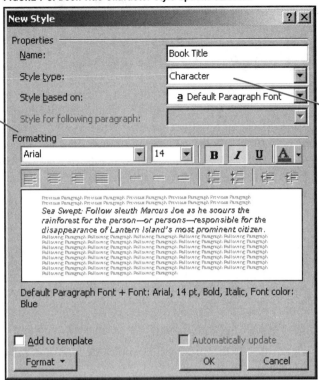

FIGURE I-10: Modified Book Title style applied

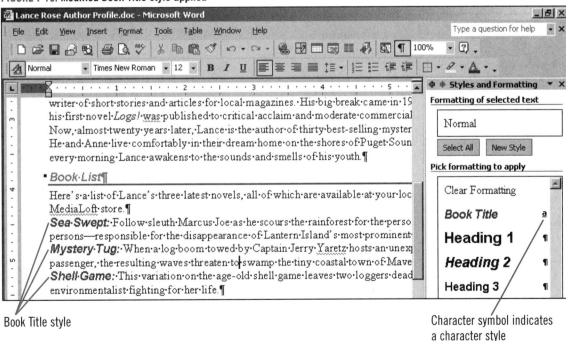

Book Title style

Character symbol indicates a character style

Creating List and Table Styles

A **list style** includes paragraph and character format settings that you use to format a series of paragraphs when you want the paragraphs to appear related in some way. For example, you can create a list style that adds bullet characters to a series of paragraphs or sequential numbers to a list of items. A **table style** includes formatting settings for both the table grid and the table text. Nazila wants to create a list style called Book List to format the list of books with a special bullet character, and then she wants to create a table style called Mystery Table to format the table at the bottom of the document.

Steps

1. Click the **New Style button** in the Styles and Formatting task pane, type **Book List** in the Name text box, click the **Style type list arrow**, then select **List**
   The New Style dialog box changes to show the formatting options for a list style, as shown in Figure I-11. You want to select a symbol as the bullet character for your bulleted list.

2. Click the **Insert Symbol button** to open the Symbol dialog box, click the **Font list arrow**, scroll down and select **Wingdings**, then click the **Book symbol** as shown in Figure I-12

3. Click **OK** to exit the Symbol dialog box, then click **OK** to exit the New Style dialog box

4. Click in the paragraph that describes **Sea Swept**, click **Book List** in the Pick formatting to apply list box, then apply the Book List style to the paragraph that describes **Mystery Tug** and the paragraph that describes **Shell Game**
   The three paragraphs in the Book List section are formatted with the new Book List style.

Trouble?

If your table does not show gridlines, click Table on the menu bar, then click Show Gridlines.

5. Press **[Ctrl][End]** to move to the bottom of the document, click anywhere in the **table**, click the **New Style button**, type **Mystery Table** in the Name text box, click the **Style type list arrow**, then select **Table**
   The New Style dialog box changes to show formatting options for a table. You can base the style on one of Word's preset table styles or you can modify the default table style.

6. Click the **Style based on list arrow**, scroll to select **Table Grid**, click the **Bold button**, click the **Font Color button list arrow**, select the **Blue** color box, click the **Fill Color button list arrow**, select the **Light Turquoise** color box, click the **Alignment button list arrow**, then click the **Align Center button**
   The format settings required for the table are identified.

7. Click **OK** to exit the New Style dialog box, then click **Mystery Table** in the Pick formatting to apply list box
   The Mystery Table style is applied to the table.

8. Scroll up until the book list and the table appear on the screen, if necessary, compare the book list and the table with Figure I-13, then save the document

FIGURE I-11: Formatting options for a list in the New Style dialog box

Insert Symbol button

Preview of current settings for a list style

List of current settings for a list style

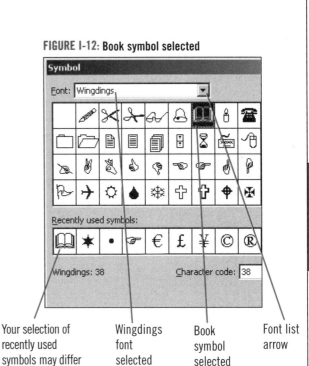

FIGURE I-12: Book symbol selected

Your selection of recently used symbols may differ

Wingdings font selected

Book symbol selected

Font list arrow

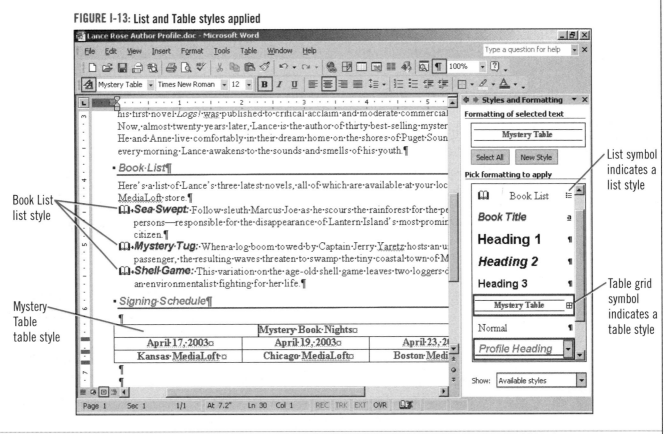

FIGURE I-13: List and Table styles applied

Book List list style

Mystery Table table style

List symbol indicates a list style

Table grid symbol indicates a table style

Renaming, Deleting, and Copying Styles

In the Styles and Formatting task pane, you can change the name of a style and even delete it altogether. Sometimes you might want the styles you've created for one document to be available in another document. In the Organizer dialog box, you can copy all the styles you've saved with one document to another document, where you can then apply those styles to selected text. Nazila decides to change the name of the Profile Title style to Author Title. She also decides to remove the Book List style. Finally, she will copy the styles to a document containing an author profile that she's written for Janice Li, a mystery author from San Francisco.

Steps

Trouble?

Use the Pick formatting to apply a scroll bar if necessary to view a style.

1. Press **[Ctrl][Home]**, click the **Profile Title list arrow** in the Pick formatting to apply list box, click **Modify**, type **Author Title**, change the font color to **Green**, then click **OK**
   The text "Lance Rose" is formatted with the Author Title style.

2. Right-click **Book List** in the Pick formatting to apply list box, click **Delete**, click **Yes** to accept the warning, then scroll down to view the list of book titles
   The book descriptions are formatted with the Normal style.

Trouble?

If text is left-aligned and there is no hanging indent, then proceed to step 4.

3. Click the **Show list arrow**, click **Formatting in use**, click the **Sea Swept paragraph**, right-click **Left: 0", Hanging: 0.25** in the Pick formatting to apply list box, click **Delete**, then click **Yes**

4. Save the document, open the file **WD I-2** from the drive and folder where your Project Files are located, then save it as **Janice Li Author Profile**
   Some of the headings in Janice's author profile are formatted with a default heading style and the book titles are formatted with a character style called Books.

5. Click **File** on the menu bar, click **Close** to close the Janice Li Author Profile document and return to the Lance Rose Author Profile, click **Tools** on the menu bar, click **Templates and Add-Ins**, then click the **Organizer button** in the Templates and Add-ins dialog box
   In the Organizer dialog box, you need to open the file called Janice Li Author Profile and make it the Target file.

QuickTip

By default only templates are listed.

6. Click **Close File** under the list box on the right side in the Organizer dialog box, then click **Open File**, click the **Files of type list arrow**, select **Word Documents**, navigate to the drive and folder where your Project Files are located, click **Janice Li Author Profile**, then click **Open**
   To see a Word file, select Word documents as the file type, and then navigate to the location of the file. The styles assigned to the Janice Li Author Profile appear in the list box on the right side.

7. Confirm that **Author Title** is selected at the top of the list of styles in the Lance Rose Author Profile document (left side of the Organizer dialog box), press and hold the **[Shift]** key, scroll down the list, click the last style listed **Table Normal** to select all the styles as shown in Figure I-14, click **Copy**, click **Yes to All**, click **Close File** on the right side, click **Yes** to save the document, then click **Close** to exit the Organizer dialog box

8. Open the file **Janice Li Author Profile**, click the **Styles and Formatting button** 🅰 on the Formatting toolbar, apply styles as shown in Figure I-15, press **[Ctrl][End]**, type **Compiled by [Your Name]**, save the document, print a copy, then close the document
   The file Lance Rose Author Profile is the active document.

FIGURE I-14: Styles selected in the Organizer dialog box

Style names
selected

Copy button

Source file

Target file

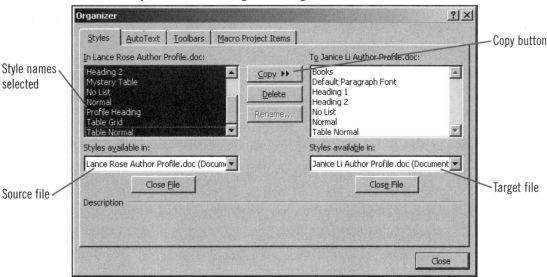

FIGURE I-15: Document modified with styles

Author
Title style

Profile
Heading
style

Book Title
style

Mystery
Table style

Document
appears in
Print Preview
so that as
much of the
document as
possible is
visible. Your
document
still appears
in the Print
Layout View.

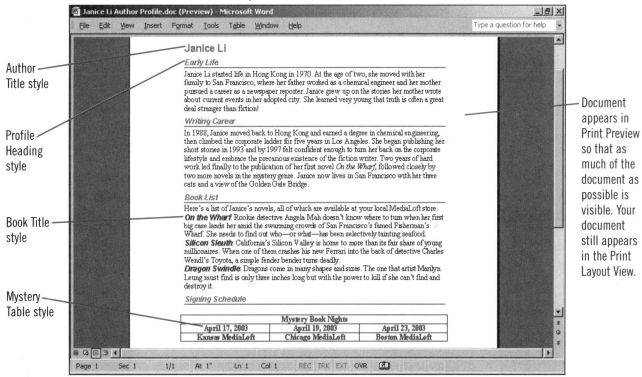

Word 2002

Working in the Organizer dialog box

You copy styles from the document shown in the left side of the Organizer dialog box to a new document that you open in the right side of the Organizer dialog box. The document in the left side is the **Source** file because it contains the styles you want to copy. The document in the right side is the **Target** file because it receives the styles you copy. By default, the Target file is the Normal template.

Creating a Template

A template is a document that contains the basic structure of a document, including all of the styles required for the text. You can create a template from an existing document, or you can create the template from scratch. Templates that you create yourself are called **user templates**. To base a document on a template, you select General Templates from the New Document task pane. A new document opens that contains all the formats stored in the template. You can enter text into the document and then save it, just as you would any document. The original template is not modified. ➤ Nazila decides to modify some of the document settings, replace text related to Lance Rose with instructions, then save the document as a template called Author Profile. She then opens a new document based on the Author Profile template and starts modifying it for a new author.

Steps

1. Click **File** on the menu bar, click **Page Setup**, click the **Margins tab** if necessary, change the **Left** and **Right** margins to 1", click the **Layout tab**, click the **Borders button**, click **Box**, verify that the border color is **Blue** and the border width is 1½ **pt**, then click **OK**

   The border setting you selected in an earlier lesson is still in effect.

   Trouble?

   If text you enter appears in a style other than Normal, select the text, then click Clear Formatting in the Pick formatting to apply list box.

2. Press **[Ctrl][Home]**, select **Lance Rose**, type **[Enter Author Title Here]**, then enter directions so the document appears as shown in Figure I-16

   The Word document is ready to save as the Author Profile template. You can save the template in the default location on your computer's hard drive or you can select a new location.

3. Minimize Word, right-click **My Computer** on your computer desktop, click **Explore**, navigate to the drive and folder where your Project Files are located, click **File** on the menu bar, point to **New**, click **Folder**, type **[Your Name] Templates** as the folder name, then press **[Enter]**

   You want this new folder to be the default location for user templates.

4. Close Explorer, return to Word, click **Tools** on the menu bar, click **Options**, click **File Locations**, click **User templates**, click **Modify**, click the **Look in list arrow**, select the location where you created the [Your Name] Templates folder, click the folder to select it, click **OK**, then click **OK**

   Now you can save the document on your screen as a template into the new folder.

   Trouble?

   Be sure Lance Rose Author Profile is the active document.

5. Click **File** on the menu bar, click **Save As**, click the **Save as type list arrow**, then click **Document Template**

   When you select Document Template as the file type, Word switches to the default location for user templates—which you set as the folder called [Your Name] Templates.

6. Type **Author Profile** as the filename, then click **Save**

   The file is saved as Author Profile.dot to your default template location. The .dot filename extension identifies this file as a template file. You can create new documents based on this template.

7. Click **File** on the menu bar, click **Close**, click **File** on the menu bar, then click **New**

8. Click **General Templates** in the New from template section, click **Author Profile.dot**, be sure Document in the Create New section is selected, then click **OK**

   The template opens as a new document. Note that Document2 appears in the title bar. You can enter text into this document just as you would any document.

9. Delete the **placeholder text**, then enter new text as shown in Figure I-17

10. Click **File**, click **Save as**, navigate to the drive and folder where your Project Files are located, type **Mary-Jo Watson Author Profile**, then click **Save**

    The file Mary-Jo Watson Author Profile is the active document.

FIGURE I-16: Template text entered

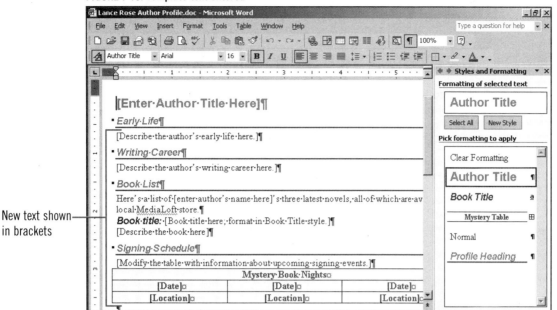

New text shown in brackets

FIGURE I-17: Information about a new author

Mary-Jo Watson

Early Life

Mary-Jo Watson was born in 1962 in Montreal, Quebec, and then moved to Toronto in 1970 with her family. Her father, a professor of English Literature, encouraged Mary-Jo's talent from a very young age.

Writing Career

In 1980, Mary-Jo attended the University of Toronto, where she earned a degree in Philosophy. She published her first novel in 1990 and has been writing steadily ever since. She is currently working on "Algonquin Mystery," which is due out in Spring of 2004.

Book List

Here's a description of Mary-Jo's latest novel. You can buy it at your local MediaLoft store.
Grains of Sand: The Pacific winds took millennia to reduce the rocks off British Columbia's west coast to impossibly fine grains of sand. Detective Marge Barrow has just a few days to shift through those sands to find the only clue that will lead her to a murderer.

Signing Schedule

Mystery Book Nights		
May 1, 2003	May 10, 2003	May 12, 2003
Seattle MediaLoft	Chicago MediaLoft	New York MediaLoft

CLUES TO USE

Setting the default file location for user and workgroup templates

By default, user templates are stored in the Templates folder. The path for this folder is: C:/Documents and settings/Administrator/ApplicationData/Microsoft/Templates. Note that a different folder might appear for "Administrator," depending on how your computer system is set up. If you change the location of a user template, you can select the default location again by selecting the Templates folder path in the File Locations tab of the Options dialog box. You can also create templates to distribute to others. These templates are called **workgroup templates.** You select the location of a workgroup template in the File Locations tab of the Options dialog box, just as you select the location of a user template. To open the Options dialog box, click Tools on the Standard toolbar, then select Options.

Revising and Attaching a Template

You can modify a template just as you would any Word document. All new documents you create from the modified template will use the new settings. All documents that you created before you modified the template are not changed unless you open the Templates and Add-ins dialog box and direct Word to update styles automatically. Note that when you attach a template to an existing document, structural settings such as margins and page layouts originally included with the template are not attached to the new document. These structural settings affect only new documents that you create from a template. Nazila decides to change the font style, size, and color of the Author Title style, update Mary-Jo Watson's author profile with the revised template, and then add the template to the author profile she's written for veteran mystery author Ron Leitz.

Steps

1. Click the **Open button** on the Standard toolbar, navigate to the location of the [Your Name] Templates folder, double-click the **folder name** to open it, click **Author Profile.dot** if necessary, then click **Open**

2. Click the **Styles and Formatting button** on the Formatting toolbar, right-click **Author Title** in the Pick formatting to apply list box, click **Modify**, change the font to **Georgia** (or a similar font), change the font size to **14 pt**, change the font color to **Dark Blue**, then click **OK**

3. Click the **Save button** on the Standard toolbar, then close the template
   The modified template is saved and the Mary-Jo Watson Author Profile document is the active document.

4. Click **Tools** on the menu bar, click **Templates and Add-Ins**, verify that the **Automatically update document styles option button** is selected, then click **OK**
   The Author Title style in the Mary-Jo Watson Author Profile is updated, as shown in Figure I-18.

Trouble?
All of the page border might not print on some printers. Remove the page border if your printer cannot accommodate it.

5. Press **[Ctrl][End]**, type **Compiled by** and enter your name, save the document, print a copy, then close the file
   The document prints and the file closes. You can also attach the template to a new document.

6. Open the file **WD I-3** from the drive and folder where your Project Files are located, then save it as **Ron Leitz Author Profile**

7. Click **Tools** on the menu bar, click **Templates and Add-Ins**, click **Attach**, select the **Author Profile.dot** template, click **Open**, click the **Automatically update document styles check box**, then click **OK**

8. Open the Styles and Formatting task pane if necessary, then apply styles as shown in Figure I-19
   The text is formatted with the styles, but the page border does not appear and the left and right margins are still set at 1.25". When you add the template to an existing document or update an existing document with a modified template, structural changes do not appear.

9. Press **[Ctrl][End]**, type **Compiled by [your name]**, save the document, print a copy, close the file, then exit Word

FIGURE I-18: Updated document

Author Title
style updated

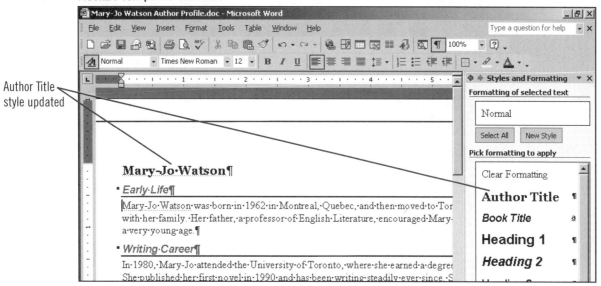

FIGURE I-19: Ron Leitz author profile formatted

Author Title style ——— **Ron Leitz**

Profile Heading style ———

Book Title style ———

Mystery Table style ———

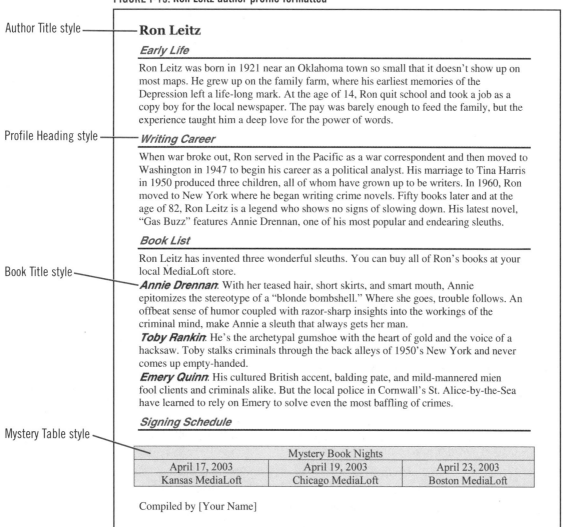

Practice

► Concepts Review

Identify each type of style shown in Figure I-20.

FIGURE I-20

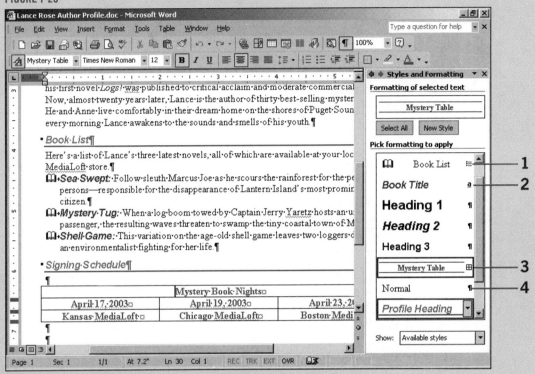

Match each term with the statement that best describes it.

5. **AutoFormat**
6. **Paragraph style**
7. **Template**
8. **Normal template**
9. **Character style**
10. **Style**

a. A combination of character and paragraph formats that are named and stored as a set
b. Character formats that you name and store as a set
c. Various formats that are combined into one set, which is named
d. A file that contains the basic structure of a document in addition to selected styles
e. A file that contains the settings available to all documents
f. Used to apply formatting quickly to a completed document

Select the best answer from the list of choices.

11. **What is the name of the template that is loaded automatically when you start a new document?**
    a. Global template
    b. User template
    c. Normal template
    d. Paragraph template

12. **What is the purpose of AutoFormat?**
    a. To remove extra spacing from a document
    b. To apply styles to text in a document
    c. To change the document type
    d. To apply a preset theme to a document

13. **Which of the following definitions best describes a paragraph style?**
    a. Format settings applied only to selected text within a paragraph
    b. Format settings applied to a table grid
    c. Format settings applied to the structure of a document
    d. Format settings applied to all the text in a paragraph

14. **How do you modify a style?**
    a. Double-click the style in the Styles and Formatting task pane.
    b. Right-click the style in the Styles and Formatting task pane, then click Modify.
    c. Right-click the style in the Styles and Formatting task pane, then click Revise.
    d. Click the style in the Styles and Formatting task pane, then click New Style.

15. **In which dialog box do you copy styles from one document to another?**
    a. Organizer dialog box
    b. New Document dialog box
    c. Styles dialog box
    d. Modify Styles dialog box

16. **Which selection from the Tools menu do you click to attach a template to a document?**
    a. Templates
    b. New templates
    c. General template
    d. Templates and Add-ins

► Skills Review

1. **Create paragraph styles.**
   a. Start Word, open the file WD I-4 from the drive and location where your Project Files are stored, save it as **Shaped Jigsaw Puzzles**, then open the Styles and Formatting task pane.
   b. Create a new paragraph style called **Puzzle Title** with **Arial Black** font, **18 pt**, and the **Brown** font color.
   c. Apply the Puzzle Title style to Shaped Jigsaw Puzzles.
   d. Click the Animal Puzzles heading, then select all the headings formatted with the Heading 3 style.
   e. Create a new style called **Puzzle Heading** that changes the font size to **14 pt**, adds **Italic**, and changes the font color to **Light Orange**.
   f. Apply the Puzzle Heading style to the three selected headings, then deselect the text to view the change.
   g. Show only the formatting currently in use in the document, then save the document.

2. **Modify paragraph styles.**
   a. Click the Puzzle Heading list arrow in the Pick formatting to apply list box, then click Modify.
   b. Click the Format button, open the Paragraph dialog box, then change the After spacing to **6 pt**.
   c. Click the Format button, open the Font dialog box, then select the **Small caps** font effect.
   d. Exit the Modify Style dialog box and check to ensure that the modified Puzzle Heading style is applied.
   e. Click any text formatted with the Puzzle Heading style, open the Reveal Formatting task pane and view the formatting currently applied to the text, then save the document.

3. **Create and modify character styles.**
   a. Show the Styles and Formatting task pane, then create a character style named **Puzzle Theme**.
   b. Select the **Arial Black** font, **Italic**, and the **Brown** font color, then exit the New Style dialog box.
   c. Show the Available styles, apply the Puzzle Theme style to the text **Elephant puzzle** and **Dolphin puzzle** in the Animal Puzzles section, and to the text **Italy puzzle** and **Great Britain puzzle** in the Map Puzzles section.
   d. Modify the Puzzle Theme style by changing the font size to **10 pt** and the color to **Orange**, then save the document.

4. **Create list and table styles.**
   a. Create a List style called **Puzzle List**.
   b. Select the right-pointing **hand symbol** from the Wingdings character set.
   c. Accept the symbol, select the **14 pt** font size for the bullet character, then apply the style to each paragraph that describes a puzzle (for example, Elephant puzzle, Dolphin puzzle).
   d. Click the table at the bottom of the document, then create a Table style called **Puzzle Table** based on the Table Grid style.
   e. Select **Brown** for the font color, select **Light Yellow** for the fill color, change the font size to **14 pt**, select **Align Top Center** alignment, then accept the style specifications to close the New Style dialog box.
   f. Apply the Puzzle Table style to the table, then save the document.

5. Rename, delete, and copy styles.

    a. Change the name of the Puzzle Title style to **Puzzle Category**, then change the font color to **Dark Red**. Check that the formatted text Shaped Jigsaw Puzzles at the beginning of the document is changed.

    b. Delete the Puzzle List style. If necessary, remove the indent formatting from the paragraphs that were formatted with the Puzzle List style. (*Note:* Remember to show Formatting in Use.)

    c. Save the document, then open the file WD I-5 from the drive and location where your Project Files are located and save it as **3-D Jigsaw Puzzles**.

    d. Close the 3-D Jigsaw Puzzle file, make sure Shaped Jigsaw Puzzles is the active document, click Tools on the menu bar, click Templates and Add-Ins, then click the Organizer button.

    e. Close the file in the right of the Organizer dialog box, then open the 3-D Jigsaw Puzzles document. Remember to change the Files of type to Word documents.

    f. Select all the styles in the Shaped Jigsaw Puzzles document, then copy them to the 3-D Jigsaw Puzzles document. Click Yes to all to overwrite existing style entries with the same name.

    g. Close the 3-D Jigsaw Puzzles document in the Organizer dialog box, click Yes to save when prompted, then close the Organizer dialog box.

    h. Open the file 3-D Jigsaw Puzzles, then open the Styles and Formatting task pane. Apply the Puzzle Category style to the document title, apply the Puzzle Heading style to all text formatted with the Heading 3 style, apply the Puzzle Theme style to the name of each individual puzzle (for example, Oak Tree puzzle), then apply the Puzzle Table style to the table.

    i. Type your name at the bottom of the document, save the document, print a copy, then close the document.

6. Create a template.

    a. Make sure that Shaped Jigsaw Puzzles is the active document, then change the Left and Right margins to **1.5"** and add a 3 pt **Brown** page border.

    b. Select Shaped Jigsaw Puzzles at the top of the page, type **[Enter Puzzle Category Here]**, then delete text and enter directions so the document appears as shown in Figure I-21.

    c. In Explorer, create a new folder called **[Your Name] Skills Review** in the drive and folder where your Project Files are located.

    d. Change the file location for user templates to the new folder you named [Your Name] Skills Review.

    e. Save the file as a template called **Puzzle Description** to the [Your Name] Skills Review folder, then close the template.

    f. Create a new file based on the Puzzle Description template.

    g. Replace the title of the document with the text **Brain Teaser Puzzles**, then save the document as **Brain Teaser Puzzles** to the drive and folder where your Project Files are located.

FIGURE I-21

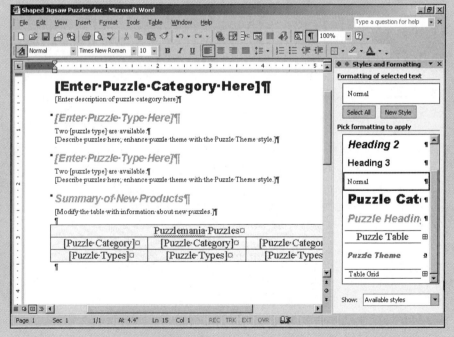

7. Revise and attach a template.

    a. Open the Puzzle Description template, change the font color in the Puzzle Category style to **Orange**, then save and close the template.

  b. With the Brain Teaser Puzzles document active, click Tools on the menu bar, click Templates and Add-ins, click the Automatically update document styles check box, then click OK.

  c. Verify that the font color of text formatted with the Puzzle Category style has changed to Orange.

  d. Save the document, then close it.

  e. Open the file WD I-6 from the drive and location where your Project Files are located, then save it as **Landscape Puzzles**.

  f. Attach the Puzzle Description template to the document. Remember to click the Automatically update document styles check box in the Templates and Add-ins dialog box to select it.

  g. Apply styles from the Puzzle Description template so that the Landscape Puzzles document resembles the other documents you have formatted for this Skills Review.

  h. Type your name at the end of the document, save the document, print a copy, close the document, then exit Word.

► Independent Challenge 1

You are the Office Manager of Digital Learning, a company that creates learning materials for delivery over the Internet. The annual company softball game is coming soon and you need to inform the employees about the date and time of the game. To save time, you've decided to type the text of the memo without formatting and then to use the AutoFormat and Style Gallery functions to format the memo attractively.

  a. Start Word, open the file WD I-7 from the drive and folder where your Project Files are located, then save it as **Softball Memo**.

  b. Use the AutoFormat feature to apply styles to the document. (*Hint:* To apply an AutoFormat, click Format on the menu bar, click AutoFormat, click the AutoFormat now option button, then click OK).

  c. Open the Style Gallery and apply the Elegant Memo template. (*Hint:* To open the Style Gallery, click Format on the menu bar, click Theme, then click the Style Gallery button. Select the Elegant Memo template from the list of templates, then click Document in the Preview section to see how the template appears when applied to the current document.)

  d. Open the Styles and Formatting task pane, then make the following changes to selected styles. (*Hint:* To identify the style assigned to specific text, click the text and then notice which style name is framed in the Pick formatting to apply list box.)

Style Name	Changes
Document Label	Verdana font, 18 pt font size
Message Header	Times New Roman font, 12 pt font size, Before paragraph spacing to 6 pt
Heading 1	Verdana font, 14 pt font size, Bold, Left alignment
Body text	Times New Roman font, 12 pt font size, Left alignment, First line indent of 0" (Check the Indents and Spacing tab in the Paragraph dialog box)

  e. Select [Your Name] in the message header, type your name, save the document, print it, close it, then exit Word.

► Independent Challenge 2

You have enrolled in a new e-commerce program at your local community college. You have volunteered to create a design for the class newsletter and another classmate has volunteered to write text for the first newsletter. First, you will create a template for the newsletter, then you will apply the template to the document containing the newsletter text.

  a. Start Word, create a document as shown in Figure I-22. Enter the content first, then create the styles shown in Figure I-22. (*Hint:* To create two columns, turn on columns, click to the left of the first occurrence of the text Section Heading, click Format on the menu bar, then click Columns. In the Columns dialog box, click two in the Presets section, click the Apply to list arrow, select This point forward, then click OK.)

FIGURE I-22

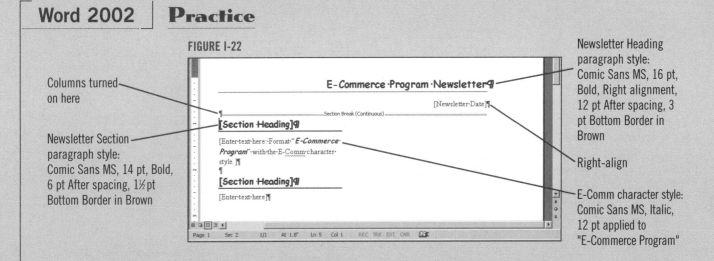

Columns turned on here

Newsletter Section paragraph style: Comic Sans MS, 14 pt, Bold, 6 pt After spacing, 1½ pt Bottom Border in Brown

Newsletter Heading paragraph style: Comic Sans MS, 16 pt, Bold, Right alignment, 12 pt After spacing, 3 pt Bottom Border in Brown

Right-align

E-Comm character style: Comic Sans MS, Italic, 12 pt applied to "E-Commerce Program"

b. Modify the default location for user templates so that they are saved in the folder you created previously named [Your Name] Templates. This folder should be in the drive and folder where your Project Files are located.

c. Save the document as a template named **E-Commerce Program Newsletter**, then close the template.

d. Open the file WD I-8 from the drive and location where your Project Files are located, then save it as **November E-Commerce Newsletter**.

e Attach the E-Commerce Program Newsletter template to the document.

f. Change the Left and Right margins to 1", then reapply the two-column format starting at the Class Projects heading. (*Note:* You need to reapply the two-column format because options related to the structure of a document saved with a template are lost when you attach the template to an existing document.)

g. Modify the following styles: Newsletter Heading style uses 18 pt, Teal font color, and Teal border line; Newsletter section uses 6 point before paragraph spacing and 1½ pt teal border line color.

h. Apply styles to the appropriate text. (*Note:* the text E-Commerce Program appears four times in the newsletter.)

i. Create a Table style called **Schedule**. Use format settings of your choice. (*Hint:* To modify just the header row, click the Apply formatting to list arrow, click Header Row, then select the formatting required.)

j. Apply the Schedule style to the table in the Class Projects section. Increase the width of column 2 so none of the dates wrap to the next line.

k. Type **Editor:** and your name so it is right-justified at the end of column 2, save the document, print a copy, close the document, then exit Word.

▶ Independent Challenge 3

As the owner of Le Bistro Café in Aspen, Colorado, you need to create two menus—one for winter and one for summer. You've already created an unformatted version of the winter menu. Now you need to format text in the winter menu with styles, open and save a new document for the summer menu, copy the styles from the winter menu document to the summer menu document, then use the styles to create a summer version of the menu. You will type your own entries for appetizers, entrees, salads, and desserts for the summer menu.

a. Start Word, open the file WD I-9 from the drive and location where your Project Files are located, then save it as **Winter Menu**.

b. Create the styles as described in Table I-1.

c. Apply the Menu Title style to the document title.

d. Apply the Menu Categories style to each menu category (for example, Appetizers, Soups and Salads)

Table I-1

Style Name and Type	Formats	Apply to
Menu Title: paragraph	Font of your choice, 18 pt font size, Bold, color of your choice, center alignment	Document title (for example, Le Bistro Café Winter Menu)
Menu Categories: paragraph	Font of your choice (should be similar to or complement the font chosen for the menu title), 14 pt font size, Bold, Italic, top and bottom border in the line width and color of your choice	Menu categories (for example, Appetizers, Entrees)
Prices: paragraph	Right tab at 6" with the 2 leader style. (*Hint:* Select Tabs from the Format menu in the New Style dialog box.)	Prices (for example, $4.95)
Menu Items: list	Bullet character of your choice	Menu items (for example, Brie baked in brioche with apple pear chutney)

e. Select all the menu items in the Appetizers category, apply the Prices style, then apply the Menu Items style. (*Note:* You must apply the styles in this order).

f. Apply the Prices and the Menu Items styles to the remaining menu items in the document.

g. Under the heading, enter your name, and type **Owner**, apply the Normal style, center the text, save the document, then print it.

h. Create a new document, save it as **Summer Menu**, then close it.

i. In the Organizer dialog box, copy the styles from the Winter Menu document to the Summer Menu document.

j. Open the Summer Menu document and create a menu similar to the winter menu, but with menu items more suitable for summer fare. For example, instead of Winter squash medley, you could include Mint-Raspberry Compote.

k. Enter your name, and type **Owner** under the heading, apply the Normal style, center-justify the text, save the documents, print them, close the documents, then exit Word.

 # Independent Challenge 4

From Microsoft's web site at www.microsoft.com, you can access a variety of templates. You can import any template from the Web site directly into Word and then modify it for your own purposes. You decide to find and then modify a template for a sales letter.

a. Start Word, open the New Document task pane, then click Templates on Microsoft.com in the New from template section.

b. In a few seconds, the Microsoft.com Web site will open to the Template Gallery. If the Template Gallery does not open, click the Try Template Gallery tab on the Microsoft Web site or search the site using the key phrase Template Gallery.

c. Explore some of the documents available, then click Sales Letters in the Letters to Customers category.

d. Scroll through the sales letters listed. You need to select one that you can adapt for a business of your choice.

e. Select the sales letter you want to adapt, then click Edit in Microsoft Word.

f. If necessary, read and accept the licensing agreement, then click the Edit in Microsoft Word button above the Preview window.

g. Modify the content of the sales letter in Microsoft Word so it contains information relevant to a company of your choice.

h. Use AutoFormat to format the document as a letter.

i. From the Style Gallery, select a letter style to apply to the letter.

j. In the Styles and Formatting task pane, modify two styles to reflect settings you prefer.

k. Save the sales letter as **Sales Letter from Online Template Gallery**, be sure your name appears in the return address block, print a copy, close the document, then exit Word.

► Visual Workshop

Create a new document, then type the price lists in tables as shown in Figure I-23. Do not include any formatting. Apply the Heading 1 style to the title, then modify it so that it appears as shown in Figure I-23. Apply the Heading 2 style to the names of the price lists, then modify them so that they appear as shown in Figure I-23. Create a table style called **Price Table** that will format each table as shown in Figure I-23. Save the price list as **Paradise Cosmetics**, be sure your name appears at the end of the document, print a copy, then close the document.

FIGURE I-23

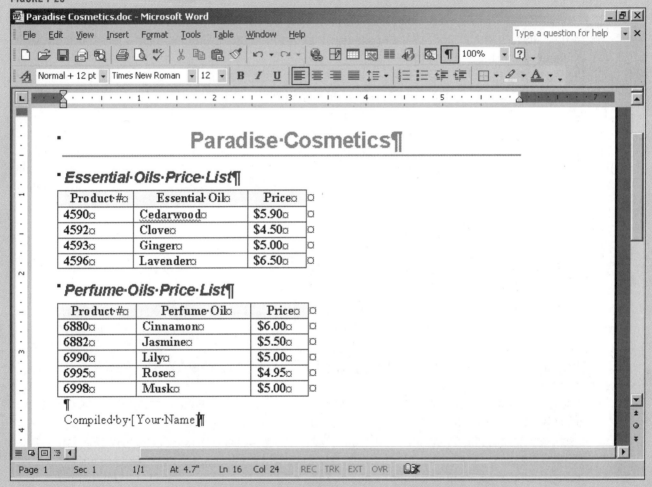

Developing
Multi-Page Documents

Objectives

► **Build a document in Outline view**
► **Work in Outline view**
MOUS ► **Add footnotes and endnotes**
MOUS ► **Navigate a document**
MOUS ► **Generate a table of contents**
MOUS ► **Generate an index**
MOUS ► **Modify pages in multiple sections**
MOUS ► **Work with master documents**

In Outline view, you use headings and subheadings to organize multi-page documents, such as reports and manuals. These documents can include footnotes, cross-references, multiple sections, and even an index. You can also combine several documents—called subdocuments—into one master document. ◢ Alice Wegman in the Marketing Department wants to develop a set of guidelines to help MediaLoft store managers host events such as book signings, readings, book clubs, and children's story time sessions. She works in Outline view to revise the structure for the guidelines and then uses Word features to format the document for publication.

Word 2002

Building a Document in Outline View

You work in Outline view to organize the headings and subheadings that identify topics and subtopics in multi-page documents. In Outline view, each heading is assigned a level from 1 to 9, with Level 1 being the highest level and Level 9 being the lowest level. In addition, you can assign the Body Text level to the paragraphs of text that expand and clarify the document headings. Each level is formatted with one of Word's preset styles. For example, Level 1 is formatted with the Heading 1 style and the Body Text level is formatted with the Normal style. ✎▬ Alice works in Outline view to develop the structure of the Book Signing Guidelines.

Steps

Trouble?

Close the New document task pane if it opens.

1. **Start Word,** then click the **Outline View button** 🔲 in the lower-left corner of the program window
   The document appears in Outline view. Notice the Outlining toolbar at the top of the program window and the minus symbol in the document window. Table J-1 describes the buttons on the Outlining toolbar.

2. Type **Author Reading Guidelines**
   Figure J-1 shows the text in Outline view. By default, the text appears at the left margin, is designated as Level 1, and is formatted with the Heading 1 style.

3. Press **[Enter]**, click the **Demote button** ⬜ on the Outlining toolbar to move to Level 2, then type **Manual Structure**
   The text is indented, designated as Level 2, and formatted with the Heading 2 style.

4. Press **[Enter]**, then click the **Demote to Body Text button** ⬜ on the Outlining toolbar

5. Type the following text: **Three principal activities relate to the organization and running of a book reading event. You need to gather the appropriate personnel, advertise the event, and arrange the physical space. This manual will cover each of these activities in turn.**, then press **[Enter]**
   The text is indented, designated as Body Text level, and formatted with the Normal style. Notice that the Level 1 and Level 2 text is preceded by a plus symbol ✚. This symbol indicates that the heading includes subtext, which could be a subheading or a paragraph of body text.

6. Click the **Promote to Heading 1 button** ⬜ on the Outlining toolbar
   The insertion point returns to the left margin and the Level 1 position.

7. Type **Personnel**, press **[Enter]**, then save the document as **Author Reading Guidelines** to the drive and folder where your Project Files are located
   When you create a long document, you often enter all the headings and subheadings first to establish the overall structure of your document.

QuickTip

You can press [Tab] to move from a higher level to a lower level and you can press [Shift][Tab] to move from a lower level to a higher level.

8. Use the **Promote, Demote,** and **Promote to Heading 1 buttons** to complete the outline so that it appears as shown in Figure J-2

9. Place the insertion point after **Guidelines**, press **[Enter]**, click ⬜, type **Prepared by [Your Name]**, save the document, print a copy, then close it
   The printed copy does not include the outline symbols.

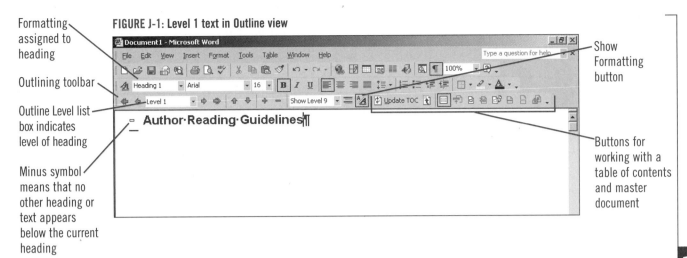

FIGURE J-1: Level 1 text in Outline view

Formatting assigned to heading

Outlining toolbar

Outline Level list box indicates level of heading

Minus symbol means that no other heading or text appears below the current heading

Show Formatting button

Buttons for working with a table of contents and master document

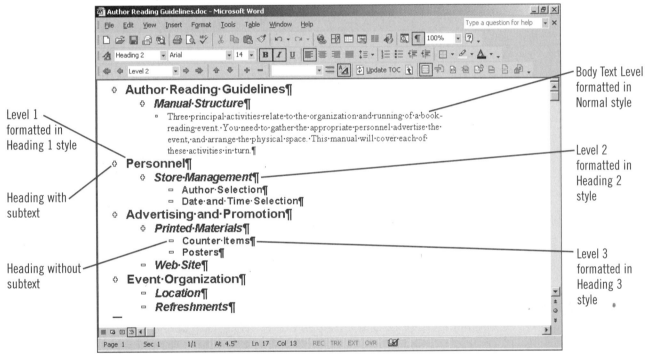

FIGURE J-2: Updated outline

Level 1 formatted in Heading 1 style

Heading with subtext

Heading without subtext

Body Text Level formatted in Normal style

Level 2 formatted in Heading 2 style

Level 3 formatted in Heading 3 style

TABLE J-1: Outlining buttons on the Outlining toolbar

button	use to	button	use to
	Promote text to Level 1		Expand text
	Promote text one level		Collapse text
	Demote text one level		Show Level
	Demote text to body text		Show only the first line of each paragraph
	Move a heading and its text up one line		Show text formatting
	Move a heading and its text down one line		

Working in Outline View

In Outline view, you can promote and demote headings and subheadings and move or delete whole blocks of text. When you move a heading, all the text and subheadings that appear under that heading also move with the heading. You also can use the Collapse, Expand, and Show Level buttons on the Outlining toolbar to view all or just some of the headings and subheadings. For example, you can choose to view just the Level 1 headings so that you can quickly evaluate the main topics of your document. Alice has written a draft of her guidelines for running a book signing event. Now she wants to work in Outline view to reorganize the structure of the document.

Steps

1. Open the file **WD J-1** from the drive and folder where your Project Files are located, save it as **Book Signing Guidelines**, scroll through the document to get a sense of its content, then click the **Outline View button**

2. Click the **Show Level list arrow** on the Outlining toolbar, then click **Show Level 1**
   Only the Level 1 headings appear, as shown in Figure J-3.

3. Click the **plus outline symbol** to the left of Advertising and Promotion
   The heading and all its subtext are selected.

4. Press and hold [**Shift**], select the headings: **Personnel**, **Event Organization**, and **Summary**, then click the **Demote button** on the Outlining toolbar
   You use [Shift] to select multiple headings at once. The selected headings are demoted one level to Level 2.

5. Press [**Ctrl**][**A**] to select all the headings, click the **Expand button** on the Outlining toolbar to expand the outline one level, then click **two** more times
   The outline expands to show all the subheadings and body text associated with each of the selected headings. You can also expand a single heading by selecting only that heading, then clicking the Expand button until all the associated subheadings and body text appear.

6. Click the **Collapse button** on the Outlining toolbar **three** times to collapse the outline, click next to **Personnel** to select it, click the **Move Up button** on the Outlining toolbar **once**, then double-click next to **Personnel**
   The outline for Personnel expands. When you move a heading in Outline view, all subtext and text associated with the heading also move.

7. Click the **Show Level list arrow**, select **Show Level 3**, double-click next to **Equipment**, then press [**Delete**]
   The Equipment heading and its associated subtext are deleted from the document. The revised outline appears, as shown in Figure J-4.

8. Click the **Show Level list arrow**, click **Show All Levels**, press [**Ctrl**][**End**] to move to the bottom of the document, press [**Enter**] twice, then type **Revised by** followed by your name.

9. Save the document

FIGURE J-3: Level 1 headings

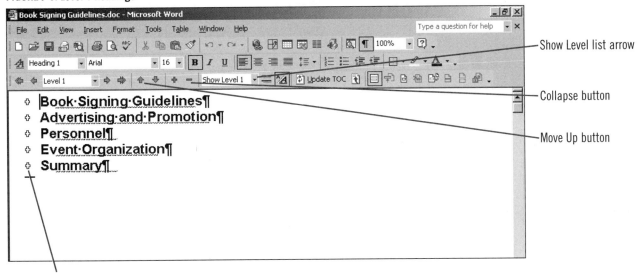

Show Level list arrow

Collapse button

Move Up button

Plus outline symbol indicates that additional levels or paragraphs of text are included under the heading

FIGURE J-4: Revised outline

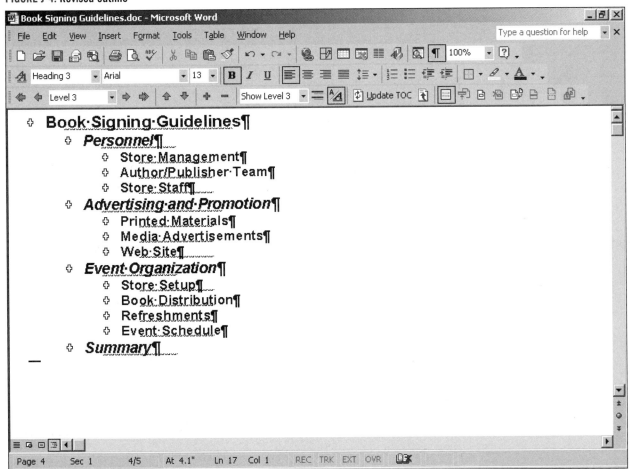

Adding Footnotes and Endnotes

Unit J
Word 2002

You use **footnotes** and **endnotes** to provide additional information or to acknowledge sources for text in a document. Footnotes appear at the bottom of the page on which the footnote reference appears; endnotes appear at the end of the document. You can use footnotes and endnotes in the same document. For example, a footnote could cite the source and an endnote could comment on information provided in the text. Every footnote and endnote consists of a **note reference mark** and the corresponding note text. When you add, delete, or move a note, any additional notes in the document are renumbered automatically. ✎ Alice works in Print Layout view to add a footnote to the book signing guidelines and to edit footnotes she inserted earlier. She uses the Find command to move quickly to the text she wants to reference.

1. Click the **Print Layout View button** ▤, press **[Ctrl][Home]** to move to the beginning of the document, click **Edit** on the menu bar, click **Find**, type **agent and/or publisher** in the Find what text box, click **Find Next**, click **Cancel** to close the Find dialog box, then click just before the **period** following publisher
   The insertion point is located next to the word publisher. Two footnotes appear in the footnote area at the bottom of the document window.

2. Click **Insert** on the menu bar, point to **Reference**, then click **Footnote**
   The Footnote and Endnote dialog box opens, as shown in Figure J-5.

3. Click **Insert**
   The insertion point moves to the footnote area at the bottom of the page, and the existing footnotes are relabeled B and C.

4. Type **You may be able to deal directly with some authors, particularly local or self-published authors.**
   The footnote reference marker appears after the word publisher, and the footnote text appears in the footnote area, as shown in Figure J-6.

5. Click anywhere in the text above the **separator line** to return to the document text, click **Edit** on the menu bar, click **Go To**, click **Footnote** in the Go to what list box, type **E** in the Enter footnote number text box, click **Go To**, then click **Close**
   The insertion point moves to the footnote reference marker for E.

6. Move the mouse over the **footnote reference marker** to view the footnote text

   Trouble?
   If the footnote does not appear in a comment text box, click Tools on the menu bar, click Options, click the ScreenTips checkbox to select it, then click OK.

7. Double-click the **footnote marker** to view the footnote at the bottom of the page, position the insertion point after the word special, press **[spacebar]**, type **sidewalk**, scroll up until the document is visible, then click anywhere in the **text** above the footnote separator

8. Press **[Ctrl][G]**, select **E** in the Enter footnote number text box, type **B**, click **Go To**, click **Close**, select the superscript **B** that appears after cookbooks, then press **[Delete]**
   The footnote reference marker and its associated footnote are deleted. The footnote reference markers and the footnotes in the footnote area are relabeled.

9. Click **Insert** on the menu bar, point to **Reference**, click **Footnote**, click the **Number format list arrow**, select the **1, 2, 3** number format, click **Apply**, then save the document
   The footnote reference markers and the footnotes are relabeled, as shown in Figure J-7.

FIGURE J-5: **Footnote and Endnote dialog box**

Footnotes selected by default ——

Click to insert a footnote at the insertion point location ——

Click list arrow to view other number formats ——

Click to apply format options ——

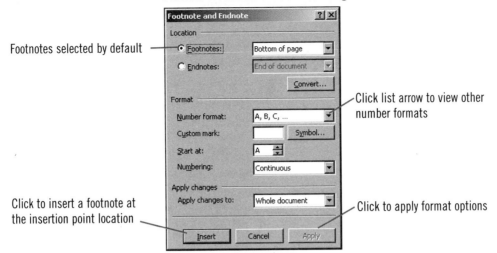

FIGURE J-6: **Footnote text inserted in the footnote area**

Footnote reference marker ——

Separator line ——

Footnotes automatically relettered sequentially ——

New footnote text ——

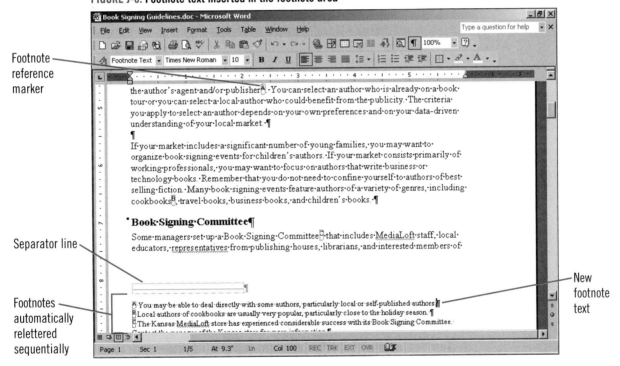

FIGURE J-7: **Revised footnotes**

New footnote format ——

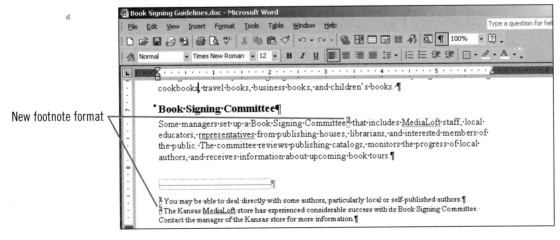

Navigating a Document

You can use the document map and cross-references to navigate through a multi-page document. The **Document Map** pane shows all the headings and subheadings in the document and opens along the left side of the document window. You can quickly move through a document by clicking headings and subheadings in the Document Map pane. A **cross-reference** is text that electronically refers the reader to another part of the document, such as a numbered paragraph, a heading, or a figure. For example, if you make the text "below" an active hyperlink in "See Figure 1 below," then when "below" is clicked, the reader moves directly to Figure 1. Alice uses the Document Map to navigate to a specific heading in the document so she can make a quick editing change. She also adds a caption to the graphic of a pie chart, then creates a cross-reference to the pie chart.

Steps

1. Press [Ctrl][Home], then click the **Document Map button** 🔲 on the Standard toolbar
   The Document Map opens in the Document Map pane.

2. Click **Counter Items** in the Document Map pane
   As shown in Figure J-8, the Counter Items subheading is selected in the Document Map pane and the insertion point moves to the subheading Counter Items in the document.

3. Select **flyers** in the first line of text under the Counter Items heading, type **author profiles**, then click 🔲 to close the Document Map pane

4. Press [Ctrl][G], scroll down the Go to what list box, click **Graphic**, click **Next**, then click **Close**

5. Click the **pie chart** to select it, click **Insert** on the menu bar, point to **Reference**, click **Caption**, then click **OK** to enter the default caption text "Figure 1"
   The caption Figure 1 appears below the pie chart and is the element you will cross-reference.

6. Press [Ctrl][F], type **children's books**, click **Find Next**, click **Cancel**, press [→] **three** times so the insertion point moves just to the left of the ¶ mark, type the text **See Figure 1** as the beginning of a new sentence, then press [**Spacebar**] once

7. Click **Insert** on the menu bar, point to **Reference**, then click **Cross-reference**
   In the Cross-reference dialog box, you select the Reference type, such as a Numbered item, or Figure, and the cross-reference text, such as the words above or below.

8. Click the **Reference type list arrow**, select **Figure**, click the **Insert reference to list arrow**, then select **Above/below**
   Figure J-9 shows the options selected in the Cross-reference dialog box.

9. Click **Insert**, then click **Close**
   The word below is inserted because the figure appears below the cross-reference.

10. Type a **period** after below, move the pointer over **below** to show the [Ctrl] + click message, press and hold [Ctrl] to show 🖑, click the **left mouse button** to move directly to the pie chart caption, scroll up to see the figure, then save the document

FIGURE J-8: Using the Document Map

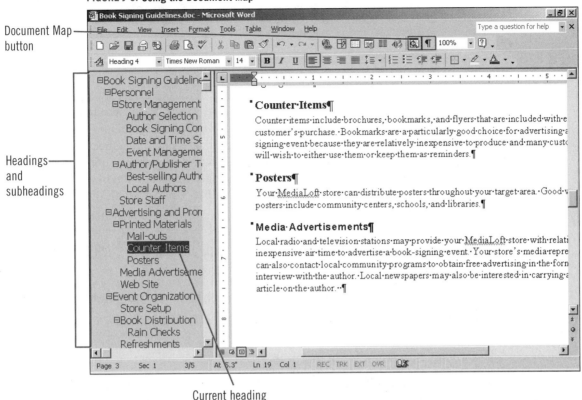

Document Map button

Headings and subheadings

Current heading

FIGURE J-9: Cross-reference dialog box

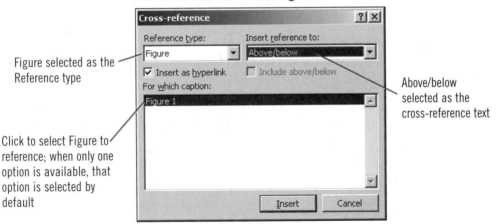

Figure selected as the Reference type

Above/below selected as the cross-reference text

Click to select Figure to reference; when only one option is available, that option is selected by default

Using bookmarks

A **bookmark** identifies a location or a selection of text in a document. To create a bookmark, you first move the insertion point to the location in the text that you want to reference. This location can be a word, the beginning of a paragraph, or a heading. Click Insert on the menu bar, then click Bookmark to open the Bookmark dialog box. In this dialog box, you type a name for the bookmark, then click Add. To find a bookmark, press [Ctrl][G] to open the Go To dialog box, click Bookmark in the Go to what list box, click the Enter bookmark name list arrow to see the list of bookmarks in the document, select the bookmark you require, click Go To, then close the Go To dialog box.

Generating a Table of Contents

Word 2002

Readers refer to a table of contents to obtain an overview of the topics and subtopics covered in a multi-page document. When you generate a table of contents, Word searches for headings, sorts them by heading levels, and then displays the completed table of contents in the document. By default, a table of contents lists the top three heading levels in a document. Consequently, before you create a table of contents, you must ensure that all headings and subheadings are formatted with heading styles. Because Alice organized her document in Outline view, she knows all headings are assigned a Word heading style. Alice is pleased with the content of her document and is now ready to create a new page that includes a table of contents.

1. Press [Ctrl][Home], click **Insert** on the menu bar, click **Break**, click the **Next page option button** in the Section break types area, then click **OK**

2. Press [Ctrl][Home], press [Enter] twice, select the **top paragraph mark**, as shown in Figure J-10, click the **Style list arrow** on the Formatting toolbar, then click **Clear Formatting**
   The formatting associated with the paragraph is removed.

3. Type **Table of Contents**, center it, select and enhance it with **Bold** and the **18 pt** font size, click after **Contents**, press [Enter] twice, then clear the current formatting
   The insertion point is positioned where the table of contents will begin.

4. Click **Insert** on the menu bar, point to **Reference**, click **Index and Tables**, then click the **Table of Contents tab**
   The Table of Contents tab in the Index and Tables dialog box opens.

5. Click the **Formats list arrow**, click **Formal**, select **3** in the Show levels text box, type **4**, compare the dialog box to Figure J-11, then click **OK**
   A complete table of contents that includes all the Level 1, 2, 3, and 4 headings appears.

6. Click the **Outline View button** 📧, click the **Show Level list arrow** 🔽, click **Show Level 3**, click the **plus outline symbol** ➕ next to the Author/Publisher Team heading, then press [Delete]
   The Author/Publisher Team heading and its related subtext are deleted from the document.

7. Click the **Print Layout View button** 📧, then press [Ctrl][Home]
   An error message appears in the Table of Contents next to each item you deleted.

8. Move the mouse to the **left** of **Book Signing Guidelines** at the top of the table of contents until the ⬚ appears, then click ⬚ to select the entire table of contents at once
   With the table of contents selected, you can update it to show the new page numbers.

9. Right-click the **table of contents**, click **Update Field**, click the **Table of Contents title** to deselect the table of contents, then save the document
   The completed table of contents appears, as shown in Figure J-12. Each entry in the table of contents is a hyperlink to the entry's corresponding heading in the document.

10. Move the mouse over the heading **Media Advertisements**, press [Ctrl], then click the **left mouse button**
    The insertion point moves automatically to the Media Advertisements heading in the document.

FIGURE J-10: Paragraph mark selected

Style list arrow

Top paragraph mark formatted with the Heading 1 style because the section break was applied just above a heading

Section break

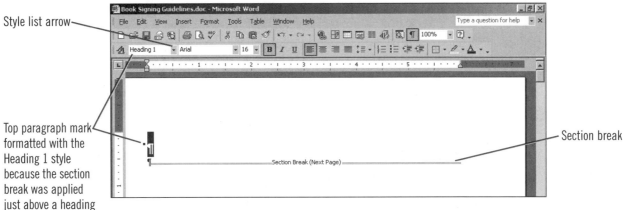

FIGURE J-11: Index and Tables dialog box

Print Preview of Formal format

Formal format selected

Table of Contents tab

Formats list arrow

Number of heading levels included in the table of contents

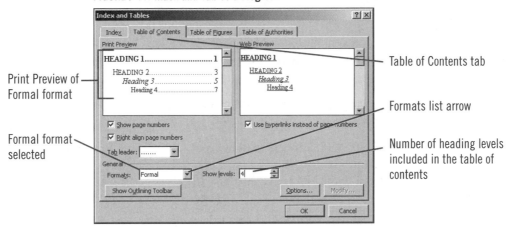

FIGURE J-12: Updated table of contents

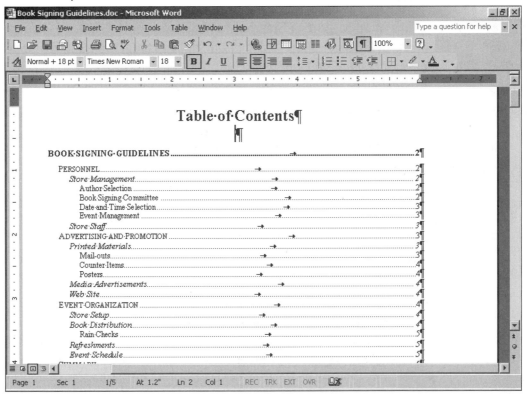

Generating an Index

An **index** lists many of the terms and topics included in a document, along with the pages on which they appear. An index can include main entries, subentries, and cross-references. Once you have marked all the index entries, you select a design for the index, and then you generate it. Alice marks terms that she wants to include in an index, creates a new last page in the document, and then she generates the index.

Steps

1. Press **[Ctrl][Home]**, press **[Ctrl]** and click **Book Signing Guidelines** in the table of contents, then select the text **book signing event** in the first paragraph

2. Click **Insert** on the menu bar, point to **Reference**, click **Index and Tables**, click the **Index tab**, then click **Mark Entry**
   The Mark Index Entry dialog box appears, as shown in Figure J-13.

3. Click **Mark All**
   All instances of "book signing event" are marked with the XE field code. "XE" stands for "Index Entry." The Mark Index Entry dialog box remains open so that you can continue to mark text for inclusion in the index.

4. Click **twice** anywhere in the document to deselect the **current index entry**, press **[Ctrl][F]**, type **store manager** in the Find what text box, click **Find Next**, click the title bar of the Mark Index Entry dialog box, then click **Mark All**
   All instances of store manager are marked for inclusion in the index. By default, selected text is entered in the Main entry text box and treated as a main entry in the index.

5. Click the **title bar** of the Find and Replace dialog box, select **store manager** in the Find what text box, type **book signing committee**, click **Find Next**, click the **title bar** of the Mark Index Entry dialog box, click the Main entry text box and verify book signing committee, then click **Mark All**

6. Follow the procedure in Step 5 to switch between the Find and Replace dialog box and the Mark Index Entry dialog box to find and mark the following main entries: **rain checks**, **author**, and **publisher**
   In addition to main entries, an index often has a subentry included under a main entry.

7. Click the **title bar** of the Find and Replace dialog box, find the text **shopping cart**, click the **title bar** of the Mark Index Entry dialog box, select **shopping cart** in the Main entry text box, type **Web site**, press **[Tab]**, type **shopping cart** in the Subentry text box, click **Mark All**, then close the Mark Index Entry and Find and Replace dialog boxes
   Shopping cart is marked as a subentry to appear following the Main entry, Web site.

8. Press **[Ctrl][End]**, click to the left of **Revised by [Your Name]**, click **Insert** on the menu bar, click **Break**, click the **Next page option button**, click **OK**, type **Index**, press **[Enter] three** times to move your name down, enhance **Index** with **18 pt** and **Bold** and **center alignment**, then click at the **left margin** above your name

9. Click **Insert** on the menu bar, point to **Reference**, click **Index and Tables**, click the **Formats list arrow**, click **Fancy**, click **OK**, then save the document
   As shown in Figure J-14, Word has collected all the index entries, sorted them alphabetically, included the appropriate page numbers, and removed duplicate entries. If you add or delete index entries, you can update the index by right-clicking the index and clicking Update Fields.

FIGURE J-13: Mark Index Entry dialog box

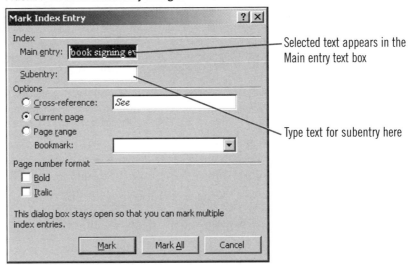

Selected text appears in the Main entry text box

Type text for subentry here

FIGURE J-14: Completed index

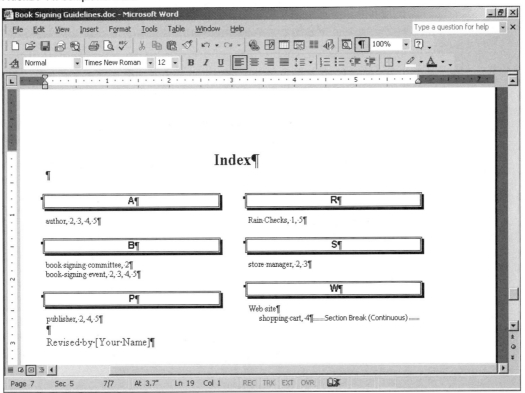

Creating a cross-reference in the index

A cross-reference in an index refers the reader to another entry in the index. For example, a cross-reference in an index might read, "London. *See* Europe." Readers then know to refer to the Europe entry in the index to find the page number that contains information about London, presented in the context of its relationship to Europe. To create a cross-reference in an index, find the text you want to cross-reference. In the Mark Index Entry dialog box, click after *See* in the Cross-reference text box, then type the text you want readers to refer to when they see the marked entry. For example, you could mark the text "London" as a main entry and then enter "Europe" after *See* in the Cross-reference text box.

Modifying Pages in Multiple Sections

Multi-page documents often consist of two or more sections—each of which can be formatted differently. For example, you can include different text in the header for each section, or change how page numbers are formatted from section to section. ✐ Alice wants to format the page number on the table of contents page in lowercase Roman numerals and format the page numbers for the guidelines in regular numbers, starting with page 1. She also wants to include a header that starts on the second page of the guidelines. The diagram in Figure J-15 shows the header and footer for each of the three document sections.

Steps

1. Press **[Ctrl][Home]**, click **Insert** on the menu bar, click **Page Numbers**, click the **Alignment list arrow**, select **Center**, click **Format**, click the **Number format list arrow**, click **i, ii, iii**, click **OK** to close the Page Number Format dialog box, click **OK** to close the Page Numbers dialog box, then scroll to the bottom of the page
   Notice the "i" inserted in the footer area at the bottom of the Table of Contents page.

QuickTip

When you want the first page in a section to be different from the other pages in the same section, you must be sure to select the Different first page option.

2. Scroll to the top of the next page, click the **Book Signing Guidelines** heading, click **View** on the menu bar, click **Header and Footer**, click the **Page Setup button** 🔲 on the Header and Footer toolbar to open the Page Setup dialog box, click the **Different first page check box** to select it, then click **OK**

3. Click the **Switch Between Header and Footer button** 🗐 on the Header and Footer toolbar, click the **Same as Previous button** 🗐 to deselect it, click the **Center button** 🗏 on the Formatting toolbar, then click the **Insert Page Number button** 🗐
   The number 2 appears in the First Page Footer because by default, the numbering is continuous from the first page in the document.

4. Click the **Format Page Number button** 🗐 on the Header and Footer toolbar, click the **Start at option button**, verify that **1** appears, click **OK**, then click the **Show Next button** 🗐
   Clicking the Show Next button moves the insertion point to the header or footer on the next page of the document when the Different first page option is selected in the Page Setup dialog box. Clicking the Show Next button moves the insertion point to the header or footer of the next section of a document when the Different first page option is *not* selected.

5. Click 🗐, click 🗐 to deselect it, type **Book Signing Guidelines**, press **[Tab]** twice, type **Reviewed by [Your Name]**, enhance the text with **Bold** and **Italic**, then click **Reviewed** to deselect the text
   The header appears as shown in Figure J-16. You deselected the Same as Previous button to make sure that the header contains only the text you type into the header in this section. You must deselect the Same as Previous button when you want the header in a section to be unique.

6. Click 🗐, click 🗐, delete **Book Signing Guidelines**, **Reviewed by [Your Name]**, then click **Close**
   When you click the Show Next button, the header for Section 3, which contains the index, appears. You delete the header text in section 3 so that it will not appear on the index page.

7. Press **[Ctrl][Home]**, right-click the **table of contents**, click **Update Field**, click the **Update entire table option button**, click **OK**, press **[Ctrl][End]**, scroll as needed to view the Index, right-click the **index**, click **Update Field**, save the document, print a copy, then close it
   The headers and footers appear in the document as indicated in Figure J-15.

FIGURE J-15: Diagram of document headers and footers

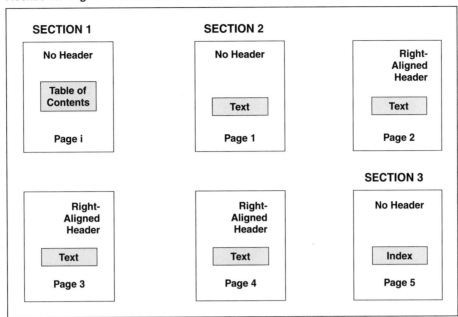

FIGURE J-16: Completed header

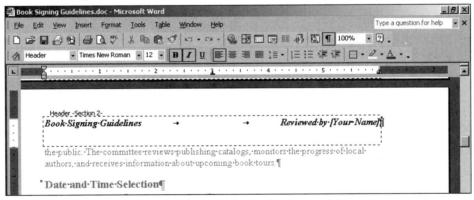

Using text flow options

You adjust text flow options to control how text in a multi-page document breaks across pages. To change text flow options, open the Paragraph dialog box from the Format menu, and then select the Line and Page Breaks tab. In the Pagination section of this tab, you can choose to select or deselect four text flow options. For example, you select the Widow/Orphan control option to prevent the last line of a paragraph from printing at the top (a widow) of a page or the first line of a paragraph from printing at the bottom (an orphan) of a page. By default, Widow/Orphan is turned on.

Working with Master Documents

A **master document** is a Word document that contains links to two or more related documents called **subdocuments**. You create a master document to organize and format long documents such as reports and books into manageable subdocuments, each of which you can open and edit directly from the master document. ✎ Alice has written guidelines for story time sessions and book clubs. She has also created a new version of the Book Signing Guidelines. Now she creates a master document that contains all three sets of guidelines.

Steps 1 2 3 4

1. Open a new blank Word document, type **MediaLoft Event Guidelines**, center the text and enhance it with **Bold** and **26 pt**, press **[Enter] two** times, change the font size to **14 pt**, type **Prepared by [Your Name]**, press **[Enter] twice**, clear the formatting, then save the document as **MediaLoft Event Guidelines** to the drive and folder where your Project Files are located

2. Open the file **WD J-2**, save it as **Guidelines_Book Signing**, close the document, open the file **WD J-3**, save it as **Guidelines_Book Club**, close the document, open the file **WD J-4**, save it as **Guidelines_Story Time**, then close the document

3. Switch to **Outline view**, click the **Insert Subdocument button** 📄 on the Outlining toolbar, click **Guidelines_Book Signing** in the list of files, then click **Open**
By default, each subdocument is contained in its own section so a section break is added automatically at the end of the Book Signing Guidelines.

4. Use 📄 to insert **Guidelines_Book Club** and **Guidelines_Story Time** as the second and third subdocuments, click the **Collapse Subdocuments button** 🔲 on the Outlining toolbar, then click **OK** to save the master document
The three subdocuments appear, as shown in Figure J-17. To make changes to a subdocument, you open the subdocument in the master document or open the subdocument file.

5. Double-click 🗒 next to **Guidelines_Book Club**, switch to **Outline view**, show the top **three** levels, delete the **Store Setup** subheading and its subtext, then close and save the document

6. Click the **Expand Subdocuments button** 🔲 on the Outlining toolbar, click the **Update TOC button** 🔲, click the **Update entire table option button**, click **OK**, switch to **Print Layout** view, then scroll to view the Table of Contents
The table of contents includes the Book Club Guidelines and the Story Time Guidelines.

7. Press **[Ctrl]** and click the **Book Club Guidelines** heading

8. Double-click in the **header**, click the **Same as Previous button** 🔲 to deselect it, change the header text to **Book Club Guidelines**, click **Close**, then repeat the procedure to change the header for the Story Time document to **Story Time Guidelines**
Each section of the guidelines now includes an appropriate header.

9. Save the document, print a copy of the title page, page 5 and page 8, close the document, then exit Word
The title page and pages 5 and 8 are printed, as shown in Figure J-18.

FIGURE J-17: Inserting a subdocument

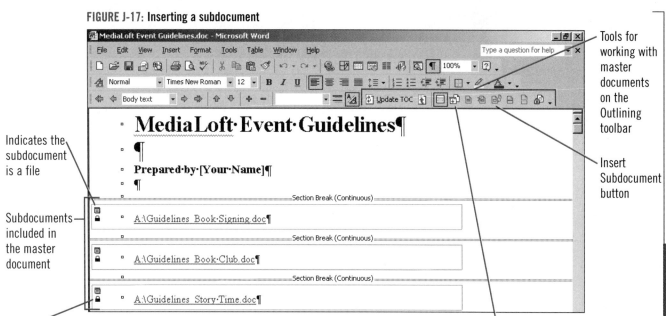

Indicates the subdocument is a file

Subdocuments included in the master document

Subdocuments are locked when the master document is collapsed

Tools for working with master documents on the Outlining toolbar

Insert Subdocument button

Expand Subdocuments button

FIGURE J-18: Pages from the printed document

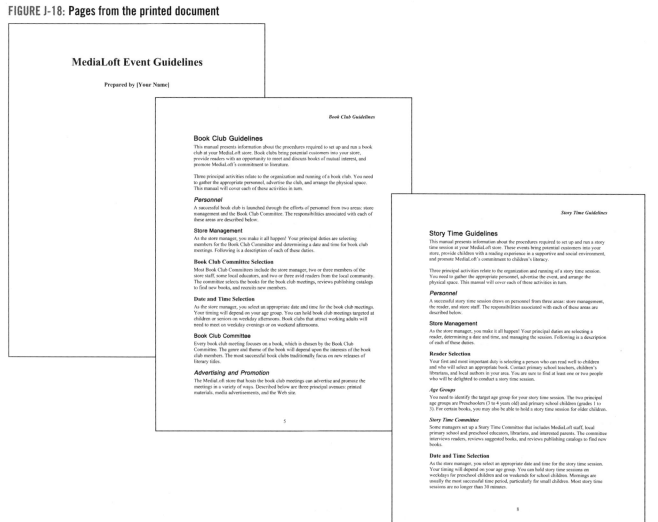

Practice

► Concepts Review

Label the numbered items on the Outlining toolbar shown in Figure J-19.

FIGURE J-19

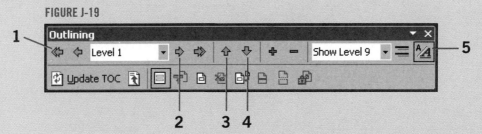

Match each term with the statement that best describes it.

6. Table of contents
7. Demote button
8. Mark Index Entry dialog box
9. Footnote
10. Insert Subdocument button
11. Cross-reference
12. Demote to Body Text button

a. Used to enter a lower-level heading in Outline view
b. Provides additional comments on information provided in the text
c. Included on the Master Document toolbar
d. Used to enter a paragraph of text in Outline view
e. List of topics and subtopics included at the beginning of a document
f. Text that refers the reader to another part of the document
g. Where you enter text for inclusion in an index

Select the best answer from the list of choices.

13. In Outline view, which button do you click to move to Level 1?
    a. Demote to Body Text button
    b. Promote to Level 1 button
    c. Promote to Heading 1 button
    d. Promote subtext button

14. Which symbol in Outline view indicates that a heading includes subtext such as subheadings or paragraphs of text?
    a. Plus outline symbol
    b. Minus outline symbol
    c. Slash outline symbol
    d. Level outline symbol

15. Which feature can you use to navigate a document?
    a. Bookmark
    b. Cross-reference
    c. Document map
    d. All of the above

16. From the Insert menu, which item do you select when you want to insert a table of contents?
    a. Tools
    b. Index and Tables
    c. Reference
    d. Supplements

17. Which button on the Header and Footer toolbar do you deselect to make sure that text you enter in a header or footer will be unique from that section forward?
    a. Same as Next button
    b. Same as Previous button
    c. Show Next button
    d. Show Formatting button

18. What is a master document?
    a. A document formatted in Outline view
    b. A short document included as part of a primary document
    c. A document containing two or more subdocuments
    d. A document containing two or more secondary documents

► Skills Review

1. Build a document in Outline view.

a. Start Word, open a new blank document, switch to Outline view, type **Introduction by [Your Name]** as a Level 1 heading, press [Enter], type **Partnership Requirements** as another Level 1 heading, then press [Enter].

b. Type **Background Information**, then use the Demote button to demote it to a Level 2 heading.

c. Type the text shown in Figure J-20 as body text under Background Information.

d. Use the Promote button to type the heading **Benefits** as a Level 2 heading, then complete the outline, as shown in Figure J-20.

FIGURE J-20

```
▫ Introduction·by·Student·Name¶
✦ Partnership·Requirements¶
    ✦ Background·Information¶
        ▫ This·section·provides·background·information·about·Apex·Training·and·
          discusses·how·the·partnership·could·benefit·both·Forward·
          Communications·and·Apex·Training.¶
    ▫ Benefits¶
    ▫ Partnership·Need¶
✦ Products·and·Services¶
    ▫ Apex·Training·Services¶
    ▫ Forward·Communications·Products¶
    ▫ Package·Opportunities¶
✦ Financial·Considerations¶
    ▫ Projected·Revenues¶
    ▫ Financing·Required¶
▫ Conclusion¶
```

e. Save the document as **Partnership Agreement Outline** to the drive and folder where your Project Files are located, print a copy, then close the document.

2. Work in Outline view.

a. Open the file WD J-5 from the drive and folder where your Project Files are located, save it as **Partnership Agreement Proposal**, switch to Outline view, then show all Level 1 headings.

b. Move the heading Financial Considerations below Products and Services.

c. Select the Partnership Requirements heading, click the Expand button twice, collapse Benefits, collapse Partnership Need, then move Benefits and its subtext below Partnership Need and its subtext.

d. Collapse the Partnership Requirements section to show Level 1 headings only.

e. Expand Products and Services, then delete Forward Communications Products and its subtext.

f. Show all levels of the outline, press [Ctrl][End], press [Enter] twice, type **Prepared by** followed by your name, then save the document.

3. Add footnotes and endnotes.

a. In Print Layout view, find the words **computer labs**, then position the insertion point before the period.

b. Insert a footnote, which will be Footnote 2, with the default settings and the text: **The principal competitor is ICC Trainers, which offers clients a choice of three computer training labs for a total of 120 workstations.**

c. In the document, go to Footnote 4, click in the footnote area, then change **Appendix B** to **Appendix C**.

d. Click in the document, then find, read, and delete Footnote 1.

e. Apply the a,b,c number format to the footnotes, view the footnote area, then save the document.

4. Navigate a document.

a. Open the Document Map and then navigate to Package Opportunities.

b. Change custom to **customizable** under the Package Opportunities heading, then close the Document Map.

c. Go to the column chart graphic, select it, then add **Figure 1** as a caption.

d. Find the text "See Figure 1," then insert a cross-reference to the figure using above/below as the reference text.

e. Insert a period after the word below, test the cross-reference, scroll to see the figure, then save the document.

5. Generate a table of contents.

  a. Press [Ctrl][Home]. Use the Next page section break command to insert a new page above the first page.

  b. Press [Ctr][Home], press [Enter] twice, select the top paragraph mark, clear the current formatting, enter **Table of Contents** at the top of the new first page, press [Enter] twice, enhance the text with 18 pt and Bold, then center it.

  c. Two lines below "Table of Contents" at the left margin, generate a table of contents using the Distinctive format and showing 2 levels.

  d. Use [Ctrl] + click to navigate to Partnership Need in the document, switch to Outline view, then delete Partnership Need and its subtext.

  e. Return to Print Layout view, update the table of contents, then save the document.

6. Generate an index.

  a. Find the words **computer labs** and mark all occurrences for inclusion in the index.

  b. Find and mark the following main entries: Web page design, Networking, and PowerPoint.

  c. Find **online publishing**, click in the Mark Index Entry dialog box, select online publishing in the Main entry text box, type **Forward Communications Products**, press [Tab], type **online publishing seminars**, in the Subentry text box, then click Mark All.

  d. Repeat the process to insert **writing seminars** as a subentry of Forward Communications Products.

  e. Insert a new page in a new section above the text Prepared by [Your Name] at the end of the document, clear the formatting, press [Enter] twice, then type **Index** at the top of the page and format it with Bold and 18 pt and center alignment.

  f. Click at the left margin above your name, press [Enter] twice, press the up arrow once, generate the index in the Bulleted format, then save the document.

7. Modify pages in multiple sections.

  a. Move to the beginning of the document, then open the Page Numbers dialog box and insert a right-aligned page number in the footer with the i, ii, iii format.

  b. Scroll down and click the title of the next page, then show the Header and Footer toolbar.

  c. Select Different first page in the Page Setup dialog box, then move to the header that will start on page 2 of the section.

  d. Deselect the Same as Previous button, type **Partnering Agreement: Apex Training** at the left margin, press [Tab] twice, type **Prepared by** followed by your name at the right margin, then format the text in Bold and Italic.

  e. Insert a right-aligned page number in the footer starting on the first page of Section 2. Use the 1, 2, 3 number format starting at 1.

  f. Remove the header from the index page.

  g. Update the table of contents and the index, save the document, print a copy, then close the document.

8. Work with master documents.

  a. In a new blank document, type **Forward Communications Partnership Agreements** as a centered title formatted with Bold and 20 pt, press [Enter] twice, type **Prepared by** followed by your name in 14 pt and centered, press [Enter] twice, then clear the formatting.

  b. Save the document as **Partnership Agreements**.

  c. Open the files from the drive and folder where your Project Files are located, save them as follows, and close them: WD J-6 as **Partnering_Apex Training**; WD J-7 as **Partnering_Speak Easy**; and WD J-8 as **Partnering_Bay Area College**.

  d. In Outline view, insert the three files as subdocuments in the following order: Apex Training, Speak Easy, and Bay Area College.

  e. Collapse and save the master document so just the filenames appear.

f. Open the subdocument Partnering_Bay Area College, remove the subheading Partnership Need and its sub-text, then save and close the document.

g. Expand the subdocuments, show all levels, then update the table of contents.

h. In Print Layout view, change the header starting on the first page of the Partnering_Speak Easy subdocument to **Partnering Agreement: Speak Easy**, then change the header starting on the first page of the Partnering_Bay Area College subdocument to **Partnering Agreement: Bay Area College**. (*Hint*: Use the Document Map to navigate to each subsection.)

i. Print a copy of the title page, the first page of the Speak Easy subdocument (page 4), and the first page of the Bay Area College subdocument (page 7), save the document, close it, then exit Word.

▶ Independent Challenge 1

You work in the Finance Department of Fitness First, a successful fitness and spa facility in Orlando, Florida. Recently, Fitness First's owners began selling franchises. Your supervisor asks you to format a report that details the development of these franchise operations.

a. Start Word, open the file WD J-9 from the drive and folder where your Project Files are located, then save it as **Fitness First Franchises**.

b. In Outline view, organize the document as shown in the following table, starting with "Introduction," followed by "Scope of the Report," and then moving column by column. Note that the headings are formatted with the green font color.

Heading	Level	Heading	Level	Heading	Level
Introduction	1	Ethan Stone	2	Naples Clientele	3
Scope of the Report	2	Franchise Locations	1	Daytona Beach	2
Owner Information	1	Tallahassee	2	Daytona Beach Clientele	3
Janice Ross	2	Tallahassee Clientele	3	Opening Schedules	1
Yolanda Watson	2	Naples	2		

c. Switch the order of Naples and its accompanying subtext so it follows Daytona Beach and its subtext.

d. Switch to Print Layout view, use the Document Map to move directly to the Opening Schedules heading, then create a bookmark called **Dates** using the first of the three dates listed. Close the Document Map. Move to the beginning of the document and go to your bookmark.

e. Insert a footnote following the text "gourmet restaurants" that reads **One of these restaurants specializes in vegetarian and health-conscious cuisines.**

f. Create an index with appropriate Main entries and subentries. You might mark all locations and owners' names as Main entries. You might enter owners' names as subentries for the Main entry owner. You might cross-reference owners with their specialities.

g. Create a new page in a new section at the end of the document, enter and format **Index** as the page title, then generate an index in the Modern format.

h. Create a footer with your name left-aligned and the page number right-aligned. The footer can print on every page.

i. Save the document, print a copy, close the document, then exit Word.

Independent Challenge 2

You work for an author who has just written a series of vignettes about her travels in France and Italy. The author hopes to publish the vignettes and accompanying illustrations in a book called "Pastel and Pen." She has written a short proposal that she plans to present to publishers. As her assistant, your job is to combine the proposal into a master document that includes three of the vignettes as subdocuments.

a. Start Word, open these files from the drive and folder where your Project Files are located, save them as follows, and close them: WD J-10 as **Pastel and Pen Proposal**, WD J-11 as **Pastel_Lavender**, WD J-12 as **Pastel_Ocher**, WD J-13 as **Pastel_Roman Rain**.

b. Open Pastel and Pen Proposal, switch to Outline view, press [Ctrl][End], then add the other three files as subdocuments under the body text for Sample Vignettes.

c. With the subdocuments expanded, switch to Print Layout view, press [Ctrl][Home], then scroll down to the list of the three titles ("Lavender," "Ocher," and "Roman Rain") under the Sample Vignettes heading.

d. Make each title a cross-reference to the corresponding subdocument title. For example, select the text "Lavender," open the Cross-reference dialog box, select Heading as the reference type, then select the "Lavender" heading as the reference text. (*Note:* Press [Enter] as needed so the titles continue to appear as a list in the document.)

e. Open the Document Map. Use [Ctrl] + click to test each of the titles in the list under the Sample Vignettes heading. Once your insertion point moves to the subdocument, use the Document Map to navigate back to the list of titles under Sample Vignettes and test the next title.

f. Insert a new page with a section break at the beginning of the document, enter and format **Table of Contents** as the page title, then generate a table of contents with two levels in the Formal style.

g. On the Table of Contents page, add your name left-aligned in the footer, and the page number "i" right-aligned in the footer. On the Proposal Overview page, add your name left-aligned in the footer, and the page number "1" right-aligned in the footer.

h. Update the table of contents, save the document, print a copy of the table of contents page and page 1 of the proposal, close the document, then exit Word.

Independent Challenge 3

As the Program Assistant at Somerset College in Victoria, British Columbia, you are responsible for creating and formatting reports about programs at the college. You work in Outline view to create one program report.

a. Create a new document and save it as **Program Information Report**.

b. In Outline view, enter the headings and subheadings for the report as shown in the table starting with "Program Overview," followed by "Career Opportunities." You will need to substitute appropriate course names for "Course 1," "Course 2," etc. For example, courses in the first term of E-Commerce Studies could be "Introduction to E-Commerce," "Online Marketing," etc.

Heading	Level	Heading	Level
Program Overview	1	[Enter name for Course 1]	3
Career Opportunities	2	[Enter name for Course 2]	3
Admission Requirements	2	Second Term	2
Program Content	1	[Enter name for Course 1]	3
First Term	2	[Enter name for Course 2]	3

c. Enter appropriate body text for each heading. For ideas, refer to college catalogs.

d. In Print Layout view, add a title page: include the name of the program, your name, and any other pertinent information. Format the title page text.

e. If necessary, insert page breaks in the body of the report to spread it over two pages. Format the title page with no header and no page number. Format Page 1 of the report with no footer and a right-aligned page number in the header with the 1,2,3 format. Format Pages 2 and the following pages of the report with the name of the program left-aligned in the footer, your name right-aligned in the footer, and a right-aligned page number in the header.

f. Save the document, print a copy, then close it.

 # Independent Challenge 4

Many large online businesses post job opportunities on their Web sites. You can learn a great deal about opportunities in a wide range of fields just by checking out the job postings on these Web sites. You decide to create a document that describes a selection of jobs available on two Web sites of your choice.

a. Find two Web sites that post jobs online. For example, you can search sites such as www.looksmart.com, www.yahoo.com and www.monster.com.

b. On two Web sites, find a page that lists current job opportunities.

c. Identify two job categories (e.g., "Marketing" and "Web Page Development.") on each Web site.

d. Create a new document in Word, then save it as **Online Job Opportunities**.

e. In Outline view, set up the document starting with name of Web site, and followed by Job Category 1 as shown in the table.

Heading	Level	Heading	Level
Name of Web site 1	1	Job Posting 2	3
(for example, Yahoo.com)		Job Category 2	2
Job Category 1	2	Job Posting 1	3
Job Posting 1	3	Job Posting 2	3

f. Repeat the outline for the other Web site. (*Note*: You need to enter specific text for headings such as "Marketing Jobs" for "Job Category 1" and "Marketing Assistant" for "Job Posting 1.")

g. Complete the Word document with information you find on the Web sites. Include a short description of each job you select.

h. Double-space the document text so that the document prints over at least two pages. Use Page Formatting options to keep headings with their paragraph text and lines of text in a paragraph together.

i. Format the document so that a header starts on page 1 and includes the text "Online Job Opportunities for [Your Name]." Include a page number on each page of the document in either the header or the footer.

j. Save the document, print a copy, close the document, then exit Word.

▶ Visual Workshop

Open the file WD J-14, then save it as E-Commerce Term Paper. Modify the outline so that it appears as shown in Figure J-21. In Print Layout view, insert a new page at the beginning of the document, clear the formatting, enter and enhance a Table of Contents, then generate a table of contents as shown in Figure J-22. Save the document, be sure your name is on the document, then print one copy of the table of contents page and one copy of the first three levels of the document in Outline view.

FIGURE J-21

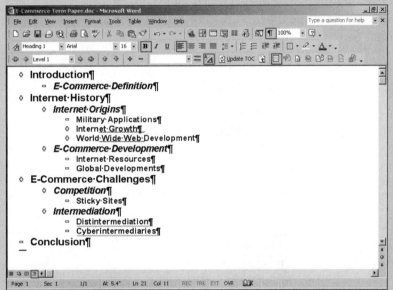

FIGURE J-22

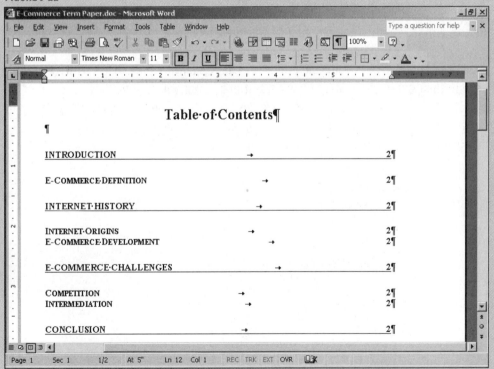

Integrating

Word with Other Programs

Objectives

- ► **Explore integration methods**
- ► **Embed an Excel worksheet**
- ► **Link an Excel chart**
- ► **Embed a PowerPoint slide**
- ► **Insert a Word file**
- ► **Import a table from Access**
- ► **Manage document links**
- ► **Merge with an Access Data Source**

The Office XP suite includes several programs, each with its own unique purpose and characteristics. Sometimes information you want to include in a Word document is stored in files created with other Office programs such as PowerPoint or Excel. For example, the report you are writing in Word might need to include a pie chart from a worksheet created in Excel. You can embed information from other programs in a Word document or you can create links between programs. ◢ Nazila Sharif in the Marketing Department has started a report on how to market MediaLoft Online, the Web site. She needs to supplement the report with information contained in another Word file and in files created in Excel, PowerPoint, and Access. She then needs to merge an Access data source with the cover letter she'll send along with the report to MediaLoft store managers.

Exploring Integration Methods

Information created with other Office XP programs can be integrated into a Word document in a variety of ways. Figure K-1 shows a five-page Word document containing shared information from PowerPoint, Excel, Access, and another Word document. The methods available for sharing information between programs include copy and paste, drag and drop, Object Linking and Embedding, and inserting files. Table K-1 describes each Office XP program and includes its associated filename extension and icon. A **filename extension** is three letters that follow the period in a filename.  Before Nazila integrates information created in other programs into her Word document, she reviews the various ways in which she can share information between programs.

► **Copy and paste**

You use the Copy and Paste commands to copy information from one program and paste it into another program, usually when you need to copy a small amount of text.

► **Drag and drop**

You can position documents created in two programs side by side in separate windows and then use drag and drop to copy or move selected text or objects from one document (the source file) into another document (the destination file).

► **Insert a Word file**

You can use the File command on the Insert menu to insert an entire file. The file types you can insert include Word documents or templates, documents saved in Rich Text Format, and documents created as .htm files for Web pages.

► **Object Linking and Embedding**

The ability to share information with other programs is called **Object Linking and Embedding** (OLE). Two programs are involved in the OLE process. The **source program** is the program in which information is originally created, and the **destination program** is the program to which the information is copied. With OLE, you use the source program to create a **source file** and you use the destination program to create a **destination file**.

► **Objects**

An **object** is defined as self-contained information that can be in the form of text, spreadsheet data, graphics, charts, tables, or even sound and video clips. Objects provide a means of sharing information between programs. You can create objects by selecting Object on the Insert menu or by selecting Paste Special on the Edit menu.

► **Embedded objects**

An **embedded object** is created within the destination file or copied from the source file. You can edit an embedded object within the destination program using the editing features of the source program. Any changes you make to an embedded object appear only in the destination file; the changes are *not* made to the information in the source file.

► **Linked objects**

A **linked object** is created in a source file, then inserted into a destination file and linked to the source file. When you link an object, changes made to the data in the source file are reflected in the destination file. In a linked object, the connection between the source file and the destination file is called a **Dynamic Data Exchange** (DDE) link.

FIGURE K-1: Word document with shared information

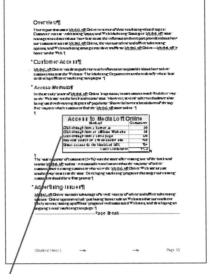

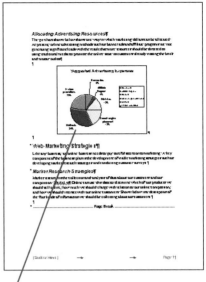

PowerPoint slide
created as an
embedded object
in Word

Excel worksheet
inserted as an
embedded object
into Word

Excel pie chart inserted into Word as a
linked object. The linked chart in Word
can be updated to reflect any changes
made to the Excel chart.

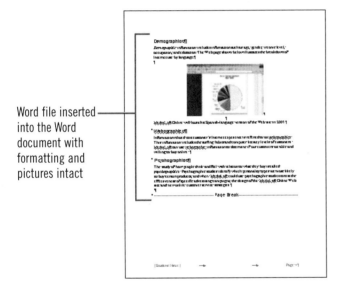

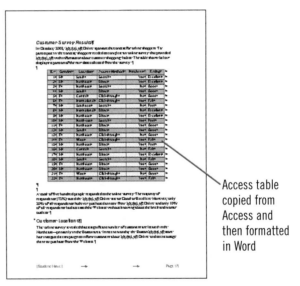

Word file inserted
into the Word
document with
formatting and
pictures intact

Access table
copied from
Access and
then formatted
in Word

TABLE K-1: Office programs

icon	program	extension	purpose
W	**Word**	.doc	To create documents and share information in print, e-mail, and on the Web
X	**Excel**	.xls	To create, analyze, and share spreadsheets and to analyze data with charts, PivotTable dynamic views, and graphs
P	**PowerPoint**	.ppt	To organize, illustrate, and deliver materials in an easy-to-understand graphics format for delivery in a presentation or over the Internet
A	**Access**	.mdb	To store, organize, and share database information
F	**FrontPage**	.htm or .html	To create and manage the files required for a Web site

Embedding an Excel Worksheet

An embedded object uses the features of another program such as Excel, but is stored as part of the Word document. You embed an object, such as an Excel worksheet or a PowerPoint slide, in Word when you do *not* need changes made in the source file to be updated in the embedded Word object. You edit an embedded object directly in Word using the source program toolbars. For example, you can embed a worksheet created in Excel into a Word document, double-click the embedded worksheet object to enter edit mode and show the Excel toolbars, and then edit the embedded object using the Excel toolbars. ◢◣◤◥ The Online Marketing Report that Nazila created in Word contains placeholder text and bookmarks to designate where she wants to insert information created in other programs. Her first task is to embed an Excel worksheet that contains data related to the top five methods customers use to find MediaLoft Online.

Steps

1. Start **Word**, open the file **WD K-1.doc** from the drive and folder where your Project Files are located, save it as **Online Marketing Report**, click the Show/Hide ¶ button ¶ to select it, then scroll through the report to note where you will insert content from other programs

2. Click **Edit** on the menu bar, click **Go To**, click **Bookmark** in the Go to what list box, verify that **Access** appears in the Enter bookmark name text box, click **Go To**, click **Close**, then delete the placeholder text **Excel Worksheet Here** but *not* the ¶ mark following Here

3. Click **Insert** on the menu bar, then click **Object**
   You use the Object dialog box to create a new object using the tools of a program other than Word or to insert an object created in another program.

4. Click the **Create from File tab**, click the **Browse button**, navigate to the drive and folder where your Project Files are located, click **WD K-2.xls**, then click **Insert**
   Figure K-2 shows that the Link to file check box is blank because you want to create an embedded object.

5. Click **OK**
   The Excel worksheet is inserted as an embedded object in Word.

6. Double-click the embedded worksheet object
   You work within the Excel object window, using the Excel toolbars, to format the cells or change the data in the Excel worksheet object.

7. Click the **value** in cell B3 as shown in Figure K-3, type **50**, click the **value** in cell B8, then click the **Bold button** B on the Excel Formatting toolbar
   The total number of customers shown in cell B8 increases by 26 from 1406 to 1432.

8. Click to the right of the embedded Excel worksheet object
   The Excel toolbars close and the Word toolbars appear.

9. Click the worksheet object again to select it, click the **Center button** ≡ on the Formatting toolbar, click the **Outside Border button** ▢ on the Formatting toolbar, click below the worksheet object, then save the document
   The modified embedded Excel worksheet object appears in the Word document, as shown in Figure K-4.

FIGURE K-2: Object dialog box

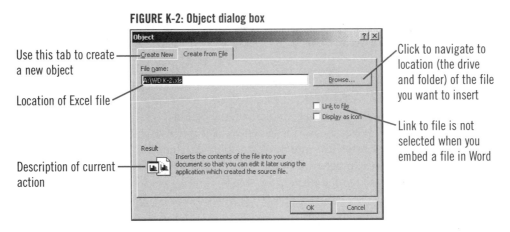

Use this tab to create a new object

Location of Excel file

Description of current action

Click to navigate to location (the drive and folder) of the file you want to insert

Link to file is not selected when you embed a file in Word

FIGURE K-3: Editing the embedded worksheet object

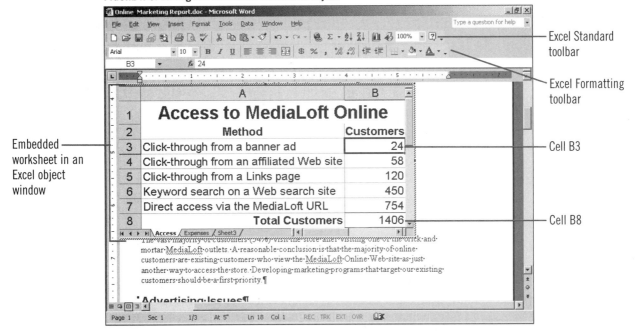

Embedded worksheet in an Excel object window

Excel Standard toolbar

Excel Formatting toolbar

Cell B3

Cell B8

FIGURE K-4: Modified embedded worksheet object

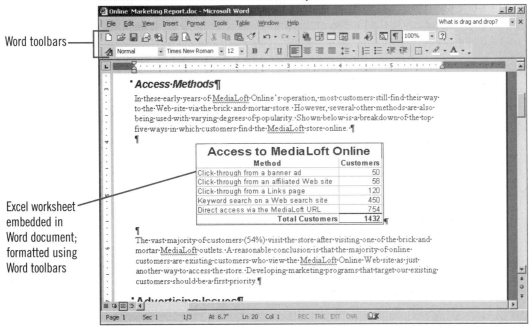

Word toolbars

Excel worksheet embedded in Word document; formatted using Word toolbars

Linking an Excel Chart

You can use the Paste Special command on the Edit menu to integrate data from a source file into a destination file. When you use the Paste Special command, you copy data from the source file in one program and paste the data into the destination file in another program. If you make a change to the object in the source program, the data in the linked object in the destination program is updated. Any changes you make to the data in the destination file are *not* made to the data in the source file. ✎ Nazila uses the Paste Special command to insert a pie chart she created in Excel into her Word report as a linked object.

Steps 1 2 3 4

QuickTip
The pie chart required for the Word document is contained in the Excel file you inserted in the previous lesson.

1. **Press [Ctrl][G], click the Enter bookmark name list arrow, select Resources, click Go To, click Close, then delete the text Excel Pie Chart Here but *not* the ¶ mark following Here**

2. **Click Start on the taskbar, point to Programs, click Microsoft Excel, open the file WD K-2.xls from the drive and folder where your Project Files are located, then save it as Online Marketing Data**
   Two programs are currently open, as indicated by the program buttons on your taskbar.

Trouble?
Be sure a border with sizing handles surrounds the pie chart and all its related components. If only one component is selected, click another area and try again to select the pie chart and all its components.

3. **Click the Expenses tab at the bottom of the Excel worksheet, click the white space in the lower-right corner of the chart area to select the pie chart and all its components, then click the Copy button 🖻 on the Standard toolbar**

4. **Click Online Marketing Report on the taskbar to return to Word, click Edit on the menu bar, then click Paste Special**
   You use the Paste Special dialog box, shown in Figure K-5, to identify whether the data you want to paste will be inserted as an embedded object or a linked object.

5. **Click the Paste link option button, then click OK**
   In the pie chart, Banner Ads account for 2% of suggested advertising expenses.

6. **Click Microsoft Excel Online Marketing Data worksheet on the taskbar to return to Excel, scroll up to see the top of the worksheet, click cell B2, type 5000, then press [Enter]**
   The Banner Ads slice increases to 8%, as shown in Figure K-6.

QuickTip
If you make changes to a source file and the destination file is not automatically updated, right-click the linked object, then click Update Link.

7. **Click Online Marketing Report on the taskbar to return to Word, then verify that the Banner Ads slice now shows 8%**

8. **Right-click the pie chart object, click Format Object, click the Size tab in the Format Object dialog box, select the contents of the Width text box in the Size and rotate area, type 3.8, then click OK**
   You use the Format Object dialog box to format embedded and linked objects.

9. **Click the Center button 🖺 on the Formatting toolbar, click away from the pie chart object to deselect it, compare the pie chart object to Figure K-7, then save the document**

10. **Click Microsoft Excel Online Marketing Data on the taskbar to return to Excel, click File on the menu bar, click Exit, then click Yes to save the updated worksheet**
    The Online Marketing Report in Word is again the active document.

FIGURE K-5: Paste Special dialog box

Use the Paste option button to create an embedded object

Use the Paste link option button to create a linked object

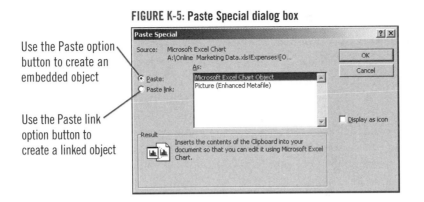

FIGURE K-6: Modified pie chart in Excel

Microsoft Excel title bar

Cell B2

Banner Ads slice increased to 8%

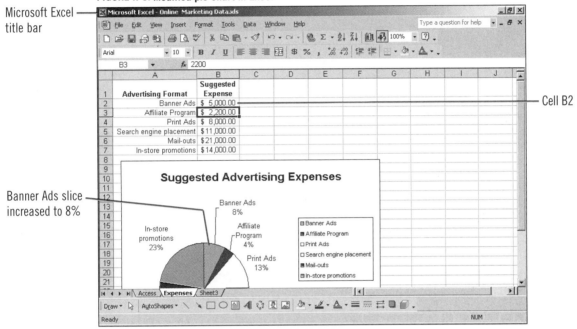

FIGURE K-7: Updated pie chart in Word

Microsoft Word title bar

Banner Ads slice increased to 8%

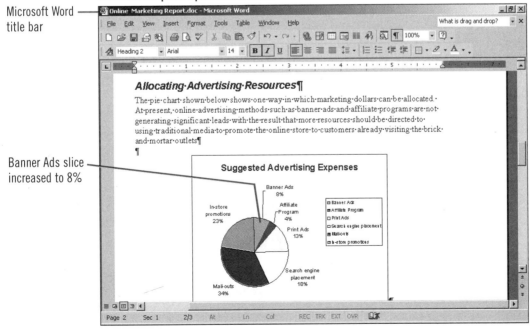

Word 2002

Embedding a PowerPoint Slide

Information can be shared between Word and PowerPoint in a variety of ways. You can use the Paste Special command to insert a slide as a linked or an embedded object into a Word document. You can use Create New to create a PowerPoint slide as an embedded object in Word and then use PowerPoint tools to modify the slide in Word. ✎ Nazila plans to distribute the Online Marketing Report at a conference where she will also deliver a PowerPoint presentation. She decides to use her PowerPoint presentation theme on the title page of her report. She creates a new PowerPoint slide and embeds it in her title page, then she uses PowerPoint tools to format the embedded object.

Steps 1234

1. **Press [Ctrl][Home], then press [Ctrl][Enter]**
   A page break appears. You want to embed a PowerPoint slide on the new blank page.

2. **Press [Ctrl][Home], click Insert on the menu bar, then click Object**
   The types of objects that you can create from new in Word are listed in the Object type list box.

3. **Scroll down, select Microsoft PowerPoint Slide in the Object type list, then click OK**
   A blank PowerPoint slide appears along with the PowerPoint toolbars.

4. **Click in the Click to add title text box, type Marketing Online Report, click in the Click to add subtitle text box, type MediaLoft Online, press [Enter], then type your name**

   > **Trouble?**
   > You may need to scroll to find crayons.pot.

5. **Click the Slide Design button 🗹 on the PowerPoint Formatting toolbar, then select the Crayons.pot design as shown in Figure K-8**

6. **Click the Zoom list arrow on the Standard toolbar, then click Whole Page**
   The document appears in Whole Page view.

7. **Click below the embedded slide object, click the object again to select it if necessary, click Format on the menu bar, click Object, click the Size tab, type 6 in the Width text box in the Size and rotate area, then click OK**

8. **Click Format on the menu bar, click Borders and Shading, click Box on the Borders tab, select the border style and width shown in Figure K-9, then click OK**

9. **Click to the right of the slide object to deselect it, then save the document**
   The embedded PowerPoint slide appears in a Word document, as shown in Figure K-10.

CLUES TO USE

Creating a PowerPoint presentation from a Word outline

When you create a PowerPoint presentation from a Word outline, the Word document is the source file and the PowerPoint document is the destination file. In the Word source file, headings formatted with heading styles are converted to PowerPoint headings in the PowerPoint destination file. To create a PowerPoint presentation from a Word outline, create the outline in Word, click File on the menu bar, point to Send To, then click Microsoft PowerPoint. In a few moments the Word outline appears in PowerPoint, where you can modify it just like any PowerPoint presentation. Any changes you make to the presentation in PowerPoint are *not* reflected in the original Word document.

FIGURE K-8: Selecting the Crayons.pot design

PowerPoint Standard toolbar

Slide Design button on the PowerPoint Formatting toolbar

Available For Use section of the Slide Design task pane

Crayons.pot selected

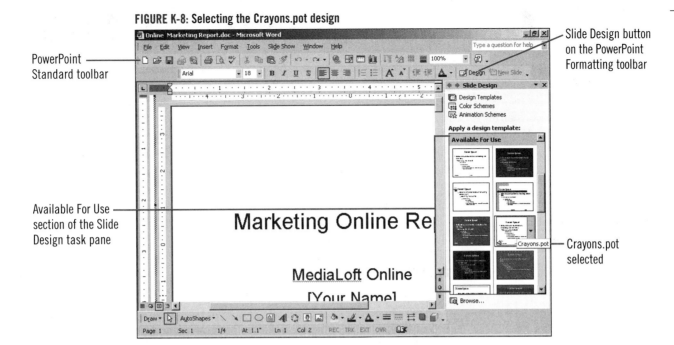

FIGURE K-9: Borders dialog box

Box border selected

Double line border style selected

1½ pt border width selected

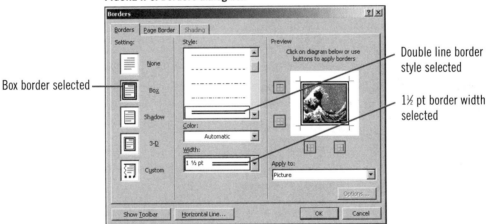

FIGURE K-10: Completed embedded PowerPoint slide object in Word

Word Standard and Formatting toolbars

PowerPoint Crayon.pot design applied to embedded PowerPoint slide using PowerPoint toolbars in Word

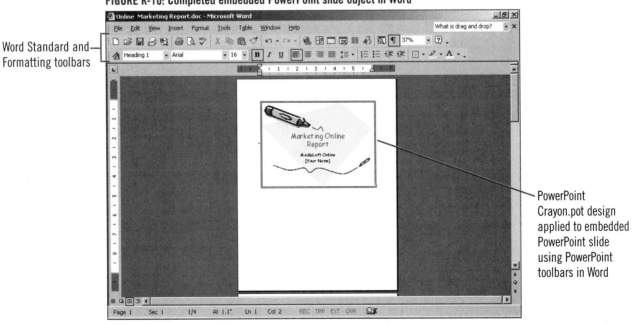

Inserting a Word File

In addition to sharing information with other programs, you can share information between Word documents. When you need the contents of an entire Word document, you can insert an entire Word file rather than copy and paste the document into your current Word document. The formatting of the current document can be applied to the text in the inserted file. When you insert a Word file into a Word document, you cannot return to the original document from the inserted file; instead, the inserted file becomes an integral part of the Word document. ▰▰▰ Nazila previously created a Word document that contains information about methods used to conduct market research. She wants to insert the entire file into her report. She uses the Office Search function to find the Word file containing the information she needs to include in her report.

Steps

1. Click the **Search button** 🔍 on the Standard toolbar
   The Basic Search task pane opens.

2. Type **Demographics** in the Search text box, click the **Results should be list arrow**, verify that a check mark appears in the Anything check box, click the **Search in list arrow**, click the **Expand button** ⊞ next to Everywhere to expand the menu if necessary, then click ⊞ next to My Computer
   By default, the Search function looks for the search text in several locations, including your computer's hard drive and any network drives. You want to search the contents of your Project Files only.

Trouble?

If your Project Files are *not* located in drive A, select the check box next to the drive where your Project Files are located.

3. Click the **check box** next to Everywhere to remove the checkmark if necessary, then click the **check box** next to 3½ (Floppy A:) to insert a checkmark as shown in Figure K-11

4. Click **Search** two times
   The filename for the Word document (WD K-3.doc) that contains the search text "demographics" appears. You can click the filename listed in the Search Results task pane to open a file in its associated program.

5. Close the Search Results task pane, press [**Ctrl**][**G**], select the **Research** bookmark, click **Go To**, then click **Close**

6. Return to 100% view, delete the text **Word File Here** but leave the ¶ mark, click **Insert** on the menu bar, click **File**, navigate to the drive and folder where your Project Files are located if necessary, click **WD K-3.doc**, then click **Insert**
   The contents of the WD K-3.doc file appear in your current document. If you make changes to the text you inserted in this destination file, the changes will *not* be reflected in the WD K-3.doc source file.

7. Scroll up and delete the title **Market Research Methods** including the ¶, select the **Demographics** heading, then apply the **Heading 3 style**

8. Scroll down and apply the **Heading 3 style** to the **Webographics** and **Psychographics** headings

9. Scroll up and insert a page break to the left of the **Demographics** heading, scroll down to view the graphic containing the pie chart, compare the document to Figure K-12, then save the document

FIGURE K-11: Selecting the Search location

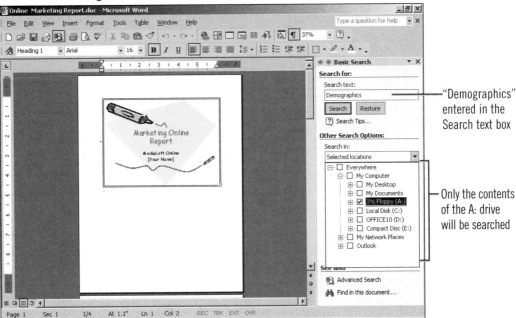

"Demographics" entered in the Search text box

Only the contents of the A: drive will be searched

FIGURE K-12: Word file inserted into a Word document and formatted

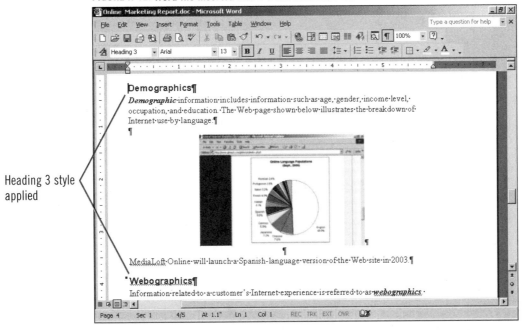

Heading 3 style applied

Conducting a search

Clicking the Search button 🔍 on the Formatting toolbar opens the Basic Search task pane, where you can search for specific text in files located on your computer hard drive, your local network, your Microsoft Outlook mailbox, and your network places. When you conduct a search from the Basic Search task pane, all the files that contain the search text you specified are displayed according to their location.

For example, a search for the text "book club" yields a list of all the files in the locations you specified that contain the text "book club" in the filename, contents, or properties. When you find the file you want, you can open and edit the file in its program, you can create a new document based on the file, you can copy a link to the file to the Office Clipboard, or you can view the file's properties.

Importing a Table from Access

Information can be shared between Access and Word in a variety of ways. The most common method is to use the Access Publish It command, which publishes an Access table into Word. When you publish an Access table, Access launches Word and then copies the Access table in a Word window in Rich Text Format (.rtf). Once the Access table is published to Word, you can use Word's table features to format it. ◆━━ Nazila has created an Access database that contains information related to online survey results. She opens the Access database, then uses the Publish It command in Access to publish one of the Access database tables into Word. Nazila then copies the Word table into the Marketing Online Report and formats it with one of Word's preset Table AutoFormats.

Steps

1. Press **[Ctrl][G]**, select the **Survey** bookmark, go to and then delete the placeholder text **Access Table Here** but *not* the ¶ mark, click **Start** on the taskbar, point to **Programs**, then click **Microsoft Access**

2. Click the **Open button** ☞ on the Standard toolbar in Access, navigate to the drive and folder where your Project Files are located, click **WD K-4.mdb**, then click **Open**
   The database file opens in Microsoft Access. You want to copy the Online Survey table from the database into Word.

3. Click **Online Survey** in the Tables window if necessary as shown in Figure K-13, click the **OfficeLinks list arrow** 🖳▾ on the Standard toolbar, then click **Publish It with Microsoft Word**
   In a few moments, a Word window opens with a new document named Online Survey.rtf, as shown in Figure K-14. The "rtf" extension stands for "Rich Text Format." Notice that the taskbar indicates you have two Word documents open. When you use the Publish It with Microsoft Word command in Access, the Access data is always copied into a new Word window.

4. Move the pointer over the upper-left corner of the table to show ⊞, click ⊞ to select the entire **table**, click **Table** on the menu bar, click **Table AutoFormat**, click **Table List 7**, then click **Apply**
   The Online Survey table is formatted with the Table List 7 style.

5. With the entire table still selected, move the pointer over any **column division** in the gray area of the first row to show ◄║►, then double-click ◄║► to automatically resize the columns to fit the data

6. With the table still selected, click the **Copy button** 🖻 on the Standard toolbar, click **Online Marketing Report** on the taskbar, then click the **Paste button** 🖺 on the Standard toolbar
   The Word table is copied into your Word document. The Word table is just that—a Word table; it is *not* an embedded object or a linked object.

QuickTip

If the gridlines on your table are *not* visible, click Table, Show Gridlines.

7. Scroll up to see the first row of the table, click ⊞ to select the entire table, click the **Center button** ▤ on the Formatting toolbar, then click away from the table to deselect it
   Figure K-15 shows the formatted table in Word.

8. Save the Word Online Marketing Report document, click **Online Survey.rtf** on the taskbar, then close the document without saving it
   You don't need to save the Online Survey.rtf file because you've already copied the table.

9. Click **Microsoft Access** on the taskbar, click **File** on the menu bar, then click **Exit**
   The Online Marketing Report is the active document.

FIGURE K-13: Online Survey table selected in Access

Open button

Tables selected

Tables window

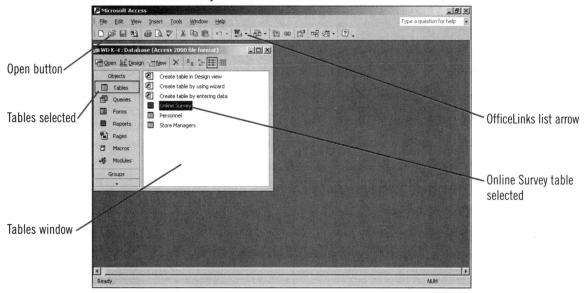

OfficeLinks list arrow

Online Survey table selected

FIGURE K-14: Online Survey.rtf file published in Word

Word document

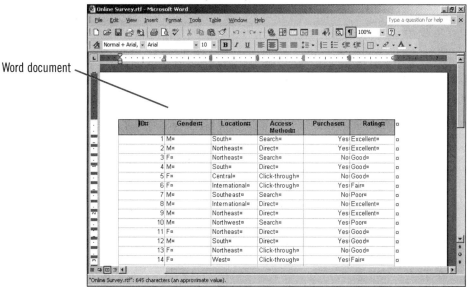

FIGURE K-15: Access table formatted and copied to Word

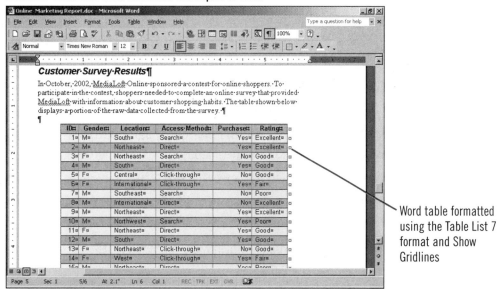

Word table formatted using the Table List 7 format and Show Gridlines

Managing Document Links

When you create a document that contains linked objects, you must include all source files when you copy the document to a new location, such as a floppy disk, or when you e-mail the document to a colleague. If you do *not* include source files, you (or your colleague) will receive error messages when trying to open the destination file. If you do *not* want to include source files when you move or e-mail a document containing links, then you should break the links before moving or e-mailing the document. After you break the links, the Update Links command cannot be used to update information in your destination file. Any changes you make to the source files after breaking the links will *not* be reflected in the destination file. The objects in the destination file will appear as they do at the time the links are broken. ✎ Nazila wants to distribute the Word report to all the MediaLoft store managers. She keeps a copy of the original report with the links intact, then saves the report with a new name and breaks the links.

Steps

1. Click **File** on the menu bar, click **Save As**, type **Online Marketing Report_Managers**, then click **Save**
   Now you can break the link you created between the Excel pie chart in the Word destination file and the Excel pie chart in the Excel source file.

2. Click **Edit** on the menu bar, then click **Links**
   The Links dialog box opens, as shown in Figure K-16. One source file is listed—the Excel file called "Online Marketing Data." You can use the Links dialog box to update links, open source files, change source files, and break existing links.

3. With the **Excel file** selected, click **Break Link**
   A message appears asking if you are sure you want to break the selected link.

4. Click **Yes**
   The link between the Excel source file and the pie chart in the Word destination file is broken. Now if you make a change to the pie chart in the Excel source file, the pie chart in Word will *not* change.

5. Scroll up until the Suggested Advertising Expenses pie chart is visible, then double-click the **pie chart**
   The Format Picture dialog box opens. When you broke the link to the source file, Word converted the pie chart from a linked object to a picture object. You can format the picture object using the Format Picture dialog box, but you cannot change the content of the pie chart.

6. Click **Cancel**, then click the **Print Preview button** 🔍 to view the document in the Print Preview screen

7. In Print Preview, click the **Multiple Pages button** ▦ on the toolbar, select **2 × 3 pages**, then compare the six pages of the report to Figure K-17

8. Click **Close**, scroll down to view the footer, double-click **[Your Name]** in the footer on any page in the report, type your name, then click **Close** on the Header and Footer toolbar to return to the document

9. Save the document, print a copy, then close it

FIGURE K-16: Links dialog box

Excel file ——

Source information for the selected link; information changes to reflect link selected in list

Break Link button

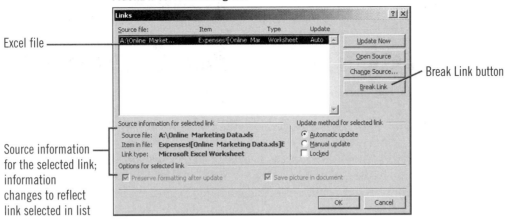

FIGURE K-17: Completed report in Print Preview

Multiple Pages button

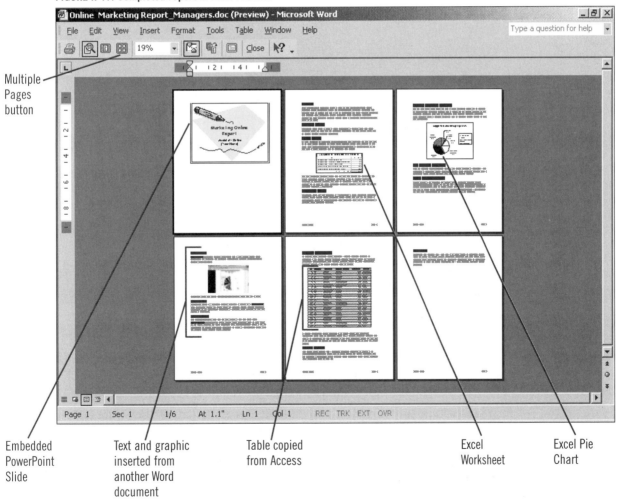

Embedded PowerPoint Slide

Text and graphic inserted from another Word document

Table copied from Access

Excel Worksheet

Excel Pie Chart

Merging with an Access Data Source

Many businesses store the names and addresses of contacts, employees, and customers in an Access database. You can merge information contained in an Access database with a letter, a sheet of labels, or any merge document that you've created in Word. The data you merge with the destination file is the **data source**. When you use an existing database as your data source, you save time because you do *not* need to create a new data source in Word. ➤ Nazila wants to mail a printed copy of the Online Marketing Report to all the MediaLoft store managers. She creates a cover letter to accompany the report and then merges the form letter with the names and addresses of the MediaLoft store managers, which are stored in an Access database.

Steps

1. Open the file **WD K-5.doc** from the drive and folder where your Project Files are located, save it as **Online Marketing Cover Letter**, scroll down the letter, then type your name in place of [Your Name] in the complimentary closing

2. Click **Tools** on the menu bar, point to **Letters and Mailings**, then click **Mail Merge Wizard**

Trouble?

If you have used Mail Merge before, Step 3 of 6 appears in the task pane.

3. If necessary, click **Next** at the bottom of the Mail Merge task pane to accept Letters as the mail merge document, click **Next** to accept the current document, then click **Next** to move to Step 3 of 6

4. Click **Browse**, navigate to the drive and folder where your Project Files are located, select the Access database called **WD K-4.mdb**, then click **Open**
   The Select Table window lists the tables available in the WD K-4 Access database.

5. Click **Store Managers** in the Select Table window, click **OK** to open the Mail Merge Recipients dialog box, then click **OK**

6. Click **Next: Write your letter** to move to Step 4 of 6, click at the **second paragraph mark** below the date in the cover letter, then click **Address block** in the Mail Merge task pane
   A preview of the default address block appears in the Preview area in the Insert Address Block dialog box.

7. Click **OK** to accept the default settings, click to the left of the **second paragraph mark** below the address block, click **Greeting line** in the Mail Merge task pane, select **Joshua** as shown in Figure K-18, then click **OK**
   The field code for the Address block and the field code for the Greeting Line are inserted in your letter.

8. Click **Next: Preview your letters** to move to Step 5 of 6, then click ⏩ to view the letters containing the name and address of each store manager
   You've successfully merged the cover letter with the names and addresses of the store managers. Now you can print just a selection of the letters.

9. Click **Next: Complete the merge** to move to Step 6 of 6, click **Print**, click the **From option button**, enter **1** in the From text box and **2** in the To text box, click **OK**, then click **OK**
   The letters to Harriet Gray and Sandra Barradas print, as shown in Figure K-19.

10. Save the document in Word, close it, then exit Word

FIGURE K-18: Greeting Line dialog box

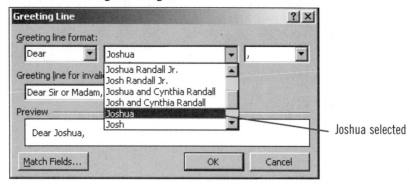

Joshua selected

FIGURE K-19: Merged cover letters

MediaLoft Corporate Headquarters
821 Post Street
San Francisco, CA 94108
(415) 555-2398
www.medialoftonline.com

February 14, 2003

Ms. Harriet Gray
MediaLoft Seattle
621 Broadway E.
Seattle, WA 98102

Dear Harriet,

The success of MediaLoft Online depends on you! The number of online sales in each region is in direct proportion to the marketing efforts of store managers. When a store encourages its customers to purchase from MediaLoft online, everyone benefits!

Enclosed is a document titled *Online Marketing Report* that discusses issues related to the marketing of MediaLoft Online. You will find suggestions for new marketing strategies you can adapt for your customers. As a company, our goal is to increase online sales by 30% within the next two years.

Please call me at (415) 555-2398 if you have any questions about the report or if you have suggestions you'd like to make with relation to marketing MediaLoft Online.

Sincerely,

[Your Name]
Marketing Assistant

Enclosure

MediaLoft Corporate Headquarters
821 Post Street
San Francisco, CA 94108
(415) 555-2398
www.medialoftonline.com

February 14, 2003

Ms. Sandra Barradas
MediaLoft San Diego
7008 Friars Road
San Diego, CA 92108

Dear Sandra,

The success of MediaLoft Online depends on you! The number of online sales in each region is in direct proportion to the marketing efforts of store managers. When a store encourages its customers to purchase from MediaLoft online, everyone benefits!

Enclosed is a document titled *Online Marketing Report* that discusses issues related to the marketing of MediaLoft Online. You will find suggestions for new marketing strategies you can adapt for your customers. As a company, our goal is to increase online sales by 30% within the next two years.

Please call me at (415) 555-2398 if you have any questions about the report or if you have suggestions you'd like to make with relation to marketing MediaLoft Online.

Sincerely,

[Your Name]
Marketing Assistant

Enclosure

Practice

► Concepts Review

Refer to Figure K-20 to answer the following questions.

FIGURE K-20

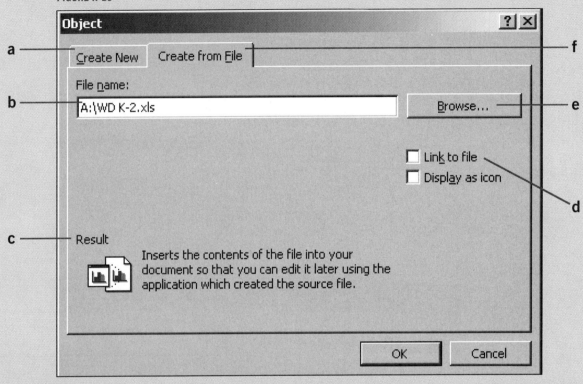

1. Which element do you click to insert a file created in another program?
2. Which element do you click to create an Excel worksheet or PowerPoint slide directly in Word?
3. Which element describes the action being taken?
4. Which element points to the name of the file that will be inserted?
5. Which element do you click to link the inserted file to its source program?
6. Which element do you click to find the file you want to insert?

Match each term with the statement that best describes it.

7. OLE
8. Object
9. DDE
10. Embedded object
11. Source program
12. Destination program

a. Related to the dynamic exchange of data
b. Program to which information is copied
c. Doesn't change if the source document is edited
d. Describes the process of how objects can be inserted in documents
e. Program from which information is copied
f. Provides a means of exchanging information between programs

Select the best answer from the list of choices.

13. What is the destination program?
   a. The program from which the information is copied
   b. The program to which the information is copied
   c. The program in which the information is created
   d. The program containing new information

14. What is the source program?
   a. The program from which the information is copied
   b. The program to which the information is copied
   c. The program containing new information
   d. None of the above

15. What does DDE stand for?
   a. Dedicated Data Exchange
   b. Dynamic Data Extension
   c. Dynamic Data Exchange
   d. Dynamic Data Enhancements

16. Which of the following statements is *not* true about an embedded object?
   a. An embedded object can be created in a source file and inserted into a destination file.
   b. An embedded object becomes part of the destination file.
   c. Changes you make to an embedded object are reflected in the destination file.
   d. Changes you make to an embedded object are reflected in the source file.

17. Which of the following statements is *not* true about a linked object?
   a. A linked object is created in a source file and inserted into a destination file, while maintaining a connection between the two files.
   b. Source files must accompany destination files with linked objects when the destination files are moved.
   c. Changes made to a linked object in the destination file are also reflected in the source file.
   d. The linked object can be updated in the destination file by right-clicking it, then clicking Update Link.

18. Which command can be used to insert a linked object?
   a. Paste
   b. Paste Special
   c. Link Paste
   d. Insert Link

19. Which command do you use in Access to create a Word version of a selected table?
   a. Publish It with Access
   b. Publish It with Microsoft Word
   c. Publish
   d. Insert

▶ Skills Review

1. Embed an Excel worksheet.
   a. Start Word, open the file WD K-6.doc from the drive and folder where your Project Files are located, then save it as **Northern Adventures Report**.
   b. Use the Go To command to find the Categories bookmark, then delete the placeholder text **Insert Excel Worksheet Here** but do *not* delete the ¶ mark.
   c. Click Insert on the menu bar, then click Object.

   d. Click the Create from File tab, then use the Browse feature to insert file WD K-7.xls from the drive and folder where your Project Files are located into the Word document.

   e. Edit the worksheet object. Change the value in cell B5 from 950 to **1200**, then enhance the value in cell B8 with Bold.

   f. In Word, center the worksheet object, apply an outside border, then save the document.

2. **Link an Excel chart**.

   a. Use the Go To command to find the Popularity bookmark, then delete the placeholder text **Insert Excel Chart Here** but *not* the ¶ mark.

   b. Start Microsoft Excel, open the file WD K-7.xls from the drive and folder where your Project Files are located, then save it as **Northern Adventures Data**.

   c. Show the Popularity worksheet, copy the column chart, switch to Word, then use the Paste Special command in Word to paste the column chart as a link in the Word document.

   d. Switch to Excel, scroll up to view the chart used to create the column chart, then change the value in cell C2 from 1800 to **2400**.

   e. Save the worksheet in Excel, then exit Excel.

   f. Notice the Available Tours for Biking is now 2400 in Word.

   g. Reduce the width of the chart in Word to **5"**, center the chart, then save the document.

3. **Embed a PowerPoint slide**.

   a. Insert a blank page at the top of the document, then insert a PowerPoint slide as an embedded object on the new blank page.

   b. Enter the text **Northern Adventures Tours** as the slide title, then enter [your name] as the subtitle.

   c. Apply the Mountain Top.pot slide design to the embedded slide object. (*Hint:* The name of the design appears as a ScreenTip when you move the pointer over a slide design. You might need to scroll down the list of options.)

   d. Switch to Whole Page view, click below the embedded slide object, then modify the width of the object to **6"**.

   e. Save the document.

4. **Insert a Word file**.

   a. Use the Office Search tool to find the Project File that contains the text **Queen Charlotte Islands**.

   b. Close the Search pane, then use the Go To command to find the Tours bookmark in the Northern Adventures Report Word document.

   c. Return to 100% view, remove the placeholder text but not the ¶, then insert the file WDK-8.doc from the drive and folder where your Project Files are located.

   d. Delete the centered title, **Northern Adventures Tours**, then remove the extra ¶ above Sea Kayaking.

   e. Apply the Heading 3 style to the five headings: Sea Kayaking, Hiking, Mountaineering, Wilderness Canoeing, and Mountain Biking.

   f. Save the document.

5. **Import a table from Access**.

   a. Use the Go To command to find the Profile bookmark, then remove the placeholder text **Insert Access Table Here**.

   b. Start Microsoft Access, then open the file WD K-9.mdb from the drive and folder where your Project Files are located.

   c. Publish the Customer Profile table to a new document in Word.

   d. Apply the Table Columns 3 AutoFormat to the table in Word, then automatically reduce the column widths.

   e. Copy the formatted table to the Northern Adventures Report Word document. (*Note:* The copied table will split across two pages. This will be fixed in a later step.)

   f. Save the Northern Adventures Report Word document, switch to and close the Customer Profile.rtf file without saving it, then switch to and exit Access.

6. **Manage document links**.

   a. Open the Links dialog box, then break the link to the Northern Adventures Data Excel file.

   b. Insert a hard page break to the left of the Tour Popularity heading.

c. Insert a page break to the left of the Customer Survey Results heading.

d. Enter your name in the document footer.

e. View all five pages of the document in Print Preview.

f. Save the document, print a copy, then close it.

7. Merge with an Access data source.

a. Open the file WD K-10.doc from the drive and folder where your Project Files are located, save it as **Northern Adventures Cover Letter**, then type your name in place of [Your Name] in the complimentary closing.

b. Open the Mail Merge task pane, then move to Step 3 of 6, if necessary.

c. Select the Access file WD K-9.mdb from the drive and folder where your Project Files are located.

d. Select the Tour Guides table from the Access database, click OK, then click OK to select all the tour guides listed in the Mail Merge Recipients dialog box.

e. Move to Step 4 of 6, insert the Address block at the second paragraph mark below the date, use the default format, then insert the Greeting line with the first name selected to follow **Dear** at the second paragraph mark below the Address block.

f. Move to Step 5 of 6, then preview each letter.

g. Move to Step 6 of 6, print a copy of letters 2 and 3, save and close the document, then exit Word.

► Independent Challenge 1

As a member of the Rainforest Recreation Commission in the Great Bear Rainforest in British Columbia, you are responsible for compiling the minutes of the monthly meetings. You have already written most of the text required for the minutes. Now you need to insert information from two sources. First, you insert a worksheet from an Excel file that shows the monies raised from various fundraising activities and then you insert a Word file that the Director of the Commission has sent you for inclusion in the minutes.

a. Start Word, open the file WD K-11.doc from the drive and folder where your Project Files are located, then save it as **Recreation Commission Minutes**.

b. Go to the Fundraising bookmark, then insert the Project File WD K-12.xls from the drive and folder where your Project Files are located as an embedded object. (*Hint:* Click the Create from File tab in the Insert Object dialog box.)

c. Edit the worksheet object in Word changing the value in cell D5 to **600**, and then enhance the contents of cells A5 and A6 with Bold.

d. Center the worksheet in Word, then enclose it with a border.

e. Go to the end of the document (press [Ctrl][End]), then insert the file WD K-13.doc from the drive and folder where your Project Files are located.

f. Use Format Painter to apply the formatting of the current headings to the text "Director's Report," then delete the paragraph mark above "Director's Report."

g. Type **Prepared by** followed by your name at the bottom of the document.

h. View the completed document in Whole Page view, then print a copy of the document.

i. Save and close the document, then exit Word.

► Independent Challenge 2

You run a summer camp in Grand Teton National Park in Wyoming for teenagers interested in taking on leadership roles at their schools and in their communities. You need to create a report in Word and a presentation in PowerPoint that describes the camp for potential investors. You start by creating an outline of the report in Word, then sending it to PowerPoint as a presentation.

a. Start Word, open a new blank document, then switch to Outline view.

b. Type the outline shown in Figure K-21. Remember to press the [Tab] key to move the insertion point to a lower heading level, then click the Promote button or press [Shift][Tab] to move the insertion point to a higher heading level.

c. Save the outline in Word as **Grand Teton Camp Report**.

d. Send the outline to PowerPoint as a presentation. (*Hint:* Click File on the menu bar, point to Send To, then click Microsoft PowerPoint.)

e. In PowerPoint, apply the Blends.pot design template. (*Hint:* The Blends design template is located in the first column of the second row of the list of design templates in the Available for Use section.)

f. In PowerPoint, click View on the menu bar, click Header and Footer, type your name in the Footer text box, then click Apply to All.

g. Print the presentation as Handouts of six handouts to each page. (*Hint:* Click File on the menu bar, click Print, click the Print what list arrow in the Print dialog box, select Handouts, click the Slides per page list arrow, select 6, then click OK.)

h. Save the PowerPoint presentation as **Grand Teton Camp Presentation**, close it, then exit PowerPoint.

i. In Word, switch to Print Layout view, insert a new page above the first page in the document, then insert an embedded PowerPoint slide formatted with the Blends design. Include **Grand Teton Camp Report** as the title and your name as the subtitle.

j. In Whole Page view, center and resize the slide object to fit the space.

k. In Word, scroll to the Student Enrollment heading toward the end of the document, click after the subheading that begins "The chart shows....", then press [Enter] twice.

l. Insert the Excel file WD K-14.xls from the drive and folder where your Project Files are located as an embedded object.

m. Double-click the worksheet object, then change the value in cell B2 from 1200 to **1400**.

n. Click away from the worksheet object, then insert a page break next to the Student Enrollment heading.

o. View the document in Print Preview, save the document, print a copy, close the document, then exit Word.

FIGURE K-21

Overview
> Mission
> History
> Programs
> Student Enrollment
> Safety

Mission
> To provide an intense learning experience for teens aged 13 to 18
> To develop valuable leadership skills

History
> Established in 1997
> 2500 students have attended
> Consistently high ratings

Programs
> Two programs are available:
>> *Leadership*
>> *Communication Skills*

Student Enrollment
> The chart shows student enrollment since 1999 in the two programs

Safety
> School personnel all have Emergency First Aid certification
> A staff doctor is on 24-hour call
> All activities are monitored for maximum safety

▶ Independent Challenge 3

You own a small Web-based business that sells art materials online. The business is growing—thanks in large part to the help you're receiving from several art stores in your area. The store managers are promoting your Web site in exchange for commissions paid to them when a customer from their target market purchases art materials from your Web site. You've decided to send a memo to the store managers every few months to keep them informed about the growth of the Web site. The memo will include a linked Excel worksheet and an Access table. Once you have completed the memo, you will merge it with a database table containing the names of all the store managers who are helping to promote the Web site.

a. Start Word, open the file WD K-15.doc from the drive and folder where your Project Files are located and save it as **Arts Online Memo**.

b. Start Access, then open the file WD K-16.mdb from the drive and folder where your Project Files are located.

c. Publish the Access table called November 1 Sales in Word.

d. In Word, apply the table AutoFormat of your choice, automatically adjust the column widths, copy the formatted table, then paste it to the second paragraph mark below the second paragraph ("The table illustrated below...") in the Arts Online Memo Word document. Center the table.

e. Start Excel and open the file WD K-17.xls from the drive and folder where your Project Files are located, then save the Excel file as **Arts Online Data**.

f. Scroll down the worksheet, click the pie chart to select it, copy the pie chart, switch to Arts Online Memo in Word, then paste the worksheet as a link at the second paragraph mark below paragraph 3 ("The pie chart below..."). Center and resize the pie chart.

g. In Excel, click cell F2, change the sale generated by the Delaware customer from 52.34 to **120.15**, press [Enter], then save and close the worksheet.

h. Switch to the Arts Online Memo Word document.

i. Scroll to the top of the document, then replace the placeholder text with your name and today's date in the Memo heading.

j. Click after the "To:" in the Memo heading, open the Mail Merge task pane, then select the file WD K-16.mdb from the drive and location where your Project Files are located. Select the Retail Outlets table and all the recipients listed in the table.

k. Insert an Address Block following To: that will contain the recipient's name. (*Hint:* Deselect the Insert postal address check box and the Insert company name check box in the Insert Address Block dialog box.)

l. View the recipients, then print copies of the memos to Tara Winston and Richard Harwood.

m. Save and close the document in Word, close the published table without saving it, then exit all open applications.

Independent Challenge 4

The Internet is a great resource for gathering information about products and services. If you are starting a new business or even if you run an established business, you can always gain new ideas by checking out the ways competing businesses use the Internet to advertise and sell products and services. You decide to evaluate the contents of a Web site that sells a product or service of your choice. You will integrate information from the Web site into your report. To integrate the information, you will use Copy and Paste commands or the drag and drop method to copy excerpts from the Web site you've selected so that you can comment on them.

a. Select a product or service that interests you and that you might even want to sell as part of your own business. For example, if you are interested in mountain biking, you could decide to find a Web site that sells mountain bikes and related equipment.

b. Open your Web browser and conduct a search for a company that sells the product or service that interests you. You can try entering project-related keywords such as "mountain biking," "cycling," and "mountain bikes" and you can try entering generic domain names such as www.bikes.com or www.mountainbiking.com in the Address box of your Web browser.

c. Open the file WD K-18.doc from the drive and folder where your Project Files are located, then save it as **Competition Research**. This document contains questions about the Web site you've selected.

d. As directed in the Competition Research document, copy the URL of the Web site to the space provided at the top of the table.

e. Complete the Competition Research document with the information requested. Note that you will be directed to integrate information from the Web site into your document. You might need to modify the formatting of the copied information.

f. Type your name at the bottom of the document, print a copy, save and close it, then exit Word.

▶ Visual Workshop

In Word, enter the headings and text for the document shown in Figure K-22. Start Excel, open the file WD K-19.xls from the drive and folder where your Project Files are located, then save it as **Cell Phone Data**. Copy the pie chart, then paste it as a link, as shown in Figure K-22. Center the pie chart in Word. In Excel, change the value in cell B2 to **180**, then save the worksheet. In Word, verify that the pie chart appears as shown in Figure K-22. Save the document as **Maryland Arts Cell Phone Report**, type your name under the chart, print a copy, then close the document and exit Word. Close the worksheet in Excel, then exit Excel.

FIGURE K-22

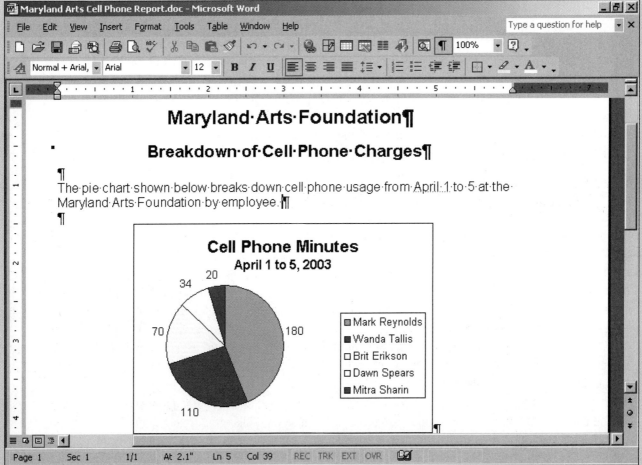

Exploring
Advanced Graphics

Objectives

- ► **Insert drop caps**
- [MOUS] ► **Edit clip art**
- ► **Work with the drawing canvas**
- [MOUS] ► **Use layering options**
- [MOUS] ► **Align, distribute, and rotate graphics**
- [MOUS] ► **Use advanced positioning options**
- [MOUS] ► **Adjust shadow and 3-D settings**
- [MOUS] ► **Insert a watermark and a page border**

Word includes features you can use to create and modify pictures and other objects such as shapes and text boxes. In addition, you can enhance a document with drop caps, a watermark, and a page border. You can use shadow and 3-D effects to add pizzazz to all kinds of graphics objects. You can also create your own pictures in the drawing canvas by modifying clip art pictures and combining them with other pictures and drawn objects. ⬤ The Seattle MediaLoft is excited about holding a series of Mystery Book Nights featuring authors who will sign their books and meet readers. Nazila Sharif in the Marketing Department has offered to provide the Seattle store with sample posters for advertising the events. Nazila has written the text for the posters. Now you will help her enhance the posters with a variety of graphics objects.

Word 2002

Inserting Drop Caps

A **drop cap** is a large dropped character that appears as the first character in a paragraph. By default, a drop cap that you insert from the Format menu is three lines high and appears in its own text box. You can modify the size of a drop cap and its position relative to the paragraph of text. You can also select a font style for the drop cap that differs from the font style of the surrounding text. ▬▬▬▬ The poster Nazila created to advertise the first Mystery Book Night featuring Janice Li includes a description of three of Ms. Li's novels. Nazila decides to make the first letter of each novel title a drop cap. She experiments with different looks for the drop caps, decides on the best drop cap format, and then edits the drop caps so that they all contain the same formatting.

QuickTip

This unit assumes Show/Hide ¶ is on.

1. **Start Word, open the file WD L-1 from the drive and folder where your Project Files are located, save the file as Mystery Book Night Poster_Janice Li**
   A WordArt object appears at the top of the poster and two clip art pictures (also called clip art objects) appear at the bottom. You will use these pictures in later lessons.

2. **Click in the paragraph that starts with the book title "On the Wharf"**
   Word automatically assigns the drop cap to the first letter of the paragraph containing the insertion point.

QuickTip

If your document is formatted in columns, the In margin option is not available.

3. **Click Format on the menu bar, then click Drop Cap**
   From the Drop Cap dialog box, you can insert a drop cap in the margin or as part of the current paragraph. You also use this dialog box to select a font style for the drop cap and to specify the number of lines to drop.

4. **Click Dropped, click the Font list arrow, select the Comic Sans MS font style, click the Lines to drop down arrow once to reduce the lines to drop to 2 as shown in Figure L-1, then click OK**
   The letter *O* in *On the Wharf* appears as a drop cap in its own text box, as shown in Figure L-2. The drop cap looks good, but you format the next drop cap differently so you can decide which effect you prefer.

5. **Click in the paragraph that begins "Silicon Sleuth," click Format, click Drop Cap, click Dropped, click the Font list arrow, select Comic Sans MS, click the Lines to drop list arrow two times to reduce the lines to drop to 1, then click OK**
   The letter *S* in *Silicon* is a drop cap that drops 1 line. You decide that dropping 1 line is not enough. You format the next drop cap as 2 lines dropped and experiment with the distance from text option.

6. **Click in the paragraph that begins "Dragon Swindle," click Format, click Drop Cap, click Dropped, select the Comic Sans MS font, select 2 for the lines to drop, click the Distance from text up arrow one time to set the distance from the text at 0.1", then click OK**
   The *D* in *Dragon Swindle* is a drop cap and exactly what you want. You modify the other two drop caps.

QuickTip

The black handles that appear around the border indicate that the drop cap is selected.

7. **Click the drop cap O, then click the shaded border**

8. **Right-click the drop cap, click Drop Cap, change the distance from text to 0.1", click OK, then revise the drop cap for Silicon Sleuth to drop 2 lines and appear 0.1" from the text**

9. **Click away from the selected drop cap, then save the document**
   The modified poster appears, as shown in Figure L-3. Notice that a portion of the paragraph mark appears next to each drop cap because the Show/Hide ¶ button on the Standard toolbar is selected. Remember that the ¶ marks do not print.

FIGURE L-1: Drop Cap dialog box

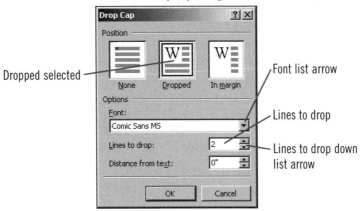

Dropped selected

Font list arrow

Lines to drop

Lines to drop down list arrow

FIGURE L-2: Drop cap inserted

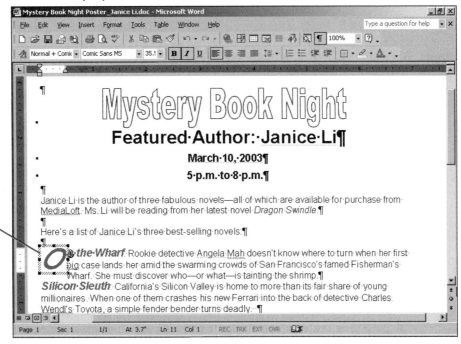

Text box containing the drop cap

FIGURE L-3: Paragraphs with drop caps

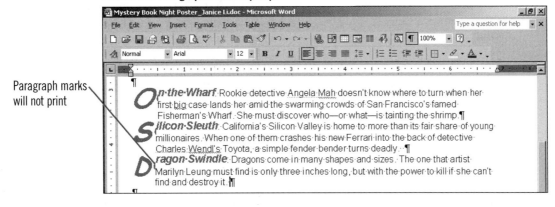

Paragraph marks will not print

Editing Clip Art

The pictures included in the artist profile document are all clip art pictures obtained from the Clip Organizer. When you first import a clip art picture into a document, all of the objects that make up the clip art picture are grouped together into one picture. When you edit a clip art picture, you are really editing the objects that make up the picture. You can use drawing tools to modify clip art pictures. Because clip art pictures are composed of many objects, you work with the Group and Ungroup commands as you edit clip art. Nazila has already inserted two clip art pictures from the Clip Organizer into the poster. She wants to combine them with some drawn objects to create a new picture. She starts by modifying the picture of the Golden Gate Bridge.

Steps

1. Scroll to the bottom of the poster, right-click the picture of the **bridge**, then click **Edit Picture**

   The picture is contained in a drawing canvas. A shaded border encloses the edge of the drawing canvas. The **drawing canvas** is an area upon which you can draw multiple shapes and insert clip art. The drawing canvas appears automatically when you edit a clip art picture.

QuickTip

Remember that you can click Edit, then click Undo if you want to undo your last action.

2. Click the **blue shape** that represents the sky as shown in Figure L-4, then press **[Delete]**

   The blue sky is removed.

3. Right-click the **border** of the drawing canvas, click **Show Drawing Canvas Toolbar** if necessary, click the **Expand Drawing button** ❏ on the Drawing Canvas toolbar **three** times, then scroll as needed to view the entire drawing canvas

   Each time you click ❏, the drawing canvas enlarges, creating more white space around the picture.

4. Click **View** on the menu bar, point to **Toolbars**, click **Drawing**, then click the **Select Objects button** ❏ on the Drawing toolbar

5. Point ❏ at the upper-left corner of the drawing canvas, then click and drag ❏ to select all the objects that make up the bridge as shown in Figure L-5

6. Click **Draw** on the Drawing toolbar to open the Draw menu, then click **Group**

   The Group command combines all the objects that make up the bridge into one object that you can move and size easily.

QuickTip

You clear the Lock aspect ratio check box when you want to specify both a height and a width that are not necessarily proportional. You select the Lock aspect ratio check box when you want to keep the correct proportions of the object once you've changed the object's height or width.

7. With the **bridge** still selected, click the right mouse button, click **Format Object**, click the **Size tab**, make sure the **Lock aspect ratio check box** is clear, enter **2.5** in the Height text box, enter **4** in the Width text box, then click **OK**

   The bridge is resized. Notice that the area under the bridge consists of several objects: one blue-green object that represents water and two black objects that represent shadows.

8. Right-click the **bridge**, point to **Grouping**, click **Ungroup**, click outside the drawing canvas to deselect all the objects, click just the **water object** (the blue-green colored object below the bridge) to select it, then press **[Delete]**

   The water object beneath the bridge is deleted, leaving only the shadow effect.

9. Click ❏ on the Drawing toolbar, drag ❏ to select all the objects in the drawing canvas again, click **Draw**, click **Regroup**, click ❏ to deselect it, then save the document

   The bridge picture appears, as shown in Figure L-6. While you can spend many hours using the tools on the Drawing toolbar to modify a clip art picture, the key concept is that every clip art picture is composed of two or more drawn objects—all of which can be modified or removed.

FIGURE L-4: Sky object selected

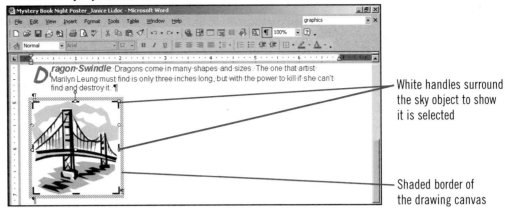

White handles surround the sky object to show it is selected

Shaded border of the drawing canvas

FIGURE L-5: Selecting the bridge objects

Expand Drawing button

Select Objects button

Draw button

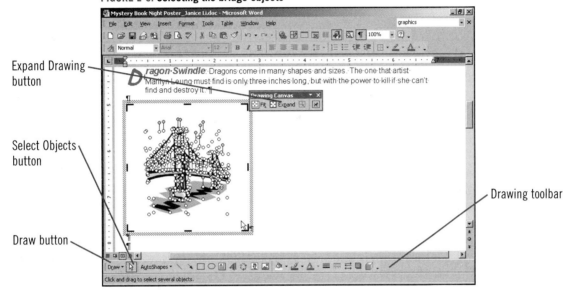

Drawing toolbar

FIGURE L-6: Modified bridge picture

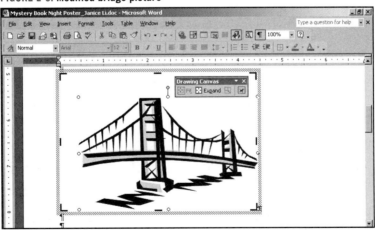

Converting clip art pictures

You can use two methods to convert a clip art picture into a drawing object. First, you can right-click a clip art picture and select Edit Picture from the menu. You used this method to convert the clip art picture of the bridge into a clip art object. Second, you can change a clip art picture from an inline graphic to a floating graphic. In the next lesson you will use this second method to convert a clip art picture of a dragon into a clip art object that you can ungroup and modify.

Working with the Drawing Canvas

The drawing canvas appears when you right-click a clip art picture and select Edit Picture or when you draw an AutoShape. You can add new objects such as clip art pictures or shapes you draw yourself to an existing drawing canvas. You also can change the size of the drawing canvas, move it anywhere in the document, and format it with an attractive fill color and border, just as you would any graphics object. When you move the drawing canvas, all the pictures and objects contained within it also move. Nazila wants to include a picture of a dragon next to the Golden Gate Bridge, draw a lightning bolt shape, and change the size and fill color of the drawing canvas.

Steps

1. With the bridge picture still selected, click the **Expand Drawing button** ▣ on the Drawing Canvas toolbar **four** times, then drag the bridge picture down and to the lower-left corner of the drawing canvas

2. Scroll down, click the **dragon** to select it, right-click the **dragon**, click **Format Picture**, click the **Layout tab** in the Format Picture dialog box, click the **Square** wrapping style, then click **OK**

3. Click the **Zoom Control list arrow** on the Standard toolbar, click **Two pages**, drag the **dragon** onto the bridge, click the **Zoom Control list arrow** and select **Page Width**, then position the bridge and dragon as shown in Figure L-7

4. Make sure the dragon picture is selected, click the **More Brightness button** ☀ on the Picture toolbar **two** times, then click a blank area in the drawing canvas to deselect the dragon
You can add objects that you draw yourself to the drawing canvas.

5. Click the **AutoShapes button** AutoShapes ▾ on the Drawing toolbar, point to **Basic Shapes**, select the **Lightning Bolt** shape, then draw a lightning bolt that appears as shown in Figure L-8

6. Right-click the **lightning bolt**, click **Format AutoShape**, click the **Size tab**, be sure the Lock aspect ratio check box is clear, change the Height to **1"** and the Width to **0.8"**, then click **OK**

7. With the **lightning bolt** selected, click the **Fill Color button list arrow** ▣ ▾ on the Drawing toolbar, click **Light Yellow** in the bottom row, position the lightning bolt relative to the bridge as shown in Figure L-9, then click a blank area of the drawing canvas

8. Right-click the **border** of the drawing canvas, click **Format Drawing Canvas**, click the **Colors and Lines tab** in the Format Drawing Canvas dialog box, click the **Color list arrow** in the Fill section, then click **Fill Effects**

9. In the Gradient tab, click the **Preset Option button**, click the **Preset colors list arrow**, select **Daybreak**, click the **upper-left square** in the Variants section, click **OK** to exit the Fill Effects dialog box, click **OK** to exit the Format Drawing Canvas dialog box, then save the document
The picture appears in the poster, as shown in Figure L-10.

FIGURE L-7: Dragon and bridge pictures positioned

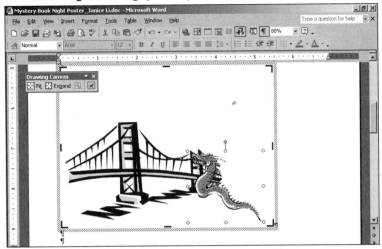

FIGURE L-8: Lightning bolt drawn

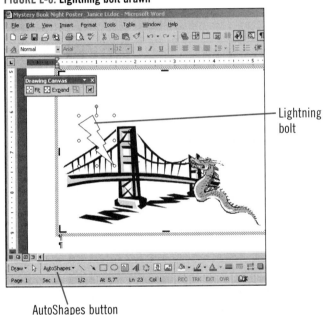

Lightning bolt

AutoShapes button

FIGURE L-9: Lightning bolt sized and positioned

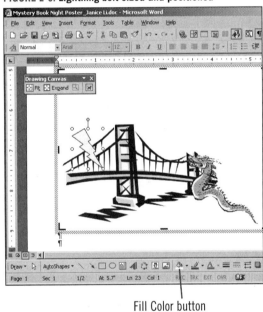

Fill Color button

FIGURE L-10: Formatted drawing canvas

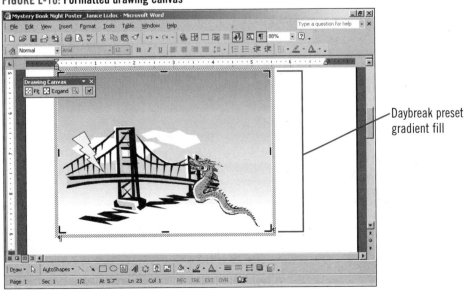

Daybreak preset gradient fill

EXPLORING ADVANCED GRAPHICS

Using Layering Options

The Draw menu includes the Order command, which in turn includes several options for specifying how objects should appear in relation to each other. For example, you can choose to show one object partially on top of another object. By using layering commands in combination with the group and ungroup commands, you can achieve some interesting effects. The layering options available in Word are explained in Table L-1. ✎ Nazila wants the lightning bolt to strike between the two suspension cables of the bridge and the dragon to slither up behind the bridge roadbed. Her first task is to use the Ungroup command to separate the bridge into its various objects.

Steps 1 2 3 4

1. Click the **bridge** to select it, click **Draw** on the Drawing toolbar, click **Ungroup**, then click a blank area in the drawing canvas to deselect the bridge objects

2. Click the lower of the two **suspension cables** as shown in Figure L-11 to select it
   You want this lower cable to appear in front of the lightning bolt.

3. Click **Draw** on the Drawing toolbar, point to **Order**, then click **Bring to Front**
   The lightning bolt appears to be striking between the suspension cables.

4. Click the **Zoom Control list arrow** on the Standard toolbar, click **200%**, then scroll down to view the bridge roadbed
   The bridge roadbed consists of three objects—two black objects, which are the black curved lines, and one wide brown object, which is the area between the two black lines. You want all three of these objects to appear in front of the dragon.

5. Click a blank area in the drawing canvas to deselect the suspension bridge, press and hold [**Ctrl**], then click the roadbed objects—the **top black object**, the **brown object**, and the **bottom black object**
   Figure L-12 shows the objects that make up the roadbed selected.

6. Click **Draw**, point to **Order**, click **Bring to Front**, then scroll to the right
   Notice that the dragon appears to slither up behind the bridge roadbed.

7. Click the **Zoom Control list arrow**, click **100%**, then use your pointer to position the dragon as shown in Figure L-13

8. Click the **Fit Drawing to Contents button** 🖾 on the Drawing Canvas toolbar, then save the document
   The contents of the drawing canvas now fit the drawing canvas.

TABLE L-1 Layering options in Word

command	function	command	function
Bring to Front	Places the object in front of all other objects	Send Backward	Moves the object backward one layer at a time
Send to Back	Places the object behind all other objects	Bring in Front of Text	Moves the object on top of text
Bring Forward	Moves the object forward one layer at a time; use to show an object overlapping one object and then being overlapped by another object	Send Behind Text	Moves the object behind text; often used to show a lightly shaded picture behind relevant text

FIGURE L-11: Lower suspension cable selected

Handles appear only around the lower suspension cable

Click here to select the correct cable

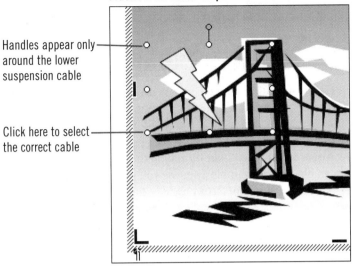

FIGURE L-12: Roadbed objects selected

Three sets of sizing handles are visible and indicate that each of the three objects that make up the bridge roadbed are selected

FIGURE L-13: Dragon positioned

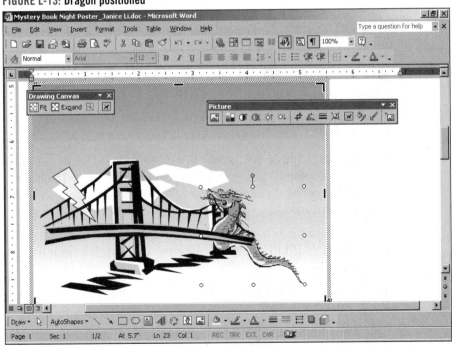

EXPLORING ADVANCED GRAPHICS

Aligning, Distributing, and Rotating Graphics

The Align and Distribute option on the Draw menu includes commands you can use to change the relative positioning of two or more objects. For example, you can use the Left Align command to align several drawn objects along their left sides. You can use the Distribute Vertically or the Distribute Horizontally command to display three or more objects so that the same amount of space appears between each object. The Rotate option on the Draw menu includes commands you can use to rotate or flip an object. For example, suppose you insert a clip art picture of a cat stalking to the right. You can use the Flip Horizontal command to flip the cat so that it stalks to the left, or you can use the Rotate option to make the cat stalk uphill or downhill. 🖉 Nazila wants to include a series of stars that are aligned and distributed vertically above the dragon along the right side of the drawing canvas. She also wants to rotate the dragon by 15 degrees.

Steps

1. Click the **AutoShapes button** AutoShapes ▼ on the Drawing toolbar, point to **Stars and Banners**, click **5-Point Star**, then draw a star similar to the star shown in Figure L-14

2. With the star selected, click the **Fill Color button list arrow** ◇▼ on the Drawing toolbar, select **Red**, click the **Line Color button list arrow** ✐▼ on the Drawing toolbar, then click **No Line**
   The star is filled with the color red and is no longer outlined in black.

3. Right-click the **star**, click **Format AutoShape**, click the **Size tab**, click the **Lock aspect ratio check box** to select it, set the Height at **0.3"**, press **[Tab]** to set the Width automatically, then click **OK** to exit the Format AutoShape dialog box
   By selecting the Lock aspect ratio check box, you make sure that the Width is calculated in proportion to the Height you enter (or vice versa).

4. Drag the **star** to the left about ½" so it appears above the dragon's head, press **[Ctrl][C]**, press **[Ctrl][V] four** times, then drag the **bottom star** down so that it appears just above the dragon's tail
   Five red stars are visible.

5. Press and hold **[Ctrl]**, then click each **star** to select all five stars, click **Draw** on the Drawing toolbar, point to **Align or Distribute**, then click **Align Right**
   The five stars are aligned along the right side of the drawing canvas.

6. With all five stars still selected, click **Draw**, point to **Align or Distribute**, then click **Distribute Vertically**
   The aligned and distributed stars appear, as shown in Figure L-15. The Distribute Vertically command places the stars so that the distance between each star is equal.

7. Click the **dragon** to select it, click **Draw**, point to **Rotate or Flip**, then click **Free Rotate**
   Green dots appear at each corner of the selected picture. To use Free Rotate, you drag a green dot to rotate the object either left or right. You can also constrain the rotation to 15-degree increments by pressing and holding the Shift key as you move the pointer up or down.

8. Press and hold **[Shift]**, point 🖑 over the **upper-left green dot**, then drag ⟳ to the left (down) once
   The dragon is rotated 15 degrees to the left, as shown in Figure L-16. When you rotate an object, you see a shadow of the object as it rotates to the new position.

9. Click away from the dragon to deselect it, then save the document

FIGURE L-14: Star drawn in the drawing canvas

When Show/Hide ¶ is active, the paragraph marks show in the document, but do not print

5-point star

FIGURE L-15: Aligned and distributed stars

FIGURE L-16: Rotated dragon

Rotate handle

Using Advanced Positioning Options

Word offers a variety of ways to position objects. You can use your pointer to position an object anywhere on the page in a Word document, including on the drawing canvas or you can use the Nudge command on the Draw menu to move an object by very small increments. You can also use the Layout tab in the Format Object dialog box to position an object precisely in relation to the page, margin, column, paragraph, or line in a Word document. Finally, you can use the Advanced Layout dialog box in the Format Drawing Canvas dialog box to position an object precisely on the drawing canvas.   Nazila wants to group the stars into one object and then position it precisely in relation to the upper-right corner of the drawing canvas. She then uses the Nudge option to position the dragon in relation to the bridge.

Steps

1. Use **[Ctrl]** to select each of the **five stars**, click **Draw**, then click **Group**
You group the stars into one object so that you can position the group of stars easily.

2. Right-click the grouped **object**, click **Format Object**, then click the **Layout tab**
The Layout tab in the Format Object dialog box appears. In this dialog box you can set an exact horizontal and vertical position for the selected object in relation to either the upper-left corner or the center of the drawing canvas.

> **Trouble?**
> If you see Format Picture instead of Format Object, close the menu and right-click the grouped object again.

3. Set the Horizontal position at **4.54**, set the Vertical position at **0.07** as shown in Figure L-17, then click **OK**
The star object is positioned precisely, based on the measurements you entered.

> **Trouble?**
> If you get a warning message regarding the measurements, click OK, then enter the maximum measurement allowed.

4. Click the **dragon** to select it, click **Draw**, point to **Nudge**, then click **Left**
The dragon moves 1 pixel to the left. The Nudge command moves an object one pixel at a time. You can also use the arrow keys to nudge an object up, down, left, or right.

5. With the dragon still selected, use the **arrow keys** to move it up, down, left, or right so that its final position appears similar to Figure L-18

6. Right-click the **border** of the drawing canvas, click **Format Drawing Canvas**, click the **Square** wrapping style, then click the **Center Option button** in the Horizontal alignment section
You select the Square wrapping style to transform the drawing canvas from an inline graphic to a floating graphic. Now you can apply advanced positioning options.

7. Click **Advanced**
The Advanced Layout dialog box opens.

8. Be sure the **Absolute Position Option button** in the Vertical section of the dialog box is selected, enter **6** in the text box, click the **below list arrow**, click **Page**, click **OK** to exit the Advanced Layout dialog box, then click **OK**
The Format Drawing Canvas dialog box closes. The drawing canvas is centered horizontally and positioned exactly six inches from the top of the page. You can use the Click and Type feature to position the insertion point below the drawing canvas.

9. Double-click below the drawing canvas, click the **Center button** 🔳 if necessary, then type and format the address of the Seattle MediaLoft as shown in Figure L-19

10. Save the document

FIGURE L-17: **Position of the stars within the diagram**

Refers to the position of the object with relation to a diagram or a drawing canvas

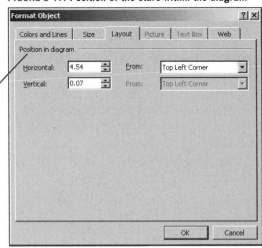

FIGURE L-18: **Dragon nudged into position**

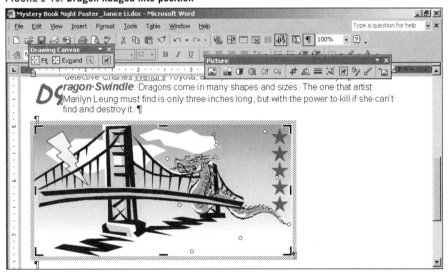

FIGURE L-19: **Address information entered**

Enhance the address with italic and enhance Seattle MediaLoft with bold and italic

Address text centered

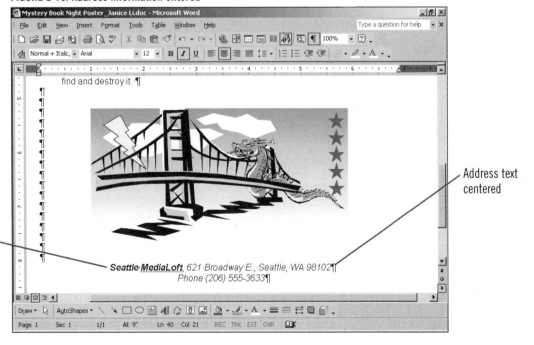

Adjusting Shadow and 3-D Settings

Word 2002

The Drawing toolbar includes the Shadow and 3-D buttons that you can use to enhance a graphics object. You can change a flat object to a 3-D object and you can add a shadow effect to an object. You can also modify the appearance of the shadow and 3-D effects you apply. ➤ The poster includes a WordArt object that Nazila wants to enhance with a textured fill and a 3-D effect. She also wants to add a blue shadow to the lightning bolt in the drawing canvas.

Steps

Trouble?

Click toward the top of the B in "Book" to select the WordArt object.

1. Scroll to the top of the document, then click the **WordArt object** to select it
   When you select the WordArt object, the WordArt toolbar appears. If the WordArt toolbar does not appear, right-click the WordArt object, then click Show WordArt Toolbar.

2. Click the **Format WordArt button** 🎨 on the WordArt toolbar, click the **Colors and Lines tab**, click the **Color list arrow** in the Fill section, click **Fill Effects**, click the **Texture tab**, select **Bouquet** as shown in Figure L-20, click **OK** to exit the Fill Effects dialog box, then click **OK**
   The Format WordArt dialog box closes and the WordArt object is formatted with the Bouquet texture.

QuickTip

As you move the pointer over the 3-D styles, the style name appears in a ScreenTip.

3. With the WordArt object selected, click the **3-D Style button** 🔲 on the Drawing toolbar, then select **3-D Style 2**

4. With the WordArt object still selected, click 🔲, then click **3-D Settings**
   The 3-D Settings toolbar appears. Table L-2 describes the buttons on the 3-D Settings toolbar. These buttons are used to change the appearance of the 3-D effect. For example, you can change the depth and lighting of the 3-D effect.

5. Click the **Depth button** 🔲 on the 3-D Settings toolbar, select **36.00 pt** in the text box, type **18**, press **[Enter]**, click the **Lighting button** 🔲 on the 3-D Settings toolbar, then click the **Lighting Direction button** in the lower-left corner
   The WordArt is modified based on the style, depth, and shadow settings you set.

6. Scroll down to view the drawing canvas, click the **lightning bolt** in the drawing canvas to select it, click the **Shadow Style button** 🔲 on the Drawing toolbar, then click **Shadow Style 1**
   One way to enhance a shadow effect is to change the shadow color.

7. Click 🔲, click **Shadow Settings**, click the **Shadow Color list arrow** 🔲, verify that **Semitransparent Shadow** is selected, then select **Dark Blue**
   Your poster is completed.

Trouble?

If necessary, reduce the font size of the text under the drawing canvas so the poster fits on one page.

8. Close the Shadow Settings, 3-D Settings, and Drawing Canvas toolbars, double-click below the address at the bottom of the document, type **Contact [Your Name] for assistance.**, then click the **Print Preview button** 🔲 on the Standard toolbar
   The completed poster appears, as shown in Figure L-21.

9. Close Print Preview, save the document, print a copy, then close the document

FIGURE L-20: Bouquet texture selected

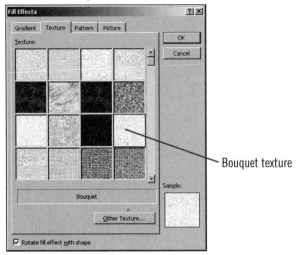

Bouquet texture

FIGURE L-21: Completed poster

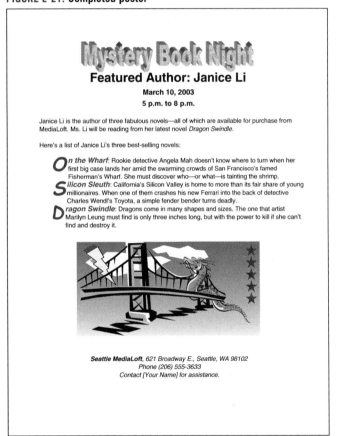

TABLE L-2: The 3-D settings toolbar

button	use to	button	use to
	Turn the 3-D effect on or off		Change the depth of the 3-D effect
	Tilt the 3-D effect down		Change the direction of the 3-D effect
	Tilt the 3-D effect up		Select a lighting direction
	Tilt the 3-D effect to the left		Select a surface texture for the 3-D effect
	Tilt the 3-D effect to the right		Select a 3-D color

Inserting a Watermark and a Page Border

You can enhance a document with a watermark and a page border. A **watermark** is a picture or other type of graphics object that appears lightly shaded behind text in a document. For example, you could include a company logo as a watermark on every page of a company report, or you could create "Confidential" as a WordArt object that appears in a very light gray behind the text of an important letter or memo. A **page border** encloses one or more pages of a document. You can select a box border in a variety of line styles and colors, or you can insert one of Word's preset art borders. ◀━━ Nazila has promised to supply the Seattle MediaLoft with two poster designs. The other poster design she created advertises Lance Rose's appearance at the Mystery Book Night hosted by the Seattle MediaLoft. To finish the poster, Nazila needs to add a watermark and a page border.

1. Open the file **WD L-2** from the drive and folder where your Project Files are located, then save it as **Mystery Book Night Poster_Lance Rose**

The picture that you want to make into a watermark appears at the bottom of the document.

Trouble?
If the Picture toolbar is not visible, click View, point to Toolbars, then click Picture.

2. Scroll to the bottom of the document, then click the picture of the **quill and ink pot** to select it

The tools you need to turn the picture into an attractive watermark are included on the Picture toolbar.

3. Click the **Color button** 🖼 on the Picture toolbar, then click **Washout**

The colors of the picture now appear very lightly tinted. You can use the More Brightness, Less Brightness, More Contrast, and Less Contrast buttons on the Picture toolbar to further modify the appearance of the picture. However, you are pleased with the default settings.

4. Click the **Text Wrapping button** 🖼 on the Picture toolbar, then click **Behind Text**

5. Use the **Zoom list arrow** to select **Whole Page**, click the **Format Picture button** 🖼 on the Picture toolbar, click the **Size tab**, click the **Lock aspect ratio button** to clear it, change the Height to **6"** and the Width to **4"**, click **OK**, then use the pointer to position the picture as shown in Figure L-22

The enlarged watermark appears behind the text.

6. Click away from the picture to deselect it, click **Format** on the menu bar, click **Borders and Shading**, then click the **Page Border tab**

In the Page Border tab of the Borders and Shading dialog box you can add a simple box border, a shadow border, or a 3-D border.

7. Click **Box**, scroll down the Style list box, select the **border style** shown in Figure L-23, click the **Color list arrow**, click the **Light Blue color box**, then click **OK**

The poster is ready to print.

Trouble?
If your page border does not print as expected, read the Clues to Use on the next page.

8. Return to **100% view**, type your name in place of [Your Name] at the bottom of the document, click the **Print Preview button** 🖾 on the Standard toolbar, then compare the completed poster to Figure L-24

9. Save the document, print a copy, close the document, then exit Word

FIGURE L-22: **Watermark sized and positioned**

Watermark

FIGURE L-23: **Borders dialog box**

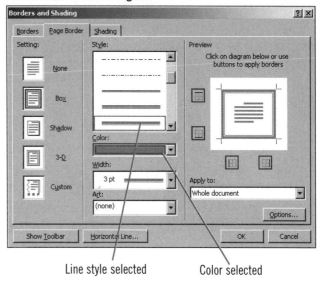

Line style selected   Color selected

FIGURE L-24: **Completed poster**

CLUES TO USE

Printing a page border

Sometimes a document formatted with a page border will not print correctly on certain printers because the page border falls outside the print area recognized by the printer. For example, the bottom border or one of the side borders might not print. To correct this problem, open the Borders and Shading dialog box, click Options on the Page Border tab, then increase the point size of the top, bottom, left, or right margins. Or, you can specify that the border be measured from the text, not from the edge of the page, and set the points to measure from the text. Experiment until you find the settings that work with your printer.

Practice

► Concepts Review

Refer to the pictures in the drawing canvas shown in Figure L-25, then answer the following questions.

FIGURE L-25

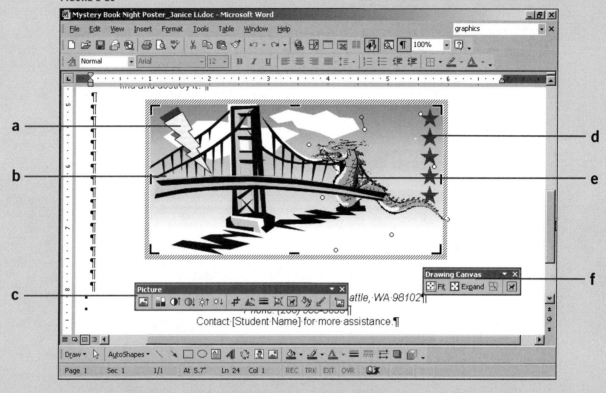

1. Which items are vertically distributed?
2. A layering option was applied to which item?
3. Which item is enhanced with a shadow?
4. Which item is currently selected?
5. Which item contains the tools used to modify a picture?
6. Which item contains the button used to expand the drawing canvas?

Match each term with the statement that best describes it.

7. Drawing canvas
8. Drop cap
9. Ungroup
10. Distribute Vertically
11. Align Left
12. Gradient fill

a. Large single letter that appears at the beginning of a paragraph
b. Color shading that ranges from light to dark in various patterns
c. Evenly spaces three or more objects
d. Used to separate a clip art picture into its component objects
e. Arrange two or more objects along the same plane
f. Enclosed box that contains a variety of graphics objects

Select the best answer from the list of choices.

13. **Which of the following options is *not* available in the Drop Cap dialog box?**
    - **a.** Distance from text
    - **b.** Vertical alignment
    - **c.** Lines to drop
    - **d.** Font style

14. **What is the purpose of the Expand button on the Drawing Canvas toolbar?**
    - **a.** To increase the size of the drawing canvas, but not the contents of the drawing canvas
    - **b.** To increase the size of the drawing canvas and its contents
    - **c.** To increase only the contents of the drawing canvas
    - **d.** To expand the contents to fit the drawing canvas

15. **Which of the following fill effects is *not* available in the Fill Effects dialog box?**
    - **a.** Texture
    - **b.** Gradient
    - **c.** Picture
    - **d.** Color

16. **How do you select two or more objects?**
    - **a.** Press and hold [Ctrl], then click each object in turn.
    - **b.** Click each object in turn.
    - **c.** Press and hold [Alt], then click each object in turn.
    - **d.** Click Edit on the menu bar, then click Select.

17. **Which option from the Draw menu do you select to modify how two or more objects appear in relation to each other?**
    - **a.** Align or Distribute
    - **b.** Nudge
    - **c.** Edit AutoShape
    - **d.** Distribute

18. **How far does a Nudge button move an object?**
    - **a.** 2 pixels
    - **b.** 1 inch
    - **c.** 1 pixel
    - **d.** 10 pixels

19. **Which option in the Color button on the Picture toolbar do you select to turn an object into a watermark?**
    - **a.** Washout
    - **b.** Grayscale
    - **c.** Watermark
    - **d.** More Brightness

▶ Skills Review

1. **Insert a drop cap.**
   a. Start Word. Open the file WD L-3 from the drive and folder where your Project Files are located, then save it as **Story Time Poster_Sally-Lou**.
   b. Click in the first paragraph (begins with the text "Sally-Lou Pearson has been delighting...").
   c. Insert a drop cap that is dropped three lines and uses the Book Antiqua font.
   d. Insert a drop cap at the beginning of the next paragraph that is dropped two lines and uses the Book Antiqua font.
   e. Insert a drop cap at the beginning of the next paragraph that is dropped two lines, uses the Book Antiqua font, and is positioned 0.1" from the text.
   f. Modify the "S" drop cap and the "M" drop cap to match the drop cap inserted in paragraph 3, then save the document.

2. **Edit clip art.**
   a. Scroll to the bottom of the poster, right-click the picture of the Eiffel Tower, then click Edit Picture.
   b. Delete the large cloud shape in the upper-right area of the picture.
   c. Use the Drawing Canvas toolbar to expand the drawing canvas four times.
   d. Use the Select Objects tool on the Drawing toolbar to select all the objects that make up the Eiffel Tower picture.
   e. Group the picture into one object.
   f. With the object selected, open the Format Object dialog box, click the Size tab if necessary, click the Lock aspect ratio check box to select it, then change the Height of the object to 2.5".

g. Ungroup the object, delete the cloud object in the upper-left area of the picture, and then delete the blue sky background.

h. Group all the objects into one picture, then save the document.

3. Work with the drawing canvas.

a. Expand the drawing canvas three times, then drag the Eiffel Tower picture up so that its upper-left sizing handle is even with the upper-left corner of the drawing canvas. (*Note:* If the entire picture does not move, use the Select Objects tool to select and group the picture again.)

b. Use the Zoom list arrow to view Two Pages, click the picture of the bicycle, then change it to an object with the Square wrapping style.

c. Drag the bicycle picture into the drawing canvas, then position the bicycle so the back wheel overlaps the far-right bush in the Eiffel Tower picture and the bicycle seat is above the bush. You don't need to be exact at this stage.

d. Increase the brightness of the bicycle three times.

e. Draw a crescent moon shape that is 0.7" high with the lock aspect ratio check box selected. Position the moon in the sky to the left of the Eiffel Tower.

f. Fill the moon shape with Gold and delete the black outline.

g. Fill the drawing canvas with the Fog preset gradient, using the top-left variant selected. Save the document.

4. Use layering options.

a. Position the bicycle behind the Eiffel Tower picture so that part of the back wheel is hidden.

b. Ungroup the Eiffel Tower picture, then bring to the front the top white line representing a cloud so that it appears in front of the Eiffel Tower.

c. Use the Fit button on the Drawing Canvas toolbar to fit the picture inside the drawing canvas. Save the document.

5. Align, distribute, and rotate graphics.

a. Draw a heart AutoShape that is 0.3" wide and 0.3" in height, then fill it with Rose.

b. Copy the heart twice so that you have a total of three hearts, then move the selected heart near the right edge of the picture.

c. Align the hearts along their bottom edges.

d. Use the Distribute Horizontally feature to distribute the hearts, then position them so that they appear about an inch above the bicycle. You do not have to position them precisely yet.

e. Select the bicycle, then flip it horizontally.

f. Select the bottom cloud, send it behind the bike basket, then save the document.

6. Use advanced positioning options.

a. Group the hearts into one object.

b. Position the grouped hearts in the drawing canvas so that the horizontal position is 2.17" from the upper-left corner and the vertical position is 0.2" from the upper-left corner. (*Note:* If a warning appears, enter the measurements suggested.) Refer to the picture of the completed drawing in Figure L-26.

c. Use the Nudge command to adjust the position of the bike so it appears as shown in Figure L-26.

d. Change the layout of the drawing canvas to select the Square wrapping style and Center horizontal alignment.

e. In the Advanced Layout dialog box, set the Absolute Vertical position of the drawing canvas to 6" below the page.

FIGURE L-26

f. Double-click below the drawing canvas, change the view to 100% if necessary, then type with center alignment the following text:

MediaLoft Houston, 2118 Westheimer Road, Houston, TX 77098

Phone: (281) 555-8233

Contact [Your Name] for assistance.

g. Enhance "MediaLoft Houston" with bold, then save the document.

7. **Adjust Shadow and 3-D settings.**

   a. Click the WordArt object at the top of the document to select it.

   b. Fill the WordArt object with the Water Droplets texture.

   c. Add the 3-D Style 3 to the WordArt object.

   d. Change the 3-D settings so that the depth is 18 points and change the lighting so it comes from the center left.

   e. Scroll down, click the crescent moon in the drawing canvas to select it, then add the Shadow Style 5.

   f. Make the shadow semitransparent and Light Yellow.

   g. Save the document, view it in Print Preview, print a copy, then close the document.

8. **Insert a watermark and a page border.**

   a. Open the file WD L-4 from the drive and folder where your Project Files are located, then save it as **Story Time Poster_Annabelle**.

   b. Click the picture at the top of the document, then use the Color button on the Picture toolbar to change its color to the Washout setting.

   c. Click the More Brightness button twice to further increase the washed out effect.

   d. Change the text wrapping of the picture to Behind Text.

   e. Use the Zoom list arrow to view Whole Page, change the Height of the picture to 5" with the Lock Aspect ratio check box selected so that the Width is calculated automatically.

   f. Center the picture and position it 4" below the top of the page.

   g. Add a Sea Green page border in the 3 pt double line box style.

   h. In 100% view, replace **[Your Name]** at the bottom of the document with your name.

   i. Save the document, print a copy, close the document, then exit Word.

▶ # Independent Challenge 1

You work as a teacher's aide at an elementary school. Your supervisor has asked you to create an attractive picture that includes a variety of elements that children can color, according to the labels. You've already downloaded the clip art pictures you plan to use to create the picture. Now you need to work in the drawing canvas to modify the pictures you've downloaded, draw some AutoShapes, then add some text objects.

   a. Start Word, open the file WD L-5 from the drive and folder where your Project Files are located, and save it as **Learning Colors Picture**.

   b. Edit the picture of the balloons, show the drawing canvas toolbar, then expand the drawing canvas eight times.

   c. Remove the colored shape from each balloon, then group the balloons into one object.

   d. Increase the Height of the balloons to 5" with the Lock aspect ratio check box selected.

   e. Scroll down the page to find the picture of the hat and balloon, edit the picture, then remove all the objects that make up the single balloon.

   f. Expand the drawing canvas containing the hat two times, then group all the objects that make up the hat into one object.

   g. Drag the grouped hat picture into the drawing canvas that contains the three balloons. Position the hat picture in the lower-left corner of the drawing canvas, then increase its Height to 3" with the Lock Aspect Ratio button selected so the Width is calculated automatically.

   h. Rotate the hat picture by 15 degrees to the left. (*Hint:* Press and hold [Shift] while dragging a rotate handle to constrain the rotation to 15-degree increments.)

i. Refer to Figure L-27 to complete the picture. Here are the tasks required:

- Add the Sun AutoShape, then use layering options to show the sun just behind the two balloons on the right.
- Position all the objects so they are placed similarly to how they are shown in Figure L-27. Use the pointer, as well as order, rotate, and size commands as needed.
- Add text boxes and draw lines. Type text in the text boxes and format it in 16-pt, Arial, and Bold. (*Note*: You can remove the border around each text box by clicking the Line button, then selecting No Line. Move text boxes as needed to be sure they do not block other parts of the picture.)

j. Click the Fit button to fit the canvas to the objects, then create a page border that is a dark red single line.

k. Change the layout of the drawing canvas to a Square floating graphic, then center the drawing canvas.

l. Use Click and Type to enter **Prepared by** followed by your name centered below the Drawing canvas.

m.View the document in Whole Page view, delete the blank drawing canvas below the picture, save the document, print a copy, close the document, then exit Word.

FIGURE L-27

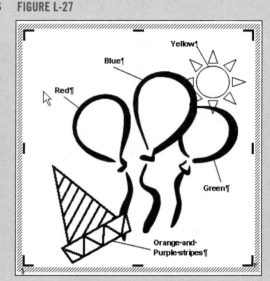

▶ Independent Challenge 2

You have just been hired to create a series of templates for the menus and other documents produced by Carrots & Beans—a new vegetarian café in your neighborhood. Your first task is to create the logo for Carrots & Beans that appears as shown in Figure L-28. Refer to this figure as you work.

FIGURE L-28

a. Start Word. Open a new blank Word document, show the Drawing toolbar, if necessary, click the Insert WordArt button on the Drawing toolbar, select the upper-left WordArt style, then enter the text C & B. Select the Impact font style.

b. Change the WordArt object to a floating graphic with the Square wrapping style and left-aligned, set the Width of the WordArt object to 2" with the Lock aspect ratio button unselected, then fill the object with the Woven Mat texture.

c. Add a semitransparent tan shadow using Shadow Style 1 to the WordArt object.

d. Refer to Figure L-28 to insert and modify the carrot clip art picture. (*Note*: Use the search term "carrot" to find the clip art picture). You need to edit the carrot picture, expand the drawing canvas, group all the objects that make up the picture into one object, then flip the carrot horizontally. You also need to change the Height of the carrot to 0.8" and the Width of the carrot to 1.5".

e. Position the drawing canvas containing the carrot as a right-aligned floating graphic with the Square layout.

f. To insert the horizontal line graphic, double-click below the WordArt object and carrot picture, open the Page Border tab in the Borders and Shading dialog box, click Horizontal Line, then select the middle line style in the first row of the line style selections. (*Note*: If the horizontal line does not extend the full width of the page, be sure you have the same number of paragraph marks as shown in Figure L-28.) Move the drawing canvas as needed to allow the horizontal line to extend the width of the page.

g. Type your name right-aligned at the bottom of the page, save the document as **Carrots and Beans Logo** to the drive and folder where you are storing your Project Files, print a copy, save and close the document, then exit Word.

▶ Independent Challenge 3

You are the owner of a small home-based business. You determine the kinds of products and services you sell. For example, you could operate a small catering business that specializes in company parties, or you could operate a Web site design service for other home-based businesses. You use Word's graphics features to create an attractive flyer to advertise your business.

a. On a piece of paper, plan the contents of your flyer. Your flyer must include four of the following five elements: WordArt object containing the name of the company or a slogan, clip art picture that has been modified in some way, three or more AutoShapes that are aligned and distributed, a formatted drawing canvas containing the modified clip art picture and AutoShapes, along with additional graphics if appropriate, and two or more drop caps used appropriately.

b. Start Word. Open a new blank Word document, show the Drawing toolbar if necessary, then create the text for your flyer. You should include the following information: company name, company address and contact information, including the URL of a Web site and the company e-mail address, and two or three short paragraphs describing the products or services offered. You might want to include some of the information in the form of a bulleted list.

c. Add the graphics objects required. Use Drawing tools as you create and edit the graphics. Experiment with some of the tools you did not use in this unit. Make sure you use at least five of the following Drawing tools: align and distribute; group and ungroup; fill colors, textures, or gradients—use at least one fill effect somewhere in your document; advanced positioning to set the position of an object within the drawing canvas; layering options; rotate; and 3-D and Shadow effect.

d. Enter your name in an appropriate location on your flyer.

e. View the flyer in Whole Page view, then make any final spacing and sizing adjustments to ensure all the text and graphics elements appear attractively on the page.

f. Save your flyer as **[Company Name] Flyer** to the drive and folder where your Project Files are located.

g. Print a copy of the flyer, close the document, then exit Word.

Independent Challenge 4

Many of the Web pages on the World Wide Web are beautifully designed with attractive graphics that entice the Web surfer to explore further. Other Web pages are less well-designed, and sometimes have clashing colors, unattractive graphics, and hard-to-read text. To increase your understanding of the role graphics play in enhancing—or detracting from—the effectiveness of a document, you decide to evaluate design elements on the home pages of two Web sites that sell similar products or services.

a. Open your Web browser and search for two companies that sell a product or service of interest to you. You can try entering product-related keywords, such as "art supplies," "pastels," and "watercolors," and you can try entering generic domain names, such as www.art.com or www.artsupplies.com, in the Address box of your Web browser.

b. Open the file WD L-6 from the drive and folder where your Project Files are located, then save it as **Web Page Design Evaluations**. This document contains criteria for ranking the design elements on the Web pages you've chosen.

c. As directed in the Web Page Design Evaluations document, enter the company name and copy the URL of each Web site to the spaces provided.

d. Assign a ranking to each site as directed, then complete the two questions at the bottom of the document.

e. Type your name at the bottom of the document, print a copy, save and close it, then exit Word.

▶ Visual Workshop

You have been hired by the Pet Place to design an attractive letterhead. The graphics you need to create the letterhead are already included in a Word file. Open the file WD L-7 from the drive and folder where your Project Files are located, then save it as **Pet Place Letterhead**. Use the graphics to create the letterhead shown in Figure L-29. Note that you need to fill the WordArt object with the Papyrus texture and then add the Shadow Style 1. You need to change the color of the shadow beneath the dog and flip the dog so that it faces to the left. Reduce the height of the dog to .9" with the Lock aspect ratio check box selected so that a proportionate width is selected. Remove the dog from the drawing canvas, delete the drawing canvas, then use the pointer to position the dog, as shown in Figure L-29. Use Click and Type to enter the contact information. Save the document, then print a copy.

FIGURE L-29

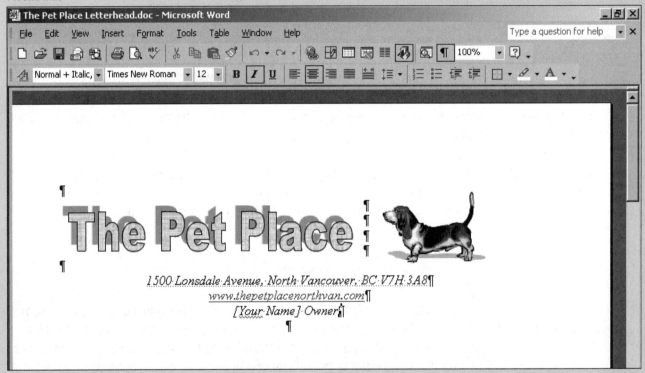

Building

Forms

Objectives

Word provides the tools you need to build forms that users can complete within a Word document. A **form** is a structured document with spaces reserved for entering information. You create a form as a template that includes labeled spaces—called **form fields**—into which users type information. The form template can include check box fields, drop-down lists, formulas in form fields to perform calculations, help messages, and other form controls to make the form interactive. Finally, you can protect a form so that users can enter information into the form but they cannot change the structure of the form itself. ◄— Alice Wegman in the Marketing Department wants to create a form to survey MediaLoft store managers. You help Alice create the form template.

Word 2002

Constructing a Form Template

A Word form is created as a **form template**, which contains all the components of the form. As you learned in an earlier unit, a template is a file that contains the basic structure of a document, such as the page layout, headers and footers, and graphic elements. In the case of a form template, the structure usually consists of a table form that contains field labels and form fields. Figure M-1 shows a completed form template containing several different types of form fields. A **field label** is a word or phrase such as "Date" or "Location" that tells users the kind of information required for a given field. A **form field** is the location where the data associated with a field label is stored. Information that can be stored in a form field includes text, an X in a check box, a number, or a selection in a drop-down list. ◄◄◄◄◄ Alice needs to create the basic structure of the form in Word and then save the document as a template located in a new folder. You help Alice by creating the form in Word, then saving it as a template to a new folder that you create in the drive and folder where your Project Files are located.

Steps 1234

1. Start **Word**

2. Click **General Templates** in the New from template section of the New Document task pane
   The Templates dialog box opens.

3. Verify **Blank Document** is selected, click the **Template option button** in the Create New section, then click **OK**
   A new document appears in the document window and Template1 appears on the title bar.

4. Type **Monthly Marketing Survey**, center the text, enhance it with **Bold** and the **16 pt** font size, press **[Enter]** twice, then clear the formatting

5. Click **Table** on the menu bar, point to **Insert**, click **Table**, enter **2** for the number of columns and **13** for the number of rows, then click **OK**

QuickTip
You will need to merge cells in four of the rows. To merge cells, click to the left of the row to select it, click Table on the menu bar, then click Merge Cells.

6. Type **Name:**, press **[Tab]**, type **Date:**, press **[Tab]**, then enter the remaining field labels as shown in Figure M-2
   Once you have created the structure for your form, you can save it as a template. First, you create a new folder to contain the template and then you specify this folder as the location of user templates so that Word can find it.

7. Minimize **Word**, right-click **My Computer** on your computer desktop, click **Explore** to open Windows Explorer, navigate to and open the drive and folder where your Project Files are located, click **File**, point to **New**, click **Folder**, type **[Your Name] Form Templates** as the folder name, then press **[Enter]**
   In order to have your templates stored in the same location, you set this new folder as the default location for user templates. A **user template** is any template that you create yourself.

8. Close **Windows Explorer**, click **Template1** on the taskbar, click **Tools** on the menu bar, click **Options**, click **File Locations**, click **User templates** in the list of File types, click **Modify**, click the **Look in list arrow**, select the **location** where you created the [Your Name] Form Templates folder, click the **folder** to select it, click **OK**, then click **OK**

9. Click the **Save button** 🖫 on the Standard toolbar, verify that "Monthly Marketing Survey.dot" appears in the File name text box as shown in Figure M-3, then click **Save**
   Word saves the template to the new folder you created.

FIGURE M-1: Form template

Text form field limited to four characters

Text form field

Drop-down form field; a list arrow appears when users move to the field

Check box form field

Form control option button

Number form field

Calculation form field

Monthly·Marketing·Survey¶

Name: °°°°° ¤	Date: °°°°° ¤
Store·Location: San Diego¤	Extension: °°°° ¤
Marketing-related·activities·(check·and·rank·the·success·of·all·that·apply): ¤	
☐·Book-signing·events¤	☐·Counter·bookmarks¤
☐·Story-telling·sessions¤	☐·Special·promotions¤
☐·Other·(please·specify): °°°°° ¤	
How·would·you·rank·the·success·of·the·activities? ○ Poor …○ Good …○ Excellent ¤	
Sales·by·Category¤	
Books¤	°°°°° ¤
CDs¤	°°°°° ¤
Café¤	°°°°° ¤
Miscellaneous¤	°°°°° ¤
Total¤	$0.00¤

FIGURE M-2: Field Labels Table form

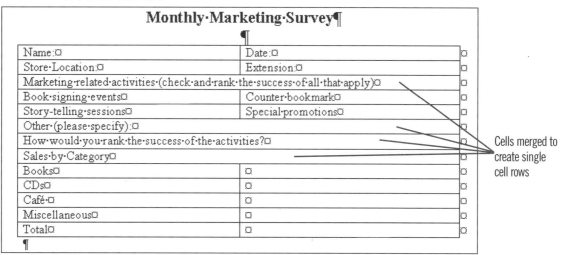

Monthly·Marketing·Survey¶

Name:¤	Date:¤
Store·Location:¤	Extension:¤
Marketing-related·activities·(check·and·rank·the·success·of·all·that·apply)¤	
Book-signing·events¤	Counter·bookmark¤
Story-telling·sessions¤	Special·promotions¤
Other·(please·specify):¤	
How·would·you·rank·the·success·of·the·activities?¤	
Sales·by·Category¤	
Books¤	¤
CDs¤	¤
Café¤	¤
Miscellaneous¤	¤
Total¤	¤

Cells merged to create single cell rows

FIGURE M-3: Saving a user template

Save location is the folder you identified as the default location

.dot extension identifies the file as a template

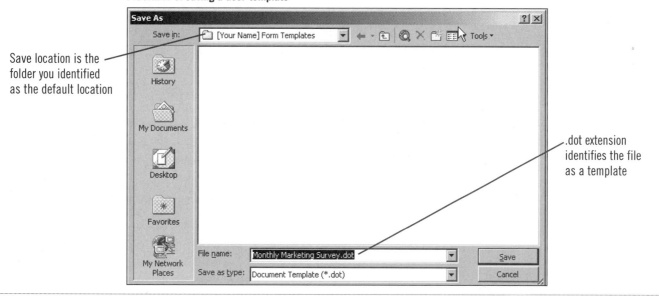

Adding and Modifying Text Form Fields

Once you have created a structure for your form, you need to designate form fields where users enter information. You insert **text form fields** in the table cells where users will enter text information, such as their names or the current date. A text form field allows you to control the kind of information users can enter. For example, you can specify that a text form field accepts only a numeric value, limits the number of characters entered, or requires dates be entered in a specified format. ✎ Alice inserts text form fields in the table cells where she needs users to enter text or numbers. She then works in the Text Form Field Options dialog box to specify the kind of information required for each text form field.

1. Click **View** on the menu bar, point to **Toolbars**, then click **Forms**

   The Forms toolbar contains the buttons used to create and modify the various elements of a form. Table M-1 describes each button on the Forms toolbar.

2. Click after **Name:**, press **[Spacebar]** one time, then click the **Text Form Field button** ab| on the Forms toolbar

   A gray shaded rectangle with five dots appears following Name. When completing the form, the user will be able to enter text into this form field.

3. Press **[Tab]**, click after **Date:**, press **[Spacebar]** one time, then click ab|

4. Insert a text form field after "Extension:," then insert a text form field after "Other (please specify):"

   Figure M-4 shows the form with text form fields inserted in four table cells. You want each user who completes the form to enter a date in a specific format in the text form field following the Date label.

5. Click the **text form field** next to Date:, then click the **Form Field Options button** 🖆 on the Forms toolbar

   The Text Form Field Options dialog box opens. In this dialog box you specify options related to the format and content of the selected text form field.

6. Click the **Type list arrow**, click **Date**, click the **Date format list arrow**, click **MMMM d, yyyy** as shown in Figure M-5, then click **OK**

   The text form field looks the same. In a later lesson, you will add a Help message that will inform users how to enter the date.

7. Click the **text form field** next to Extension:, then click 🖆

8. Click the **Maximum length up arrow** until "4" appears, then click **OK**

   You specify the number of characters a field can contain when you want to restrict the length of an entry. For example, a user completing this form can enter a phone extension of no more than four digits.

9. Click the **Save button** 🖫 on the Standard toolbar to save the template

FIGURE M-4: Text form fields inserted

Forms toolbar

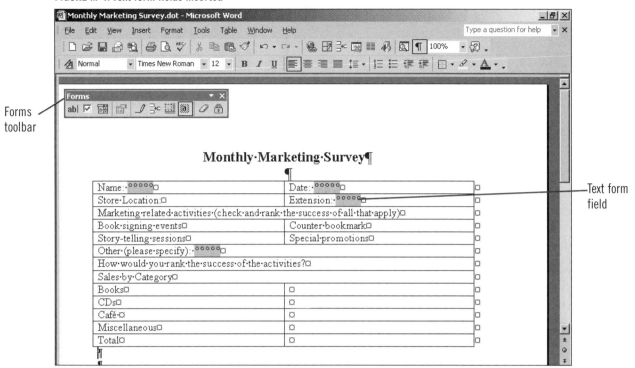

Text form field

FIGURE M-5: Text Form Field Options dialog box

Type list arrow

Date format list arrow

Date format selected

Shows the number of the text form field in the form. Text2 indicates that the current text form field was the second field you entered while creating the form

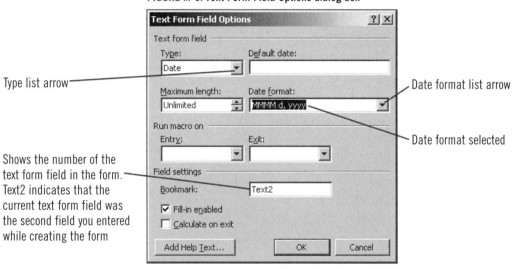

TABLE M-1: Buttons on the Forms Toolbar

button	use to	button	use to
ab|	Insert a text form field		Insert a table to contain form fields
☑	Insert a check box form field		Insert a frame to contain a form
	Insert a drop-down form field		Insert or remove shading from form fields
	Open the Form Field Options dialog box, then modify the options of an inserted form field		Reset form fields to their default settings
	Draw a table to contain form fields		Protect a form so that users can enter only data required for the form fields

Word 2002

Adding Drop-Down and Check Box Form Fields

In addition to text form fields, Word forms can include check box form fields and drop-down form fields. Users can use the pointer to make selections in check box or drop-down form fields. For example, users can click a check box to select it or they can select an item from a drop-down list. ◄◢▬▬ Alice wants to provide store managers an easy way to select the location of their MediaLoft store. She decides to provide a drop-down list of the MediaLoft store locations so that store managers can select the location of their MediaLoft store. Alice also wants the store managers to identify which marketing-related activities listed in the form they engaged in during the past month. She provides check boxes next to the activities so store managers can quickly make their selections.

1. Click after **Store Location:** in the second row of the table form, press **[Spacebar]** one time, then click the **Drop-Down Form Field button** 🔲 on the Forms toolbar
   A gray shaded rectangle without dots appears, indicating that the field is a drop-down form field and not a text form field.

2. Click the **Form Field Options button** 🔲 on the Forms toolbar
   The Drop-Down Form Field Options dialog box opens. In this dialog box, you enter the selections required for the drop-down list.

3. Type **Boston** in the Drop-down item text box, then click **Add**
   Boston becomes the first entry in the drop-down list.

QuickTip

You can press [Enter] after typing each entry, or you can click Add.

4. Repeat step 3 to enter these store locations in the Drop-down item text box: **Chicago, Houston, Kansas City, New York, San Diego, San Francisco, Toronto,** and **Seattle**
   Figure M-6 shows the MediaLoft store locations entered in the Drop-Down Form Field Options dialog box. You can change the order in which the locations are presented so that the entire list appears in alphabetical order.

5. Be sure **Seattle** is still selected in the Items in drop-down list box, then click the **Move Up button** 🔼
   Seattle moves above Toronto in the list and the list is in alphabetical order.

6. Click **OK**
   Boston appears in the form field because it is the first item in the drop-down form field list. In a later lesson, you will protect the form. When you open the protected form to complete it as a user, a list arrow will appear next to Boston to indicate that other selections are available.

7. Click to the left of **Book signing events**, click the **Check Box Form Field button** ☑ on the Forms toolbar, then press **[Spacebar]** one time to insert a space between the check box and the text
   A gray shaded box appears before the text "Book signing events." After the form is protected, an X will appear in the box when a user selects it.

8. Repeat step 7 to insert check boxes next to **Story-telling sessions, Counter bookmarks, Special promotions,** and **Other (please specify):**
   Figure M-7 shows the form with the text form fields, a drop-down form field, and check box form fields.

9. Save the template

FIGURE M-6: Drop-Down Form Field Options dialog box

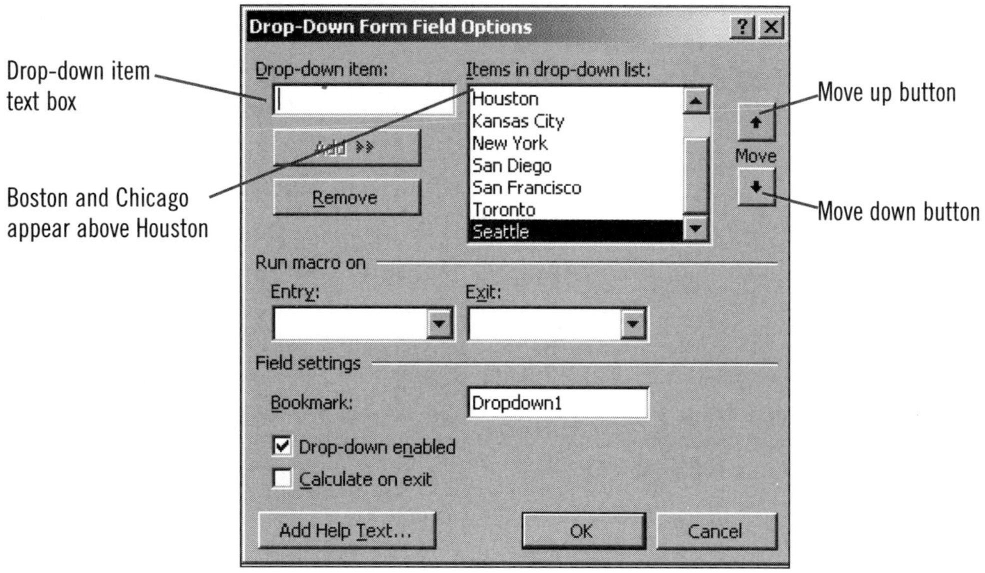

Drop-down item text box ———

Boston and Chicago appear above Houston

Move up button

Move down button

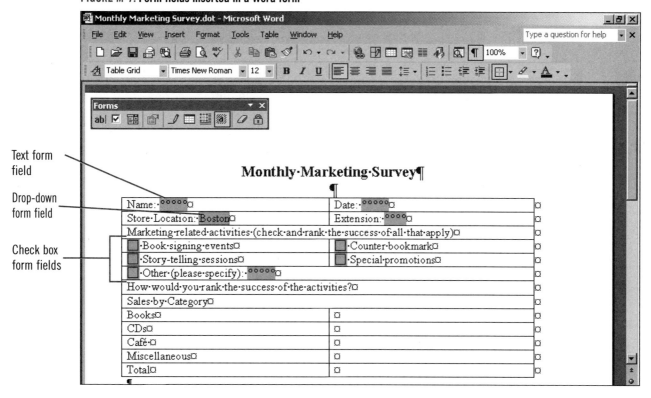

FIGURE M-7: Form fields inserted in a Word form

Text form field

Drop-down form field

Check box form fields

Using Calculations in a Form

A Word form can be designed to perform calculations. For example, you can specify that a text form field should add a series of numbers. To perform calculations in a form, you must follow two steps. First, you specify each text form field that will be used to perform the calculation as the Number type so that a user can only enter numbers. Second, you specify the form field that contains the result of the calculation as Calculation type and you type the mathematical formula that will perform the calculation. ◀━━ Alice wants the store managers to enter the dollar amounts generated in the current month from the sale of Books, CDs, Café products, and Miscellaneous products. She then wants the form to calculate the total sales automatically.

Steps 1 2 3 4

1. Click the blank **cell** to the right of Books in the table form, then click the **Text Form Field button** abl on the Forms toolbar

2. Click the **Form Field Options button** on the Forms toolbar, click the **Type list arrow**, then select **Number**
   You change the text form field type to Number because you want users to be able to enter only a number.

3. Click the **Number format list arrow**, select the number format as shown in Figure M-8, click the **Calculate on exit check box**, then click **OK**
   You select the Calculate on exit check box because you want the number that users enter into the text form field to be included as part of a calculation. The three table cells under the current cell require the same text form field as the one you just created. You can save time by copying and pasting the text form field you just created.

QuickTip
To check the properties of a form field, right-click the form field, then click Properties on the shortcut menu.

4. With the **form field** selected, click the **Copy button** on the Standard toolbar, click the blank **cell** to the right of CDs, click the **Paste button** on the Standard toolbar, then paste the text form field into the blank cells to the right of Café and Miscellaneous
   You want the cell to the right of Total to display the total of the values users enter in the four cells immediately above it.

5. Click the blank **cell** next to Total, click abl, click to open the Text Form Field Options dialog box, click the **Type list arrow**, then click **Calculation**

Trouble?
The calculation expression must begin with =.

6. Click in the **Expression text box**, then type **SUM(ABOVE)** next to =
   The formula =SUM(ABOVE) is a standard calculation expression that is recognized by programs such as Word and Excel. The =SUM(ABOVE) calculation expression calculates all the values entered in the designated text form fields. The designated text form fields must be above the text form field that contains the calculation expression, and the text form fields must use a Number format.

7. Click the **Number format list arrow**, select the number format as shown in Figure M-8, then click the **Calculate on exit check box** to select it
   Figure M-9 shows the completed Text Form Field Options dialog box.

8. Click **OK**
   The $0.00 entered next to Total indicates that the cell contains a calculation form field.

9. Compare your form to Figure M-10, then save the template

FIGURE M-8: Number format selected

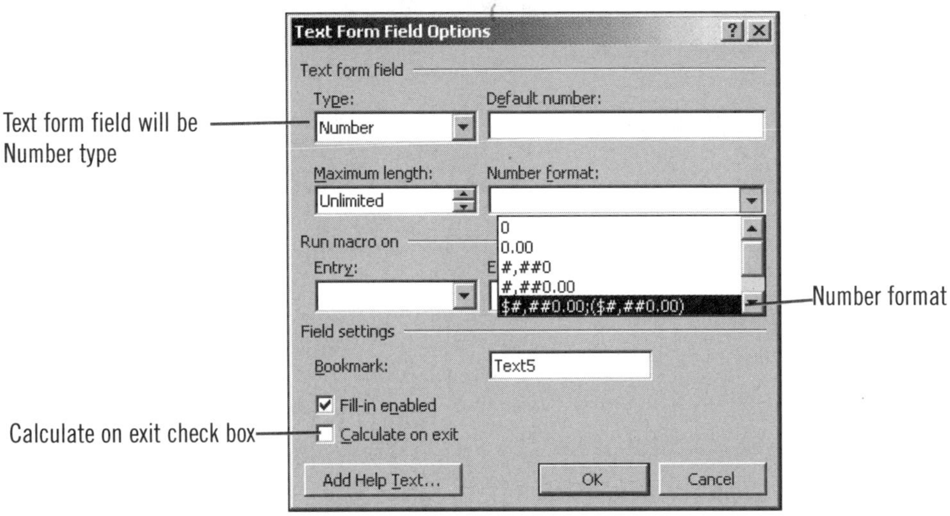

Text form field will be Number type

Number format

Calculate on exit check box

FIGURE M-9: Calculation options selected

FIGURE M-10: Calculation form field inserted

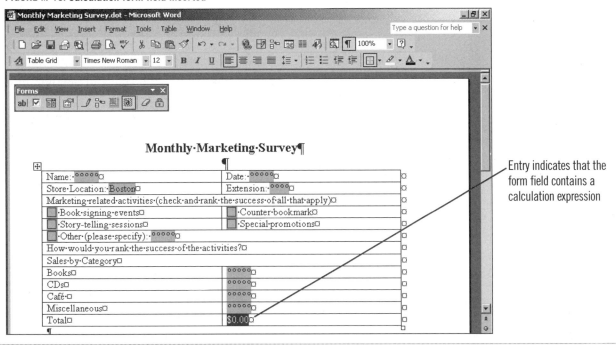

Entry indicates that the form field contains a calculation expression

Adding Help to a Form

You can help users fill in a form quickly and easily by attaching help messages to selected form fields. For example, you can include a help message in the Date form field that advises users how to enter a correctly formatted date. Help messages can appear on the status bar or when the user presses the [F1] function key. Alice wants to include instructions that advise store managers how to enter the date. She also wants to add instructions to the Other (please specify): form field.

Steps

1. Click the **text form field** for the Date field label, then click the **Form Field Options button** 🖹 on the Forms toolbar

2. Click **Add Help Text**, then verify that the **Status Bar tab** is selected
   You can choose to include an AutoText entry such as a page number or the word "Confidential," or you can type your own Help message.

3. Click the **Type your own option button**, then enter the text: **Type the date as Month, day, year; for example, March 18, 2003.** as shown in Figure M-11
   The text entered in the Status Bar text box will appear in the Status Bar when a user clicks the text form field next to Date.

4. Click **OK** to exit the Form Field Help Text dialog box, then click **OK** to exit the Text Form Field Options dialog box

5. Click the **text form field** next to the Other (please specify): field label, click 🖹, click **Add Help Text**, then click the **Help Key (F1) tab**
   You can enter a help message containing up to 225 characters in the Help Key (F1) text box.

6. Click the **Type your own option button**, then type the Help text as shown in Figure M-12

7. Click **OK**, then click **OK**
   The form fields to which you have added Help messages do not appear to change. You will see the Help messages only when you fill in the form as a user.

8. With the **text form field** next to the Other (Please specify): field label still selected, click the **Italic button** 𝐼 on the Formatting toolbar, then click to the right of the text form field
   The text form field does not appear to have changed. However, the Italic button on the Formatting toolbar is selected to indicate that any text entered in the text form field will appear in italic.

9. Save the template

FIGURE M-11: Status Bar help

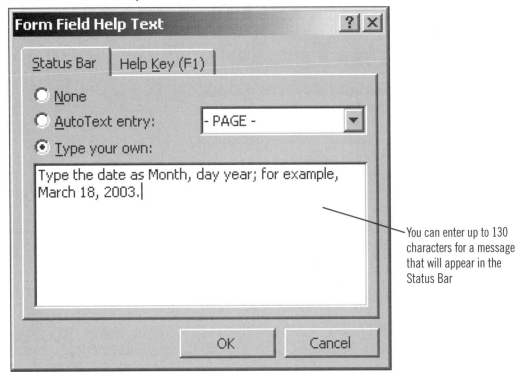

You can enter up to 130 characters for a message that will appear in the Status Bar

FIGURE M-12: Help Key (F1) text

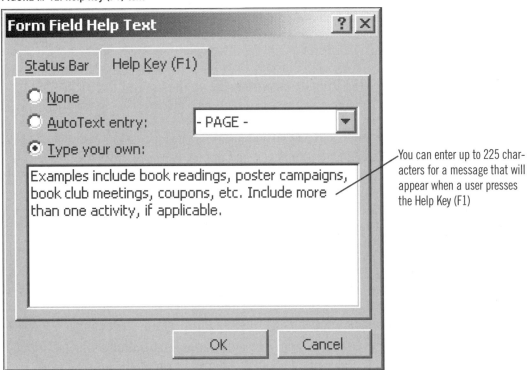

You can enter up to 225 characters for a message that will appear when a user presses the Help Key (F1)

Word 2002

Inserting Form Controls

The Forms toolbar contains the tools most commonly used to create a form that users complete in Word. You can further enhance a form by including some of the controls available on the Control Toolbox toolbar. These controls are referred to as Active X controls and are used to offer options to users or to run macros or scripts that automate specific tasks. One of the easiest controls to use in a form that users complete in Word is the Option button control. You insert a series of Option button controls when you want users to select just one of the available options. Alice wants the store managers to rank the effectiveness of the month's marketing activities. She decides to create a series of labeled Option buttons that store managers can select to indicate if the marketing activities yielded Poor, Good, or Excellent results.

Steps

QuickTip

Some controls in the Control Toolbox, such as the check box control, are also available on the Forms toolbar. To use most Control Toolbox controls, however, you need knowledge of Visual Basic.

1. Click **View** on the menu bar, point to **Toolbars**, then click **Control Toolbox**
   The Control Toolbox toolbar appears.

2. Click the **Design Mode button** on the Control Toolbox toolbar, then click the **blank area** to the right of How would you rank the success of the activities?
   The Design Mode button becomes a floating toolbar, indicating that you are in Design Mode. You must be in Design Mode when you want to insert a control from the Control Toolbox toolbar to a selected cell.

3. Click the **Option Button button** on the Control Toolbox toolbar to insert an option button control into the selected cell
   Figure M-13 shows the option button with the button caption "OptionButton1" inserted in the selected cell. You need to change the properties of the control so that the label next to the option button shows the caption "Poor." A **property** is a named attribute of a control that you set to define one of the control's attributes such as its size, its color, and its behavior in response to user input.

QuickTip

You can move and resize the Properties window. To move the window, click the title bar and drag the window to its new location. To resize the window, move ↖ over the lower-right corner of the Properties window, then click and drag ↖ to resize the Properties window.

4. Click the **Properties button** on the Control Toolbox toolbar
   The Properties window opens with the Alphabetic tab selected. The properties are listed in alphabetical order on the Alphabetic tab. In this window, you can identify properties such as the height and width of the option button and designate the label text to appear next to the option button.

5. Select **OptionButton1** next to Caption, type **Poor**, select **21.75** next to Height, type **17.25**, scroll down the Properties window if necessary, select **108** next to Width, then type **50.25**
   The Properties window is shown in Figure M-14, and the caption "Poor" appears next to the option button in the Word form. The measurements are in pixels.

6. Click the **option button** in the form
   The size of the option button changes to match the Properties (Height = 17.25 and Width = 50.25) that you entered in the Properties window.

7. With the option button box still selected, press [➜] once, press [**Spacebar**] two times, click ◉, replace **OptionButton2** next to Caption in the Properties window with the word **Good**, change the Height to **17.25**, then change the Width to **50.25**

8. Repeat steps 6 and 7 to enter an option button with the caption text **Excellent**, a Height value of **17.25**, and a Width value of **75**
   The three option buttons appear, as shown in Figure M-15.

9. Close the Properties window, click the **Exit Design Mode button** on the Design Mode floating toolbar, close the Control Toolbox toolbar, then save the template
   You must exit Design Mode after you insert a form control so that you can continue working with the form.

FIGURE M-13: Option Button 1 inserted

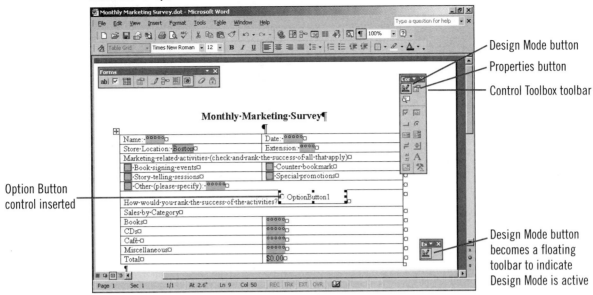

Option Button
control inserted

Design Mode button
Properties button
Control Toolbox toolbar

Design Mode button
becomes a floating
toolbar to indicate
Design Mode is active

FIGURE M-14: Properties window

Alphabetic tab selected

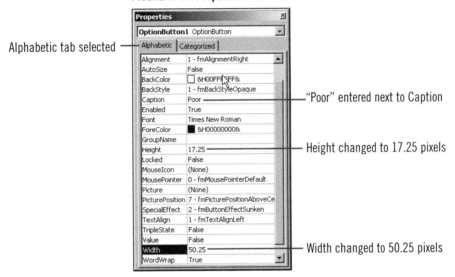

"Poor" entered next to Caption

Height changed to 17.25 pixels

Width changed to 50.25 pixels

FIGURE M-15: Option buttons inserted

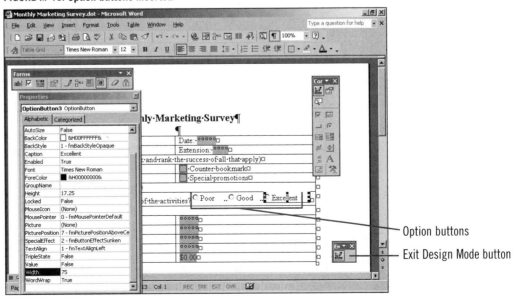

Option buttons

Exit Design Mode button

Formatting and Protecting a Form

Forms should be easy to read onscreen so that users can fill them in quickly and accurately. You can enhance a table containing form fields and you can modify the magnification of a document containing a form so that users can easily see the form fields. Finally, you can protect a form so that users can enter only the data required and *not* be able to change the structure of the form. When a form is protected, information can be entered only in form fields. ✐ Alice enhances the field labels, adds shading to the form, and changes the background color of the option button controls. Finally, she protects and then saves the form template.

Steps

1. Select **Name** in the first cell of the table, click the **Bold button** B on the Formatting toolbar, then enhance the following field labels with bold: **Date**, **Store Location**, **Extension**, and **Sales by Category**

Trouble?

You must be in Page Layout view to see ⊞.

2. Move your pointer over the upper-left corner of the table to show ⊞, click ⊞ to select the table, click **Table** on the menu bar, click **Table Properties**, click the **Row tab**, click the **Specify height check box**, enter **.3** in the text box, then click **OK**

3. Click **View** on the menu bar, point to **Toolbars**, then click **Tables and Borders**
   The Tables and Borders toolbar appears. You can use this toolbar to fill the entire table with light yellow shading.

4. With the entire table still selected, click the **Shading Color button list arrow** 🎨▾ on the Tables and Borders toolbar, click **More Fill Colors**, click the **Custom tab**, enter settings in the Red, Green, and Blue text boxes as shown in Figure M-16, then click **OK**

5. With the entire table still selected, click the **Align Top Left button list arrow** ▦▾ on the Tables and Borders toolbar, click the **Align Center Left button** ▦, click away from the table to deselect it, then close the Tables and Borders toolbar
   The option buttons still have white backgrounds. You can change the background color of an Active X form control in the Properties window.

6. Click **View** on the menu bar, point to **Toolbars**, click **Control Toolbox**, click the **Design Mode button** 🖾, click the **Poor option button** to select it, then click the **Properties button** 🖾 on the Control Toolbox toolbar to open the Properties window for the Poor option button

Trouble?

After changing a control property, click the option button, then press [➡] to deselect the option button.

7. Click the **cell** to the right of BackColor, click the **list arrow**, select the **Light Yellow color box** as shown in Figure M-17, then change the back color of the **Good** and **Excellent** option buttons to light yellow

8. Close the Properties window, click the **Exit Design Mode button** 🖾 on the Control Toolbox toolbar, then close the Control Toolbox toolbar
   After you modify an Active X control, you need to exit Design Mode so that you can pro-tect the form. When the Design Mode button is selected, you cannot protect a form.

9. Click the **Protect Form button** 🔒 on the Forms toolbar, then save and close the template
   The completed form template appears, as shown in Figure M-18.

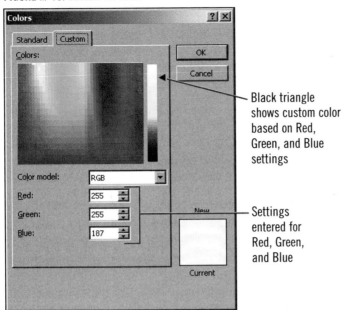

Black triangle
shows custom color
based on Red,
Green, and Blue
settings

Settings
entered for
Red, Green,
and Blue

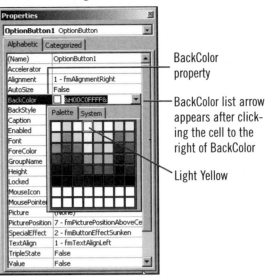

BackColor
property

BackColor list arrow
appears after click-
ing the cell to the
right of BackColor

Light Yellow

FIGURE M-18: **Completed form template**

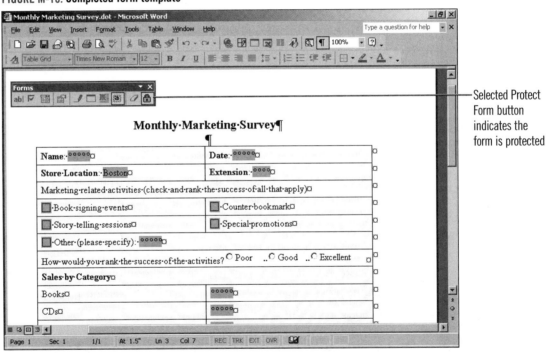

Selected Protect
Form button
indicates the
form is protected

Locking form fields

When you protect a form using the Protect Form button on the Forms toolbar, the form information, such as field labels, is protected or locked. A user can input information only in form fields and the input information must match the type specified by the person who originated the form. Sometimes, however, instead of protecting an entire form, you might want to lock certain form fields. For example, if you are entering numbers in a form for a budget and you want to be sure that the numbers do not inadvertently get changed, you can lock the form field after you enter the numbers. To lock a form field, and prevent changes to the current field results, click the field, then press [Ctrl] F11. If you need to unlock a field to update the field results, click the field, then press [Ctrl][Shift]F11.

Filling in a Form as a User

Before you distribute a form template to users, you need to test it to ensure that all the elements work correctly. For example, you want to make sure the total is calculated properly when numbers are entered in the form fields formatted with the Number type. You also want to make sure that selections appear in the list box, the correct help messages appear, and that you can easily select the check boxes and option buttons. ▰▰▰▰ Alice opens a new document based on the template, then fills in the form as if she were the San Diego store manager.

Steps 1234

1. **Click File on the menu bar, then click New**
   The New Document task pane opens.

2. **Click General Templates in the New Document task pane, click Monthly Marketing Survey.dot, verify that the Document option button in the Create New section of the Templates window is selected, then click OK**
   Notice that the Monthly Marketing Survey.dot file opens as a Word document, as indicated by the filename that appears on the title bar. The insertion point highlights the space following Name. The form is protected, so you can enter information only in spaces that contain text form fields, check boxes, drop-down lists, or option buttons.

3. **Type your name, then press [Tab]**
   The insertion point moves to the space following Date. Notice the Help message that appears in the Status Bar, telling you how to enter the date.

4. **Enter the current date in the required format, press [Tab], click the list arrow next to Boston, scroll down the list of store locations, click San Diego, then press [Tab]**

5. **Type 4455, press [Tab], then click the check box next to Book signing events, the check box next to Counter bookmark, and the check box next to Other (please specify):**

6. **Press [Tab], then press F1**
   The Help message appears, as shown in Figure M-19.

7. **Click OK, type Mystery Book Night readings by Lance Rose, click the Good option button, press [Tab] two times to move the insertion point to the text form field next to Books, type 48000, then press [Tab]**
   The amount is automatically formatted with a dollar sign and the amount in the cell to the right of Total is updated automatically when you press [Tab] to move the insertion point out of the cell.

8. **Enter the remaining sales amounts shown in the completed form in Figure M-20; press [Tab] after you enter each value**
   The total—$93,000—is calculated automatically because this text field is a calculation type with the =SUM(ABOVE) formula. When you press [TAB] after entering the last value, the insertion point moves to the next text form field that will accept user input, which is the form field after Name.

9. **Save the document with the name San Diego Survey to the drive and folder where your Project Files are located, print a copy, then close the document**

FIGURE M-19: F1 Help message

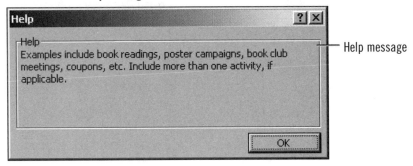

Help message

FIGURE M-20: Sales amounts entered

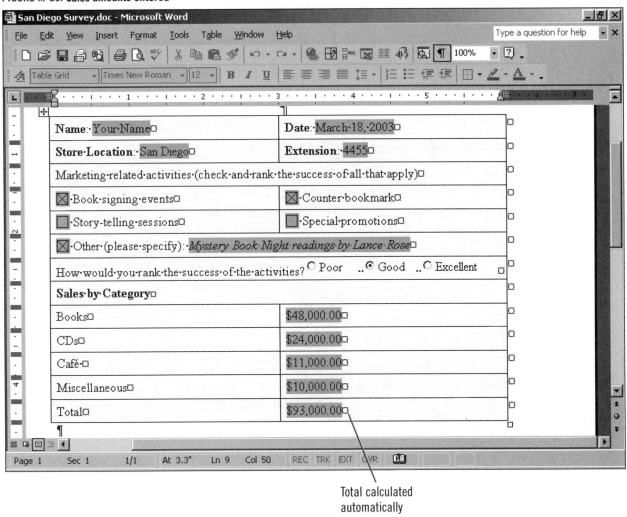

Total calculated automatically

Editing a form template

To edit the structure of a form, you need to open the template, then click the Protect Form button on the Forms toolbar to deselect it. You can then make changes to the form by adding or removing form fields and modifying the appearance of the form. When you have finished modifying the form template, click the Protect Form button again, then save the template.

Practice

▶ Concepts Review

Identify each of the numbered buttons on the Forms toolbar shown in Figure M-21.

FIGURE M-21

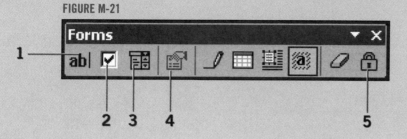

Match each term with the statement that best describes it.

6. **Drop-down form field**
7. **Control Toolbox**
8. **Text form field**
9. **Option button**
10. **Calculation form field**
11. **F1**

a. An area of a form into which users can enter information
b. A list of options in a form
c. Contains a mathematical expression
d. Contains a selection of ActiveX controls that can be inserted in a form
e. One type of ActiveX control
f. Help key

Select the best answer from the list of choices

12. **What is a field label?**
    a. A space for users to enter variable information
    b. A placeholder for text such as a user's name or the current date
    c. A word or phrase, such as the user's current address, that is entered into a blank cell
    d. A word or phrase such as "Date" or "Location" that tells users the kind of information required for a given field

13. **What happens when you insert a text form field into a table cell?**
    a. A blank check box appears.
    b. A shaded rectangle with five dots appears.
    c. A blank bar outlined in black appears.
    d. A Help message appears to inform users what information to enter in the form field.

14. **How do you view the list of choices available in a drop-down form field?**
    a. Double-click the drop-down form field to insert a list arrow.
    b. Open the form as a user, click the drop-down form field, then click the list arrow.
    c. Right-click the drop-down form field, then click Activate.
    d. View the form in the Print Preview screen.

15. **How would you enter a Help message containing 200 characters?**
    a. Enter the Help message in the Type your own text box in the Status Bar tab of the Help Text dialog box.
    b. Enter the Help message in the form field.
    c. Edit the Help message so it contains only 130 characters, the accepted limit.
    d. Enter the Help message in the Type your own text box in the Help Key (F1) tab of the Help Text dialog box.

1. Construct a form template.

a. Start Word, open the New Document task pane if necessary, open the General Templates dialog box, then create a new blank document as a template.

b. Check to ensure that [Your Name] Form Templates is designated as the folder to contain user templates.

c. Type **Change of Grade Notification** as the title, then center the text and enhance it with Bold and 18 pt.

d. Two lines below the title, clear the formatting, then create a table consisting of 4 columns and 13 rows.

e. Type the text as shown in Figure M-22. (*Note*: Merge selected cells in rows 2, 10, 11, and 13. Apply bold to selected field labels, as noted in Figure M-22. Do *not* apply alignment at this time.)

f. Save the template as **Change of Grade Notification** to the [Your Name] Form Templates folder.

FIGURE M-22

Student·Number◻	◻	Date◻	◻	◻
Student·Name◻	◻			◻
Course·Title◻	◻	Course·Number◻	◻	◻
Original·Letter Grade◻	Revised·Letter Grade◻	Courses◻	Points◻	◻
A·—·4◻	A·—·4◻	Accounting◻	◻	◻
B·—·3◻	B·—·3◻	Business·Math◻	◻	◻
C·—·2◻	C·—·2◻	Computer·Basics◻	◻	◻
D·—·1◻	D·—·1◻	English◻	◻	◻
F·—·0◻	F·—·0◻	Office·Procedures◻	◻	◻
		Grade·Point·Average◻	◻	◻
Reason·for·Grade·Change·(check·one):◻				◻
◻		◻		◻
Other·(specify):◻	◻			◻

2. Add and modify text form fields.

a. Show the Forms toolbar, if necessary.

b. Insert a text form field in the blank cell to the right of Student Number.

c. Insert text form fields in the blank cells to the right of the following field labels: Date, Student Name, Course Number, and Other (specify).

d. Modify the text form field next to Student Number so that users can enter up to six numbers.

e. Modify the text form field next to Date so that users must enter a date formatted as M/d/yy, then save the template.

3. Add drop-down and check box form fields.

a. Insert a drop-down form field after Course Title.

b. In the Drop-Down Form-Field Options dialog box, enter the following list of items: **Accounting**, **Computer Basics**, **English**, **Business Math**, and **Office Procedures**.

c. Move Business Math up so that it appears immediately after Accounting.

d. Insert a check box form field and a space to the left of each letter grade in the Original Letter Grade and Revised Letter Grade columns, then save the template.

4. Use calculations in a form.

a. Insert a text form field in the blank cell to the right of Accounting with the Number format set to 0 and the Calculate on exit check box selected.

b. Copy the text form field with number formatting to the next four cells (Business Math through Office Procedures).

c. Insert a text form field with the type set to Calculation in the blank cell to the right of Grade Point Average. Type the expression **=SUM(ABOVE)/5** and set the Number format to 0. This formula will add the numbers in the Points cells, then divide the total by 5 to determine the average. Make sure the Calculate on exit check box is selected before you exit the Text Form Field Options dialog box, then save the template.

5. Add help to a form.

a. Add a Status Bar help message in the Date form field that states: **Type the date in numerals as month, day, year; for example, 03/18/03.**

b. Add a Help Key (F1) help message in the Other (specify): field that states: **Acceptable reasons include completion of work outstanding and acceptance of medical documentation**, then save the template.

6. **Insert form controls.**

a. Show the Control Toolbox toolbar. Make sure the Design Mode button is selected, then click the blank cell below the Reason for Grade Change field label.

b. Insert an Option Button control with the following properties: Caption is **Calculation Error** and height is **18**.

c. Insert an Option Button control in the next blank cell with the caption **Exam Retake** and a height of **18**.

d. Close the Properties window, exit Design Mode, close the Control Toolbox toolbar, then save the template.

7. **Format and protect a form.**

a. With the table selected, change the row height to **.35"**

b. Show the Tables and Borders toolbar, then change the alignment for the entire table so all the text is aligned center-left.

c. Align top-center all four field labels in the row beginning with Original Letter Grade.

d. Align center all the form fields in the six cells under the cell with the Points label.

e. Align center-right the Grade Point Average field label.

f. Select the table again, then change the colors in the Custom tab of the Colors dialog box to Red: **255**, Green: **225**, and Blue: **195**. (*Hint:* You should see a light tan color.)

g. View the Control Toolbox toolbar, then select Design Mode

h. With the Calculation Error option button selected, change the BackColor in the Properties window to beige (third color box from the left in the top row of the color selections).

i. Repeat the preceding procedure to change the BackColor to beige for the Exam Retake option button.

j. Close the Properties window, exit Design Mode, then protect the form. (*Note:* You must click the Design Mode button to exit Design Mode.)

k. Close the Forms toolbar, the Tables and Borders toolbar, and the Control Toolbox toolbar.

l. Save and close the template.

8. **Fill in a form as a user.**

a. Open a new document based on the Change of Grade Notification template. (*Hint:* Make sure the Document option button in the Create New section of the Templates dialog box is selected.)

b. Type **567888** as the Student Number, press [Tab], type the **current date**, press [Tab], type your name, select **Computer Basics** as the Course Title, enter **334** as the Course Number, select **B** as the Original Letter Grade, then select **A** as the Revised Letter Grade.

c. Enter the points for each course as follows: Accounting: **3**, Business Math: **3**; Computer Basics: **4**; English: **4**; and Office Procedures: **2**.

d. Press [Tab] and verify that the value in the Grade Point Average cell is 3.

e. Select the Calculation Error option button.

f. Check the F1 Help Message in the Other (specify): field.

g. Save the document with the filename **Computer Basics Grade Change** to the drive and folder where your Project Files are located, print a copy, close the document, then exit Word.

► Independent Challenge 1

You work for the owner of Fly Me to the Snow—a new company that sells skiing and snowboarding equipment. The owner and some of the sales representatives have begun taking frequent business trips to ski resorts around North America to meet with ski shop owners interested in carrying the company's products. Your boss asks you to help expedite the bookkeeping by creating an expense report form that can be completed online in Word.

a. Start Word and open the file WD M-1 from the drive and folder where your Project Files are located. Save it as a template called **Expense Report Form** to the [Your Name] Form Templates folder that you created to complete the lessons in this unit. (Refer to the first lesson in this unit, if necessary.)

b. View the Forms toolbar.

c. Insert text form fields for the Name, Report Date, Extension, and Purpose of Travel field labels.

d. Specify the date format of your choice for the Report Date form field.

e. Change the type of the text form field next to Extension to Number and specify a maximum of four numbers.

f. Add a Status Bar help message to the Purpose of Travel form field that states: **Specify the location(s) you visited and the business goals accomplished**.

g. Insert a drop-down form field in the blank cell to the right of Department that includes the following entries: **Management**, **Marketing**, and **Sales**.

h. Insert a text form field in the first blank cell in the Date column, select Date as the type, specify the M/d/yy date format, then copy the text form field and paste it to all the blank cells in the Date column.

i. Insert a drop-down form field in the first blank cell in the Category column. Include the following entries in the drop-down list: **Mileage**, **Meals**, **Hotel**, **Air Fare**, and **Other**. Put the entries in alphabetical order.

j. Copy the drop-down form field and paste it to all the blank cells in the Category column.

k. Insert a text form field in the first blank cell in the Details column, then copy the text form field and paste it to all the blank cells in the Details column.

l. Insert a text form field in the blank cell below Amount, then change the text form field options so the type is Number, the format is 0.00, and the Calculate on exit check box is selected. Copy the text form field with Number formatting and paste it to all the blank cells in the Amount column, except the cell next to Total.

m. Insert a text form field in the blank cell to the right of Total, then change the form field options so the type is Calculation, the format is 0.00, the Expression is =SUM(ABOVE), and the Calculate on exit check box is selected.

n. Right-align the form fields in the Amount column and Total cell.

o. Protect the form, then save and close the template.

p. Open a new document based on the template, then complete the form as a user. Type your name and the **current date**, select the "Marketing" department, type any **four-digit extension**, then after Purpose for Travel type **Setting up contact with ski shops in Whistler and Blackcomb in British Columbia**.

q. Enter expense amounts appropriate for a three-day trip a few days before the current date from Seattle, WA to Whistler, BC (use a distance of 130 miles). Include expenses for mileage at 10¢ a mile for a total of 260 miles, a hotel room for three nights at the Whistler Chateau at $200 per night, and meals for three days at various locations at $100 per day. Enter appropriate details and select the correct category for each expense. (*Hint:* You should enter the date of the first day of the trip for the mileage expense and the date of the last day of the trip for the hotel and meals expenses.) Your total expenses should be $926.00.

r. Save the document as **Completed Expense Report** to the drive and folder where your Project Files are located, print a copy, close the document, then exit Word.

▶ Independent Challenge 2

You are the Office Manager at Great Northern Securities, a company that has just instituted parking regulations for staff wishing to park in the new staff parking lot. Any staff member who wants to park in the lot must purchase a parking permit. You decide to create a Word form that staff members complete to purchase a parking permit. You will create the form as a Word template saved on the company's network. Staffers can open a new Word document based on the template, then complete the form in Word, or they can print the form and fill it in by hand.

   a. Start Word, open the file WD M-2 from the drive and folder where your Project Files are located, and save it as a template called **Parking Permit Requisition** to the [Your Name] Form Templates folder that you created to complete the lessons in this unit. (Refer to the first lesson in this unit, if necessary.)

   b. View the Forms toolbar.

   c. Insert a text form field in the blank cell to the right of Date. Format the text form field to accept dates entered in the format you prefer. Include a Help message that appears on the Status bar and tells users how to enter the date.

   d. Enter a text form field in the blank cell to the right of Name.

   e. Insert a drop-down form field in the blank cell to the right of Department that includes the following entries: **Accounting**, **Administration**, **Investments**, **Marketing**, **Sales**, and **Information Technology**.

   f. Move entries so they appear in alphabetical order.

   g. Insert a text form field in the blank cell to the right of Extension, then modify the text form field so that it accepts a maximum of four numbers. Include a Status Bar Help message that advises users to enter their four-digit telephone extension.

   h. Insert check box form fields to the left of the selections in the fourth column (Full-time, Part-time, etc.). Leave a space between the check box and the first letter of each selection.

   i. Insert an option button control in each of the blank cells in the last row of the form. The captions for the option buttons are as follows: **Check**, **Cash**, and **Pay Debit**.

   j. Click the Exit Design Mode button on the Control Toolbox, then close the Control Toolbox.

   k. Apply the Table Columns 5 Table AutoFormat to the table.

   l. Show the Tables and Borders toolbar, then remove the shading from the cell that contains the Cash option button.

   m. Protect the form, then save and close the template.

   n. Open a new document based on the template, then complete the form as a user. Type the **current date** and your name, select "Executive" status, select the "Information Technology" department, enter any **four-digit extension**, then select "Cash" as the payment method.

   o. Save the document as **Completed Parking Requisition** to the drive and folder where your Project Files are located, print a copy, close the document, then exit Word.

▶ Independent Challenge 3

You work for a company that specializes in taking small groups of people on educational tours. Your job is to design tours based on a theme and location of your choice. For example, you might design an art tour of Italy or a history tour of Southeast Asia. One way you can measure the success of the tours you design is to ask customers to complete a feedback form after participating in a tour. You decide to create a Word form that you can e-mail to customers. Your customers can complete the form in Word, then send it back to you as an e-mail attachment.

   a. Start Word, then create a new template.

   b. Think of a company name, then type the **name of your company** as the title and **Tour Feedback** as the subtitle. Enhance both titles attractively.

   c. Save the template as **Tour Feedback Form** to the [Your Name] Form Templates folder you created to contain the form templates you created in this unit.

d. Plan a form that will contain the following field labels: **Name**, **Tour Date**, **Tour Guide**, and **Tour Name** and a section for ranking tour components, as shown in Figure M-23. (*Hint:* Create a table with 6 columns and 11 rows. Merge cells as needed.)

e. Enter text form fields in the Name, Tour Date, and Tour Guide cells, then enter a drop-down form field in the Tour Name cell that lists five tours. Type sample tour names such as "Florence Fantasy," "Venice Dream," and "Tuscany Treat." Use tour names appropriate to your company. Be sure the names appear in alphabetical order in the drop-down list.

FIGURE M-23

⌂	1⌂	2⌂	3⌂	4⌂	5⌂	⌂
Meals⌂	⌂	⌂	⌂	⌂	⌂	⌂
Accommodations⌂	⌂	⌂	⌂	⌂	⌂	⌂
Tour·Guide·⌂	⌂	⌂	⌂	⌂	⌂	⌂
Educational·Interest⌂	⌂	⌂	⌂	⌂	⌂	⌂
Overall⌂	⌂	⌂	⌂	⌂	⌂	⌂

¶

f. Insert check box form fields in the ranking section of your form. Add a sentence above the ranking section that tells users what the rankings mean: for example, 1 is poor and 5 is outstanding.

g. After the section where users rank tour components, include the following: one row with the field label **Additional Comments** followed by a text form field; and one row with the question: **May we contact you regarding new tours as information about them becomes available?** Follow the question with option control buttons: one labeled **YES!** and one labeled **No thanks**. Format the option buttons so that they fit the table cell.

h. Format the form attractively, using one of the Table AutoFormats if you wish. (*Hint:* You might need to increase the row height so that the option buttons fit.)

i. Protect the form, save it, then close the template.

j. Open a new document based on the form template, then save it as **Completed Feedback Form** to the drive and folder where your Project Files are located.

k. Fill in the form as if you had participated in one of your tours. Enter your name in the Name field.

l. Save the form, print a copy, close the form, then exit Word.

ⓔ Independent Challenge 4

Many companies and organizations that maintain Web sites include online forms that visitors can complete to participate in a survey, provide payment information, select products or services, and request information. You can learn a great deal about form design by studying some of the forms included on Web sites. You decide to search for Web sites that conduct surveys, then evaluate two survey forms.

a. Open your Web browser and conduct a search for companies that conduct online surveys or provide tools for creating online surveys. Search terms you can use include "online surveys," "survey forms," and "online survey companies." If your search does *not* result in links to appropriate sites with online surveys, try the following sites: www.zoomerang.com (click Test Drive Zoomerang, then pick a survey), or www.quask.com (click Samples, then pick a survey).

b. Select two Web sites that include online surveys that users can complete. Many of the online companies that provide online survey tools include a sample survey that users can complete to evaluate the survey tool.

c. Open the file WD M-3, then save it as **Survey Form Evaluation** to the drive and folder where your Project Files are located. This document contains criteria for ranking the survey forms on the Web sites you've chosen.

d. Type your name and the **current date** in the spaces provided.

e. As directed in the Survey Form Evaluation document, type the company name and copy the URL of the Web site to the spaces provided.

f. Follow the directions on the Survey Form Evaluation and complete the form at the bottom of the document.

g. Save the document as **Survey Form Evaluation**, print a copy, then close it.

▶ Visual Workshop

You are in charge of the audio-visual department at a local community college. Faculty members come to you to borrow TVs, VCRs, projectors, and laptop computers to use in class presentations. You decide to make up a simple form that faculty members can complete online and then e-mail to you when they want to borrow audio-visual equipment. Create and enhance a form template, as shown in Figure M-24. Save the template as **Audio Visual Request Form** to the [Your Name] Form Templates folder containing all the form templates you've created for this unit. The items in the drop-down list for Department are **Arts**, **Sciences**, **Business**, **Education**, and **Technology**. The items in the drop-down list for Equipment are **Laptop Computer**, **Television**, **VCR**, and **Projector**. Protect the form, close the template, then open a new document based on the template. Complete the form entering your name in the Name field. Save the completed form as **My Audio Visual Form** to the drive and folder where your Project Files are located, print a copy, and close the document.

FIGURE M-24

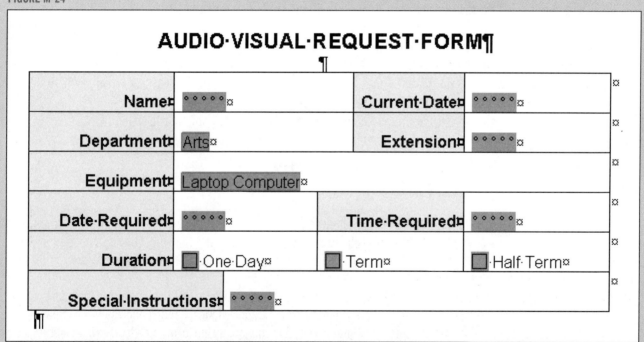

Working
with Charts and Diagrams

Objectives

- [MOUS] ▶ **Define charts and diagrams**
- [MOUS] ▶ **Create a column chart**
- [MOUS] ▶ **Edit a chart**
- [MOUS] ▶ **Create a pie chart**
- [MOUS] ▶ **Import spreadsheet data into a chart**
- [MOUS] ▶ **Create a diagram**
- [MOUS] ▶ **Create an organization chart**
- [MOUS] ▶ **Modify an organization chart**

Word provides the tools you need to create and modify numerically-based charts, such as bar charts, pie charts, and area charts. You can also create and modify diagrams such as Venn diagrams and cycle diagrams to show conceptual relationships that are not numerically based. Finally, you can create and modify an organization chart that shows hierarchical relationships, such as those among employees in a corporation. ◣ Graham Watson has just started working in the Marketing Department at MediaLoft. One of his first jobs is to prepare an analysis for MediaLoft management that highlights the success of online marketing efforts for MediaLoft Online. Most of the data he needs is already entered in a Word document. You will help him present the information in chart and diagram form.

Word 2002

Defining Charts and Diagrams

A **chart** illustrates the trends, relationships, or patterns represented by a series of numbers in various combinations. Charts should clarify data for the reader. For example, when viewing a column chart about sales, a reader can see at a glance the relationship between the column representing the current year's sales and the column representing the previous year's sales, and then make decisions and draw conclusions accordingly. You can create different kinds of charts in Word, as shown in Figure N-1. You can also create six types of diagrams, as shown in Figure N-2. The Drawing toolbar includes the Insert Diagram or Organization Chart button, which you use to create diagrams and organization charts.  Graham is intrigued by the various charts and diagrams available in Word. He decides to investigate the purpose of each type of chart and diagram so that he can make appropriate choices when working with the data in the Marketing report.

Details

▶ **Charts**

Column charts compare values side by side, usually over time. For example, you can use a column chart to show total sales generated in each of four years, with each year represented by one column. Several variations on the column chart are available. You can select a **Bar chart** to show values as horizontal bars; you can select **Cylinder**, **Cone**, and **Pyramid charts** to show values in either horizontal or vertical format, similar to the rectangles used in column and bar charts.

Circular charts show how values relate to each other as parts of a whole. For example, you can create a **Pie chart** to show the breakdown of sales by product category for a store that specializes in sporting goods. Each product category, such as skis, boots, snowboards, and clothing, is represented by a slice of the pie chart. The most commonly used circular charts are pie charts and 3-D pie charts.

Line style charts illustrate trends, where each value is connected to the next value by a line. An **Area chart** shows data similarly to a line chart, except that the space between the lines and the bottom of the chart is filled, and a different band of color represents each value.

Point-to-point charts are used to identify patterns or to show values as clusters. **XY charts** (also called **Scatter charts**) are the most commonly used point-to-point charts.

▶ **Diagrams**

An **Organization chart** illustrates a hierarchy, most often in terms of how functional areas in a company or organization relate to each other. For example, you can use an organization chart to show relationships among executives, managers, supervisors, and employees in a company.

A **Venn diagram** illustrates areas of overlap between two or more elements. You can use a Venn diagram to show how three departments in a company have individual responsibilities in addition to shared responsibilities.

A **Cycle diagram** illustrates a process that has a continuous cycle. You can use a Cycle diagram to show the life cycle of a product from manufacturing to sales to consumer use to recycling into raw materials to manufacturing back into the same or a new product.

A **Pyramid diagram** illustrates a hierarchical relationship. Probably the most familiar pyramid diagram is the food diagram, which shows the foods you should eat the most of at the base of the pyramid and the foods you should eat the least of at the top.

A **Target diagram** illustrates steps toward a goal. You can use a Target diagram to show the steps required to complete a specific project represented by the target area of the diagram.

A **Radial diagram** illustrates the relationships of several related elements to a core element. You can use a Radial diagram to show how a group of individuals all report to the same supervisor.

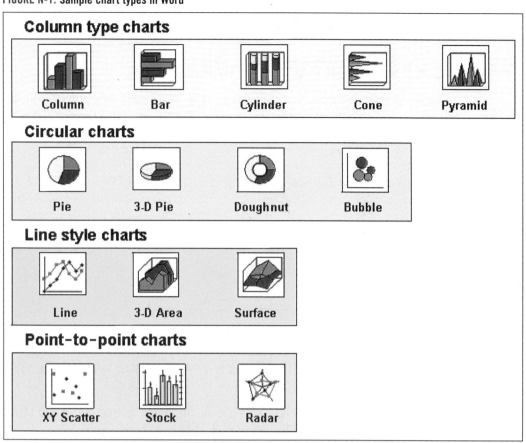

FIGURE N-2: Diagram Gallery

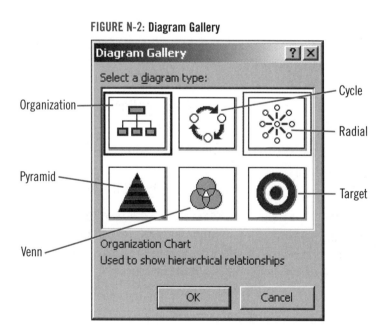

Creating a Column Chart

A column chart—or any of the charts available in Word—can be created from data you have entered into a Word table or from data you enter directly into a datasheet. A **datasheet** is a table grid that opens when you insert a chart in Word. The datasheet contains the values and labels that appear in the chart. A **value** is a number and a **label** is a word or two of text that describes the significance of the number. When you create a chart from data that you have entered into a Word table, the datasheet that appears contains the same information. However, any changes you make to the labels or values in the datasheet are not reflected automatically in the table—and vice versa. ▶ Graham has created a Word table that shows the sales for each quarter of 2002 and each quarter of 2003. He uses the data in this Word table to create a column chart.

Steps

1. Start **Word**, open the file **WD N-1.doc** from the drive and folder where your Project Files are located, save it as **Online Marketing Analysis**, then scroll through the document to get a sense of its contents

   The data you want to chart is contained in a table under the Sales heading. You can create a chart from all the data in the table or just a portion of the data.

2. Press **[Ctrl][Home]**, move the pointer over the upper-left corner of the table below the Sales paragraph to display ⊞, then click ⊞ to select the entire table

Trouble?

If the datasheet covers the chart, click the datasheet title bar and drag the datasheet to a new location.

3. Click **Insert** on the menu bar, point to **Picture**, then click **Chart**

   A column chart opens in the document, as shown in Figure N-3, because the default chart type is column. In addition, a datasheet opens that contains the same data shown in the Word table. The buttons required for working with charts appear on the Standard toolbar.

4. Click **Chart** on the menu bar, click **Chart Options**, click the **Titles tab** if necessary, click in the **Chart title text box**, type **MediaLoft Online Sales**, then press **[Tab]**

   The Chart title appears in the preview window in the Chart Options dialog box, as shown in Figure N-4.

5. Click the **Legend tab**, click the **Bottom option button**, then click **OK**

   The **legend** identifies the patterns or colors assigned to the data series in a chart.

6. Click **cell B1** in the datasheet (contains $50,000), type **$40,000**, then click an **empty cell** in the datasheet

   The chart column that illustrates the data in cell B1 changes to reflect the new data.

7. Click outside the chart area to return to your Word document, click the **cell** below 2nd Quarter in the table, then change $50,000 to **$40,000**

   You change the value in the Word table because the values in the table do not update automatically to reflect changes made to the datasheet.

QuickTip

If necessary, click View, then click ruler to show the ruler bars.

8. Click the **chart** to select it, then drag the lower-right corner down until the bottom of the chart aligns approximately with 6.3 on the vertical ruler

9. Click the **Outside Border button** ▢ on the Formatting toolbar, click away from the chart, then save the document

   Figure N-5 shows the completed column chart.

FIGURE N-3: Inserted column chart

Menu bar includes the Chart menu item

Table in the Datasheet contains the same data as the Word table

Word table containing data for the chart

Column chart based on data in Word table; column chart is default chart type

Buttons for working with charts added to Standard toolbar

All labels appear when you resize the chart

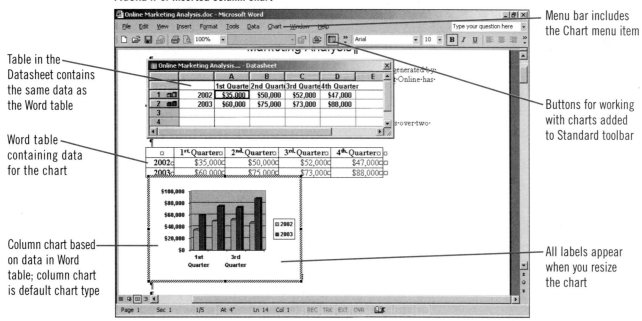

FIGURE N-4: Chart Options dialog box

Chart title entered

Chart updated in the preview window

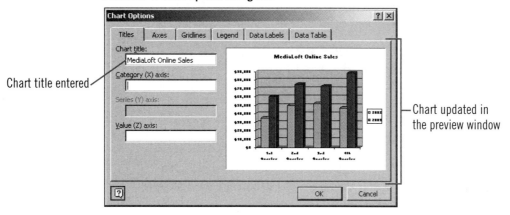

FIGURE N-5: Completed column chart

6.3 on the vertical ruler

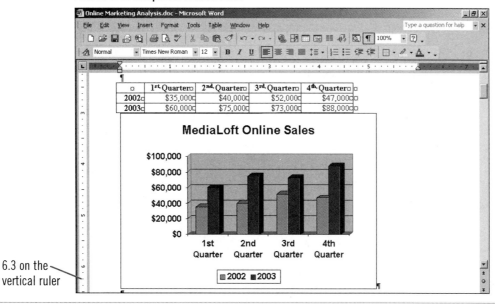

Editing a Chart

You can edit a chart in a variety of ways. For example, you can change the appearance of the columns representing each data series and you can change the font sizes of the various chart labels. You can also change the scale and appearance of each chart axis. In a two-dimensional chart, the **Y-axis** is the vertical axis and the **X-axis** is the horizontal axis. ▬▬▬▬ Graham modifies the Y-axis and the X-axis of the chart and then changes the font size of selected data labels. He also changes the color of one of the data series and then changes the column chart into a cylinder chart.

Steps 1 2 3 4

Trouble?

If the size of your chart changed, you can resize your chart after editing it.

1. Right-click the **column chart**, point to **Chart Object**, then click **Edit**
   The chart and datasheet open so that you can modify the chart. The Y-axis of the chart is represented by the numbers to the left of the chart and the X-axis is represented by the text below the chart (1st Quarter, 2nd Quarter, and so forth).

2. Right-click the **Y-axis**, click **Format Axis**, then click the **Scale tab**
   In the Scale tab of the Format Axis dialog box, you can change the values shown on the Y-axis by changing the value of the major and minor units. For example, you can select the maximum value to appear on the Y-Axis and then you can set unit increments such as 5,000 or 50 between each value.

3. Select the contents of the **Major unit text box**, then type **15000** as shown in Figure N-6
   The check mark is removed from the Major unit check box when you set a specific unit.

4. Click the **Font tab** in the Format Axis dialog box, change the font size to **10**, then click **OK**
   The information in the Y-axis changes to reflect the settings you selected.

5. Right-click the **X-axis**, click **Format Axis**, select the **10 pt** font size, then click **OK**
   The information in the X-axis changes to reflect the settings you selected.

QuickTip

The maroon bars represent the year 2003.

6. Click one of the **maroon bars** in the Column chart
   All the maroon bars are selected. When you point to a bar in a column chart a ScreenTip appears with information about what that bar represents.

7. Click **Format** on the menu bar, then click **Selected Data Series**
   You use the Format Data Series dialog box to modify the appearance of a data series. For example, you can select a new fill color or pattern.

QuickTip

You can also convert a column chart into a pyramid chart or a cone chart.

8. In the Format data series dialog box, select the **Orange color box** as shown in Figure N-7, then click **OK**
   The bars representing the selected data series are now orange.

9. Click **Chart** on the menu bar, click **Chart Type**, scroll down the Chart type list box, then click **Cylinder**

10. Click **OK** to exit the Chart Type dialog box, click outside the chart to exit Edit mode, then save the document
    The modified cylinder chart appears, as shown in Figure N-8. Notice that the columns representing each data series now appear as 3-D cylinders.

FIGURE N-6: **Format Axis dialog box**

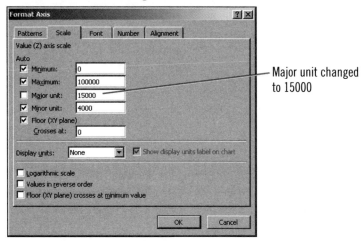

Major unit changed
to 15000

FIGURE N-7: **Format Data Series dialog box**

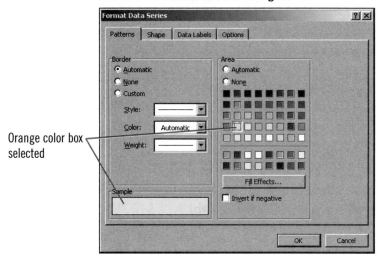

Orange color box
selected

FIGURE N-8: **Modified cylinder chart**

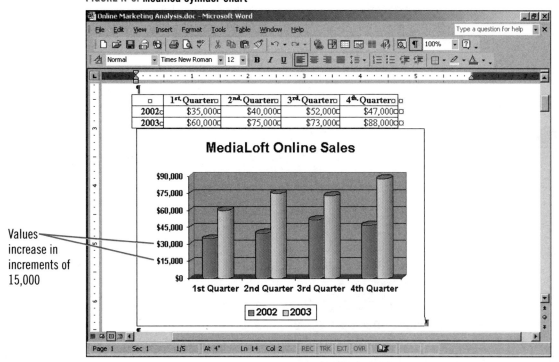

Values
increase in
increments of
15,000

Word 2002

Creating a Pie Chart

Pie charts show data as parts of a whole. For example, you could create a pie chart to show the various expenses included in a budget. Each pie wedge would represent a specific expense, such as Rent or Salaries. The size of the wedge depends on its numerical relationship to the overall budget. Taken together, all the wedges of a pie chart add up to 100%. ✎ Graham creates a pie chart to show the breakdown by category of the marketing expenses incurred in 2003.

Steps

Trouble?

Click Show/Hide ¶ to show formatting marks.

1. Scroll down to the top of page 2, click the **second paragraph mark** below the paragraph on Marketing Expenses, click **Insert** on the menu bar, point to **Picture**, then click **Chart**

   The default chart type opens and a datasheet with placeholder data and labels appears.

2. Click **Chart** on the menu bar, click **Chart Type**, click **Pie**, then click **OK**

   A pie chart based on the default data in the datasheet appears. In a pie chart, only the column labels and the values in the first row of the datasheet will be used.

QuickTip

You use the same methods to work in a datasheet (for example, adjust column and rows or move from cell to cell) that you use when you work in a Word table.

3. Click the **upper-left cell** in the datasheet, drag to select all the content, press **[Delete]**, click the **cell** directly below "A" on the datasheet, type **Brochures**, press **[Tab]**, type **Magazine Ads**, press **[Tab]**, type **Flyers**, press **[Tab]**, type **Radio Ads**, press **[Tab]**, type **E-Mail Marketing**, then press **[Tab]**

   The pie chart will include five wedges—one for each value represented by the labels.

4. Drag the **horizontal scroll bar** on the datasheet window to the left, click the **cell** below "Brochures," type **$15,000**, press **[Tab]**, type **$10,000**, press **[Tab]**, type **$5,000**, press **[Tab]**, type **$1,400**, press **[Tab]**, type **$1,000**, then press **[Enter]**

   Figure N-9 shows the completed datasheet.

5. Click **Chart** on the menu bar, click **Chart Options**, click the **Data Labels tab**, click the **Percentage check box**, then click **OK**

   The size of the pie chart is reduced and labels appear to indicate the percentage represented by each pie wedge. For example, the $15,000 Brochure expense is converted to 47%.

6. Click any white space in the chart area, click the **Chart Area list arrow** on the Standard toolbar, select **Plot Area** as shown in Figure N-10, then press **[Delete]**

   You can select any component of a chart by clicking it or by selecting it from the Chart Area list.

Trouble?

If a warning message appears, click Yes.

7. Click **Chart** on the menu bar, click **Chart Type**, select the **middle chart** in the top row of the Chart sub-type section, then click **OK**

   After changing a pie chart from a two-dimensional to a three-dimensional view, you can modify the appearance of the 3-D view.

8. Click **Chart** on the menu bar, click **3-D View**, type **45** in the Elevation text box, then click **OK**

9. Click outside the chart area, click the **pie chart** to select it, click **Format** on the menu bar, click **Object**, click the **Size tab**, change the Width to 4", click **OK**, click the **Center button** 📄 on the Formatting toolbar, click the **Outside Border button** 📄, click away from the pie chart, then save the document

   The completed pie chart is shown in Figure N-11.

FIGURE N-9: Data labels and values entered

The color wedge matches the color in the legend and the pie chart

Use the scroll bar to view all columns

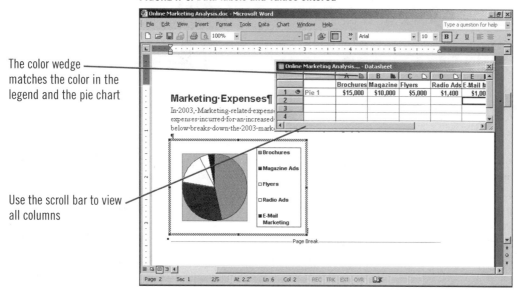

FIGURE N-10: Selecting the plot area

Chart Area list arrow

Pie chart components

Plot Area is the gray shaded square behind the pie chart.

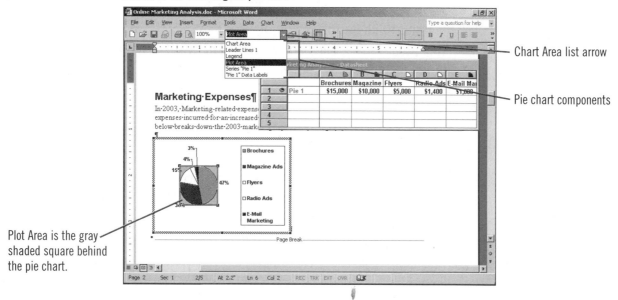

FIGURE N-11: Completed pie chart

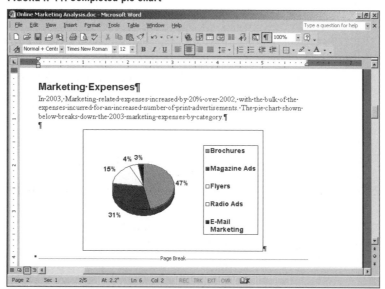

Importing Spreadsheet Data into a Chart

As you have learned, you can create a chart from data entered into a Word table or from data you enter in a datasheet. You can also create a chart from data you import from an Excel worksheet. You often choose this option when you have used Excel to enter data suitable for a chart and do not wish to re-create the data in Word. You save time by importing the data in the Excel worksheet directly into the datasheet for a chart you create in Word. Graham has created an Excel worksheet containing data about the number of visitors MediaLoft Online has attracted over a two-year period. He imports the Excel file into a datasheet for a chart he creates in Word. He then changes the chart type to a Line chart.

Steps

1. Scroll down to the top of page 3, click the **second paragraph mark** below the Web Site Visitors paragraph, click **Insert** on the menu bar, point to **Picture**, then click **Chart**

QuickTip
You can also choose to import specific cells from an Excel worksheet by selecting the Range Option button and identifying the cells to import.

2. Click the **Import File button** on the Standard toolbar, navigate to the drive and folder where your Project Files are located, click **WD N-2.xls**, click **Open**, verify that **Web Site** in the Import Data Options dialog box is selected, then click **OK**
The Web Site worksheet from the WD N-2.xls file is imported into the Word datasheet and the column chart changes to reflect the information in the datasheet.

3. As shown in Figure N-12, use ✛ to select the **framed cells** (three rows of five cells each) in the datasheet

4. Move the pointer over the left edge of the selected cells to show ↖, use ↖ to drag the selected cells left one column, click the **top border** of column E, then press **[Delete]**
The placement of the columns shifts to reflect the change in the datasheet.

5. Click **Chart** on the menu bar, click **Chart Type**, click **Line**, then click **OK** to accept the default line chart style
The column chart changes to a Line chart with markers at each data value.

6. Right-click the **pink line** in the Line chart, then click **Format Data Series**
The Format Data Series dialog box opens with the Patterns tab selected.

7. Refer to Figure N-13: in the Line section select the **bright red** color for the Line color, in the Marker section select the **triangle** style and the **bright red** color for both the foreground and the background color of the marker, then click **OK**
With the chart data completed, you can format the chart object so that it appears attractively in the Word document.

8. Click outside the chart area, right-click the **chart**, click **Format Object**, click the **Size tab**, change the Height to **3"**, then click **OK**

9. Center the chart and add an outside border, click away from the chart, then save the document
The completed line chart is shown in Figure N-14.

FIGURE N-12: Moving imported data in the chart datasheet

Select framed cells

Drag selected cells
to the left

Top border of
column E

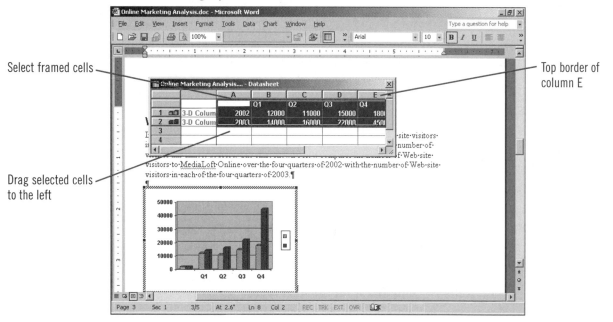

FIGURE N-13: Selecting options in the Format Data Series dialog box

Bright red Line color
selected

Triangle Marker style selected

Bright red Foreground and
Background colors selected

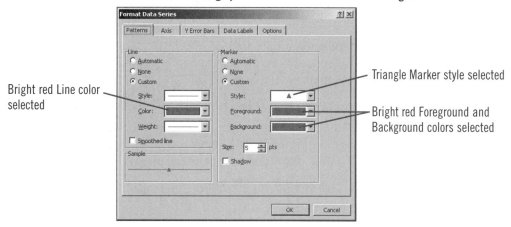

FIGURE N-14: Completed line chart

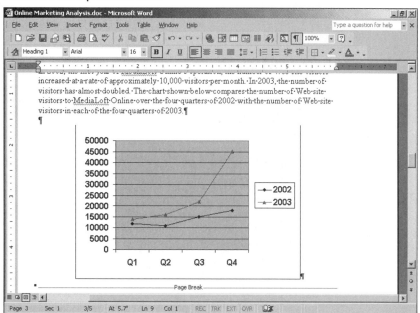

Creating a Diagram

You can create six kinds of diagrams with the Diagram tool. After you select a diagram type, you can enter text into the various sections of the diagram, then modify the size and fill color of the diagram. The diagram appears in a drawing canvas that you can size and position, just like you would any graphics object. ✐ Graham wants to provide MediaLoft management a visual comparison of the four ways in which users access MediaLoft Online. He starts by showing the Drawing toolbar and then creating and labeling a pyramid diagram.

Steps

1. Scroll down to the top of page 4, click the **second paragraph mark** below the Access Methods paragraph, show the Drawing toolbar, then click the **Insert Diagram or Organization Chart button** ⊠ on the Drawing toolbar
   The Diagram Gallery dialog box opens.

2. Click the **Pyramid Diagram**, then click **OK**
   A pyramid diagram opens and the Diagram toolbar appears. Table N-1 describes the buttons on the Diagram toolbar for pyramid diagrams. The pyramid diagram consists of a series of shapes. The Insert Shape and Move Shape buttons change, depending on the diagram you create.

3. Scroll down to see the bottom layer of the pyramid diagram, click the **bottom layer**, then type **MediaLoft Online URL** as shown in Figure N-15
   Each shape in a diagram includes a text box, into which you can enter and then format text just as you would in any text box.

4. Click the next **layer**, type **Keyword Search**, then click the **Insert Shape button** ▲ on the Diagram toolbar
   The new shape is inserted to fit automatically under the shape that contains the insertion point. The Pyramid diagram now contains four shapes.

5. Click in the **text box** for the new shape, type **Banner Ad**, scroll up and click the **top layer**, then type **Links**

6. Click **Keyword Search** to select that shape, then click the **Move Shape Forward button** ▤ on the Diagram toolbar
   You use the Move Shape Forward button to switch the positions of the Keyword Search and Banner Ad layers so that the Banner Ad layer appears above the Keyword Search layer.

7. Click the **AutoFormat button** ⊠ on the Diagram toolbar, select **Thick Outline**, then click **Apply**
   In the AutoFormat dialog box, you can select from a variety of interesting diagram formats. When you select a format, a preview of the selected format appears to the right of the Diagram Style list.

8. Click the **Layout button** Layout ▾ on the Diagram toolbar, click **Scale Diagram**, then drag the **right-middle sizing handle** to the right approximately ½"
   Links now appears on one line.

9. Click outside the drawing canvas, click the **zoom list arrow**, click **50%** and scroll to view the pyramid, then save the document
   The completed pyramid diagram appears, as shown in Figure N-16.

FIGURE N-15: Text entered in the bottom layer of the pyramid diagram

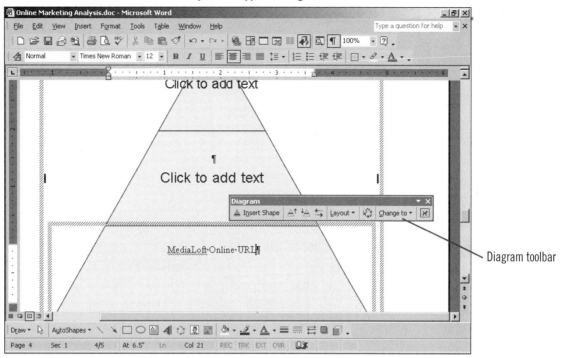

Diagram toolbar

FIGURE N-16: Completed pyramid diagram

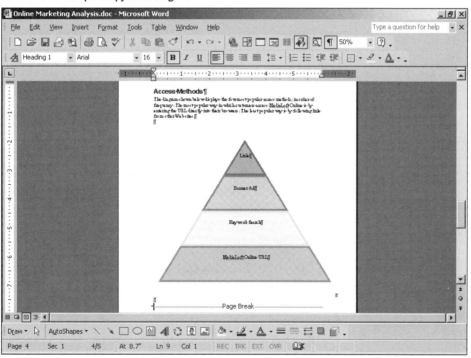

TABLE N-1: Buttons on the Diagram toolbar

Button	Use to	Button	Use to
⬛	Insert a new shape in the diagram	Layout ▾	Change the layout of the diagram
⬛	Move a selected shape backward	🔄	Apply an AutoFormat
⬛	Move a selected shape forward	Change to ▾	Change the diagram to another diagram type
↩	Reverse the diagram	🖼	Adjust the text wrapping

Word 2002

Creating an Organization Chart

An organization chart shows information in the form of a hierarchy—the top box in the organization chart represents a top position, such as a president or supervisor, and the subordinate boxes represent secondary positions, such as vice-presidents or clerks. You can also create an organization chart to show the relationships among related components, such as Web pages in a Web site. ◀◀◀ Graham wants to create a visual representation of the marketing activities related to the MediaLoft Online Web site. He creates an organization chart to show two principal activities and their subactivities.

QuickTip

The buttons on the Organization Chart toolbar are similar to the buttons on the Diagram toolbar.

1. Click the **zoom list arrow**, click **100%**, scroll to the top of page 5, click the **second paragraph mark** below the Marketing Activities paragraph, click the **Insert Diagram or Organization Chart button** on the Drawing toolbar, verify that the **Organization chart** in the upper-left corner is selected, then click **OK**

   An organization chart with two levels opens in a drawing canvas and the Organization Chart toolbar appears. The boxes in the Organization chart contain placeholder text.

2. Click in the **top box**, then type **Marketing Activities**

3. Click in the **far left box**, type **Print**, click in the **middle box**, then type **Online**

4. Click the **far right box**, click the **border** of the box to show the handles as in Figure N-17, then press **[Delete]**

   When you delete a box in an organization chart, the remaining boxes shift position and are centered under the top box.

5. Click the **box** containing the text "Print," click the **Insert Shape button list arrow** on the Organization Chart toolbar, then click **Subordinate** as shown in Figure N-18

   A new box appears under the Print box. You select Subordinate when you want to show a component beneath another component in the organization chart. You select Coworker when you want to show a component on the same level as another component. You select Assistant when you want a component to appear off to the side, indicating a supportive role, rather than a subordinate or equal role.

Trouble?

If you insert a Subordinate below the Brochures text box, click Edit, then click Undo.

6. Click the **new box**, type **Brochures**, click the **Insert Shape button list arrow**, select **Coworker**, click in the **new box**, then type **Bookmarks**

7. Click the **box** containing the text "Online," then add a Subordinate box with the text **E-Mail Marketing** and a Coworker box with the text **Affiliate Programs**

8. Click the **Layout button** on the Organization Chart toolbar, then click **Fit Organization Chart to Contents**

9. Click outside the drawing canvas, then save the document

   The organization chart appears, as shown in Figure N-19.

FIGURE N-17: Organization chart box selected

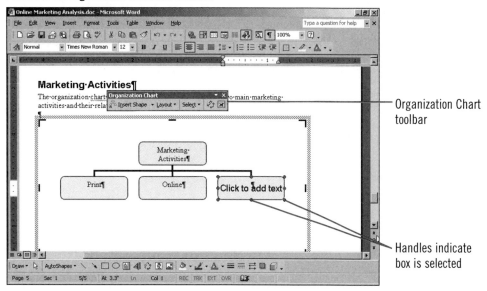

Organization Chart toolbar

Handles indicate box is selected

FIGURE N-18: Insert Shape menu options

Diagrams show placement of shape boxes in relation to other boxes in the chart

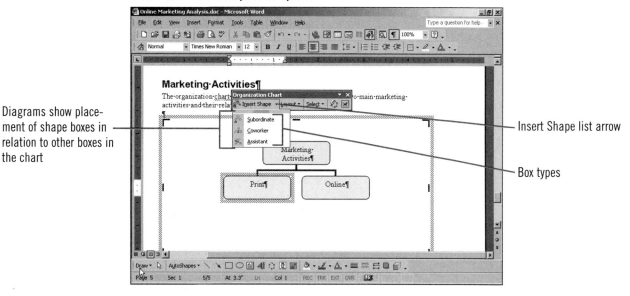

Insert Shape list arrow

Box types

FIGURE N-19: Completed organization chart

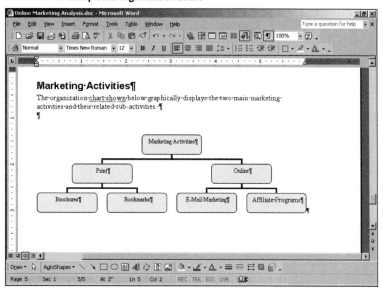

Word 2002

Modifying an Organization Chart

You can modify an organization chart by adding boxes to represent new coworkers or subordinates, or by removing boxes. You can also change the fill color of the boxes and modify the text. Finally, you can increase or decrease the size of the organization chart. ✏️ Graham applies one of the AutoFormats to the organization chart and then modifies the text in the various boxes. He then increases the size of the chart and changes the color of selected boxes so that all the information is displayed clearly.

Steps

1. Click the **chart** to select it, then click the **AutoFormat button** 🔄 on the Organization Chart toolbar
   The Organization Chart Style Gallery opens. You can choose from a variety of interesting styles.

2. Click **Primary Colors** as shown in Figure N-20, then click **Apply**
   The Primary Color style is applied to the organization chart.

Trouble?

The newly formatted text does not fit in the box. You will scale the chart in a later step so that all text can be read.

3. Select the text **Marketing Activities** in the top box, click the **Bold button** 🅱 on the Formatting toolbar, then select the **12 pt** font size
   You use the buttons on the Formatting toolbar to modify text in an organization chart box, just as you would modify any text in a Word document.

4. With the text still selected, double-click the **Format Painter button** 🖌 on the Standard toolbar, then apply Format Painter to the text in all of the chart boxes
   You can use the Format Painter button to modify text in an organization chart, just as you would in a regular Word document.

5. Click 🖌 to deselect the Format Painter, click the **Layout button** [Layout ▾] on the Organization Chart toolbar, then click **Scale Organization Chart**
   Round sizing handles appear at the corners and midpoints of the drawing canvas.

Trouble?

If the formatting of any of the text is altered, use buttons on the Formatting toolbar to reapply the correct formatting.

6. Click the **lower-middle sizing handle**, then drag it down about **1"** to the **4"** marker on the vertical ruler as shown in Figure N-21

7. Click outside the drawing canvas, press **[Ctrl][Home]**, then create a header containing the text **Prepared by** followed by your name at the left margin and the page number at the right margin

8. Click the **Print Preview button** 🔍 on the Standard toolbar, click the **Multiple Pages button** ▦, then click **2 × 3 pages**
   The completed marketing analysis document appears on five pages, as shown in Figure N-22.

9. Click **Close** on the Print Preview toolbar, save the document, print a copy, close the document, then exit Word

FIGURE N-20: Organization Chart Style Gallery

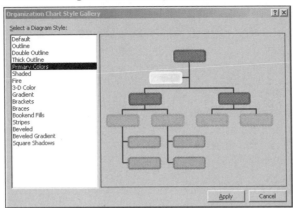

FIGURE N-21: Organization chart resized

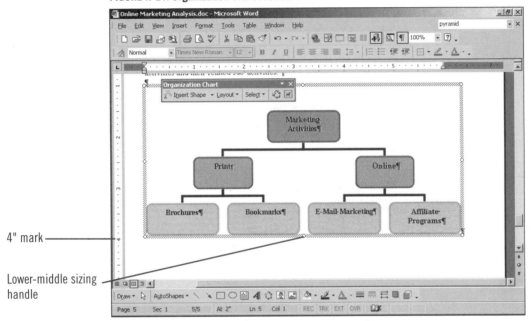

4" mark

Lower-middle sizing handle

FIGURE N-22: Completed document in Print Preview

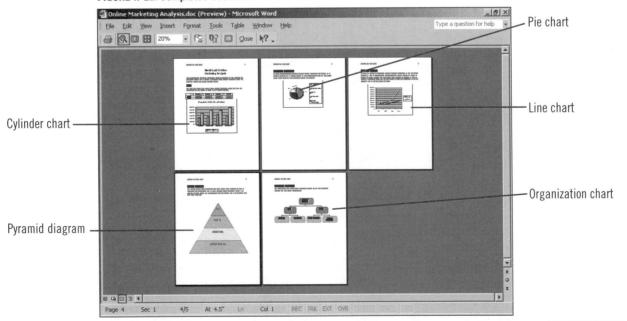

Pie chart

Cylinder chart

Line chart

Organization chart

Pyramid diagram

Practice

▶ Concepts Review

Label each of the elements in Figure N-23.

FIGURE N-23

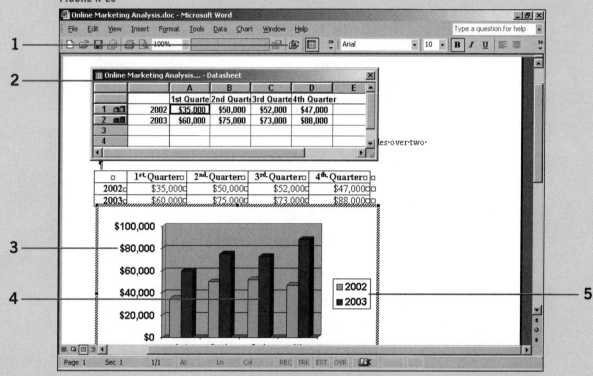

Match each term with the statement that best describes it.

6. Cone	a. Contains the data for a chart
7. Radial	b. Type of column chart
8. Legend	c. The key to the chart data
9. Label	d. A diagram that shows relationships to a core element
10. Datasheet	e. A kind of box included in an organization chart
11. Coworker	f. Describes the significance of a value

Select the best answer from the list of choices.

12. **Which of the following chart types shows data as part of a whole?**
    a. Column chart
    b. Pie chart
    c. Scatter XY chart
    d. Cylinder chart

13. **Which term refers to a number represented by a data series in a chart?**
    a. label
    b. legend
    c. value
    d. datasheet

14. **Which tab in the Format Axis dialog box do you select to change the increments shown on an X-axis or Y-axis?**
    a. Scale
    b. Font
    c. Data series
    d. Legend

15. **How many rows or columns of data can be represented in a pie chart?**
    a. one
    b. two
    c. three
    d. four

16. **How do you import Excel spreadsheet data into a chart you create in Word?**
    a. Click Insert on the menu bar, then select Chart Data.
    b. Click the Import file button on the Standard toolbar.
    c. Click the Insert file button on the Standard toolbar.
    d. Right-click a chart, then click Insert Data.

17. **Which type of diagram do you use to show areas of overlap between elements?**
    a. Venn diagram
    b. Target diagram
    c. Organization chart
    d. Pyramid diagram

18. **Where does a Subordinate shape appear in an organization chart?**
    a. above the selected shape
    b. below the selected shape
    c. to the right of the selected shape
    d. to the left of the selected shape

19. **How do you enhance an organization chart with a preset format?**
    a. Click the AutoFormat button on the Organization Chart toolbar.
    b. Click the Format Chart button on the Organization Chart toolbar.
    c. Double-click the top box in the organization chart, then click AutoFormat.
    d. Double-click the organization chart to enter Edit mode, then select a format from the AutoFormat gallery.

Skills Review

1. Create a column chart.

a. Start Word, open the file WD N-3.doc from the drive and folder where your Project Files are located, then save it as **Asia Pacific Trading Report**.

b. Select the table below the Sales paragraph at the top, then insert a column chart.

c. Open the Chart Options dialog box, then enter Asia Pacific Trading Sales as the chart title.

d. Move the legend to the bottom of the chart.

e. Change the 1st Quarter sales for 2001 to $25,000 in the datasheet and in the table.

f. Drag the lower-right corner sizing handle down to approximately the 7" mark on the vertical ruler bar and the 5" mark on the horizontal ruler.

g. Enclose the chart with an outside border, deselect the chart, then save the document

2. Edit a chart.

a. Double-click the chart, then change the Major unit of the Y-axis from 20000 to **30000** and change the font size of the Y-axis to 10 pt.

b. Change the font size of the X-axis to 10 pt.

c. Change the color of the data series representing 2003 to light green or a color of your choice.

d. Change the chart to a Cone chart, then save the document.

3. Create a pie chart.

a. Insert a chart below the Sales Expenses paragraph on the second page of the document.

b. Convert the chart to a pie chart, then clear the placeholder data.

c. Click Slice 1 in the datasheet, type Web Site, then enter Print Ads, Radio Ads, Travel Expenses, and Special Events as the labels for columns B through E.

d. Click the cell below Web Site, type **$45,000**, then enter **$20,000**, **$15,000**, **$10,000**, and **$5,000** as the values for columns B through E.

e. Open the Chart Options dialog box, then show the data labels as percentages.

f. Click any white area in the chart, select Plot Area from the Chart Area list, then delete the plot area.

g. Convert the pie chart to a 3-D chart.

h. Change the 3-D elevation of the chart to 35 degrees.

i. Use the Format Object dialog box to change the width to **4"**, center the chart, add a border, then save the document.

4. Import spreadsheet data into a chart.

a. Insert a chart at the second paragraph below the Retail Outlet Visitors paragraph on page 3 of the document.

b. Import the file WD N-4.xls from the drive and folder where your Project Files are located, verify that the Visitors worksheet is selected, then click **OK**.

c. Use the pointer to select cells with data under the columns labeled A–E in the datasheet (15 cells total), move the selected cells to the left, then delete column E.

d. Convert the chart to a Line chart. Accept the default chart subtype for a Line chart.

e. Format the data series that represents 2002 so that the line color and the foreground and background marker colors are bright green and the marker style is a square.

f. Use the Format Object dialog box to change the height of the chart to **3"**, center the chart, apply a border, then save the document.

5. Create a diagram.

    a. Scroll down to the top of page 4, click the second paragraph mark below the Supplier Countries paragraph, then show the Drawing toolbar, if necessary.

    b. Insert a Radial Diagram.

    c. Click the top circle, type **Japan**, then click the Insert Shape button twice so that the total number of circles is six, including the middle circle.

    d. Enter text in the circles, as shown in Figure N-24.

    e. Click the China circle, then click the Move Shape Forward button so that China and South Korea change places.

    f. Change the AutoFormat style to Double Outline.

    g. Change Asia Pacific Trading to Bold, 14 pt, then use the Format Painter to format the text in the remaining circles.

    h. Save the document.

FIGURE N-24

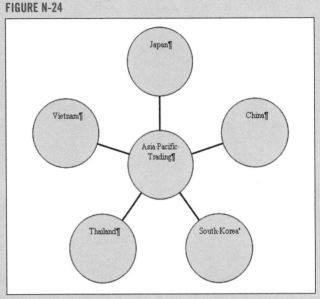

6. Create an organization chart.

    a. Scroll to the top of page 5, click the second paragraph mark below the Store Management Structure paragraph, then insert an organization chart.

    b. In the top box, type **Dawn Lu**, press [Enter], then type **Store Manager**.

    c. In the leftmost box, type **George West** followed by **Day Supervisor**; in the middle box, type **Yolanda Smith** followed by **Evening Supervisor**, then delete the far right box.

    d. Insert a Subordinate below the George West box that contains the text **Martin Lee** followed by **Clerk**.

    e. Insert a Coworker next to Martin Lee that contains the text **Sara Ng** followed by **Clerk**.

    f. Insert a Subordinate below the Yolanda Smith box that contains the text **Sam Ramos** followed by **Clerk**.

    g. Click the Layout button, then click Fit Organization Chart to Contents.

    h. Save the document.

7. Modify an organization chart.

    a. Open the Organization Chart Style Gallery, then select the Beveled Gradient style.

    b. Apply Bold and 14 pt to each name in the organization chart. Use the Format Painter to automate the process.

    c. Scale the organization chart, then drag to enlarge the chart as needed.

    d. Move to the top of the document, create a header that includes the text **Prepared by** followed by your name at the left margin and the page number at the right margin, then view all five pages in the Print Preview screen.

    e. Close the Print Preview screen, print a copy of the document, save and close it, then exit Word.

► Independent Challenge 1

As the assistant manager of a local art gallery, you are responsible for keeping track of how many people visit the gallery each month. At the end of six months, you compile the results into a column chart that you include in the gallery's semiannual report. The data for the column chart is already contained in an Excel worksheet.

    a. Start Word, open a new blank document, then save it as **Gallery Attendance** to the drive and folder where your Project Files are located.

    b. Enter the text **Prairie View Art Gallery** as a heading formatted with Bold, 16 pt, and center alignment.

c. Press [Enter] twice after the heading, clear the formatting, then enter the following sentence: **The column chart shown below presents the gallery attendance figures for adults and children from January to June, 2003**.

d. Press [Enter] twice after the sentence, then create a column chart with the default settings.

e. Click the Import file button, then import the data from the Attendance worksheet in the file WD N-5.xls, which is stored in the drive and folder where your Project Files are located.

f. Edit the chart to change the color of the Adults data series to light pink.

g. Change the chart type to Pyramid.

h. Enter **Gallery Attendance 2003** as the chart title, then move the legend to the bottom of the chart.

i. Use the Format Object dialog box to change the width to **5"** wide, then include a border line.

j. Edit the chart, change the font size of the Y-axis to 10 pt, the font size of the X-axis to 8 pt, and the font size of the Legend text to 10 pt, if necessary.

k. Remove the gray walls from the chart. (*Hint*: Right-click an area of the gray wall, click Format Walls, then change the color to None.)

l. Double-click two lines below the chart, type **Prepared by** followed by your name left-aligned, save the document, print a copy, close the document, then exit Word.

▶ Independent Challenge 2

Six months ago, you started a new online business called Net Linens that sells designer towels and linens. As part of a report for your investors, you want to include a pie chart that shows online sales of your products by category.

a. Start Word, open a new document, then save it as **Net Linens Sales** to the drive and folder where your Project Files are located.

b. Create a 3-D pie chart based on the data in the table that follows.

Category	Sales
Bath Towels	$67,000
Bed Linens	$41,000
Bedspreads	$26,000
Hand Towels	$21,000
Bath Accessories	$13,000

c. Add the title **Online Sales by Category**, position the legend at the top of the chart, below the title, then add data labels to show the percentage represented by each slice of the pie.

d. Remove the shaded plot area, then change the color of the Bath Towels data point to bright pink. (*Hint*: You need to click the pie chart, then click just the pie slice that represents Bath Towels.)

e. Increase the 3-D tilt to 45 degrees.

f. Use the Format Object dialog box to increase the width of the chart to **5"**, enclose the chart in an outside border, then center the chart.

g. Edit the chart by changing Bath Accessories to **$18,000**, then change the font size of the Legend text to 10 pt and the data labels to 9 point.

h. Double-click below the chart, type **Prepared by** followed by your name left-aligned, save the document, print a copy, close the document, then exit Word.

▶ Independent Challenge 3

You have just started working for Jasper Tours, a heli-skiing tour company based in Jasper in the Canadian Rockies. One of your jobs is to help prepare the company's annual report. Included in the report will be a page that describes the company personnel. You suggest creating an organization chart to show the hierarchy of positions.

a. Start Word, open a new document, then save it as **Jasper Tours Organization** to the drive and folder where your Project Files are located.

b. Enter Jasper Tours Organization Chart as a title enhanced with 18 pt, Bold, and center alignment.

c. Two blank lines below the title, insert an organization chart.

d. Refer to Figure N-25 to enter the text and add the boxes required for your Organization chart.

e. Apply the Shaded AutoFormat.

f. Apply Bold to the names.

g. Scale the Organization chart, then increase its height so that the bottom edge of the chart is even with the 5" mark on the vertical scroll bar.

h. Double-click below the Organization chart, type **Prepared by** followed by your name left-aligned, print a copy of the document, save and close the document, then exit Word.

FIGURE N-25

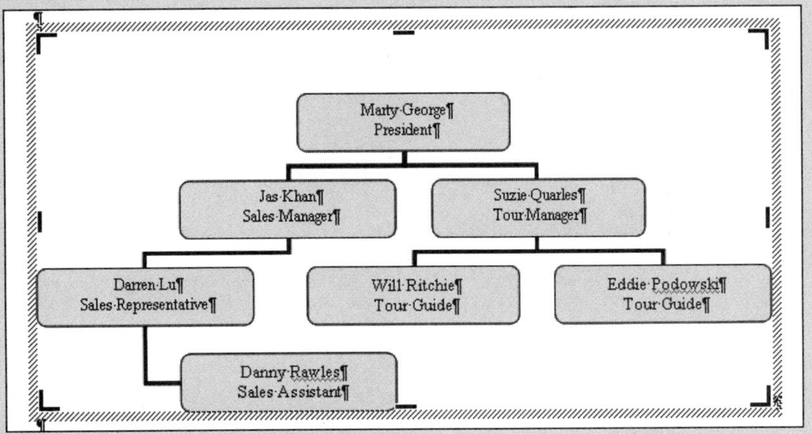

Marty George¶
President¶

Jas Khan¶
Sales Manager¶

Suzie Quarles¶
Tour Manager¶

Darren Lu¶
Sales Representative¶

Will Ritchie¶
Tour Guide¶

Eddie Podowski¶
Tour Guide¶

Danny Rawles¶
Sales Assistant¶

Independent Challenge 4

You use Radial diagrams to illustrate relationships of several related elements to a core element. As a Web designer in the process of designing a new Web site for a company of your choice, you have been checking out your competitors' Web sites. To help you determine the contents of your new Web site, you create a Radial diagram that shows six features included on a Web site that sell similar products or services.

a. Open your Web browser and conduct a search for a company that sells a product or service that interests you. You can try entering keywords related to the project, such as **lawn furniture**, **garden tools**, and **hiking tours**, and you can try entering generic domain names such as **www.garden.com** or **www.hiking.com** in the Address box of your Web browser.

b. Explore the Web site you have selected and identify six features. Features include a search tool, shopping cart, free gift offer, product-related content, and a Frequently Asked Questions page.

c. Start Word. In a new Word document, enter a title such as **Radial Diagram of an Online Garden Store**. In place of the word "Garden" use a word that describes the type of stores you researched.

d. Insert a Radial diagram that contains the name of the Web site in the center circle and one feature in each of the six surrounding circles. (*Note:* You need to add three new circles).

e. Format the diagram with the AutoFormat of your choice.

f. Format the text so that it appears attractive and easy to read. (*Note:* You might need to scale the diagram and then drag the sizing handles so that text in the circles doesn't wrap inappropriately.)

g. Type your name below the diagram.

h. Save the document as **Web Site Radial Diagram** to the drive and folder where your Project Files are located, print a copy, close the document, then exit Word.

▶ Visual Workshop

You are working with the Web Development Group at ZooAnimals.com to plan and launch a new Web site that sells a wide assortment of exotic stuffed animals—from panthers to pelicans. To help your investors understand the development process, you've created a Target diagram that illustrates the steps toward the goal of launching the Web site. The largest circle of the target diagram represents the first step in the process and the target area of the diagram represents the final goal. In a new Word document, enter the title and create the Target diagram shown in Figure N-26. The 3-D Color AutoFormat has been applied. Save the document with the name **Web Launch Target Diagram**, print a copy, then close the document.

FIGURE N-26

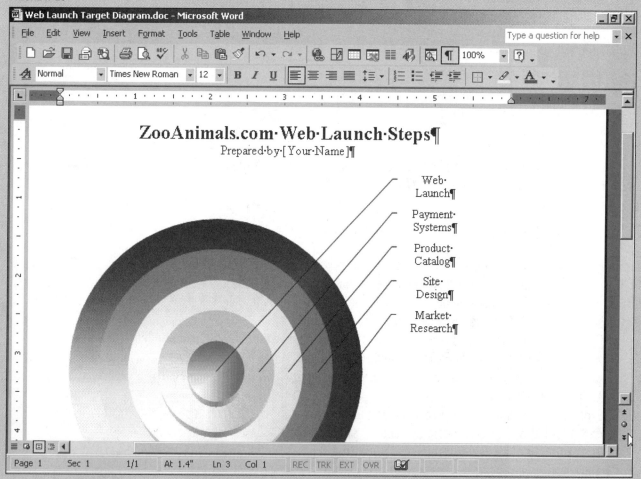

Unit O

Collaborating
with Workgroups

Objectives

► **Explore collaboration options**

[MOUS] ► **Include comments in a document**

[MOUS] ► **Track changes**

[MOUS] ► **Accept and reject changes**

[MOUS] ► **Create document versions**

[MOUS] ► **Compare documents and merge changes**

► **Use Find and Replace options**

[MOUS] ► **Protect documents**

Word includes a variety of functions designed to let you work on a document as part of a team. You can include comments in a document, highlight the changes you've made to the document text, create different versions of a document, compare these versions, and then merge changes to create a finished document that all members of the team can approve. You can also use Find and Replace options to find special characters and formatting. Finally, you can protect documents against unauthorized changes. ✎ Nazila Sharif in the Marketing Department at MediaLoft has written several questions for an online survey that visitors to MediaLoft's Web site can complete. You collaborate with Nazila and her colleague, Graham Watson, to develop a version of the survey that she can submit to Alice Wegman, the department manager, for final approval.

Exploring Collaboration Options

Word 2002

You can collaborate with colleagues in different ways. For example, you can distribute printed documents that show all the changes made by one or more colleagues, along with the comments they've made, or you can share the electronic file of the document, which also shows the changes and comments. Before they start working together to develop questions for an online survey, Nazila and Graham investigate collaborative features available in Word.

Details

► Reviewing toolbar
You use the buttons on the Reviewing toolbar to access commands that allow you to share a document between two or more people. Table O-1 describes the buttons on the Reviewing toolbar.

► Insert Comments
You insert comments into a document when you want to ask questions or provide additional information. When several people work on the same document, their comments appear in different colored balloons along the right side of the document in Print Layout view. Figure O-1 shows a document containing comments made by two people.

► Track Changes
When you share documents with colleagues, you need to be able to show them where you have inserted and deleted text. In Word, inserted text appears in the document as underlined text in the color assigned to the person who made the insertion. This same color identifies that person's deletions and comment text. For example, if Nazila's comment balloons are blue, then the text she inserts in a document will also be blue. Text that is deleted appears in a balloon along the right side of the document in Print Layout view, along with the comment balloons. Figure O-1 includes new text inserted in the document and two balloons containing deleted text.

► View Markup
When you open a document in which the Track Changes feature has been active, you can see the tracked changes and comments by selecting Markup on the View menu. When Markup is active and you are in Page Layout or Web view, the comments and tracked changes balloons appear in the right margin, the inserted text appears in colored text in the document, and the Reviewing toolbar is open. When Markup is active and you are in Normal view, tracked changes appear in colored text in the document, comment markers appear in the document at the location where comments were inserted, the comments and tracked changes appear in the Reviewing pane, and the Reviewing toolbar is open. As you work with tracked changes and comments, experiment with the different views to decide which view best meets your needs. The lessons in this unit use Page Layout view to provide practice using the Comment and Track Changes balloons.

► Create Versions
Sometimes you might want to maintain two or three versions of the same document so you can keep an ongoing record of changes. To save disk space, you can save several versions of one document within the same document file. You can then view each version of the document at any time.

► Compare and Merge Documents
You use the Compare and Merge Documents feature to determine where changes have been made to a document when the Track Changes feature has not been turned on, and then to merge changes from two or more reviewers into one document. You can choose one of three locations, as shown in Figure O-2, to display the compare and merge results.

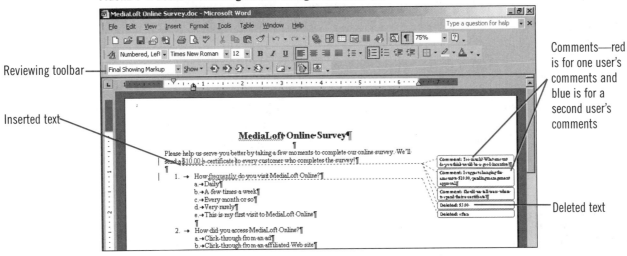

FIGURE O-1: Document showing tracked changes and comments

Reviewing toolbar

Inserted text

Comments—red is for one user's comments and blue is for a second user's comments

Deleted text

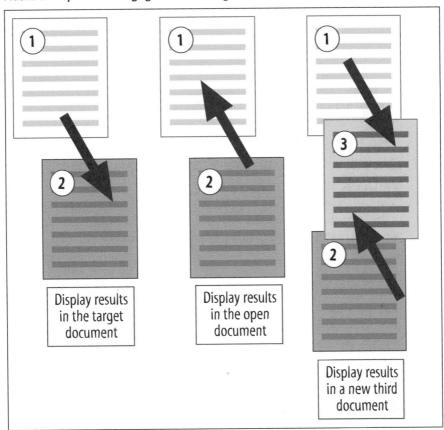

FIGURE O-2: Options for merging document changes

Display results in the target document

Display results in the open document

Display results in a new third document

TABLE O-1: Buttons on the Reviewing toolbar

button	use to	button	use to
	Show the previous change in a document		Insert a new comment
	Show the next change in a document		Turn on/off Track Changes
	Accept the highlighted change		Open the Reviewing Pane
	Reject the highlighted change or delete the currently selected comment		

Including Comments in a Document

Word 2002

Sometimes when you review a document that someone else has written, you want to insert a comment relating to the document text, the document formatting, or any number of related issues. When working in Page Layout view, a **comment** is text you insert in a comment balloon that appears, by default, along the right side of your document. A comment mark appears in the document at the point where you inserted the comment. A line leads from the comment mark to the comment balloon. Nazila has already inserted some comments in the document containing the list of survey questions. She sends the document to Graham, who asks you to add a new comment and to edit one of the comments that Nazila inserted. You work in Page Layout view so you can see the comments in comment balloons in the right margin.

Steps 1234

1. Start Word, open the file **WD O-1** from the drive and folder where your Project Files are located, then be sure the Show/Hide ¶ button ¶ is selected

2. Verify that you are in Print Layout view, click **View** on the menu bar, click **Markup**, click the **Zoom list arrow** on the Standard toolbar, click **Page Width**, scroll the document to view its contents, then save it as **MediaLoft Online Survey**
   The Reviewing toolbar appears above the document window and the two comments that Nazila inserted appear in shaded balloons in the right margin of the document. Comment markers appear in the document itself. Even if comment balloons are hidden, the comment markers associated with a comment continue to be visible in the document to indicate that a comment has been made.

> **QuickTip**
>
> In Normal view, the comment will appear in a ScreenTip when you move the insertion point over the area enclosed by the comment markers.

3. Select the word **e-certificate** in the first paragraph, then click the **New Comment button** on the Reviewing toolbar
   Comment markers appear around the word "e-certificate" and a comment balloon appears in the right margin in a color that is different from Nazila's comment. You select a word or two when inserting a comment so that the comment markers enclose the words you selected.

4. Click the **Zoom list arrow**, click **100%**, then scroll right to view the comment balloon

5. Type **Should we tell users where to spend their e-certificate?**, then click **visit** in the first question to exit the comment balloon
   You increase the zoom percentage so you can read text in a balloon. Your comment appears in a new balloon, as shown in Figure O-3.

> **QuickTip**
>
> When you click in a comment balloon, the balloon becomes a darker shade of its original color.

6. Click after **incentive** in the first comment balloon, click, in the new balloon type **I suggest changing the amount to $10.00, pending management approval.**, then click **visit** in the first question to exit the comment balloon
   A comment balloon with your response appears between the two existing comments. You click in a comment balloon and then click to keep the original comment and the response together.

7. Scroll down, click in Nazila's **second comment balloon**, click, then in the new balloon type **I suggest changing URL to Web site address.**
   You can also choose to view comments in the Reviewing Pane.

8. Click the **Reviewing Pane button** on the Reviewing toolbar, then scroll down the Reviewing Pane to view the comments
   Figure O-4 shows comments in the Reviewing Pane.

9. Click to close the Reviewing Pane, then save the document

FIGURE O-3: Comment balloons

Reviewing toolbar; location of your toolbar might differ

New Comment button

Comment marker in text

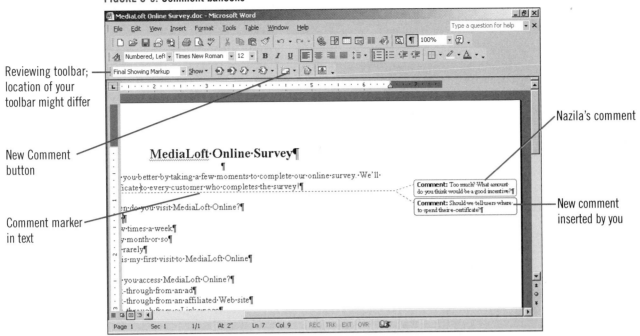

Nazila's comment

New comment inserted by you

FIGURE O-4: Comments in the Reviewing Pane

The name that appears here depends on the User Information settings

Inserted comment

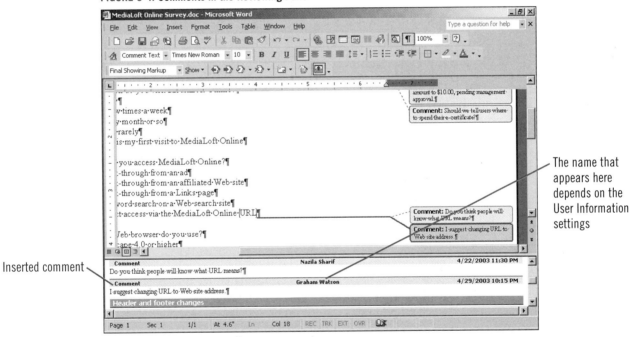

Changing User Information

The name that appears in the Reviewing Pane when you enter or edit a document with the Track Changes feature turned on is based on the content of User Information. To change this information, open the Tools menu, click Options, then click the User Information tab. In this tab, you can enter a name in the Name text box and the corresponding set of initials in the Initials text box. You modify user information when two or more people share access to the same computer and you want each person's comments and changes to appear in separate colors. If you are working in a lab setting, do not change the user information without permission.

Tracking Changes

When you work on a document with two or more people, you want to be able to see where changes have been made. You use the Track Changes command to show inserted text and deleted text. In Page Layout view, the deleted text appears in a balloon, similar to a comment balloon, and the inserted text appears in a new color and underlined in the document. ✎ Graham goes through the survey that Nazila prepared and makes some editing changes. He then reviews changes by type and reviewer.

Steps

1. **Press [Ctrl][Home], then click the Track Changes button 📖 on the Reviewing toolbar**
   Now that Track Changes is turned on, every change you make to the document will appear in colored text.

2. **Select $5.00 in the first paragraph, then press [Delete]**
   The deleted text appears in a balloon in the right margin. You can view the balloon by scrolling right or by changing the Zoom percentage to Page Width.

3. **Type $10.00, then press [Spacebar]**
   As shown in Figure O-5, the inserted text appears underlined and in the same color as the color of the comment you inserted in the previous lesson.

4. **Select often in question 1, then type frequently**
   The deleted text appears in a new balloon and the text "frequently" appears in colored underlined text.

5. **Scroll down the document to question 6, select all the text (Have you...No ¶) included with question 6, then press [Delete] twice**
   The deleted text appears in a balloon in the right margin along with a balloon that shows the formatting associated with the deleted text.

6. **Click Show on the Reviewing toolbar, click Comments to deselect it, click Show, click Insertions and Deletions to deselect it, click Show, then click Formatting to deselect it**
   You deselect all tracked changes and comment balloons so that you can review changes by type and reviewer.

7. **Click Show, then point to Reviewers**
   A menu opens listing the reviewers and showing the color assigned to each, as shown in Figure O-6. You can choose to view comments either for all reviewers or for individual reviewers. Only the comments and tracked changes associated with each reviewer listed next to a selected check box appear. You leave All Reviewers selected.

8. **With Show still active, select Comments, then scroll up to view the comment balloons**
   Since you left All Reviewers selected, comment balloons for all reviewers appear in the right margin. The different colors match the colors assigned to the reviewers in the reviewers list.

9. **Click Show, click Insertions and Deletions, click Show, click Formatting, scroll down to view the balloon next to question 6, then save the document**
   The insertions appear as underlined text in the document and the deletions appear in balloons in the right margin. Formatting changes appear in their own balloons.

FIGURE O-5: Text inserted with Track Changes feature active

New text inserted

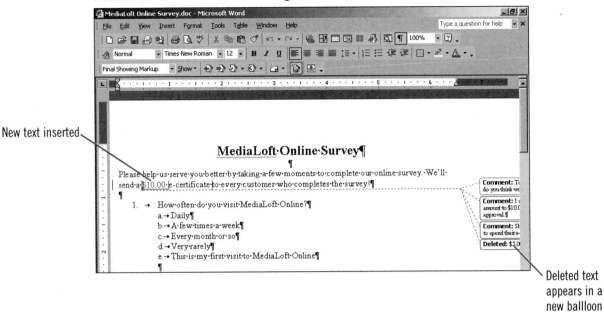

Deleted text
appears in a
new ballloon

FIGURE O-6: List of Reviewers

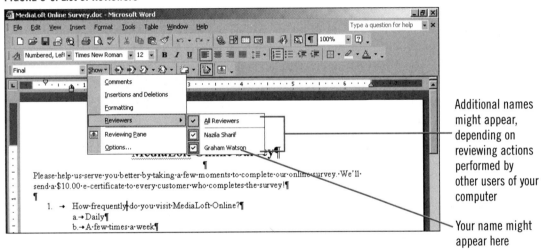

Additional names
might appear,
depending on
reviewing actions
performed by
other users of your
computer

Your name might
appear here

CLUES TO USE

Modifying Tracked Changes options

You modify the appearance of tracked changes in the Track Changes dialog box, which is shown in Figure O-7. To open this dialog box, click Show on the Reviewing toolbar, then click Options. In the Track Changes dialog box, you can change the formatting of insertions and select a specific color for them, and you can modify the appearance of the comment balloons. For example, you can increase or reduce the width of the balloons and you can choose to display the balloons in either the left or the right margin of the document.

FIGURE O-7: Track Changes dialog box

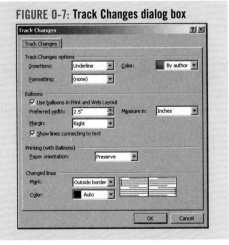

Word 2002

Accepting and Rejecting Changes

When you receive a document containing tracked changes, you will want to accept or reject the changes before you print the document as a final copy. When you accept a change, inserted text becomes part of the document and deleted text is permanently removed. You use the Reviewing toolbar to accept and reject changes in a document and to find and remove comments. ▰▰▰ Graham uses the Reviewing toolbar to accept or reject the tracked changes and to remove the comments.

Steps 1234

Trouble?

Be sure your insertion point is before MediaLoft in the title.

1. Press [Ctrl][Home], click the **Zoom list arrow** on the Standard toolbar, click **Page Width**, click the **list arrow** next to Final Showing Markup on the Reviewing toolbar, then click **Original Showing Markup**

The inserted text appears in a balloon, as shown in Figure O-8.

Trouble?

If your insertion point does not move to the balloon with $5.00, click Edit on the menu bar, click Undo, then repeat the steps starting with Step 1 and following the directions exactly.

2. Click the **list arrow** next to Original Showing Markup, click **Final Showing Markup**, then click the **Next button** 🔲 on the Reviewing toolbar to move to the first tracked change ($5.00) in the document

The insertion point moves to the balloon containing the deleted text $5.00.

3. Click the **Accept Change button** 🔲 on the Reviewing toolbar

The balloon with deleted text is removed from the right margin and the insertion point appears in the document before the next tracked change.

4. Click 🔲 to select the next tracked change ($10.00), click 🔲, then click **e-certificate** to deselect the text

The amount $10.00 appears in black text in the document, which indicates it has been accepted as the new amount.

5. Click 🔲 to move to the next tracked change which is the comment you inserted in a previous lesson, then click the **Reject Change/Delete Comment button** 🔲 on the Reviewing toolbar to remove the comment and balloon from the right margin

6. Click 🔲 to move to the next change (often), click 🔲 to restore the word "often", click 🔲, then click 🔲 to reject the insertion of the text "frequently"

Question 1 is restored to its original state. You can continue to review and accept or reject changes, or you can choose to accept the remaining changes in the document.

7. Click the **Accept Change button list arrow** 🔲, then click **Accept All Changes in Document**

All the tracked changes in the document are accepted.

QuickTip

You can choose to delete each comment individually, or you can remove all of the comments at once.

8. Click the **Reject Change/Delete Comment button list arrow** 🔲, then click **Delete All Comments in Document**

As shown in Figure O-9, all tracked changes and comments are removed from the document.

9. Click the **Track Changes button** 🔲 on the Reviewing toolbar to turn off Track Changes, then save the document

FIGURE O-8: Original Showing Markup view

Original Showing Markup selected

Deleted text appears in strike-through formatting

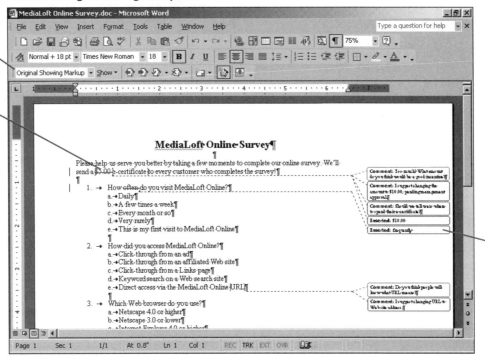

Inserted text appears in a balloon

FIGURE O-9: Tracked changes and comments accepted and removed

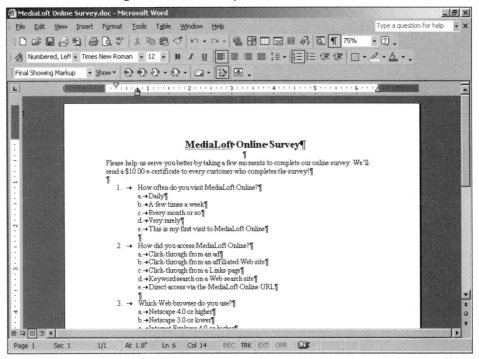

Display options for viewing tracked changes

You can choose from four different displays for reviewing a document containing tracked changes. In the Original Showing Markup view, the deleted text appears in strike-through text that ~~looks like this~~. You can use Original view to see how the document looked before changes were made, and Final view to see how the document will look after changes have been accepted or rejected and all markup formatting has been removed. You can use Final Showing Markup view to see all changes before accepting or rejecting them.

Creating Document Versions

You can use the Versions command to create two or more versions of a document. Each version can contain text that differs from every other version. You create versions of a document when you want to keep a record of the changes you've made to a document and store all versions of the document within the same filename. ◄━━━ Although Nazila and Graham are pleased with the revised questions, they want Alice to see two versions of the survey document. One version will contain the changes Graham has just accepted and the other version will contain a new question.

Steps 1234

Trouble?

Files must be saved to the hard drive to create document versions. If you are not saving your files to the hard drive, you can read the steps to understand how to create document versions, but you will not be able to complete the steps.

1. Click **File** on the menu bar, then click **Versions**
The Versions in MediaLoft Online Survey.doc dialog box opens.

2. Click **Save Now**
The Save Version dialog box opens. In this dialog box, you can type a short description of the version.

3. Type **Survey with 6 questions** as shown in Figure O-10, then click **OK**
The Versions dialog box closes and the version of the document containing six survey questions is saved to the drive and folder where the original document is located.

4. Switch to **100% view**

5. Click at the end of item **e.** in Question 2, press **[Enter]** twice, type **3.**, press **[Tab]**, type **Have you ever visited a MediaLoft real world store?**, press **[Enter]**, press **[Tab]**, type **Yes**, press **[Enter]**, then type **No**
The new question appears in the document, as shown in Figure O-11.

6. Click **File** on the menu bar, then click **Versions**
The Versions in MediaLoft Online Survey.doc dialog box opens and information about the document version you've already saved appears in the Existing versions area.

7. Click **Save Now**, type **Survey with 7 questions**, then click **OK**
A second version of the MediaLoft Online Survey document is saved.

8. Click **File** on the menu bar, then click **Versions**
Both versions of the document appear in the Versions in MediaLoft Online Survey.doc dialog box, as shown in Figure O-12.

9. Click **Close**, then save the document

FIGURE O-10: **Save Version dialog box**

Shows the current date and time

The name assigned to User Information in the Options dialog box appears here

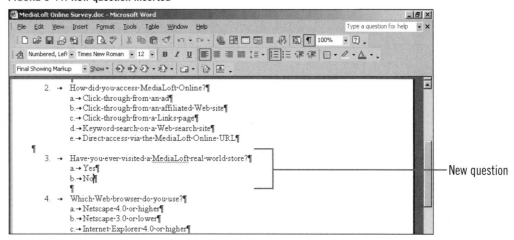

FIGURE O-11: **New question inserted**

New question

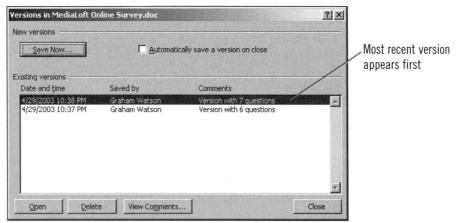

FIGURE O-12: **Versions in MediaLoft Online Survey.doc dialog box**

Most recent version appears first

Using Versions

To work on an earlier version of a document, click File on the menu bar, then click Versions to open the Versions dialog box. In the Versions dialog box, all versions of the document that you've saved are listed. The versions are listed with the most recently saved version first. You select the version you want to work on and then click Open.

Word 2002

Comparing Documents and Merging Changes

The Compare and Merge Documents feature in Word allows you to compare two or more documents to determine where changes have been made, and then to merge the changes to create a final version of the document. Word shows the differences between the documents as tracked changes. You use the Compare and Merge Documents feature to compare files of the same document saved using different filenames. You cannot use the feature to compare two or more versions of the document saved within the same filename. ✎ Alice sent Nazila her revision of the survey questions. In addition, Chris Williams in Customer Service sent Nazila his revision of the survey questions. Nazila opens these documents and saves them with new filenames. She then uses the Compare and Merge Documents features to determine what additional changes Alice and Chris have made.

1. Open the file **WD O-2** from the drive and folder where your Project Files are located, save the document as **MediaLoft Online Survey_Alice**, then scroll through the document and read Alice's changes

QuickTip

In order to merge these documents, these files must be saved to the drive and folder that contains the MediaLoft Online Survey document.

2. Open the file **WD O-3**, save it as **MediaLoft Online Survey_Chris**, then scroll through the document and read the changes Chris made

   The last file you saved, MediaLoft Online Survey_Chris, is the active document. In the Compare and Merge process, the active document is called the current document.

3. Click **Tools** on the menu bar, then click **Compare and Merge Documents**

   The three survey documents appear in the Compare and Merge Documents dialog box. You want to merge the changes from Alice and Chris with the MediaLoft Online Survey document, which has the seven questions.

4. Click **MediaLoft Online Survey_Alice**, then click the **list arrow** next to Merge

   A list of merge options appears, as shown in Figure O-13. You use the Merge command to display results in the target document. You use the Merge into current document command to display the results in the currently open document.

QuickTip

To view which reviewer is associated with which color, click the Show list arrow on the Reviewing toolbar, then point to Reviewers.

5. Click **Merge into current document**, then scroll down the merged document and identify what changes have been made

   Word merges the current document (MediaLoft Online Survey_Chris) and the target document (MediaLoft Online Survey_Alice) and then displays the differences between the two documents as tracked. See Figure O-14.

6. Click **Tools**, click **Compare and Merge Documents**, click **MediaLoft Online Survey**, click the **Merge list arrow**, then click **Merge into new document**

   The three files are merged into one new document. Tracked changes and comments from the three files appear in the right margin.

7. Click the **Accept Change button list arrow** 🖉▾ on the Reviewing toolbar, click **Accept All Changes in Document**, click the **Reject Change/Delete Comment button list arrow** 🖉▾, then click **Delete All Comments in Document**

   After accepting the combined tracked changes, the new document contains five questions.

8. Scroll to the bottom of the document, type your name where indicated, save the document as **MediaLoft Online Survey_Final**, close and save the survey documents from Alice and Chris, then close but do not save the first compare document

   MediaLoft Online Survey_Final is the only active Word document.

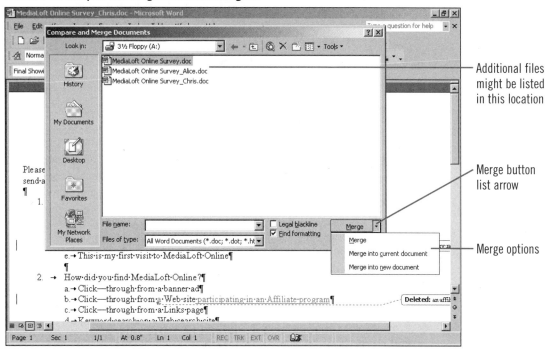

Additional files might be listed in this location

Merge button list arrow

Merge options

FIGURE O-14: Document showing merged changes

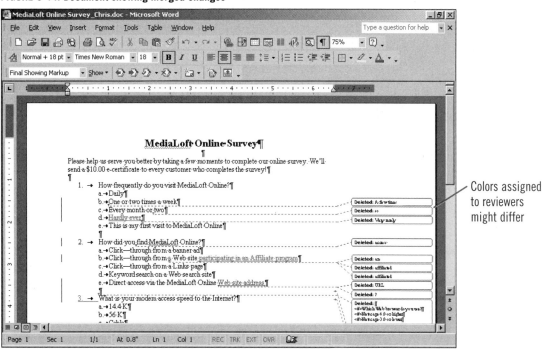

Colors assigned to reviewers might differ

Distributing documents for revision via e-mail

When you work with several people on a document, you can e-mail each person a copy of the document and ask for their input. To save time, you can use the Send To command that automatically asks a recipient to review the attached document. To send the active document, click File on the menu bar, point to Send To, then click Mail Recipient (for Review). In a few moments, the default e-mail client window appears. If you are already connected to the Internet, you just enter the e-mail address of the recipient in the To: text box and then click Send.

Using Find and Replace Options

Word's advanced find and replace options allow you to search for and replace formats, special characters, and even nonprinting elements such as paragraph marks (¶) and section breaks. For example, you can direct Word to find every occurrence of a word or phrase of unformatted text and then replace it with the same text formatted in a different font style and font size. Nazila is pleased with the final version of the survey questions. Now she needs to consider how best to format the questions for delivery over the Internet. She decides that every instance of the company name MediaLoft Online should appear in bold and italic. She uses the Find and Replace feature to find every instance of MediaLoft Online and replace it with *MediaLoft Online*. She then notices that an em dash (—) appears between the words Click and through in three entries in question 2. She decides to replace the em dash with the smaller en dash (–).

Steps

1. Click **Edit** on the menu bar, click **Replace**, then type **MediaLoft Online** in the Find what text box

2. Press [**Tab**], type **MediaLoft Online** in the Replace with text box, then click **More**
   The Find and Replace dialog box expands.

3. Click in the Replace with text box

QuickTip
You can also click Format on the menu bar and then click Font to open the Font dialog box.

4. Click **Format** at the bottom of the Find and Replace dialog box, click **Font** to open the Font dialog box, select **Bold Italic** in the Font style list, then click **OK**
   The Find and Replace dialog box appears, as shown in Figure O-15.

5. Click **Find Next**, click **Replace All**, click **OK**, click **Close**, then click the **first paragraph** to deselect the text
   All instances of MediaLoft Online are replaced with *MediaLoft Online*.

6. Press [**Ctrl**][**F**] to open the Find and Replace dialog box, click the **Replace tab**, then press [**Delete**] to remove **MediaLoft Online** from the Find what text box

7. Click **Special**, click **Em Dash**, press [**Tab**], click **Special**, then click **En Dash**
   Codes representing the em dash and en dash are entered in the Replace dialog box, as shown in Figure O-16.

8. Click the **No Formatting** button at the bottom of the Find and Replace dialog box to remove the formatting assigned to the text in the Replace with text box, click **Find Next**, then click **Replace All**

9. Click **OK**, click **Close**, then save the document

FIGURE O-15: Expanded Find and Replace dialog box

Clicking Less returns the dialog box to its original size

Formatting assigned to text in the Replace with text box

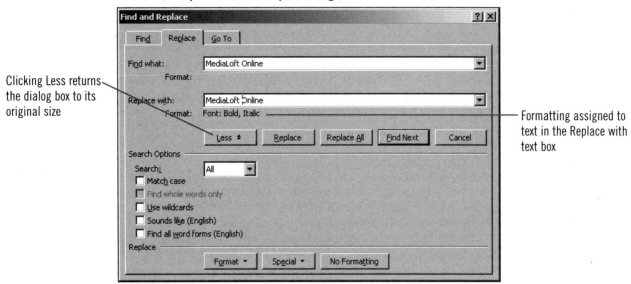

FIGURE O-16: Special characters inserted in the Find and Replace dialog box

Em dash code

En dash code

No Formatting button

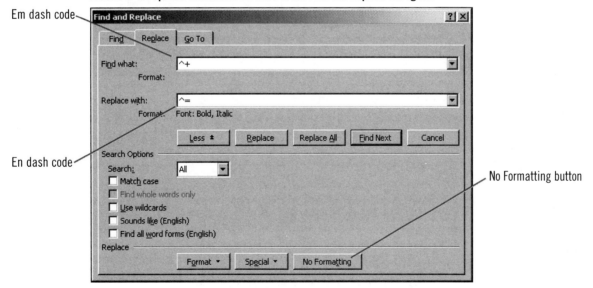

Protecting Documents

You can protect a document so that no one else can make changes or insert comments. When you protect a document, you can choose to enter a password. A user then needs to enter this password to use the Track Changes feature to accept or reject changes made to the document. You can also authenticate yourself as the author of a document by inserting a digital signature. A **digital signature** is an electronic stamp that you attach to a document to authenticate the document. The highest-level digital signature is encryption-based and secure, which assures the recipient that the document originated from the signer and has not been altered. Nazila makes one more change to the document and protects the document against tracked changes so that any user who opens the document cannot accept or reject the new change she made. Finally, she reviews the process required to insert a digital signature.

Steps

1. Click the **Track Changes button** to turn on the Track Changes feature, click immediately after **e-certificate** in the first paragraph, press **[Spacebar]**, then type **redeemable for any book in our online store**

2. Click **Tools** on the menu bar, click **Protect Document**, verify that Tracked changes is selected, enter **mrk2$7#** as the password, compare the Protect Document dialog box to Figure O-17, click **OK**, type **mrk2$7#** again, then click **OK**

   For security reasons, the password you entered appears as a series of asterisks. Now that you have protected the document, the Track Changes button on the Reviewing toolbar is dimmed. With the document protected, users can no longer accept or reject changes.

3. Save and close the document, open the document again (MediaLoft Online Survey_Final), click the **Next button** on the Reviewing toolbar to move to the change you made, click the **Accept Change button**, then click **visit** in the first question to deselect the text

   The change is not accepted because the document is protected.

4. Click **Tools** on the menu bar, click **Unprotect Document**, type **mrk2$7#**, click **OK**, click the **Previous button**, click, then deselect the text

   With the document unprotected, you can again accept or reject changes. In addition to protecting a document, you can also sign your document with a digital signature.

5. Click **Tools** on the menu bar, click **Options**, click the **Security tab**, click **Digital Signatures** to open the Digital Signature dialog box, click **Add**, click **OK** to accept the warning, click **Yes** to save the document, click **OK** to accept the default certificate, then click **View Certificate**

   Information about the default certificate attached to the digital signature appears, as shown in Figure O-18.

6. Click **OK** to exit the Certificate dialog box, click **OK** to exit the Digital Signature dialog box, then click **OK** to exit the Options dialog box

   The digital signature you have created is generated by Microsoft Office and might not constitute a legally binding signature. You decide to remove the signature you've attached until you can attach a digital signature that has been generated by a digital certificate issued by a recognized certificate authority.

7. Click **Tools** on the menu bar, click **Options**, then click **Digital Signatures**

   The digital signature currently attached to the document is listed.

8. Be sure the digital signature viewed in step 5 is selected, click **Remove**, click **OK** to return to the Security tab of the Options dialog box, then click **OK** to return to the document

9. Save the document, print a copy, close the document, then exit Word

FIGURE O-17: Protect Document dialog box

FIGURE O-18: Digital signature information

The default digital signature is not trusted, which means it can't guarantee the identity of the person who created the document

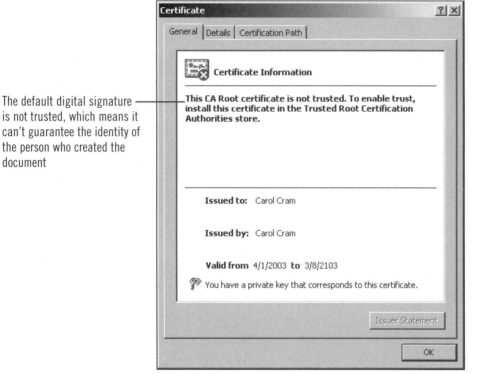

Obtaining a digital signature or certificate

You can create your own trusted digital signature by running the Selfcert.exe program included with Office XP. This program allows you to create a digital signature that will identify a document as yours; however, this type of signature is considered unauthenticated, which means the digital signature is not secure. When you e-mail a document that includes this type of digital signature, a warning message will appear in the Security Warning box if the recipient's security level is set to medium or high. If you need a secure digital signature, you can obtain a digital certificate from a certificate authority such as Verisign, Inc. A **digital certificate** is an attachment for a file that vouches for the authenticity of the file, provides secure encryption, or supplies a verifiable signature. You or your organization must submit an application to obtain a digital certificate from a commercial certification authority. You must obtain a digital certificate in order to generate an authenticated digital signature.

Practice

▶ Concepts Review

Label each of the elements in Figure O-19.

FIGURE O-19

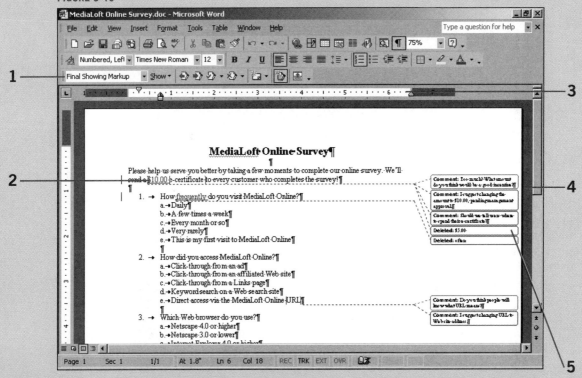

Match each term with the statement that best describes it.

6. Balloon
7. Next button
8. Original Showing Markup
9. Digital signature
10. Reviewing Pane
11. Show button

a. Use to move to another change
b. View that shows deleted text in strike-through form
c. Contains a comment and appears in the right margin
d. Use to verify the identity of the person who created the document
e. Use to view comments at the bottom of the document window
f. Click to select what type of changes you want to view

Select the best answer from the list of choices.

12. How are comments inserted by two or more individuals differentiated in a document?
- **a.** The initials of the individual are inserted next to the comment.
- **b.** The comment balloon is a different color for each individual.
- **c.** The comment balloon appears in a different location for each individual.
- **d.** The full name of the individual appears at the end of the comment text.

13. Which view do you choose when you want the text of the document and the comment balloons to be visible on the screen at the same time?
- **a.** Original Showing Markup view
- **b.** Final Showing Markup view
- **c.** Page Width view
- **d.** 100% view

14. Where can you see the name of an individual associated with a specific comment?
- **a.** In the Reviewing Pane
- **b.** In the comment balloon
- **c.** At the location where the comment was inserted
- **d.** In the Track Changes pane

15. How is deleted text shown in the Final Showing Markup view?
- **a.** As strike-through text that ~~looks like this~~
- **b.** In a balloon along the right side of the document
- **c.** As double-underlined text in the document
- **d.** As bold and colored text in the document

16. Which of the following merge options do you select when you want to display results in the target document?
- **a.** Merge
- **b.** Merge into current document
- **c.** Merge into target document
- **d.** Merge into new document

17. How do you e-mail document revisions to a colleague?
- **a.** Select Mail Recipient from the Send To menu.
- **b.** Select Mail Recipient (for Review) from the Send To menu.
- **c.** Select Reviewers from the Show menu.
- **d.** Select Mail Reviewers from the File menu.

18. How do you protect a document against tracked changes?
- **a.** Select Document Protection from the File menu.
- **b.** Select Protect Document from the Tools menu.
- **c.** Select Protect Document from the Edit menu.
- **d.** Select Protect Document on the Security tab in the Options dialog box.

19. Which of the following statements best describes a digital signature?

   a. It confirms that the document originated from the signer and has not been altered.

   b. It confirms that the document originated from a certification authority.

   c. It confirms that the document is password-protected.

   d. It confirms that the document has been approved by VeriSign.

Skills Review

1. Include comments in a document.

   a. Start Word, open the file WD O-4 from the drive and folder where your Project Files are located.

   b. Use the View menu to turn on Markup, change the zoom to Page Width, and then scroll to view the two comments.

   c. Select **service** at the end of the second line, return to 100% view, then insert a comment that states: **We need to change this sentence to mention Devaux Designs.**

   d. Scroll to the end of the paragraph in the Company Background section, click in the comment, then insert a new comment with the text **Good idea.**

   e. View the reviewers in the Reviewing Pane, then close the Reviewing Pane.

   f. Save the file as **Image Makers Company Description**.

2. Track changes.

   a. Press [Ctrl][Home], then turn on Track Changes.

   b. Delete **no other design consultation services operates** in the first paragraph, then type **the only local competition comes from Devaux Designs, a small consulting firm that opened just three months ago.**

   c. Replace "objects d'art" at the end of the first paragraph with **collectibles**.

   d. Scroll down to the Expansion Plans section of the document, then replace $50,000 with **$75,000**.

   e. Save the document.

3. Accept and reject changes.

   a. Switch to Page Width zoom.

   b. Change the Display for Review view to Original Showing Markup view, note the deletions made to the document, then return to Final Showing Markup view.

   c. Use the Reviewing toolbar to accept the changes in the first paragraph and to delete the comment associated with the first paragraph.

   d. Delete the comments associated with the Company Background paragraph.

   e. Reject deleting the original amount of $50,000 and reject inserting $75,000 in the third paragraph.

   f. Save the document.

4. Create document versions.

   a. Save the active document as a version with the comment **Three new employees**. (*Note:* You will be able to save document versions only if you are saving to a hard drive.)

   b. Switch to 100% view, if necessary, scroll to the Expansion Plans sections, then select the text **two apprentice designers and an administrative assistant** and type **three designers and an office manager**.

   c. Save the document as a version with the comment **Four new employees**.

   d. Accept all tracked changes, save the document, then close the document.

5. Compare documents and merge changes.

   a. Open the file WD O-5 from the drive and folder where your Project Files are located and save the document as **Image Makers_Donald**, open WD O-6.doc, then save it as **Image Makers_Julia**.

   b. Be sure Image Makers_Julia is the active document, then select **Compare and Merge Documents** from the Tools menu.

   c. Select the document **Image Makers Company Description**, use the Merge list arrow, then select **Merge into new document**.

d. With the new document the active document, select **Compare and Merge Documents** from the Tools menu, select **Image Makers_Donald**, then select **Merge into current document**. (*Note:* If a warning box appears, be sure Current Document is selected, then click Continue with Merge to continue.)

e. Show all the reviewers who have worked on the document.

f. Show changes by type: comments only, insertions and deletions only, formatting only, and then all three types again.

g. Accept all the changes to the document, then proofread the document and add spaces and punctuation as needed.

h. Scroll to the bottom of the document, then insert your name where indicated.

i. Reduce the top and bottom margins to **.5** so that all the text fits on one page.

j. Save the document as **Image Makers_Final**.

k. Close and do not save the other Word documents so that Image Makers_Final is the only Word document open.

6. Use Find and Replace options.

a. Open the Find and Replace dialog box, type **Image Makers** in the Find what text box, expand the Find and Replace dialog box if necessary, then assign Italic formatting to the text in the Find what text box.

b. Type **Image Makers** in the Replace with text box, then assign Bold Italic formatting to the text in the Replace with text box.

c. Find and replace all instances of Image Makers formatted in Italic with Image Makers formatted in Bold and Italic.

d. Click in the Find what text box, delete **Image Makers**, show the list of Special characters, select **Manual Line Break**, then clear the formatting assigned to text in the Find what text box. (*Hint*: Click the No Formatting button at the bottom of the Find and Replace dialog box.)

e. Click in the Replace with text box, delete **Image Makers**, show the list of Special characters, select **Paragraph Mark**, then clear the formatting assigned to text in the Replace with text box.

f. Find and replace all instances of a Manual Line Break with a Paragraph Mark. (*Note:* If a message box appears, click Yes to continue the search.)

g. Close the Find and Replace dialog box, then save the document.

7. Protect documents.

a. Turn on Track Changes, then delete **freelance** in the Company Background section.

b. Protect the document for Tracked changes with the password **R2D3%12**.

c. Save the document.

d. Press [Ctrl][Home], then move to the tracked change and try to accept it.

e. Unprotect the document with the R2D3%12 password, then accept the change.

f. Save the document, print a copy, close the document, then exit Word.

▶ Independent Challenge 1

You work for Adelphi Solutions, a large Application Service Provider based in Reading, England. The company is sponsoring a conference called E-Business Solutions for local businesses interested in developing or enhancing their online presence. Two of your co-workers have been working on a preliminary schedule for the conference. They ask for your input.

a. Start Word, open the file WD O-7 from the drive and folder where your project files are located, then save it as **E-Business Solutions Conference**.

b. Save a version of the document with the comment **Changes by Mark and Winnifred**. (*Note:* You will be able to save document versions only if you are saving to a hard drive.)

c. Scroll through the document to read the comments and view the changes made by Mark Smythe and Winnifred Reese.

d. In the 9:00 to 10:00 entry, select E-Payment Systems, then insert a comment with the text **I suggest we change the name of this session to "E-Cash in the New Millennium."**

e. Be sure the Track Changes feature is active. In the 3:00 to 4:00 entry, delete the text Nirvana, then type **Heaven**.

f. Type your name where indicated at the bottom of the document, then accept all the changes, but do not delete the comments.

g. Print a copy of the document, save a new version of the document with the comment **Changes by** followed by your name, then close the document.

h. Open the document, show the version with the comment Changes by Mark and Winnifred, then maximize the window containing the version. (*Note:* A new window opens containing the version. The title bar of the window containing the version includes the date and time the version was created.)

i. Enter your name where indicated at the bottom of the document, then print a copy of the document.

j. Close both versions of the document without saving changes, then exit Word.

▶ Independent Challenge 2

You work as an editor for Rex Harding, a freelance author currently writing a series of articles related to e-commerce. Rex sent you the first draft of his article titled "Internet Security Issues." You edited the article, then sent it back to Rex, who reviewed your changes, accepted or rejected them, inserted some new changes of his own, responded to some of your comments, and then added some new comments. You've just received this latest revision of the article. Now you need to review Rex's new changes and then prepare the final document. Rex has also asked you to use the Find and Replace feature to apply formatting to selected text included throughout the article.

a. Start Word, open the file WD O-8 from the drive and folder where your project files are located, then save it as **Internet Security Issues Article**.

b. Turn on Track Changes, then scroll through the document to get a feeling for its contents.

c. Open the Reviewing Pane to review two sets of changes. One set of changes was made by Rex and the other set was made by you, as indicated by Your Name in the Reviewing Pane. Close the Reviewing Pane.

d. Find and accept the first change (the formatting of Rex's name as the author of the article at the top of the document).

e. Move to the first comment, read it, delete it, then move to the next comment and delete it. Move the last sentence in paragraph 1 to the end of the article as shown in Figure O-20. (*Hint*: Select the sentence, click the Cut button, move to the bottom of the document, then click the Paste button.)

FIGURE O-20

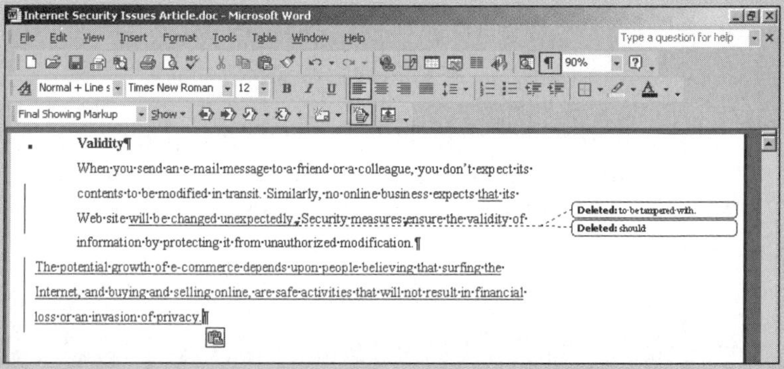

f. Move to the comment that states "Could you switch the Protection and Access Control sections?", then perform the action requested. (*Hint:* Select the Protection section (including the heading), press [Ctrl][X], click to the left of the Access Control section, then press [Ctrl][V].)

g. Delete the two paragraph marks that appear above the Validity section.

h. Accept all the remaining changes in the document, delete all the comments from the document, then turn off the Track Changes feature.

i. Scroll to the top of the document, then use the Find and Replace feature to find all instances of Web and replace it with Web formatted in Italic.

j. Take a moment to review the document and make any other changes to enhance it. For example, check the spelling and grammar or use paragraph formatting to keep headings and subheading with their paragraphs—keep the subheading Protection with the rest of its paragraph. (*Hint*: Select text you want to keep together, click Format, Paragraph, Line and Page Breaks, then activate Keep lines together and Keep with next.)

k. Create a header that includes your name and the date, save the document, print a copy, close the document, then exit Word.

► Independent Challenge 3

The Rocky Mountain Center in Boulder, Colorado, offers teens and young adults courses in various winter and summer mountain sports. As the course programmer, you are responsible for approving all the course descriptions included on the school's Web site. Three of your colleagues, Malcolm Pascal, Teresa Lopez, and Gregg Luecke have each revised descriptions of the three summer courses offered at the school. You use the Compare and Merge Documents feature to merge the documents so that you can see the changes made by the reviewers. You review the changes and add some additional changes. Finally, you protect the document so that only you or your colleagues with access to your password may accept or reject your changes.

a. Start Word, open these files from the drive and folder where your Project Files are located, then save them as indicated: WD O-9 as **Summer Courses_Malcolm**, WD O-10 as **Summer Courses_Teresa**, and WD O-11 as **Summer Courses_Gregg**.

b. Use the Compare Documents and Merge feature to merge the Summer Courses_Malcom (target file) and the Summer Courses_Gregg (active) documents into the current document, then merge Summer Courses_Teresa into a new document.

c. Review the changes in the merged version of the document.

d. Accept all the changes and delete any comments, then save the document as **Summer Courses_Final**.

e. If you have e-mail capability, e-mail this revision to yourself and then continue revising the e-mailed document, starting with step f. If you do not have e-mail access, continue with step f.

f. Be sure the Track Changes feature is active, then change the name of the Mountaineering Course to **Wilderness Survival**.

g. Attach a digital signature, if available.

h. Password-protect the document for Tracked changes with a password of your choice, then try to accept the tracked change to verify that the file is protected.

i. Unprotect the document, then accept the change.

j. Create a header containing your name and the date, save the document (which removes the digital signature), print a copy, close all documents without saving changes, then exit Word.

Independent Challenge 4

You are thinking about launching a small business that sells a product or service of your choice. As part of your start up, you decide to find out more about digital signatures and digital certificates.

a. Open your Web browser and conduct a search for information on digital signatures and digital certificates. You can try entering the keywords, "digital signature" and "digital certificate." If your search is unproductive, you can try entering www.webopedia.com and then searching the site for the keywords. Webopedia is an online glossary of terms related to the Internet. You can also check out www.verisign.com, which is a certificate authority.

b. Start Word, open the file WD O-12 from the drive and folder where your Project Files are located, then save it as **Digital Signatures**.

c. Use information from the Web sites you accessed as well as the Word Help system to answer the questions.

d. Type your name and today's date in the header section.

e. Close your browser when you have completed your research.

f. Print a copy of the Word document, close the document, then exit Word.

▶ Visual Workshop

You work for a company called Calm Oasis that sells gardening supplies and plants. Your co-worker has prepared a mission statement for the company and she asks you to edit it. Open the Project File WD O-13, then save it as **Calm Oasis Mission Statement**. Turn on the Track Changes feature, then insert comments and add changes so that the edited mission statement appears as shown in Figure O-21. Ensure that your name and date are in the footer, save the document, print a copy, then close the document.

FIGURE O-21

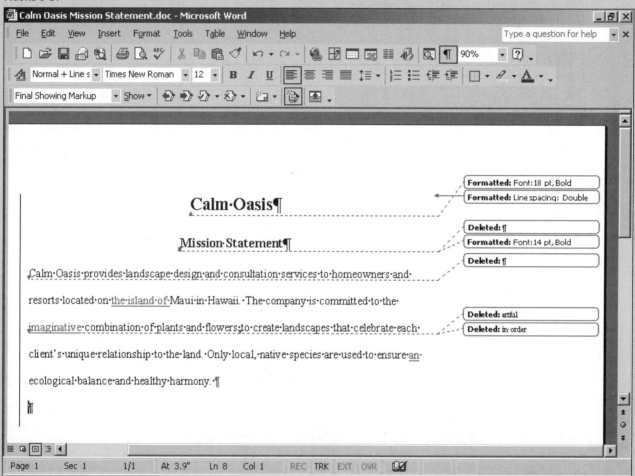

Customizing
Word

Objectives

- ► **Plan a macro**
- [MOUS] ► **Create a macro**
- [MOUS] ► **Run a macro**
- [MOUS] ► **Edit a macro in Visual Basic**
- [MOUS] ► **Rename, delete, and copy macros**
- [MOUS] ► **Create a custom toolbar**
- [MOUS] ► **Customize menus**
- ► **Modify options**

You can create macros in Word to automate a series of tasks and procedures that you perform frequently. You can also copy macros to other documents and add macros to custom toolbars. You can further customize Word to suit your working style by selecting the options you want to include on menus and by changing the default options related to elements such as measurement units and editing options. ⬛ Graham Watson in the Marketing Department at MediaLoft wants to produce a booklet containing extracts from novels featured at book signing events. He has already received extracts from several authors, but each extract is formatted differently. He decides to create a macro to automate the formatting and saving tasks. Then he will modify menus and default settings to help him work more efficiently.

Planning a Macro

If you perform a task repeatedly in Microsoft Word, you can automate the task by using a macro. A **macro** is a series of Word commands and instructions that you group together as a single command to accomplish a task automatically. You create a macro when you want to quickly perform multiple tasks. For example, you can create a macro that inserts a table with a specific number of rows and columns and with a particular border style, or you can create a macro to perform a series of complex tasks that involve multiple keystrokes. ━━━ Graham carefully plans the steps he will perform to create a macro that he will apply to each of the three documents containing book extracts. He wants the macro to format each document consistently, enter a title at the top of each document, and then save and close each document.

Details

► Macro tasks

When planning a macro, you first need to determine the tasks you want the macro to accomplish. For example, the macro could apply consistent formatting to a series of graphics in a document and then perform a series of functions such as saving, printing, and closing the document. As you learned in a previous unit, you use templates and styles to apply consistent formatting to documents. You create a macro to accomplish these tasks when you also want to include a series of specific procedures such as saving or inserting a special Word field. Table P-1 lists all the tasks that Graham wants his macro to perform when he opens a document containing a book extract.

► Macro steps

Table P-1 also lists all the steps required to accomplish each task. You plan and practice these steps before you create a macro so that you can perform the steps without error when you create the macro. If you make an error while recording the steps in the macro, you usually need to stop recording and start over. By rehearsing the steps required, you can save time. You can only use keystrokes or mouse clicks to complete all the macro steps. You cannot use a mouse to select text while recording a macro. To select all the text in a document, you use the [Ctrl][A] or Edit, Select All commands. To select just a portion of text, first you use arrow keys to move the insertion point to the text, then you press the F8 key to turn on select mode, and finally you use arrow keys to select the required text.

► Macro information

Once you have listed the steps required for the macro, you are ready to determine the information related to the macro. Figure P-1 shows the Record Macro dialog box. You use this dialog box to name the macro, assign the macro to a button to be placed on a toolbar or to a keyboard shortcut, and enter a short description of the macro. This description is usually a summary of the tasks you listed while planning the macro. You also use this dialog box to assign the location where the macro should be stored. The default location is in the Normal template so that the macro is accessible in all documents that use the Normal template. The date and name of the person who created the macro appear in the description section. The name of the person is based on the User Information associated with the computer. In Figure P-1, the macro is created by Graham Watson.

► Record macro procedure

When you click OK after completing the Record Macro dialog box, the Stop Recording toolbar opens, as shown in Figure P-2. The buttons on the Stop Recording toolbar are toggle buttons. You click the Pause button if you want to pause recording temporarily to fix an error; you click the Stop button when you have completed all the steps required for the macro. You must click the Stop button before you close the Stop Recording toolbar because simply closing it does not stop the macro recording function.

FIGURE P-1: Record Macro dialog box

By default, Macro1 is entered as the macro name the first time you open the Record Macro dialog box

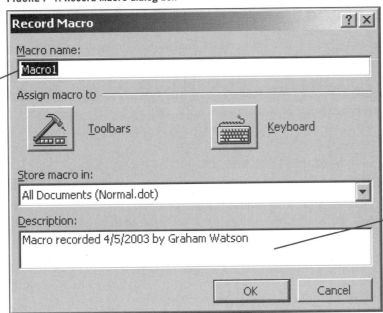

The Description information is entered by default; you can also enter a more detailed description of the macro in the Description text box

FIGURE P-2: Stop Recording toolbar

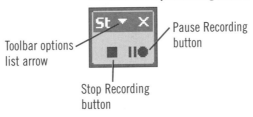

Toolbar options list arrow

Pause Recording button

Stop Recording button

TABLE P-1: Macro tasks and steps to complete the tasks

tasks	steps
Select all the text	Press [Ctrl][A]
Change the line spacing to double	Click Format on the menu bar, click Paragraph, click the Line spacing list arrow, click Double, click OK
Select the Arial font and 16 pt	Click Format on the menu bar, click Font, select the Arial font, select 16 pt, click OK
Insert a fill-in field text box into which a page title can be typed	Press the up arrow once to deselect the text and move to the top of the document, click Insert on the menu bar, click Field, scroll down the list of Field names, click Fill-in, click OK, click OK
Save and close the document	Click the Save button, click File on the menu bar, click Close

Creating a Macro

You can create a macro by using the macro recorder or by entering codes into the Visual Basic Editor. For most routine macros, you use the macro recorder. For complex macros, you use the Visual Basic Editor and enter macro steps as a series of Visual Basic codes. In this lesson, you use the macro recorder to create a macro. The macro recorder actually records each step you perform as a sequence of Visual Basic codes. ➤ Now that Graham has planned the macro, he is ready to create and record the macro steps. He creates the macro in a new blank document.

1. Start Word, close the New Document task pane, verify that the **Show/Hide ¶ button ¶** on the Standard toolbar is selected, save the blank document as **Macro Setup** to the drive and folder where your Project Files are located, then press **[Enter]** four times
With the paragraph marks visible, you can see the formatting changes you make as part of your macro steps.

2. Click Tools on the menu bar, point to **Macro,** then click **Record New Macro**
The Record Macro dialog box opens. In this dialog box, you enter information about the macro, including the name, the location where the macro is stored, and a description.

3. Type FormatExtracts, then press **[Tab]** three times to move to the Store macro in text box
You can store the macro in the Normal.dot template so that it is available to all new documents or you can store the macro in the current document. Since you want the new macro to format several different documents, you accept the default storage location, which is the Normal.dot template.

4. Press [Tab] to move to the Description box, then type the description shown in Figure P-3
By default, the Description box contains the name of the person who is recording the macro and the date the macro is recorded. You can keep this information, you can add to it, or you can overwrite it as you did in Step 4.

5. Click OK
The Stop Recording toolbar opens, the pointer changes to ▯, which indicates that you are in record macro mode.

6. Press [Ctrl][A], click **Format** on the menu bar, click **Paragraph,** click the **Line spacing list arrow,** click **Double,** then click **OK**
The line spacing between the paragraph marks changes to double spacing.

7. Click Format on the menu bar, click **Font,** select the **Arial** font, select **16 pt,** then click **OK**
The size of the paragraph marks changes to show 16 pt Arial.

8. Press the [▲] once to move to the top of the document, click **Insert** on the menu bar, click **Field,** select **Fill-in** from the list of Field names, then click **OK**
A fill-in field textbox appears, as shown in Figure P-4. When you run the macro, you will enter text in the fill-in field text box.

9. Click OK, click the **Save button** ▯ on the Standard toolbar, click **File** on the menu bar, click **Close,** then click the **Stop Recording button** ▮ on the Stop Recording toolbar
The Macro Setup file is saved and closed. The macro steps are completed and the Stop Recording toolbar closes. When you run the macro on a document that you open, the Save command saves the document with the filename already assigned to it. When you run the macro on a document that has not been saved, the Save command opens the Save As dialog box so that you can enter a filename in the File name text box, click Save, and then continue running the macro.

FIGURE P-3: Description entered in the Record Macro dialog box

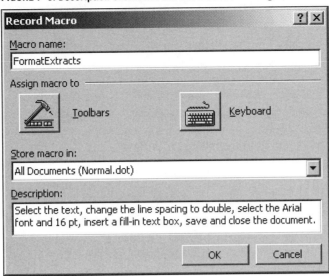

FIGURE P-4: Fill-in field text box

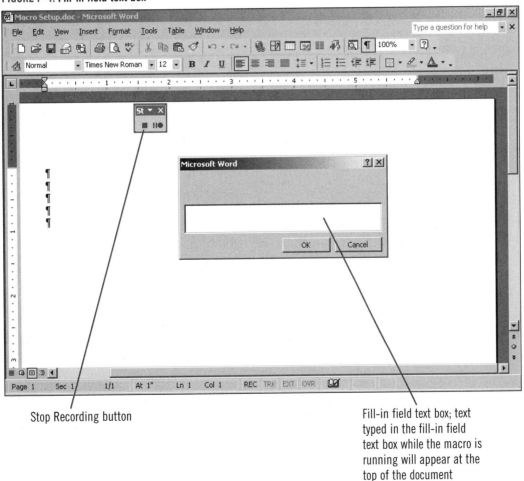

Stop Recording button

Fill-in field text box; text typed in the fill-in field text box while the macro is running will appear at the top of the document

Running a Macro

When you run a macro, the steps you recorded are performed. You can choose to run a macro in three different ways. You can select the macro name in the Macro dialog box and click the Run button, you can click a button on a toolbar if you have assigned a toolbar button to the macro, or you can press a keystroke combination if you have assigned shortcut keys to the macro. Graham opens one of the novel extracts he wants to format and runs the FormatExtracts macro by selecting the macro name in the Macro dialog box and clicking Run. He then decides to assign a keyboard shortcut to the macro.

Steps

QuickTip

The document contains spelling errors that you will correct later.

1. **Open the file WD P-1 from the drive and folder where your Project Files are located, then save it as Novel Extract_Janice Li**
   The file contains an extract from Janice Li's new novel *Dragon Swindle*.

2. **Click Tools on the menu bar, point to Macro, then click Macros**
   The Macros dialog box opens. In this dialog box, you select a macro and then the action you want to perform such as running, editing, or deleting the macro. The FormatExtracts macro is listed, as well as any other macros you have created. The name of the macro selected in the list box appears in the Macro name text box.

3. **Be sure FormatExtracts is selected, then click Run**
   The macro selects all the text, changes the line spacing to double, selects the Arial font and 16 pt, then opens a fill-in field text box.

4. **Type Janice Li's Dragon Swindle in the fill-in field text box, then click OK**
   The macro saves and then closes the document.

5. **Open the file Novel Extract_Janice Li from the drive and folder where your Project Files are located, then compare it to Figure P-5**
   The text you entered in the fill-in field text box appears at the top of the page. The document text is double-spaced and formatted in 16-pt Arial. The title text you entered appears shaded because you entered it in a fill-in field text box. The shading will not appear in the printed document.

6. **Close the document, click Tools on the menu bar, click Customize, then click Keyboard at the bottom of the Customize dialog box**
   The Customize Keyboard dialog box opens. In this dialog box, you can assign a keystroke combination to a macro or you can create a button for the macro and identify on which toolbar to place the button.

7. **In the Categories list, scroll to and click Macros, verify that FormatExtracts is selected, click in the Press new shortcut key text box, then press [Alt][E]**
   Figure P-6 shows the settings you will assign to the FormatExtracts macro to create a keyboard shortcut.

8. **Click Assign, click Close, then click Close**

9. **Open the file WD P-2 from the drive and folder where your Project Files are located, save it as Novel Extract_Lance Rose, then press [Alt][E]**
   The macro runs to the point where the fill-in field text box appears.

10. **Enter Lance Rose's Sea Swept in the fill-in field text box as shown in Figure P-7, then click OK**
    The macro saves and closes the document.

FIGURE P-5: Document formatted with the FormatExtracts macro

Font formatting, Arial font and 16 pt applied to the text

Text entered in the fill-in field text box appears here

Double spacing applied

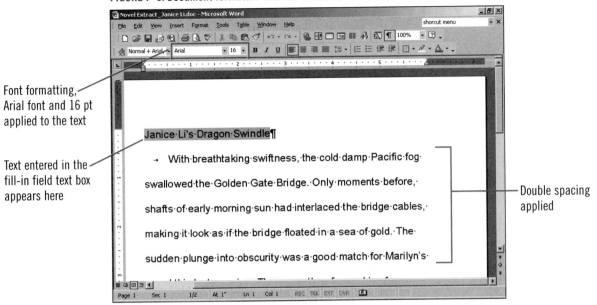

FIGURE P-6: Customize Keyboard dialog box

Macro that will run when the assigned keystroke is implemented

Shortcut key combination assigned to the macro

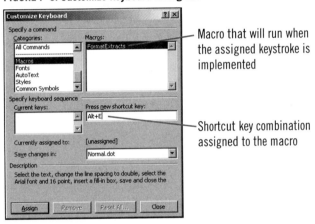

FIGURE P-7: Fill-in field text box

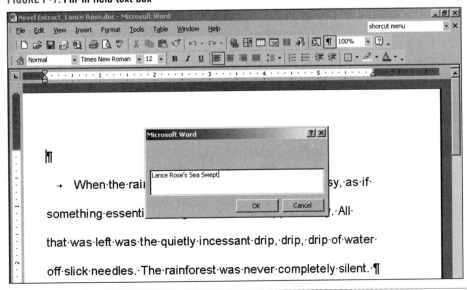

Editing a Macro in Visual Basic

You can make changes to a macro in two ways. First, you can delete the macro and record the steps again, or second, you can edit the macro in the Microsoft Visual Basic window. You use the second method when the change you want to make to the macro is relatively minor—such as changing the font style or font size, or removing one of the commands. Graham decides to reduce the font size from 16 pt to 12 pt and then remove the close document command.

Steps 1234

1. **Click Tools on the menu bar, point to Macro, then click Macros**
   The FormatExtracts macro appears in the list of available macros in the Macros dialog box.

2. **Verify that FormatExtracts is selected, then click Edit**
   The Microsoft Visual Basic window opens. The green text in the main pane is the description of the macro you entered when you created the macro. A list of codes appears in the main pane below the description. These codes are inserted as you perform the steps in the FormatExtracts macro. The text that appears to the left of the equal sign represents the code for a specific attribute such as SpaceBefore or Keep With Next. The text to the right of the equal sign represents the attribute setting.

3. **Maximize the Microsoft Visual Basic window if necessary, scroll down the page to the With Selection.Font section, then find the line .Size = 16 as shown in Figure P-8**

4. **Select 16, then type 12**

5. **Scroll down to the last End With section, then find the ActiveDocument.Close command shown in Figure P-9**

6. **Select the ActiveDocument.Close command, then press [Delete]**
   With the Close document command removed from the Visual Basic window, the macro will no longer close the document after saving it.

7. **Click the Save Normal button 🖫 on the Standard toolbar in the Microsoft Visual Basic window, then click the View Microsoft Word button 🗐 on the Standard toolbar**

8. **Open the file Novel Extract_Lance Rose from the drive and folder where your Project Files are located, click No to cancel the Merge warning if necessary, press [Alt][E] to run the macro, then click Cancel to close the fill-in field text box**
   The second time you run the macro you don't need to enter a title in the fill-in field text box. The font size of the document is now reduced to 12 pt and the document is saved, but not closed.

9. **Click Microsoft Visual Basic on the taskbar, then click the Close button in the Microsoft Visual Basic window**

10. **Type Formatted by followed by your name at the bottom of the Novel Extract_Lance Rose document, print a copy, then save and close the document**

FIGURE P-8: Font size entry in Visual Basic

With Selection.Font section

Code to change the font size to 16

All codes in this section relate to font selection attributes

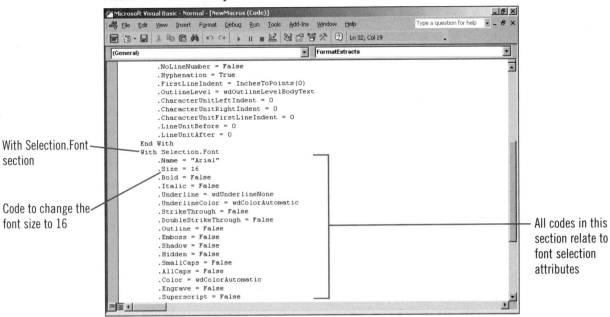

FIGURE P-9: ActiveDocument.Close command in Visual Basic

View Microsoft Word button

Save Normal button

Code to save the active document

Code to close the active document

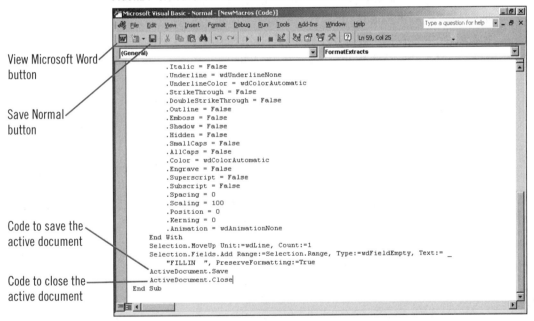

Locating Visual Basic codes

Sometimes you might want to insert a Visual Basic code into a macro. You find the correct code by searching Microsoft Visual Basic Help. To access Help, click Tools on the menu bar, click Macro, click Visual Basic Editor, then click the Microsoft Visual Basic Help button on the Standard toolbar in the Microsoft Visual Basic window. You are then prompted to install the required Help files. Once these files are installed, you can type a brief description of the action you want to perform and then search for the required codes. You must paste a code above the "End Sub" code and either above or below any of the codes related to other tasks. All codes related to a specific task, such as format paragraph spacing, must stay together in their own section.

Renaming, Deleting, and Copying Macros

Word 2002

If you save a macro in the current document, you can choose to copy the macro to other documents in which you wish to run the macro. You can also choose to copy the macro to the Normal.dot template so that the macro is available to all documents. You use the Organizer dialog box to copy macros from one document to another document. ✎ Alice Wegman, Graham's supervisor, suggests he use a different macro to format the novel extracts. She sends him a document containing a new macro, which Graham copies to an unformatted novel extract

Steps

QuickTip

If the security setting was not Medium when you opened the Security dialog box, you can return to the original security setting when you have completed this lesson.

1. Click **Tools**, point to **Macro**, click **Security**, then click the **Medium option button**
   With the security level set to Medium, you can choose whether or not to open documents containing macros.

2. Click **OK**, open the file **WD P-3** from the drive and folder where your Project Files are located, click **Enable Macros**, save the document as **Novel Extract Macro**, open the file **WD P-4**, save it as **Novel Extract_Ron Leitz**, then close the document
   The Novel Extract Macro document is the active document. You will copy the macro from the Novel Extract Macro document to the Novel Extract_Ron Leitz document.

3. Click **Tools** on the menu bar, point to **Macro**, click **Macros**, then click **Organizer**
   In the Organizer dialog box, shown in Figure P-10, you copy macros from a source file to a target file.

QuickTip

If you save your solution files in a location that is different from where your Project Files are located, navigate to that location.

4. Click **Close File** under the right-hand list in the Organizer dialog box, click **Open File**, navigate to the drive and folder where your Project Files are located, click the **Files of type list arrow**, click **All Word Documents**, click **Novel Extract_Ron Leitz**, then click **Open**

5. Be sure **NewMacros** in the list box on the left (see Figure P-10) is selected, click **Copy**, click **Close**, then click **Yes** to save the document

QuickTip

The NovelExtractMacro formats the document with 1.5 spacing, the Arial Narrow font, and 14 pt, and then saves the document.

6. Close the **Novel Extract Macro** document, open the **Novel Extract_Ron Leitz** document, click **Enable Macros**, click **Tools** on the menu bar, point to **Macro**, click **Macros**, select **NovelExtractMacro**, then click **Run**

7. Press **[Alt][E]**, type **Ron Leitz's Spade Murders**, then click **OK**

8. Click **Tools** on the menu bar, point to **Macro**, click **Macros**, click **NovelExtractMacro**, click **Delete**, then click **Yes**

9. Click **FormatExtracts**, click **Edit**, refer to Figure P-11 to replace **FormatExtracts** in two places with **Book**, then close Microsoft Visual Basic to return to Word
   The FormatExtracts macro is renamed Book and no longer appears in the Macro dialog box.

10. Press **[Ctrl] [End]**, type **Formatted by** followed by your name, print a copy, then save and close the document

FIGURE P-10: Organizer dialog box

Name of active document

Macro to be copied

Source file (file to copy macro from)

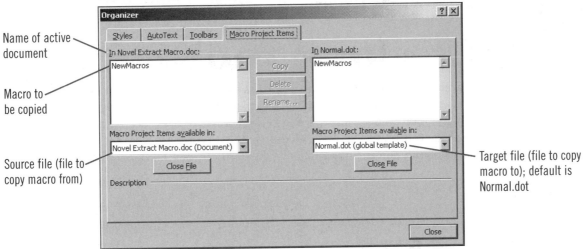

Target file (file to copy macro to); default is Normal.dot

FIGURE P-11: Renaming the macro in Visual Basic

FormatExtracts selected; replace with Book

Also replace FormatExtracts here with Book

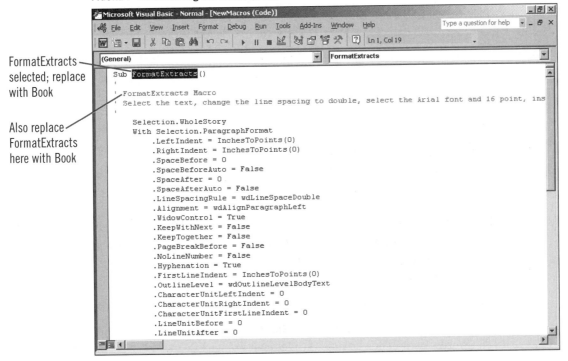

Setting security levels

If you frequently receive documents containing macros, you might need to change the security level, depending on the source of the macros. A macro can introduce a virus into your system. As a result, you want to ensure that any macro included with documents you open in Word are created by sources you trust. You can select three security levels. A High security level (the default setting) allows you to open only digitally signed macros from trusted sources. Any macro that is not digitally signed will be automatically disabled. A Medium security level provides you with a prompt when you open a document containing a macro. You can then choose to enable or disable the macros. A Low security level accepts any document containing any number of macros, and you are not protected from unsafe macros.

Creating a Custom Toolbar

You can create a custom toolbar that contains only the buttons you want to use to perform a specific number of tasks. The custom toolbar can include a button that you click to run a macro, along with buttons for other functions such as checking spelling or drawing an AutoShape. Graham decides to create a toolbar that includes a button to count the words in the document, a button to add an outside border at the position of the insertion point, and a button to run the Book macro.

Steps

1. Click **View** on the menu bar, point to **Toolbars**, click **Customize**, click the **Toolbars tab** if necessary, then click **New**
   In the New Toolbar dialog box, you type a name for the new toolbar and you assign a location in which to store the toolbar.

2. Type **Novel Extracts**, then click **OK**
   The new toolbar appears next to the Customize dialog box and contains no buttons.

3. Click the **Commands tab** in the Customize dialog box, select **Tools** in the Categories list, scroll down the list of commands, click **Word Count**, then drag **Word Count** to the Novel Extract toolbar as shown in Figure P-12

4. Scroll down the Categories list, click **Borders**, scroll down the Commands list, click **Outside Borders**, then drag the **Outside Borders button** to the Novel Extracts toolbar

5. Scroll down the Categories list, click **Macros**, click **Normal.NewMacros.Book** in the Commands list, then drag **Normal.NewMacros.Book** to the Novel Extracts toolbar

6. Click **Modify Selection** in the Customize dialog box, point to **Change Button Image**, click the **red diamond** shape, click **Modify Selection**, click **Text Only (in Menus)**, then click **Close** to close the Customize dialog box
   Figure P-13 shows the Novel Extracts custom toolbar.

7. Open the file **Novel Extract_Janice Li** from the drive and folder where your project files are located, then click **Word Count** on the Novel Extracts toolbar
   The Word Count dialog box opens, as shown in Figure P-14.

8. Click **Close** to close the Word Count dialog box, click the **red diamond** on the Novel Extracts toolbar to run the macro, click **Cancel** to close the fill-in field text box, select **Janice Li's Dragon Swindle** including the paragraph mark, click the **Outside Border button** 🔲 on the Novel Extracts toolbar, click **breathtaking**, save the document, then compare it to Figure P-15

9. Click **View** on the menu bar, point to **Toolbars**, click **Customize**, click the **Toolbars tab**, click **Novel Extracts** at the bottom of the list, click the **check box** to deselect it, click **Delete**, click **OK**, then click **Close**
   You decide to delete the macros you have created before you exit Word.

10. Click **Tools**, point to **Macro**, click **Macros**, select **Book** if necessary, click **Delete**, click **Yes**, then close the dialog box

FIGURE P-12: Word Count dragged to the Novel Extracts toolbar

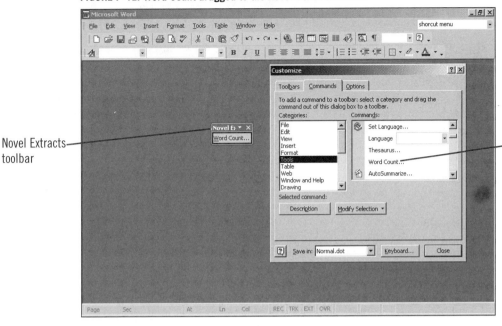

Novel Extracts toolbar

Word Count in the Commands list

FIGURE P-14: Word Count dialog box

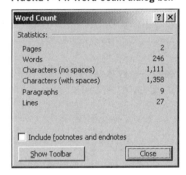

FIGURE P-13: Novel Extracts custom toolbar

FIGURE P-15: Title enhanced with an outside border

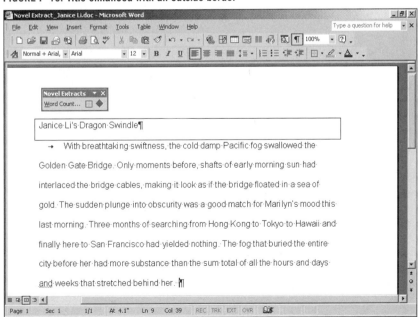

Word 2002

Customizing Menus

You can customize any menu in Word by removing commands, by renaming commands, and by displaying an icon and text for a command. You can also copy a command from one menu to another menu. You can choose to customize a menu on the menu bar, or you can customize a shortcut menu. ◤━━━ Graham decides that he wants the Spelling command to appear on the shortcut menu when he clicks the right-mouse button. Then he can quickly check the spelling in each novel extract he formats.

Steps 1 2 3 4

1. Click **Tools** on the menu bar, then click **Customize**

2. Scroll down the list of toolbars, then click the check box next to **Shortcut Menus**
   The Shortcut Menus toolbar appears, as shown in Figure P-16. You can modify Text, Table, and Draw shortcut menus.

3. Click **Text** on the Shortcut Menus toolbar, scroll down the list of shortcut menus that appears, then click **Text** as shown in Figure P-17
   The Text shortcut menu appears when you right-click a line of text.

4. Drag the **title bar** of the Customize dialog box as needed so you can see the Commands tab, then click the **Commands tab** in the Customize dialog box

QuickTip
Be sure to select Spelling, not Spelling and Grammar, in the list of commands.

5. Click **Tools** in the Categories list, scroll down the Commands list, then click **Spelling** in the list of commands

6. Drag **Spelling** to below Hyperlink in the shortcut menu as shown in Figure P-18, then click **Close** in the Customize dialog box

7. Right-click anywhere in the document to show the modified shortcut menu, then click **Spelling**

8. Correct the two spelling errors ("sholders" and "radioe"), then save the document
   Notice that the word "copyright" is misspelled as COPYWRIGHT. That is because one of the default options in Word is to not check a word's spelling if it is in all uppercase letters. You will change the option setting and correct this spelling error in the next lesson.

FIGURE P-16: Shortcut Menus toolbar

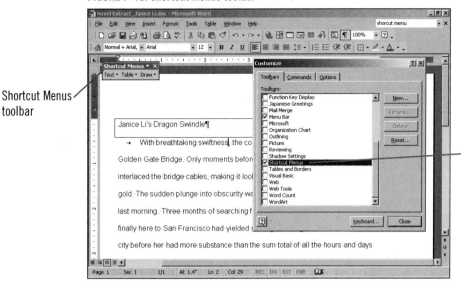

Shortcut Menus toolbar

Shortcut Menus selected in the list of toolbars

FIGURE P-17: Text shortcut menu selected

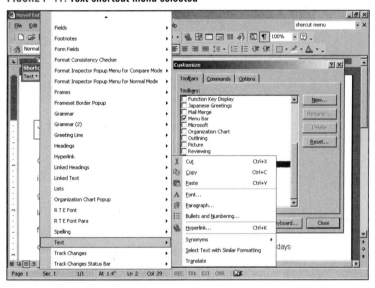

FIGURE P-18: Spelling added to the Text shortcut menu

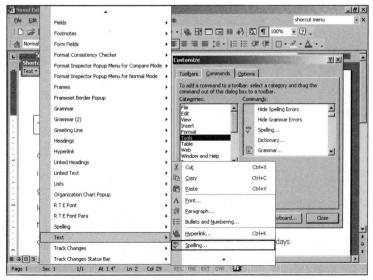

Modifying Options

Word includes many default settings designed to meet the needs of most users. For example, the default setting for entering text is black text on a white background. You can change this default to enter text another way, such as white text on a blue background. You modify default settings by selecting or deselecting options in the Options dialog box from the Tools menu. After working with Word for several months, Graham has identified some default options that do not suit his working style. He decides to change these options in the Options dialog box. First, he modifies one of the Spelling options and then he deselects the option that automatically creates a drawing canvas each time he inserts an AutoShape.

Steps

1. Click **Tools** on the menu bar, then click **Options**

   In the Options dialog box, you can change settings in eleven categories. For example, you can enter new information in the User Information, you can change the location where files are stored in the File Locations tab, and you can modify how a document is printed in the Print tab.

2. Click the **Spelling & Grammar tab**, then click the **Ignore words in UPPERCASE check box** to deselect it

   Now when you use the Spelling command to check the spelling of a document, Word will check the spelling of words entered in uppercase.

3. Click the **General tab**, click the **Automatically create drawing canvas when inserting AutoShapes check box** to deselect it, then click **OK**

   Now you can draw an AutoShape independent of the drawing canvas—something you often need to do when you want to draw just one AutoShape such as a horizontal line or a small geometric shape.

4. Right-click anywhere in the document, click **Spelling**, then change COPYWRIGHT to the correct spelling—**COPYRIGHT**

5. Move to the top of the document, show the **Drawing toolbar** if necessary, click **AutoShapes** on the Drawing toolbar, point to **Callouts**, click the **Rounded Rectangular Callout**, then draw a callout shape as shown in Figure P-19

6. Type **Nominated for Mystery Book of the Year!**, size and position the callout shape as shown in Figure P-20, enhance the text with **Bold**, center it, then click outside the text box

   If you are working on a computer that other users access, you should restore the default options and remove the Spelling command from the shortcut menu.

7. Click **Tools** on the menu bar, click **Options**, click the **Automatically create drawing canvas when inserting AutoShapes check box** to select it, click the **Spelling & Grammar tab**, click the **Ignore words in UPPERCASE check box** to select it, then click **OK**

8. Click **Tools** on the menu bar, click **Customize**, click the **Toolbars tab**, click the **Shortcut Menus check box**, click **Text** on the Shortcut Menus toolbar, select the **Text shortcut menu**, click **Spelling** in the shortcut menu, drag it to a blank area of the screen, then click **Close** in the Customize dialog box

9. Move to the bottom of the document, press [**Enter**] after the last line, type **Formatted by** followed by your name, print a copy, save and close the document, then exit Word

FIGURE P-19: Callout shape drawn

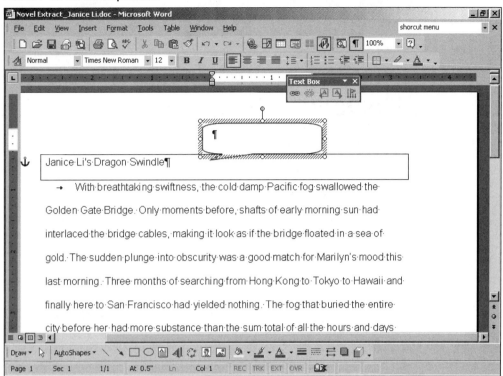

FIGURE P-20: Completed callout shape

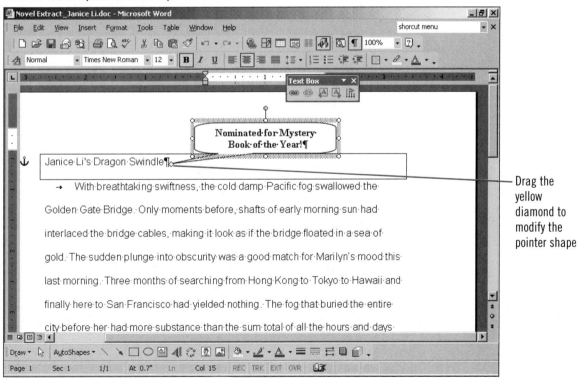

Drag the yellow diamond to modify the pointer shape

Practice

► Concepts Review

Label each of the elements in Figure P-21.

FIGURE P-21

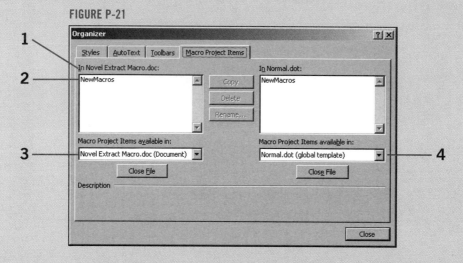

Match each term with the statement that best describes it.

5. **Stop Recording toolbar**
6. **Attribute setting**
7. **Custom toolbar**
8. **Customize**
9. **Options**
10. **Macros dialog box**

a. Contains the buttons of your choice
b. Appears to the right of the equal sign in the Visual Basic window
c. Contains the buttons used to stop and pause a macro
d. Command selected to modify a shortcut menu
e. Used to run macros
f. Selection on the Tools menu used to modify default settings

Select the best answer from the list of choices.

11. **What is a macro?**
   a. A series of procedures
   b. A series of Word commands and instructions that you group together as a single command
   c. Tasks that you cannot perform manually
   d. A series of tasks that Word performs when you select Run Macro from the Tools menu

12. **What information is *not* included in the Record Macro dialog box?**
   a. Name of the person who created the macro
   b. Name of the macro
   c. Number of the macro
   d. Location where the macro is stored

13. **Which Visual Basic code is inserted when you include the Save Document command in a macro?**
   a. SaveDocument
   b. ActiveDocument.Save
   c. ActiveDocument.SaveClose
   d. Document=Save

14. **Which dialog box do you open when you want to copy a macro from one document to another document?**
   a. Organizer dialog box
   b. Organizing Macros dialog box
   c. Record Macro dialog box
   d. Copy Macro dialog box

15. **What security level should you select if you want to be warned when a document contains macros so you can enable or disable them?**
   a. High
   b. Medium
   c. No Security
   d. Low

► Skills Review

1. Create a macro.

a. Start Word, Open the file **WD P-5** from the drive and folder where your Project Files are located, then save it as **Press Release_Bay Street Hotel**.

b. Open the Record New Macro dialog box, then type **PressReleaseFormat** as the macro name.

c. Enter the following description after the identification information: **Select all the text, change the Before and After spacing to 6 pt, enhance the title with Arial Black, 24 pt, Bold, then apply the Table Simple 3 AutoFormat to the table.**

d. Click OK, press [Ctrl][A] to select all the text, open the Paragraph dialog box, then change the Before spacing to **6 pt** and the After spacing to **6 pt**.

e. Exit the Paragraph dialog box, press [▲] once, press F8 to turn on text select mode, then press [End] to select the document title (Bay Street Hotel).

f. Open the Font dialog box, then select the Arial Black font, 24 pt, and Bold.

g. Exit the Font dialog box, press [Ctrl][End], press [▲] to move into the table, click Table on the menu bar, click Table AutoFormat, then apply the Table Simple 3 AutoFormat.

h. Click [▼] once, then click the Stop Recording button on the Stop Recording toolbar.

i. Scroll up to view the formatted document, then save and close the document.

2. Run a macro.

a. Open the file **WD P-6** from the drive and folder where your Project Files are located, then save it as **Press Release_Regina Classic Hotel**.

b. Open the Macros dialog box, select the PressReleaseFormat macro, then click Run.

c. Type **Formatted by** followed by your name at the bottom of the document, scroll up and view the formatted document, print a copy, then save and close it.

d. Open the Customize dialog box from the Tools menu, click Keyboard, select Macros from the Categories list, select the PressReleaseFormat macro if necessary, assign the [Alt][H] keystrokes to the FormatPressRelease macro, then close the Customize dialog box.

e. Open the file **WD P-7** from the drive and folder where your Project Files are located, save it as **Press Release_Royal Maritime Hotel**, press [Alt][H] to run the macro, scroll up to view the formatted document, then save the document.

3. Edit a macro in Visual Basic.

a. Open the Macros dialog box, verify the FormatPressRelease macro is selected, then click Edit.

b. Find the line SpaceAfter = 6, then change the spacing to **12**.

c. Scroll down as needed to find the line Size = 24, then change the size to **22**.

d. Save the macro, close Visual Basic and return to Microsoft Word, then use the [Alt][H] keystrokes to run the revised macro on the Press Release_Royal Maritime Hotel document.

e. Save the document, then close it.

4. Rename, delete, and copy macros.

a. Verify that the security level for macros is set to Medium. (*Note:* If the security setting was *not* Medium, return to the original security setting when you have completed this Skills Review.)

b. Open the file **WD P-8** from the drive and folder where your Project Files are located, click Enable Macros, then save the document as **Hotel Macro Sample**.

c. Open the Macros dialog box, then open the Organizer dialog box.

d. Close the file in the list on the right side, then open the **Press Release_Royal Maritime Hotel** file. (*Note:* You must change the Files of type to All Word Documents.)

e. Copy the macro from the Hotel Macro Sample file to the Press Release_Royal Maritime Hotel file, then close the Organizer dialog box and click Yes to save the Press Release_Royal Maritime Hotel file.

    f. Close the Hotel Macro Sample file, open the **Press Release_Royal Maritime Hotel** file, click Enable Macros, then run the HotelMacro.

    g. Scroll through the document to view the results of the HotelMacro, then run the [Alt][H] macro.

    h. Delete the HotelMacro macro from the Macros dialog box.

    i. Click PressReleaseFormat in the Macro name list if necessary, click Edit, change the name of the macro to **Hotel** in two places, then close Visual Basic to return to Word.

    j. Type **Formatted by** followed by your name at the bottom of the Press Release_Royal Maritime Hotel document, print a copy, then save and close the document.

5. Create a custom toolbar.

    a. Click View on the menu bar, point to Toolbars, click Customize, click the Toolbars tab if necessary, then click New.

    b. Enter **Hotels** as the name of the new custom toolbar.

    c. From the Commands tab, select Drawing in the Categories list, scroll down the list of commands, then drag the Shadow Style button to the Hotels toolbar. (*Note*: When you drag a button that includes a black list arrow at the right side of the Commands list, the options associated with the list arrow move with the button.)

    d. Select Macros in the Categories list, then select Normal.NewMacros.Hotel in the Commands list and drag it to the toolbar.

    e. Modify the Macro button so that it shows the key shape and appears as text only in menus, then close the Customize dialog box.

    f. Open the file **Press Release_Bay Street Hotel** from the drive and folder where your Project Files are located, click the picture, click the Shadow Style button on the Hotel toolbar, then select Shadow Style 2.

    g. Click the Hotel macro button on the Hotel toolbar to run the revised macro.

    h. Delete the Hotel toolbar from the Customize Toolbars dialog box, then save the document.

6. Customize menus.

    a. Open the Customize dialog box from the Tools menu, then click the check box next to Shortcut Menus in the Toolbars tab to select it.

    b. Click Table on the Shortcut Menus toolbar, then select the Table Text shortcut menu.

    c. Click the Commands tab in the Customize dialog box, click Table in the Categories list, select the Sort Ascending button from the list of commands, drag it to the Table Text shortcut menu so that it appears above Borders and Shading, then close the Customize dialog box.

    d. Scroll to the bottom of the document, click anywhere in the Price column (contains the room rates) of the table, right-click to show the modified Table Text shortcut menu, click Sort Ascending, then save the document.

7. Modify options.

    a. Open the Options dialog box from the Tools menu, click the General tab, click the Measurement units list arrow, then select Centimeters.

    b. Close the Options dialog box, right-click the picture at the top of the document, click Format Picture, click the Size tab, change the Height of the picture to **3** centimeters, then exit the Format Picture dialog box.

    c. Open the Options dialog box from the Tools menu, then change the Measurement unit in the General tab back to inches.

    d. Open the Customize dialog box from the Tools menu, then remove the Sort Ascending button from the Table Text shortcut menu. (*Hint*: Repeat steps 6a–6b. When the Table Text shortcut menu appears, drag Sort Ascending to a blank area of the screen.)

    e. Scroll to the bottom of the document, type **Formatted by** followed by your name, print a copy of the document, then save and close it.

    f. Open the Macros dialog box, delete the Hotel macro, close the Macros dialog box, then exit Word.

▶ Independent Challenge 1

You've just started working for Organics Forever. With each delivery, customers receive the price list for the coming week. Your supervisor asks you to create a macro that will speed up the tasks required to prepare each week's price lists.

a. Start Word, type **Starting Date**, press [Enter], type **Date**, press [Enter] two times, type **Special of the Week**, press [Enter], type **Special**, then press [Enter]. This text is sample text that you can use as you create the macro.

b. Press [Ctrl][Home], open the Record Macro dialog box, then enter **PriceList** as the macro name.

c. Click the Store macro in list arrow and select Document1 (document).

d. Enter the following description for the macro: **Macro created by [your name] on [the current date]. Select Date, insert the current date, select the Special, then insert a fill-in text box**.

e. Click Keyboard in the Record Macro dialog box and assign the [Alt][P] shortcut key combination.

f. Click Assign and Close, then perform the steps required for the macro as follows:
   - Press the [▼] key once, press [F8], then press [End] to select Date.
   - Press [Delete], click Insert on the menu bar, click Date and Time, click the format corresponding to March 29, 2003, verify that the Update automatically check box is selected, then click OK.
   - Press [Enter], press the[▼] twice, press [F8], press [End] to select Special, click Insert on the menu bar, scroll down to click Field, click Fill-in, click OK, then click OK.
   - Click the Stop Recording button on the Stop Recording toolbar.

g. Save the document as **Price List Macro**.

h. Open the file **WD P-9** from the drive and folder where your Project Files are located, save it as **Organics Forever Price List_[Current Date]**, then close the document.

i. Copy the macro in the Price List Macro document to the Organics Forever Price List_[Current Date] document.

j. Close the Price List Macro document, set the Security setting to Medium if necessary, open the file **Organics Forever Price List_[Current Date]**, click Enable Macros, then run the [Alt][P] macro. In the fill-in box, type **Mangoes on sale: $3.00 per pound**, then click OK.

k. Open the Macros dialog box, select PriceList in the list of macros if necessary, click Edit to enter the Visual Basic window, click File on the menu bar, then click Print to print a copy of the PriceList macro codes.

l. Close Visual Basic and return to the document, type **Formatted by** followed by your name at the bottom of the document, print a copy of the document, save it, close it, then exit Word.

▶ Independent Challenge 2

As the office manager of the Black Belt Academy, you prepare a gift certificate that you can give to new members. Since you will need to create several of these certificates each week, you decide to create a custom toolbar that contains the buttons you'll use most often to personalize each certificate.

a. Start Word, open the Customize dialog box.

b. Click the Toolbars tab, then create a new toolbar named **Gift Certificate** and saved in the Normal.dot template. See Figure P-22.

c. Click the Command tab. From the Drawing category, add the Fill Color button and the Change AutoShape button; from the AutoShapes category, add the Text Box button and the Lines button. (*Note*: Make sure you select the "Lines" button, *not* the Line button.

FIGURE P-22

d. Open the Options dialog box from the Tools menu, click the General tab if necessary, then click the Automatically create drawing canvas when inserting AutoShapes check box to deselect it.

e. Open the file **WD P-10**, then save it as **Gift Certificate_John Marks**.

f. Click the hexagon shape, click the Change AutoShape button on the Gift Certificate toolbar, point to Stars and Banners, then select the Change Shape to Explosion 2 shape.

g. Click the Text Box button on the Gift Certificate toolbar, click in the explosion shape, type **John Marks** on two lines, then enhance the text with Bold, 14 pt, and center alignment.

h. Click the Fill Color button list arrow on the Gift Certificate toolbar, then select the Light Turquoise fill color.

i. Click next to To:, click the Lines button, click the straight line, press and hold the [Shift] key, draw a line approximately six inches from To: to the right margin, then repeat the process to draw a line next to Date:.

j. Click next to To:, then type **John Marks, 202 West 4th Street, Milwaukee, WI**.

k. Click next to Date:, then type the current date. If necessary, adjust the line so that it appears under the date.

l. Type **Prepared by** followed by your name at the left margin at the bottom of the document, save the document, print a copy, then close the document.

m. Open the file **WD P-10**, then save it as **Gift Certificate_Helga Bruin**.

n. Use the Gift Certificate toolbar to create a second gift certificate for Helga Bruin, 180 Maple Avenue, Milwaukee, WI. Follow steps f-l, but use different shapes and colors.

o. Delete the Gift Certificate toolbar from the toolbars list in the Customize dialog box, close the document, then exit Word.

▶ Independent Challenge 3

You work for Blossom Inc., a florist shop in Nashville, Tennessee. The company has moved recently. As a result, several letters include an incorrect address in the letterhead. You decide to create a macro that replaces the address, phone number, and fax number of the old location with the correct contact information.

a. Start Word, open the file **WD P-11** from the drive and folder where your Project Files are located, then save it as **Catalogue Request_Farrell**.

b. Open the Record Macro dialog box, name the new macro **BlossomLetterhead**, then enter the following text in the Description text box: **Select the address, type a new address, change the zip code, change the phone and fax numbers, apply italic**. Close the dialog box.

c. Press [↓] once, then press [←] once to position the insertion point at the beginning of the address line.

d. Press F8 to turn on select mode, then press [→] repeatedly to select just 1801 Bower Avenue.

e. Press [Delete], then type **150 Mainline Avenue**.

f. Press [→] to move just before the 0 in the zip code, type **22**, then press [Delete] two times to delete 01.

g. Press [↓] two times, then press [Home] to move to the beginning of the Phone number line.

h. Press [→] to move to the last four digits of the phone number (7766), type **4455**, press [Delete] four times to delete 7766, press [→] to move to the last four digits of the fax number (7768), type **6641**, then press [Delete] four times to delete 7768.

i. Press [Home] to move to the beginning of the line, press F8, then press [End].

j. Press [Ctrl][I] to turn on italic, press [→] once, then click the Stop Recording button on the Stop Recording toolbar.

k. Enter your name in the closing where indicated, print a copy of the letter, then save and close it.

l. Open the Macros dialog box, click BlossomLetterhead in the list of macros, click Edit to enter the Visual Basic window, then change the name of the macro to **Letterhead** (in two places).

m. Scroll down toward the end of the Letterhead code to find the code Selection.Font.Italic = wdToggle, then delete the line of code. (*Note*: If you make a mistake, click Edit Undo.)

n. Save the revised macro, then close the Visual Basic window.

o. Open the file **WD P-12** from the drive and folder where your Project Files are located, save it as **Catalogue Request_Deville**, run the Letterhead macro, enter your name in the complimentary closing, print a copy of the letter, save, then close the document.

p. Delete the Letterhead macro, then exit Word.

Independent Challenge 4

You decide to search the Microsoft Design Gallery Live for four pieces of clip art related to a theme of your choice. You will insert the clip art images into a Word document, then customize a Drawing shortcut menu with the commands required to quickly modify each image. You will also change the default measurement unit to centimeters.

a. Select a theme for your catalog of online clip art. For example, you could search for images of objects such as flowers or dogs or images of places such as France or China.

b. Start Word, in a new blank Word document, enter and enhance a title such as **Clip Art Images of [Theme]**, then on the next line enter **Compiled by** followed by your name.

c. Press [Enter] two times, clear the formatting, then create a table consisting of two rows and two columns.

d. Click the Insert Clip Art button on the Drawing toolbar, click Clips Online, then click Accept to open Microsoft's Design Gallery Live. (*Note*: If the Web site is not available, use the Clip Organizer.)

e. Enter a keyword related to your theme in the Search for text box, click Go, then download the first image that suits your theme. (*Hint*: To download an image, click the Click to Download icon below the picture. When the picture appears in the Microsoft Clip Organizer dialog box, click the list arrow next to the picture, click Copy, click the Word document button on the taskbar, click in the first cell of the table, then click the Paste button on the Standard toolbar.)

f. Download three more images to complete the table. Note that the images probably will be different sizes. You will modify the images to make them a standard height after you modify the Table Pictures shortcut menu.

g. Close the Design Gallery Live (or the Clip Organizer). (*Note*: Click no if a warning box opens.)

h. Change the measurement unit to centimeters on the General tab in the Options dialog box.

i. Open the Customize dialog box from the Tools menu, select Shortcut Menus from the Toolbars tab, show the Draw shortcut menus, then click the Table Pictures shortcut menu.

j. In the Commands tab of the Customize dialog box, select Format, then drag the Center command below Borders and Shading in the Table Pictures shortcut menu.

k. In the Commands tab, select Drawing, drag the Fill Color command below the Center command, then drag the Flip Horizontal command below the Fill Color command. Close the Customize dialog box.

l. Click the first image you inserted, click the right-mouse button to show the modified Table Pictures shortcut menu, click Center, right-click the picture again, point to Fill Color, then select a color you think will complement the image.

m. With the image still selected, right-click it again, then click Flip Horizontal. (*Note*: By flipping the image, you convert it to a floating picture. When you right-click the image again, the Floating Picture shortcut menu will appear.)

n. Right-click the image, click Format Picture from the Floating Picture shortcut menu, click the Size tab, deselect the Lock aspect ratio check box, then set the Height at 7 cm and the Width at 7 cm. (*Note*: Some pictures appear slightly distorted if the Height and Width are set to the same measurement. If you prefer to resize your figures proportionally to the original figure, then select the Lock aspect ratio check box and type 7 cm in the Height box.)

o. Repeat steps k through m to format the remaining three clip art images.

p. Print a copy of the document, then save it as **Clip Art for [Your Name]**.

q. Remove the Center, Fill Color, and Flip Horizontal commands from the Tables Pictures shortcut menu.

r. Change the measurement unit back to inches, close the document, then exit Word.

► Visual Workshop

Open the file **WD P-13** from the drive and folder where your Project Files are located, click Enable Macros, then save the file as **Birthday Card_Jason**. The file contains text and a macro called BirthdayCard. Open the Visual Basic window for the BirthdayCard macro, then edit the code as follows: Change the font attribute from "Arial" to **Georgia**, scroll down, then change the line spacing attribute from wdLineSpaceDouble to wdLineSpaceSingle. (*Note*: You only need to replace Double with Single in the attribute code.) Save the revised macro, close the Visual Basic window, then run the revised macro and enter **Jason** in the fill-in box. Switch to Whole Page view, then compare the completed birthday card to Figure P-23. Enter **Formatted by** followed by your name at the bottom of the document, print a copy, then save and close the document.

FIGURE P-23

Formatting

a Disk

A **disk** is a device on which you can store electronic data. Disks come in a variety of sizes and have varying storage capacities. Your computer's **hard disk**, one of its internal devices, can store large amounts of data. **Floppy disks**, on the other hand, are smaller, inexpensive, and portable. Most floppy disks that you buy today are 3½" (the diameter of the inside, circular part of the disk). Disks are sometimes called **drives**, but this term really refers to the name by which the operating system recognizes the disk (or a portion of the disk). The operating system typically assigns a drive letter to a drive (which you can reassign if you want). For example, on most computers the hard disk is identified by the drive letter "C" and the floppy drive by the drive letter "A." The amount of information a disk can hold is called its **capacity**, usually measured in megabytes (Mb). The most common floppy disk capacity is 1.44 Mb. Newer computers come with other disk drives, such as a **Zip drive**, a kind of disk drive made to handle **Zip disks**. These disks are portable like floppy disks, but they can contain 100 Mb, far more than regular floppy disks.  In this appendix, you will prepare a floppy disk for use.

Windows 2000

Formatting a Disk

In order for an operating system to be able to store data on a disk, the disk must be formatted. **Formatting** prepares a disk so it can store information. Usually, floppy disks are formatted when you buy them, but if not, you can perform this function yourself using Windows 2000. ➤ To complete the following steps, you need a blank floppy disk or a disk containing data you no longer need. Do not use your Project Disk for this lesson, as all information on the disk will be erased.

Steps

Trouble?

This unit assumes that the drive that will contain your floppy disks is drive A. If not, substitute the correct drive any time you are instructed to use the 3½ Floppy (A:) drive.

1. Start Windows if necessary, then place a 3½" floppy disk in drive A

2. Double-click the **My Computer icon** on the desktop
My Computer opens, as shown in Figure AP-1. This window lists all the drives and printers that you can use on your computer. Because computers have different drives, printers, programs, and other devices installed, your window will probably look different.

3. Right-click the **3½ Floppy (A:) icon**
When you click with the right mouse button, a pop-up menu of commands that apply to the item you right-clicked appears. Because you right-clicked a drive, the Format command is available.

Trouble?

Windows cannot format a disk if it is write-protected; therefore, you may need to slide the write-protect tab over until it clicks to continue. See Figure AP-3 to locate the write-protect tab on your disk.

4. Click **Format** on the pop-up menu
The Format dialog box opens, as shown in Figure AP-2. In this dialog box, you specify the capacity of the disk you are formatting, the File system, the Allocation unit size, the kind of formatting you want to do, and if you want, a volume label. You are doing a standard format so you will accept the default settings.

5. Click **Start**, then, when you are warned that formatting will erase all data on the disk, click **OK** to continue
Windows formats your disk. After the formatting is complete, you will probably see a summary about the size of the disk; it's okay if you don't.

6. Click **OK** when the message telling you that the format is complete appears, then click **Close** in the Format dialog box

QuickTip

Once a disk is formatted, you do not need to format it again. However, some people use the Quick Format option to erase the contents of a disk quickly, rather than having to select the files and then delete them.

7. Click the **Close button** in the My Computer window
My Computer closes and you return to the desktop.

FIGURE AP-1: My Computer window

Drive containing your disk →

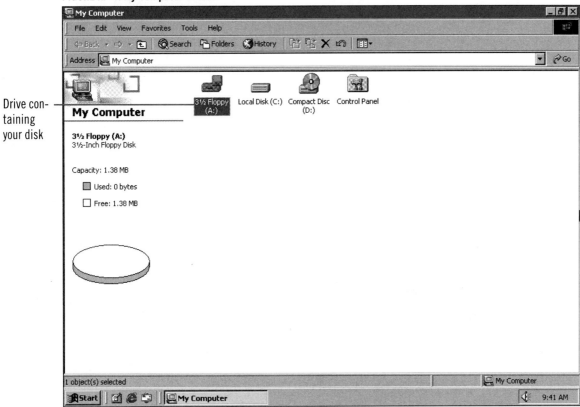

FIGURE AP-2: Format dialog box

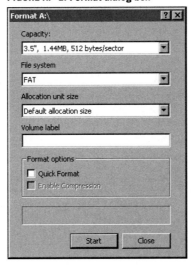

FIGURE AP-3: Write-protect tab

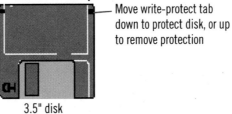

Move write-protect tab down to protect disk, or up to remove protection

3.5" disk

Project Files List

Read the following information carefully!

It is very important to organize and keep track of the files you need for this book.

1. Find out from your instructor the location of the Project Files you need and the location where you will store your files.

- To complete many of the units in this book, you need to use Project Files. Your instructor will either provide you with a copy of the Project Files or ask you to make your own copy.
- If you need to make a copy of the Project Files, you will need to copy a set of files from a file server, stand-alone computer, or the Web to the drive and folder where you will be storing your Project Files.
- Your instructor will tell you which computer, drive letter, and folders contain the files you need, and where you will store your files.
- You can also download the files by going to www.course.com. See the inside back cover of the book for instructions on how to download your files.

2. Copy and organize your Project Files.

Floppy disk users

- If you are using floppy disks to store your Project Files, the list on the following pages shows which files you'll need to copy onto your disk(s).
- Unless noted in the Project Files List, you will need one formatted, high-density disk for each unit. For each unit you are assigned, copy the files listed in the **Project File Supplied column** onto one disk.
- Make sure you label each disk clearly with the unit name (e.g., Word Unit A).
- When working through the unit, save all your files to this disk.

Users storing files in other locations

- If you are using a zip drive, network folder, hard drive, or other storage device, use the Project Files List to organize your files.
- Create a subfolder for each unit in the location where you are storing your files, and name it according to the unit title (e.g., Word Unit A).
- For each unit you are assigned, copy the files listed in the **Project File Supplied column** into that unit's folder.
- Store the files you modify or create for each unit in the unit folder.

3. Find and keep track of your Project Files and completed files.

- Use the **Project File Supplied column** to make sure you have the files you need before starting the unit or exercise indicated in the **Unit and Location column**.
- Use the **Student Saves File As column** to find out the filename you use when saving your changes to a Project File that was provided.
- Use the **Student Creates File column** to find out the filename you use when saving a file you create new for the exercise.

Unit and Location	Project File Supplied	Student Saves File As	Student Creates Files
Windows 2000 Unit A	(No files provided or created)		
Windows 2000 Unit B			
DISK 1			
Lessons	Win_B-1.bmp		
DISK 2			
Skills Review	Win_B-2.bmp		
Word Unit A			
Lessons			Marketing Memo.doc
Skills Review			Lacasse Fax.doc
Independent Challenge 1			Zobel Letter.doc
Independent Challenge 2			Smart Tags Memo.doc
Independent Challenge 3			Komata Letter.doc
Independent Challenge 4			Business Letters.doc
Visual Workshop			Publishing Cover Letter.doc
Word Unit B			
Lessons	WD B-1.doc	NY Press Release.doc	NYT Fax.doc
Skills Review	WD B-2.doc	CAOS Press Release.doc	CAOS Fax.doc
Independent Challenge 1	WD B-3.doc	Lyric Theatre Letter.doc	
Independent Challenge 2			Global Dynamics Letter.doc
Independent Challenge 3	WD B-4.doc	Computer Memo.doc	
Independent Challenge 4	WD B-5.doc	Web References.doc	
Visual Workshop			Visa Letter.doc
Word Unit C			
Lessons	WD C-1.doc	Chicago Marketing Report.doc	
Skills Review	WD C-2.doc	EDA Report.doc	
Independent Challenge 1	WD C-3.doc	Zakia Construction.doc	
Independent Challenge 2	WD C-4.doc	Membership Flyer.doc	
Independent Challenge 3	WD C-5.doc	Solstice Memo.doc	
Independent Challenge 4	WD C-6.doc	Fonts.doc	
Visual Workshop	WD C-7.doc	Rosebud Specials.doc	
Word Unit D			
Lessons	WD D-1.doc	MediaLoft Buzz.doc	
Skills Review	WD D-2.doc	Amherst Fitness.doc	
Independent Challenge 1	WD D-3.doc	Bon Appetit.doc	

Unit and Location	Project File Supplied	Student Saves File As	Student Creates Files
Independent Challenge 2	WD D-4.doc	Parking FAQ.doc	
Independent Challenge 3	WD D-5.doc	Stormwater.doc	
Independent Challenge 4	WD D-6.doc	MLA Style.doc	
			MLA Sample Format.doc
Visual Workshop	WD D-7.doc	Gardener's Corner.doc	
Word Unit E			
Lessons		.	Boston Ad Budget.doc
Skills Review			Mutual Funds.doc
Independent Challenge 1	WD E-1.doc	40K Relay.doc	
Independent Challenge 2			Business Cards.doc
Independent Challenge 3	WD E-2.doc	Ad Dimensions.doc	
Independent Challenge 4			My Resume.doc
Visual Workshop			March 2003.doc
Word Unit F			
Lessons	WD F-1.doc Mloft.jpg	Ad Tips.doc	
			Genre Sales.doc
	WD F-2.doc	Age and Gender.doc	
Skills Review	WD F-3.doc Farm.jpg	Farm Flyer.doc	
			Realty Sales.doc
Independent Challenge 1			Letterhead.doc
Independent Challenge 2			GoTropper Ad.doc
	Vacation.jpg		
Independent Challenge 3			Bookmarks.doc
Independent Challenge 4	WD F-4.doc	Copyright Info.doc	
Visual Workshop			Surf Safe.doc
	WD F-5.doc Surfing.jpg		

Word Unit G: If you are saving your solution files to a floppy disk, then the files for the Lessons, Skills Review, each Independent Challenge, and the Visual Workshop must be stored on separate disks. Copy the files you need for the exercise you are completing onto one disk, and label it clearly (e.g. Word Unit G Lessons).

Unit and Location	Project File Supplied	Student Saves File As	Student Creates Files
Lessons			swfhome.htm
	mloft.jpg WD G-1.doc	swfevent.htm	
Skills Review			literacy.htm
	WD G-2.doc reader.gif		
	WD G-3.doc	whattodo.htm	
Independent Challenge 1			longwalk.htm
	WD G-4.doc rwolf.jpg jackson.jpg		

Unit and Location	Project File Supplied	Student Saves File As	Student Creates Files
Independent Challenge 2			default.htm
			Monet's Garden Home.htm
	WD G-5.doc	Products and Prices.htm	
Independent Challenge 3	WD G-6.doc	tri_home.htm	
	WD G-7.doc	tri_view.htm	
	WD G-8.doc	tri_get.htm	
	WD G-9.doc	tri_athl.htm	
Independent Challenge 4			my_page.htm
Visual Workshop			azulhome.htm
			azulexhb.htm
	rest.jpg		
	bridge.jpg		
	studlamp.jpg		
Word Unit H			
Lessons	WD H-1.doc	Coffee Letter Main.doc	
			New Coffee Club Data.mdb
			Coffee Letter Merge.doc
			Coffee Labels Main.doc
	WD H-2.mdb		US Coffee Labels Zip Code Merge.doc
Skills Review			Donor Labels Main.doc
			Donor Thank You Main.doc
			Donor Data.mdb
			Donor Thank You Merge.doc
			NH Donor Labels Merge.doc
Independent Challenge 1	WD H-3.doc	Member Letter Main.doc	
	WD H-4.mdb		
			Member Letter Merge.doc
Independent Challenge 2			Employee Data.mdb
			Business Cards Main.doc
			Business Cards Merge.doc
Independent Challenge 3			Softball Team Data.mdb
			Softball Roster Merge.doc
			Softball Labels Merge.do
Independent Challenge 4			5160 Labels Memo.doc
Visual Workshop			Party Data.mdb
			Party Card Main.doc
			Party Card Merge.doc
Unit I			
Lessons	WD I-1.doc	Lance Rose Author Profile.doc	
	WD I-2.doc	Janice Li Author Profile.doc	
	WD I-3.doc	Ron Leitz Author Profile.doc	
			Author Profile.dot
			Mary-Jo Watson Author Profile.doc
Skills Review	WD I-4.doc	Shaped Jigsaw Puzzles.doc	
	WD I-5.doc	3-D Jigsaw Puzzles.doc	
	WD I-6.doc	Landscape Puzzles.doc	
			Puzzle Description.dot
			Brain Teaser Puzzles.doc
Independent Challenge 1	WD I-7.doc	Softball memo.doc	

Unit and Location	Project File Supplied	Student Saves File As	Student Creates Files
Independent Challenge 2			E-Commerce Program Newsletter.dot
	WD I-8.doc	November E-Commerce Newsletter.doc	
Independent Challenge 3	WD I-9.doc	Winter Menu.doc	
			Summer Menu.doc
Independent Challenge 4			Sales Letter from Online Template
		Gallery.doc	
Visual Workshop			Paradise Cosmetics.doc
Unit J			
Lessons			Author Reading Guidelines.doc
	WD J-1.doc	Book Signing Guidelines.doc	
	WD J-2.doc	Guidelines_Book Signing.doc	
	WD J-3.doc	Guidelines_Book Club.doc	
	WD J-4.doc	Guidelines_Story Time.doc	
			MediaLoft Event Guidelines.doc
Skills Review			Partnership Agreement Outline.doc
	WD J-5.doc	Partnership Agreement Proposal.doc	
	WD J-6.doc	Partnering_Apex Training.doc	
	WD J-7.doc	Partnering_Speak Easy.doc	
	WD J-8.doc	Partnering_Bay Area College.doc	
			Partnership Agreements.doc
Independent Challenge 1	WD J-9.doc	Fitness First Franchises.doc	
Independent Challenge 2	WD J-10.doc	Pastel and Pen Proposal.doc	
	WD J-11.doc	Pastel_Lavendar.doc	
	WD J-12.doc	Pastel_Ocher.doc	
	WD J-13.doc	Pastel_Roman Rain.doc	
Independent Challenge 3			Program Information Report.doc
Independent Challenge 4			Online Job Opportunities.doc
Visual Workshop	WD J-14.doc	E-Commerce Term Paper.doc	
Unit K – Disk 1 *			
Lessons	WD K-01.doc	Online Marketing Report.doc	
	WD K-02.xls	Online Marketing Data.xls	
	WD K-03.doc		
	WD K-04.mdb		
			Online Marketing Report_Managers.doc
	WD K-05.doc	Online Marketing Cover Letter.doc	
Unit K – Disk 2			
Skills Review	WD K-06.doc	Northern Adventures Report.doc	
	WD K-07.xls	Northern Adventures Data.xls	
	WD K-08.doc		
	WD K-09.mdb		
	WD K-10.doc	Northern Adventures Cover Letter.doc	
Unit K – Disk 3			
Independent Challenge 1	WD K-11.doc	Recreation Commission Minutes.doc	
	WD K-12.xls		
	WD K-13.doc		

Unit and Location	Project File Supplied	Student Saves File As	Student Creates File
Independent Challenge 2			Grand Teton Camp Report.doc Grand Teton Camp Presentation.ppt
	WD K-14.xls		
Independent Challenge 3	WD K-15.doc WD K-16.mdb	Arts Online Memo.doc	
	WD K-17.xls	Arts Online Data.xls	
Independent Challenge 4	WD K-18.doc	Competition Research.xls	
Visual Workshop	WD K-19.xls	Cell Phone Data.xls	
			Maryland Arts Cell Phone Report.doc

* Because the files created in the unit are large, you will need to organize the files onto three floppy disks if you are using floppies and completing all the exercises. Copy the files as outlined above, and label each disk clearly (e.g., Word Unit K Disk 1).

Unit and Location	Project File Supplied	Student Saves File As	Student Creates File
Unit L			
Lessons	WD L-1.doc	Mystery Book Night Poster_Janice Li.doc	
	WD L-2.doc	Mystery Book Night Poster_Lance Rose.doc	
Skills Review	WD L-3.doc	Story Time Poster_Sally-Lou.doc	
	WD L-4.doc	Story Time Poster_Annabelle.doc	
Independent Challenge 1	WD L-5.doc	Learning Colors Picture.doc	
Independent Challenge 2			Carrots and Beans.doc
Independent Challenge 3			[Company Name] Flyer.doc
Independent Challenge 4	WD L-6.doc	Web Page Design Evaluations.doc	
Visual Workshop	WD L-7.doc	Pet Place Letterhead.doc	
Unit M			
Lessons			San Diego Survey.doc
Skills Review			Computer Basics Grade Change.doc
Independent Challenge 1	WD M-1.doc	Completed Expense Report.doc	
Independent Challenge 2	WD M-2.doc	Completed Parking Requisition.doc	
Independent Challenge 3			Completed Feedback Form.doc
Independent Challenge 4	WD M-3.doc	Survey Form Evaluation.doc	
Visual Workshop			My Audio Visual Form.doc
Unit N			
Lessons	WD N-1.doc WD N-2.xls	Online Marketing Analysis.doc	
Skills Review	WD N-3.doc WD N-4.xls	Asia Pacific Trading Report.doc	
Independent Challenge 1			Gallery Attendance.doc
	WD N-5.xls		
Independent Challenge 2			Net Linen Sales.doc
Independent Challenge 3			Jasper Tours Organization.doc
Independent Challenge 4			Web Site Radial Diagram.doc
Visual Workshop			Web Launch Target Diagram.doc

Unit and Location	Project File Supplied	Student Saves File As	Student Creates File
Unit O			
Lessons	WD O-1.doc	MediaLoft Online Survey.doc	
	WD O-2.doc	MediaLoft Online Survey_Alice.doc	
	WD O-3.doc	MediaLoft Online Survey_Chris.doc	
			MediaLoft Online Survey_Final.doc
Skills Review	WD O-4.doc	Image Makers Company Description.doc	
	WD O-5.doc	Image Makers_Donald.doc	
	WD O-6.doc	Image Makers_Julia.doc	
			Images Makers_Final.doc
Independent Challenge 1	WD O-7.doc	E-Business Solutions Conference.doc	
Independent Challenge 2	WD O-8.doc	Internet Security Issues Article.doc	
Independent Challenge 3	WD O-9.doc	Summer Courses_Malcolm.doc	
	WD O-10.doc	Summer Courses_Teresa.doc	
	WD O-11.doc	Summer Courses_Gregg.doc	
			Summer Courses_Final.doc
Independent Challenge 4	WD O-12.doc	Digital Signatures.doc	
Visual Workshop	WD O-13.doc	Calm Oasis Mission Statement.doc	
Unit P			
Lessons			Macro Setup.doc
	WD P-1.doc	Novel Extract_Jancie Li.doc	
	WD P-2.doc	Novel Extract_Lance Rose.doc	
	WD P-3.doc	Novel Extract Macro.doc	
	WD P-4.doc	Novel Extract_Ron Leitz.doc	
Skills Review	WD P-5.doc	Press Release _Bay Street Hotel.doc	
	WD P-6.doc	Press Release _Regina Classic Hotel.doc	
	WD P-7.doc	Press Release_Royal Maritime Hotel .doc	
	WD P-8.doc	Hotel Macro Sample.doc	
Independent Challenge 1			Price List Macro.doc
	WD P-9.doc	Organics Forever Price List_[Current Date] .doc	
Independent Challenge 2	WD P-10.doc	Gift Certificate_John Marks.doc	
		Gift Certificate_Helga Bruin.doc	
Independent Challenge 3	WD P-11.doc	Catlogue Request_Farrell.doc	
	WD P-12.doc	Catalogue Request_Deville.doc	
Independent Challenge 4			Clip Art for [Your Name] .doc
Visual Workshop	WD P-13.doc	Birthday Card_Jason.doc	

Microsoft Word 2002 MOUS Certification Core Objectives

Below is a list of the Microsoft Office User Specialist program objectives for the Core Word 2002 skills, showing where each MOUS objective is covered in the Lessons and Practice. For more information on which Illustrated titles meet MOUS certification, please see the inside cover of this book.

MOUS Standardized Coding Number	Activity	Lesson page where skill is covered	Location in lesson where skill is covered	Practice
W2002-1	**Inserting and Modifying Text**			
W2002-1-1	Insert, modify, and move text and symbols	WORD B-4	Steps 1–8	Skills Review
		WORD B-5	Clues to Use	Independent Challenges 1–4
		WORD B-6	Steps 1–7	Visual Workshop
		WORD B-7	Clues to Use	
		WORD B-8	Steps 1–8	
		WORD B-9	Clues to Use	
		WORD B-10	Steps 1–9	
		WORD B-11	Clues to Use	
		WORD B-14	Steps 1–9	
		WORD B-15	Clues to Use	
		WORD D-12	Steps 2–3	Skills Review
				Independent Challenges 2, 3
W2002-1-2	Apply and modify text formats	WORD C-2	Steps 2–9	Skills Review
		WORD C-3	Clues to Use	Independent Challenges 1–3
		WORD C-4	Steps 1–9	Visual Workshop
		WORD C-5	Clues to Use	
W2002-1-3	Correct spelling and grammar usage	WORD B-12	Steps 1–9	Skills Review
				Independent Challenges 1–4
				Visual Workshop
W2002-1-4	Apply font and text effects	WORD C-4	Steps 1–9	Skills Review
		WORD C-5	Clues to Use	Independent Challenges 1–3
		WORD C-16	Clues to Use	Visual Workshop
W2002-1-5	Enter and format date and time	WORD D-8	Clues to Use	Skills Review
		WORD D-10	Steps 2–3, Quick Tip	Independent Challenge 3
		WORD D-11	Clues to Use	
W2002-1-6	Apply character styles	WORD C-3	Clues to Use	Independent Challenge 3
		WORD C-7	Clues to Use	
W2002-2	**Creating and Modifying Paragraphs**			
W2002-2-1	Modify paragraph formats	WORD C-6	Steps 1–9	Skills Review
		WORD C-7	Clues to Use	Independent Challenges 1–3
		WORD C-8	Steps 1–9	Visual Workshop
		WORD C-9	Clues to Use	
		WORD C-10	Steps 1–9	
		WORD C-12	Steps 1–6, Table	
		WORD C-16	Steps 1–8	
W2002-2-2	Set and modify tabs	WORD C-10	Steps 1–9	Skills Review
				Independent Challenges 1–3
W2002-2-3	Apply bullet, outline, and numbering format to paragraphs	WORD C-14	Steps 1–8	Skills Review
		WORD C-15	Clues to Use	Independent Challenges 1–3
W2002-2-4	Apply paragraph styles	WORD C-7	Clues to Use	Independent Challenge 3
W2002-3	**Formatting Documents**			
W2002-3-1	Create and modify a header and footer	WORD D-10	Steps 1–7, Quick Tip	Skills Review
		WORD D-11	Table	Independent Challenges 1–4
		WORD D-12	Steps 1–9	

MOUS Standardized Coding Number	Activity	Lesson page where skill is covered	Location in lesson where skill is covered	Practice
W2002-3-2	Apply and modify column settings	WORD D-4 WORD D-5 WORD D-6 WORD D-14	Steps 4–5 Clues to Use Clues to Use Steps 1–8, Quick Tip	Skills Review Independent Challenges 1, 2 Visual Workshop
W2002-3-3	Modify document layout and Page Setup options	WORD D-2 WORD D-3 WORD D-4 WORD D-5 WORD D-6 WORD D-7 WORD D-8	Steps 1–6 Clues to Use Steps 1–6, Quick Tip Clues to Use Steps 1–5, Clues to Use Table Steps 1–6, Quick Tip	Skills Review Independent Challenges 1–4 Visual Workshop
W2002-3-4	Create and modify tables	WORD C-11 WORD E-2 WORD E-3 WORD E-4 WORD E-5 WORD E-6 WORD E-10 WORD E-14 WORD E-15 WORD E-16 WORD E-17	Clues to Use Steps 1–8 Clues to Use Steps 1–9 Clues to Use Steps 1–8 Steps 1–9 Steps 1–5 Clues to Use Steps 3–9 Clues to Use	 Skills Review Independent Challenges 1–4 Visual Workshop
W2002-3-5	Preview and Print documents, envelopes, and labels	WORD A-12 WORD H-14 WORD H-16 WORD H-17	Steps 1–4, 6–7 Steps 1–6 Steps 1–10 Clues to Use	Skills Review Independent Challenges 1–4 Visual Workshop Skills Review Independent Challenges 1–3 Visual Workshop
W2002-4	**Managing Documents**			
W2002-4-1	Manage files and folders for documents	WORD B-3	Clues to Use	Independent Challenge 2
W2002-4-2	Create documents using templates	WORD B-16 WORD I-2 WORD I-14 WORD I-15 WORD I-16	Steps 1–9 Details Steps 1–10 Clues to Use Steps 1–9	Skills Review Independent Challenge 3 Visual Workshop Skills Review Independent Challenges 1–4
W2002-4-3	Save documents using different names and file formats	WORD A-10 WORD A-11 WORD B-2 WORD B-3	Steps 1–5 Table Steps 5–6 Clues to Use	Skills Review Independent Challenges 1–4 Visual Workshop Skills Review Independent Challenges 1–4 Visual Workshop
W2002-5	**Working with Graphics**			
W2002-5-1	Insert images and graphics	WORD D-16 WORD F-2 WORD F-3 WORD F-4 WORD F-5 WORD F-6 WORD F-8	Steps 1–8 Steps 1–8 Clues to Use Steps 1–6, Table Clues to Use Steps 1–8 Steps 1–10	Skills Review Independent Challenges 1, 2 Visual Workshop Skills Review Independent Challenges 1–4 Visual Workshop

MOUS Standardized Coding Number	Activity	Lesson page where skill is covered	Location in lesson where skill is covered	Practice
W2002-5-1 (continued)		WORD F-10 WORD F-12 WORD F-13 WORD F-14	Steps 1–8 Steps 1–8 Clues to Use Steps 1–8	
		WORD L-2 WORD L-4 WORD L-5 WORD L-6 WORD L-8 WORD L-10 WORD L-12 WORD L-14 WORD L-15 WORD L-16	Steps 1–10 Steps 1–9 Clues to Use Steps 1–9 Steps 1–8 Steps 1–9 Steps 1–9 Steps 1–8 Clues to Use Steps 1–8	Skills Review Independent Challenges 1–3 Visual Workshop
W2002-5-2	Create and modify diagrams and charts	WORD F-16 WORD F-17	Steps 1–10 Clues to Use	Skills Review
		WORD N-2 WORD N-4 WORD N-6 WORD N-8 WORD N-10 WORD N-12 WORD N-14 WORD N-16	Details Steps 1–9 Steps 1–10 Steps 1–9 Steps 1–9 Steps 1–9 Steps 1–9 Steps 1–9	Skills Review Independent Challenges 1–4 Visual Workshop
W2002-6	**Workgroup Collaboration**			
W2002-6-1	Compare and Merge documents	WORD H-2 WORD H-3 WORD H-4 WORD H-5 WORD H-6 WORD H-7 WORD H-8 WORD H-10 WORD H-11 WORD H-12 WORD H-13 WORD H-17	Details Clues to Use Steps 1–7 Clues to Use Steps 1–8 Clues to Use Steps 1–8 Steps 1–9 Clues to Use Steps 1–9 Table Clues to Use	Skills Review Independent Challenges 1–3 Visual Workshop
W2002-6-2	Insert, view, and edit comments	WORD G-14	Clues to Use	Independent Challenge 2
W2002-6-3	Convert documents into web pages	WORD G-2 WORD G-3 WORD G-4 WORD G-5 WORD G-6 WORD G-7 WORD G-8 WORD G-9 WORD G-10 WORD G-11 WORD G-12 WORD G-13 WORD G-14 WORD G-16 WORD G-17	Steps 7–10 Clues to Use Steps 1–10 Clues to Use Steps 1–9 Clues to Use Steps 1–6 Clues to Use Steps 1–7 Table Steps 1–9 Clues to Use Steps 1–6, Clues to Use Steps 1–10, Clues to Use	Skills Review Independent Challenges 1–4 Visual Workshop

Microsoft Word 2002 MOUS Certification Expert Objectives

Below is a list of the Microsoft Office User Specialist program objectives for the Expert Word 2002 skills, showing where each MOUS objective is covered in the Lessons and Practice. For more information on which Illustrated titles meet MOUS certification, please see the inside cover of this book.

MOUS Standardized Coding Number	Activity	Lesson page where skill is covered	Location in lesson where skill is covered	Practice
W2002E-1	**Customizing Paragraphs**			
W2002E-1-1	Control Pagination	WORD D-6	Steps 1–5, Table	Independent Challenge 4
		WORD J-15	Clues to Use	Skills Review Independent Challenges 1, 2
W2002E-1-2	Sort paragraphs in lists and tables	WORD E-8 WORD E-9	Steps 1–7 Clues to Use	Skills Review
W2002E-2	**Formatting documents**			
W2002E-2-1	Create and format document sections	WORD D-3 WORD D-5 WORD D-12	Clues to Use Clues to Use Steps 7–8	Skills Review Independent Challenges 1–4 Visual Workshop
		WORD J-10 WORD J-14	Step 2 Steps 3–4	Skills Review Independent Challenges 2–4 Visual Workshop
		WORD I-2 WORD I-6	Details Step 7, Clues to Use	Skills Review Independent Challenge 1
W2002E-2-2	Create and apply character and paragraph styles	WORD I-2 WORD I-4 WORD I-6 WORD I-8 WORD I-12	Details Steps 1–9 Steps 1–6 Steps 1–9 Steps 1–10	Skills Review Independent Challenges 1–3 Visual Workshop
W2002E-2-3	Create and update document indexes and tables of contents, figures, and authorities	WORD J-10 WORD J-12	Steps 1–9 Steps 1–9	Skills Review Independent Challenge 1 Visual Workshop
W2002E-2-4	Create cross-references	WORD J-8 WORD J-13	Steps 7–10 Clues to Use	Skills Review Independent Challenges 1, 2
W2002E-2-5	Add and revise endnotes and footnotes	WORD J-6	Steps 1–9	Skills Review Independent Challenge 1
W2002E-2-6	Create and manage master documents and subdocuments	WORD J-16	Steps 1–9	Skills Review Independent Challenge 2
W2002E-2-7	Move within documents	WORD J-8 WORD J-9	Steps 1–3 Clues to Use	Skills Review Independent Challenges 1, 2
W2002E-2-8	Create and modify forms using various form controls	WORD M-2 WORD M-4 WORD M-6 WORD M-8 WORD M-10 WORD M-12	Steps 1–9 Steps 1–8 Steps 1–8 Steps 1–8 Steps 1–8 Steps 1–9	Skills Review Independent Challenges 1–3 Visual Workshop

MOUS Standardized Coding Number	Activity	Lesson page where skill is covered	Location in lesson where skill is covered	Practice
W2002E-2-9	Create forms and prepare forms for distribution	WORD M-14	Steps 8–9, Clues to Use	Skills Review Independent Challenges 1–3 Visual Workshop
W2002E-3	**Customizing Tables**			
W2002E-3-1	Use Excel data in tables	WORD K-2 WORD K-4	Details Steps 2–9	Skills Review Independent Challenges 1–3 Visual Workshop
W2002E-3-2	Perform calculations in Word tables	WORD E-10 WORD E-12 WORD E-16	Steps 1–9 Steps 1–7 Step 1	Skills Review Independent Challenges 3, 4 Visual Workshop
		WORD L-8	Steps 1–8	Skills Review Independent Challenge 1
W2002E-4	**Creating and Modifying Graphics**			
W2002E-4-1	Create, modify, and position graphics	WORD F-2 WORD F-4 WORD F-5 WORD F-8 WORD F-10 WORD F-12 WORD F-14	Steps 1–8, Clues to Use Steps 1–6, Table Clues to Use Steps 1–8 Steps 1–9 Steps 1–8, Clues to Use Steps 1–8	Skills Review Independent Challenges 1–4 Visual Workshop
		WORD L-2 WORD L-4 WORD L-5 WORD L-6 WORD L-8 WORD L-10 WORD L-12 WORD L-14 WORD L-15 WORD L-16	Steps 1–10 Steps 1–9 Clues to Use Steps 1–9 Steps 1–8 Steps 1–9 Steps 1–9 Steps 1–8 Clues to Use Steps 1–8	Skills Review Independent Challenges 1–3 Visual Workshop
W2002E-4-2	Create and modify charts using data from other applications	WORD K-6 WORD K-12	Steps 1–10 Steps 1–8	Skills Review Independent Challenges 2, 3 Visual Workshop
W2002E-4-3	Align text and graphics	WORD F-6	Steps 1–8	Skills Review
		WORD L-10 WORD L-12	Steps 1–9 Steps 1–9	Skills Review Independent Challenges 1–3 Visual Workshop
W2002E-5	**Customizing Word**			
W2002E-5-1	Create, edit, and run macros	WORD P-2 WORD P-4 WORD P-6 WORD P-8 WORD P-10	Details, Table Steps 1–9 Steps 1–10 Steps 1–9 Steps 1–9	Skills Review Independent Challenges 1, 3 Visual Workshop
W2002E-5-2	Customize menus and toolbars	WORD P-12 WORD P-14 WORD P-16	Steps 1–9 Steps 1–8 Steps 1–9	Skills Review Independent Challenges 2, 4
W2002E-6	**Workgroup Collaboration**			
W2002E-6-1	Track, accept, and reject changes to documents	WORD O-2 WORD O-4 WORD O-6 WORD O-7 WORD O-8	Details Steps 6–9 Steps 1–9 Clues to Use Steps 1–9	Skills Review Independent Challenges 1–3 Visual Workshop

MOUS Standardized Coding Number	Activity	Lesson page where skill is covered	Location in lesson where skill is covered	Practice
W2002E-6-2	Merge input from several reviewers	WORD G-15	Clues to Use	
		WORD O-12	Steps 1–8	Skills Review Independent Challenge 3
W2002E-6-3	Insert and modify hyperlinks to other documents and web pages	WORD G-12 WORD G-13 WORD G-14	Steps 1–9 Clues to Use Steps 1–6	Skills Review Independent Challenges 1–4 Visual Workshop
W2002E-6-4	Create and edit Web documents in Word	WORD G-2 WORD G-3 WORD G-4 WORD G-5 WORD G-6 WORD G-7 WORD G-8 WORD G-9 WORD G-10 WORD G-11 WORD G-12 WORD G-13 WORD G-14 WORD G-16 WORD G-17	Steps 7–10 Clues to Use Steps 1–10 Clues to Use Steps 1–9 Clues to Use Steps 1–6 Clues to Use Steps 1–7 Table Steps 1–9 Clues to Use Steps 1–6, Clues to Use Steps 1–10 Clues to Use	Skills Review Independent Challenges 1–4 Visual Workshop
W2002E-6-5	Create document versions	WORD O-10	Steps 1–9	Skills Review Independent Challenge 1
W2002E-6-6	Protect documents	WORD O-16	Steps 2–4	Skills Review Independent Challenge 3
W2002E-6-7	Define and modify default file locations for workgroup templates	WORD I-14 WORD I-15	Steps 3–10 Clues to Use	Skills Review
		WORD M-2	Steps 7–9	Skills Review Independent Challenges 1–3 Visual Workshop
W2002E-6-8	Attach digital signatures to documents	WORD O-16 WORD O-17	Steps 5–8 Clues to Use	Independent Challenge 3
W2002E-7	**Using Mail Merge**			
W2002E-7-1	Merge letters with a Word, Excel, or Access data source	WORD H-2 WORD H-3 WORD H-4 WORD H-5 WORD H-6 WORD H-7 WORD H-8 WORD H-10 WORD H-11 WORD H-12	Details Clues to Use Steps 1–7 Clues to Use Steps 1–8 Clues to Use Steps 1–8 Steps 1–9 Clues to Use Steps 1–9	Skills Review Independent Challenges 1–3 Visual Workshop
		WORD K-16	Steps 1–9	Skills Review Independent Challenge 3
W2002E-7-2	Merge labels with a Word, Excel, or Access data source	WORD H-14 WORD H-16 WORD H-17	Steps 1–6 Steps 1–10 Clues to Use	Skills Review Independent Challenges 1–3 Visual Workshop
W2002E-7-3	Use Outlook data as a mail merge data source	WORD H-6	Clues to Use	Independent Challenge 1

Glossary

Accessories Built-in programs that come with Windows 2000.

Active Desktop The screen that appears when you first start Windows 2000, providing access to your computer's programs and files and to the Internet. *See also* Desktop.

Active program The program that you are using, differentiated from other open programs by a highlighted program button on the taskbar and a differently colored title bar.

Active window The window that you are currently using, differentiated from other open windows by a differently colored title bar.

Address Bar The area below the toolbar in My Computer and Windows Explorer that you use to open and display a drive, folder, or Web page.

Back up To save files to another location in case you have computer trouble and lose files.

Browser A program, such as Microsoft Internet Explorer, designed to access the Internet.

Bullet mark A solid circle that indicates that an option is enabled.

Capacity The amount of information a disk can hold, usually measured in megabytes (Mb).

Cascading menu A list of commands from a menu item with an arrow next to it; pointing at the arrow displays a submenu from which you can choose additional commands.

Check box A square box in a dialog box that you click to turn an option on or off.

Check mark A mark that indicates that a feature is enabled.

Classic style A Windows 2000 setting in which you single-click to select items and double-click to open them.

Click To press and release the left mouse button once.

Clipboard Temporary storage space on your computer's hard disk containing information that has been cut or copied.

Close To quit a program or remove a window from the desktop. The Close button is usually located in the upper-right corner of a window.

Command A directive that provides access to a program's features.

Command button In a dialog box, a button that carries out an action. A command button usually has a label that describes its action, such as Cancel or Help. If the label is followed by an ellipses (…), clicking the button displays another dialog box.

Context-sensitive help Help that is specifically related to what you are doing.

Control Panel Used to change computer settings such as desktop colors or mouse settings.

Copy To place information onto the Clipboard in order to paste it in another location, but also leaving it in the original location.

Cut To remove information from a file and place it on the Clipboard, usually to be pasted into another location.

Default Settings Preset by the operating system or program.

Delete To place a file or folder in the Recycle Bin, where you can either remove it from the disk permanently or restore it to its original location.

Desktop The screen that appears when you first start Windows 2000, providing access to your computer's programs and files and to the Internet. *See also* Active Desktop.

Dialog box A window that opens when more information is needed to carry out a command.

Document A file that you create using a program such as WordPad.

Double-click To press and release the left mouse button twice quickly.

Drag To move an item to a new location using the mouse.

Drive A device that reads and saves files on a disk and is also used to store files; floppy drives read and save files on floppy disks, whereas hard drives read and save files on your computer's built-in hard disk.

Edit To change the content or format of an existing file.

Explorer Bar The pane on the left side of the screen in Windows Explorer that lists all drives and folders on the computer.

File An electronic collection of information that has a unique name, distinguishing it from other files.

File hierarchy A logical structure for folders and files that mimics how you would organize files and folders in a filing cabinet.

File management The process of organizing and keeping track of files and folders.

Floppy disk A disk that you insert into a disk drive of your computer (usually drive A or B) to store files.

Folder A collection of files and/or other folders that helps you organize your disks.

Font The design of a set of characters (for example, Times New Roman).

Format To enhance the appearance of a document by, for example, changing the font or font size, adding borders and shading to a document.

Graphical user interface (GUI) An environment made up of meaningful symbols, words, and windows in which you can control the basic operation of a computer and the programs that run on it.

Hard disk A disk that is built into the computer (usually drive C) on which you store files and programs.

Highlighting When an icon is shaded differently, indicating it is selected. *See also* Select.

Icon Graphical representation of computer elements such as files and programs.

Inactive Refers to a window or program that is open but not currently in use.

Input device An item, such as a mouse or keyboard, that you use to interact with your computer.

Insertion point A blinking vertical line that indicates where text will appear when you type.

Internet A worldwide collection of over 40 million computers linked together to share information.

Internet style A Windows 2000 setting in which you point to select items and single-click to open them. *See also* Web style.

Keyboard shortcut A keyboard alternative for executing a menu command (for example, [Ctrl][X] for Cut).

List box A box in a dialog box containing a list of items; to choose an item, click the list arrow, then click the desired item.

Maximize   To enlarge a window so it fills the entire screen. The Maximize button is usually located in the upper-right corner of a window.

Menu   A list of related commands in a program (for example, the File menu).

Menu bar   A bar near the top of the program window that provides access to most of a program's features through categories of related commands.

Minimize   To reduce the size of a window. The Minimize button is usually located in the upper-right corner of a window.

Mouse   A hand-held input device that you roll on your desk to position the mouse pointer on the Windows desktop. *See also* Mouse pointer.

Mouse buttons   The two buttons on the mouse (right and left) that you use to make selections and issue commands.

Mouse pointer   The arrow-shaped cursor on the screen that follows the movement of the mouse. The shape of the mouse pointer changes depending on the program and the task being executed. *See also* Mouse.

Multi-tasking   Working with more than one window or program at a time.

My Computer   A program that you use to manage the drives, folders, and files on your computer.

Open   To start a program or open a window; also used to describe a program that is running but not active.

Operating system   A computer program that controls the basic operation of your computer and the programs you run on it. Windows 2000 is an example of an operating system.

Option button   A small circle in a dialog box that you click to select an option.

Paint   A drawing program that comes with Windows 2000.

Pane   A section of a divided window.

Point   To position the mouse pointer over an item on your computer screen; also a unit of measurement (1/72nd inch) used to specify the size of text.

Pointer trail   A shadow of the mouse pointer that appears when you move the mouse; helps you locate the pointer on your screen.

Pop-up menu   A menu that appears when you right-click an item on the desktop.

Program   Task-oriented software that you use for a particular kind of work, such as word processing or database management. Microsoft Access, Microsoft Excel, and Microsoft Word are all programs.

Program button   A button on the taskbar that represents an open program or window.

Properties   Characteristics of a specific computer element (such as the mouse, keyboard, or desktop display) that you can customize.

Quick Launch toolbar   A toolbar located next to the Start button on the taskbar that contains buttons to start Internet-related programs and show the desktop.

Random access memory (RAM)   The memory that programs use to perform necessary tasks while the computer is on. When you turn the computer off, all information in RAM is lost.

Recycle Bin   An icon that appears on the desktop that represents a temporary storage area on your computer's hard disk for deleted files, which remain in the Recycle Bin until you empty it.

Restore   To reduce the window to its previous size before it was maximized. The Restore button is usually located in the upper-right corner of a window.

Right-click   To press and release the right mouse button once.

ScreenTip   A description of a toolbar button that appears when you position the mouse pointer over the button.

Scroll bar   A bar that appears at the bottom and/or right edge of a window whose contents are not entirely visible; you click the arrows or drag the box in the direction you want to move. *See also* Scroll box.

Scroll box   A rectangle located in the vertical and horizontal scroll bars that indicates your relative position in a window. *See also* Scroll bar.

Select   To click and highlight an item in order to perform some action on it. *See also* Highlighting.

Shortcut   A link that you can place in any location that gives you instant access to a particular file, folder, or program on your hard disk or on a network.

Shut down   The action you perform when you have finished working with Windows 2000; after you shut down it is safe to turn off your computer.

Slider   An item in a dialog box that you drag to set the degree to which an option is in effect.

Spin box   A box with two arrows and a text box; allows you to scroll in numerical increments or type a number.

Start button   A button on the taskbar that you use to start programs, find and open files, access Windows Help and more.

Tab   A place in a dialog box where related commands and options are organized.

Taskbar   A strip at the bottom of the screen that contains the Start button, Quick Launch toolbar, and shows which programs are running.

Text box   A rectangular area in a dialog box in which you type text.

Title bar   The area along the top of the window that indicates the filename and program used to create it.

Toolbar   A strip with buttons that allow you to activate a command quickly.

Web page   A document that contains highlighted words, phrases, and graphics that link to other documents on the Internet.

Web site   A computer on the Internet that contains Web pages.

Web style   A Windows 2000 setting in which you point to select items and single-click to open them. *See also* Internet style.

Window   A rectangular frame on a screen that can contain icons, the contents of a file, or other usable data.

Windows Explorer   A program that you use to manage files, folders, and shortcuts; allows you to work with more than one computer, folder, or file at once.

Windows Help   An online "book" stored on your computer, complete with an index and a table of contents, that contains information about Windows 2000.

WordPad   A word processing program that comes with Windows 2000.

World Wide Web   Part of the Internet that consists of Web sites located on different computers around the world.

Zip disk   A portable disk that can contain 100 Mb, far more than a regular floppy disk.

Zip drive   A drive that can handle Zip disks.

Glossary

Word 2002

Adjustment handle Used to change the shape, but not the size, of many Autoshapes.

Alignment The position of text in a document relative to the margins.

Anchored The state of a floating graphic that will move with a paragraph if the paragraph is moved; an anchor symbol appears with the floating graphic when formatting marks are displayed.

Application *See* Program.

Area chart A chart similar to a line chart; however the space between the lines and the bottom of the chart is filled, and a different band of color represents each value.

Ascending order Lists data alphabetically or sequentially (from A to Z, 0 to 9, or earliest to latest).

Ask a Question box The list box at the right end of the menu bar in which you can type or select questions for the Help system.

AutoComplete A feature that automatically suggests text to insert.

AutoCorrect A feature that automatically detects and corrects typing errors, minor spelling errors, and capitalization, or inserts certain typographical symbols as you type.

Autoshapes Drawing objects, such as rectangles, ovals, triangles, lines, block arrows, stars, banners, lightning bolts, hearts, and suns, that you create using the tools on the Drawing toolbar.

AutoText A feature that stores frequently used text and graphics so they can be easily inserted into a document.

Bar chart A chart that shows values as horizontal bars. Cylinder, Cone, and Pyramid charts can also show values in horizontal format, similar to the rectangles used in bar charts.

Bitmap graphic A graphic that is composed of a series of small dots called "pixels."

Boilerplate text Text that appears in every version of a merged document.

Bold Formatting applied to text to make it thicker and darker.

Bookmark Text that identifies a location or a selection of text in a document.

Border Lines that can be added above, below, or to the sides of paragraphs, text, and table cells; lines that divide the columns and rows and help you see the grid-like structure of a table.

Browser A software program used to access and display Web pages.

Bullet A small graphic symbol used to identify items in a list.

Cell reference Identifies a cell's position in a table. Each cell reference contains a letter (A, B, C, and so on) to identify its column and a number (1, 2, 3, and so on) to identify its row.

Center Alignment in which an item is centered between the margins.

Character spacing Formatting that changes the width or scale of characters, expands or condenses the amount of space between characters, raises or lowers characters relative to the line of text, and adjusts kerning (the space between standard combinations of letters).

Character style A named set of character format settings that can be applied to text to format it all at once.

Chart A visual representation of numerical data, which is usually used to illustrate trends, patterns, or relationships.

Circular chart A chart that shows how values relate to each other as parts of a whole. A pie chart is an example of a circular chart.

Click and Type pointer A pointer used to move the insertion point and automatically apply the paragraph formatting necessary to insert text at that location in the document.

Clip art A collection of graphic images that can be inserted into documents, presentations, Web pages, spreadsheets, and other Office files.

Clipboard A temporary storage area for items that are cut or copied from any Office file and are available for pasting. *See also* Office Clipboard and System Clipboard.

Column break A break that forces text following the break to begin at the top of the next column.

Column chart A chart that compares values side-by-side, usually over time. Cylinder, Cone, and Pyramid charts can also show values in vertical format, similar to the rectangles used in column charts.

Comment Text that appears in a comment balloon when working in Page Layout view.

Cone chart A type of column chart.

Copy To place a copy of an item on the Clipboard without removing it from a document.

Cross-reference Text that electronically refers the reader to another part of the document.

Cut To remove an item from a document and place it on the Clipboard.

Cut and paste To move text or graphics using the Cut and Paste commands.

Cycle diagram A diagram that illustrates a process that has a continuous cycle.

Cylinder chart A type of column chart.

Data field A category of information, such as last name, first name, street address, city, or postal code.

Data record A complete set of related information for a person or an item, such as a person's name and address.

Data source In a mail merge, the file with the unique data for individual people or items; the data merged with a main document to produce multiple versions.

Datasheet A table grid that opens when a chart is inserted in Word.

Delete To permanently remove an item from a document.

Destination file The file to which data is copied.

Destination program The program to which the data is copied.

Descending order Lists data in reverse alphabetical or sequential order (Z to A, 9 to 0, or latest to earliest).

Dialog box A window that opens when a program needs more information to carry out a command.

Digital certificate An attachment for a file that vouches for the authenticity of the file, provides secure encryption, or supplies a verifiable signature.

Digital signature An electronic stamp attached to a document to authenticate the document.

Document The electronic file you create using Word.

Document Map A pane that shows all the headings and subheadings in a document.

Document window The workspace in the program window that displays the current document.

Drawing canvas A workspace for creating your own graphics; an area within which multiple shapes can be drawn and clip art or pictures inserted.

Drop cap A large dropped character that appears as the first character in a paragraph.

Dynamic Data Exchange (DDE) The connection between the source file and the destination file.

Embedded object An object contained in a source file and inserted into a destination file. An embedded object becomes part of the destination file that is no longer linked to the source file.

Endnote Text that provides additional information or acknowledges sources for text in a document and appears at the end of a document.

Field A code that serves as a placeholder for data that changes in a document, such as a page number.

Field label A word or phrase that tells users the kind of information required for a given field.

Field name The name of the data field.

File An electronic collection of information that has a unique name, distinguishing it from other files.

Filename The name given to a document when it is saved.

Filename extension Three letters that follow the period in the filename. Examples include .doc for a Word file and .xls for an Excel file.

Filtering In mail merge, pulls out records that meet specific criteria and includes only those records in the merge.

First line indent A type of indent in which the first line of a paragraph is indented more than the subsequent lines.

Floating graphic A graphic to which a text wrapping style has been applied which makes the graphic independent of text and able to be moved anywhere on a page.

Font The typeface or design of a set of characters (letters, numbers, symbols, and punctuation marks).

Font effects Font formatting that applies special effects to text, such as shadow, outline, small caps, or superscript.

Font size The size of characters, measured in points (pt).

Footnote Text that provides additional information or acknowledges sources for text in a document and appears at the bottom of the page on which the footnote reference appears.

Footer Text or graphics that appears at the bottom of every page in a document or a section.

Form A structured document with spaces reserved for entering information.

Form field The location where the data associated with a field label is stored.

Format Painter A feature used to copy the format settings applied to text to other text.

Form template A file that contains the structure of a form. Users create new forms from a form template. Data entered into new forms based on a form template do not affect the structure of the template file.

Formatting marks Nonprinting characters that appear on-screen to indicate the ends of paragraphs, tabs, and other formatting elements.

Formatting toolbar A toolbar that contains buttons for frequently used formatting commands.

Frame A section of a Web page window in which a separate Web page can be displayed.

Gutter Extra margin space left for a binding at the top or left side of a document.

Hanging indent A type of indent in which the second and subsequent lines of a paragraph are indented more than the first.

Hard page break A page break inserted to force the text following the break to begin at the top of the next page.

Header Text or graphics that appears at the top of every page in a document or a section.

Highlighting Transparent color that can be applied to text to call attention to it.

Home page The main page of a Web site and the first page Web page viewers see when they open a site.

Horizontal ruler A ruler that appears at the top of the document window in Print Layout, Normal, and Web Layout view.

HTML (Hypertext Markup Language) The programming language used to code how each element of a Web page should appear when viewed with a browser.

Hyperlink Text or a graphic that opens a file, Web page, or other item when clicked. Also known as a link.

I-beam pointer The I pointer, used to move the insertion point and select text.

Indent The space between the edge of a line of text or a paragraph and the margin.

Indent markers Markers on the horizontal ruler that show the indent settings for the active paragraph.

Index Text that lists many of the terms and topics in a document, along with the pages on which they appear.

Inline graphic A graphic that is part of a line of text in which it was inserted.

Insertion point The blinking vertical line that shows where text will appear when you type in a document.

Italic Formatting applied to text to make the characters slanted.

Justify Alignment in which an item is flush with both the left and right margins.

Keyboard shortcut A combination of keys or a function key that can be pressed to perform a command.

Label Text that describes the significance of a value in a chart.

Landscape orientation Page orientation in which the page is wider than it is tall.

Left-align Alignment in which the item is flush with the left margin.

Left indent A type of indent in which the left edge of a paragraph is moved in from the left margin.

Legend A chart element that identifies the patterns or colors that are assigned to the data series or categories in a chart.

Line spacing The amount of space between lines of text.

Line style chart A chart that illustrates trends, where each value is connected to the next value by a line.

Linked object An object created in a source file and inserted into a destination file that maintains a connection between the two files; changes made to the data in the source file are reflected in the destination file.

List style A style that allows the formatting of a series of lines with numbers or bullets and with selected font and paragraph formats.

Macro A series of Word commands and instructions grouped together as a single command to accomplish a task automatically.

Main document In mail merge, the document with the standard text.

Margin The blank area between the edge of the text and the edge of a page.

Master document A Word document that contains links to two or more related documents called subdocuments.

Menu bar The bar beneath the title bar that contains the names of menus, that when clicked, open menus from which you can choose program commands.

Merge To combine adjacent cells into a singer larger cell.

Merge field A placeholder that you insert in the main document to indicate where the data from each record should be inserted when you perform the merge.

Mirror margins Margins used in documents with facing pages, where the inside and outside margins are mirror images of each other.

Negative indent A type of indent in which the left edge of a paragraph is moved to the left of the left margin.

New Document task pane A task pane that contains shortcuts for opening documents and for creating new documents.

Normal style The paragraph style that is used by default to format text typed into a blank document.

Normal template The template that is loaded automatically when a new document is inserted in Word.

Normal view A view that shows a document without margins, headers and footers, or graphics.

Note reference mark A number or character that indicates additional information is contained in a footnote or endnote.

Nudged The action of moving a graphic a small amount in one direction; use the arrow keys to nudge a graphic.

Object Self-contained information that can be in the form of text, spreadsheet data, graphics, charts, tables, or sound and video clips.

Object Linking and Embedding (OLE) The ability to share information with other programs.

Office Assistant An animated character that appears to offer tips, answer questions, and provide access to the program's Help system.

Office Clipboard A temporary storage area shared by all Office programs that can be used to cut, copy and paste multiple items within and between Office programs. The Office Clipboard can hold up to 24 items collected from any Office program. *See also* Clipboard and System Clipboard.

Open To use one of the methods for opening a document to retrieve it and display it in the document window.

Organization chart A chart that illustrates a hierarchy, most often showing how functional areas in a company or organization relate to each other.

Outline view A view that shows the headings of a document organized as an outline.

Overtype mode A feature that allows you to overwrite existing text as you type.

Page border A graphical line that encloses one or more pages of a document.

Paragraph spacing The amount of space between paragraphs.

Paragraph style A named set of paragraph and character format settings that can be applied to a paragraph to format it all at once.

Paste To insert items stored on the Clipboard into a document.

Pie chart A type of circular chart.

Pixels Small dots that define color and intensity in a graphic.

Point The unit of measurement for text characters and the space between paragraphs and characters; 1/72 of an inch.

Point-to-point chart A chart used to identify patterns or to show values as clusters. The most commonly used point-to-point chart is the XY chart, also known as a Scatter chart.

Portrait orientation Page orientation in which the page is taller than it is wide.

Print Layout view A view that shows a document as it will look on a printed page.

Print Preview A view of a file as it will appear when printed.

Program Task-oriented software (such as Excel or Word) that enables you to perform a certain type of task such as data calculation or word processing.

Property A named attribute of a control set to define one of the control's attributes such as its size, its color, and its behavior in response to user input.

Pyramid chart A type of column chart.

Pyramid diagram A diagram that illustrates a hierarchical relationship.

Radial diagram A diagram that illustrates the relationships of several related elements to a core element.

Reset usage data An option that allows adapted toolbars and menus to be returned to their default settings.

Right-align Alignment in which an item is flush with the right margin.

Right indent A type of indent in which the right edge of a paragraph is moved in from the right margin.

Sans serif font A font, such as Arial, whose characters do not include serifs.

Save To store a file permanently on a disk or to overwrite the copy of a file that is stored on a disk with the changes made to the file.

Save As Command used to save a file for the first time or to create a new file with a different filename, leaving the original file intact.

Scale Describes the way a graphic can be resized so the height to width ratio remains the same.

Scatter chart A type of point-to-point chart.

ScreenTip A label that appears on the screen to identify a button or to provide information about a feature.

Scroll To use the scroll bars or the arrow keys to display different parts of a document in the document window.

Scroll arrows The arrows at the ends of the scroll bars that are clicked to scroll a document one line at a time.

Scroll bars The bars on the right and bottom edges of the document window that are used to display different parts of the document in the document window.

Scroll box The box in a scroll bar that can be dragged to scroll a document.

Section A portion of a document that is separated from the rest of the document by section breaks.

Section break A formatting mark inserted to divide a document into sections.

Word 2002

Select To click or highlight an item in order to perform some action on it.

Serif font A font, such as Times New Roman, whose characters include serifs—small strokes—at the ends.

Shading A background color or pattern that can be applied to text, tables, or graphics.

Shortcut key *See* Keyboard shortcut.

Sizing handles The black squares or white circles that appear around a graphic when it is selected; used to change the size or shape of a graphic.

Smart tag A purple dotted line that appears under text that Word identifies as a date, name, address, or place.

Smart Tag Actions button The button that appears when you point to a smart tag.

Soft page break A page break that is inserted automatically at the bottom of a page.

Sorting In mail merge, determines the order in which records are merged.

Source file The file in which data is originally saved.

Source program The program in which data is originally created.

Standard toolbar A toolbar that contains buttons frequently used for operating and editing commands.

Status bar The bar at the bottom of the Word window that shows the vertical position, section, and page number of the insertion point, the total number of pages in a document, and the on/off status of several Word features.

Style A named collection of character and/or paragraph formats that are stored together and can be applied to text to format it quickly.

Subdocument A document contained within a master document.

Subscript A font effect in which text is formatted in a smaller font size and placed below the line of text.

Superscript A font effect in which text is formatted in a smaller font size and placed above the line of text.

Symbols Special characters that can be inserted into a document using the Symbol command.

System Clipboard A clipboard that stores only the last item cut or copied from a document. *See also* Clipboard and Office Clipboard.

Tab *See* Tab stop.

Tab leaders Lines that appear in front of tabbed text.

Tab stop A location on the horizontal ruler that indicates where to align text.

Table A grid made up of rows and columns of cells that you can fill with text and graphics.

Table style A style that specifies how both the table grid and the text in the table will appear.

Tags HTML codes placed around the elements of a Web page to describe how each element should appear when viewed with a browser.

Target diagram A diagram that illustrates steps toward a goal.

Template A formatted document that contains placeholder text you can replace with your own text.

Text box A container that you can fill with text and graphics.

Text form field A location in a form where users enter text.

Theme A set of complementary design elements that you can apply to Web pages, e-mail messages, and other documents that are viewed on-screen.

Title bar The bar at the top of the program window that indicates the program name and the name of the current file.

Toggle button A button that turns a feature on and off.

Toolbar A bar that contains buttons that you can click to perform commands.

Undo To reverse a change by using the Undo button or command.

URL (Uniform Resource Locator) A Web address.

User template Any template created by the user.

Value A number in a chart.

Venn diagram A diagram that illustrates areas of overlap between two or more elements.

Vertical alignment The position of text in a document relative to the top and bottom margins.

Vertical ruler A ruler that appears on the left side of the document window in Print Layout view.

View A way of displaying a document in the document window; each view provides features useful for editing and formatting different types of documents.

View buttons Buttons on the horizontal scroll bar that are used to change views.

Watermark A picture or other type of graphics object that appears lightly shaded behind text in a document.

Web Layout view A view that shows a document as it will look when viewed with a Web browser.

Web page A document that can be stored on a computer called a Web server and viewed on the World Wide Web or on an intranet using a browser.

Web site A group of associated Web pages that are linked together with hyperlinks.

Wizard An interactive set of dialog boxes that guides you through a task.

WordArt A drawing object that contains text formatted with special shapes, patterns, and orientations.

Word processing program A software program that includes tools for entering, editing, and formatting text and graphics.

Word program window The window that contains the Word program elements, including the document window, toolbars, menu bar, and status bar.

Word wrap A feature that automatically moves the insertion point to the next line as you type.

Workgroup template A templates created for distribution to others.

X-axis The horizontal axis in a two-dimensional chart.

XY chart A type of point-to-point chart.

Y-axis The vertical axis in a two-dimensional chart.

Index

Index

Index